DB2 9 for Linux, UNIX, and Windows
Advanced Database Administration
Certification Study Guide

DB2 9

for Linux, UNIX, and Windows
Advanced Database Administration
Certification Study Guide

Roger E. Sanders & Dwaine R. Snow

MC Press Online, LP

Lewisville, TX 75077

DB2 9 for Linux, UNIX, and Windows Advanced Database Administration Certification Study Guide
Roger E. Sanders and Dwaine R. Snow

First Edition

First Printing—October 2008

MC Press offers excellent discounts on this book when ordered in quantity for bulk purchases or special sales, which may include custom covers and content particular to your business, training goals, marketing focus, and branding interest.

For information regarding permissions or special orders, please contact:
  MC Press
  Corporate Offices
  125 N. Woodland Trail
  Lewisville, TX 75077 USA

For information regarding sales and/or customer service, please contact:
  MC Press
  P.O. Box 4300
  Big Sandy, TX 75755-4300 USA

ISBN: 978-158347-080-0

To my loving family, Kristen, Tyler, and Beth.
                                                    —*Roger*

To my loving family, Alyssa and Linda.
                                                    —*Dwaine*

Acknowledgments

A project of this magnitude requires both a great deal of time and the support of many different individuals. The authors would like to express their gratitude to the following people for their contributions:

Susan Dykman—Information Management Certification Program Manager
IBM Information Management

Susan invited us to participate in the DB2 9 exam development process and provided screen shots of the IBM Certification Exam Testing software. Susan also reviewed the first chapter of the book and provided valuable feedback.

Susan Visser—IBM Press, Data Management Program Manager
IBM Toronto Lab

Once again, Susan's help was invaluable—without her help, this book would not have been written. Among other things, Susan found several subject-matter experts at IBM who were willing to review the manuscript before it went into production and coordinated the whole review process.

Dr. Arvind Krishna – Vice President,
IBM Data Servers and Worldwide Information Management Development

Dr. Krishna provided us with the Foreword for this book.

Reed M. Meseck – Senior Competitive Specialist,
IBM Information Management Software

Reed provided some valuable insights on using multidimensional clustered (MDC) tables and materialized query tables (MQTs).

Bill Minor—Manager, Data Management Services
IBM Toronto Lab

Bill provided detailed information on how Deep Compression works and reviewed the section in this book on deep compression for accuracy and completeness.

Kelly Schlamb—Manager, Data Protection Services (DPS)
and Backup/Restore (BAR) Development
IBM Toronto Lab

Kelly provided detailed examples illustrating how a table space's high-water mark is affected by reorganization and compression operations and reviewed the section in this book on deep compression for accuracy and completeness.

Dale McInnis—Sr. Technical Staff Member, DB2 High Availability
IBM Toronto Lab

Dale reviewed the material in Chapter 4—High Availability and Diagnostics for accuracy and completeness; the valuable feedback he provided was incorporated into the chapter.

Kevin Yeung-Kuen See—Certified Information Systems Security Professional
IBM Toronto Lab

Kevin reviewed the material in Chapter 6—Security for accuracy and completeness; the valuable feedback he provided was incorporated into the chapter.

Rebecca Bond—Senior DB2 Consultant
R. Bond Consulting, Inc.

Rebecca provided material on encrypting data from her book, *Understanding DB2 9 Security*. Some of the material she provided was incorporated into Chapter 6—Security.

Linda Snow—Executive IT Specialist
IBM Information Management

Linda not only reviewed the book for accuracy, but she helped ensure that this book is easy for you to read and understand, so that you will not only pass the test, but will use the book as your DB2 Bible.

The authors would also like to thank the following people for reviewing the manuscript and providing feedback:

Bob Bernard—Senior Education Specialist
Education Planning and Development
IBM Data Management

Melanie Stopfer
Consulting Learning Specialist
Data Management, IBM Software Group

Adil Sardar
DB2 Data Movement Utilities
IBM Toronto Lab

Matthew Rhea
Data Services IT Specialist
IBM Information Management

Dan Tuck
Senior Technical Advisor
Mar-Dale LLC

Tariq Al-Omari, PhD
Software Performance Analyst
DB2 OLTP Performance Benchmarks and Solution Development

Roger Archambault
Advisory Instructor
Data Management Education
IBM Software Group

Nick (N.V.) Tchervenski
Software Developer, DPS & BAR Team, DB2 Kernel Development
IBM Software Group, Information Management

Emilia (E.T.) Cifani
DB2 UDB Support
IBM Software Group, Information Management

About The Authors

Roger E. Sanders is the President of Roger Sanders Enterprises, Inc. He has been designing and developing database applications for more than 20 years and has been working with DB2 and its predecessors since it was first introduced on the IBM PC (as part of OS/2 Extended Edition). He has written articles for publications such as *Certification Magazine* and *IDUG Solutions Journal,* authored tutorials for IBM's developerWorks Web site, presented at numerous International DB2 User's Group (IDUG) and Regional DB2 User's Group (RUG) conferences, taught classes on DB2 fundamentals and database administration (DB2 for Linux, UNIX, and Windows), writes a regular column called *Distributed DBA* in *IBM Database Magazine,* and is the author of the following books:

- *Deploying DB2 for Linux, UNIX, and Windows on EMC Symmetrix DMX* (EMC TechBook; co-author)

- *Using the IBM System Storage N Series with Databases* (IBM RedBook; co-author)

- *DB2 9 for Linux, UNIX, and Windows Database Administration Upgrade Certification Study Guide*

- *DB2 9 for Linux, UNIX, and Windows Database Administration Certification Study Guide*

- *DB2 9 Fundamentals Certification Study Guide*

- *Integrating IBM DB2 with the IBM System Storage N Series* (IBM RedBook; co-author)

- *Using IBM DB2UDB with IBM System Storage N Series* (IBM RedBook; co-author)

- *DB2 Universal Database V8.1 Certification Exam 703 Study Guide*

- *DB2 Universal Database V8.1 Certification Exam 701 and 706 Study Guide*

- *DB2 Universal Database V8.1 Certification Exam 700 Study Guide*

- *DB2 UDB Exploitation of NAS Technology* (IBM RedBook; co-author)

- *All-In-One DB2 Administration Exam Guide*

- *DB2 Universal Database SQL Developer's Guide*

- *DB2 Universal Database API Developer's Guide*

- *DB2 Universal Database Call Level Interface Developer's Guide*

- *ODBC 3.5 Developer's Guide*

- *The Developer's Handbook to DB2 for Common Servers*

Roger holds the following DB2 9 professional certifications:

- IBM Certified Solutions Developer – DB2 9.5 SQL Procedure Developer

- IBM Certified Advanced Database Administrator – DB2 9 for Linux, UNIX, and Windows

- IBM Certified Application Developer – DB2 9

- IBM Certified Database Administrator – DB2 9 DBA for Linux, UNIX, and Windows

- IBM Certified Database Associate – DB2 9 Fundamentals

Dwaine R. Snow is a Senior DB2 Technical Evangelist for IBM and is one of the senior product managers responsible for charting the features and functions in the new releases of DB2 for Linux, UNIX, and Windows. Dwaine has also been working with DB2 since its days as part of OS/2, and was part of the development team responsible for DB2 version 1. He has written articles for a number of publications, authored tutorials for IBM's developerWorks Web site, presented at numerous International DB2 User's Group

(IDUG) and Regional DB2 User's Group (RUG) conferences, taught classes on DB2 around the world, and is the author of the following books:

- *Understanding DB2: Learning Visually with Examples –1st and 2nd Editions*

- *DB2 Universal Database Certification Guide – 2nd Edition*

- *The DB2 Cluster Certification Guide*

- *The Universal Guide to DB2 for Windows NT*

- *DB2 Viper Strikes Again*

Dwaine holds the following DB2 9 professional certifications:

- IBM Certified Advanced Database Administrator – DB2 9 for Linux, UNIX, and Windows

- IBM Certified Application Developer – DB2 9

- IBM Certified Database Administrator – DB2 9 DBA for Linux, UNIX, and Windows

- IBM Certified Database Associate – DB2 9 Fundamentals

Contents

Foreword

Data is moving faster than ever, the volume of data is exploding, the expectation is moving rapidly toward real-time, all the time, and users want access to data quicker and more easily.

Yesterday's data is no longer good enough, and business decisions are moving from being made day to day, to minute by minute and even down to milliseconds in the case of leading edge stream and event processing.

A new generation of data is being unleashed, from XML to Web Services to Stream and Event processing. So how do we stay ahead of this tidal wave of data?

At IBM, we continue to invest in DB2 to stay ahead of your needs. The revolutionary pureXML capabilities we first shipped in DB2 9 continue to be extended, and are enabling the rapid and easy development of a whole new generation of pureXML applications. We continue to enhance our already industry leading compression and performance.

In years past, the primary purpose of a relational database management system was to reliably store data in a machine independent manner. With the demands of today's global businesses, the demands on data to be available 24 x 7 x 365 are greater than ever, and increasingly we live in an Internet connected, "Always on, always available" world. Today, data has to be secure and privacy must be preserved, while at the same time making it more available than ever to a broader audience of users than ever.

Data must flow more easily and dynamically to applications, processes and people than ever before. It must support flexible architectures, like Services Oriented Architecture, provide optimized support for new data types, like XML, and embrace new developer communities and development paradigms, like Ruby or PHP. And it must do all of this while reducing the cost of operations to allow people to create business value in other ways.

DB2 9.5 continues to advance the goals of providing high performance, optimized access to data, and the new challenges of ever higher availability, ease of use, security and privacy, as well. And as DB2 celebrates its 25th year, it is only fitting that two of the most prolific DB2 authors, Roger Sanders and Dwaine Snow, come to together to guide you through this latest version of DB2. I encourage you to take advantage of the tremendous insights that these two authors provide into DB2 9.5. You will be learning skills you can both leverage across many technology settings and use to deliver more value to your business. Enjoy the experience and the insights herein.

IBM Corporation
Vice President
Data Servers and Information Management Development

Preface

One of the biggest challenges computer professionals face today is keeping their skill sets current with the latest changes in technology. When the computing industry was in its infancy, it was possible to become an expert in several different areas because the scope of the field was relatively small. Today, our industry is both widespread and fast paced, and the skills needed to master a single software package can·be quite complex. Because of this complexity, many application and hardware vendors have initiated certification programs to evaluate and validate an individual's knowledge of their technology. Businesses benefit from these programs because professional certification gives them confidence that an individual has the expertise needed to perform a specific job. Computer professionals benefit because professional certification allows them to deliver high levels of service and technical expertise, and more importantly, professional certification can lead to advancement and/or new job opportunities within the computer industry.

If you bought this book (or if you are thinking about buying this book), chances are you have already decided you want to acquire the most advanced IBM DB2 Professional Certification available. Let me assure you that the exams you must pass in order to become a certified DB2 professional are not easy. IBM prides itself on designing comprehensive certification exams that are relevant to the work environment that an individual holding a particular certification will have had some exposure to. As a result, all of IBM's certification exams are designed with the following items in mind:

- What are the critical tasks that must be performed by an individual who holds a particular professional certification?

- What skills must an individual possess in order to perform each critical task identified?

- How frequently will an individual perform each critical task identified?

You will find that to pass a DB2 certification exam, you must possess a solid understanding of DB2—and for the Advanced Database Administrator certification, you must understand many of its nuances as well.

Now for the good news. You are holding in your hands what we consider to be the best tool you can use to prepare for the DB2 9 for Linux, UNIX, and Windows Advanced Database Administration exam (Exam 734). When IBM began work on the DB2 9 certification exams, both of the authors of this book were invited once again to participate in the exam development process. In addition to helping define the exam objectives, we authored several exam questions and provided feedback on many more before the final exams went into production. Consequently, we have seen every exam question you are likely to encounter, and we know every concept you will be tested on when you take the DB2 9 for Linux, UNIX, and Windows Advanced Database Administration exam (Exam 734). Using this knowledge, along with copies of the actual exam questions, we developed this study guide, which not only covers every concept you must know in order to pass the DB2 9 for Linux, UNIX, and Windows Advanced Database Administration exam (Exam 734) but also covers the exam process itself and the requirements for each DB2 9 certification role available. In addition, you will find at the end of each chapter sample questions that are worded just like the actual exam questions. In short, if you see it in this book, count on seeing it on the exam; if you don't see it in this book, it won't be on the exam. If you become familiar with the material presented in this book, you should do well on the exam.

About this Book

This book is divided into two parts:

- Part 1—DB2 UDB Certification (Chapter 1)

  This section consists of one chapter (Chapter 1), which is designed to introduce you to the DB2 Professional Certification Program that is available from IBM. In this chapter you will learn about the different certification roles available, along with the basic prerequisites and requirements for each role. This chapter also explains what's involved in the certification process, and it includes a tutorial on the IBM Certification Exam testing software, which you will encounter when you go to take any IBM certification exam.

- Part 2—DB2 9 for Linux, UNIX, and Windows Advanced Database Administration (Chapters 2–7)

This section consists of six chapters (Chapters 2 through 7), which are designed to provide you with the concepts you will need to master before you can pass the DB2 9 for Linux, UNIX, and Windows Advanced Database Administration exam (Exam 734).

Chapter 2 is designed to introduce you to the various aspects of database design. In this chapter you will learn how to create both a non-partitioned and a partitioned DB2 9 database, as well as how to design, create, and manage buffer pools and table spaces. You will also be introduced to the concept of federated databases and you will be shown how to configure federated database access.

Chapter 3 is designed to teach you everything you need to know about data partitioning and clustering. In this chapter you will learn about parallelism and partitioned databases and you will learn about partition groups, partitioning keys, and partitioning maps, as well as the process used to add new database partitions to an existing partitioned database. You will also learn how to design and construct range-clustered tables, range-partitioned tables, and multi-dimensional clustered tables, as well as use the Design Advisor to identify indexes, materialized query tables (MQTs), and multidimensional clustering tables that could help improve query performance in your database environment. This chapter concludes with an introduction to the IBM InfoSphere Balanced Warehouse—also known as the Balanced Configuration Unit or BCU.

Chapter 4 is designed to introduce you to the concept of database backup and recovery and to the various tools available with DB2 9 that can be used to return a damaged or corrupted database to a useable and consistent state. In this chapter you will learn what transaction logging is, how transaction logging is performed, and how log files are used to restore a damaged database. You will also learn how to make backup images of a database or a table space using the Backup utility, how to perform version recovery using the Restore utility, how to reapply transaction records stored in logs to perform a roll-forward recovery operation using the Rollforward utility, and how to restore a database using information stored in the recovery history log file using the Recover utility. You will also learn how to set up a High

Availability Disaster Recovery (HADR) environment and how to configure a database for log mirroring.

Chapter 5 is designed to provide you with an inside-out look at performance tuning, starting with the DB2 registry variables and configuration parameters that have the greatest impact on performance. In this chapter, you will learn how to use the self-tuning memory manager, how to take advantage of parallelism, how to create appropriate indexes, how to control locking at the application level, and how to take control of a server. You will also learn how the DB2 optimizer works, how to analyze data access plans created by the optimizer, and how to take advantage of Deep Compression.

Chapter 6 is designed to introduce you to the concept of database security and to the various authorization levels and privileges that are recognized by DB2. In this chapter, you will learn how and where users are authenticated, how authorities and privileges determine what a user can and cannot do while working with a database, and how authorities and privileges are given to and taken away from individual users and/or groups of individual users. You will also learn how to use encryption to further protect sensitive data, how to implement Label-Based Access Control (LBAC) to control access to columns and rows in a table, and how to track all data access using an audit trail.

Chapter 7 is designed to provide you with everything you need to know about configuring communications. In this chapter, you will learn how to catalog remote databases, remote servers (nodes), and Database Connection Services (DCS) databases. You will also learn how to configure and use DB2 Discovery and how to manage connections to System z and System i host databases. And finally, you will learn how the fast communications manager (FCM) is used to handle communications between database partitions in a partitioned database environment.

This book is written primarily for IT professionals who have a great deal of experience working with DB2 9, have already acquired the DB2 9 for Linux, UNIX, and Windows Database Administration certification, and would like to take (and pass) the DB2 9 for Linux, UNIX, and Windows Advanced Database Administration exam (Exam 734). However, any individual who would like to learn some of the more complex skills needed to administer one or more DB2 9 databases will benefit from the information found in this book.

Conventions Used

Many examples of DB2 9 administrative commands and SQL statements can be found throughout this book. The following conventions are used whenever a DB2 command or SQL statement is presented:

[ ] Parameters or items shown inside of brackets are required and must be provided.

< > Parameters or items shown inside of angle brackets are optional and do not have to be provided.

| Vertical bars are used to indicate that one (and only one) item in the list of items presented can be specified

,... A comma followed by three periods (ellipsis) indicates that multiple instances of the preceding parameter or item can be included in the DB2 command or SQL statement

The following examples illustrate each of these conventions:

Example 1

```
REFRESH TABLE [TableName ,...]
<INCREMENTAL | NON INCREMENTAL>
```

In this example, at least one *TableName* value must be provided, as indicated by the brackets ([ ]), and more than one *TableName* value can be provided, as indicated by the comma-ellipsis (, . . .) characters that follow the *TableName* parameter. INCREMENTAL and NON INCREMENTAL are optional, as indicated by the angle brackets (< >), and either one or the other can be specified, but not both, as indicated by the vertical bar (|).

Example 2

```
CREATE SEQUENCE [SequenceName]
<AS [SMALLINT | INTEGER | BIGINT | DECIMAL]>
<START WITH [StartingNumber]>
<INCREMENT BY [1 | Increment]>
<NO MINVALUE | MINVALUE [MinValue]>
<NO MAXVALUE | MAXVALUE [MaxValue]>
<NO CYCLE | CYCLE>
<NO CACHE | CACHE 20 | CACHE [CacheValue]>
<NO ORDER | ORDER>
```

In this example, a *SequenceName* value must be provided, as indicated by the brackets ([ ]). However, everything else is optional, as indicated by the angle brackets (< >), and in many cases, a list of available option values is provided (for example, NO CYCLE and CYCLE); however, only one can be specified, as indicated by the vertical bar (|). In addition, when some options are provided (for example, START WITH, INCREMENT BY, MINVALUE, MAXVALUE, and CACHE), a corresponding value must be provided, as indicated by the brackets ([ ]) that follow the option.

SQL is not a case-sensitive language, but for clarity, the examples provided are shown in mixed case—command syntax is presented in uppercase whereas user-supplied elements such as table names and column names are presented in lowercase. However, the examples shown can be entered in any case.

Although basic syntax is presented for most of the DB2 commands and SQL statements covered in this book, the actual syntax supported may be much more complex. To view the complete syntax for a specific command or to obtain more information about a particular command, refer to the *IBM DB2, Version 9 Command Reference* product documentation. To view the complete syntax for a specific SQL statement or to obtain more information about a particular statement, refer to the *IBM DB2, Version 9 SQL Reference, Volume 2* product documentation.

CHAPTER 1

IBM DB2 9 Certification

Recognized throughout the world, the Professional Certification Program from IBM offers a range of certification options for IT professionals. This chapter is designed to introduce you to the various paths you can take to obtain DB2 9 Certification from IBM and to describe the testing software you will use when you sit down to take your first DB2 9 certification exam.

DB2 9 Certification Roles

One of the biggest trends in the IT industry today is certification. Many application and software vendors now have certification programs in place that are designed to evaluate and validate an individual's proficiency at using the vendor's latest product release. In fact, one of the reasons the Professional Certification Program from IBM was developed was to provide a way for skilled technical professionals to demonstrate their knowledge and expertise with a particular version of an IBM product.

The Professional Certification Program from IBM is made up of several distinct certification roles that are designed to guide you in your professional development. You begin the certification process by selecting the role that's right for you and familiarizing yourself with the certification requirements for that role. The following subsections are designed to help get you started by providing you with the prerequisites and requirements associated with each DB2 9 certification available.

IBM Certified Database Associate – DB2 9 Fundamentals

The *IBM Certified Database Associate – DB2 9 Fundamentals* certification is intended for entry-level DB2 9 users who are knowledgeable about the fundamental concepts of DB2 9 for Linux, UNIX, and Windows; DB2 9 for zSeries (OS/390); or DB2 9 for iSeries (AS/400). In addition to having some hands-on experience or some formal training, or both, in DB2 9, individuals seeking this certification should:

- Know what DB2 9 products are available, and be familiar with the various ways DB2 9 is packaged.

- Know what DB2 9 products must be installed in order to create a desired environment.

- Know what features and functions are provided by the various tools that are shipped with DB2 9.

- Possess a strong knowledge about the mechanisms DB2 9 uses to protect data and database objects against unauthorized access and/or modification.

- Know how to create, access, and manipulate basic DB2 objects, such as tables, views, and indexes.

- Be familiar with the different types of constraints that are available, and know how each is used.

- Be familiar with how XML data can be stored and manipulated.

- Possess an in-depth knowledge of the Structured Query Language (SQL), Data Definition Language (DDL), Data Manipulation Language (DML), and Data Control Language (DCL) statements that are available with DB2 9.

- Possess a basic understanding of the methods used to isolate transactions from each other in a multi-user environment.

- Be familiar with the methods used to control the manner in which locking is performed.

In order to acquire the IBM Certified Database Associate – DB2 9 Fundamentals certification, candidates must take and pass one exam: the **DB2 9 Family Fundamentals** exam (Exam 730). The roadmap for acquiring the IBM Certified Database Associate – DB2 9 Fundamentals certification is illustrated in Figure 1–1.

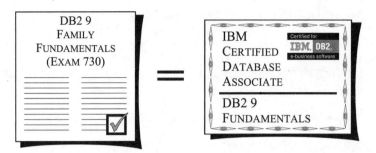

Figure 1–1: IBM Certified Database Associate – DB2 9 Fundamentals
certification roadmap.

IBM Certified Database Administrator – DB2 9 for Linux, UNIX, and Windows

The *IBM Certified Database Administrator – DB2 9 for Linux, UNIX, and Windows* certification is intended for experienced DB2 9 users who possess the knowledge and skills necessary to perform the day-to-day administration of DB2 9 instances and databases residing on Linux, UNIX, or Windows platforms. In addition to being knowledgeable about the fundamental concepts of DB2 9 and having significant hands-on experience as a DB2 9 Database Administrator (DBA), individuals seeking this certification should:

- Know how to configure and manage DB2 9 instances.

- Know how to configure client—server connectivity.

- Be able to obtain and modify the values of environment/registry variables.

- Be able to obtain and modify DB2 Database Manager (instance) and database configuration file parameter values.

- Know how to use Automatic Maintenance and self-tuning memory.

- Know how to create DB2 9 databases.

- Possess a strong knowledge about SMS, DMS, and automatic storage table spaces, as well as be familiar with the management requirements of each.

- Know how to create, access, modify, and manage the different DB2 9 objects available.

- Know how to manage XML data.

- Be able to create constraints on and between table objects.

- Know how to capture and interpret snapshot monitor data.

- Know how to create and activate event monitors, as well as capture and interpret event monitor data.

- Know how to capture and analyze Explain information.

- Know how to use the DB2 Control Center and the other GUI tools available to manage instances and databases, create and access objects, create tasks, schedule jobs, and view Explain information.

- Possess an in-depth knowledge of the Export, Import, and Load utilities.

- Know how to use the REORGCHK, REORG, REBIND, RUNSTATS, db2look, db2move, and db2pd commands.

- Know how to perform database-level and table space-level backup, restore, and roll-forward recovery operations.

- Have a basic understanding of transaction logging.

- Be able to interpret information stored in the administration notification log.

- Possess a strong knowledge about the mechanisms DB2 9 uses to protect data and database objects against unauthorized access and/or modification.

Candidates who have either taken and passed the **DB2 V8.1 Family Fundamentals exam** (Exam 700) or acquired the IBM Certified Database Administrator – DB2 V8.1 for Linux, UNIX, and Windows certification (by taking and passing Exams 700 and 701) must take and pass the **DB2 9 for Linux, UNIX, and Windows Database Administration** exam (Exam 731) to acquire the IBM Certified Database Administrator—DB2 9 for Linux, UNIX, and Windows certification. All other candidates must take and pass both the **DB2 9 Family Fundamentals** exam (Exam 730) and the **DB2 9 for Linux, UNIX, and Windows Database Administration** exam (Exam 731). The roadmap for acquiring the IBM Certified Database Administrator – DB2 9 for Linux, UNIX, and Windows certification can be seen in Figure 1–2.

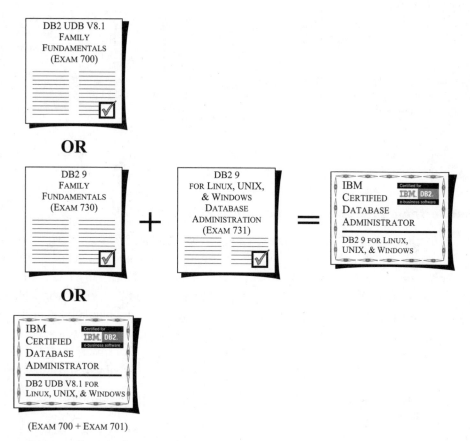

Figure 1–2: IBM Certified Database Administrator – DB2 9 for Linux, UNIX, and Windows certification roadmap.

Candidates who already hold the IBM Certified Database Administrator – DB2 V8.1 for Linux, UNIX, and Windows certification may opt to take the **DB2 9 for Linux, UNIX, and Windows Database Administration Upgrade** exam (Exam 736) to acquire the IBM Certified Database Administrator – DB2 9 for Linux, UNIX, and Windows certification. This exam, which is half the length and half the cost of the **DB2 9 for Linux, UNIX, and Windows Database Administration** exam (Exam 731), is designed to test a candidate's knowledge of the new features and functions that are provided in DB2 9. Essentially, the upgrade exam provides certified DB2 Version 8.1 DBAs an accelerated approach for acquiring an equivalent Version 9 certification. This accelerated approach is outlined in Figure 1–3.

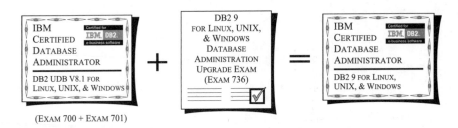

*Figure 1–3: The accelerated approach for acquiring IBM Certified Database .
Administrator – DB2 9 for Linux, UNIX, and Windows certification.*

IBM Certified Database Administrator – DB2 9 for z/OS

The *IBM Certified Database Administrator – DB2 9 for z/OS* certification is
intended for experienced DB2 9 users who possess the knowledge and skills
necessary to perform the day-to-day administration of DB2 9 instances and
databases residing on OS/390 platforms. In addition to being knowledgeable about
the fundamental concepts of DB2 9 and having significant hands-on experience as a
DB2 9 Database Administrator, individuals seeking this certification should:

- Know how to convert a logical database design to a physical database design.

- Know how to create, access, modify, and manage the various DB2 9 objects
  available.

- Know how to interpret the contents of system catalogs and directories.

- Possess a strong knowledge about the activities associated with enabling
  stored procedures.

- Be familiar with the different types of constraints available and know how
  each is used.

- Possess an in-depth knowledge of the Structured Query Language (SQL),
  Data Definition Language (DDL), Data Manipulation Language (DML), and
  Data Control Language (DCL) statements that are available with DB2 9.

- Know the difference between static and dynamic SQL.

- Know how to manage storage allocation with tools such as VSAM DELETE,
  VSAM DEFINE, and STOGROUP.

- Be familiar with DB2 Disaster Recovery.

- Possess a basic understanding of the different object statuses available (for example: RECP, GRECP, LPL, and RESTP).

- Be able to describe the effects of COMMIT frequency.

- Know how to capture and analyze Explain information.

- Know how to capture and analyze DB2 Trace data.

- Be able to determine the best characteristics for an index.

- Be able to describe the benefits of data sharing.

- Be able to describe the features that enable around-the-clock availability.

- Know how to use the REORG, BIND, REPAIR, UNLOAD, RUNSTATS, LOAD, and MODIFY utilities, including being able to restart a failed utility.

- Know how to use the DISPLAY, START, STOP, ALTER, RECOVER, and TERM UTILITY commands.

- Possess a basic understanding of the CHECK DATA/INDEX/LOB utility.

- Be able to demonstrate how DB2I is used.

- Be able to identify the functions of the Control Center.

- Possess a strong knowledge about the mechanisms DB2 9 uses to protect data and database objects against unauthorized access and/or modification.

Candidates who have either taken and passed the **DB2 V8.1 Family Fundamentals** exam (Exam 700) or acquired the IBM Certified Database Administrator – DB2 V8.1 for z/OS and OS/390 certification (by taking and passing Exams 700 and 702) must take and pass the **DB2 9 for z/OS Database Administration** exam (Exam 732) to acquire the IBM Certified Database Administrator – DB2 9 for z/OS certification. All other candidates must take and pass both the **DB2 9 Family Fundamentals** exam (Exam 730) and the **DB2 9 for z/OS Database Administration** exam (Exam 732). The roadmap for acquiring the IBM Certified Database Administrator–DB2 9 for z/OS certification can be seen in Figure 1–4.

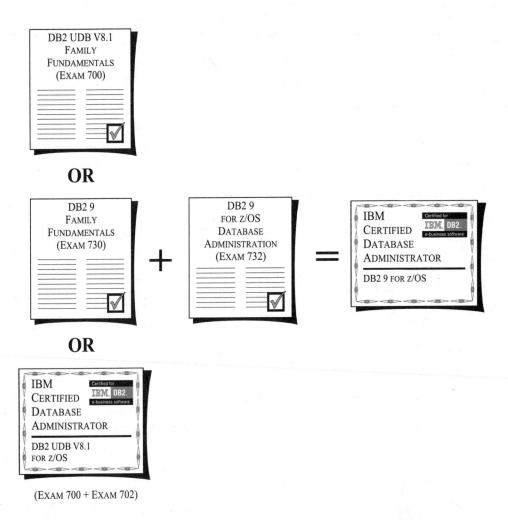

Figure 1–4: IBM Certified Database Administrator – DB2 9 for z/OS and OS/390 certification roadmap.

IBM Certified Application Developer – DB2 9 Family

The *IBM Certified Application Developer – DB2 9 Family* certification is intended for intermediate- to advanced-level application developers who possess the knowledge and skills necessary to create applications that interact with DB2 9 databases residing on supported platforms, including Linux, AIX, HP-UX, Sun Solaris, Windows, zSeries (z/OS, OS/390), and iSeries (AS/400). In addition to being knowledgeable about the fundamental concepts of DB2 9 and having strong skills in Embedded SQL programming, ODBC/CLI programming, JDBC programming, or SQLJ and .NET programming, individuals seeking this certification should:

- Be familiar with the naming conventions used to identify DB2 9 objects.

- Know what authorities and privileges are needed in order to access data with an application.

- Possess an in-depth knowledge of the complex database objects available with DB2 9.

- Possess an in-depth knowledge of the Structured Query Language (SQL), Data Definition Language (DDL), Data Manipulation Language (DML), and Data Control Language (DCL) statements that are available with DB2 9.

- Know the difference between static and dynamic SQL.

- Possess an in-depth knowledge of the SQL functions available.

- Know when to use Embedded SQL, CLI/ODBC, JDBC, SQLJ, PHP, Perl, Python, .NET, and XML.

- Be able to execute queries across multiple tables and/or views.

- Be able to identify the types of cursors available, as well as know when to use cursors in an application and what their scope will be.

- Be able to work with materialized query tables (MQTs).

- Be able to identify the results of XML parsing and XML serialization.

- Possess an in-depth knowledge of XML document encoding management.

- Know how XML schemas are validated.

- Be able to execute and identify the results of an XQuery expression.

- Be familiar with the SQL/XML functions that are available with DB2 9.

- Be able to establish a connection to a database within an Embedded SQL, CLI/ODBC, JDBC, SQLJ, or .NET application.

- Be able to analyze the contents of an SQL Communications Area (SQLCA) data structure.

- Be able to obtain and analyze CLI/ODBC diagnostic information.

- Be able to obtain and analyze JDBC trace, SQL exception, and JDBC error log information.

- Be able to obtain and analyze .NET diagnostic information.

- Be able to query tables across multiple databases, including federated databases.

- Be able to create triggers and identify their results.

- Know how to cast data types.

- Know when to use compound SQL, parameter markers, and distributed units of work.

- Know when to use user-defined functions (UDFs) and stored procedures.

- Know how to create user-defined functions (UDFs) and stored procedures.

- Be familiar with the DB2 Developer Workbench.

Candidates who have either taken and passed the **DB2 V8.1 Family Fundamentals** exam (Exam 700) or acquired the IBM Certified Application Developer – DB2 V8.1 Family certification (by taking and passing Exams 700 and 703) must take and pass the **DB2 9 Family Application Development** exam (Exam 733) to acquire the IBM Certified Application Developer – DB2 9 Family certification. All other candidates must take and pass both the **DB2 9 Family Fundamentals** exam (Exam 730) and the **DB2 9 Family Application Development** exam (Exam 733). The roadmap for acquiring the IBM Certified Application Developer – DB2 9 Family certification can be seen in Figure 1–5.

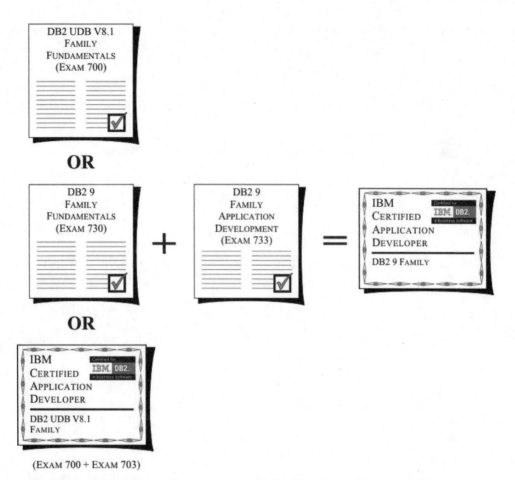

Figure 1–5: IBM Certified Application Developer – DB2 9 Family certification roadmap.

IBM Certified Advanced Database Administrator – DB2 9 for Linux, UNIX, and Windows

The *IBM Certified Advanced Database Administrator – DB2 9 for Linux, UNIX, and Windows* certification is intended for lead database administrators who possess extensive knowledge about DB2 9 and who have extensive experience using DB2 9 on one or more of the following supported platforms: Linux, AIX, HP-UX, Sun Solaris, and Windows. In addition to being knowledgeable about the more complex concepts of DB2 9 and having significant experience as a DB2 9 Database Administrator, individuals seeking this certification should:

- Know how to design, create, and manage SMS, DMS, and automatic storage table spaces.

- Know how to design, create, and manage buffer pools.

- Be able to take full advantage of intra-partition parallelism and inter-partition parallelism.

- Be able to design and configure federated database access.

- Know how to manage distributed units of work.

- Be able to develop a logging strategy.

- Be able to create constraints on and between table objects.

- Know how to perform database-level and table space-level backup, restore, and roll-forward recovery operations.

- Be able to use the advanced backup and recovery features available.

- Know how to implement a standby database using log shipping, replication, failover, and fault monitoring.

- Be able to identify and modify the DB2 Database Manager and database configuration file parameter values that have the greatest effect on performance.

- Possess a strong knowledge of query optimizer concepts.

- Be able to correctly analyze, isolate, and correct database performance problems.

- Know how to manage a large number of users and connections, including connections to host systems.

- Know how to create, configure, and manage a partitioned database spanning multiple servers.

- Be able to create and manage multidimensional clustered tables.

- Know when the creation of an index will improve database performance.

- Be able to identify and resolve database connection problems.

- Possess a strong knowledge about the external authentication mechanisms that DB2 9 uses to protect data and database objects against unauthorized access and/or modification.

- Know how to implement data encryption using Label-Based Access Control (LBAC).

To acquire the IBM Certified Advanced Database Administrator – DB2 9 for Linux, UNIX, and Windows certification, candidates must hold the IBM Certified Database Administrator – DB2 9 for Linux, UNIX, and Windows certification, and they must take and pass the **DB2 9 for Linux, UNIX, and Windows Advanced Database Administration** exam (Exam 734). The roadmap for acquiring the IBM Certified Advanced Database Administrator – DB2 9 for Linux, UNIX, and Windows certification can be seen in Figure 1–6.

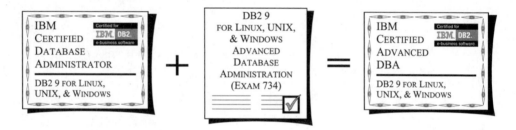

Figure 1–6: IBM Certified Advanced Database Administrator – DB2 9 for Linux, UNIX, and Windows certification roadmap.

IBM Certified Solution Designer – DB2 Data Warehouse Edition V9.1

The *IBM Certified Solution Designer – DB2 Data Warehouse Edition V9.1* certification is intended for individuals who are knowledgeable about the fundamental concepts of IBM's DB2 Data Warehouse Edition (DWE), Version 9.1. In addition to having the knowledge and skills necessary to design, develop, and support DB2 data warehouse environments using DB2 DWE, anyone seeking this certification should:

- Be able to explain how data warehouse and front-end analytics impact Business Intelligence Analytics architecture.

- Know the difference between a multidimensional database and a relational database warehouse.

- Know how metadata affects analytical queries.

- Be able to select appropriate front-end features based on criteria such as presentation needed, level of interactivity required, Web versus FAT client, static versus dynamic, and end user skill level.

- Know how to translate data warehouse-based analytics into schemas, aggregations, and SQL.

- Know when to use the DB2 Design Advisor versus the CV Advisor.

- Be able to explain how the DB2 Query Patroller fits into warehouse-based analytics.

- Be able to distinguish between logical and physical data models.

- Be able to describe the architecture of DB2 DWE in terms of its components.

- Be able to describe the architecture of DB2 DWE in terms of the three physical nodes used and where they are installed.

- Be able to identify the hardware needed to install DB2 Data Warehouse Edition.

- Know how to create a Data Design Project in the Project Engineer as a container for physical data modeling.

- Know how to reverse-engineer an existing DB2 schema (or a schema subset).

- Know how to design or modify a physical data model that describes a data warehouse (including constraints), as well as perform an impact analysis to identify all model-database dependencies.

- Be able to view the contents of database objects.

- Be able to identify candidate fact and dimension tables in a data warehouse.

- Be able to create cube models and cubes.

- Know how to define levels and hierarchies.

- Know how to define and create a dimension object.

- Know how to create materialized query tables (MQTs), as well as how to troubleshoot ineffective MQTs.

- Know how to perform Import and Export operations.

- Be able to create a data-mining project in the Project Explorer.

- Know how to formulate a data-mining task from a business problem, define a preprocessing function to prepare data for data mining, edit properties of mining operators, apply a visualizer operator to a data-mining flow, run a data-mining flow against a data warehouse, and view the results of any data-mining flow run.

- Be able to describe use cases for the SQL Warehousing Tool.

- Know how to create, set up, and navigate a Data Warehouse Project using the DB2 DWE Design Studio.

- Be able to describe the concepts of dataflows, subflows, and control flows, as well as build dataflows and subflows by adding, connecting, and defining properties of SQL Warehousing Dataflow Operators.

- Know why, when, and how to use a data station in a dataflow.

- Be able to prepare and deploy a Data Warehouse Project application to a test or production environment using the DB2 DWE Administration Console.

- Be able to set up and perform Query Workload Management.

- Know how to set up and perform Historical Analysis.

- Know how to administer, maintain, and tune the Query Patroller.

In order to acquire the IBM Certified Solution Designer – DB2 Data Warehouse Edition V9.1 certification, candidates must take and pass one exam: the **DB2 Data Warehouse Edition V9.1** exam (Exam 716). The roadmap for acquiring the IBM Certified Solution Designer – DB2 Data Warehouse Edition V9.1 certification is illustrated in Figure 1–7.

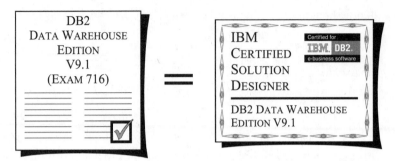

Figure 1–7: IBM Certified Solution Designer – DB2 Data Warehouse Edition
V9.1 certification roadmap.

IBM Certified Solution Developer – DB2 9.5 SQL Procedure Developer

The *IBM Certified Solution Developer – DB2 9.5 SQL Procedure Developer*
certification is intended for intermediate- to advanced-level developers who
possess the knowledge and skills necessary to create stored procedures, user-
defined functions, and triggers using DB2's SQL Procedural Language (SQL PL)
and tools such as IBM Data Studio. In addition to being knowledgeable about the
fundamental concepts of DB2 9.5 and having strong skills in DB2 SQL Procedural
Language programming, individuals seeking this certification should:

- Know how to code and use the DECLARE statement.

- Be able to code assignment statements.

- Know how to use SQL Control statements.

- Be familiar with SQL procedure error handling.

- Be able to identify when it is appropriate to use SQL procedures.

- Be able to use the CREATE PROCEDURE statement to create an SQL procedure.

- Know the proper structure of an SQL procedure body.

- Know how to return values and result sets from SQL procedures.

- Know how to code and use nested SQL procedures.

- Be able to test and deploy an SQL procedure.

- Be able to identify when it is appropriate to use SQL functions.

- Be able to use the CREATE FUNCTION statement to create an SQL function.

- Know the proper structure of a function body.

- Know how to return values and a table from an SQL function.

- Be able to test and deploy an SQL function.

- Be able to identify when it is appropriate to use a trigger.

- Be able to use the CREATE TRIGGER statement to construct a trigger.

- Be able to identify the actions of a trigger.

- Be able to test and deploy triggers.

- Know how to create and use Declared Global Temporary Tables.

- Be able to describe how to use system features.

- Be familiar with application development tools such as IBM Data Studio and the Explain facility.

In order to acquire the IBM Certified Solution Developer – DB2 DB2 9.5 SQL Procedure Developer certification, candidates must take and pass both the **DB2 9 Family Fundamentals** exam (Exam 730) and the **DB2 9.5 SQL Procedure Developer** exam (Exam 735). The roadmap for acquiring the IBM Certified Solution Developer – DB2 DB2 9.5 SQL Procedure Developer certification can be seen in Figure 1–8.

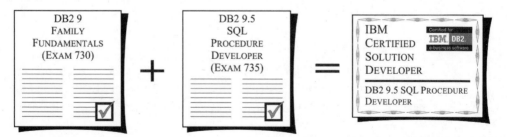

Figure 1–8: IBM Certified Solution Developer – DB2 9.5 SQL Procedure Developer certification roadmap.

The Certification Process

A close examination of the IBM certification roles available quickly reveals that, in order to obtain a particular DB2 9 certification, you must take and pass one or more exams that have been designed specifically for that certification role. (Each exam is a software-based exam that is neither platform- nor product-specific.) Thus, once you have chosen the certification role you wish to pursue and have familiarized yourself with the requirements for that particular role, the next step is to prepare for and take the appropriate certification exam or exams.

Preparing for the Certification Exams

If you have experience using DB2 9 in the context of the certification role you have chosen, you may already possess the skills and knowledge needed to pass the exam(s) required for that role. However, if your experience with DB2 9 is limited (or even if it is not), you can prepare for any of the certification exams available by taking advantage of the following resources:

- Formal Education

  IBM Learning Services offers courses that are designed to help you prepare for DB2 9 certification. A listing of the courses recommended for each certification exam can be found using the Certification Navigator tool provided on IBM's "Professional Certification Program from IBM" Web site (*www.ibm.com/certify*). Recommended courses can also be found at IBM's "DB2 Data Management" Web site (*www.ibm.com/software/data/education/learningcontent.html*). For more information on course schedules, locations, and pricing, contact IBM Learning Services or visit their Web site.

- Online Tutorials

  IBM offers a series of seven interactive online tutorials designed to prepare you for the DB2 9 Fundamentals exam (Exam 730). These tutorials can be found at *www-128.ibm.com/developerworks/offers/lp/db2cert/db2-cert730.html*.

  IBM also offers a series of interactive online tutorials designed to prepare you for the DB2 9 for Linux, UNIX, and Windows Database Administration exam (Exam 731) and the DB2 9 Family Application Development exam (Exam 733).

These tutorials can be found at *www-128.ibm.com/developerworks/offers/lp/ db2cert/db2-cert731.html* and *www-128.ibm.com/developerworks/offers/lp/ db2cert/db2-cert733.html*.

- Publications

  All the information you need to pass any of the available certification exams can be found in the documentation provided with DB2 9. A complete set of manuals comes with the product, and the manuals are accessible through the Information Center once you have installed the DB2 9 software. DB2 9 documentation can also be downloaded from IBM's Web site in both HTML and PDF formats. (The IBM Web site containing the DB2 9 documentation can be found at *www.ibm.com/software/data/db2/library*.)

  Self-study books (such as this one) that focus on one or more DB2 9 certification exams or roles are also available. Most of these books can be found at your local bookstore or can be ordered from many online book retailers. (A listing of possible reference materials for each certification exam can be found using the Certification Navigator tool provided on IBM's "Professional Certification Program from IBM" Web site [*http://www.ibm. com/certify*]).

  In addition to the DB2 9 product documentation, IBM often produces manuals, known as "RedBooks," that cover advanced DB2 9 topics (as well as other topics). These manuals are available as downloadable PDF files on IBM's RedBook Web site (*www.redbooks.ibm.com*). Or, if you prefer to have a bound hard copy, you can obtain one for a modest fee by following the appropriate links on the RedBook Web site. (The downloadable PDF files are available at no charge.)

  A list of possible reference materials for each certification exam can be found using the Certification Navigator tool provided on IBM's "Professional Certification Program from IBM" Web site (*www.ibm.com/certify*). Ordering information is often included with the listing.

- Exam Objectives

    Objectives that provide an overview of the basic topics covered on a particular certification exam can be found using the Certification Navigator tool provided on IBM's "Professional Certification Program from IBM" Web site (*www.ibm.com/certify*). Exam objectives for the DB2 9 for Linux, UNIX, and Windows Advanced Database Administration exam (Exam 734) can also be found in Appendix A of this book.

- Sample Questions and Exams

    Sample questions and sample exams allow you to become familiar with the format and wording used on the actual certification exams. They can help you decide whether you possess the knowledge needed to pass a particular exam. Sample questions, along with descriptive answers, are provided at the end of every chapter and in Appendix F of this book. Sample exams for each DB2 9 certification role available can be found using the Certification Exam tool provided on IBM's "Professional Certification Program from IBM" Web site (*www.ibm.com/software/data/education/cert/assessment.html*). There is a $10 charge for each exam taken.

It is important to note that the certification exams are designed to be rigorous. Very specific answers are expected for most exam questions. Because of this, and because the range of material covered on a certification exam is usually broader than the knowledge base of many DB2 9 professionals, you should take advantage of exam preparation resources if you want to guarantee your success in obtaining the certification(s) you desire.

Arranging to Take a Certification Exam

When you are confident that you are ready to take a specific DB2 9 certification exam, your next step is to contact an IBM-authorized testing vendor. The DB2 9 certification exams are administered by Pearson VUE, by Thompson Prometric, and, in rare cases, by IBM (for example, IBM administers the DB2 9 certification exams free of charge at some of the larger database conferences, such as the International DB2 User's Group North American conference). However, before you contact either testing vendor, you should visit their Web site (*www.vue.com/ibm* and *www.2test.com*, respectively) and use the navigation tools provided there to locate a testing center that is convenient for you. Once you have located a testing center, you can then contact the vendor and make arrangements to take the certification exam. (Contact information for the testing vendors can also be found on their respective Web sites; in some cases, you can schedule an exam online.)

You must make arrangements to take a certification exam at least 24 hours in advance, and when you contact the testing vendor, you should be ready to provide the following information:

- Your name (as you want it to appear on your certification certificate)

- An identification number (if you have taken an IBM certification exam before, this is the number assigned to you at that time; if not, the testing vendor will supply one)

- A telephone number where you can be reached

- A fax number

- The mailing address to which you want all certification correspondence, including your certification welcome package, to be sent

- Your billing address, if it is different from your mailing address

- Your email address

- The number that identifies the exam you wish to take (for example, Exam 734)

- The method of payment (credit card or check) you wish to use, along with any relevant payment information (such as credit card number and expiration date)

- Your company's name (if applicable)

- The testing center where you would like to take the certification exam

- The date when you would like to take the certification exam

Before you make arrangements to take a certification exam, you should have paper and pencil or pen handy so that you can write down the test applicant identification number the testing center will assign you. You will need this information when you arrive at the testing center to take the certification exam. (If time permits, you will be sent a letter of confirmation containing the number of the certification exam you have been scheduled to take, along with corresponding date, time, and location information; if you register within 48 hours of the scheduled testing date, you will not receive a letter.)

> If you have already taken one or more of the certification exams offered, you should make the testing vendor aware of this and ask them to assign you the same applicant identification number that was used before. This will allow the certification team at IBM to quickly recognize when you have met all the exam requirements for a particular certification role. (If you were assigned a unique applicant identification number each time you took an exam, you should go to the IBM Professional Certification Member Web site (*www.ibm.com/certify/members*) and select Member Services to combine all of your exam results under one ID.)

With the exception of the DB2 9 for Linux, UNIX, and Windows Database Administration Upgrade Exam (Exam 736), each certification exam costs $150 (in the United States). Scheduling procedures vary according to how you choose to pay for the exam. If you decide to pay by credit card, you can make arrangements to take the exam immediately after providing the testing vendor with the appropriate information. However, if you elect to pay by check, you will be required to wait until the check has been received and payment has been confirmed before you will be allowed to make arrangements to take the exam. (Thompson Prometric recommends that if you pay by check, you write your registration ID on the front and contact them seven business days after the check is mailed. By that time, they should have received and confirmed your payment, and you should be able to make arrangements to take the exam for which you have paid.)

If, for some reason, you need to reschedule or cancel your testing appointment after it is made, you must do so at least 24 hours before your scheduled test time. Otherwise, you will still be charged the price of the exam.

Taking an IBM Certification Exam

On the day you are scheduled to take a certification exam, you should arrive at the testing center at least 15 minutes before the scheduled start time to sign in. As part of the sign-in process, you will be asked to provide the applicant identification number you were assigned when you made arrangements to take the exam, as well as two forms of identification. One form of identification must feature a recent photograph, and the other must feature your signature. Examples of valid forms of identification include a driver's license (photograph) and a credit card (signature).

Once you are signed in, the exam administrator will instruct you to enter the testing area and select an available workstation. The exam administrator will then enter your name and identification number into the workstation you have chosen, provide you with a pencil and some paper, and instruct you to begin the exam when you are ready. At that point, the title screen of the IBM Certification Exam testing software should be displayed on the computer monitor in front of you. Figure 1–9 illustrates what this screen looks like.

TITLE SCREEN

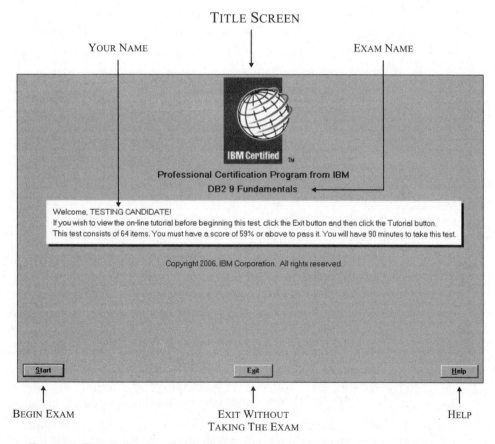

Figure 1–9: Title screen of the IBM Certification Exam testing software.

As you can see in Figure 1–9, the title screen of the IBM Certification Exam testing software consists of the IBM Certification Logo along with the title "Professional Certification Program from IBM," the name of the exam that is about to be administered (for example, the title screen shown in Figure 1–9 indicates that the DB2 9 Family Fundamentals exam is about to be administered), and a welcome message containing your name and some basic information on how to get started. Before proceeding, you should do the following:

- Verify that the exam you are about to take is indeed the exam you expected to take. If the name of the exam shown on the title screen is different from the name of the exam you had planned to take, bring this to the attention of the exam administrator immediately.

- Verify that your name is spelled correctly. The way your name appears in the welcome message shown on the title screen reflects how it has been stored in the IBM Certification database. This is how all correspondence to you will be addressed, and more importantly, this is how your name will appear on the certification credentials you will receive if you pass the exam.

In addition to telling you which exam is about to be administered, the title screen of the IBM Certification Exam testing software lets you know how many questions you can expect to see on the exam you are about to take, what kind of score you must receive in order to pass, and the time frame in which the exam must be completed. With one exception, each exam contains between 50 and 70 questions and is allotted 90 minutes for completion. The DB2 9 for Linux, UNIX, and Windows Database Administration Upgrade exam (Exam 736) contains 38 questions and is allotted 60 minutes for completion. Although each certification exam must be completed within a predefined time limit, you should never rush through an exam just because the "clock is running"; the time limits imposed are more than adequate for you to work through the exam at a relaxed, steady pace.

When you are ready, begin by selecting the "Start" push button located in the lower left corner of the screen (refer to Figure 1–9). If, instead, you would like a quick refresher course on how to use the IBM Certification Exam testing software, select the "Help" push button located in the lower right corner of the screen. (If you panic and decide you're not ready to take the exam, you can select the "Exit" push button located between the "Start" and "Help" push buttons at the bottom of the screen to get out of the testing software altogether, but you should talk with the exam administrator about your concerns before selecting this push button.)

If you plan to take a quick refresher course on how to use the IBM Certification Exam testing software, make sure you do so before you select the "Start" push button to begin the exam. Although help is available at any time, the clock does not start running until the "Start" push button is selected. By viewing help information before the clock is started, you avoid spending what could prove to be valuable testing time reading documentation instead of answering test questions.

Once the "Start" button on the title screen of the IBM Certification Exam testing software is selected, the clock will start running, and the first exam question will be presented in a question panel that looks something like the one shown in Figure 1–10.

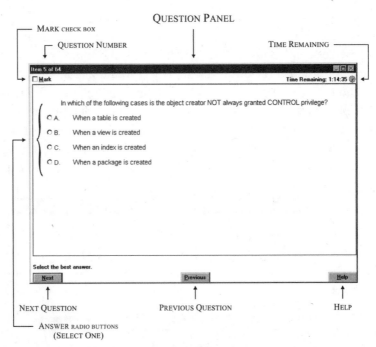

Figure 1–10: Typical question panel of the IBM Certification Exam testing software.

Aside from the question itself, one of the first things you may notice when you examine the question panel of the IBM Certification Exam testing software is the question number displayed in the top left corner of the screen. If you answer each question in the order they are presented, this portion of the screen can act as a progress indicator because the current question number is displayed along with the total number of questions contained in the exam.

Immediately below the question number, you will find a special check box that is referred to as the "Mark" check box. If you would like to skip the current question for now and come back to it later, or if you're uncertain about the answer(s) you have chosen and would like to look at this question again after you have completed the rest of the exam, you should mark this check box (by placing the mouse pointer over it and pressing the left mouse button). When every question has been viewed once, you will be given the opportunity to review just the marked questions again. At that time, you can answer any unanswered questions remaining and reevaluate any answers about which you have some concerns.

Another important feature found on the question panel is the "Time Remaining" information displayed in the top right corner of the screen. This area of the question panel provides continuous feedback on the amount of time you have available in which to finish and review the exam. If you would like to see more detailed information, such as the current wall-clock time and the time frame within which you are expected to complete the exam, you can view that information by selecting the clock icon located just to the right of the "Time Remaining" information. When you select this icon (by placing the mouse pointer over it and pressing the left mouse button), a dialog similar to the one shown in Figure 1–11 is displayed.

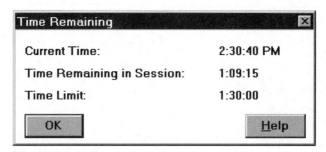

Figure 1–11: Time Remaining dialog.

The most important part of the question panel, however, is the exam question and the corresponding list of possible answers provided. Take time to read each question carefully. When you have located the correct answer in the list provided, mark it by selecting the answer radio-button positioned just to the left of the answer text (by placing the mouse pointer over the desired answer radio-button and pressing the left mouse button). Once you have selected an answer for the question being displayed (or marked it with the "Mark" check box), you can move to the next question by selecting the "Next" push button, which is located in the lower left corner of the screen (refer to Figure 1–10).

If at any time you would like to return to the previous question, you can do so by pressing the "Previous" push button, located at the bottom of the screen, just to the right of the "Next" push button. If you would like help on how to use the IBM Certification Exam testing software, select the "Help" push button located in the lower right corner of the screen. It is important to note that although the "Next" and "Previous" push buttons can be used to navigate through the questions, the navigation process itself is not cyclic in nature—that is, when you are on the first question, you cannot go to the last question by selecting the "Previous" push button (in fact, the "Previous" push button will not be displayed if you are on the first question). Likewise, when you are on the last question, you cannot go to the first question simply by selecting the "Next" push button. However, there is a way to navigate quickly to a specific question from the item review panel, which we will look at shortly.

Although in most cases only one answer in the list provided is the correct answer to the question shown, there are times when multiple answers are valid. On those occasions, the answer radio-buttons will be replaced with answer check boxes, and the question will be worded in such a way that you will know how many answers are expected. An example of such a question can be seen in Figure 1–12.

These types of questions are answered by selecting the answer check box positioned just to the left of the text *for every correct answer found*. (Again, do this by placing the mouse pointer over each desired answer check box and pressing the left mouse button.)

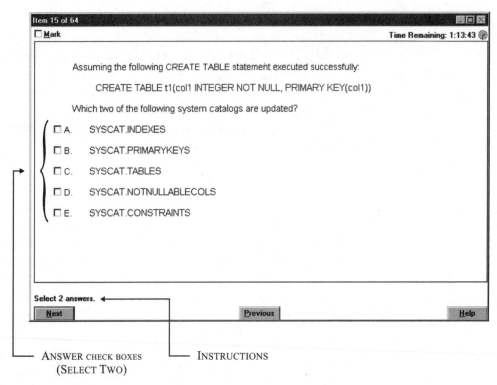

Figure 1–12: Question panel for questions expecting multiple answers.

On occasion, an illustration or the output from some diagnostic tool will accompany a question. You will be required to view that illustration or output (referred to as an exhibit) before you can successfully answer the question presented. On those occasions, a message instructing you to display the exhibit for the question will precede the actual test question, and a special push button called the "Exhibit" push button will be positioned at the bottom of the screen between the "Previous" push button and the "Help" push button. An example of such a question can be seen in Figure 1–13.

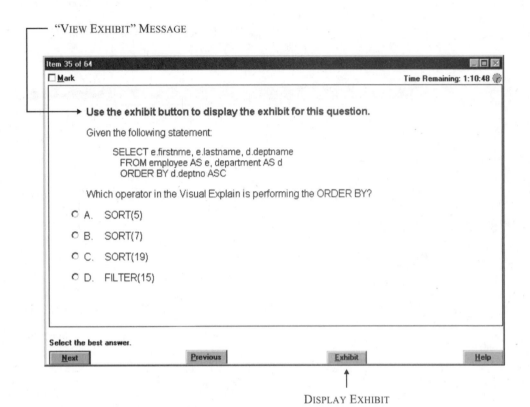

"VIEW EXHIBIT" MESSAGE

Figure 1–13: Question panel for questions that contain an exhibit.

To view the exhibit associated with such a question, simply select the "Exhibit" push button located at the bottom of the screen. This action will cause the corresponding exhibit panel to be displayed. (A sample exhibit panel can be seen in Figure 1–14.)

Exhibit panels are relatively simple. In fact, once an exhibit panel is displayed, there are only two things you can do with it: You can close it by selecting the "Close" push button located at the bottom of the screen, or you can tile it (i.e., make it share screen real estate) with its corresponding question panel by selecting the "Tile" push button, which is located beside the "Close" push button. Aside from having to view the exhibit provided, the process used to answer questions that have exhibits is no different from the process used to answer questions that do not.

EXHIBIT PANEL

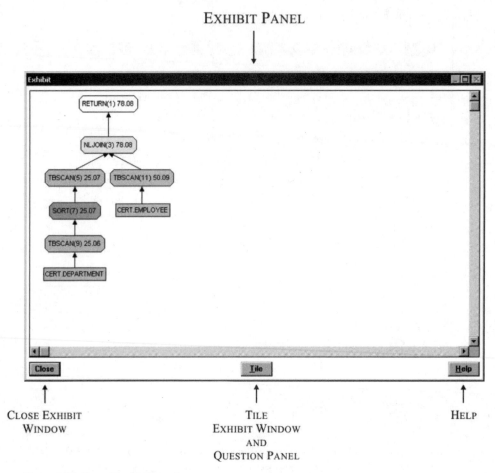

CLOSE EXHIBIT
WINDOW

TILE
EXHIBIT WINDOW
AND
QUESTION PANEL

HELP

Figure 1–14: Sample exhibit panel.

When you have viewed every exam question available (by selecting the "Next" push button on every question panel shown), an item review panel that looks something like the panel shown in Figure 1–15 will be displayed.

ITEM (QUESTION) REVIEW PANEL

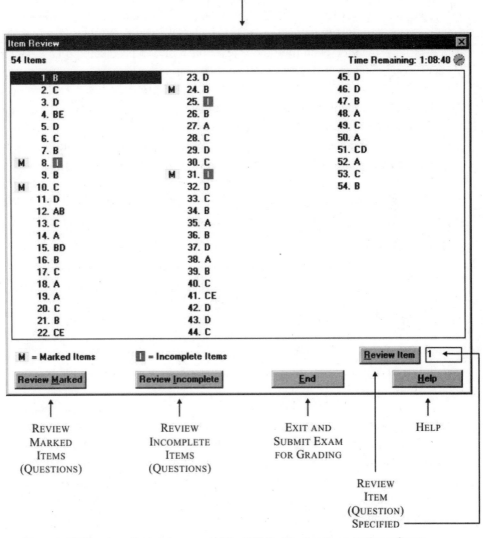

Figure 1–15: Item (question) review panel of the IBM Certification Exam testing software.

As you can see in Figure 1–15, the item review panel contains a numerical listing of the questions that make up the certification exam you are taking, along with the answers you have provided for each. Questions that you marked (by selecting the "Mark" check box) are preceded by the letter "M," and questions that you skipped or did not provide the correct number of answers for are assigned the answer "I" to indicate they are incomplete. By selecting the "Review Marked" push button located in the lower left corner of the screen (refer to Figure 1–15), you can quickly go back through just the questions that have been marked. When reviewing marked items in this manner, each time the "Next" push button is selected on a question panel, you are taken to the next marked question in the list until eventually you are returned to the item review panel. Likewise, by selecting the "Review Incomplete" push button located just to the right of the "Review Marked" push button, you can go back through just the questions that have been identified as being incomplete. (Navigation works the same as when the "Review Marked" push button is selected.) If, instead, you would like to review a specific question, you can do so by highlighting that question's number or typing that question's number in the entry field provided just to the right of the "Review Item" push button (which is located just above the "Help" push button in the lower right corner of the screen) and selecting the "Review Item" push button.

••

If you elect to use the "Review Item" push button to review a particular question, the only way you can return to the item review screen is by selecting the "Next" push button found on that question panel and every subsequent question panel presented until no more question panels exist.

••

One of the first things you should do when the item review panel is displayed is resolve any incomplete items found. (When the exam is graded, each incomplete item found is marked incorrect, and points are deducted from your final score.) Then, if time permits, you should go back and review the questions that you marked. It is important to note that when you finish reviewing a marked question, you should unmark it (by placing the mouse pointer over the "Mark" check box and pressing the left mouse button) before going on to the next marked question or returning to the item review panel. This will make it easier for you to keep track of which questions have been reviewed and which have not.

As soon as every incomplete item found has been resolved, the "Review Incomplete" push button is automatically removed from the item review panel. Likewise, when there are no more marked questions, the "Review Marked" push button is removed from the item review panel. Thus, when every incomplete and marked item found has been resolved, the item review panel will look similar to the one shown in Figure 1–16.

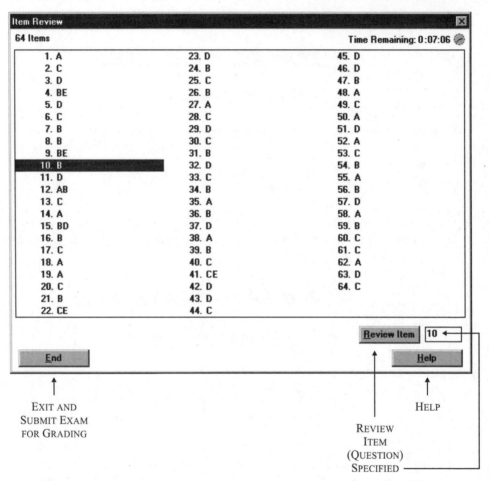

Figure 1–16: Item (question) review panel with all incomplete and marked items (questions) resolved.

Keep in mind that even when the "Review Incomplete" and "Review Marked" push buttons are no longer available, you can still go back and review a specific question by highlighting that question's number or typing that question's number in the entry field provided and selecting the "Review Item" push button (refer to Figure 1–16).

As soon as you feel comfortable with the answers you have provided, you can end the exam and submit it for grading by selecting the "End" push button, which should now be located in the lower left corner of the item review panel. After you select this push button (by placing the mouse pointer over it and pressing the left mouse button), a dialog similar to the one shown in Figure 1–17 should be displayed.

Figure 1–17: End exam session confirmation dialog.

If you select the "End" push button on the item review panel before all incomplete items found have been resolved, a dialog similar to the one shown in Figure 1–18 will be displayed instead.

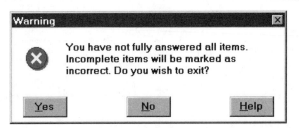

Figure 1–18: Ending exam with incomplete items warning dialog.

Both of these dialogs give you the opportunity to confirm your decision to end the exam and submit it for grading or to reconsider and continue resolving and/or reviewing exam questions. If you wish to do the former, you should select the "OK" or the "Yes" push button when one of these dialogs is presented; if you wish to do the latter, you should select the "Cancel" or "No" push button, in which case you will be returned to the item review panel. Keep in mind that if you select the "Yes" push button when the dialog shown in Figure 1–18 is displayed, all incomplete items found will be marked as being wrong, which will detract from your final score.

As soon as you confirm that you do indeed wish to end the exam, the IBM
Certification Exam testing software will evaluate your answers and produce a
score report that indicates whether you passed the exam. This report will then be
displayed on an exam results panel that looks something like the panel shown in
Figure 1–19, and a corresponding hard copy (printout) will be generated.

EXAM RESULTS PANEL

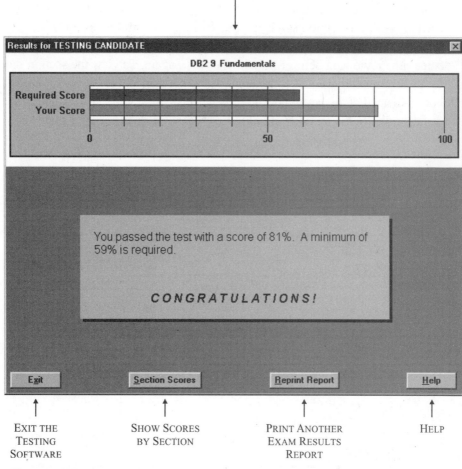

Figure 1–19: Exam results panel of the IBM Certification Exam testing software.

As you can see in Figure 1–19, the exam results panel shows the required score
along with your actual score in a horizontal percentage bar graph. Directly below

this graph is a message that contains the percentage score you received, along with the percentage score needed to pass the exam. If you received a passing score, this message will end with the word "Congratulations!" However, if you received a score that is below the score needed to pass, the message you see will begin with the words "You did not pass the test," and your score will follow.

Each certification exam is broken into sections, and regardless of whether you pass or fail, you should take a few moments to review the score you received for each section. This information can help you evaluate your strengths and weaknesses; if you failed to pass the exam, it can help you identify the areas you should spend some time reviewing before you take the exam again. To view the section scores for the exam you have just completed, you simply select the "Section Scores" push button located at the bottom of the screen. This action will cause a section scores panel similar to the one shown in Figure 1–20 to be displayed.

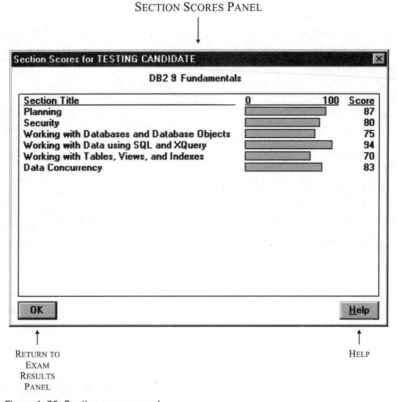

Figure 1–20: Section scores panel.

When you have finished reviewing your section scores, you may return to the exam results panel by selecting the "OK" push button located at the bottom left corner of the screen. From there, you can exit the IBM Certification Exam testing software by selecting the "Exit" push button, which is also located at the bottom left corner of the screen.

Shortly after you take a certification exam (usually within five working days), the testing vendor sends your results, along with your demographic data (e.g., name, address, phone number) to the IBM Certification Group for processing. If you passed the exam, you will receive credit toward the certification role the exam was designed for, and if the exam you took completes the requirements that have been outlined for a particular certification role, you will receive an email (at the email address you provided during registration) containing a copy of the IBM Certification Agreement and a welcome package that includes a certificate suitable for framing (in the form of a PDF file), camera-ready artwork of the IBM certification logo, and guidelines for using the "IBM Certified" mark. (If this email cannot be delivered, the welcome package will be sent to you via regular mail.) You can also receive a printed certificate, along with a wallet-sized certificate, via regular mail by going to the Web site referenced in the email you receive and requesting it—you will be asked to provide your Fulfillment ID and Validation Number (also provided in the email) as verification that you have met the requirements for certification.

Upon receipt of the welcome package, you are officially certified and may begin using the IBM Professional Certification title and trademark. (You should receive the IBM Certification Agreement and welcome package within four to six weeks after IBM processes the exam results.) However, if you failed to pass the exam and you still wish to become certified, you must make arrangements to retake the exam (including paying the testing fee again). There are no restrictions on the number of times you can take a particular certification exam, but you may not take the same certification exam more than two times within a 30-day period.

CHAPTER 2

Database Design

Fourteen percent (14%) of the DB2 9 for Linux, UNIX, and Windows Advanced Database Administration exam (Exam 734) is designed to test your ability to create a DB2 database, as well as to test your knowledge of the methods used to create and manage table spaces, buffer pools, and federated databases. The questions that make up this portion of the exam are intended to evaluate the following:

- Your ability to create a DB2 database

- Your ability to design, create, and manage buffer pools

- Your knowledge of the characteristics of SMS, DMS, and Automatic Storage table spaces

- Your ability to design, create, and manage table spaces

- Your ability to design and configure a federated database server

This chapter is designed to introduce you to instances and databases, to walk you through the database creation process in both partitioned and non-partitioned environments, and to provide you with a detailed overview of buffer pools and table spaces. This chapter is also designed to introduce you to the concept of federated databases, as well as show you how to configure federated database access.

Servers, Instances, and Databases

DB2 sees the world as a hierarchy of objects. Workstations (or servers) on which DB2 has been installed occupy the highest level of this hierarchy. Instances occupy the second level in the hierarchy and are responsible for managing system resources and databases that fall under their control. (When any edition of DB2 is installed on a workstation, program files for a background process known as the DB2 Database Manager (or DB2 system controller) are physically copied to a specific location on that workstation, and by default, a DB2 instance is created.) Databases make up the third level in the hierarchy and are responsible for managing the storage, modification, and retrieval of data. Each database has its own environment (controlled by a set of configuration parameters), as well as its own set of grantable authorities and privileges to govern how users interact with the data and database objects it controls. From a user's perspective, a database is a collection of tables (preferably related in some way) that are used to store data. However, from a database administrator's viewpoint, a DB2 database is much more; a database is an entity composed of many physical and logical components. Some of these components help determine how data is organized, and others determine how and where data is physically stored.

Creating a Non-partitioned DB2 Database

There are two ways to create a non-partitioned DB2 9.x database: by using the Create Database Wizard or by using the CREATE DATABASE command. Because the Create Database Wizard is essentially a graphical user interface (GUI) for the CREATE DATABASE command, we will look at the command method first.

In its simplest form, the syntax for the CREATE DATABASE command is:

```
CREATE [DATABASE | DB] [DatabaseName]
```

where:

DatabaseName   Identifies a unique name that is to be assigned to the database once it is created.

The only value you must provide when executing this command is a name to assign to the new database. This name:

- can consist of only the characters **a** through **z**, **A** through **Z**, **0** through **9**, @, #, $, and _ (underscore);

- cannot begin with a number;

- cannot begin with the letter sequences "SYS," "DBM," or "IBM";

- cannot exceed eight characters in length; and

- cannot be the same as the name already assigned to another database within the same instance.

A much more complex form of the CREATE DATABASE command that provides you with a great deal more control over database parameters is available, and we will examine it shortly. But for now, let's look at what happens when this form of the CREATE DATABASE command is executed.

What Happens When a DB2 9.x Database Is Created

Regardless of how the process is initiated, whenever a new DB2 9.x database is created, the following tasks are performed, in the order shown:

1. All directories and subdirectories needed are created in the appropriate location.

   Information about every DB2 database is stored in a special hierarchical directory tree. Where this directory tree is actually created is determined by information provided with the CREATE DATABASE command—if no location information is specified, this directory tree is created in the location identified by the *dftdbpath* DB2 Database Manager configuration parameter associated with the instance under which the database is being created. The root directory of this hierarchical tree is assigned the name of the instance with which the database is associated. This directory will contain a subdirectory that has been assigned a name corresponding to the partition's node. If the database is a partitioned database, this directory will be named NODExxxx, where xxxx is the unique number that has been assigned to the partition; if the database is a non-partitioned database, this directory will always be named NODE0000. The node-name directory, in turn, will contain one subdirectory for each database that has been created on that path, along with one subdirectory that includes the table space containers that are used to hold the database's data (if you do not explicitly define the containers when you create the database).

The name assigned to the subdirectory that holds the containers used to house the database's data is the same as that specified for the database; the name assigned to the subdirectory that contains the base files for the database corresponds to the database token that is assigned to the database during the creation process (the subdirectory for the first database created will be named SQL00001, the subdirectory for the second database will be named SQL00002, and so on). Figure 2–1 illustrates how this directory hierarchy typically looks in a non-partitioned database environment.

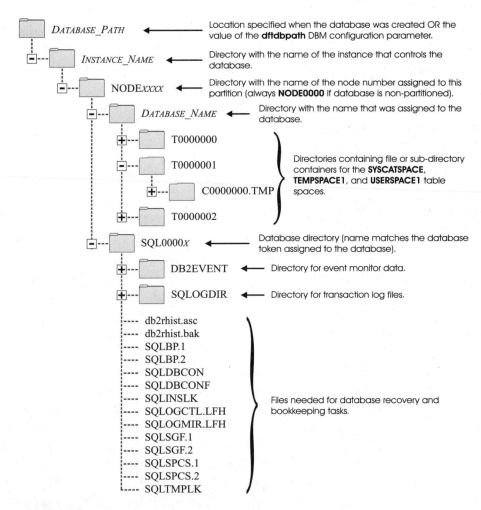

Figure 2–1: Typical directory hierarchy tree for a non-partitioned database.

Never attempt to modify this directory structure or any of the files stored in it. Such actions could destroy one or more databases or make them unusable.

2. Files needed for management, monitoring, and database recovery are created.

After the subdirectory that was assigned the name of the database's token is created, the following files are created in it:

db2rhist.asc This file contains historical information about backup operations, restore operations, table load operations, table reorganization operations, table space alterations, and similar database changes (in other words, the recovery history file).

db2rhist.bak This file is a backup copy of db2rhist.asc.

SQLBP.1 This file contains buffer pool information.

SQLBP.2 This file is a backup copy of SQLBP.1.

SQLDBCON This file contains database configuration information.

SQLDBCONF This file is a backup copy of SQLDBCON.

SQLINSLK This file contains information that is used to ensure that the database is assigned to only one DB2 instance.

SQLOGCTL.LFH This file contains information about active transaction log files. Recovery operations use information stored in this file to determine how far back in the logs to begin the recovery process.

SQLOGMIR.LFH This file is a mirrored copy of SQLOGCTL.LFH.

SQLSGF.1 This file contains storage path information associated with automatic storage.

SQLSGF.2 This file is a backup copy of SQLSGF.1.

SQLSPCS.1 This file contains table space information.

SQLSPCS.2 This file is a backup copy of SQLSPCS.1.

SQLTMPLK This file contains information about temporary table spaces.

Two subdirectories named DB2EVENT and SQLOGDIR are also created; a detailed deadlocks event monitor is created and stored in the DB2EVENT subdirectory, and three files named S0000000.LOG, S0000001.LOG, and S0000002.LOG are created and stored in the SQLOGDIR subdirectory. These three files are used to store transaction log records as SQL operations are performed against the database.

3. A buffer pool is created for the database.

During the database creation process, a buffer pool is created and assigned the name IBMDEFAULTBP. (A buffer pool is an area of main memory that has been allocated to DB2 for the purpose of caching table and index data pages as they are read from disk or modified. By default, on Linux and UNIX platforms, this buffer pool is 1,000 4K (kilobyte) pages in size; on Windows platforms, this buffer pool is 250 4K pages in size. The actual memory used by this buffer pool (and for that matter, by any other buffer pools that may exist) is allocated when the database is activated and freed when the database is deactivated. A database can be explicitly activated by executing the ACTIVATE DATABASE command or implicitly activated when a connection to the database is established.

4. One regular table space, one large table space, and one system temporary table space are created.

Table spaces are used to control where data is physically stored and to provide a layer of abstraction between database objects (such as tables, indexes, and views) and one or more containers (i.e., directories, files, or raw devices) in which the object's data actually resides. Immediately after the buffer pool IBMDEFAULTBP is created, three table spaces are created and associated with this buffer pool. These three table spaces are as follows:

- A regular table space named SYSCATSPACE, which is used to store the system catalog tables and views associated with the database

- A large table space named USERSPACE1, which is used to store all user-defined objects (tables, indexes, and so on) along with user data, index data, LOB data, and long value data

- A system temporary table space named TEMPSPACE1, which is used as a temporary storage area for operations such as sorting data, reorganizing tables, and creating indexes

Unless otherwise specified, SYSCATSPACE and USERSPACE1 will be DMS FILE table spaces, and TEMPSPACE1 will be an SMS table space. (The database itself will use automatic storage, so these table spaces will have the characteristics of automatic storage table spaces.) Specific characteristics for each of these table spaces can be provided as input to the CREATE DATABASE command or the Create Database Wizard.

5. The system catalog tables and views are created.

After the table space SYSCATSPACE is created, a special set of tables, known as the system catalog tables, is constructed within that table space. DB2 uses the system catalog tables to keep track of such information as database object definitions, database object dependencies, database object privileges, column data types, table constraints, and object relationships. A set of system catalog views is created along with the system catalog tables, and these views are typically used when accessing data stored in the system catalog tables. The system catalog tables and views cannot be modified with SQL DML statements (however, their contents can be viewed). Instead, they are modified by DB2 whenever one of the following events occurs:

- A database object (such as a table, view, or index) is created, altered, or dropped.

- Authorizations or privileges are granted or revoked.

- Statistical information is collected for a table.

- Packages are bound to the database.

In most cases, the complete characteristics of a database object are stored in one or more system catalog tables when the object is created. However, in some cases, such as when triggers and constraints are defined, the actual SQL used to create the object is stored instead.

6. The database is cataloged in the system and local database directory (a system or local database directory is created first if it does not already exist).

   DB2 uses a set of special files to keep track of where databases are stored and to provide access to those databases. Because the information stored in these files is used in the way that the information stored in an office-building directory is used, the files are referred to as directory files. Whenever a database is created, these directories are updated with the database's name and alias. (If these directories do not exist, they are created automatically and populated with the appropriate information.) If specified, a comment and/or code set value is also stored in the system and local database directory. On Linux or UNIX, the system database directory is stored in the file **sqldbdir**, which is located in the **sqllib** directory under your home directory or under the directory where DB2 was installed. On Windows, the system database directory is located in the instance directory.

7. The database configuration file for the database is initialized.

   Some of the parameters in the database configuration file (such as code set, territory, and collating sequence) will be set using values that were specified as input for the CREATE DATABASE command or the Create Database Wizard; others are assigned system default values.

8. Four schemas are created.

   Schemas are objects that are used to logically classify and group other objects in the database. Once the system catalog tables and views are created, the following schemas are created: SYSIBM, SYSCAT, SYSSTAT, and SYSFUN. A special user named SYSIBM is made the owner of each.

9. A set of utility programs is bound to the database.

   Before some of the DB2 utilities available can work with a database, the packages needed to run those utilities must be created. Such packages are created by binding a set of predefined DB2 bind files to the database. The bind files used are stored in the utilities bind list file *db2ubind.lst*.

10. Authorities and privileges are granted to the appropriate users.

To connect to and work with a particular database, a user must have the authorities and privileges needed to use that database. Therefore, unless otherwise specified, whenever a new database is created, the following authorities and privileges are granted:

- Database Administrator (DBADM) authority as well as CONNECT, CREATETAB, BINDADD, CREATE_NOT_FENCED, IMPLICIT_SCHEMA, and LOAD privileges are granted to the user who created the database.

- USE privilege on the table space USERSPACE1 is granted to the group PUBLIC.

- CONNECT, CREATETAB, BINDADD, and IMPLICIT_SCHEMA privileges are granted to the group PUBLIC.

- SELECT privilege on each system catalog table and view is granted to the group PUBLIC.

- EXECUTE privilege on all procedures found in the SYSIBM schema is granted to the group PUBLIC.

- EXECUTE WITH GRANT privilege on all functions found in the SYSFUN schema is granted to the group PUBLIC.

- BIND and EXECUTE privileges for each successfully bound utility are granted to the group PUBLIC.

11. Several autonomic features are enabled.

To help make management easy, whenever a new database is created, the following autonomic features are enabled:

- Automatic Maintenance (database backups, table and index reorganization, data access optimization, and statistics profiling)

- Self-Tuning Memory Manager (package cache, locking memory, sort memory, database shared memory, and buffer pool memory)

- Utility throttling

- The Health Monitor

12. The Configuration Advisor is launched.

The Configuration Advisor is a tool designed to help you tune performance and balance memory requirements for a database by suggesting which configuration parameters to modify based on information you provide about the database. In DB2 9.x, the Configuration Advisor is automatically invoked whenever you create a database, unless the default behavior is changed by assigning the value NO to the DB2_ENABLE_AUTOCONFIG_DEFAULT registry variable.

The Complete CREATE DATABASE Command

When the simplest form of the CREATE DATABASE command is executed, the characteristics of the database created, such as the code page and storage method used, are determined by several predefined defaults. If you wish to change any of the default characteristics, you must specify one or more options available when executing the CREATE DATABASE command. The complete syntax for this command is:

```
CREATE [DATABASE | DB] [DatabaseName] <AT DBPARTITIONNUM>

or

CREATE [DATABASE | DB] [DatabaseName]
<AUTOMATIC STORAGE [YES | NO]>
<ON [StoragePath ,...] <DBPATH [DBPath]>>
<ALIAS [Alias]>
<USING CODESET [CodeSet] TERRITORY [Territory]>
<COLLATE USING [CollateType]>
<PAGESIZE [4096 | Pagesize <K>]>
<NUMSEGS [NumSegments]>
<DFT_EXTENT_SZ [DefaultExtSize]>
<RESTRICTIVE>
<CATALOG TABLESPACE [TS_Definition]>
<USER TABLESPACE [TS_Definition]>
<TEMPORARY TABLESPACE [TS_Definition]>
<WITH "[Description]">
<AUTOCONFIGURE <USING [Keyword] [Value] ,...>
<APPLY [DB ONLY | DB AND DBM | NONE>>
```

where:

DatabaseName   Identifies the unique name that is to be assigned to the database to be created.

StoragePath	If AUTOMATIC STORAGE YES is specified (the default), identifies one or more storage paths that are to be used to hold table space containers used by automatic storage. Otherwise, identifies the location (drive or directory) where the directory hierarchy and files associated with the database to be created are to be physically stored.
DBPath	If AUTOMATIC STORAGE YES is specified (the default), identifies the location (drive or directory) where the directory hierarchy and metadata files associated with the database to be created are to be physically stored. (If this parameter is not specified, and automatic storage is used, the metadata files will be stored in the first storage path specified in the *StoragePath* parameter.)
Alias	Identifies the alias to be assigned to the database to be created.
CodeSet	Identifies the code set to be used for storing data in the database to be created. (In a DB2 9.x database, each single-byte character is represented internally as a unique number between 0 and 255. This number is referred to as the code point of the character; the assignments of code points to every character in a particular character set are called the code page; and the International Organization for Standardization term for a code page is code set.)
Territory	Identifies the territory to be used for storing data in the database to be created.
CollateType	Specifies the collating sequence (i.e., the sequence in which characters are ordered for the purpose of sorting, merging, and making comparisons) that is to be used by the database to be created. The following values are valid for this parameter: COMPATABILITY, IDENTITY, IDENTITY_16BIT, UCA400_NO, UCA400_LSK, UCA400_LTH, NLSCHAR, and SYSTEM.
PageSize	Specifies the page size of the default buffer pool and the three default table spaces (SYSCATSPACE, TEMPSPACE1, USERSPACE1) that are created when the database is created. This also specifies the default page size to be used whenever a buffer pool or table space is created and no page size is specified during the creation process. The following values are valid for this parameter: 4,096;

8,192; 16,384 or 32,768 bytes—if the suffix K (for kilobytes) is provided, this parameter must be set to 4, 8, 16, or 32.

NumSegments   Specifies the number of directories (table space containers) that will be created and used to store data for any default SMS table spaces created. This parameter does not affect automatic storage table spaces, DMS table spaces, any SMS table spaces with explicit creation characteristics that are created when the database is created, or any SMS table spaces explicitly created after the database is created.

DefaultExtSize   Specifies the default extent size to be used whenever a table space is created and no extent size is specified during the creation process.

Description   A comment used to describe the database entry that will be made in the database directory for the database to be created. The description must be enclosed by double quotation marks.

Keyword   One or more keywords recognized by the AUTOCONFIGURE command. Valid values include mem_percent, workload_type, num_stmts, tpm, admin_priority, is_populated, num_local_apps, num_remote_apps, isolation, and bp_resizable. Refer to the DB2 9 Command Reference for more information on how the AUTOCONFIGURE command is used.

Value   Identifies the value that is to be associated with the *Keyword* specified.

TS_Definition   Specifies the definition that is to be used to create the table space that will be used to hold the system catalog tables (SYSCATSPACE), user-defined objects (USERSPACE1), and/or temporary objects (TEMPSPACE1).

The syntax used to define a system managed (SMS) table space is:

```
MANAGED BY SYSTEM
USING ('[Container]' ,...)
<EXTENTSIZE [ExtentSize]>
<PREFETCHSIZE [PrefetchSize]>
<OVERHEAD [Overhead]>
<TRANSFERRATE [TransferRate]>
```

The syntax used to define a database managed (DMS) table space is:

```
MANAGED BY DATABASE
USING ([FILE | DEVICE] '[Container]' NumberOfPages ,...)
<EXTENTSIZE [ExtentSize]>
<PREFETCHSIZE [PrefetchSize]>
<OVERHEAD [Overhead]>
<TRANSFERRATE [TransferRate]>
<AUTORESIZE [NO | YES]>
<INCREASESIZE [IncreaseSize] <PERCENT | K | M | G>>
<MAXSIZE [NONE | MaxSize <K | M | G>]>
```

And the syntax used to define an automatic storage table space is:

```
MANAGED BY AUTOMATIC STORAGE
<EXTENTSIZE [ExtentSize]>
<PREFETCHSIZE [PrefetchSize]>
<OVERHEAD [Overhead]>
<TRANSFERRATE [TransferRate]>
<AUTORESIZE [NO | YES]>
<INITIALSIZE [InitialSize] <K | M | G>>
<INCREASESIZE [IncreaseSize] <PERCENT | K | M | G>>
<MAXSIZE [NONE | MaxSize <K | M | G>]>
```

where:

Container Identifies one or more containers to be used to store data that will be assigned to the table space specified. For SMS table spaces, each container specified must identify a valid directory; for DMS FILE containers, each container specified must identify a valid file; for DMS DEVICE containers, each container specified must identify an existing device.

NumberOfPages Specifies the number of pages to be used by the table space container.

ExtentSize Specifies the number of pages of data that will be written in a round-robin fashion to each table space container used.

PrefetchSize Specifies the number of pages of data that will be read from the specified table space when data prefetching is performed.

Overhead	Identifies the input/output (I/O) controller overhead and disk-seek latency time (in number of milliseconds) associated with the containers that belong to the specified table space.
TransferRate	Identifies the time, in milliseconds, that it takes to read one page of data from a table space container and store it in memory.
InitialSize	Specifies the initial size that an automatic storage table space should be.
IncreaseSize	Specifies the amount by which a table space that has been enabled for automatic resizing will be increased when the table space becomes full and a request for space is made.
MaxSize	Specifies the maximum size to which a table space that has been enabled for automatic resizing can be increased to.

If the RESTRICTIVE clause is specified, the RESTRICT_ACCESS database configuration parameter for the database being created will be set to YES, and no privileges will be granted to the group PUBLIC.

Suppose you wanted to create a database that has the following characteristics:

- Will be physically located on drive E:

- Will not use automatic storage

- Will be assigned the name SAMPLEDB

- Will recognize the United States/Canada code set (The code page, along with the territory, is used to convert alphanumeric data to binary data that is stored in the database.)

- Will use a collating sequence that is based on the territory used (which in this case is United States/Canada)

- Will not automatically be accessible to the group PUBLIC

- Will store the system catalog in a DMS table space that uses the file SYSCATSPACE.DAT as its container (This file is stored on drive E: and is capable of holding up to 5,000 pages that are 4K in size.)

To construct such a database, you would execute a CREATE DATABASE command that looks something like this:

```
CREATE DATABASE sampledb
AUTOMATIC STORAGE NO
ON E:
USING CODESET 1252 TERRITORY US
COLLATE USING SYSTEM
PAGESIZE 4096
RESTRICTIVE
CATALOG TABLESPACE MANAGED BY DATABASE
   (FILE 'E:\syscatspace.dat', 5000)
```

Creating a DB2 Database with the Create Database Wizard

If you prefer using graphical user interfaces to typing long commands, you can use the Create Database Wizard to construct a DB2 database. The Create Database Wizard is designed to collect information that defines the characteristics of a database—and then create a database that has those characteristics. These same characteristics can be specified through the various options that are available with the CREATE DATABASE command. The Create Database Wizard is invoked by selecting the appropriate action from the Databases menu found in the Control Center. Figure 2–2 shows the Control Center menu items that must be selected to activate the Create Database Wizard; Figure 2–3 shows what the first page of the Create Database Wizard looks like when it is first initiated.

Once the Create Database Wizard is displayed, you simply follow the directions shown on each panel presented to define the characteristics of the database that is to be created. When you have provided enough information for DB2 to create a database, the "Finish" push button displayed in the lower right corner of the wizard (see Figure 2–3) will be enabled. Once this button is selected, a database will be created using the information provided.

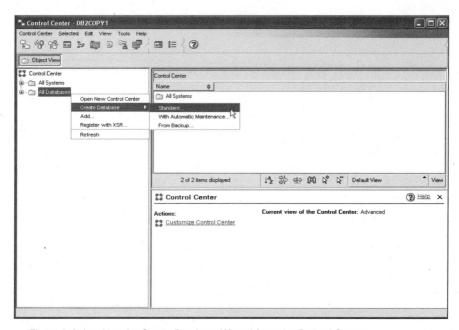

Figure 2–2: Invoking the Create Database Wizard from the Control Center.

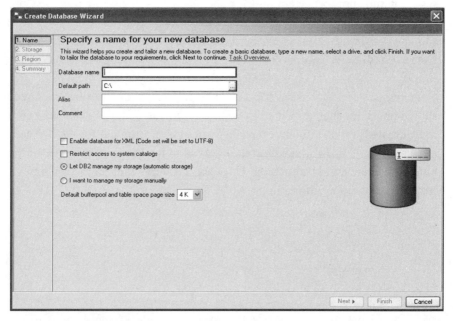

Figure 2–3: The first page of the Create Database Wizard.

Creating a Partitioned DB2 Database

As the name implies, a partitioned database is a database that spans two or more database partitions, allowing data to be distributed across each partition used. Sometimes called a database node or node, a database partition contains its own data, indexes, configuration files, and transaction log files and holds just a portion of a much larger database. Data retrieval and update requests are decomposed automatically into sub-requests and executed in parallel among all applicable database partitions. The fact that a database is split across multiple database partitions is transparent to users issuing SQL statements.

Partitioned databases are created in the same way that non-partitioned databases are created—by using the Create Database Wizard or by executing the CREATE DATABASE command. In a partitioned environment, the resulting database is automatically created across all database partitions defined in the db2nodes.cfg file. (The db2nodes.cfg file is used to define the database partitions and servers that participate in a DB2 instance. We'll take a closer look at the db2nodes.cfg file in Chapter 3—"Data Partitioning and Clustering.") When creating a partitioned database, you must decide which partition will act as the catalog partition and then create the database directly from that partition or from a remote client that is attached to that partition. The catalog partition is the database partition on which all system catalog tables are stored; all access to system tables must go through this partition. (The database partition to which you attach and execute the CREATE DATABASE command—or invoke the Create Database Wizard—becomes the catalog partition for the new database.)

Automatic Storage and Partitioned Databases

Earlier, we saw that when a database is created, automatic storage is enabled by default (but can be explicitly disabled by specifying the AUTOMATIC STORAGE NO option with the CREATE DATABASE command). Automatic storage is comprised of a collection of storage paths on which table spaces can be created without having to explicitly specify container definitions. In most cases, the same storage paths must be used by every database partition in a multi-partition database, and the paths used must exist before a partitioned database can be created. The one exception to this rule is when database partition expressions are used in the storage path definitions provided. Using database partition expressions allows the database partition number to be reflected in the storage path such that the resulting path name is different on each partition.

The argument " $N" ([blank]$N) is used to indicate a database partition expression; when used, it is replaced with the actual partition number. Table 2.1 shows the only forms of the database partition expression argument that are recognized by DB2.

Table 2.1 Recognized Forms of the Database Partition Expression Argument and their results.		
Syntax	Example	Result (on partition 10)
[blank]$N	" $N"	10
[blank]$N+[number]	" $N+100"	110
[blank]$N%[number]	" $N%4"	2
[blank]$N+[number]%[number]	" $N+1%5"	1
[blank]$N%[number]+[number]	" $N%4+2"	4
+ represents the addition operator; % represents the modulus operator		
Adapted from table on page 405 of the DB2 9 Command Reference manual		

A database partition expression can be used anywhere in the storage path specified, and multiple database partition expressions are allowed. However, you must terminate any database partition expression used with a space character—whatever follows the space is appended to the storage path after the database partition expression is evaluated. If there is no space character in the storage path after the database partition expression, it is assumed that the rest of the string is part of the expression.

Thus, if you wanted to create a partitioned database named SAMPLE that uses automatic storage and you wanted the storage path for the first partition to be "/mydata0", the storage path for the second partition to be "/mydata1", and so on, you could do so by executing a CREATE DATABASE command that looks something like this:

```
CREATE DATABASE sample
AUTOMATIC STORAGE YES
ON "/mydata $N"
```

The Directory Tree for a Partitioned Database

As with non-partitioned databases, information about partitioned databases is stored in a special hierarchical directory tree. Once again, the location where this directory tree is actually created is determined by information provided with the CREATE DATABASE command—if no location information is specified, this directory tree is created in the location identified by the *dftdbpath* DB2 Database Manager configuration parameter associated with the instance under which the database is being created. The root directory of this hierarchical tree is assigned the name of the instance with which the database is associated and will contain a subdirectory that has been assigned a name corresponding to the database partition's node—this directory will be named NODExxxx, where xxxx is the unique four-digit partition number that has been assigned to the partition, as designated in the db2nodes.cfg file. For example, for partition number 43, this directory would be NODE0043. The node-name directory, in turn, will contain one subdirectory for each database that has been created, along with one subdirectory that includes the default containers that are to be used to hold the database's data.

The name assigned to the subdirectory that holds the containers used to house the database's data is the same as that specified for the database; the name assigned to the subdirectory that contains the base files for the database corresponds to the database token that is assigned to the database during the creation process (the subdirectory for the first database created will be named SQL00001, the subdirectory for the second database will be named SQL00002, and so on). Figure 2–4 illustrates how this directory hierarchy would look for a database that spans two partitions.

As with a non-partitioned database, when a partitioned database is created, information about the database is cataloged in the system and local database directories. (As mentioned earlier, if these directories do not exist, they are created automatically and populated with the appropriate information.) On UNIX, the system database directory must reside on a shared file system (for example, NFS), because only one system database directory exists for all database partitions that make up the partitioned database environment. Additionally, when a partitioned database is created, a file named sqldbins is created and is used to ensure that all of the database partitions remain synchronized. This file is shared by all the database partitions that make up the database and thus also must reside on a shared file system, because there is only one file for all database partitions.

Several DB2 Database Manager configuration parameters usually have to be modified to take advantage of database partitioning. The DB2 Database Manager configuration parameters that affect a partitioned database environment include: *conn_elapse, fcm_num_buffers, fcm_num_channels, max_connretries, max_coordagents, max_time_diff, num_poolagents,* and *stop_start_time.*

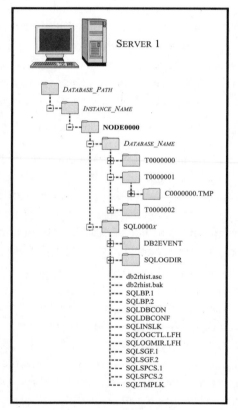

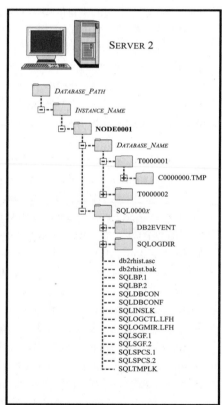

DATABASE PARTITION 0   DATABASE PARTITION 1
(CATALOG PARTITION)

Figure 2–4: Typical directory hierarchy tree for a DB2 9 database that spans two partitions.

Buffer Pools

A buffer pool is an area of main memory that has been allocated to DB2 for the purpose of caching table and index data pages as they are read from disk and/or modified. Memory for a database's buffer pools is allocated when the database is activated or the first time a connection to the database is established. Buffer pool memory is freed and returned to the operating system when all connections have been terminated and the database is deactivated. The purpose of buffer pools is to improve overall database performance by reducing disk I/O—data can be accessed much faster from memory than from disk. Because most data manipulation takes place in buffer pools, creating the right amount of buffer pools and managing their usage is the single most important tuning area for DB2 9 databases.

Earlier, we saw that a buffer pool named IBMDEFAULTBP is created automatically as part of the database creation process. The overall size of this buffer pool is determined by the page size specified when the database was created and the operating system used. By default, on Linux and UNIX platforms, this buffer pool is 1,000 pages in size (or about 4MB if 4K pages are used; on Windows platforms, this buffer pool is 250 pages in size (or about 1MB if 4K pages are used). Once created, this buffer pool cannot be dropped, but its size and attributes can be changed using the ALTER BUFFERPOOL SQL statement, which we will look at shortly. A database must have at least one buffer pool associated with it but can use multiple buffer pools if a sufficient amount of memory is available.

When a DB2 agent acting on behalf of an application retrieves a row of data for the first time, DB2 retrieves the page that contains the data from disk and copies it to the appropriate buffer pool before passing it on to the application or user that requested it. The next time that any application requests data, every available buffer pool is searched to see if the data already resides in memory. If the requested data is found it is immediately passed to the appropriate application or user; if the data is not found, DB2 retrieves it from disk and copies it to a buffer pool before passing it on.

Before a page can be copied into a buffer pool, an empty page must be available in the pool. If the buffer pool is full (i.e., there are no empty pages available), DB2 will determine which page(s) are to be removed from the buffer pool (referred to as "victim" pages) to make room for new pages by examining:

- When the page was last referenced

- The likelihood that the page will be referenced again by the last agent that accessed it

- The type of data on the page (index or data)

- Whether the page in the buffer pool has been changed but has not yet been written to disk

In order to guarantee the integrity of data and transactions, changed pages must first be written to disk before they can be replaced in the buffer pool. As a result, transactions may need to wait for pages to be written to disk. To overcome this condition and improve performance, DB2 uses buffer pool cleaners to periodically scan the buffer pool for "dirty" pages (i.e. pages that have changed since they were read into the buffer pool) and asynchronously write them to disk. To optimize access to the data on these pages, they are not removed from the buffer pool after they have been written to disk. However, if at some point these pages become victim pages, they can quickly be removed from the buffer pool, because they have already been flushed to disk.

Reading individual pages from disk and storing them in memory can be an expensive, time-consuming operation if you are reading entire tables or indexes. On the other hand, reading several consecutive pages from disk using a single I/O operation can greatly reduce the amount of overhead required. Because of this, in most situations, whenever a page of data is requested, DB2 uses a set of heuristic algorithms to try to determine which pages will be needed next by the requesting user/application. Once this determination is made, both the requested page and a predefined number of additional pages are copied to a buffer pool in a single I/O operation. This behavior is referred to as prefetching. Prefetching index and data pages into a buffer pool can help improve performance by reducing I/O wait time.

Creating New Buffer Pools

Earlier, we saw that by default, one buffer pool (named IBMDEFAULTBP) is automatically created as part of the database creation process. Additional buffer pools can be created by executing the CREATE BUFFERPOOL SQL statement. The basic syntax for this statement is:

```
CREATE BUFFERPOOL [BufferPoolName]
<IMMEDIATE | DEFERRED>
<ALL DBPARTITIONNUMS |
  DATABASE PARTITION GROUP [PartitionGroup ,...]>
<SIZE AUTOMATIC |
  SIZE 1000 AUTOMATIC |
  SIZE [NumberOfPages] |
  SIZE [NumberOfPages] AUTOMATIC>
<EXCEPT ON DBPARTITIONNUMS ( [PartitionNum]
  <TO [LastPartitionNum]> SIZE [NumberOfPages] ,...)
<NUMBLOCKPAGES 0 |
  NUMBLOCKPAGES [NumBlockPages] <BLOCK SIZE [BlockSize]>>
<PAGESIZE [PageSize] <K>>
```

where:

BufferPoolName	Identifies the name that is to be assigned to the buffer pool to be created. (This name must be unique and cannot begin with the characters "SYS" or "IBM.")
PartitionGroup	Identifies the database partition group or groups that the buffer pool will be created on.
NumberOfPages	Enables or disables self-tuning OR identifies the number of pages (of *PageSize* size) that are to be allocated for the buffer pool to be created. (In a partitioned database, this will be the default size for all database partitions where the buffer pool exists.)
PartitionNum	Identifies, by partition number, one or more database partitions where the buffer pool to be created is to be sized differently.
LastPartitionNum	Identifies, by partition number, a database partition that, together with the database partition identified in the *PartitionNum* parameter, identifies a range of database partitions where the buffer pool to be created is to be sized differently. (When specifying a range of partitions, the second database partition

number specified must be higher than the first database partition number specified.)

NumBlockPages   Specifies the number of pages that are to be created in the block-based area of the buffer pool. (The block-based area of a buffer pool cannot consume more than 98 percent of the total buffer pool.) Enabling block-based I/O by setting this parameter to a value greater than zero can help improve performance for applications that do sequential prefetching. However, if there are no applications that perform sequential prefetching, setting this parameter to a value greater than zero will result in wasted space.

BlockSize   Specifies the number of pages that can be stored within a block in the block-based area of the buffer pool. (The *BlockSize* value specified must be between 2 and 256 pages; the default value is 32 pages.)

PageSize   Specifies the size that each page will be that will be used by the buffer pool to be created. (Valid values include 4096, 8192, 16384, or 32768 bytes—if the suffix K (for kilobytes) is provided, this parameter must be set to 4, 8, 16, or 32.) If no page size is specified, the default value used is provided by the *pagesize* database configuration parameter, which is set when a database is created; by default, this value is 4K. Note that the page size used by a buffer pool determines which table spaces can be used with it—a buffer pool can only be used by a table space that has a corresponding page size.

If the DEFERRED clause is specified with the CREATE BUFFERPOOL statement, the buffer pool will be created, but no memory will be allocated until all connections to the database for which the buffer pool is to be created have been terminated and the database has been deactivated (i.e. the database is stopped and restarted). If the IMMEDIATE clause is specified instead, or if neither clause is specified, the buffer pool will be created and the amount of memory needed will be allocated immediately unless the amount of memory required is unavailable—in which case a warning message will be generated and the buffer pool creation process will behave as if the DEFERRED clause were specified.

Thus, if you wanted to create a buffer pool that has the name DEV_BP, consists of 100 pages that are 8K in size, and is to be created immediately (assuming enough free memory is available), you could do so by executing a CREATE BUFFERPOOL SQL statement that looks something like this:

```
CREATE BUFFERPOOL dev_bp
SIZE 100
PAGESIZE 8 K
```

On the other hand, if you wanted to create a buffer pool that has the name PROD_BP, is 650MB in size, holds pages that are 16K in size, but not allocate memory for it until the database has been stopped and restarted, you could do so by executing a CREATE BUFFERPOOL SQL statement that looks more like this:

```
CREATE BUFFERPOOL prod_bp
DEFERRED
SIZE 40000
PAGESIZE 16 K
```

In this case, because the DEFERRED option is specified with the CREATE BUFFERPOOL statement, the buffer pool will not be allocated until the database is stopped and restarted. (40,000 16K pages = approximately 650MB)

And finally, if you wanted to create a buffer pool that has the name BLOCK_BP, is 400 MB in size, will hold pages that are 4K in size, is to have 128MB set aside for block-based I/O (to help optimize sequential prefetch activity), and is to be created immediately—assuming enough free memory is available—you could do so by executing a CREATE BUFFERPOOL SQL statement that looks something like this:

```
CREATE BUFFERPOOL block_bp
SIZE 102400
NUMBLOCKPAGES 32768
BLOCKSIZE 256
```

In this case, because the page size is not specified, the buffer pool will use the default page size of 4K. And because the DEFERRED option was not specified, memory for the buffer pool will be allocated immediately, provided enough memory is available to fulfill the request. (100,000 4K pages = approximately 400MB).

When using block-based buffer pools, it is a good idea to set the extent size for every table space assigned to the buffer pool to the block size of the buffer pool, whenever possible.

Buffer pools can also be created using the Create Buffer Pool dialog, which can be activated by selecting the appropriate action from the Buffer Pools menu found in the Control Center. Figure 2–5 shows the Control Center menu items that must be selected to activate the Create Buffer Pool dialog; Figure 2–6 shows how the Create Buffer Pool dialog looks when it is first activated.

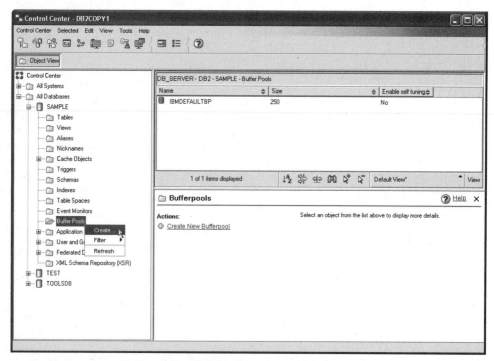

Figure 2–5: Invoking the Create Buffer Pool dialog from the Control Center.

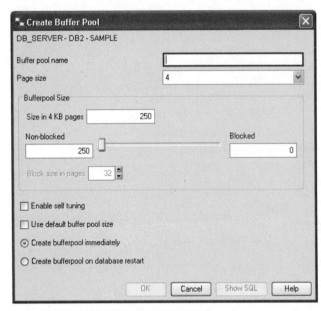

Figure 2–6: The Create Buffer Pool dialog.

Modifying Existing Buffer Pools

From a database performance perspective, buffer pools are probably the single most important database object. Because of this, and because data constantly changes, it is easy to see how it may be necessary to modify the sizes of existing buffer pools many times in order to maintain optimal performance. The characteristics of an existing buffer pool can be modified by executing the ALTER BUFFERPOOL SQL statement. The syntax for this statement is:

```
ALTER BUFFERPOOL [BufferPoolName]
<IMMEDIATE | DEFERRED>
<DBPARTITIONNUM [PartitionNum]>
SIZE [AUTOMATIC |
  [NumberOfPages] |
  [NumberOfPages] AUTOMATIC]
```

or

```
ALTER BUFFERPOOL [BufferPoolName]
ADD DATABASE PARTITION GROUP [PartitionGroup]
```

or

```
ALTER BUFFERPOOL [BufferPoolName]
NUMBLOCKPAGES [NumBlockPages] <BLOCK SIZE [BlockSize]>
```

or

```
ALTER BUFFERPOOL [BufferPoolName]
BLOCK SIZE [BlockSize]
```

where:

BufferPoolName	Identifies, by name, the buffer pool whose characteristics are to be modified.
PartitionNum	Identifies the database partition on which the size of the buffer pool is to be altered.
NumberOfPages	Enables or disables self-tuning OR identifies the new number of pages to be allocated for the buffer pool.
PartitionGroup	Identifies a new database partition group to be added to the list of database partition groups to which the buffer pool definition is applicable.
NumBlockPages	Specifies the number of pages to be created in the block-based area of the buffer pool. (The block-based area of a buffer pool cannot consume more than 98 percent of the total buffer pool.)
BlockSize	Specifies the number of pages that can be stored within a block in the block-based area of the buffer pool. (The *BlockSize* value specified must be between 2 and 256 pages; the default is 32 pages.)

If the DEFERRED clause is specified with the ALTER BUFFERPOOL statement, changes made to the characteristics of the buffer pool will not take effect until all connections to the database for which the buffer pool is to be altered have been terminated and the database has been deactivated (i.e. the database is stopped and restarted). Until then, the original attributes of the altered buffer pool will persist; there will not be any impact on the buffer pool during the interim. If the

IMMEDIATE clause is specified instead, or if neither clause is specified, changes to the buffer pool will take effect immediately unless the amount of memory needed is unavailable, in which case a warning message will be generated and the existing buffer pool will remain unaltered until the database is stopped and restarted.

Thus, if you wanted to change the size of a buffer pool named DEV_BP that holds data pages that are 4K in size, from 100MB to 200MB—and you wanted the change to take place immediately provided enough free memory is available—you could do so by executing an ALTER BUFFERPOOL SQL statement that looks something like this:

```
ALTER BUFFERPOOL dev_bp
SIZE 51200
```

Before altering the number of pages in a buffer pool, it is important to assess the effect the change will have on applications that are accessing the database. In some cases, a change in buffer pool size can result in the selection of different access plans.

On the other hand, if you wanted to change the block-based area of a buffer pool named PROD_BP that holds data pages that are 4K in size, from 100MB to 200MB, you could do so by executing an ALTER BUFFERPOOL SQL statement that looks more like this:

```
ALTER BUFFERPOOL prod_bp
NUMBLOCKPAGES 51200
```

Changes to the size of the block-based area of a buffer pool will not take effect until the database is stopped and restarted.

Finally, if you wanted to create a buffer pool named PARTGRP_BP on the database partitions found in a partition group named PGRP2 that has the same characteristics as a buffer pool named PARTGRP_BP that was created on a different database partition group earlier, you could do so by executing an ALTER BUFFERPOOL SQL statement that looks something like this:

```
ALTER BUFFERPOOL partgrp_bp
ADD DATABASEPARTITIONGROUP pgrp2
```

For this example, assume the buffer pool PARTGRP_BP was created using the
following CREATE BUFFERPOOL SQL statement:

```
CREATE BUFFERPOOL partgrp_bp
DATABASEPARTITIONGROUP pgrp1
SIZE 25000
PAGESIZE 32K
```

Buffer pools can also be altered using the Alter Buffer Pool dialog, which can be
activated by selecting the appropriate action from the Buffer Pools menu found in
the Control Center. Figure 2–7 shows the Control Center menu items that must be
selected in order to activate the Alter Buffer Pool dialog; Figure 2–8 shows how the
first page of the Alter Buffer Pool dialog might look when it is first activated.

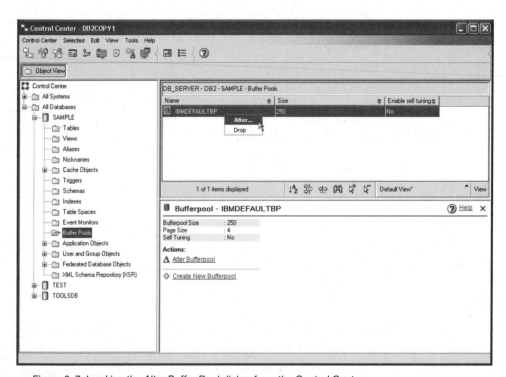

Figure 2–7: Invoking the Alter Buffer Pool dialog from the Control Center.

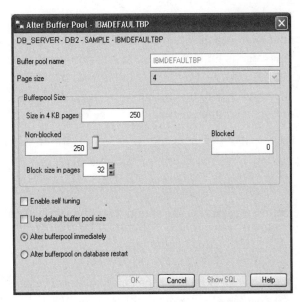

Figure 2–8: The first page of the Alter Buffer Pool dialog.

DB2's Hidden Buffer Pools

When a database is activated, or the first time a connection to a database is established, DB2 automatically creates four hidden buffer pools (in addition to the IBMDEFAULTBP buffer pool and any other user-defined buffer pools that may exist). Because these buffer pools are hidden, they do not have entries in the system catalog tables and cannot be used directly (by assigning them to table spaces) or altered.

Each hidden buffer pool uses one of the supported page sizes (i.e., 4K, 8K, 16K and 32K) and exists to ensure that a buffer pool will always be available to handle any situation. Specifically, DB2 will use these buffer pools under the following conditions:

- When the CREATE BUFFERPOOL statement is executed with the IMMEDIATE option specified, but there is not enough memory available to create the buffer pool immediately. If this occurs, a message is written to the administration notification log, and any table spaces that are using the buffer pool will be remapped to the hidden buffer pool having the same page size.

- When memory for the IBMDEFAULTBP and/or any of the user-defined buffer pools cannot be allocated when the database is activated or started. If this occurs, a message is written to the administration notification log, and any table space that is using a buffer pool that was not allocated will be remapped to the hidden buffer pool having the same page size. If this occurs, DB2 will be fully functional, but performance will be drastically reduced.

- When a table space is created and its page size does not correspond to the page size of any of the user-defined buffer pools.

- During a roll-forward operation, if a buffer pool is created and the DEFERRED option is specified. Any user-created table spaces assigned to this buffer pool will be remapped to the hidden buffer pool having the same page size for the duration of the roll-forward operation.

By default, each hidden buffer pool is capable of holding 16 pages of data. This can be changed by assigning a different number to the DB2_OVERRIDE_BPF registry variable. For example, if you wanted to change the capacity of the hidden buffer pools from 16 pages to 64 pages, you could do so by executing the following command:

```
db2set -g DB2_OVERRIDE_BPF=64
```

How Many Buffer Pools Should a Database Have?

Because the way in which buffer pools are used can have a significant effect on database performance, deciding how many buffer pools are needed for a particular implementation and sizing each buffer pool can be a daunting task. When it comes to deciding how many buffer pools to create, there are two main schools of thought:

- Use one big buffer pool and let DB2 take care of moving older pages out of the buffer pool to make room for new ones.

- Use several small buffer pools and assign them to specific table spaces to ensure that highly active pages always remain in memory.

The advantage of using a single large buffer pool is that, other than choosing an appropriate size, no additional tuning is needed. That's because DB2 has a highly optimized algorithm for aging pages that uses several techniques designed to optimize the buffer pool hit ratio by favoring important pages (such as index pages) and placing pages deemed unlikely to be accessed again on "hate stacks" which are used to quickly identify victim pages that can be removed to free up space.

On the other hand, when properly sized and assigned to the right table spaces, multiple smaller buffer pools provide better overall performance than one large buffer pool. Use of multiple buffer pools, however, requires constant monitoring and tuning in order to keep performance optimal.

In most environments, the number of buffer pools that can be used effectively depends on the amount of system memory available. If the total amount of memory available can hold only 10,000 4K pages (or less), it's often better to use a single large buffer pool than several small buffer pools—the later can cause frequently accessed pages to be swapped in and out of memory more often, in turn leading to I/O contention for storage objects—such as the system catalog tables and/or user tables and indexes—that are accessed repeatedly.

If sufficient memory is available, you should consider creating individual buffer pools for the following:

- Temporary table spaces
- Table spaces containing tables that are accessed consistently and repeatedly by many short-duration update transactions
- Table spaces containing tables and indexes that are updated frequently
- Table spaces containing tables and indexes that are queried frequently but updated infrequently
- Table spaces containing tables that are queried frequently in a random manner
- Table spaces containing data that is accessed by infrequently used applications
- Any table space containing data and indexes you want to favor

Here are some other rules of thumb to follow when contemplating whether to use multiple buffer pools:

- Use multiple buffer pools if multiple applications are accessing the database and you want to favor a particular application.

- If tables are usually scanned concurrently, separate them into their own dedicated table spaces and buffer pools. (DB2 will try to keep these pages in memory, but if stored in a single buffer pool, this could quickly saturate the buffer pool, interfering with access to other objects.)

- Use multiple buffer pools to isolate high-priority or high-usage tables and/or indexes from other database activity.

- If large reports are run occasionally on OLTP systems that do large joins, sorts, etc. that result in the creation of large temporary tables, create a dedicated buffer pool for the table space used to hold the temporary tables so that report generation will have less effect on the overall performance of the online system. (Size this buffer pool according to the "typical" sorting done under normal operations; this buffer pool typically does not need to be large, because it is normally accessed sequentially.)

In most cases, larger buffer pools are better than small buffer pools. However, you must take into account the total amount of memory available as well as how the buffer pool(s) you create will be used. Some tables do not need large buffer pools, for example:

- Tables that are always appended to, such as journal or history tables.

- Huge tables (i.e., bigger than the buffer pool) that are rarely fully scanned. These tables will likely always require disk I/O regardless of how big the buffer pool associated with them is. (Assign these tables to a dedicated buffer pool, or when they are scanned they may cause other important pages to be flushed from memory; be careful to make the dedicated buffer pool large enough to make prefetching effective.)

- Large tables that are predominately accessed by applications performing random access operations. In this case, there's no need to keep a lot of data pages in the buffer pool once they've been used to resolve a query.

DB2 creates a 100-byte page descriptor in the database heap for each buffer pool page used. (In a 64-bit instance, this page descriptor occupies 150 bytes.) Therefore, before creating large buffer pools, it may be necessary to increase the size of the database heap (*dbheap*) database configuration parameter to hold the descriptors for the buffer pool pages. For example, 262,144 pointers must be allocated in the data base heap for a 1GB buffer pool with a 4K page size—this will use approximately 25MB of database heap; 8,388,608 pointers must be allocated for a 32GB buffer pool with a 4K page size of 4K—this will use approximately 800MB of database heap.

Block-Based Buffer Pools

Earlier, we saw that when there are no empty pages available in a buffer pool, DB2 will pick one or more "victim" pages and remove them to make room for others. As a result, when contiguous pages on disk are prefetched, they most likely will be placed into non-contiguous pages within a buffer pool. If however, contiguous pages can be read from disk and stored in contiguous pages within a buffer pool, sequential prefetch and sequential read operations will execute faster.

That's where block-based buffer pools come in. A block-based buffer pool contains both a page-based area and a block-based area—the size of each area is determined by options specified with the CREATE BUFFERPOOL SQL statement. The page-based area is used for any I/O operation that is not performed using sequential prefetching; the block-based area, on the other hand, is made up of a number of "blocks," each of which will contain a set number of contiguous pages that are retrieved using sequential prefetching.

When block-based buffer pools are used, prefetch operations attempt to read data from a table space, one extent at a time, and write the data read into a block in the buffer pool. Thus, to make block-based I/O as efficient as possible, it is important to try to match the extent size for any table spaces using the buffer pool with the block size that has been defined for the buffer pool. DB2 will still use the block-based area of the buffer pool for prefetching if the extent size is larger or smaller than the block size of the buffer pool; if there is too much difference between the extent and block sizes, DB2 may choose to use the page-based area of the buffer pool instead.

If some of the pages requested in a prefetch request have already been read into the page-based area of the buffer pool using page-based I/O, the prefetcher may or may not read the data into the block-based area, depending on how much of the block would be wasted. The I/O server allows some wasted pages in each buffer pool block, but if too much of a block would be wasted, the I/O server will prefetch the data into the page-based area of the buffer pool. Space is considered wasted if the page would be empty because the extent size is smaller than the block size or if the page already exists in the page-based area of the buffer pool.

A Word About Page Cleaners

Earlier, we saw that when an agent acting on behalf of an application attempts to access table or index pages, it looks for those pages in the appropriate buffer pool first; if they cannot be found, they are read from disk and copied to the buffer pool before being passed on to the application. Once a buffer pool becomes full, if new pages need to be brought in, DB2 must select one or more "victim" pages to discard in order to make room for the new pages. If a victim page is "dirty" (i.e., has been changed since it was read into the buffer pool, but the changes have not yet been written to disk) it must be written to disk before it can be discarded. To reduce the likelihood that the victim page(s) selected will be dirty, DB2 uses one or more page cleaners to asynchronously write dirty pages to disk before space in a buffer pool is requested. This reduces or eliminates the amount of time applications might otherwise have to wait for changed pages to be written to disk before deleting them, which in turn improves overall performance.

One of three different events can cause the page cleaners for a buffer pool to be triggered:

- **Dirty Page Threshold Exceeded.** Each time a page in the buffer pool is changed, that page is added to what is known as a "dirty list," which is nothing more than a list of every dirty page in the buffer pool. Each time a page is added to the dirty list, DB2 checks to see whether the number of pages on the list exceeds the changed page threshold that has been established for the database—if so, the page cleaners are triggered and all changed pages are written to disk. (The *chngpgs_thresh* database configuration parameter is used to specify a percentage of the buffer pool that can be dirty before the page cleaners are triggered.)

- **Dirty Page Steals.** When an agent requests a page that must be read from disk and DB2 chooses a victim page that is dirty, the page must first be written to disk before its space can be used to store the new page that the agent has requested. After a dirty victim page has been selected, DB2 will automatically trigger the page cleaners to write all remaining dirty pages to disk.

- **LSN Gap Situation.** When the amount of log space used, starting from the time a log record for the oldest dirty page in the buffer pool was written, exceeds the percentage of log file data that can be written before a soft checkpoint will be established, it is said that the database is in an "LSN gap" situation. When the logger detects than an LSN gap has occurred, it will trigger the page cleaners to write out all dirty pages contributing to the LSN gap situation. (That is, it will write out those pages which are older than what is allowed by the *softmax* database configuration parameter.)

When any of these three triggering events occur, all of the page cleaners for the database are fired simultaneously. Each page cleaner then gathers up to 400 pages from the dirty lists *for every buffer pool in the database* and writes them to disk, one page at a time. (Page cleaner writes happen asynchronously.) Once a page cleaner has finished writing its pages, it will check to see whether more pages are waiting to be written. If so, it will gather a new list of pages to process; if not, it will wait for the next page cleaner trigger event to occur.

Choosing the right number of page cleaners

Because all page cleaners are started whenever a page cleaner trigger event takes place, using a large number of page cleaners can overwhelm the run queue on a server and significantly degrade performance. When choosing an appropriate number of page cleaners to use, a good rule of thumb is to pick a number that is equal to the number of CPUs found on the database server.

The number of asynchronous page cleaners available to a database is controlled by the value assigned to the *num_iocleaners* database configuration parameter. If this configuration parameter is assigned the value zero (0), no page cleaners are started, and as a result, database agents will perform all of the page writes from the buffer pool to disk. If this parameter is assigned the value AUTOMATIC (the default), the number of page cleaners started will be based on the number of CPUs configured on the current machine, as well as the number of local logical database partitions available (if the database is a partitioned database). At least one page cleaner will be started when this configuration parameter is set to AUTOMATIC.

Setting the right changed pages threshold value

By default, the value assigned to the *chngpgs_thresh* database configuration parameter is 60%. This value works fine for smaller buffer pools; however, for systems with large buffer pools, this setting can cause a noticeable dip in performance each time the page cleaners are activated. For example, if a 2GB buffer pool is used, a changed pages threshold setting of 60% will cause the page cleaners to be started when there are 1.2GB of dirty pages in the buffer pool. Starting up several page cleaners asynchronously to write 1.2GB of data to disk can cause a very noticeable slowdown. Setting the changed page threshold to a smaller value (i.e., 20–30%) will cause the page cleaners to be triggered more frequently, but because they will have a much smaller amount of data to write to disk, the negative impact on system performance will be minimized.

Table Spaces

Table spaces are used to control where data is physically stored and to provide a layer of abstraction between database objects (such as tables, indexes, and views) and one or more containers in which the object's data actually resides. Whereas a table space is a logical database entity, containers represent the physical storage associated with table spaces. The container used is dependant upon the type of table space being created and can be an operating system directory, an individual file, or a raw logical volume/disk partition. When a table space is created, it must have at least one container associated with it. A single table space can span many containers, but each container can belong to only one table space.

The basic unit of storage in a DB2 database is a page, and pages can be 4K (kilobytes), 8K, 16K, or 32K in size. When pages are written to a container, they are grouped into contiguous ranges called extents; the extent size is specified during the table space creation process and cannot be changed once the table space has been constructed. When a table space spans multiple containers, data is written in a round-robin fashion (one extent at a time) to each container assigned to that table space. This helps balance data across all containers belonging to a given table space. Figure 2–9 shows the relationship between pages, extents, and table space containers.

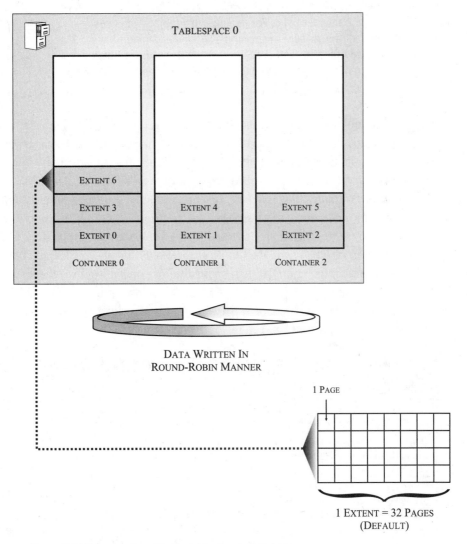

Figure 2–9: How data is written to table space containers.

When multiple containers are used to store table space data in an SMS table space, the maximum amount of data that each container can hold is determined by the smallest container used. For example, if a table space uses one container that is 10M in size and a second container that is 12M in size, 2M of the second container will not be useable; the maximum amount of storage available to the table space will be 20M.

Two types of table spaces can exist: system managed space (SMS) table spaces and database managed space (DMS) table spaces. With SMS table spaces, only directory containers can be used for storage, and the operating system's file manager is responsible for controlling how that space is utilized. The SMS storage model consists of many files (each representing a table, index, or long data object) that reside within the file system space—the user decides on the location of the files, DB2 assigns the files their names, and the file system is responsible for managing their growth. With DMS table spaces, only file and/or device containers can be used for storage and DB2 is responsible for controlling how the space is used. In DB2 9, the initial allocation of space for an object in an SMS table space is one extent; in a DMS table space it is two extents. Other differences between SMS and DMS table spaces can be seen in Table 2.3.

Table 2.3 Differences Between SMS and DMS Table Spaces	
SMS Table Spaces	**DMS Table Spaces**
Storage space is allocated and managed by the operating system's file manager.	Storage space is allocated, if so specified, and managed by DB2.
Only directory containers can be used for storage; file and device containers cannot be used.	File or device containers can be used as storage; directory containers cannot be used.
No additional containers can be added to a table space (using the ALTER TABLESPACE SQL statement) once it has been created.	Additional containers can be added to a table space after it has been created. When new containers are added, existing data can automatically be rebalanced across the new set of containers to retain optimal I/O efficiency.
Storage space is allocated as needed.	Storage space is pre-allocated.
A container's size is not specified when the table space is created; therefore, it cannot be changed.	A container's size can be increased or decreased after a table space has been created.

Table 2.3 Differences Between SMS and DMS Table Spaces (Continued)	
SMS Table Spaces	**DMS Table Spaces**
Regular data and long data are stored in the same table space.	Regular data and long data can be split across multiple table spaces (regular data can reside in one table space while long data resides in another).
Table spaces are easier to create and manage.	Table access is slightly faster, making overall performance better.

A Word about Storage Containers

With SMS table spaces, only operating system directories can be used as storage containers. If a directory specified as a storage container does not exist, DB2 will create it; if it does exist, it must be empty—if it contains any files or subdirectories, DB2 will not be able to use it. Because containers cannot be dynamically added to an existing SMS table space, it is important to know the anticipated storage space requirements before the table space is created.

During the SMS table space creation process, DB2 creates a special file named SQLTAG.NAM and stores it inside each container used to uniquely identify it. This file is called the container tag file (or the container tag) and contains information that identifies the container by a unique number, information about the table space to which the container belongs, and information about the database to which the table space belongs. This information is used to ensure that no other table space will be able to use the container, even if the table space resides in a different database.

As objects are created in an SMS table space, DB2 stores their corresponding data in individual files, within the directories used as storage containers. Names for these files are assigned by DB2, based on the ID given to the associated table when it was created. The naming convention used is as follows:

- The file name for the data part of the table will be "SQL[*ObjectID*].DAT"

- The file name for the indexes for the table will be "SQL[*ObjectID*].INX"

- The file name for any long varchar columns in the table will be "SQL[*ObjectID*].LF"

- The file name for any LOB columns in the table will be "SQL[*ObjectID*].LB" For each LOB object there is also a LOB allocation object needed; this will be stored in a file named "SQL[*ObjectID*].LBA"

- The file name for XML columns in the table will be "SQL[*ObjectID*].XDA"

- The file name for the block map for any MDC table will be "SQL[*ObjectID*].BKM"

- The file name for temporary data will be "SQL[*ObjectID*].TDA"

For example, for a table with an object ID of 14, the following files may be created:

- SQL00014.DAT   - Normal data records
- SQL00014.INX   - Indexes
- SQL00014.LF   - Long varying character column data
- SQL00014.LB   - LOB column data
- SQL00014.LBA   - LOB allocation information
- SQL00014.XDA   - XML column data
- SQL00014.BKM   - Block information for MDC tables
- SQL00014.TDA   - Temporary data

With DMS table spaces, a storage container can be either a file, a raw device or raw logical volume, or a disk partition. A file container is an operating system file of a given size. If a file is specified as a DMS table space storage container and the file itself does not exist, DB2 will create it and initialize it to the size specified. If an existing file is specified, DB2 will check it to verify that it is not already being used for some other purpose. If its contents can be overwritten, DB2 will expand it or shrink it to the size specified and initialize it for use. The file size can be specified in number of pages, KB, MB, or GB.

In Linux and UNIX environments, raw device containers are mapped to underlying logical volumes. In Windows, a raw device container is mapped to an unformatted disk partition. If a device is specified as a DMS table space storage container, it cannot be used for any other purpose—in fact, it can not contain a file system and it should not be formatted. When specifying the size of a device container, it is a good idea to use all the space available, because any unused space will not be accessible for other applications. (Unused space can be used at a later date if the table space container is extended or resized.) Like file sizes, device sizes can be specified in number of pages, KB, MB, or GB.

As with SMS table space containers, DB2 generates container tag information for each container used by a DMS table space. However, in the case of DMS table spaces, container tag information is recorded in the first extent of each container—not in a special file.

Raw Devices Versus Files

Within the database community a long-running debate has surrounded the use of raw devices versus files for data storage. Advocates of raw devices stress the performance gains that can be realized through their use; file supporters emphasize the ease of use and manageability features of file systems. As with other aspects of database system design, it must be decided which is more important: performance or manageability.

In order to better understand the performance advantages associated with raw devices, it helps to understand the impact of the file system cache. Most Linux and UNIX file systems set aside an area of memory to hold recently accessed files, which can subsequently allow physical I/O requests to be satisfied from memory instead of from disk. If DB2 requests data that is not already in the cache, the operating system will read the data from disk into the cache and then copy the data to a buffer pool so that it can be used. Thus, each read request translates into a disk read followed by a copy of the data from the cache to the database buffer pool.

When data is read from the cache, I/O requests can be satisfied in nanoseconds instead of the milliseconds that would be required to retrieve the data from disk. In addition, most Linux and UNIX file systems employ the use of a sequential read-ahead mechanism to prefetch data into the cache when it detects that a file is being accessed sequentially.

In non-database environments, the file system cache can significantly reduce I/O wait time for heavily accessed files. However, the performance benefits of file system caching in database environments are not as clear. This is because most relational database management systems, including DB2, also allocate a region of memory for caching frequently accessed data (i.e., the database buffer pools). This results in double buffering of data in the file system cache and in a DB2 buffer pool.

In 64-bit systems, the memory used by the file system cache could be better used by the database buffer pools. In 32-bit systems, with their associated shared memory limits, the file system cache can provide benefit for some workloads.

The primary benefit of raw devices is that they bypass the file system cache by directly accessing the underlying logical device. The extra memory saved by eliminating the file system cache can then be allocated to the database buffer pools. In addition, overall CPU utilization is decreased because the system no longer has to copy the data from the file system cache to the database buffer pools. Another benefit of raw logical volumes in AIX is that there is no inode management overhead, unlike file systems in which the inode is locked when the file is accessed.

With DB2 9, it is possible have the best of both worlds (performance and manageability)—by using the NO FILE SYSTEM CACHING option when creating DMS table spaces. This option provides a way to bypass the file system cache when using file containers for storage.

Table Space Types

Both SMS and DMS table spaces are classified according to the type of data they are intended to store. Three classifications exist:

- Regular
- Large
- Temporary

Regular Table Spaces

Regular table spaces are used to store both table data and index data. The maximum size of a regular table space depends on the page size used for the table space. For a table space with 4K pages, the maximum size is 64GB (gigabytes). For a table space with 32K pages, the maximum size is 512GB. This is the only table space type allowed for SMS table spaces, and it is also the default type for SMS table spaces when no type is specified

Large Table Spaces

Large table spaces are used to store regular and index data as well as long and large object (LOB) data. (The use of large table spaces is optional given that large data can reside in regular table spaces as well.) The maximum size of a large table space is 16 TB (terabytes). If a table contains long varying-length character string, long varying-length double-byte character string, or large object columns, the table's data may be stored in such a way that regular data resides in a regular table space and long/large object data resides in a large table space. However, this method of storage must be specified at the time the table is created; once the table is created, it cannot be changed. Beginning with DB2 Version 9.1, DMS table spaces are created as large table spaces by default. (Prior to this release, DMS table spaces were created as regular table spaces by default.) In this release, the record identifier (RID) length has been increased so that large table spaces allow more data pages per table object and more records per page.

By default, every DB2 9 (or later) database has at least one regular table space named USERSPACE1. This table space is normally created as a DMS table space but can be created as a SMS table space if so desired. (The USERSPACE1 table space can also be dropped once another regular table space has been created.)

Temporary Table Spaces

Temporary table spaces are further classified as being either system temporary or user temporary. The maximum size of a temporary table space is 2 TB.

System temporary table spaces are used by DB2 to hold transient data (such as intermediate tables) during sort operations and table reorganization operations, and to aid in SQL statement processing when creating indexes and joining tables. A database must have at least one system temporary table space—by default, a system temporary table space named TEMPSPACE1 is created when a database is created. However, this table space can be dropped once another system temporary table space with the same page size has been created.

User temporary table spaces are used to store declared global temporary tables, which in turn are used to store application-specific data for a brief period of time. Because a database is not required to have a user temporary table space, one is not automatically created as part of the database creation process. However, before a declared global temporary table can be created, a user temporary table space must exist in the database.

In the event that a system temporary table is needed, DB2 will create it in the system temporary table space with the largest buffer pool that has a page size large enough to hold the temporary table. The largest buffer pool is based on total size, not the number of pages. For example, a 1,000 page 4K buffer pool is smaller than a 1,000 page, 8K buffer pool. If there are multiple system temporary table spaces with the same page size and the same size buffer pool, DB2 will choose the system temporary table space to use in a round-robin manner.

Automatic Storage Table Spaces

If a database is enabled for automatic storage, one other type of table space—an automatic storage table space—can exist. Automatic storage table spaces use space in the storage paths that have been defined for the database and grow automatically as the table space begins to fill up.

Although at first glance, automatic storage table spaces appear to be a third type of table space, they are really just an extension of SMS and DMS table spaces: regular and large table spaces are created as DMS table spaces with one or more file containers; system and user temporary table spaces are created as SMS table spaces with one or more directory containers.

Unlike when SMS and DMS table spaces are defined, no container definitions are needed for automatic storage table spaces; DB2 assigns containers to automatic storage table spaces automatically. However, an initial size can be specified as part of the table space creation process. (If an initial size is not specified, DB2 will use a default value of 32 megabytes.)

A Word about the System Catalog Table Space

As part of the database creation process, a table space named SYSCATSPACE is created and used to hold a special set of tables known as the system catalog tables. (The system catalog tables are used to store metadata about objects that have been created in the database.) The SYSCATSPACE table space is a regular table space but is only used to store the database catalog tables; once created, it cannot be dropped. By default, the SYSCATSPACE table space is created as an automatic storage DMS table space but can be created as an SMS table space if so desired.

The system catalog table space contains many tables of varying lengths and sizes, and when a DMS table space is used, a minimum of two extents are allocated for each table in the system catalog. Depending upon the extent size, a significant amount of allocated and unused space may result. Therefore, when using a DMS table space for the system catalog (the default behavior in DB2 Version 9.1), it is recommended that you use a small extent size (i.e., 2–4 pages) to minimize the amount of space wasted.

In a partitioned database, there is only one set of system catalogs; they are located on the catalog partition for the database.

Creating New Table Spaces

Earlier, we saw that when a DB2 database is created, one buffer pool named IBMDEFAULTBP is created, and three table spaces are created and associated with this buffer pool as part of the database initialization process. These three table spaces are sufficient for small databases, but large databases are usually composed of many different buffer pool and table space objects.

Additional table spaces can be created by executing the CREATE TABLESPACE SQL statement. The basic syntax for this statement is:

```
CREATE
<REGULAR | LARGE | SYSTEM TEMPORARY | USER TEMPORARY>
TABLESPACE [TablespaceName]
<IN DATABASE PARTITION GROUP [PartitionGroup]>
```

```
<PAGESIZE [PageSize] <K>>
MANAGED BY SYSTEM USING ('[Container]' ,...)
<ON DBPARTITIONNUM<S> ([DBPartition]
     <TO [DBPartitionEnd]>>
<EXTENTSIZE [ExtentPages | ExtentSize <K | M | G>]>
<PREFETCHSIZE [AUTOMATIC | PrefetchPages |
     PrefetchSize <K | M | G>]>
<BUFFERPOOL [BufferPoolName]>
<<NO> FILE SYSTEM CACHING>
<DROPPED TABLE RECOVERY <ON | OFF>>
```

or

```
CREATE
<REGULAR | LARGE | SYSTEM TEMPORARY | USER TEMPORARY>
TABLESPACE [TablespaceName]
<IN DATABASE PARTITION GROUP [PartitionGroup]>
<PAGESIZE [PageSize] <K>>
MANAGED BY DATABASE USING ([FILE | DEVICE] '[Container]'
 [ContainerPages | ContainerSize <K | M | G>] ,...)
<ON DBPARTITIONNUM<S> ([DBPartition]
     <TO [DBPartitionEnd]>>
<AUTORESIZE [YES | NO]>
<INCREASESIZE [IncSize <PERCENT | K | M | G>]>
<MAXSIZE [NONE | MaxSize <K | M | G>]>
<EXTENTSIZE [ExtentPages | ExtentSize <K | M | G>]>
<PREFETCHSIZE [AUTOMATIC | PrefetchPages |
     PrefetchSize <K | M | G>]>
<BUFFERPOOL [BufferPoolName]>
<<NO> FILE SYSTEM CACHING>
<DROPPED TABLE RECOVERY <ON | OFF>>
```

or

```
CREATE
<REGULAR | LARGE | SYSTEM TEMPORARY | USER TEMPORARY>
TABLESPACE [TablespaceName]
<IN DATABASE PARTITION GROUP [PartitionGroup]>
<PAGESIZE [PageSize] <K>>
MANAGED BY AUTOMATIC STORAGE
<AUTORESIZE [YES | NO]>
<INITIALSIZE [InitSize <K | M | G>]>
<INCREASESIZE [IncSize <PERCENT | K | M | G>]>
<MAXSIZE [NONE | MaxSize <K | M | G>]>
<EXTENTSIZE [ExtentPages | ExtentSize <K | M | G>]>
<PREFETCHSIZE [AUTOMATIC | PrefetchPages |
     PrefetchSize <K | M | G>]>
<BUFFERPOOL [BufferPoolName]>
<<NO> FILE SYSTEM CACHING>
<DROPPED TABLE RECOVERY <ON | OFF>>
```

where:

TablespaceName	Identifies the name that is to be assigned to the table space to be created.
PartitionGroup	Identifies, by name, the database partition group in which the table space is to be created. If no database partition group is specified, the default database partition group IBMDEFAULTGROUP is used for REGULAR, LARGE, and USER TEMPORARY table spaces and the default database partition group IBMTEMPGROUP is used for SYSTEM TEMPORARY table spaces.
PageSize	Specifies the size that each page used by the table space being created is to be. The following values are valid for this parameter: 4,096; 8,192; 16,384, or 32,768 bytes—if the suffix K (for kilobytes) is provided, this parameter must be set to 4, 8, 16, or 32. Unless otherwise specified, pages used by table spaces are 4K in size.
Container	Identifies, by name, one or more containers that are to be used to store the data associated with the table space to be created.
ContainerPages	Identifies, by number of pages, the amount of storage to be pre-allocated for the container(s) identified in the *Container* parameter.
ContainerSize	Identifies the amount of storage to be pre-allocated for the container(s) identified in the *Container* parameter. The value specified for this parameter is treated as the total number of bytes unless the letter K (for kilobytes), the letter M (for megabytes), or the letter G (for gigabytes) is specified. (If a *ContainerSize* value is specified, it is converted to a *ContainerPages* value using the *PageSize* value provided.)
DBPartition	Identifies a specific database partition or the beginning partition of a range of database partitions on which the table space container(s) specified reside or are to be created.

DBPartitionEnd   Identifies the ending partition of a range of database partitions on which the table space container(s) specified reside or are to be created.

InitSize   Identifies the amount of storage to be pre-allocated for an automatic storage table space.

IncSize   Identifies the amount by which a table space enabled for automatic resizing will automatically be increased when the table space is full and a request for more space is made.

MaxSize   Identifies the maximum size to which a table space enabled for automatic resizing can automatically be increased.

ExtentPages   Identifies the number of pages of data to be written to a single table space container before another container will be used.

ExtentSize   Identifies the amount of data to be written to a single table space container before another container will be used. The value specified for this parameter is treated as the total number of bytes unless the letter K (for kilobytes), the letter M (for megabytes), or the letter G (for gigabytes) is specified. (If an *ExtentSize* value is specified, it is converted to an *ExtentPages* value using the *PageSize* value provided.)

PrefetchPages   Identifies the number of pages of data to be read from the table space when data prefetching is performed (prefetching allows data needed by a query to be read before it is referenced, so that the query spends less time waiting for I/O).

PrefetchSize   Identifies the amount of data to be read from the table space when data prefetching is performed. The value specified for this parameter is treated as the total number of bytes unless the letter K (for kilobytes), the letter M (for megabytes), or the letter G (for gigabytes) is specified. (If a *PrefetchSize* value is specified, it is converted to a *PrefetchPages* value using the *PageSize* value provided.)

BufferPoolName   Identifies the name of the buffer pool to be used by the table space to be created. (The page size of the buffer pool specified must match the page size of the table space to be created, or else the CREATE TABLESPACE statement will fail.)

If the MANAGED BY SYSTEM version of this statement is executed, the resulting table space will be an SMS table space. On the other hand, if the MANAGED BY DATABASE version is executed, the resulting table space will be a DMS table space.

If the DROPPED TABLE RECOVERY ON option is specified (the default), dropped tables in the specified table space can be recovered using the RECOVER DROPPED TABLE option of the ROLLFORWARD DATABASE command—provided the table space is a regular table space. This option cannot be used when creating large or temporary table spaces.

If the FILE SYSTEM CACHING option is specified (the default), all I/O for the table space will be buffered by the file system. If, instead, the NO FILE SYSTEM CACHING option is specified, I/O for the table space will not be buffered by the file system (i.e., the table space will use direct I/O). In most cases, not buffering I/O will cause a DMS file table space to have performance characteristics that are similar to a DMS raw table space.

In DB2 9.5, if neither the FILE SYSTEM CACHING option nor the NO FILE SYSTEM CACHING option is specified, FILE SYSTEM CACHING is the default for JFS on AIX, Linux System z, all non-VxFS file systems on Solaris, HP-UX, SMS temporary table space files on all platforms, and all LOB and large data. NO FILE SYSTEM CACHING is the default on all other platforms and file system types.

Thus, if you wanted to create an SMS table space that has the name SALES_TS; consists of pages that are 4 kilobytes in size; uses the directories C:\TBSP1, C:\TBSP2, and C:\TBSP3 as its storage containers; and uses the buffer pool IBMDEFAULTBP, you could do so by executing a CREATE TABLESPACE SQL statement that looks something like this:

```
CREATE REGULAR TABLESPACE sales_ts
PAGESIZE 4096
MANAGED BY SYSTEM USING
 ('C:\tbsp1', C:\tbsp2', 'C:\tbsp3')
EXTENTSIZE 32
PREFETCHSIZE 96
BUFFERPOOL ibmdefaultbp
```

On the other hand, if you wanted to create a DMS table space that has the name PAYROLL_TS, consists of pages that are 8 kilobytes in size, uses the file DMS_TBSP. TSF, (which is 1,000 megabytes in size and resides in the directory C:\TABLESPACES) as its storage container, and uses the buffer pool PAYROLL_BP, you could do so by executing a CREATE TABLESPACE SQL statement that looks more like this:

```
CREATE REGULAR TABLESPACE payroll_ts
PAGESIZE 8K
MANAGED BY DATABASE USING
 (FILE 'C:\TABLESPACES\dms_tbsp.tsf' 1000 M)
BUFFERPOOL PAYROLL_BP
```

Finally, if you wanted to create an automatic storage table space that has the name HR_TS and uses the buffer pool IBMDEFAULTBP, you could do so by executing a CREATE TABLESPACE SQL statement that looks something like this:

```
CREATE REGULAR TABLESPACE payroll_ts
MANAGED BY AUTOMATIC STORAGE
```

If a database is enabled for automatic storage, the MANAGED BY AUTOMATIC STORAGE clause can be left out completely—its absence implies automatic storage. No container definitions are provided in this case, because DB2 assigns containers automatically.

Table spaces can also be created using the Create Table Space Wizard, which can be activated by selecting the appropriate action from the Table Spaces menu found in the Control Center. Figure 2–10 shows the Control Center menu items that must be selected to activate the Create Table Space Wizard; Figure 2–11 shows how the first page of the Create Table Space Wizard might look when it is first activated.

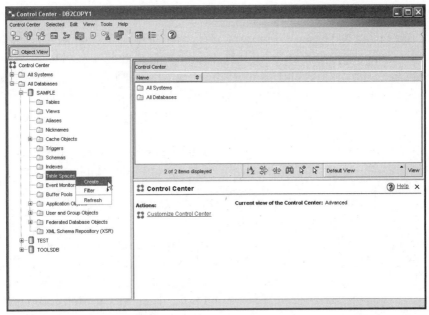

Figure 2–10: Invoking the Create Table Space Wizard from the Control Center.

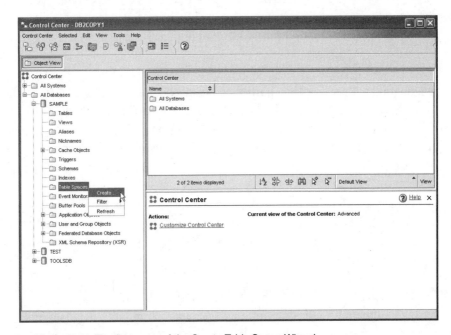

Figure 2–11: The first page of the Create Table Space Wizard.

Creating Table Spaces That Span Multiple Database Partitions

In a partitioned database environment, it is possible to define named subsets of one or more database partitions. Each subset you define is known as a database partition group; each subset that contains more than one database partition is known as a multi-partition database partition group. A database partition group can contain as few as one database partition, or it can span all the database partitions in a database.

In order to create tables for a partitioned database, you must first create one or more database partition groups that will be used to control where table spaces will be stored and then you create the table space(s) where the tables will be stored. Finally, you create the tables and assign them to the appropriate table space(s).

When a partitioned database is created, three database partition groups are created automatically. One is named IBMCATGROUP and is the database partition group that is used by the table space that contains the system catalogs (SYSCATSPACE). Another is named IBMDEFAULTGROUP and is the database partition group that is used, by default, for table spaces that contain user-defined tables. A third, named IBMTEMPGROUP, is the database partition group that is used by default for system temporary table spaces. (A user temporary table space for a declared temporary table can be created in IBMDEFAULTGROUP or any user-created database partition group, but not in IBMTEMPGROUP.)

When creating table spaces in a partitioned database, the partition group in which the table space is created determines which database partition(s) the table space will be physically created on. A table space can only belong to one partition group, but a partition group can contain more than one table space. Figure 2–12 shows the one-to-many relationship between database partitions, partition groups, and table spaces.

Once a table space has been created, there is no way to dynamically change the partition group it belongs to. If you want to change the partition group for which a table space has been created, you must drop the table space and recreate it using the new partition group.

Due to the increased popularity of SAN and NAS disk subsystems, as well as the trend toward creating multiple database partitions within large SMP servers, it is important to identify the database partition to which the table space containers used

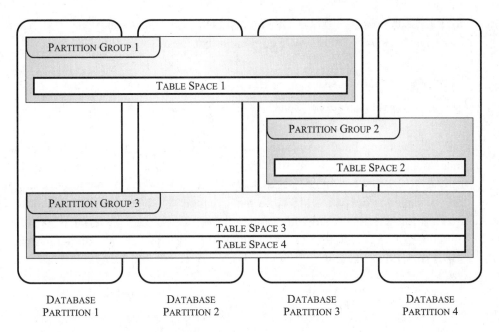

Figure 2–12: Table spaces and partition groups.

belong. To aid in this, DB2 allows the use of a database partition expression in the container name when creating either SMS or DMS containers.

Earlier, we saw that the argument " $N" ([blank]$N) is used to indicate a database partition expression and that when this argument is used, it is replaced with the actual partition number. (Table 2.1 shows the only forms of the database partition expression argument that are recognized by DB2.) A database partition expression can be used anywhere in a container name, and expressions can be specified within the same name. To use a partition expression, there must be a space after the container name, followed by the expression. The result of the expression following the space will then be appended to the container name. If there is no space character in the container name after the database partition expression, it is assumed that the rest of the string is part of the expression.

Thus, if you wanted to create a DMS table space named TBSP1 in a partitioned database that has five partitions numbered 0 through 4, and you wanted the storage container for the first partition to be a file named CONT1P0, the storage container

for the second partition to be a file named CONT1P1, and so on, you could do so by
executing a CREATE TABLESPACE command that looks something like this:

```
CREATE TABLESPACE tbsp1
MANAGED BY DATABASE
USING (FILE 'cont1P $N' 5000)
```

DB2 also allows a database administrator to individually control the creation and
placement of containers within database partitions through the use of the the ON
DBPARTITIONNUM option of the CREATE TABLESPACE SQL statement. For example,
if you wanted to create a DMS table space named TBSP1 in a partitioned database
that has four partitions and you wanted to use a file on each partition as its storage
containers, you could do so by executing a CREATE TABLESPACE command that
looks something like this:

```
CREATE TABLESPACE tbsp1
MANAGED BY DATABASE
USING (FILE '/tbspcs/cont1' 25000) ON DBPARTITONNUM(0)
USING (FILE '/tbspcs/cont1' 25000) ON DBPARTITONNUM(1)
USING (FILE '/tbspcs/cont1' 25000) ON DBPARTITONNUM(2)
USING (FILE '/tbspcs/cont1' 25000) ON DBPARTITONNUM(3)
```

Modifying Existing Table Spaces

Because SMS table spaces rely on the operating system for physical storage space
management, they rarely need to be modified after they have been successfully
created. DMS table spaces, on the other hand, have to be monitored closely to ensure
that the fixed-size pre-allocated file(s) or physical raw device(s) that they use for
storage always have enough free space available to meet the database's needs. When
the amount of free storage space available to a DMS table space becomes dangerously
low (typically less than 10 percent), you can add more free space either by increasing
the size of one or more of its existing containers or by adding one or more new
containers to it. That's where the ALTER TABLESPACE SQL statement comes in. Using
the ALTER TABLESPACE statement, an existing table space can be modified as follows:

- A container can be added to an SMS table space on a database partition that
  currently has no containers.

- Containers can be added to, or dropped from a DMS table space.

- The size of an existing container in a DMS table space can be changed.

- The buffer pool used to cache data for a table space can be changed.

- The amount of data that gets prefetched from a table space can be changed.

- The I/O controller overhead and disk seek latency time for a table space can be changed.

- The time it takes to transfer one page of data from the table space to memory can be changed.

- The file system caching policy used by a table space can be changed.

The basic syntax for the ALTER TABLESPACE SQL statement is:

```
ALTER TABLESPACE [TablespaceName]
ADD ('[Container]' ,...)
ON DBPARTITIONNUM<S> ([DBPartition]
<TO [DBPartitionEnd]>
```

or

```
ALTER TABLESPACE [TablespaceName]
[ADD | EXTEND | REDUCE | RESIZE]
  ([FILE | DEVICE] '[Container]'
  [ContainerPages | ContainerSize <K | M | G>] ,...)
```

or

```
ALTER TABLESPACE [TablespaceName]
[EXTEND | REDUCE | RESIZE]
  (ALL <CONTAINERS>
  [ContainerPages | ContainerSize <K | M | G>])
```

or

```
ALTER TABLESPACE [TablespaceName]
DROP ([FILE | DEVICE] '[Container]' ,...)
```

or

```
ALTER TABLESPACE [TablespaceName]
<PREFETCHSIZE AUTOMATIC |
 PREFETCHSIZE [PrefetchPages | PrefetchSize <K | M | G>]>
<BUFFERPOOL [BufferPoolName]>
<<NO> FILE SYSTEM CACHING>
<AUTORESIZE [NO | YES]>
<INCREASESIZE [IncSize <PERCENT | K | M | G>]>
<MAXSIZE [NONE | MaxSize <K | M | G>]>
<DROPPED TABLE RECOVERY [ON | OFF]>
<CONVERT TO LARGE>
```

where:

TablespaceName   Identifies the name assigned to the table space to be altered.

DBPartition   Identifies a specific database partition or the beginning partition of a range of database partitions on which the table space container(s) specified reside.

DBPartitionEnd   Identifies the ending partition of a range of database partitions on which the table space container(s) specified reside.

Container   Identifies one or more containers that are to be added to, resized, or removed from the DMS table space specified.

ContainerPages   Identifies, by number of pages, the amount of storage to be added to, removed from, or allocated for all containers or the container(s) identified in the *Container* parameter.

ContainerSize   Identifies the amount of storage to be added to, removed from, or allocated for all containers or the container(s) identified in the *Container* parameter. The value specified for this parameter is treated as the total number of bytes unless the letter K (for kilobytes), the letter M (for megabytes), or the letter G (for gigabytes) is specified. (If a *ContainerSize* value is specified, it is converted to a *ContainerPages* value using the *PageSize* value provided.)

PrefetchPages   Identifies the number of pages of data to be read from the table space when data prefetching is performed.

PrefetchSize   Identifies the amount of data to be read from the table space when data prefetching is performed. The value specified for this parameter is treated as the total number of bytes unless the letter K (for kilobytes), the letter M (for megabytes), or the letter G (for gigabytes) is specified. (If a *PrefetchSize* value is specified, it is converted to a *PrefetchPages* value using the page size of the table space being altered.)

BufferPoolName Identifies the name of the buffer pool to be used by the table space to be altered. (The page size of the buffer pool specified must match the page size used by the table space to be altered.)

IncSize Identifies the amount by which a table space enabled for automatic resizing will automatically be increased when the table space is full and a request for more space is made.

MaxSize Identifies the maximum size to which a table space enabled for automatic resizing can automatically be increased.

Thus, if you wanted a fixed-size pre-allocated file named NEWFILE.TSF that is 1,000 megabytes in size and resides in the directory C:\TABLESPACES, to be used as a new storage container for an existing DMS table space named PAYROLL_TS, you would execute an ALTER TABLESPACE SQL statement that looks like this:

```
ALTER TABLESPACE payroll_ts
ADD (FILE 'C:\tablespaces\newfile.tsf' 1000 M)
```

On the other hand, if you wanted to expand the size of all containers associated with an existing DMS table space named PAYROLL_TS by 200 megabytes, you could do so by executing an ALTER TABLESPACE SQL statement that looks like this:

```
ALTER TABLESPACE payroll_ts
EXTEND (ALL CONTAINERS 200 M)
```

Table spaces can also be altered using the Alter Table Space dialog, which can be activated by selecting the appropriate action from the Table Spaces menu found in the Control Center. Figure 2–13 shows the Control Center menu items that must be selected in order to activate the Alter Table Space dialog; Figure 2–14 shows how the first page of the Alter Table Space dialog might look when it is first activated.

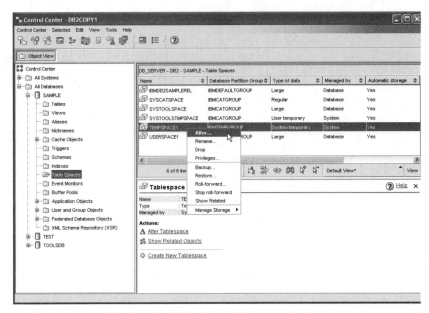

Figure 2–13: Invoking the Alter Table Space dialog from the Control Center.

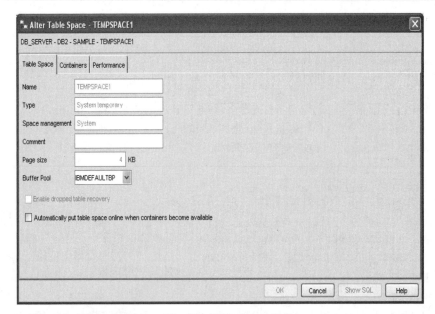

Figure 2–14: The first page of the Alter Table Space dialog.

Adding new containers to existing automatic storage table spaces

Earlier, we saw that if a database is enabled for automatic storage, the container- and space- management characteristics of its table spaces are determined by DB2. And we have just seen that although the ALTER TABLESPACE command can be used to add new containers to existing DMS table spaces, it cannot be used to add new containers to automatic storage table spaces. So how can you add new storage paths to the collection of paths used for automatic storage table spaces once a database has been created? To perform this type of operation, you must use the ALTER DATABASE statement. The basic syntax for this statement is:

```
ALTER DATABASE [DatabaseName]
ADD STORAGE ON '[Container]' ,...)
```

where:

DatabaseName   Identifies, by name, the database that is to have new containers added to its pool of containers that are used for automatic storage.

Container   Identifies one or more new storage locations (containers) to be added to the collection of storage locations that are used for automatic storage table spaces.

Thus, if you wanted to add the storage locations /data/path1 and /data/path2 to a database named SAMPLE, that is configured for automatic storage and resides on a UNIX system, you could do so by executing an ALTER DATABASE SQL statement that looks like this:

```
ALTER DATABASE sample
ADD STORAGE '/data/path1', '/data/path2'
```

On the other hand, if you wanted to add the storage locations D: and E: to a database named SAMPLE that is configured for automatic storage and resides on a Windows system, you could do so by executing an ALTER DATABASE SQL statement that looks like this:

```
ALTER DATABASE sample ADD STORAGE ON 'D:', 'E:'
```

The Table Space High-Water Mark

The basic premise behind DMS table space storage is that storage is pre-allocated in advance in order to avoid the performance cost associated with allocating storage on demand. As a database evolves over time, it typically grows in size, which naturally leads to a demand for increased storage capacity, something that can in turn translate into a desire to increase the size of an existing table space. The high-water mark represents the first page after the highest page number that has been allocated in a table space. The high-water mark is a DMS-only concept that also includes automatic storage table spaces. The high-water mark is not necessarily the same as the number of pages used, since objects that may have been deleted from within a table space will not have an effect on the high-water mark.

Whenever a row of data is stored in a table, DB2 assigns that row a unique record identifier known as a row ID (or RID). Prior to DB2 9, RIDs consisted of a three-byte page number and a one-byte slot number. The slot number is an array entry into a slot directory, which in turn contains the offset into the data page where the row's data physically resides; the page number identifies the data page itself. DB2 9 has the ability to support both four-byte RIDs as well as larger six-byte RIDs that consist of a four-byte page number and a two-byte slot number (tables that reside in a DMS LARGE table space use these). As a result, you can now have data pages that contain more than 255 rows (the old limit with four-byte RIDs) and a single table partition can grow to 2TB in size when a 4K page is used (16TB when a 32K page is used). In DB2 9, six-byte RIDs are used by default for any new automatic storage table spaces and DMS table spaces created, because the default table space type has been changed from Regular to Large.

DB2 indexes use table space–relative RIDs to reference base table records. (An index is an ordered set of pointers that refer to rows in a base table.) This means that every key in an index points to slot X in page Y in a table space—not to slot X in page Y of a base table. As a result, DB2 can't freely move extents around in a table space; if it did, RIDs stored in indexes would point to the wrong data and every index that referenced data in the table space would have to be rebuilt any time a move occurred.

Using table space–relative RIDs improves performance because the extra step of figuring out where a particular page of a table resides in a table space (which would have to be done by scanning the table's extent map pages) is eliminated. However, because DB2 can't alter the placement of extents in a table space, only unused storage space that comes after the high-water mark can be freed.

To illustrate this concept further, let's look at what happens when a table is reorganized to compress a table's data (using the deep compression technology that was introduced in DB2 9). In DB2, table reorganization processing is shadow copy-based—a new reorganized copy of the original table is built, and that copy becomes the table; the original version is dropped. If a temporary table space is used to reorganize the data the resulting version of the table is constructed in the temporary table space, its data pages are copied over the original table object in the original table space, and the storage space that was used by the table is truncated. Figure 2–15 shows how a table space containing four tables (named TABLE_1, TABLE_2, TABLE_3, and TABLE_4) might look before and after all four tables in it have been reorganized and compressed using a temporary table space.

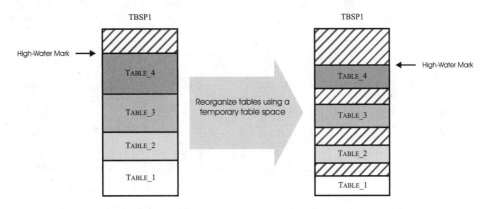

Figure 2–15: How a table space's high-water mark is affected by table reorganization/ compression operations that use a temporary table space.

In this example, once the data in all four tables has been compressed, more free space is available; however, that free space is scattered throughout the table space and the high-water mark was not lowered significantly.

If the shadow copy is built in the table space where the table resides (i.e., no temporary table space is used), new extents must be allocated or assigned within the table space. These shadow copy extents can extend the table space's high-water mark if there are not a sufficient number of free extents available below the current high-water mark. (Freed extents below the high-water mark result from operations such as dropping a table, truncating data in a table (via an Import or Load operation), and performing a table reorganization operation (with or without compression).

The order in which tables are reorganized and compressed, as well as where these tables are placed within the table space, will impact the table space's high-water mark. Figure 2–16 shows how our original table space containing four tables (TABLE_1, TABLE_2, TABLE_3, and TABLE_4) might look before and after all four tables in it have been reorganized and compressed (without using a temporary table space) in the following order: TABLE_1, TABLE_2, TABLE_3, and TABLE_4.

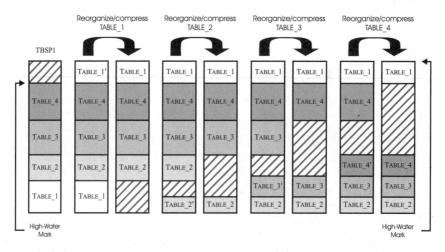

*Figure 2–16: How a table space's high-water mark is affected by table reorganization/
compression operations that do not use a temporary table space.*

In this case, we end up with a high-water mark that is higher than it was when we began the reorganization and compression operations. However, if we were to reorganize and compress table TABLE_1 again, the table would be moved to the beginning of the free space in the table space and the high-water mark would be lowered significantly. Figure 2–17 shows how the table space would look after a second reorganization and compression of table TABLE_1 is performed.

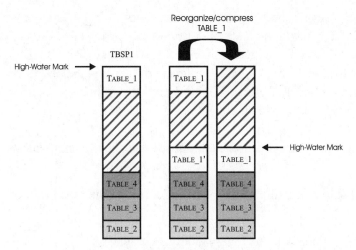

Figure 2–17: How a table space's high-water mark is lowered by performing a second reorganization/compression operation on table TABLE_1.

It is important to note that the examples shown in Figures 2–15, 2–16, and 2–17 are based on the assumption that TABLE_1, TABLE_2, TABLE_3, and TABLE_4 were created and populated one at a time and that the table space TBSP1 has been fully compacted. In reality, this example represents the worse-case scenario. When more than one table exists in a single table space, it's more common to have extents from different tables interleaved throughout the table space. Assessing the degree of extent fragmentation that exists becomes more complex, but is probably less drastic than depicted in these illustrations. Therefore, the actual high-water mark impact made will most likely be significantly less. When you start adding things like index objects and large objects (LOBs) to the same table space, things get even more confusing, and it becomes difficult to predict exactly what will happen.

Lowering the Table Space High-Water Mark

If there are no unused extents below the current high-water mark for a table space, the high-water mark cannot be lowered without dropping one or more objects stored in the table space.

However, as we have just seen, the high-water mark for a table space could be lowered by reorganizing an existing table or by exporting an existing table, dropping it, recreating it, and then importing or loading the exported data back into the new table. In both of these cases, however, it is important to know which object is holding the high-water mark so that the correct table can be reorganized or unloaded/dropped/reloaded. This information can be obtained by executing the GET SNAPSHOT FOR TABLESPACES command or by using the db2dart command. If the db2dart command is executed with the /DHWM option specified, the following information will be provided:

- A map of the extents in the table space that shows which objects own which extents

- The object ID and object type of the object holding the high-water mark extent

- Information about the high-water mark extent

- The number of free and used extents below the high-water mark

Once this information has been obtained, the db2dart command can be executed with the /LHWM option specified to interpret this information and generate a set of steps you can follow (i.e. reorg, export, load) to lower the high-water mark. When this option is specified, the table space ID and a desired high-water mark for the table space must also be specified. Although there is no guarantee that the current high-water mark will be able to be lowered to the desired value, using a value of "0" tells DB2 to determine the lowest value possible.

For each step presented in the list returned, there will be an estimate of the number of used and free extents below the high-water mark so that the benefits of each step in the process can be evaluated and a decision can be made whether or not to perform all of the steps. Because the DB2DART tool makes some assumptions about the affects of the suggested operations, the resulting high-water mark may be higher or lower than the specified value.

• •

In a partitioned database, db2dart collects information about table spaces and high-water marks only on the partition where it is run.

• •

If the db2dart command is executed with the /RHWM option specified, db2dart will remove all space map extents within a table space that are no longer required. (DB2 places a space map extent at regular intervals within a DMS table space to record the extent usage for a set of extents within the table space.) If a table space has had a lot of data deleted from it, there may be space map pages that no longer point to used pages in the table space, but they are not removed when the data is deleted. The /RHWM option tells db2dart to look for any unneeded space map pages and remove them from the table space to potentially reduce the high-water mark.

In is important to note that the dropping of existing table space containers is only allowed if the number of extents in the container(s) being dropped is less than or equal to the number of free extents available above the high-water mark in the table space. The number of free extents available above the high-water mark is important because all extents up to and including the high-water mark must be able to fit in the same logical position within the table space. In other words, the table space must have enough space available to hold all of the data in the container being dropped.

A Closer Look at Prefetching

Earlier, we saw that when an agent acting on behalf of a user or an application needs to access table or index pages, it will look for the pages in the buffer pool area first. If the desired pages cannot be found in the buffer pool area, they will be read from disk into the buffer pool. Unfortunately, disk I/O can be very expensive and in this case, the agent is forced to wait for the read request to finish before it can access the page. These types of read operations are typically done one page at a time, and if the user/application needs to access subsequent pages in the table or index, this approach to reading pages can become very inefficient.

In many situations DB2 can anticipate the pages that will be requested by an application and read them into the buffer pool before the agent actually attempts to access them. This is referred to as prefetching and can improve read performance since chances are good that the desired pages will be found in the buffer pool when the agent attempts to access them, reducing or eliminating the time the application must wait for pages to be read from disk. (This is more relevant to decision support system–type workloads that scan large indexes and tables than it is for OLTP-type workloads that require less scanning and contain more random insert/update/delete activity.)

Prefetching can be enabled by the DB2 Optimizer when it is building the access plan for an SQL statement if it determines that a large portion of a table or index will be scanned when the statement is executed. Prefetching can also be triggered when DB2 is executing an access plan and detects that it has read a number of pages in sequence and will most likely continue to do so. This is known as sequential detection and this behavior can be enabled or disabled using the *seqdetect* database configuration parameter. (Restart recovery will automatically use prefetchers to minimize restart time; prefetching during restart recovery can be disabled by setting the DB2 registry variable DB2_AVOID_PREFETCH to ON.)

How Does Prefetching Work?

When DB2 makes the determination that prefetching should be performed, a DB2 agent will make prefetch requests, and these requests are sent to a queue where they are examined by the prefetch manager. (There is only one prefetch queue and it can hold up to 100 prefetch requests.) The prefetch manager examines every request to determine whether any of the prefetch requests from different applications can be combined and processed in a single prefetch operation. Otherwise, requests in the queue are assigned to DB2 I/O servers (also known as prefetchers) in a first in, first out (FIFO) manner.

Eventually each prefetch request is broken up into a number of smaller I/O requests. By default, the number of I/O requests will be determined by the number of containers used by a table space. However, if the DB2_PARALLEL_IO registry variable has been set, DB2 will start up a number of prefetchers that is equal to the prefetch size divided by the extent size. This allows multiple prefetchers to be working on requests in parallel.

To ensure that the prefetchers do not retrieve data into a buffer pool too aggressively, overwriting existing pages before they can be accessed, the amount of prefetching performed is controlled by the size of the buffer pool, as well as the prefetch size and the access plan generated by the DB2 Optimizer. For smaller buffer pools, prefetching may be scaled back to ensure that prefetched pages do not flood the buffer pool and kick out pages that are currently being used or that have been copied into the buffer pool but have not yet been accessed.

Two types of prefetch operations can be performed in DB2: range and list. Range prefetching is used to prefetch a sequential range of data pages from storage; range prefetching is used during table scans and when prefetching is triggered by sequential detection. When it is determined that a large amount of sequential data needs to be prefetched, it is not all prefetched at once, since this could potentially flood a buffer pool and force important pages to be removed. Instead, it is prefetched in stages, each time a trigger point page is read by an agent. (Trigger point pages are located every multiple of the prefetch size within the table.)

For example, if a table scan is initiated, a trigger point will be hit when the first page in the table is read. This trigger point will then request that DB2 prefetch the first two prefetch-sized blocks from the table. The first block will actually be one page less than the regular prefetch size and will start on the second page in the table to avoid prefetcher/agent contention on the first page. All subsequent trigger points will make a prefetch request to bring in the next prefetch-sized block of pages. If a system is configured and tuned properly, the agent should never have to wait on I/O as the prefetcher will have already read the page into the buffer pool. Figure 2–18 illustrates how prefetching would be done in response to a table scan if the prefetch size used were four times the extent size.

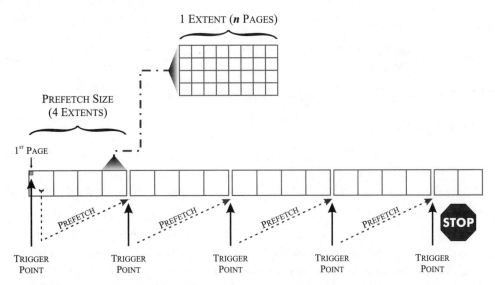

Figure 2–18: How range prefetching is performed in response to a table scan. In this case, prefetching stops after the last trigger point because there are not enough pages remaining to satisfy a prefetch request.

If there is more than one container in the table space and/or DB2_PARALLEL_IO is enabled, it is much more efficient to have multiple prefetchers performing the I/O, rather than a single prefetcher. In this case, each prefetch request is broken up into smaller requests, and each of these smaller requests is placed onto the prefetch queue. The prefetchers can then service the requests in parallel, potentially performing much faster than a single prefetcher.

If a block-based area is set aside in the buffer pool, DB2 will perform a big block read to move a contiguous series of pages into a single private memory buffer and then copy the block of pages to the block-based area of the buffer pool with one memory copy operation. Internally, the mechanism used is "big block" read or "vectored" read (on platforms that support an efficient vectored read API). A "big block" read involves reading a contiguous block of pages into a single, private memory buffer. Each individual page is then copied into its own buffer pool slot (these slots are likely to be scattered throughout the buffer pool). A vectored read API will read a contiguous block of pages from disk into different memory buffers (a different memory buffer for each page of the block). In this case, those memory buffers can actually be the individual buffer pool slots, and the overhead of the copy from one memory buffer to another is avoided (hence an efficient vectored read API is preferred over big block read). The block-based area of a buffer pool overcomes this by setting aside contiguous blocks of the buffer pool equal in size to the extent size to make prefetching more efficient, especially on operating systems that do not support vectored reads.

List prefetching is used to prefetch a list of pages into a buffer pool after an index scan has produced a list of record IDs (RIDs) that identify individual data pages that might be needed. List prefetching is normally decided on by the DB2 Optimizer and specified in the access plan when an SQL statement is prepared for execution. A list prefetch request may be converted to a range prefetch request if the data pages needed are found to be sequential.

Other Roles of the Prefetchers (I/O Servers)

In addition to performing prefetch work, prefetchers perform other key functions, including:

- **Dropping temporary objects**: During query processing, one or more system temporary tables may be created to hold intermediate or final result data sets. When a system temporary table is no longer required, it is dropped. This involves purging (removing) its pages from the buffer pool and can take a relatively long time. Thus, rather than an agent dropping the table and waiting for the drop operation to complete, it requests that a prefetcher handle the drop table work. This reduces the agent's response time, because it does not have to do the work itself.

- **Adding containers to DMS table spaces**: When more than one container is added to a DMS table space with a single ALTER TABLESPACE statement, the prefetchers assist an agent in allocating the disk space needed for those containers. Specifically, the agent handles the allocation for one container and requests that prefetchers handle the allocation for the remaining containers. This allows the container allocation process to be done in parallel, speeding up the overall process.

- **Resizing containers in DMS table spaces**: This request is similar to that of adding containers to DMS table spaces; it requests that prefetchers handle the allocation of new space when the RESIZE or EXTEND options of the ALTER TABLESPACE statement are used.

- **Traversing index leaf pages**: This request is mainly used by the REORG utility when scanning an index object. Given the root page of an index, the leaf level is traversed using prefetchers.

Choosing the Optimal Prefetch Size

Earlier, we saw that the prefetch size for a table space can be specified when the table space is created. We also saw that the ALTER TABLESPACE statement can be used to adjust the prefetch size for a table space if the prefetchers are over-prefetching or under-prefetching. Over-prefetching results in wasted space in the buffer pool and/or in overwriting pages in the buffer pool that are likely to be reused by other applications. Under-prefetching results in high prefetch wait times and usually causes the DB2 agents to perform the I/O themselves.

As a general rule, the best prefetch size to use for a table space with multiple containers can be determined using the following formula:

```
Prefetch size = Extent size * Number of containers
```

On the other hand, the best prefetch size to use for a table space with a single container that resides on a RAID striped disk can be determined with the following equation:

```
Prefetch size = Extent size * Number of disks in the stripe set
```

(In this case, the DB2_PARALLEL_IO registry variable should be set as well.)

If the table space contains multiple containers and the containers reside on separate physical disks, parallel I/O will enable the prefetchers to read all extents simultaneously. So, in this case, prefetching can be made more aggressive by increasing the prefetch size to be a value that is a multiple of the first formula. However, for this to be effective, disk bandwidth must be sufficient to support the I/O. In addition, the number of prefetchers available may need to be increased (but only if the DB2_PARALLEL_IO registry variable has been enabled), because the number of requests will be equal to the prefetch size divided by the extent size. With the DB2_PARALLEL_IO registry variable disabled (the default), the number of requests will be based solely on the number of containers in the table space, which means that increasing the prefetch size will not result in more prefetch requests. It will only increase the amount of I/O needed to satisfy each request.

Consider the following example. A table space has two containers and a prefetch size that is twice the extent size. With the DB2_PARALLEL_IO registry variable disabled, there will be two prefetch requests, because there are two containers in the table space; each request will be for one extent. If the DB2_PARALLEL_IO registry variable is enabled, there will two prefetch requests, because the prefetch size divided by the extent size equals two; each request will be for one extent.

If the prefetch size is increased to four times the extent size and the DB2_PARALLEL_IO the registry variable is disabled, there will still only be two prefetch requests, because there are two containers in the table space. But now each prefetch request will be for two extents—and if the DB2_PARALLEL_IO registry variable is enabled, there will be four prefetch requests, because the prefetch size divided by the extent size equals four; each request will still be for one extent.

Choosing the Optimum Number of Prefetchers (I/O Servers)

If prefetch size is set as suggested (i.e., Prefetch size = Extent size * Number of containers) for every table space in a database, and if all of the table spaces are scanned at the same time, the number of prefetchers used should be equal to the number of disks belonging to the database. (In order to fully exploit all the I/O devices in the system, a good value to use is generally one or two more than the number of physical devices on which the database resides. It is better to configure additional prefetchers, since there is minimal overhead associated with each I/O server and any unused I/O servers will remain idle.)

However, if one or more of the table spaces has been set up to use more aggressive prefetching (i.e., the prefetch size is a multiple of the Extent size * Number of containers value) and/or some of the table spaces are not scanned at the same time as others, the calculation becomes more complicated. In this case, to determine the number of prefetchers needed, you must:

- Identify the table spaces that will potentially be scanned at the same time.

- Determine the number of prefetchers required to service a scan of each of these table spaces (using the formula Prefetch size = Extent size * Number of containers).

- Add these values together to determine the total number of prefetchers required.

In either case, once the number of prefetchers needed has been determined, the number of prefetchers required should be assigned to the *num_ioservers* database configuration parameter. (If this parameter is set to AUTOMATIC, the number of prefetchers started will be based on the parallelism settings of the table spaces in the current database partition.)

Expanding a Database's Boundaries with Federated Systems

A federated system is a special type of distributed database management system that allows you to send requests to multiple data sources with a single SQL statement. For example, you can join data that is stored in a DB2 table, an Oracle table, and an Informix view using one statement.

So just what is a federated system? A federated system is a computing system that consists of the following:

- A DB2 instance that operates as a federated server.

- One or more data sources to which the federated server can forward SQL operations. Each data source consists of an instance of a relational database management system, along with a database that the instance supports.

- A DB2 database that acts as the federated database.

- One or more clients.

To end users and client applications, data sources in a federated system appear as a single collective database. In reality, users and applications actually interface with a federated database that contains catalog entries that identify data sources and their characteristics. Specifically, federated database catalog entries contain information such as: what a data source object is called, what information it contains, and information about the conditions under which the data source can be used. The actual relational database management system being referenced, the modules used to communicate with the data source, and the data objects (such as tables and views) to be accessed reside outside of the federated database.

To retrieve data from a federated data source, users/applications connect to the federated database just as they would connect to any other database and submit queries written using DB2 SQL that reference tables and views in the data source by the nicknames that they were assigned. DB2 then optimizes and distributes the queries to the appropriate data sources for processing, collects the data requested as it is returned from the data source, and returns it to the user/application.

To send data values to a federated data source (i.e., to perform insert, update, and/or delete operations on a data source table), users/applications connect to the federated database just as they would connect to any other database and submit queries that have been written using the data source's SQL dialect—not DB2's SQL dialect— in a special mode called *pass-through* mode. In a pass-through mode session, an SQL statement is sent to the data source for processing if it is dynamically prepared and executed during the session through the execution of either (1) an EXECUTE IMMEDIATE statement or (2) a PREPARE statement followed by an EXECUTE statement. Pass-through mode can also be used to submit queries to a data source in that data source's SQL dialect.

Federated Servers

A federated server is a DB2 instance to which application processes can connect and submit requests to one or more data sources. (The DB2 instance that manages the federated system is called a server because it responds to requests from end users and client applications.) Any number of DB2 instances can be configured to function as federated servers; however, two main features distinguish federated servers from other DB2 instances:

- A federated server is configured to receive requests that might be partially or entirely intended for data sources. It is a federated server's responsibility to push part or all of the requests is receives down to the data sources for processing.

- Like other application servers, a federated server uses DRDA communication protocols (over TCP/IP) to communicate with other DB2 family instances. However, unlike other application servers, a federated server uses the native client of the data source to access that data source. For example, a federated server uses the Sybase Open Client to access Sybase data sources and a Microsoft SQL Server ODBC Driver to access Microsoft SQL Server data sources.

Data Sources

Typically, a federated system data source is a relational DBMS instance (such as Oracle, Informix, Microsoft SQL Server, or Sybase) and one or more databases that are supported by the instance. However, data sources can be non-relational is well (for example, a BLAST search algorithm or an XML tagged file). And in some cases, you use one data source to access other data sources. For example, using an ODBC data source, you can access WebSphere Classic Federation server for z/OS data sources such as DB2 for z/OS, IMS, CA-IDMS, CA-Datacom, Software AG Adabas, and VSAM.

Data sources are autonomous. This means that a federated server can send queries to them at the same time that other applications are accessing them. Aside from performing integrity checking and applying locking constraints, a federated system neither monopolizes nor restricts access to any data source used.

Federated Databases

A federated database is a special DB2 database whose system catalog contains entries that identify data sources and their characteristics. The catalog in a federated database is called the global catalog because it contains information about the entire federated system. The information stored in the global catalog includes remote and local information, such as column names, column data types, column default values, and index information. (Remote catalog information is the name used by the data source; local catalog information is the name used by the federated database.)

For relational data sources, the information stored in the global catalog includes both remote and local information. For non-relational data sources, the information stored in the global catalog varies from data source to data source.

The DB2 optimizer uses the information stored in the global catalog to plan the best way to process SQL statements; in a federated system, SQL statements are processed as if the data from the data sources were ordinary relational tables or views within the federated database. As a result, a federated system can correlate relational data with data in non-relational formats. This is true even when the data sources use different SQL dialects, or do not support SQL at all. (When there are differences between the characteristics of the federated database and the characteristics of the data sources, the characteristics of the federated database take precedence.)

Query results conform to DB2 semantics, even if data from other non-DB2 data sources is used to produce the query result.

Wrappers

Wrappers are mechanisms by which a federated database interacts with data sources. Wrappers are implemented as a set of library files and a federated database uses routines stored in these library files to perform such tasks as:

- Connecting to a data source

- Submitting queries to the data source (For data sources that support SQL, the query is submitted in SQL; for data sources that do not support SQL, the query is translated into the native query language of the data source or into a series of data source API calls.)

- Retrieving result data sets from the data source

- Responding to federated database queries about the default data type mappings used by a data source (The wrapper contains the default type mappings that are used when nicknames are created for a data source object. For relational wrappers, you can create data type mappings that override the default data type mappings.)

- Responding to federated database queries about the default function mappings used by a data source (A federated database needs data type mapping information for query planning purposes. The wrapper contains information that the federated database needs to determine whether DB2 functions are mapped to functions of the data source and, if so, how they are mapped. This information is used by the SQL Compiler to determine whether the data source is able to perform the query operations. You can create function mappings for relational wrappers to override the default function mappings.)

Before a wrapper can be used, it must first be registered on a federated server. Wrappers can be registered on a federated server by executing the CREATE WRAPPER SQL statement. The basic syntax for this statement is:

```
CREATE WRAPPER [WrapperName]
<LIBRARY [LibraryName]>
<OPTIONS (ADD [Option] '[Value]' ,...)>
```

where:

WrapperName   Identifies the name to be assigned to the wrapper that is to be created. Table 2.4 contains a list of the predefined wrapper names that are provided with DB2 9.

LibraryName   Identifies, by name, the file that contains the wrapper library module. This option is only used if a user-supplied wrapper name is specified; this option should not be used if a predefined wrapper name is provided in the *WrapperName* parameter.

Option   Identifies one or more options to be used to configure the wrapper or to define how DB2 uses the wrapper.

Value   Identifies the value to be assigned to the wrapper option specified.

It is important to note that when you register a wrapper by using one of the predefined wrapper names, the federated server automatically uses the appropriate wrapper library for the operating system on which it is running.

Table 2.4 Predefined Wrapper Names	
Data Source	**Wrapper Name**
DB2 Version 9.x for Linux, UNIX, and Windows	DRDA
DB2 Universal Database for z/OS	DRDA
DB2 Universal Database for iSeries	DRDA
DB2 Server for VM and VSE	DRDA
Informix	INFORMIX
Microsoft SQL Server	MSSQLODBC3
ODBC	ODBC
OLE DB	OLEDB
Oracle	NET8
Sybase	CTLIB
Teradata	TERADATA

Thus, if you wanted to register the appropriate predefined wrapper on a federated server so that you could access one or more Oracle data sources, you could do so by executing a CREATE WRAPPER SQL statement that looks something like this:

```
CREATE WRAPPER NET8
```

You must register one wrapper for each type of data source you want to have access to. Therefore, if you wanted to access three DB2 for z/OS database tables, one DB2 for iSeries table, two Informix tables, and one Oracle view, you would need to create one wrapper for the DB2 data source objects, one wrapper for the Informix data source objects, and one wrapper for the Oracle data source object. After these wrappers have been registered in the federated database, they can be used to access other objects in those data sources.

Server Definitions

After one or more wrappers have been registered in a federated database, the name used to identify a data source that is associated with a particular wrapper, along with other pertinent information, must be supplied before the data source can be accessed. The data source name, along with other information such as the type and version of the data source, the database name for a relational data source, and metadata that is specific to the data source are collectively called a server definition.

A server definition for a relational data source usually represents a remote database. Because a DB2 family data source can have multiple databases within a single instance, the corresponding server definition must specify the database to which the federated server can connect. In contrast, some relational database management systems, such as Oracle, do not allow multiple databases within each instance. In this case, the federated server can connect to it without knowing its name so the database name does not have to be included in the server definition.

The purpose of a server definition for non-relational data sources varies from data source to data source. Some server definitions map to a search type and daemon, a Web site, or a Web server. For other non-relational data sources, a server definition is created, because the hierarchy of federated objects requires that data source files be associated with a specific server object.

Server definitions are created by executing the CREATE SERVER SQL statement. The basic syntax for this statement is:

```
CREATE SERVER [ServerName]
<TYPE [ServerType]>
<VERSION [Version] <.[Release] <.[Modification]>>>
WRAPPER [WrapperName]
<AUTHORIZATION [RemoteAuthID] PASSWORD [Password]>
<OPTIONS (ADD [Option] '[Value]' ,...)>
```

where:

ServerName	Identifies, by name, the data source to be defined.
ServerType	Identifies the type of data source to be defined.
Version	Identifies the version number of the data source being defined.
Release	Identifies the version-release number of the data source being defined.
Modification	Identifies the version-modification number of the data source being defined.
WrapperName	Identifies, by name, the wrapper that the federated server is to use to interact with the data source being defined.
RemoteAuthID	Specifies the authorization ID under which any necessary actions are to be performed at the data source when the CREATE SERVER statement is processed. This authorization ID is only required for DB2 family data sources and is not used when establishing subsequent connections to the server.
Password	Specifies the password associated with the authorization ID provided in the *RemoteAuthID* parameter.
Option	Identifies one or more options to be used to either configure or provide information about the data source being defined.
Value	Identifies the value to be assigned to the server option specified.

Thus, if you wanted to create a server definition for an Oracle 9 data source, assign it the name CUSTOMERS, and associate with the predefined wrapper NET8, you could do so by executing a CREATE SERVER SQL statement that looks something like this:

```
CREATE SERVER customers
TYPE ORACLE
VERSION 9
WRAPPER NET8
```

You must create one server for every data source that you want to access. Therefore, if you wanted to access three Oracle instances and one DB2 for z/OS data source, you would need to create three Oracle servers—one for each Oracle instance—and one server for the DB2 for z/OS database.

Nicknames

A nickname is an identifier that an application uses to reference a data source object, such as a table or view. Users and applications reference nicknames in SQL statements just as they would an alias, a base table, or a view. However, nicknames are not alternative names for data source objects in the same way that aliases are. Instead, they are pointers by which the federated server references these objects.

Nicknames are created by executing the CREATE NICKNAME SQL statement. There are two forms of this statement—one for relational data sources and one for non-relational data sources. The basic syntax for the relational data source form of this statement is:

```
CREATE NICKNAME [Nickname]
FOR [DataSourceName].[SchemaName].[ObjectName]
<OPTIONS (ADD [Option] '[Value]' ,...)>
```

or

```
CREATE NICKNAME [Nickname]
FOR [DataSourceName].[ObjectName]
<OPTIONS (ADD [Option] '[Value]' ,...)>
```

where:

Nickname   Identifies the name to be used by the federated server for the data source object specified.

DataSourceName Identifies, by name, the data source that contains the object (i.e., table or view) for which the nickname is being created. The *DataSourceName* must be the same name that was assigned to the server with the CREATE SERVER SQL statement.

SchemaName   Identifies, by name, the schema to which the object (i.e., table or view) belongs. If the schema name contains any special or lowercase characters, it must be enclosed by double quotation marks.

ObjectName   Identifies, by name, the object (i.e., table or view) for which the nickname is being created. If the object name contains any special or lowercase characters, it must be enclosed by double quotation marks.

Option   Identifies one or more options to be enabled when the nickname is created.

Value   Identifies the value to be assigned to the nickname option specified.

For data sources that support schema names, the data source name, schema name, and object name must be provided. For data sources that do not support schema names, only the data source name and object name are required.

Thus, if you wanted to create a nickname for a table named EMPLOYEE, which resides in a schema named PAYROLL, that is in a DB2 for z/OS data source called OS390A, and assign it the name EMP_INFO, you could do so by executing a CREATE NICKNAME SQL statement that looks something like this:

```
CREATE NICKNAME emp_info
FOR os390a.payroll.employee
```

And if you wanted to retrieve the data that is stored in this table, you could do so by executing a query that looks something like this:

```
SELECT * FROM emp_info
```

Of course, before the EMP_INFO nickname can be created, a server definition named OS390A would have to exist for the DB2 for z/OS data source. Such a server definition could be created by executing a CREATE SERVER statement that looks something like this:

```
CREATE SERVER os390a
TYPE DB2/ZOS
VERSION 7.1
WRAPPER DRDA
```

When you create a nickname for a data source object, metadata about that object is added to the global catalog. The DB2 Optimizer then uses this metadata, along with information in the wrapper, to facilitate access to the data source object. If after a nickname has been created, the definition of a remote data source object is changed (for example, a column is deleted or a data type is changed), the nickname should be dropped and recreated; otherwise, errors might occur when the nickname is used in SQL statements.

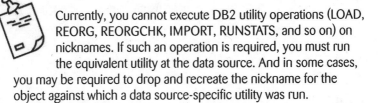

Currently, you cannot execute DB2 utility operations (LOAD, REORG, REORGCHK, IMPORT, RUNSTATS, and so on) on nicknames. If such an operation is required, you must run the equivalent utility at the data source. And in some cases, you may be required to drop and recreate the nickname for the object against which a data source-specific utility was run.

Data Type Mappings

In order for a federated server to retrieve data from a data source, the data types used by the data source must map to corresponding DB2 data types. Data type mappings are used to identify how data source-specific data types are to be mapped to DB2 data types. For example, by default:

- The Oracle FLOAT data type maps to the DB2 type DOUBLE.

- The Oracle DATE data type maps to the DB2 type TIMESTAMP.

- The Informix INTEGER data type maps to the DB2 type INTEGER.

- The DB2 for z/OS DATE data type maps to the DB2 type DATE.

For most relational data sources, default type mappings are included in the wrapper. Thus, the default type mappings for DB2 data sources are in the DRDA wrapper, the default type mappings for Informix are in the INFORMIX wrapper, and so on. If you want to override the default data type mappings provided, you can do so by executing one or more CREATE TYPE MAPPING SQL statements.

For some non-relational data sources, you must specify data type information when a nickname is created with the CREATE NICKNAME statement. In this case, corresponding DB2 data types must be specified for each column of the data source object when the nickname is created. Each column must be mapped to a particular field or column in the data source object.

· ·

If you change one or more type mappings for a relational data source after a nickname for an object in that data source has been created, you will need to drop the nickname and recreate it before the type mapping changes will take effect.

· ·

Function Mappings

In order for a federated server to recognize a data source function, the function must be mapped to an existing counterpart function in DB2. Function mappings are used to identify how data source-specific functions are to be mapped to DB2's built-in functions.

For most data sources, default function mappings are included along with default type mappings in the wrapper. Thus, the default function mappings to DB2 for z/OS functions are in the DRDA wrapper, the default function mappings to Sybase functions are in the CTLIB wrapper, and so forth.

If you want to disable one or more default data type mappings provided for a relational data source or if you want to use a data source-specific function that the federated server does not recognize, you can do so by creating one or more new function mappings. Function mappings are created by executing the CREATE FUNCTION MAPPING SQL statement. (The mapping that you create is between the data source function and a DB2 counterpart function at the federated database.)

Function mappings are typically created when a new built-in function or a new user-defined function becomes available at the data source. Function mappings are also used when a DB2 counterpart function does not exist. In this case, you must also create a function template. A function template is a function declaration that contains no executable code. You create a function template by executing the CREATE FUNCTION statement with the AS TEMPLATE option specified.

After the function mapping is created, the function template can be used in queries that are submitted to the federated server. When such a query is processed, the federated server will invoke the data source function to which the template is mapped and return values whose data types correspond to those in the RETURNS portion of the template's definition.

When you create a function mapping, it is possible that the return values from a function evaluated at the data source will be different from the return values from a compatible function evaluated at the DB2 federated database. If that is the case, DB2 will attempt to use the function mapping, but it may result in an SQL syntax error or unexpected results.

Index Specifications

When you create a nickname for a table in a data source, information about any indexes that have been defined for that table is added to the global catalog. This information is known as an index specification and is used by the DB2 Optimizer to improve performance when processing distributed requests.

When you create a nickname for a table that has no indexes or a data source object for which the federated server is unable to obtain corresponding index information, an index specification is not created. Similarly, when a nickname is created for a view, the federated server is unaware of the underlying table (and its indexes) from which the view was generated; thus, no index specifications are created. In this case, it would be probably be beneficial to tell the federated server that indexes exist.

The same is true if a nickname is created for a table that has no indexes and one or more indexes are created later, or if a nickname is created for a table that has indexes and one or more new indexes are added after the nickname is created. Otherwise, the federated server will be unaware that these indexes exist.

In these situations, you can supply the necessary index information to the global catalog by manually creating one or more index specifications. This is done by executing the CREATE INDEX SQL statement; the CREATE INDEX statement that you create will reference the nickname for the table and contain the information about the index of the data source table. If a nickname is created for a view, the CREATE INDEX statement that you create will reference the nickname for the view and contain information about the index of the underlying table for the view.

User Mappings

User mappings identify how DB2 authentication information is to be customized for a particular data source. To maintain the security of a remote data source, you can create one or more user mappings, which map a federated user ID and password to a data source user ID and password. Then, when the federated server connects to the data source and the data source requests a user ID and password, the federated server can provide the data source user ID and password rather than the user ID and password that were used to gain access to the federated server itself.

The CREATE USER MAPPING SQL statement can be used to create user mappings.

A Word about Pass-through Sessions

In addition to retrieving data from a data source using a nickname, you can also submit SQL statements directly to a data source using a special mode called pass-through. Currently, the data sources that support pass-through only do so via SQL. (In the future, it is possible that data sources will support pass-though using a data source language other than SQL.)

When you use pass-through to submit SQL statements directly to a data source, the statements must be coded in the SQL dialect used by the data source—not in the dialect recognized by DB2. Therefore, you should use a pass-through session when you want to perform an operation that cannot be conducted using the DB2 SQL/API. For example, you would use a pass-through session to create a procedure, create an index, or perform queries in the native dialect of the data source.

Similarly, you can use a pass-through session to perform actions that are not supported by SQL, such as certain administrative tasks. However, you cannot use a pass-through session to perform all administrative tasks. For example, you can create or drop tables at the data source, but you cannot start or stop the remote database.

Practice Questions

Question 1

Which CREATE TABLESPACE statement option is used to enable non-buffered I/O?

- ○ A. CONCURRENT IO
- ○ B. NO FILE SYSTEM CACHING
- ○ C. USE DIRECT IO
- ○ D. NO FILE BUFFERING

Question 2

A database named MYDB was created using automatic storage and a table space in the database named MY_TBSP is running out of space. Which command will provide more storage space to the table space so more data can be added to it?

- ○ A. ALTER DATABASE ADD STORAGE ON '/db2/dbspace1'
- ○ B. ALTER TABLESPACE my_tbsp EXTEND 100 MB
- ○ C. ALTER DATABASE EXTEND STORAGE FOR my_tbsp 100 MB
- ○ D. ALTER TABLESPACE my_tbsp ADD STORAGE ON '/db2/dbspace1'

Question 3

A table space named MY_TBSP was created in a database partition group named DBPG1. Later, a decision is made to move this table space to a database partition group named DBPG2. How can this change be made?

- ○ A. Change the partition group associate with the table space by executing the ALTER TABLESPACE statement.
- ○ B. Detach the table space from the DBPG1database partition group and attach it to the DBPG2 database partition group using the DETACH PARTITION and ATTACH PARTITION statements.
- ○ C. Drop the table space using the DROP statement and recreate it in database partition DBPG2 using the CREATE TABLESPACE statement.
- ○ D. Move the table space from the database DBPG1 partition group to the DBPG2 database partition group using the REDISTRIBUTE PARTITION GROUP statement.

Question 4

If the SQL statement shown below is executed:

```
CREATE REGULAR TABLESPACE sales_ts
MANAGED BY DATABASE USING
    (FILE 'C:\TABLESPACES\dms_tbsp.tsf' 1000 M)
```

Assuming DB2 9 is being used, which of the following is NOT a characteristic of the resulting table space?

- ○ A. The page size used is 4K.
- ○ B. File system caching is enabled.
- ○ C. The table space resides in the IBMTEMPGROUP database partition group.
- ○ D. Dropped tables in the specified table space can be recovered using the RECOVER DROPPED TABLE option of the ROLLFORWARD DATABASE command.

Question 5

Which two of the following can be successfully performed using the ALTER TABLESPACE statement? (Select two)

- ❏ A. Convert an SMS table space to a DMS table space.
- ❏ B. Change the extent size for a DMS table space.
- ❏ C. Change the prefetch size for an automatic storage table space.
- ❏ D. Resize the containers used by an SMS table space.
- ❏ E. Add a container to an SMS table space on a database partition that currently has no containers.

Question 6

Which of the following commands will create a DMS table space named TBSP1 on all database partitions used by a multi-partition database?

- ○ A. CREATE TABLESPACE tbsp1 MANAGED BY DATABASE USING (FILE '/db2files/tbsp1/cont1P $N' 5000)
- ○ B. CREATE TABLESPACE tspc1 MANAGED BY DATABASE USING (FILE '/db2files/ tbsp1/cont1P $NODE' 5000)
- ○ C. CREATE TABLESPACE tspc1 MANAGED BY DATABASE USING (FILE /db2files/ tbsp1/cont1P $P' 5000)
- ○ D. CREATE TABLESPACE tspc1 MANAGED BY DATABASE USING (FILE '/db2files/ tbsp1/cont1P $DBPARTITIONNUM' 5000)

Question 7

Given the following statements:

```
CREATE TABLESPACE payroll MANAGED BY DATABASE USING
   (FILE '\home\myfile1' 200 FILE '\home\myfile2' 400);
ALTER TABLESPACE payroll EXTEND (FILE '\home\myfile2' 1000
   FILE '\home\myfile1' 1200);
```

How large are the containers MYFILE1 and MYFILE2?

○ A. MYFILE1 = 200 pages, MYFILE2 = 400 pages

○ B. MYFILE1 = 1200 pages, MYFILE2 = 1000 pages

○ C. MYFILE1 = 1400 pages, MYFILE2 = 1400 pages

○ D. MYFILE1 = 1200 pages, MYFILE2 = 1600 pages

Question 8

If no initial size is specified for a table space that is created in a database that is using automatic storage, how much storage space is preallocated for the table space?

○ A. 32 pages

○ B. 32 MB

○ C. 64 pages

○ D. 64 MB

Question 9

Given the following sequence of SQL statements:

1) CREATE DATABASE test ON C:

2) CONNECT TO test

3) CREATE BUFFERPOOL bp1 SIZE 2000

4) CREATE TABLESPACE ts1 MANAGED BY DATABASE USING (FILE 'C:\ts1data. dat' 10 M) BUFFERPOOL bp1

5) CREATE TABLE employees(empid INT, fname CHAR(30), lname CHAR(30))

Which two statements are not required in order to create the table named EMPLOYEES? (Select two)

☐ A. 1

☐ B. 2

☐ C. 3

☐ D. 4

☐ E. 5

Question 10

While connected to a database that has four partitions, a database administrator executes the following command:

```
CREATE BUFFERPOOL mybp SIZE 3000
```

If 8 MB of memory is available at the time the command is executed, how much memory is immediately consumed?

○ A. 0 MB
○ B. 6 MB
○ C. 8 MB
○ D. 12 MB

Question 11

Given the following table spaces, their associated page size, and number of pages:

```
TBSP1        - 16K  page size, 150000 pages
TBSP2        - 8K   page size, 100000 pages
TBSP3        - 4K   page size, 200000 pages
USERSPACE1   - 4K   page size, 500000 pages
```

How many buffer pools must be created before the table spaces listed can be created?

○ A. 1
○ B. 2
○ C. 3
○ D. 4

Question 12

Given a newly created database and sufficient memory, if the following statements are successfully executed on a UNIX server:

```
CREATE BUFFERPOOL bp1 SIZE 60 MB;
CREATE BUFFERPOOL bp2 SIZE 20000 PAGESIZE 16K;
CREATE BUFFERPOOL bp3 SIZE 2000 PAGESIZE 8K;
```

How much memory will be allocated for all buffer pools used by the database?

○ A. 320 MB
○ B. 396 MB
○ C. 400 MB
○ D. 401 MB

Question 13

Which two of the following are valid ALTER BUFFERPOOL statements? (Select two)

- ❏ A. ALTER BUFFERPOOL mybp NUMBLOCKPAGES 32000
- ❏ B. ALTER BUFFERPOOL mybp TABLESPACE tbsp1
- ❏ C. ALTER BUFFERPOOL mybp PAGESIZE 8 K
- ❏ D. ALTER BUFFERPOOL mybp BLOCKSIZE 32
- ❏ E. ALTER BUFFERPOOL mybp SIZE -1

Question 14

A database administrator needs to create a federated database and configure access to join data from two Oracle instances, one SQL Server instance, and one DB2 database.

Which objects are needed to establish the specified connections?

- ○ A. 2 Oracle servers, 2 Oracle wrappers, 1 SQL Server server, 1 SQL Server wrapper, and nicknames for all databases.
- ○ B. 2 Oracle servers, 1 Oracle wrapper, 1 SQL Server server, 1 SQL Server wrapper, and nicknames for all databases.
- ○ C. 2 Oracle servers, 2 Oracle wrappers, 1 SQL Server server, 1 SQL Server wrapper, 1 DB2 server, 1 DB2 wrapper, and nicknames for all databases.
- ○ D. 2 Oracle servers, 1 Oracle wrapper, 1 SQL Server server, 1 SQL Server wrapper, 1 DB2 server, 1 DB2 wrapper, and nicknames for all databases.

Question 15

Last week, a database administrator configured a SQL Server data source in a federated database (that references a table named HISTORY). Yesterday, insert operations caused the HISTORY table to double in size. Which of the following steps must be performed in order to update the statistics for the HISTORY table at the federated server?

- ○ A. Perform the SQL Server equivalent of RUNSTATS on the HISTORY table at the SQL Server server.
- ○ B. Perform the SQL Server equivalent of RUNSTATS on the HISTORY table at the SQL Server server; then perform RUNSTATS on the nickname for the HISTORY table at the federated server.
- ○ C. Perform the SQL Server equivalent of RUNSTATS on the HISTORY table at the SQL Server server; then drop and re-create the HISTORY nickname at the federated server.
- ○ D. Perform the SQL Server equivalent of RUNSTATS on the HISTORY table at the SQL Server server; then use the "db2updfedstat" tool to update the statistics at the federated server.

Question 16

A database administrator created all of the necessary federated objects for an Oracle data source in a federated system.

Given the following set of steps:

1) Drop the current user mapping
2) Drop the current data type mapping
3) Drop the nickname to the table
4) Create the new user mapping
5) Create the new data type mapping
6) Re-create the nickname to the table

Which steps must be performed if the data types of several columns in the Oracle data source are changed?

○ A. 2, 5

○ B. 3, 5, 6

○ C. 2, 5, 3, 6

○ D. 1, 2, 4, 5, 6

Answers

Question 1

The correct answer is **B**. If the NO FILE SYSTEM CACHING option is used with the CREATE TABLESPACE or ALTER TABLESPACE statement, I/O for the specified table space will not be buffered by the file system (i.e., the table space will use direct I/O). It is important to note that the registry variable DB2_DIRECT_IO, introduced in Version 8.1 FixPak 4, enabled no file system caching for all SMS containers except for long field data, large object data, and temporary table spaces on AIX JFS2. Setting this registry variable in Version 9.1 or later is equivalent to altering all table spaces – SMS and DMS – and specifying the NO FILE SYSTEM CACHING clause. However, using the DB2_DIRECT_IO registry variable is not recommended. Instead, you should enable NO FILE SYSTEM CACHING at the table space level.

Question 2

The correct answer is **A**. If a database is enabled for automatic storage, the container- and space- management characteristics of its table spaces are determined by DB2. Therefore, although the ALTER TABLESPACE command can be used to add new containers to existing DMS table spaces, it cannot be used to add new containers to automatic storage table spaces. Instead, to add new storage paths to the collection of paths that are used for automatic storage table spaces once a database has been created, you must use the ALTER DATABASE statement. The basic syntax for this statement is:

```
ALTER DATABASE [DatabaseName]
ADD STORAGE ON '[Container]' ,...)
```

where:

DatabaseName	Identifies the database, by name, that is to have new containers added to its pool of containers that are used for automatic storage.
Container	Identifies one or more new storage locations (containers) that are to be added to the collection of storage locations that are used for automatic storage table spaces.

Thus, if you wanted to add the storage locations /data/path1 and /data/path2 to a database named SAMPLE that is configured for automatic storage and resides on a UNIX system, you could do so by executing an ALTER DATABASE SQL statement that looks like this:

```
ALTER DATABASE sample
ADD STORAGE '/data/path1', '/data/path2'
```

Question 3

The correct answer is **C**. Once a table space has been created, there is no way to dynamically change the partition group to which it belongs. Therefore, if you want to change the partition group associated with an existing table space, you must drop the table space (using the DROP statement) and recreate it (using the CREATE TABLESPACE statement) in the new database partition group.

Question 4

The correct answer is **C**. If no database partition group is specified, the default database partition group IBMDEFAULTGROUP is used for REGULAR, LARGE, and USER TEMPORARY table spaces and the default database partition group IBMTEMPGROUP is used for SYSTEM TEMPORARY table spaces. Unless otherwise specified, pages used by table spaces are 4K in size. If the FILE SYSTEM CACHING option is specified (the default in DB2 9), all I/O for the table space will be buffered by the file system. If the DROPPED TABLE RECOVERY ON option is specified (the default), dropped tables in the specified table space can be recovered using the RECOVER DROPPED TABLE option of the ROLLFORWARD DATABASE command – provided the table space is a regular table space.

Question 5

The correct answers are **C** and **E**. Using the ALTER TABLESPACE statement, an existing table space can be modified as follows:

- A container can be added to an SMS table space on a database partition that currently has no containers.
- Containers can be added to, or dropped from a DMS table space.
- The size of an existing container in a DMS table space can be changed.
- The buffer pool used to cache data for a table space can be changed.
- The amount of data that gets prefetched from a table space (prefetch size) can be changed.
- The I/O controller overhead and disk seek latency time for a table space can be changed.
- The time it takes to transfer one page (4K or 8K) of data from the table space to memory can be changed.
- The file system caching policy used by a table space can be changed.

Question 6

The correct answer is **A**. The argument " $N" ([blank]$N) is used to indicate a database partition expression; when used, it is replaced with the actual partition number. A database partition expression can be used anywhere in a container name and expressions can be specified within the same name. To use a partition expression, there must be a space after the container name followed by the expression. The result of the expression following the space will then be appended to the container name. If there is no space character in the container name after the database partition expression, it is assumed that the rest of the string is part of the expression.

Thus, if you wanted to create a DMS table space named TBSP1 in a partitioned database that has five partitions numbered 0 through 4 and you wanted the storage container for the first partition to be a file named CONT1P0, the storage container for the second partition to be a file named CONT1P1, and so on, you could do so by executing a CREATE TABLESPACE command that looks something like this:

```
CREATE TABLESPACE tbsp1
MANAGED BY DATABASE
USING (FILE 'cont1P $N' 5000)
```

Question 7

The correct answer is **C**. If you wanted to increase the size of all containers associated with an existing DMS table space named PAYROLL by 200 megabytes, you could do so by executing an ALTER TABLESPACE SQL statement that looks like this:

```
ALTER TABLESPACE payroll_ts EXTEND (ALL CONTAINERS 200 M)
```

On the other hand, if you wanted to increase the size of individual containers, you could do so by executing an ALTER TABLESPACE SQL statement that looks like this:

```
ALTER TABLESPACE payroll EXTEND (FILE '\home\myfile2' 1000
    FILE '\home\myfile1' 1200);
```

The order of the container names does not matter, so in this example the resulting container sizes would be 200 + 1200 pages or 1400 pages (MYFILE1) and 400 + 1000 or 1400 pages (MYFILE2).

Question 8

The correct answer is **B**. Unlike when SMS and DMS table spaces are defined, no container definitions are needed for automatic storage table spaces; DB2 assigns containers to automatic storage table spaces automatically. However, an initial size can be specified as part of the table space creation process - if an initial size is not specified, DB2 will use a default value of 32 megabytes.

Question 9

The correct answers are **C** and **D**. The database must exist and a connection must be made to it before the EMPLOYEE table can be created with the CREATE TABLE SQL statement shown. However, since no table space is specified with the CREATE TABLE statement used in the sequence of statements provided, the EMPLOYEE table will be created in the USERSPACE1 table space by default. This table space uses the buffer pool IBMDEFAULTBP, so the steps that create a buffer pool named BP1 and a table space named TS1 are unnecessary.

Question 10

The correct answer is **A**. If the DEFERRED clause is specified with the CREATE BUFFERPOOL statement, the buffer pool will be created, but no memory will be allocated until all connections to the database the buffer pool is to be created for have been terminated and the database has been deactivated (i.e. the database is stopped and restarted). If the IMMEDIATE clause is specified instead, or if neither clause is specified, the buffer pool will be created and the amount of memory needed will be allocated immediately unless the amount of memory required is unavailable, in which case a warning message will be generated and the buffer pool creation process will behave as if the DEFERRED clause were specified. In this scenario, approximately 12 MB of memory is needed but only 8 MB is available, so no memory will be allocated until the database is stopped and restarted.

Question 11

The correct answer is **B**. The page size used by a buffer pool determines which table spaces can be used with it – a buffer pool can only be used by a table space that has a corresponding page size. Since one buffer pool with a page size of 4K is created by default (IBMDEFAULTBP), only two additional buffer pools, one with a page size of 8 K and one with a page size of 16K, must exist before the table spaces listed can be created.

Question 12

The correct answer is **D**. The amount of memory that will be allocated for all buffer pools is calculated as follows:

Buffer pools specified:

Buffer pool BP1 = 60 MB	= **60 MB**
Buffer pool BP2 = 20,000 pages * 16 KB = 320,000 KB	= **320 MB**
Buffer pool BP3 = 2000 pages * 8 KB = 16,000 KB	= **16 MB**

Default buffer pool (1000 4K pages on UNIX):
Buffer pool IBMDEFAULTBP = 1000 pages * 4KB = 4000 KB =   **4 MB**

DB2's hidden buffer pools:
Hidden buffer pool 1 = 16 pages * 4 KB = 64 KB   = **.064 MB**
Hidden buffer pool 2 = 16 pages * 8 KB = 128 KB   = **.128 MB**
Hidden buffer pool 3 = 16 pages * 16 KB = 256 KB   = **.256 MB**
Hidden buffer pool 4 = 16 pages * 32 KB = 512 KB   = **.512 MB**

Total: **400.96 MB**

The db2mtrk utility can be used to verify the allocation.

Question 13

The correct answers are **A** and **D**. The basic syntax for the ALTER BUFFERPOOL statement is:

```
ALTER BUFFERPOOL [BufferPoolName]
<IMMEDIATE | DEFERRED>
<DBPARTITIONNUM [PartitionNum]>
SIZE [AUTOMATIC |
  [NumberOfPages] |
  [NumberOfPages] AUTOMATIC]
```

or

```
ALTER BUFFERPOOL [BufferPoolName]
ADD DATABASE PARTITION GROUP [PartitionGroup]
```

or

```
ALTER BUFFERPOOL [BufferPoolName]
NUMBLOCKPAGES [NumBlockPages] <BLOCK SIZE [BlockSize]>
```

or

```
ALTER BUFFERPOOL [BufferPoolName]
BLOCK SIZE [BlockSize]
```

where:

BufferPoolName   Identifies the buffer pool, by name, whose characteristics are to be modified.

PartitionNum   Identifies the database partition on which the size of the buffer pool is to be altered.

NumberOfPages	Enables or disables self-tuning OR identifies the new number of pages that are to be allocated for the buffer pool.
PartitionGroup	Identifies a new database partition group that is to be added to the list of database partition groups to which the buffer pool definition is applicable.
NumBlockPages	Specifies the number of pages that are to be created in the block-based area of the buffer pool. (The block-based area of a buffer pool cannot consume more than 98 percent of the total buffer pool.)
BlockSize	Specifies the number of pages that can be stored within a block in the block-based area of the buffer pool. (The *BlockSize* value specified must be between 2 and 256 pages; the default value is 32 pages.)

Therefore, the ALTER BUFFERPOOL statement can be used to change the block size and number of block pages used, but not the table space(s) that use the buffer pool nor the page size. And a size of -1 is not valid.

Question 14

The correct answer is **D**. Wrappers are mechanisms by which a federated database interacts with data sources. You must register one wrapper for each type of data source you want to have access to. Therefore, if you wanted to access two Oracle database tables, one SQL Server table, and one DB2 for z/OS view, you would need to create one wrapper for the Oracle data source objects, one wrapper for the SQL Server data source object, and one wrapper for the DB2 data source object.

After one or more wrappers have been registered in a federated database, the name used to identify a data source that is associated with a particular wrapper, along with other pertinent information, must be supplied before the data source can be accessed. The data source name, along with other information such as the type and version of the data source, the database name for a relational data source, and metadata that is specific to the data source are collectively called a server definition (or server). You must create one server for every data source that you want to access. Therefore, if you wanted to access two Oracle instances, one SQL Server data source, and one DB2 for z/OS data source, you would need to create one server for each Oracle instance, one server for the SQL Server data source, and one server for the DB2 for z/OS database.

A nickname is an identifier that an application uses to reference a data source object, such as a table or view. Users and applications reference nicknames in SQL statements just as they would reference an alias, a base table, or a view. However, nicknames are not alternative names for data source objects in the same way that aliases are. Instead, they are pointers by which the federated server references these objects. So in order to reference two Oracle database tables, one SQL Server table, and one DB2 for z/OS view in a join operation, you would need to create one nickname for each database (so each database can be referenced in the query performing the join operation).

Question 15

The correct answer is **C**. Currently you cannot execute DB2 utility operations (LOAD, REORG, REORGCHK, IMPORT, RUNSTATS, and so on) on nicknames. If such an operation is required, you must run the equivalent utility at the data source. And in some cases, you may be required to drop and re-create the nickname for the object against which a data source-specific utility was run. In this case, dropping and re-creating the nickname after statistics have been updated at the SQL Server data source will cause DB2 to update the statistics on the federated server.

Question 16

The correct answer is **B**. In order for a federated server to retrieve data from a data source, the data types used by the data source must map to corresponding DB2 data types. Data type mappings are used to identify how data source-specific data types are to be mapped to DB2 data types. For most relational data sources, default type mappings are included in the wrapper. If you want to override the default data type mappings provided, you can do so by executing one or more CREATE TYPE MAPPING SQL statements.

If after a nickname has been created, the definition of a remote data source object is changed (for example, a column is deleted or a data type is changed), the nickname should be dropped and recreated; otherwise, errors might occur when the nickname is used in SQL statements. Likewise, if you change one or more type mappings for a relational data source after a nickname for an object in that data source has been created, you will need to drop the nickname and recreate it before the type mapping changes will take effect. Thus, in this scenario, you must drop the nickname to the Oracle table, create a new data type mapping to reflect the changes made to the data types used by the Oracle data source, and then re-create the nickname.

CHAPTER 3

Data Partitioning and Clustering

Fifteen percent (15%) of the DB2 9 for Linux, UNIX, and Windows Advanced Database Administration exam (Exam 734) is designed to test your knowledge of database partitioning, as well as your ability to create and manage range-partitioned and multidimensional clustered (MDC) tables. The questions that make up this portion of the exam are intended to evaluate the following:

- Your ability to design, create, and manage a partitioned database

- Your ability to design, create, and manage range-clustered and range-partitioned tables

- Your ability to design, create, and manage multidimensional clustered (MDC) tables

- Your ability to use the Design Advisor

- Your knowledge of the Balanced Configuration Unit (BCU) design for data warehouses

This chapter is designed to introduce you to parallelism and partitioned databases, to walk you through the process used to add new database partitions to a partitioned database, and to provide you with an overview of partition groups, partitioning keys, and partitioning maps. This chapter is also designed to show you how to design and construct range-clustered tables, range-partitioned tables, and multidimensional clustered tables, as well as how to use the Design Advisor to identify indexes, materialized query tables (MQTs), and multidimensional clustering tables that could help improve query performance in your database environment. This chapter concludes with an introduction to the IBM InfoSphere Balanced Warehouse—also known as the Balanced Configuration Unit or BCU.

Parallelism

Many DB2 tasks (such as query execution) can be performed in parallel to dramatically enhance performance. The nature of the task, the database configuration, and the hardware environment used determine, to some extent, how DB2 will take advantage of parallelism. Three types of parallelism are supported by DB2:

- Input/Output
- Query
- Utility

Input/Output Parallelism

Parallel I/O refers to the process of writing to, or reading from, two or more I/O devices simultaneously; its use can result in significant improvements in throughput. When reading data from or writing data to a table space, DB2 will attempt to use parallel I/O if the table space spans more than one container. However, there are situations when it would be beneficial to have parallel I/O enabled for a table space that only uses one storage container. For example, if the container resides on a RAID device that consists of more than one physical disk, performance may be improved if read and write operations are performed in parallel.

The DB2_PARALLEL_IO registry variable is used to force DB2 to use parallel I/O for table spaces that only have one container, or for table spaces whose containers reside on more than one physical disk. If this registry variable is not set, the level of I/O parallelism used is equal to the number of containers used by the table space. If this registry variable is set, the level of I/O parallelism used is equal, at most, to the result of the table space's prefetch size divided by the table space's extent size. For example, if the DB2_PARALLEL_IO registry variable is not set and a table space using two containers has a prefetch size four times the extent size, each prefetch request for the table space will be broken into two requests (and each request will be for two extents). Therefore, assuming prefetchers are available, both requests can be executed in parallel. In the case where the DB2_PARALLEL_IO registry variable has been set, each prefetch request for the table space will be broken into four requests (this time, each request will be for one extent) and four prefetchers can service the requests in parallel. If, in this example, each table space container resided on a single, dedicated disk, setting the DB2_PARALLEL_IO registry variable could result in contention on both disks, because two prefetchers could be attempting to access both disks used at the same time. On the other hand, if both table space containers were striped across multiple disks, setting the DB2_PARALLEL_IO registry variable could potentially allow access to multiple disks at the same time.

Query Parallelism

Parallel query execution refers to the ability to execute queries using multiple CPUs simultaneously. When used, query parallelism can reduce the amount of time required to execute large queries by increasing the number of CPUs used to process the query. Two types of query parallelism are available with DB2: inter-query parallelism and intra-query parallelism. Inter-query parallelism refers to the ability of the database to accept queries from multiple applications at the same time. Each query runs independently of the others, but DB2 runs all of them simultaneously. Intra-query parallelism refers to the simultaneous processing of parts of a single query, using either intra-partition parallelism, inter-partition parallelism, or both.

Intra-partition Parallelism

Intra-partition parallelism refers to the ability to break up a database operation into multiple parts and execute those parts simultaneously within a single DB2 instance. This type of parallelism subdivides what is usually considered a single database operation, such as the creation of an index, the bulk loading of a table, or the execution of an SQL query, into multiple parts, many or all of which can be executed in parallel within a single database partition. When this happens, the operation can be completed more quickly than if it had been run serially. Intra-partition parallelism is often used to take advantage of multiple processors found in a symmetric multi-processor (SMP) server. Figure 3–1 illustrates how intra-partition parallelism is used to process an SQL query that has been broken into four parts, each of which is executed in parallel, working with a subset of the data stored in a table.

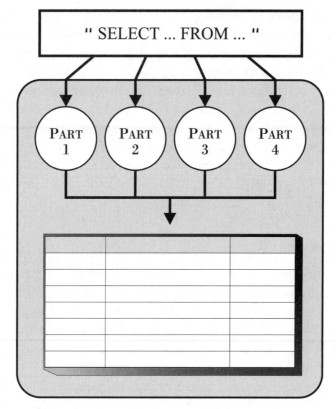

SINGLE DATABASE PARTITION

Figure 3—1: Intra-partition parallelism.

To take advantage of intra-partition parallelism, a database used must be configured as follows:

- The INTRA_PARALLEL database manager configuration parameter must be set to YES.

- The MAX_QUERYDEGREE database manager configuration parameter must be assigned a value greater than 1 or the value ANY. (The value ANY tells the DB2 Optimizer to choose the degree of parallelism to use based on cost.)

- The DFT_DEGREE database configuration parameter or the CURRENT DEGREE, DEGREE, or the RUNTIME DEGREE special register must be assigned a value greater than 1 or the value ANY. (The value ANY indicates that the default level of intra-partition parallelism to use is to be equal to the number of processors found on the computer. The CURRENT DEGREE special register sets the degree of parallelism for dynamic SQL statements, the DEGREE special register sets the degree of parallelism for static SQL statements, and the RUNTIME DEGREE special register sets the degree of parallelism for running applications.)

For example, to enable intra-partition parallelism for a DB2 database stored on a 32-way SMP server and divided among eight database partitions such that the maximum degree of parallelism for each partition is limited to four, you would execute the following commands:

```
UPDATE DBM CFG USING INTRA_PARALLEL YES;
UPDATE DBM CFG USING MAX_QUERYDEGREE 4;
```

However, suppose you had a single DB2 instance that has intra-partition parallelism enabled, and suppose that two databases existed under the instance. Assuming one database is a data warehouse that supports large, complex queries that scan large amounts of data and the other database acts as a journal that is the target of insert operations but is seldom queried, the intra-partition parallelism requirements for each database would be very different. In this case, the default degree of parallelism to use for each database could be specified by executing a set of commands that look more like this:

```
UPDATE DB CFG FOR dbase1 USING DFT_DEGREE 8;
UPDATE DB CFG FOR dbase2 USING DFT_DEGREE 1;
```

Intra-partition parallelism can take advantage of either data parallelism or pipeline parallelism. Data parallelism is normally used when scanning large indexes or tables—when data parallelism is used as part of the access plan for an SQL statement, the index or data will be dynamically partitioned and each of the executing parts of the query (known as package parts) is assigned a range of data to act upon. For an index scan, data will be partitioned based on index key values; for a table scan, data will be partitioned based on the actual data pages.

Pipeline parallelism is normally used when distinct operations on the data can be executed in parallel. For example, pipeline parallelism might be used if a table was scanned and the results of the scan were immediately fed into a sort operation. This would allow the sort operation to be executed in parallel without waiting for all the data to be scanned.

··

When intra-partition parallelism is enabled (by setting the INTRA_PARALLEL DB2 Database Manager configuration parameter to YES), an instance level control block is set up by DB2; each database operation performed on databases controlled by the instance will require a check of this control block during optimization and execution. Even if intra-partition parallelism is disabled at the database level by setting the maximum degree of parallelism or default degree of parallelism to one (1), this control block will still be checked. Therefore, it is best to disable intra-partition parallelism at the instance level rather than at the database level, if possible.

··

Inter-partition Parallelism

Inter-partition parallelism refers to the ability to break up a database operation into multiple parts, many or all of which can be run in parallel across multiple partitions of a partitioned database. Inter-partition parallelism can be used to take advantage of multiple processors of a symmetric multi-processor (SMP) server, or to take advantage of multiple processors spread across multiple servers. (Database partitions may physically reside on one workstation or can be distributed across several workstations.) Figure 3–2 illustrates how inter-partition parallelism is used to process an SQL query that has been broken into four parts, each of which is executed in parallel, on a separate database partition.

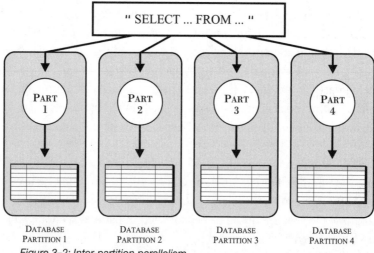

Figure 3–2: Inter-partition parallelism.

To take advantage of inter-partition parallelism, a database must be a partitioned database. The degree of parallelism used is largely determined by the number of database partitions created and by how database partition groups have been defined.

Intra-partition Parallelism and Inter-partition Parallelism

In a partitioned database, intra-partition parallelism and inter-partition parallelism can be combined to provide, in effect, two dimensions of parallelism. This combination results in an even more dramatic increase in the speed at which some database operations are performed. Figure 3–3 illustrates how intra-partition parallelism and inter-partition parallelism can be used together to process an SQL query.

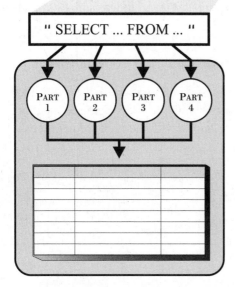
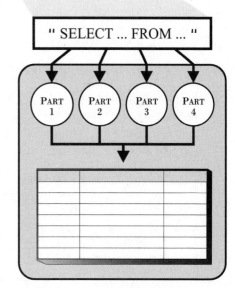

DATABASE PARTITION 1   DATABASE PARTITION 2

Figure 3—3: Intra-partition and inter-partition parallelism.

Utility Parallelism

Many DB2 utilities attempt to take advantage of intra-partition parallelism. In cases in which multiple database partitions exist, utilities can also take advantage of inter-partition parallelism by executing simultaneously at each database partition. Take, for example, the Load utility. Loading data is a CPU-intensive task, so whenever possible, the Load utility will take advantage of multiple processors for tasks such as parsing and formatting data. The Load utility will also use parallel I/O servers to write the data being loaded to containers in parallel.

The Backup utility is another utility that takes advantage of parallelism whenever possible. Backing up data is a heavily I/O-bound task. The Backup utility exploits I/O parallelism by reading from multiple table space containers in parallel and asynchronously writing to multiple backup media in parallel.

DB2 will also exploit both intra-partition parallelism and inter-partition parallelism when creating an index; during index creation, the scanning and subsequent sorting of data occurs in parallel. This helps to speed up the index creation process when an index is created initially, during an index restart (if an index is marked invalid), and during the reorganization of data.

Types of Parallelism Supported by Common Hardware Configurations

So far, we have looked at the different types of parallelism available, but we have not discussed where each type of parallelism should be used. Some of the more common hardware configurations available, along with the types of parallelism best suited for each, can be seen in Table 3.1.

Table 3.1 Types of Parallelism Possible in Common Hardware Environments			
Hardware Configuration	I/O Parallelism	Intra-partition Parallelism	Inter-partition Parallelism
Single database partition, single processor	Yes	No	No
Single database partition, multiple processors (SMP)	Yes	Yes	No
Multiple database partitions, one processor (MPP)	Yes	No	Yes
Multiple database partitions, multiple processors (cluster of SMPs)	Yes	Yes	Yes
Logical database partitions	Yes	Yes	Yes

Keep in mind that each database partition can reside on its own machine and have its own processor, memory, and disks. A logical database partition differs from a physical partition in that it is not given control of an entire machine—although the machine has shared resources, logical database partitions do not share these resources. Processors are shared, but disks and memory are not. The ability to have two or more database partitions coexist on the same machine (regardless of the number of processors available) allows greater flexibility in designing high availability configurations and failover strategies.

Partitioned Databases—A Closer Look

In Chapter 2, "Database Design," we saw that a partitioned database is a database that spans two or more database partitions, allowing data to be distributed across all of the partitions used. Sometimes called a database node or node, a database partition contains its own data, indexes, configuration files, and transaction log files and holds just a portion of a much larger database. Data retrieval and update requests are decomposed automatically into sub-requests and executed in parallel among all applicable database partitions. The fact that a database is split across multiple database partitions is transparent to users issuing SQL statements.

Partitioned databases are created in the same way that non-partitioned databases are created—by using the Create Database Wizard or by executing the CREATE DATABASE command. In a partitioned environment, the resulting database is automatically created across all database partitions defined in a special file known as the DB2 node configuration file. (Therefore, the DB2 node configuration file must be created and populated appropriately before a partitioned database is created.)

The DB2 Node Configuration File (db2nodes.cfg)

The DB2 node configuration file (a file named db2nodes.cfg) is used to define the database partitions and servers that participate in a DB2 instance. The db2nodes.cfg file is also used to specify the IP address or host name of a high-speed interconnect, if you want to use a high-speed interconnect for database partition server communication. The db2nodes.cfg file must contain one entry for each server participating in the instance; when a DB2 instance is created, a db2nodes.cfg file is also created in the instance owner's home directory, and an entry for the instance-owning server is added to the file. To scale your partitioned database system, simply add an entry for each database partition server to the db2nodes.cfg file.

On Linux and UNIX, the db2nodes.cfg file is located in the instance owner's home directory, and each record stored in it must be formatted as follows:

```
[PartitionNumber]  [HostName]  [LogicalPort]  [NetName]  [ResourceSetName]
```

where:

PartitionNumber Is a unique number between 0 and 999, inclusively, that identifies a database partition server in a partitioned database system. The value that you specify for additional database partition servers must be in ascending order, but gaps can exist in the sequence. (You may elect to put a gap between *PartitionNumber* values if you plan to add logical partition servers and wish to keep the partitions logically grouped in the file.)

HostName Identifies the TCP/IP host name of the database partition server. (The host name specified must be defined in the /etc/ hosts file on the server.)

LogicalPort Identifies the logical port number that will be used by the database partition server. During installation, DB2 reserves a port range (for example, 60000–60003) in the etc/services file on the server, to be used for inter-partition communications. The *LogicalPort* value specifies which port in that range you want to assign to a particular logical partition server. If a value is not provided for this field, the default value, 0, is used; if you are using logical database partitions, the value specified must start at 0 and continue in ascending order (for example, 0, 1, 2). Furthermore, if you specify a *LogicalPort* value for one database partition server, you must provide a value for each database partition server listed in the db2nodes.cfg file. This field is optional if you are not using logical database partitions or a high-speed interconnect.

NetName Identifies the host name or IP address of the high-speed interconnect to be used for FCM communication. This field is required only if you are using a high-speed interconnect for database partition communications. (If a *NetName* value is provided, a corresponding *LogicalPort* value must be provided.)

ResourceSetName   Defines the operating system resource that the node should be started in. This field is for process affinity support and is only supported on AIX, HP-UX, and Solaris. (If a *ResourceSetName* value is provided, a corresponding *NetName* value must be provided.)

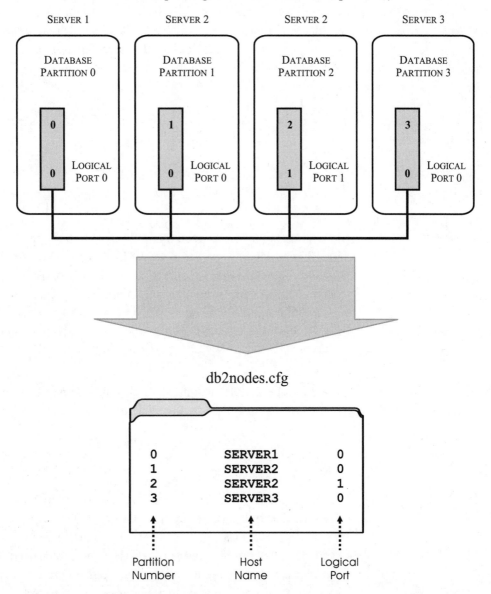

Figure 3—4: A partitioned database configuration and its corresponding DB2 node configuration file.

Figure 3–4 illustrates how a db2nodes.cfg file would be coded to correspond to a database with four database partitions residing on three different UNIX servers. When there is only one database partition per server, the partition will use logical port zero (0) for communications; in this example, because two database partitions reside on the second server used, logical port zero (0) is reserved for the first partition and logical port one (1) for the second. (When there is only one partition on each server, the logical port number does not have to be specified in the db2nodes.cfg file; the logical port number is only required when multiple partitions reside on the same server.)

On Windows, the db2nodes.cfg file is slightly different and must be formatted as follows:

    [PartitionNumber] [HostName] [ComputerName] [LogicalPort] [NetName]

where:

PartitionNumber   Is a unique number between 0 and 999, inclusively, that identifies a database partition server in a partitioned database system. The value you specify for additional database partition servers must be in ascending order, but gaps can exist in the sequence. (You may elect to put a gap between *PartitionNumber* values if you plan to add logical partition servers and wish to keep the partitions logically grouped in the file.)

HostName   Identifies the TCP/IP host name of the database partition server. (The host name specified must be defined in the file C:\winnt\ system32\drivers\etc\hosts.)

ComputerName   Identifies the name assigned to the workstation the database partition is created on.

LogicalPort   Identifies the logical port number that will be used by the database partition server. During installation, DB2 reserves a port range (for example, 60000–60003) in the c:\winnt\ system32\drivers\etc\services file on the server, to be used for inter-partition communications. The *LogicalPort* value specifies which port in that range you want to assign to a particular logical partition server. If a value is not provided for this field, the default value, 0, is used; if you are using logical database partitions, the value specified must start at 0 and continue in ascending order (for example, 0, 1, 2). Furthermore, if you specify a *LogicalPort* value for one database partition server, you must provide a value for each database partition server listed in the db2nodes.cfg file. This field is optional if you are not using logical database partitions or a high-speed interconnect.

NetName   Identifies the host name or the IP address of the high-speed interconnect to be used for FCM communication. This field is required only if you are using a high-speed interconnect for database partition communications. (If a *NetName* value is provided, a corresponding *LogicalPort* value must be provided.)

Thus, the db2nodes.cfg file on a Windows server will look something like this:

```
0    host1    server1    0    net1
1    host1    server1    1    net1
2    host2    server2    0    net2
```

On Windows operating systems, process affinity for a logical node is defined through the DB2PROCESSORS registry variable instead of through the db2nodes.cfg file. With DB2 for Windows you can:

- Use the db2nlist command to list all database partitions in a database partition server.

- Use the db2ncrt command to add a database partition server to an instance.

- Use the db2ndrop command to drop a database partition server from an instance.

- Use the db2nchg command to modify a database partition server configuration, including moving the database partition server from one machine to another, changing the TCP/IP host name, or selecting a different logical port or network name.

•••
In a Windows environment, you should never attempt to manually edit the DB2 node configuration file (db2nodes.cfg), because this can introduce inconsistencies into the file.
•••

The Default Port Range

To enable DB2's Fast Communications Manager (FCM), a port or range of ports must be reserved in the services file on each server in a partitioned database system. At a minimum, the services file must contain one entry for each database partition within a particular server. Each entry made in the services file must be formatted as follows:

    [PortName] [PortNumber]

where:

PortName   Identifies the name of the partitioned instance. For the first port
                  entry, the port name must be the name of the instance preceded
                  by the characters "DB2_". For subsequent port entries *except* the
                  last port entry, the port name must be the name of the instance
                  preceded by the characters "DB2_" and followed by "_*n*" where
                  n begins with 1 and is incremented by 1 for each successive port
                  specified. For the last port entry, the port name must be the name
                  of the instance preceded by the characters "DB2_" and followed
                  by the characters "_END".

PortNumber   Identifies the port number that is to be reserved for database
                  partition server communications. The port number specified for
                  each port entry must be followed by the characters "/tcp".

Thus, to reserve four ports for database partition server communications, you would add a set of entries to the services file on each server that looks something like this:

```
DB2_v9inst        60000/tcp
DB2_v9inst_1      60001/tcp
DB2_v9inst_2      60002/tcp
DB2_v9inst_END    60003/tcp
```

At a minimum, you should reserve one port number for each database partition per server (host name). Keep in mind that the same port(s) must be reserved on all servers that participate in the partitioned database environment. In order to avoid conflict with other applications, it is recommended to use high values for DB2 port numbers and reserve two or three more ports than needed, to allow for future growth.

The Catalog Partition

In Chapter 2, "Database Design," we saw that before you create a partitioned database, you must decide which partition will act as the catalog partition for the database. Once the partition that will serve as the catalog partition has been selected, you must create the database directly from that partition or from a remote client that is attached to that partition—the database partition to which you attach and execute the CREATE DATABASE command (or invoke the Create Database Wizard) becomes the catalog partition for the new database. The catalog partition is the database partition on which all system catalog tables are stored; all access to system tables must go through this partition.

Coordinator Partitions

In a partitioned database, the partition or partitions that will accept connection requests from clients are known as *coordinator partitions*. Because DB2 automatically routes all requests to the appropriate database partitions, all partitions need not be configured as coordinator partitions. In fact, when DB2 is configured with multiple database partitions within a single server, only one database partition per server can be a coordinator. The first database partition listed in the db2nodes. cfg file is the only database partition that can be a coordinator partition. (Because database partitions share a common install path and home directory, the listener port for partitions, as defined in the database manager configuration file, is the same for all database partitions that reside on the same server. Furthermore, because database partitions cannot use the same listener process, only one partition per server can be a coordinator.) When choosing where to create database partitions groups within the database, this should be taken into consideration.

Database partition groups that will be created on a single partition may benefit from being placed on database partitions that can act as coordinators. Accessing tables in a single partitioned database partition group that is not a coordinator requires the coordinator to receive the SQL statement and then pass it to the database partition where the SQL statement will be executed. The extra overhead of the coordinator partition "handling" the request and sending it to the affected database partition is insignificant if the operation is complex and accesses a large amount of data. However, for simple operations like single-row selects or updates, this overhead can become significant.

If there are multiple partitions on a single server, the partition listed in the db2nodes.cfg that is assigned port 0 on that server is the only partition that can act as a coordinator within that server.

Adding Database Partitions to a Partitioned Database System

Once a partitioned database system has been established, at some point it may become necessary to add additional database partitions to it. You can add database partitions to a partitioned database system both when it is running and when it is stopped. However, because adding a new server can be a time-consuming process, many elect to add servers/partitions while the instance is running.

New database partitions can be added to a partitioned database system by executing the ADD DBPARTITIONNUM command. The syntax for this command is:

```
ADD DBPARTITIONNUM
<LIKE DBPARTITIONNUM [DBPartitionNum] |
  WITHOUT TABLESPACES>
```

where:

DBPartitionNum   Identifies a database partition server, by partition number, that is to be used as a reference when defining containers for new system temporary table spaces on the partition being added. (The containers for the new system temporary table spaces will be the same as the containers of the database at the database partition server specified.) The database partition server specified must already be defined in the db2nodes.cfg file.

New database partitions can also be created by starting an instance in such a way that a new database partition is defined at instance startup. This is done by executing a special form of the START DATABASE MANAGER command; the basic syntax for this form of the START DATABASE MANAGER command is:

```
START [DATABASE MANAGER | DB MANAGER | DBM]
ADD DBPARTITIONNUM
HOSTNAME [HostName] PORT [LogicalPort]
<COMPUTER [ComputerName]>
<NETNAME [NetName]>
<LIKE DBPARTITIONNUM [DBPartitionNum] |
 WITHOUT TABLESPACES>
```

or

```
db2start </D>
ADD DBPARTITIONNUM
HOSTNAME [HostName] PORT [LogicalPort]
<COMPUTER [ComputerName]>
<NETNAME [NetName]>
<LIKE DBPARTITIONNUM [DBPartitionNum] |
 WITHOUT TABLESPACES>
```

where:

HostName Identifies the TCP/IP host name of the database partition server that is to be added to the db2nodes.cfg file.

LogicalPort Identifies the logical port number that is to be added to the db2nodes.cfg file.

ComputerName Identifies the computer name for the machine on which the new database partition is to be created. (This parameter is mandatory on Windows but is ignored on all other operating systems.)

NetName Identifies the host name or the IP address of the high-speed interconnect (to be used for FCM communication) that is to be added to the db2nodes.cfg file. (If a host name or IP address is not provided, this parameter defaults to the value specified for HostName.)

DBPartitionNum Identifies a database partition server, by partition number, that is to be used as a reference when defining containers for new system temporary table spaces on the partition being added. (The containers for the new system temporary table spaces will be the same as the containers of the database at the database partition server specified.) The database partition server specified must already be defined in the db2nodes.cfg file.

If the WITHOUT TABLESPACES option is specified, containers for system temporary table spaces are not created for the database partition being added; if this option is used, the ALTER TABLESPACE statement must be executed in order to add system temporary table space containers to each database partition created—before the database can be used. If neither the LIKE DBPARTRTIONNUM option nor the WITHOUT TABLESPACES option is specified, the containers used for system temporary table spaces on the database partition being created will be the same as the containers used by system temporary table spaces on the catalog partition. Both options are ignored for system temporary table spaces that have been defined to use automatic storage. In this case, containers will be assigned automatically by DB2, based on the storage paths associated with the database.

When you use the ADD DBPARTITIONNUM command or the ADD DBPARTITIONNUM option of the START DATABASE MANAGER command to add a new database partition to the system, all existing databases in the instance are expanded to the new database partition. However, data cannot be stored on the new partition until one or more database partition groups have been altered to include the new partition. (New partitions are added to an existing database partition group by executing the ALTER DATABASE PARTITION GROUP command.) Furthermore, when a new database partition is added, the instance must determine whether or not each database in the instance is enabled for automatic storage. (This is done by communicating with the catalog partition for each database.) If automatic storage is enabled, then the storage path definitions are retrieved as part of that communication.

When the ADD DBPARTITIONNUM option is used with the START DATABASE MANAGER command to add a new database partition to an instance that spans multiple partitions, the db2nodes.cfg file is not updated with information about the new database partition until the instance is stopped and restarted; likewise, the new database partition does not become part of the partitioned database system until the instance is stopped and re-started.

Thus, if you wanted to add a new database partition to a system at instance startup, you could do so by executing a command that looks something like this:

```
START DATABASE MANAGER ADD DBPARTITIONNUM HOSTNAME server2 PORT 1
```

On the other hand, if you wanted to add a new database partition to a system such that the containers for the new system temporary table spaces are the same as the containers of the database at the database partition number 2, you could do so by executing a command that looks something like this:

```
ADD DBPARTITIONNUM LIKE DBPARTITIONNUM 2
```

You cannot change a single-partition database to a multi-partition database by simply adding a database partition to your system. This is because the redistribution of data across database partitions requires a distribution key on each affected table. Distribution keys are automatically generated when a table is created in a multi-partition database. (In a single-partition database, distribution keys can be explicitly created with the CREATE TABLE or ALTER TABLE SQL statements.)

If you prefer using graphical user interfaces to typing commands, you can use the Add Database Partitions Launchpad to add new database partitions to a system. The Add Database Partitions Launchpad is invoked by selecting the appropriate action from the Instances menu found in the Control Center. Figure 3–5 shows the Control Center menu items that must be selected to activate the Add Database Partitions Launchpad; Figure 3–6 shows what the first page of the Add Database Partitions Launchpad looks like when it is first initiated.

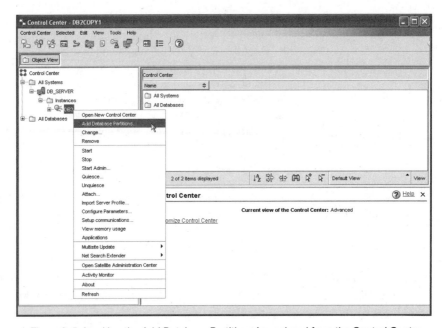

Figure 3–5: Invoking the Add Database Partitions Launchpad from the Control Center.

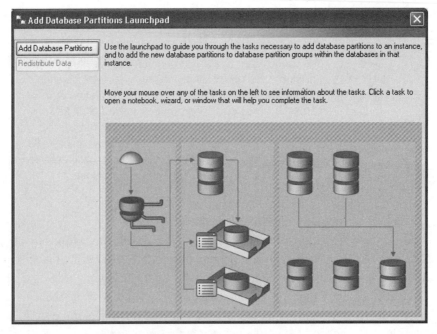

Figure 3–6: The first page of the Add Database Partitions Launchpad.

Once the Add Database Partitions Launchpad is displayed, simply follow the directions shown on each panel presented to define the characteristics of one or more database partitions to be added. When you have provided enough information for the instance to add the new partitions, the "Finish" push button displayed at the bottom of all but the first panel will be enabled. Once this button is selected, the database partitions specified will be added to the system.

A Word About Creating Multiple Database Partitions Within a Single Server

When configuring multiple database partitions on the same server, it is important to make sure that each database partition has a sufficient amount of system resources available to it. Because each database partition is required to execute a number of different processes (or threads in DB2 9.5), there must be enough CPU cycles available to handle the workload. To guarantee that sufficient CPU resources are available, it is recommended that the ratio of database partitions to CPUs not exceed 1 to 1. In other words, do not create more database partitions on a server than there are CPUs in that server.

Depending on the speed and relative processing power of the CPUs on the server, a ratio of CPUs to database partitions of 1:1 or 2:1 will normally give the best performance. For most servers a ratio of CPUs to database partitions of 2:1 will provide the best performance, but with faster processors such as the IBM pSeries P690 it is possible to reduce this ratio to 1:1 if needed.

For a database with multiple database partitions on the same server, DB2 can use shared memory to communicate between the database partitions instead of using the network interconnect. The usage of shared memory improves the performance of inter-partition communication but must be enabled using the DB2 registry variable DB2_FORCE_FCM_BP. Any inter-partition communication between database partitions on different servers will still use the dedicated interconnect; however, all inter-partition communication between database partitions on the same server will use shared memory.

One of the features available with the IBM pSeries P690 server is the ability to create logical servers within a large SMP server using logical partitions (LPARs). (The Sun E10000 and E15000 servers support a concept similar to LPARs, called domains.) This is a good way to separate different DB2 instances within a single server and ensure that each partition is given its own dedicated resources. But this may not necessarily be an optimal way of separating database partitions for the same database that reside on the same server. Currently the only way to communicate between LPARs on the same server is by using a network interconnect—at present, LPARs cannot communicate using optimized methods such as shared memory. When creating multiple database partitions on the same IBM pSeries P690 server, it is normally best not to use LPARs, so that inter-partition communication can benefit from the use of shared memory. An additional benefit of this approach is that when some database partitions are not as busy as others, they can take advantage of all of the resources available on the server and not be constrained to the resources that have been assigned to the LPAR.

Why Partition a Database on a Large SMP Server?

Although DB2 can break a query into a number of pieces that can be executed in parallel, the scalability of DB2 with intra-partition parallelism can be restricted by the operating system and hardware that DB2 is installed on. Creating multiple database partitions within a larger SMP server has proven to provide better scalability than intra-partition parallelism alone; as the number of CPUs grows, the scalability decreases when just intra-partition parallelism is used. By creating multiple database partitions within an SMP server, scalability will remain almost linear. In a recent test of DB2 with multiple database partitions on a single SMP server growing from 6 to 24 CPUs, DB2 was able to deliver a 23.9-fold increase on query response time.

Partition Groups

In Chapter 2, "Database Design," we saw that in a partitioned database environment, it is possible to define named subsets of one or more database partitions. Each subset you define is known as a database partition group. Database partition groups are important because they provide a way to decluster the data; tables do not have to be distributed across all of the database partitions in the system. A database partition group can contain as few as one database partition, or it can span all of the database partitions in a database. Partition groups that reside on a single database partition are known as single-partition partition groups, whereas partition groups that span more than one database partition are known as multipartition database partition groups. (Each database partition that a database partition group is to span must be defined in the db2nodes.cfg node configuration file.)

When table spaces are created in a partitioned database, the partition group in which the table space is defined determines which database partition(s) the table space will be physically created on. A table space can only belong to one partition group, but a partition group can contain more than one table space. Figure 3–7 shows the relationship between database partitions, partition groups, and table spaces.

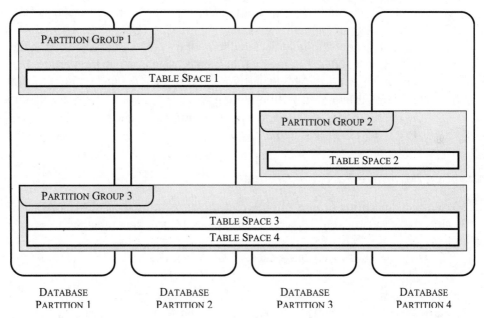

Figure 3—7: Table spaces and partition groups.

When a partitioned database is created, the following three database partition groups are created automatically:

- A partition group named IBMCATGROUP, which is used to store the system catalog tables and views associated with the database. This partition group is restricted to the catalog partition and cannot be altered to span additional database partitions. Additionally, this partition group cannot be dropped using the DROP DATABASE PARTITION GROUP statement.

- A partition group named IBMDEFAULTGROUP, which is used to store user-defined objects. (This is the partition group used when the CREATE TABLESPACE statement is executed and no partition group is specified.) By default, this partition group spans all database partitions identified in the db2nodes.cfg file. However, it can be modified at any time to span fewer or additional database partitions. Like the IBMCATGROUP partition group, this partition group cannot be dropped using the DROP DATABASE PARTITION GROUP statement.

- A partition group named IBMTEMPGROUP, which is used, by default, for system temporary table spaces that are used for operations such as sorting data, reorganizing tables, and creating indexes. (User temporary table spaces designed to hold declared temporary tables can be created in the IBMDEFAULTGROUP or in any user-created database partition group, but not in the IBMTEMPGROUP partition group.) Like the IBMDEFAULTGROUP partition group, this partition group spans all database partitions identified in the db2nodes.cfg file and cannot be dropped using the DROP DATABASE PARTITION GROUP statement.

Creating Database Partition Groups

Additional partition groups can be created by executing the CREATE DATABASE PARTITION GROUP SQL statement. The syntax for this statement is:

```
CREATE DATABASE PARTITION GROUP [PartGroupName]
ON ALL DBPARTITIONNUMS
```

or

```
CREATE DATABASE PARTITION GROUP [PartGroupName]
ON DBPARTITIONNUM<S> ([StartPartitionNum] <TO [EndPartitionNum]> ,...)
```

where:

PartGroupName   Identifies a unique name that is to be assigned to the database partition group once it is created.

StartPartitionNum   Identifies, by partition number, one or more database partitions that are to be spanned by the database partition group being created. (The database partitions specified must already be defined in the db2nodes.cfg file.)

EndPartitionNum   Identifies, by partition number, a database partition that, together with the database partition number specified in the *StartPartitionNum* parameter, identifies a range of database partitions to be spanned by the database partition group being created. (The partition number specified in this parameter must be greater than the partition number specified in the *StartPartitionNum* parameter.)

Thus, if you wanted to create a database partition group that has the name LARGE_ DPG on database partitions 0, 1, 2, 5, and 8, you could do so by executing a CREATE DATABASE PARTITION GROUP SQL statement that looks something like this:

```
CREATE DATABASE PARTITION GROUP large_dpg
ON DBPARTITIONNUMS (0 TO 2, 5, 8)
```

Modifying Existing Database Partition Groups

Earlier, we saw how three database partition groups are created automatically when a partitioned database is constructed, and we have just seen how additional database partition groups can be created. But what if you want to add or remove database partitions to or from an existing partition group? Such modifications can be made by executing the ALTER DATABASE PARTITION GROUP SQL statement. The syntax for this statement is:

```
ALTER DATABASE PARTITION GROUP [PartGroupName]
ADD DBPARTITIONNUM<S>
    ([StartPartitionNum] <TO [EndPartitionNum]> ,...)
<LIKE DBPARTITIONNUM [SrcPartitionNum] |
 WITHOUT TABLESPACES>
```

or

```
ALTER DATABASE PARTITION GROUP [PartGroupName]
DROP DBPARTITIONNUM<S>
    ([StartPartitionNum] <TO [EndPartitionNum]> ,...)
```

where:

PartGroupName   Identifies, by name, the database partition group to be modified.

StartPartitionNum   Identifies, by partition number, one or more database partitions to be added to or dropped from the database partition group specified.

EndPartitionNum   Identifies, by partition number, a database partition that, together with the database partition number specified in the

StartPartitionNum parameter, identifies a range of database partitions to be added to or dropped from the database partition group specified. (The partition number specified in this parameter must be greater than the partition number specified in the *StartPartitionNum* parameter.)

SrcPartitionNum   Identifies, by partition number, a database partition to be used as a reference when defining containers on the database partition being added for table spaces that already exist in the partition group being altered. (The database partition number specified must correspond to a partition that existed in the database partition group being altered before the ALTER DATABASE PARTITION GROUP statement was executed.)

If the WITHOUT TABLESPACES option is specified, containers for table spaces in the database partition group being altered are not created for the database partition(s) added; if this option is used, the ALTER TABLESPACE statement must be executed in order to define table space containers to be used by the table spaces that have been defined in the partition group—before the table spaces can be used. If neither the LIKE DBPARTRTIONNUM option nor the WITHOUT TABLESPACES option is specified when adding a database partition to a database partition group, the containers used for table spaces on the database partition(s) being added will be the same as the containers found on the lowest numbered database partition in the partition group. For example, if the lowest numbered database partition in a database partition group was 2 and neither the LIKE DBPARTITIONNUM option nor the WITHOUT TABLESPACES option is specified, new database partitions will be added as if the option LIKE DBPARTITIONNUM 2 had been specified.

Thus, if you wanted to add database partition number 6 to an existing database partition group named SMALL_DPG that spans database partitions 3, 4, and 5, you could do so by executing an ALTER DATABASE PARTITION GROUP SQL statement that looks something like this:

```
ALTER DATABASE PARTITION GROUP small_dpg
ADD DBPARTITIONNUM (6)
```

When this statement is executed, the table space containers on database partition number 3 will be used as a model for the table space containers created on database partition number 6.

Partitioning Keys and Partitioning Maps

After one or more database partition groups have been defined, table spaces that span all database partitions within the partition group can be created, and tables can be created in the table spaces. When a table is created in a table space that spans multiple database partitions, a special key known as a partitioning key (or distribution key) must exist before its data can be distributed evenly across all database partitions used. A table partitioning key is an ordered set of one or more columns in a table; values in partitioning key columns are used to determine to which database partition each table row is to belong. (DB2 uses a hashing algorithm to assign a given row of a table to a corresponding database partition.)

The partitioning key for a table is defined as part of the table creation process by using the PARTITION BY clause of the CREATE TABLE SQL statement. If a partitioning key is not explicitly specified (and the table is being created in a table space that resides in multi-partition database partition group), the partitioning key for the table will be defined as follows:

- If a primary key is defined for the table, the first column of the primary key will be the partitioning key.

- If the table is a typed table, the object identifier column for the table will be the partitioning key.

- The first column whose data type is not a LOB, LONG VARCHAR, LONG VARGRAPHIC, XML, structured data type, or distinct data type based on one of these data types will be the partitioning key.

- Otherwise, the table will be created without a partitioning key—in this case, the table can only be created in a table space that has been defined on a single-partition database partition group. (A single-partition database partition group is a partition group that only spans one database partition.)

Tables containing only long data and/or large object columns cannot have partitioning keys and can only be stored in table spaces that reside in single-partition partition groups.

For tables in table spaces defined on single-partition database partition groups, any collection of columns whose data type is not a LOB, LONG VARCHAR, LONG VARGRAPHIC, XML, structured data type, or a distinct data type based on one of these data types can be used to define the partitioning key; if no partitioning key is specified, a partitioning key will not be created.

Choosing a Partitioning Key

Choosing an effective partitioning key is crucial if you want to take full advantage of the benefits of table partitioning. When deciding which columns to use for a table's partitioning key, the following should be taken into consideration:

- Use the smallest number of columns possible.
- Character columns are more efficient than decimal columns; integer columns are more efficient than character columns.
- The column(s) used should contain a high proportion of different values.
- Whenever possible, columns that are frequently joined should be used.
- If possible, the column(s) used should assist in partition elimination.

Changing the Partitioning Key

So far, we have talked about things to keep in mind when defining a partitioning key for a table, but how do you determine what columns make up the partitioning key of an existing table, and how can you change the partitioning key if you are not happy with the way it has been defined? The easiest way to find out which columns make up the partitioning key of a partitioned table is by executing a query that looks something like this:

```
SELECT COLNAME, PARTKEYSEQ
FROM SYSCAT.COLUMNS
WHERE TABNAME = '[TableName]'
  AND PARTKEYSEQ != 0
ORDER BY PARTKEYSEQ
```

where:

TableName   Identifies, by name, the table that partitioning key information is to be obtained for.

Thus, if you wanted to obtain information about the partitioning key that has been defined for a table named EMPLOYEES, you could do so by executing the following query:

```
SELECT COLNAME, PARTKEYSEQ
FROM SYSCAT.COLUMNS
WHERE TABNAME = 'EMPLOYEES'
  AND PARTKEYSEQ != 0
ORDER BY PARTKEYSEQ
```

Assuming the table EMPLOYEES was created by executing the following CREATE TABLE SQL statement:

```
CREATE TABLE employees (
    empid       INTEGER NOT NULL
    name        VARCHAR(75),
    ssn         CHAR(12),
    dept        CHAR(3),
    salary      DECIMAL(8,2),
    hire_date   DATE)
  PARTITIONING KEY (empid, ssn)
```

the results produced by the query should look something like this:

```
COLNAME                     PARTKEYSEQ
--------------------------  ----------
EMPID                       1
SSN                         2

  2 record(s) selected.
```

This indicates that the partitioning key for the EMPLOYEES table is comprised of the columns EMPID and SSN.

Once a partitioning key has been defined for a table that resides in a multi-partition database partition group, it cannot be changed; to change such a table's partitioning key, the table must be dropped and recreated. (If the table has been populated, its data will need to be exported before the table is dropped and reloaded after the table has been recreated.)

However, if a table resides in a single-partition partition group, its partitioning key can be dropped and recreated by executing two special forms of the ALTER TABLE SQL statement. (If an attempt is made to drop the partitioning key of a table stored in a multi-partition database partition group, an error will be returned.) The syntax for the form of the ALTER TABLE statement that is used to drop a table's partitioning key is:

```
ALTER TABLE [TableName]
[DROP DISTRIBUTION | DROP PARTITIONING KEY]
```

where:

TableName   Identifies, by name, the table that the partitioning key is to be
                dropped from.

The syntax for the form of the ALTER TABLE statement that is used to create a new table partitioning key is:

```
ALTER TABLE [TableName]
[ADD DISTRIBUTE BY HASH | ADD PARTITIONING KEY]
([ColumnName],...)
```

where:

TableName   Identifies, by name, the table that a partitioning key is to be
                created for.
ColumnName   Identifies one or more columns that are to be used to create the
                table partitioning key.

Thus, to change the partitioning key for a single-partition table named TAB1 from a column named COL1 to a column named COL2, you would execute two ALTER TABLE statements that look like this:

```
ALTER TABLE tab1 DROP PARTITIONING KEY;
ALTER TABLE tab1 ADD PARTRTIONING KEY(col2);
```

A Word About Indexes and Partitioning Keys

Indexes defined on a partitioned table are partitioned according to the partitioning key of the table. Whenever an index is created, it is created on the same database partitions that the underlying table occupies. On each database partition, the index will only have entries for the rows of the table that are located in the same database partition. Non-unique indexes can be created on any columns of a table, regardless of whether or not the table is partitioned. However, any unique index or primary key created on a partitioned table must include the columns found in the partitioning key.

> For partitioned databases, the clustering index should be created with the partitioning key(s) as its first column(s) so that the query can be directed to the partitions where it needs to run rather than running on all partitions unnecessarily.

Partitioning (Distribution) Maps

As data gets distributed across database partitions in a partitioned database environment, the instance must have a way to find the data it needs. To aid in this endeavor, a special map, called a partitioning map (or distribution map) is used to both store and retrieve data in a partitioned database. A partitioning map is an internally generated array (or vector) that contains a single entry for single-partition database partition groups, or 4,096 entries for multiple-partition database partition groups. Each entry in the array corresponds to a specific database partition.

Earlier, we saw that DB2 uses a hashing algorithm to assign a given row of a table to a corresponding database partition. A row's partitioning key is the input for this hashing algorithm; the output is a specific position (displacement) in a partitioning map. The value found at the specified position in the map represents the database partition to which the row of data is to be physically stored. (For a single-partition database partition group, the partitioning map has only one entry containing the number of the database partition where all the rows of a database table are stored. For multiple-partition database partition groups, the numbers of the database partition groups are specified in such a way that each database partition is used one after the other to ensure an even distribution across the entire map.) Figure 3–8 shows how partitioning keys, DB2's hashing algorithm, and a partitioning/distribution map is used to determine which database partition a particular row is to be stored on.

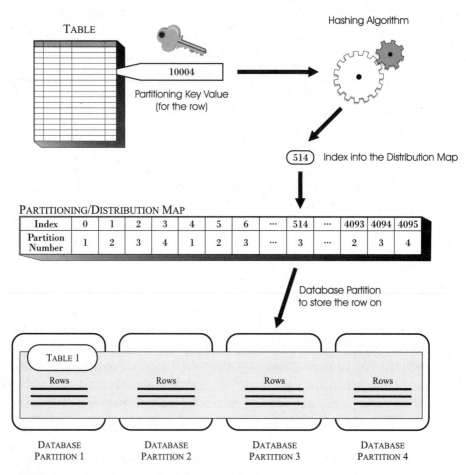

Figure 3—8: Hashing data rows using a partitioning/distribution map.

A partitioning map corresponds to a database partition group and is created when that database partition group is created (and updated when data is redistributed). All tables in a database partition group use the same partitioning map. By default, the partitioning map created contains the database partition numbers of the partition group, assigned in a round-robin fashion (as shown in Figure 3–8.) It is also possible to create and use partitioning maps that do not use this round-robin approach. Such maps are known as customized partitioning or distribution maps and may be required to achieve an even distribution of a table's data across the database partitions used.

A special command, db2gpmap, can be used to extract and display the partitioning/ distribution map for a partition group. (This information is obtained from the SYSCAT.PARTITIONMAPS catalog view.) The syntax for this command is:

```
db2gpmap
<-d [DatabaseName]>
<-g [PartitionGroup]>
<-m [MapFileName]>
<-t [TableName]>
<-h>
```

where:

DatabaseName Identifies, by name, the database for which a distribution (partitioning) map is to be generated. If a database name is not specified, the value of the DB2DBDFT environment variable is used. (If this environment variable has not been set, the SAMPLE database is used.)

PartitionGroup Identifies, by name, the database partition group, for which a distribution map is to be generated. If a database partition group is not specified, the database partition group IBMDEFAULTGROUP is used.

MapFileName Specifies the fully qualified file name where the distribution map generated is to be saved. If no file name is specified, the file db2split.map is used by default.

TableName Identifies, by name, the table for which a distribution map is to be generated.

Thus, to generate a partitioning (distribution) map for a partition group named PG_123 in a database named TEST and write it to a file named PG_123map.txt, you would execute a db2gpmap command that looks something like this:

```
db2gpmap -d TEST -g PG_123 -m PG_123map.txt
```

And, assuming the partition group named PG_123 spans three database partitions, the first eight lines of the output file produced (PG123map.txt) would look like this:

```
1 2 3 1 2 3 1 2 3 1 2 3 1 2 3 1 2 3 1 2 3 1 2 3 1 2 3 1 2 3
1 2 3 1 2 3 1 2 3 1 2 3 1 2 3 1 2 3 1 2 3 1 2 3 1 2 3 1 2 3
1 2 3 1 2 3 1 2 3 1 2 3 1 2 3 1 2 3 1 2 3 1 2 3 1 2 3 1 2 3
1 2 3 1 2 3 1 2 3 1 2 3 1 2 3 1 2 3 1 2 3 1 2 3 1 2 3 1 2 3
1 2 3 1 2 3 1 2 3 1 2 3 1 2 3 1 2 3 1 2 3 1 2 3 1 2 3 1 2 3
1 2 3 1 2 3 1 2 3 1 2 3 1 2 3 1 2 3 1 2 3 1 2 3 1 2 3 1 2 3
1 2 3 1 2 3 1 2 3 1 2 3 1 2 3 1 2 3 1 2 3 1 2 3 1 2 3 1 2 3
1 2 3 1 2 3 1 2 3 1 2 3 1 2 3 1 2 3 1 2 3 1 2 3 1 2 3 1 2 3
```

(The upper-left corner corresponds to the partition ID at element 0 of the partitioning map. The map is read by moving from left to right and down, line-by-line.)

A Word About Collocated Tables

Often, there are tables in a database that are frequently joined by applications. If the database is partitioned, it is good practice to try to avoid sending data between the partitions in order to satisfy these join requests. With DB2, this can be achieved by exploiting what is known as table collocation. Collocation between two joined tables occurs when the matching rows of the two tables are stored in the same database partitions, so that data does not have to be sent between partitions. Figure 3–9 illustrates two tables that are collocated.

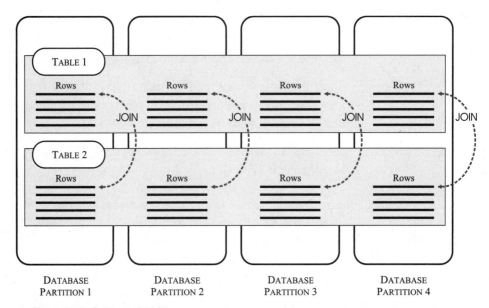

Figure 3–9: Collocated tables.

In order for two tables to be considered collocated, when they must satisfy all of the following conditions:

- The partition groups of both tables must have the same partitioning map.

- The partitioning key from both tables must have the same number of columns.

- Corresponding partitioning key columns must be partition-compatible (use the same or similar base data type).

- For tables in multi-partition partition groups, the two tables must be in the same partition group.

- For tables in single-partition partition groups, the two tables can be in different partition groups, but these partition groups must include the same (single) database partition.

A collocated join will occur if two collocated tables are joined using all of the columns in the partitioning key. If two tables can be joined using a collocated join, the query can be performed much more efficiently than a join that sends data between database partitions. (Collocated joins and other join techniques for partitioned tables are covered in detail in Chapter 5, "Performance and Scalability".)

Range Clustering and Range Partitioning

In Chapter 2, "Database Design," we saw that table spaces are used to control where data is physically stored and to provide a layer of abstraction between database objects (such as tables, indexes, and views) and one or more containers in which the object's data actually resides. Consequently, how database objects are assigned to table spaces when they are created determines how data is physically stored on disk. The physical storage of table data can be controlled even further by creating range-clustered tables or by taking advantage of a new feature introduced in DB2 9 known as range partitioning.

Range-Clustered Tables

A range-clustered table (RCT) is a table whose data is organized in ascending key sequence with a fixed size based on the specified range of key sequence values. Range-clustered tables are useful when data is tightly clustered across one or more columns in a table—the smallest and largest values in select columns define the range of possible values. Each possible key value in the defined range has a predetermined location in the physical table. Thus, the storage required for a range-clustered table must be pre-allocated and available when the table is created, and it must be sufficient to store the number of rows found in the specified range multiplied by the row size.

Range-clustered tables can bring about significant performance advantages during query processing, because fewer input/output (I/O) operations are required. Additionally, range-clustered tables require less cache buffer allocation, because there are no secondary objects to maintain; clustering indexes are not only not required, they are not supported.

Range-clustered tables are created by specifying the ORGANIZE BY KEY SEQUENCE clause of the CREATE TABLE SQL statement when a table is created. The syntax for this optional clause is:

```
ORGANIZE BY KEY SEQUENCE
([ColumnName]
  <STARTING <FROM> [Start]>
  ENDING <AT> [End] ,...)
<ALLOW OVERFLOW | DISALLOW OVERFLOW>
<PCTFREE [PercentFree]>
```

where:

ColumnName	Identifies one or more columns, by name, whose values are to be used to determine the sequence of the range-clustered table.
Start	Specifies the low end of the range of values allowed. (Values less than the starting value specified are allowed only if the ALLOW OVERFLOW option is specified.)
End	Specifies the high end of the range of values allowed. (Values greater than the ending value specified are allowed only if the ALLOW OVERFLOW option is specified.)
PercentFree	Specifies the percentage of each page to be left as free space. (The first row on each page is added without restriction; when additional rows are added to a page, a check is performed to ensure that the specified percentage of the page is left free.)

If the DISALLOW OVERFLOW clause is specified, key values will not be allowed to exceed the defined range. On the other hand, if the ALLOW OVERFLOW clause is specified, key values will be allowed to exceed the defined range, in which case overflow data will be placed in an overflow area, which is dynamically allocated. A range-clustered table that overflows data that falls outside the predefined range will suffer from poor performance.

Thus, if you wanted to create a range-clustered table named CUSTOMERS that has two columns named CUSTOMER_ID and CUSTOMER_NAME, where the CUSTOMER_ID column will become the unique key that determines how records are physically stored and where only unique values between 1 and 100, inclusively, can be assigned to the CUSTOMER_ID column, you could do so by executing a CREATE TABLE SQL statement that looks something like this:

```
CREATE TABLE customers
   (customer_id   INTEGER NOT NULL,
    customer_name VARCHAR(80))
  ORGANIZE BY KEY SEQUENCE (customer_id
    STARTING FROM 1 ENDING AT 100)
    DISALLOW OVERFLOW
```

Once this table is created and populated, if an application needs to access the row for the customer whose ID is 2, the instance will look for the second row in the CUSTOMERS table, using a predetermined offset from the logical start of the table. If a row is updated in such a way that the key column values are modified, the updated row is copied to the new location, and the old copy of the row is deleted, maintaining the clustering of data in the table.

The ORGANIZE BY KEY SEQUENCE clause of the CREATE TABLE SQL statement cannot be used in conjunction with any other clause that controls how table data is to be organized (for example, ORGANIZE BY DIMENSIONS and PARTITION BY RANGE.)

Range-Partitioned Tables

Table partitioning (also referred to as range partitioning) is a data organization scheme in which table data is divided across multiple storage objects called data partitions or ranges based on values in one or more columns. Each data partition is stored separately, and the storage objects used can reside in different table spaces, in the same table space, or in a combination of the two. Table partitioning improves performance by eliminating large amounts of I/O.

Other advantages of using table partitioning include:

Easy roll-in and roll-out of data. Rolling in partitioned table data allows a new range to be easily incorporated into a partitioned table as an additional data partition. Rolling out partitioned table data allows you to easily separate ranges of data from a partitioned table for subsequent purging or archiving. Data can be quickly rolled in and out by using the ATTACH PARTITION and DETACH PARTITION clauses of the ALTER TABLE statement.

Easier administration of large tables. Table-level administration becomes more flexible because administrative tasks can be performed on individual data partitions. Such tasks include detaching and reattaching of a data partition, backing up and restoring individual data partitions, and reorganizing individual indexes. In addition, time-consuming maintenance operations can be shortened by breaking them down into a series of smaller operations. For example, backup operations can be performed at the data-partition level when each data partition is placed in a separate table space. Thus, it is possible to back up one data partition of a partitioned table at a time.

Flexible index placement. With table partitioning, indexes can be placed in different table spaces, allowing for more granular control of index placement.

Faster query processing. In the process of resolving queries, one or more data partitions may be automatically eliminated based on the query predicates used. This functionality, known as Partition Elimination, improves the performance of many queries because less data has to be analyzed before a result data set can be returned. In addition, queries can be automatically directed to just the partition(s) where the desired data resides. For example, if you partitioned a table based on month, and a query that is designed to calculate the total sales for March 2008 is executed, the query need only access the data for March 2008, not the data for other months and years.

Data from a given table is partitioned into multiple storage objects based on the specifications provided in the PARTITION BY clause of the CREATE TABLE statement. The syntax for this optional clause is:

```
PARTITION BY <RANGE>
  ([ColumnName] <NULLS LAST | NULLS FIRST> ,...)
  (
  STARTING <FROM> [Start | MINVALUE | MAXVALUE] |
     STARTING <FROM> ([Start | MINVALUE | MAXVALUE] ,...)
  <INCLUSIVE | EXCLUSIVE>
  ENDING <AT> [End | MINVALUE | MAXVALUE] |
     ENDING <AT> ([End | MINVALUE | MAXVALUE] ,...)
  <INCLUSIVE | EXCLUSIVE>
  EVERY <(>[Constant] <DurationLabel> <)>
    ,...)
```

or

```
PARTITION BY <RANGE>
  ([ColumnName] <NULLS LAST | NULLS FIRST> ,...)
  (
  <PARTITION [PartitionName]>
  STARTING <FROM> [Start | MINVALUE | MAXVALUE] |
     STARTING <FROM> ([Start | MINVALUE | MAXVALUE] ,...)
  <INCLUSIVE | EXCLUSIVE>
  ENDING <AT> [End | MINVALUE | MAXVALUE] |
     ENDING <AT> ([End | MINVALUE | MAXVALUE] ,...)
  <INCLUSIVE | EXCLUSIVE>
  <IN [TableSpaceName]>
  ,... )
```

where:

ColumnName	Identifies one or more columns (up to 16), by name, whose values are to be used to determine which data partition a particular row is to be stored in. (The group of columns specified make up the partitioning key for the table.) No column with a data type that is a LONG VARCHAR, LONG VARGRAPHIC, BLOB, CLOB, DBCLOB, a distinct type based on any of these data types, or a structured data type can be used as part of a data partitioning key.
PartitionName	Identifies the unique name to be assigned to the data partition to be created.
Start	Specifies the low end of the range for each data partition.

End   Specifies the high end of the range for each data partition.

Constant   Specifies the width of each data-partition range when the
                 automatically generated form of the syntax is used. Data partitions
                 will be created starting at the STARTING FROM value and will
                 contain this number of values in the range. This form of the syntax is
                 supported only if the partitioning key is made up of a single column
                 that has been assigned a numeric, date, time, or timestamp data type.

DurationLabel Identifies the duration that is associated with the *Constant* value
                 specified if the partitioning key column has been assigned a
                 date, time, or timestamp data type. The following values are
                 valid for this parameter: YEAR, YEARS, MONTH, MONTHS, DAY,
                 DAYS, HOUR, HOURS, MINUTE, MINUTES, SECOND, SECONDS,
                 MICROSECOND, and MICROSECONDS.

TableSpaceName Identifies the table space in which each data partition is to be stored.

Thus, if you wanted to create a table named SALES that is partitioned such that each
quarter's data is stored in a different data partition, and such that each partition
resides in a different table space, you could do so by executing a CREATE TABLE
SQL statement that looks something like this:

```
CREATE TABLE sales
    (sales_date     DATE,
     sales_amt      NUMERIC(5,2))
    IN tbsp0, tbsp1, tbsp2, tbsp3
    PARTITION BY RANGE (sales_date NULLS FIRST)
        (STARTING '1/1/2008' ENDING '12/31/2008'
         EVERY 3 MONTHS)
```

By default, the range boundaries defined are inclusive; to prevent specific records
from being stored at a particular partition, you can create the ranges using the
EXCLUSIVE option for the ending boundary as follows:

```
CREATE TABLE sales
    (sales_date     DATE,
     sales_amt      NUMERIC(5,2))
    IN tbsp0, tbsp1, tbsp2, tbsp3
    PARTITION BY RANGE(sales_date NULLS FIRST)
          (STARTING '1/1/2008'    ENDING '3/31/2008' EXCLUSIVE,
           STARTING '3/31/2008'   ENDING '6/30/2008' EXCLUSIVE,
           STARTING '6/30/2008'   ENDING '9/30/2008' EXCLUSIVE,
           STARTING '9/30/2008'   ENDING '12/31/2008')
```

In this example, because the EXCLUSIVE option was specified, a record with a sales date of 3/31/2008 won't be stored in table space TBSP0. Instead, it will be stored in table space TBSP1. Had the EXCLUSIVE option not been specified, the record would have been stored in table space TBSP0.

If you wanted to create a table named DEPARTMENTS that is partitioned such that rows with numerical values that fall in the range of 0 to 9 are stored in one partition that resides in one table space, rows with numerical values that fall in the range of 10 to 19 are stored in another partition that resides in another table space, and so on, you could do so by executing a CREATE TABLE SQL statement that looks something like this:

```
CREATE TABLE departments
    (dept_no   INT
     desc      CHAR(3))
    PARTITION BY (dept_no NULLS FIRST)
        (STARTING   0 ENDING  9 IN tbsp0,
         STARTING 10 ENDING 19 IN tbsp1,
         STARTING 20 ENDING 29 IN tbsp2,
         STARTING 30 ENDING 39 IN tbsp3)
```

A table with the same partitioning scheme could also be created by executing a CREATE TABLE SQL statement that looks something like this:

```
CREATE TABLE departments
    (dept_no   INT
     desc      CHAR(3))
    IN tbsp0, tbsp1, tbsp2, tbsp3
    PARTITION BY (dept_no NULLS FIRST)
        (STARTING FROM(0) ENDING(39) EVERY(10))
```

In both cases, rows with a DEPT_NO value from 0 to 9 will be stored in table space TBSP0, rows with a DEPT_NO value from 10 to 19 will be stored in table space TBSP1, and so on. Figure 3–10 illustrates how such a partitioned table would look.

It is important to note that when an index is created for a range-partitioned table, the data for that index will be stored in the table space that is used to hold the first partition's data, unless otherwise specified. For example, suppose the following CREATE INDEX SQL statement is used to create an index for the DEPARTMENTS table just created:

```
CREATE INDEX dept_idx ON departments (dept_no)
```

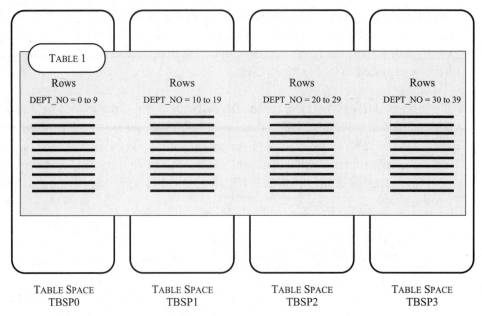

Figure 3—10: A simple range-partitioned table.

After this statement is executed, data for the index named DEPT_IDX will be stored in the table space named TBSP0. If you wanted this to be stored in the table space used to hold the last partition's data (the table space named TBSP3), the following CREATE INDEX SQL statement would have to be executed instead:

```
CREATE INDEX dept_idx ON departments (dept_no) IN tbsp3
```

Roll-In and Roll-Out of Data

Earlier, we saw that table partitioning allows for the efficient roll-in and roll-out of table data. Rolling-out partitioned table data allows you to easily separate ranges of data from a partitioned table. Once a data partition is detached into a separate table, the table can be handled in several ways—you can drop the separate table (whereby, the data from the data partition is destroyed), archive it or otherwise use it as another table, attach it to another partitioned table such as a history table, or manipulate, cleanse, and transform the data stored in it before reattaching it to the original or some other partitioned table. Rolling in partitioned table data allows you to easily incorporate a new range into a partitioned table as an additional data partition.

Partitioned table data can be rolled in or out of a partitioned table by executing an ALTER TABLE SQL statement with either the ATTACH PARTITION or the DETACH PARTITION option specified. For example, suppose you wanted to update the information stored in a table named INVENTORY by removing the data for December 2006 and replacing it with data for December 2007. To perform this roll-out and roll-in of data, you would complete the following steps in the order shown:

1. Remove the December 2006 data from the INVENTORY table and copy it to another table by executing an ALTER TABLE statement that looks something like this:

   ```
   ALTER TABLE inventory DETACH PARTITION dec06 INTO temptable
   ```

2. Load the data for December 2007 into the table used to store the data for December 2006 by executing a LOAD command that looks like this:

   ```
   LOAD FROM dec07 OF DEL REPLACE INTO temptable
   ```

   (Executing the LOAD command with the REPLACE option causes existing data to be overwritten; you must run the SET INTEGRITY statement to disable constraint checking before you can load the detached table.)

3. If appropriate, perform any data cleansing activities needed. Data cleansing activities include:

   - Filling in missing values

   - Deleting inconsistent and incomplete data

   - Removing redundant data arriving from multiple sources

   - Transforming data

     o Normalization (Data from different sources that represents the same value in different ways must be reconciled as part of rolling the data into a data warehouse.)

     o Aggregation (Raw data that is too detailed to store in a data warehouse must be pre-aggregated during roll-in.)

4. Attach the table containing the data for December 2007 (TEMPTABLE) to the INVENTORY table as a new partition by executing an ALTER TABLE statement that looks something like this:

```
ALTER TABLE inventory
ATTACH PARTITION dec07
STARTING '12/01/2007' ENDING '12/31/2007'
FROM temptable
```

(Attaching a data partition terminates queries and invalidates packages.)

5. Update indexes and other dependent objects by executing a SET INTEGRITY SQL statement that looks something like this:

```
SET INTEGRITY FOR inventory
ALLOW WRITE ACCESS
IMMEDIATE CHECKED FOR EXCEPTION IN inventory
  USE inventory_ex;
```

Multidimensional Clustering

Multidimensional clustering (MDC) provides an elegant method for clustering data in tables along multiple dimensions in a flexible, continuous, and automatic way. Prior to Version 8, DB2 only supported single-dimensional clustering of data using clustering indexes; when a clustering index was defined on a table, DB2 attempted to maintain the physical order of the data on pages as records were inserted and updated in the table, based on the key order of the clustering index used. This could significantly improve the performance of queries that contained predicates that referenced keys of the clustering index, because, with good clustering, only a portion of the physical table needed to be accessed. Furthermore, because pages were stored sequentially on disk, more efficient prefetching could be performed. (Support for single-dimensional clustering remains available in DB2 9.1 and 9.5.)

Essentially, MDC allows a table to be physically clustered on more than one key, or dimension, simultaneously. Like any other table, an MDC table can be partitioned with a partitioning key, and that partitioning key may or may not also be one of the table's dimensions. Like any other table, an MDC table can have, among other things, views, MQTs, referential integrity, triggers, RID indexes, and replication defined upon it. In the case of query performance, range queries involving any combination of the specified dimensions of the clustered table will benefit, because they will need to access only those pages that have records with the specified dimension values. (The qualifying pages will be grouped together in extents.) A table with a clustering index can become unclustered over time as available space is filled. However, an MDC table is able to maintain its clustering over the specified dimensions automatically and continuously, eliminating the need to reorganize the table in order to restore the physical order of the data. Thus, MDC can significantly reduce the overhead of data maintenance, such as reorganization and index maintenance operations during insert, update, and delete operations. MDC is primarily intended to be used with large tables in data warehousing and large database environments.

When an MDC table is created, the dimensional key (or keys) along which to cluster the table's data are specified. Each of the specified dimensions can be defined with one or more columns, the same as an index key. A dimension block index will be automatically created for each of the dimensions specified, and will be used to quickly and efficiently access data along each of the specified dimensions. (Dimension block indexes point to extents instead of individual rows and are thus much smaller than regular indexes. These dimension block indexes can be used to very quickly access only those extents of the table that contain particular dimension values.) In addition, a block index will also be automatically created, containing all dimension key columns. The block index will be used to maintain the clustering of the data during insert and update activity as well as to provide quick and efficient access to the data. A composite block index containing all dimension key columns is also created automatically. The composite block index is used to maintain the clustering of data during insert and update activity. The composite block index is also used in query processing to access data in the table having particular dimension values. Figure 3–11 shows a simple MDC table and its associated indexes.

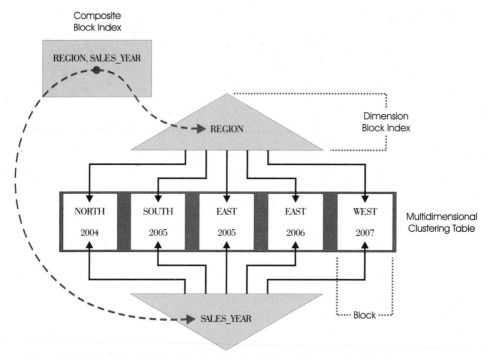

Figure 3–11: A simple multidimensional clustering table and its associated indexes.

Every unique combination of the table's dimension values forms a logical cell, which is physically comprised of blocks of pages, where a block is a set of consecutive pages on disk. The set of blocks that contain pages with data having the same key value of one of the dimension block indexes is called a slice. Every page of the table will be stored in only one block, and all blocks of the table will consist of the same number of pages, a value known as the blocking factor. The blocking factor is equal to the table space's extent size, making the block boundaries line up with extent boundaries.

In an environment with referential integrity relationships, the parent, the child, or both tables may benefit from block level clustering, depending on the query workload against the tables, and upon the nature of the data stored in them. Similarly, in a star-schema environment, the fact table may benefit from block-level clustering, as may one or more of the dimension tables. Each table should be evaluated separately, and dimensions should be chosen based on the query workload, data distribution, and expected cell density.

Multidimensional clustering tables are created by specifying the ORGANIZE BY DIMENSIONS clause of the CREATE TABLE SQL statement when a table is created. The syntax for this optional clause is:

```
ORGANIZE BY DIMENSIONS
( <(>[ColumnName] ,...<)> ,...)
```

where:

ColumnName   Identifies one or more columns, by name, whose values are to be used to cluster the table's data. The use of parentheses within the column list specifies that a group of columns is to be treated as a single dimension.

Thus, if you wanted to create an MDC table named SALES in such a way that its data is organized into extents based on unique combinations of values found in the CUSTOMER, REGION, and YEAR columns, you could do so by executing a CREATE TABLE SQL statement that looks something like this:

```
CREATE TABLE sales
    (customer   VARCHAR(80),
     region     CHAR(5),
     year       INTEGER)
ORGANIZE BY(customer, region, year)
```

Figure 3–12 illustrates how the resulting MDC table would be dimensioned.

One thing you may notice immediately about the multidimensional clustering table depicted in Figure 3–12 is that an MDC table can be divided into "slices" that contain all the blocks of data that have the same dimension value. For example, the slice that contains all blocks in which the CUSTOMER column contains the value "Widgets Inc." in the MDC table created earlier can be seen in Figure 3–13.

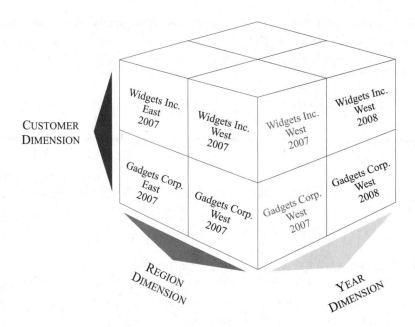

Figure 3—12: A simple multidimensional clustering table.

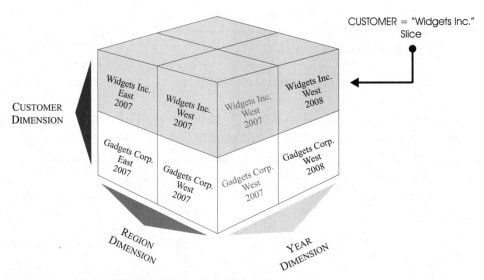

Figure 3—13: The CUSTOMER "slice" in a MDC table.

The slice that contains all blocks where the REGION column contains the value "West" can be seen in Figure 3–14.

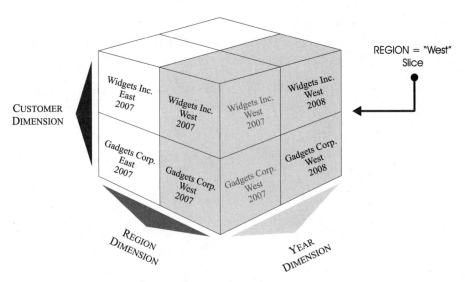

Figure 3—14: The REGION slice in a MDC table.

And finally, the slice that contains all blocks where the YEAR column contains the value 2007 can be seen in Figure 3–15.

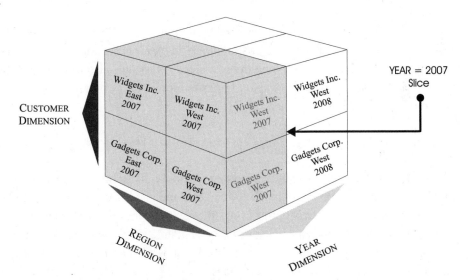

Figure 3—15: The YEAR slice in a MDC table.

Each unique attribute value combination of the dimensions used in an MDC table identifies a possible cell. For example, all rows where the CUSTOMER column contains the value "Widgets Inc.", the REGION column contains the value "West", and the YEAR column contains the value 2007 are stored in the same cell, as shown in Figure 3–16. Each cell may have zero or more blocks of data.

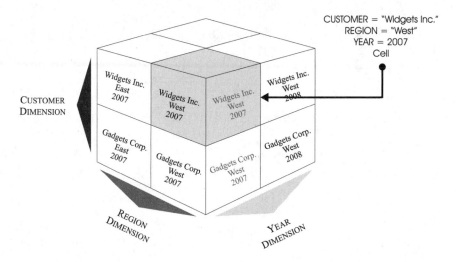

Figure 3–16: A cell in a MDC table.

When a MDC table is created, a dimension block index is automatically created for each dimension key used. This dimension block index identifies the list of blocks available for a given key value. A composite block index will also be created if the table has more than one dimension; a composite block index contains pointers to individual cells with block entries.

Guidelines for Designing MDC Tables

When designing an MDC table, it is important to choose the right set of dimensions (for clustering) and the optimum block (extent) size and page size (for space utilization). If these two items are selected appropriately, the resulting clustering can translate into significant performance increases and ease of maintenance. On the other hand, if an incorrect dimension and/or block size is chosen, performance can be negatively impacted and the space required to store the table's data could increase dramatically.

The best criteria to use for determining which clustering dimensions are ideal for a given table is a set of frequently executed queries that might benefit from clustering at the block level. Columns involved in equality or range predicate queries—especially those with low cardinalities—will show the greatest benefit from, and should be considered as candidates for, clustering dimensions. Foreign keys in a fact table that is involved in star joins with other dimension tables are also good candidates for clustering.

Another very important aspect that must be taken into consideration when designing an MDC table is the expected density of cells in the table (based on present and anticipated data). The extent size used, together with the clustering dimensions selected, determines an MDC table's cell density. The number of possible cells in an MDC table is equal to the Cartesian product of the cardinalities of each of the dimensions used. For example, if you cluster a table on the dimensions DAY, REGION, and PRODUCT, and the data covers 5 years, you might have 1821 days * 12 regions * 5 products = 109,260 different possible cells in the table. Because an extent is allocated for every cell, regardless of the number of records recorded in it, if the block size is large and the cells are not fully populated, the table could end up being much larger than it needs to be. Thus, to get the most benefit from multidimensional clustering and to get optimal space utilization, it is important to have densely filled blocks. Several design factors can be used to obtain optimal cell density, including:

- Varying the number of dimensions used

  Analysis of a set of frequently executed queries may identify multiple potential dimension keys. If that is the case, two or more dimension keys can be combined to form a composite set. For example, columns named CITY and STATE could be combined to form one aggregate dimension instead of two individual dimensions. If city and state are always used together in a query workload, using an aggregate dimension set is a good choice, because this will result in slices based on the combination of these values. However, if city or state is used independently, it is better to have two separate dimensions so that each slice can be examined independently.

- Varying the granularity of one or more dimensions used

  If one of the candidate dimension keys has too many possible unique values, a rollup technique can be used to decrease the granularity or cardinality of the dimension candidate. For example, if a candidate column (dimension) named SHIPPEDDATE has a cardinality that is quite high, a generated expression based on the YEARANDMONTH of the SHIPPEDDATE can be added to the table and used as a clustering dimension.

Keep in mind that the rolled-up granularity must remain useful as a dimension that helps the query workload. For example, if most queries on SHIPPEDDATE request ranges within a month, then rolling up to years might not be useful for improving the performance of these queries—the overhead of scanning a whole year to find a specific month will typically be too large.

It is also important for monotonic expressions or functions to produce the generated expression that will be used as a clustering dimension. (Monotonic means that an increasing range of values on the base column corresponds to a range of values on the generated column that never decreases.) For example, the YEAR() function is a monotonic function; the MONTH() function is not as it provides duplicate values for different years. If the DB2 Optimizer determines that the expression involved in a generated column is not monotonic, it will not be able to generate corresponding predicates on the generated column for range predicates on the base column, but it will be able to generate predicates on the generated column for equality and IN predicates.

- Varying the block (extent) size and page size of the table space that is used to house the MDC table

Given a value for the space occupied per cell (SPC), it is possible to adjust the page size and extent size for the table space to arrive at an optimal number of full blocks. In order to realize the full flexibility possible in the design of an MDC table, the table space's parameters may also need to be set accordingly. For example, if the SPC is relatively low and does not even fill a block when the default values for the page size (4K) and extent size (16 or 32 pages) are used, the extent size can be reduced to a lower number (say 8 pages) and the SPC recalculated to see whether this results in better block space occupancy. Although further reductions in the extent size—all the way to the smallest value of two—could help, it is important to consider the tradeoff of I/O overhead when using very small extent sizes. In these cases, all the other techniques, such as varying the granularity or reducing the number of dimensions, should be considered as well. If the value of SPC is relatively large and can accommodate several blocks, consider increasing the page size and extent size used to arrive at an optimal value of blocks per cell.

If the value of SPC is high, it might also be possible to add another dimension to the table to obtain additional performance benefits.

Choosing the Optimum MDC Table Design

To create the best design for an MDC table, perform the following tasks in the order shown:

1. Identify candidate dimensions for the table by examining typical workload queries. Columns that are referenced in one or more of the following ways should be considered:

   - Range, equality, or IN-list predicates

   - Roll-in or roll-out of data

   - Group-by and order-by clauses

   - Join clauses (especially in star schema environments)

   A set of queries may reference several columns that satisfy these criteria. If that is the case, it is important to rank the candidate columns based on the workload characteristics in order to choose an appropriate subset of the candidates for consideration. Once the list of candidate columns has been narrowed down, iterate through the remaining steps with variations of the set of dimension candidates available before deciding on a final selection.

2. Identify how many potential cells are possible if the table is organized along a set of candidate dimensions identified in Step 1. (In other words, determine the number of unique combinations of the dimension values that can occur in the data. If the table already exists, an exact number can be determined for the current data simply by selecting the number of distinct values in each of the columns that will be used as dimensions for the table. If the table does not exist, an approximation can be determined, if you have statistics for the table, by multiplying the column cardinalities for the dimension candidates. (Keep in mind that this estimate can be inaccurate if there are correlations among the dimension columns used.)

   It is important to note that if your table resides in a partitioned database, and the distribution key is not related to any of the dimensions considered, you will have to determine an average amount of data per cell by taking all the data and dividing it by the number of database partitions.

3. Estimate the space occupancy (cell density).

    Assuming that on average, each cell will have one partially filled block where only a few rows are stored, more partially filled blocks will exist as the number of rows per cell becomes smaller. In most cases, the number of records per cell can be found by dividing the number of records in the table by the number of cells used. However, if your table is in a partitioned database environment, you need to consider how many records there are per cell on each database partition, because blocks are allocated for data on a database partition basis. When estimating the space occupancy and density in a partitioned database environment, consider the number of records per cell on average on each database partition, not across the entire table.

    To improve cell density:

    - Reduce the size of each block by making the extent size appropriately small (so that partially filled blocks take up less space). Each cell that has a partially filled block, or that contains only one block with a few records in it, wastes less space. The trade-off, however, is that more blocks are needed to store those cells that contain many records. This increases the number of block identifiers (BIDs) needed in the block indexes, making these indexes larger and potentially causing more inserts and deletes to these indexes as blocks are emptied and filled. It also results in more small groupings of clustered data in the table for these more populated cell values, versus a smaller number of larger groupings of clustered data.

    - Reduce the number of cells by reducing the number of dimensions, or by increasing the granularity of the cells with a generated column. (You can roll up one or more dimensions to a coarser granularity in order to give a dimension a lower cardinality. For example, you could cluster data using a dimension of YEAR_AND_MONTH instead of a dimension of DAY. Each cell would then hold a greater range of values and would be less likely to contain only a few records.

4. Take the following items into consideration:

- When identifying candidate dimensions, search for attributes that are not too granular, thereby enabling more rows to be stored in each cell. This will make better use of block level indexes.

- Higher data volumes may improve population density.

- It may be beneficial to load the data into a non-MDC table for analysis before creating and loading an MDC table.

- The table space extent size and page size are critical parameters for efficient space usage.

- Although a smaller extent size will provide the most efficient use of disk space, the I/O for the queries should also be considered.

- A larger extent will normally reduce I/O cost, because more data will be read at a time, all other things being equal. This, in turn, makes for smaller dimension block indexes, because each dimension value will need fewer blocks. In addition, inserts will be quicker, because new blocks will be needed less often.

- Although an MDC table may require a greater initial understanding of the data, the payoff is that query times will likely improve.

- Some data may be unsuitable for MDC tables and would be a better candidate for a standard clustering index.

"Natural" Uses for MDC Tables

There are many "natural" uses for MDC tables that are often ignored. For instance, time in the general sense of date and time, is a dimension of practically every data warehouse. And questions typically asked of a data warehouse involve domains of time such as "TODAY", "YESTERDAY", "THIS WEEK", "LAST WEEK", "THIS MONTH", "LAST MONTH", etc. Such questions (queries), which specify a subdomain of rows qualified by time can benefit from MDC.

Let's look at this in terms of percentage of data accessed. Suppose you have a data warehouse that is used to store a rolling 2 years or 24 months worth of data. That represents about 100 weeks. If the data were collected via user transactions and simply placed in the data warehouse, chances are that the data will be clustered by customer. This clustering is great for a transaction system where queries about a single customer are typically performed, but brutal in a data warehouse where queries are more typically about a set of customers within a given time frame. For example, a query designed to obtain information about all sales for LAST MONTH will touch a large number of pages that have few rows of interest—what is often referred to as a hollow or low-yield page read.

To provide fast, efficient response to a query, a database needs to read as few pages as possible and ideally, the pages read need to be populated with as many qualifying rows as possible. Reading an entire page from disk and transferring it to memory just to retrieve one or two rows from the page can congest even the most robust storage subsystem. Remember, it isn't just about reading fast and in parallel; it is also about being frugal and smart. And this is where MDC can really help.

Let's go back to our query designed to obtain information about all sales for LAST MONTH from a data warehouse containing two years worth of data. If the database does not have a dimension defined on time, then it is very likely that the query will touch all 100 weeks worth of data, or 100 percent of the data. No matter how fast the server is, 100 percent of the data must be accessed, most likely resulting in a significant amount of low-yield page reads. Put an MDC in place, and you are guaranteed that the actual pages that must be accessed is limited to the time domain specified, in this case "LAST MONTH", which is less than 5 percent of the data or 20 times more efficient!

The impact of this simple use of MDC does not apply just to this query, but virtually to every query run in the data warehouse, since data warehouses by definition are time variant. So when looking to deploy MDC tables, start simple and start with the obvious and reap the benefits immediately instead of looking for the perfect set of dimensions. While you are busy seeking perfection, there are a lot of queries that can benefit from even the simplest single MDC dimension—the dimension of time.

Combining Database Partitioning, Table Partitioning, and Multidimensional Clustering

For ultimate flexibility and maximum performance, you can combine database partitioning, table partitioning, and MDC. Database partitioning will parallelize everything across all database partitions used, while table partitioning and MDC will drastically reduce the I/O required to scan the data and build a result data set.

For example, if you wanted to create a table named ORDERS with key columns ORDER_ID, SHIP_DATE, CATEGORY, and PRICE, such that the table is partitioned by the column SHIP_DATE with four months residing on its own table partition, and data is organized by columns CATEGORY and PRICE such that all rows within any four month date range are clustered together based on twelve months of data, you would execute a CREATE TABLE statement that looks something like this:

```
CREATE TABLE orders
    (order_id       INTEGER,
     ship_date      DATE,
     category       VARCHAR(20),
     price          DECIMAL(5,2))
  IN tbsp0, tbsp1, tbsp2, tbsp3
  DISTRIBUTE BY (order_id)
  PARTITION BY RANGE (ship_date NULLS FIRST)
      (STARTING '01-01-2007' ENDING '12-31-2007'
       EVERY 4 MONTHS)
  ORGANIZE BY DIMENSIONS(category, price);
```

Once this table is created and populated, if a query looking only for a specific category or price of an order shipped in a specific month, (for example electronics goods priced at $250.00 shipped in February, 2007) is executed, the query will run automatically, and in parallel, across all database partitions used. But within each database partition, only the data in the February table partition needs to be accessed—and then only the data block(s) containing the values "Electronics" and "250.00". Data blocks for other categories or prices do not have to be read. Figure 3–17 illustrates how these partitioning schemes work together to optimize data access.

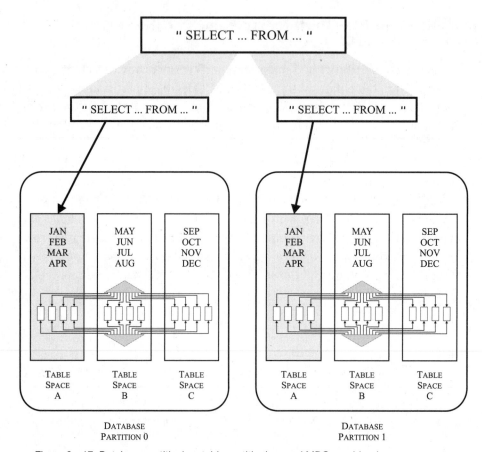

Figure 3—17: Database partitioning, table partitioning, and MDC combined.

A Word About the Design Advisor

Even if you have a lot of experience with database and database application design, the task of selecting which indexes, clustering dimensions, or database partitions to create for a complex workload can be a daunting task. That's where the Design Advisor can help. The Design Advisor is a special tool that is designed to identify indexes, materialized query tables (MQTs), and multidimensional clustering tables that could help improve query performance in your database environment. Using current database statistics, the DB2 Optimizer, snapshot monitor information, and/or a specific query or set of SQL statements (known as a workload) that you provide, the Design Advisor recommends one or more indexes that would improve query/workload performance. In addition, the indexes/MQTs/MDCs recommended, the statistics derived for them, and the data definition language (DDL) statements required to create them can be written to a user-created table named ADVISE_INDEX, if so desired.

The Design Advisor is invoked by executing the db2advis command. The basic syntax for this command is:

```
db2advis [-d | -db] [DatabaseName]
<-w [WorkloadName]>
<-s "[SQLStatement]">
<-i [InFile]>
<-g>
<-qp>
<-a [UserID] </[Password]>
<-m [AdviseType ,...]>
<-l [DiskLimit]>
<-t "[MaxAdviseTime]">
<-k [HIGH | MED | LOW | OFF]>
<-h>
<-p>
<-o [OutFile]>
```

where:

DatabaseName	Identifies, by name, the database with which the Design Advisor is to interact.
WorkloadName	Identifies the name of a workload that is to be analyzed to determine whether new indexes/MQTs/MDCs should be created.
SQLStatement	Identifies a single SQL statement that is to be analyzed to determine whether new indexes/MQTs/MDCs should be created.
InFile	Identifies the name assigned to an ASCII format file that contains a set of SQL statements that are to be analyzed to determine whether new indexes/MQTs/MDCs should be created.
UserID	Identifies the authentication ID (or user ID) that is to be used to establish a connection to the database specified.
Password	Identifies the password that is to be used to establish a connection to the database specified.
AdviseType	Specifies one or more types of recommendations for which the Design Advisor is to analyze. Valid values for this parameter

include the following: I (index), M (materialized query tables [MQTs] and indexes on the MQTs), C (convert standard tables to multidimensional clustering [MDC] tables), and P (repartitioning of existing tables).

DiskLimit Identifies the maximum amount of storage space, in megabytes, that is available for all indexes/MQTs/MDCs in the existing schema.

MaxAdviseTime Identifies the maximum amount of time, in minutes, in which the Design Advisor will be allowed to conduct an analysis. When this time limit is reached, the Design Advisor will stop all processing.

OutFile Identifies the name of the file to which the DDL that is needed to create the indexes/MQTs/MDCs recommended is to be written.

All other options shown with this command are described in Table 3.2.

Table 3.2 db2advis Command Options	
Option	**Meaning**
-g	Specifies that the SQL statements that make up the workload are to be retrieved from a dynamic SQL snapshot. If combined with the -p parameter, the SQL statements are kept in the ADVISE_WORKLOAD table.
-qp	Specifies that the workload is coming from the DB2 Query Patroller query history table.
-k	Specifies to what degree the workload will be compressed. Compression is done to allow the advisor to reduce the complexity of the advisor's execution while achieving results similar to those the advisor could provide when the full workload is considered. HIGH indicates that the advisor will concentrate on a small subset of the workload. MED indicates that the advisor will concentrate on a medium-sized subset of the workload. LOW indicates that the advisor will concentrate on a larger subset of the workload. OFF indicates that no compression will occur, and every query is considered.
-p	Specifies that the plans that were generated while running the Design Advisor are to be kept in the explain tables. This option causes the workload for -qp and -g to be saved in the ADVISE_WORKLOAD table and the workload query plans that use the final recommendation to be saved in the Explain tables.
-h	Displays help information. When this option is specified, all other options are ignored, and only the help information is displayed.

The easiest way to determine whether an index, MQT, and/or MDC would improve the performance of a workload is by constructing a file that contains one or more queries that represent a typical workload, and providing that file's contents as input to the db2advis command. Such a file might look something like this:

```
-- File Name: wkload.sql
-- Execution Command:
--      db2advis -d sample -i db2advis.sql -t 5

-- Evaluate the following set of statements 100 times
--#SET FREQUENCY 100
SELECT COUNT(*) FROM employee;
SELECT * FROM employee WHERE lastname='HAAS';

-- Evaluate the following statement once
--#SET FREQUENCY 1
SELECT AVG(bonus), AVG(salary) FROM employee
   GROUP BY workdept ORDER BY workdept;
```

Once such a file is created, analysis can be conducted by executing a db2advis
command that looks something like this (assuming the file containing the workload is
named WKLOAD.SQL, and the workload is to be run against a database named SAMPLE):

```
db2advis -d sample -i db2advis.sql -t 5
```

When this command is executed, the results produced might look something like this:

```
Using user id as default schema name. Use -n option to specify schema
execution started at timestamp 2007-05-13-10.27.28.134000
found [3] SQL statements from the input file
Recommending indexes...
total disk space needed for initial set [   0.017] MB
total disk space constrained to         [  11.439] MB
Trying variations of the solution set.
Optimization finished.
  1 indexes in current solution
 [1520.9002] timerons  (without recommendations)
 [820.9002] timerons   (with current solution)
 [46.03%] improvement


--
-- LIST OF RECOMMENDED INDEXES
-- ===========================
-- index[1],    0.017MB
   CREATE INDEX "RSANDERS"."IDX705131427300000" ON "RSANDERS"."EMPLOYEE"
   ("LASTNAME" ASC, "COMM" ASC, "BONUS" ASC, "SALARY"
   ASC, "BIRTHDATE" ASC, "SEX" ASC, "EDLEVEL" ASC, "JOB"
   ASC, "HIREDATE" ASC, "PHONENO" ASC, "WORKDEPT" ASC,
   "MIDINIT" ASC, "FIRSTNME" ASC, "EMPNO" ASC) ALLOW
   REVERSE SCANS ;
   COMMIT WORK ;
RUNSTATS ON TABLE "RSANDERS"."EMPLOYEE" FOR INDEX "RSANDERS"."IDX705131
  427300000" ;
   COMMIT WORK ;
```

```
--
-- RECOMMENDED EXISTING INDEXES
-- ============================
-- RUNSTATS ON TABLE "RSANDERS"."EMPLOYEE" FOR INDEX "RSANDERS"."XEMP2" ;
-- COMMIT WORK ;

--
-- UNUSED EXISTING INDEXES
-- ============================
-- ============================
--

31 solutions were evaluated by the advisor
DB2 Workload Performance Advisor tool is finished.
```

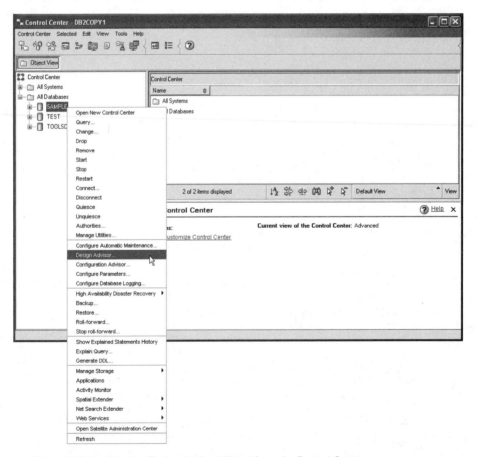

Figure 3–18: Invoking the Design Advisor Wizard from the Control Center.

A GUI version of the Design Advisor (known as the Design Advisor Wizard) is also available. The Design Advisor Wizard can be activated by selecting the appropriate action from the Databases menu found in the Control Center. Figure 3–18 shows the Control Center menu items that must be selected in order to activate the Design Advisor Wizard; Figure 3–19 shows how the second page of the Design Advisor Wizard typically looks after it has been activated.

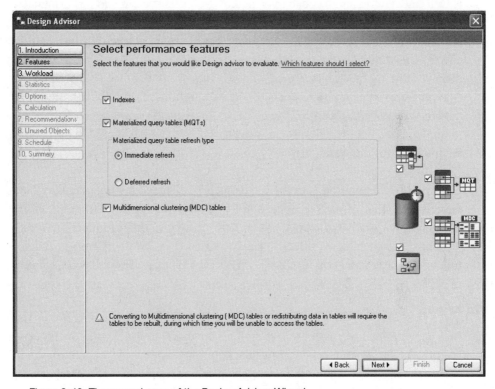

Figure 3–19: The second page of the Design Advisor Wizard.

The Balanced Configuration Unit (BCU)

The IBM Data Warehousing Balanced Configuration Unit (BCU) (renamed "InfoSphere Balanced Warehouse" with the release of DB2 9.5) combines IBM hardware and software to form a single, scalable solution for data warehouse systems. The purpose of the BCU is to provide a carefully balanced combination of resources—including processors, memory, I/O, storage, DB2 database partitions, and DB2 configuration parameters—to create a single, modular node or "building block" that can be used to start or expand a data warehouse system. The term balance indicates that the resources used are known to function well together without significant CPU, I/O, or network bottlenecks.

Large data warehouse systems are created by linking BCU nodes together to form a single system image. Because the operation of the individual components is well understood and has been verified by rigorous system and performance testing, it is possible to make recommendations regarding the number of building blocks required to build a data warehouse based on the projected volume of data and workload that the data warehouse is expected to hold. Knowing the capacity of each building block in advance allows business intelligence (BI) architects to convert the expected requirements of a data warehouse into a BCU building-block model. With careful planning, the tendency to overestimate the resources required to implement a data warehouse are greatly reduced, which should, in turn, reduce the total cost of the warehouse.

Each BCU configuration is evaluated using a BI-focused testing plan that includes three stages: quality, performance, and BI solution testing; a certified BCU solution must comply exactly with a prescribed IBM design. In order to meet the needs of different customers, IBM offers several certified BCU configurations on each of the following platforms: AIX (E-Class), Linux (D-Class), and Windows (C-Class).

BCU Layers

BCUs are defined as a part of an overall architectural hierarchy that includes several layers or levels. Each level describes the solution components, capabilities, and performance appropriate to the level. The primary reason for the existence of these levels is to provide the necessary information required for an architect or system designer to size and understand performance expectations for a data warehouse.

The lowest-level building block for the BCU is a virtual entity known as a Balanced Partition Unit (BPU). The BPU is a logical construct that includes the set of related functions performed in a DB2 database partition, and the system resources that support them. A BPU can be described in terms of the number of processors, the amount of memory, the I/O performance, and the storage capacity required to support a single DB2 database partition. Several types of BPUs are available:

- **Catalog BPU.** The catalog BPU is the database partition in a BCU environment where the DB2 system catalog resides.

- **Coordinator BPU.** A coordinator BPU is the coordinator partition in a BCU environment. It is responsible for managing user connections and coordinating queries.

- **Data BPU.** A data BPU is a database partition that is used primarily for storing partitioned database data. There are two types of data BPUs: those that support data that resides in a single database partition, and those that support data that has been partitioned into multiple database partitions.

Although a single DB2 database partition could host all of these BPU types (catalog, coordinator, single-partition data, and multi-partition data), it is good practice when designing a database to separate administration-related BPUs (catalog and coordinator) from data BPUs.

BCUs occupy the second level in the BCU architectural hierarchy. At a physical level, a BCU refers to the hardware and software components that are associated with a single operating system image—that operating system image can be provided either by an individual server or by a logical partition (LPAR). At a logical level, a BCU consists of one or more BPUs. Two types of BCU nodes are available:

- **Administration BCU.** An administration BCU is one or more database partitions that encompass the DB2 catalog and coordinator partitions. The administration BCU may also contain nonpartitioned table data (that is, tables stored in single-partition database partition groups).

- **Data BCU.** A data BCU is a collection of database partitions or data BPUs that is dedicated to managing and processing a part of the user data within the database. (That is, the data BCU contains the tables that reside in multiple-partition database partition groups.)

Depending on the particular BCU configuration, additional servers might be recommended for a complete data warehouse solution. These servers include DB2 Data Warehouse Edition application servers, ETL servers (sometimes referred to as ETL BCUs), cluster management servers, and storage management servers.

Regardless of the type, each BCU node contains a balanced amount of disk space, processing power and memory to help optimize both cost-effectiveness and throughput.

A high-availability BCU is an optional element in a BCU design and, if used, occupies the third level in the BCU architectural hierarchy. The basic BCU design provides robust availability through the use of reliable technology, hardware component redundancy, and fault-tolerant design. However, in situations in which the highest possible level of availability is required, a HA-BCU is recommended. In an HA-BCU solution, BCUs are grouped together to provide recoverability from a single point of failure.

The BCU for AIX, Version 2.1

The BCU for AIX, Version 2.1 has two configurations: one uses an IBM DS4800 for storage; the other uses an IBM DS8100. The required components for the BCU for AIX v2.1, using the IBM System Storage DS4800, are as follows:

- **Administration BCU:** The administration BCU uses an IBM System p5 or p6 server or logical partition (LPAR) and requires a minimum of 2 processors and 8 GB of memory.

- **Data BCU:** The data BCU uses an IBM System p5 575 server with 8 POWER5+ processors and 32 GB of memory. It is available in two configurations that vary in the amount of storage they are allocated: with the first configuration, the data BCU is allocated eighty-four 73 GB, 15,000 RPM drives; with the second configuration, the data BCU is allocated one hundred sixty-eight 73 GB, 15,000 RPM drives.

- **Network:** Three physical networks are required: one network for DB2 fast communications manager (FCM) communication, one network for corporate users and cluster management, and one network for the Hardware Management Console (HMC).

- **Software:** The following software is required: AIX 5.3, DB2 Data Warehouse Edition (DB2 DWE) V9.1.1 or V9.5, and DS4000 Storage Manager V9.16.

Optional components include:

- **Storage Area Network (SAN) and high-availability configuration:** Customers with high availability requirements can use a SAN. They can also implement a high-availability configuration that uses IBM Tivoli System Automation for Multiplatforms to automate failover within each HA-BCU unit.

- **Cluster management server:** A cluster management server can be used to simplify cluster setup and administration.

- **DB2 DWE application server:** Several DB2 DWE components require an application server.

- **Extract, transform and load (ETL) server:** A dedicated server can be used for transformation work outside of the DB2 database.

- **Tivoli Storage Manager (TSM) server:** All customers should implement some form of backup solution. To provide this functionality, a TSM server is recommended.

The required components for the BCU for AIX v2.1, using the IBM System Storage DS8100 are very similar. The differences are as follows:

- **Administration BCU:** The administration BCU uses an IBM System p5 server or logical partition (LPAR) and requires a minimum of 2 processors and 8 GB of memory. The first administration BCU, which hosts two database partitions, is allocated thirty-two 146 GB, 15,000 RPM drives on an IBM System Storage DS8100. The storage requirements for additional administration BCUs are dependant upon how many database partitions are hosted.

- **Data BCU:** The data BCU uses an IBM System p5 575 server with 8 POWER5+ processors and 32 GB of memory. The first data BCU, which hosts six database partitions because it shares an IBM System Storage DS8100 with the first administration BCU, is allocated ninety-six 146 GB, 15,000 RPM drives. The storage requirements for additional data BCUs depend on how many database partitions they host. In general, data BCUs host eight database partitions and are allocated one hundred twenty-eight 146 GB, 15,000 RPM drives on a DS8100.

The BCU for Linux, Version 2.1

The BCU for Linux is based on the IBM eServer 326m, which is a 1U server that uses two AMD dual-core Opteron CPUs. This server supports technology to enable 64-bit operation and memory support for DB2. Users may upgrade from the IBM eServer 326m to the IBM System x3455; model 2218 (2.6 GHz AMD dual-core Opteron CPUs) has been validated with the BCU for Linux, but models with the faster 2.8 GHz processors are also supported.

Unlike the AIX BCU, the Linux BCU uses both internal and external storage. The internal storage for each IBM eServer e326m (data BCU, administration BCU, or management node) consists of two RAID-1 mirrored SCSI disks, each with 146 GB capacity. The external storage for each pair of data BCUs is provided by one DS4800. The DS4800 is configured with 8 shelves containing 14 disks, each with a capacity of 73 GB. The external storage for either a single administration BCU or a pair of administration BCUs is provided by one DS4300 configured with 14 internal disks, each with a capacity of 73 GB.

Two networks are also recommended. One network is used for the fast communication manager (FCM), which is responsible for internal communications between database partitions on different servers. (This network is also used for cluster management.) It resides on the two integrated Gigabit Ethernet ports that come with the IBM eSeries e326m server, which are bonded together in active backup mode. This network must use a non-blocking configuration to allow for high-speed network communication between the database partitions. The other network is used by applications and clients to access and query the database. It resides on an additional PCI-Express network adapter.

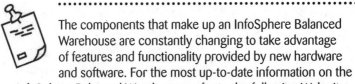

The components that make up an InfoSphere Balanced Warehouse are constantly changing to take advantage of features and functionality provided by new hardware and software. For the most up-to-date information on the InfoSphere Balanced Warehouse, refer to the following Web site:

http://www-306.ibm.com/software/data/infosphere/balanced-warehouse/

Practice Questions

Question 1

A partitioned instance named DB2INST1 uses the following db2nodes.cfg file:

```
 0   Svr1  0
 1   Svr1  1
 2   Svr1  2
 3   Svr1  3
 4   Svr2  0
 5   Svr2  1
 6   Svr2  2
 7   Svr2  3
 8   Svr3  0
 9   Svr4  0
10   Svr4  1
11   Svr4  2
```

If the CREATE DATABASE command is executed from the server Svr2, which partition will be the catalog partition?

○ A. 0
○ B. 4
○ C. 5
○ D. 6

Question 2

Which of the following node configuration files (db2nodes.cfg) indicates that both intra-partition parallelism and inter-partition parallelism is being used?

- O A.   0 Srv1 0
          1 Srv2 1
          2 Srv3 2
          3 Srv4 3

- O B.   0 Srv1 0
          1 Srv2 0
          2 Srv3 0
          3 Srv4 0

- O C.   0 Srv1 0
          1 Srv1 1
          2 Srv1 2
          3 Srv1 3

- O D.   0 Srv1 0
          1 Srv1 1
          2 Srv2 0
          3 Srv2 1

Question 3

A database administrator needs to add a new database partition to an existing DB2 instance. Which two of the following SQL statements must be executed before data can be stored in the new partition? (Select two)

- ❏ A.   ADD PARTITION
- ❏ B.   ADD DBPARTITIONNUM
- ❏ C.   ALTER INSTANCE ADD DBPARTITION
- ❏ D.   ALTER DATABASE PARTITION GROUP
- ❏ E.   REDISTRIBUTE DATABASE PARTITION GROUP

Question 4

An active partitioned instance named DB2INST1 uses the following db2nodes.cfg file:

0 server1 0
1 server1 1
2 server2 0
3 server2 1

If the following command executes without errors:

```
db2start DBPARTITIONNUM 4
    ADD DBPARTITIONNUM HOSTNAME server2 PORT 2
```

Which of the following statements is NOT true regarding instance DB2INST1?

○ A. Instance DB2INST1 was started on hosts named SERVER1 and SERVER2.

○ B. Partitions 0, 1, 2, and 3 are active and available; partition 4 is not.

○ C. An entry for partition 4 was automatically added to the db2nodes.cfg file before the instance DB2INST1 was started.

○ D. An entry for partition 4 will not be added to the db2nodes.cfg file until the instance DB2INST1 is stopped and restarted.

Question 5

A database named SALES has a database partition group named PG1 that has been defined across partitions 2, 3, 4, and 5.

If the commands shown below are executed:

```
CONNECT TO sales;
ALTER DATABASE PARTITION GROUP pg1 ADD DBPARTITIONNUM (6)
```

Which database partition will DB2 use as a model for table spaces created on partition 6?

○ A. Partition 2

○ B. Partition 3

○ C. Partition 4

○ D. Partition 5

Question 6

If the following statement is used to create a table in a multi-partitioned database:

```
CREATE TABLE employee
     (fname      CHAR(30) NOT NULL,
      lname      CHAR(30) NOT NULL,
      empno      INT NOT NULL,
      dept       INT NOT NULL,
      ssn        INT,
   PRIMARY KEY (empno, dept))
```

Which column(s) will be chosen by DB2 to be the table's partitioning key?

- ○ A. FNAME
- ○ B. EMPNO
- ○ C. SSN
- ○ D. EMPNO, DEPT

Question 7

If the following SQL statements are executed:

```
CREATE TYPE yearday AS INTEGER WITH COMPARISONS;

CREATE TABLE sales
     (year_day        YEARDAY,
      item_number     CHAR(10),
      po_number       CHAR(12),
      amount          NUMERIC(9, 2))
PARTITION BY RANGE (year_day)
     (STARTING 200801 ENDING 200812 EVERY 3)
ORGANIZE BY DIMENSIONS (item_number));
```

Which statement correctly describes the resulting table?

- ○ A. The table SALES will be partitioned by YEAR_DAY such that 3 days of data will reside on its own partition. Additionally, data will be organized by ITEM_NUMBER such that all rows within any 3 day period are clustered together based on 3 months of data.
- ○ B. The table SALES will be partitioned by YEAR_DAY such that 3 months of data will reside on its own partition. Additionally, data will be organized by ITEM_NUMBER such that all rows within any 3 day period are clustered together based on 3 months of data.
- ○ C. The table SALES will be partitioned by YEAR_DAY such that 3 years of data will reside on its own partition. Additionally, data will be organized by ITEM_NUMBER such that all rows within any 3 year period are clustered together based on 12 months of data.
- ○ D. The table SALES will be partitioned by YEAR_DAY such that 3 months of data will reside on its own partition. Additionally, data will be organized by ITEM_NUMBER such that all rows within any 3 month period are clustered together based on 12 months of data.

Question 8

Given the following CREATE TABLE statement:

```
CREATE TABLE camera_sales
      (model              CHAR(20) NOT NULL,
       price              DECIMAL(9,2) NOT NULL,
       year               CHAR(4) NOT NULL,
       manufacturer       CHAR(20))
```

If the following queries are executed against the resulting table on a regular basis:

```
SELECT * FROM camera_sales WHERE model = 'D300';
SELECT * FROM camera_sales WHERE price < 2000.00;
SELECT * FROM camera_sales WHERE manufacturer = 'NIKON';
```

Which clause could be added to the CREATE TABLE statement to improve performance of the queries shown?

- ○ A. ORGANIZE BY DIMENSIONS (model)
- ○ B. ORGANIZE BY DIMENSIONS (model, price)
- ○ C. ORGANIZE BY DIMENSIONS (price)
- ○ D. ORGANIZE BY DIMENSIONS (model, manufacturer)

Question 9

In which environment should you consider replacing an existing base table with a multidimensional clustered (MDC) table?

- ○ A. In an OLTP environment to speed up access to large tables.
- ○ B. In a data warehouse environment to improve performance and reduce data maintenance overhead for large tables.
- ○ C. In an OLTP to speed up access to small tables.
- ○ D. In a data warehouse environment to improve performance and reduce data maintenance overhead for small tables.

Question 10

A table named TAB1 has the following columns and cardinalities:

```
COL1  -  Cardinality 100,000
COL2  -  Cardinality 10,000
COL3  -  Cardinality 1,000
COL4  -  Cardinality 100
```

Which column is NOT a good dimensional candidate for MDC?

- ○ A. COL1
- ○ B. COL2
- ○ C. COL3
- ○ D. COL4

Question 11

Your company is required to keep exactly 7 years worth of sales history data available in a table named SALES_RECORDS. It is now midnight on April 30th 2008, and you need to remove the data for May 2001 from the table and begin storing sales records for May 2008. Which of the following set of statements will accomplish this?

○ A. ALTER TABLE sales_records DETACH PARTITION may01 INTO tab0501;
LOAD FROM may08.del OF DEL REPLACE INTO tab0501;
ALTER TABLE sales_records ATTACH PARTITION may08 STARTING
    05/01/2008' ENDING '05/31/2008' FROM tab0501;
SET INTEGRITY FOR sales_records ALLOW WRITE ACCESS IMMEDIATE
    CHECKED FOR EXCEPTION IN sales_records USE salesrecs_ex;

○ B. ALTER TABLE sales_records DETACH PARTITION may01 INTO tab0501;
LOAD FROM may08.del OF DEL REPLACE INTO tab0501;
ALTER TABLE sales_records ATTACH PARTITION may08 STARTING
    01/01/2008' ENDING '05/31/2008' from tab0501;

○ C. ALTER TABLE sales_records DETACH PARTITION may01 into tab0501
LOAD FROM may08.del OF DEL INSERT INTO tab0501;
ALTER TABLE sales_records ATTACH PARTITION may08 STARTING
    05/01/2008' ENDING '05/31/2008' FROM tab0508;
SET INTEGRITY FOR sales_records ALLOW WRITE ACCESS IMMEDIATE
    CHECKED FOR EXCEPTION IN sales_records USE salesrecs_ex;

○ D. ALTER TABLE sales_records DETACH PARTITION may01 into tab0501;
LOAD FROM may08.del OF DEL INSERT INTO tab0501;
ALTER TABLE sales_records ATTACH PARTITION may08 STARTING
    01/01/2008' ENDING '05/31/2008' FROM tab0508;

Question 12

Which of the following data organization schemes is NOT supported by DB2?

○ A. Partition by range
○ B. Partition by dimensions
○ C. Organize by key sequence
○ D. Organize by dimensions

Question 13

Which of the following is NOT a true statement about creating distribution keys?

○ A. A distribution key should include columns with low cardinality.
○ B. A distribution key should include columns most often used in equality or range predicate queries.
○ C. A distribution key should include columns most often used in sort operations.
○ D. A distribution key should include columns most often used in join operations.

Question 14

A database administrator captured the entire SQL workload against a database named SALES into an ASCII file names WKLD.SQL. What is the proper command to use to run the Design Advisor so that it will evaluate all information stored in the file WKLD.SQL, and give advice on converting standard tables to multidimensional clustering (MDC) tables?

- ○ A. db2advis –d sales –i wkld.sql –m C
- ○ B. db2advis –d sales –i wkld.sql –CLUSTERING
- ○ C. db2advis –d sales –i wkld.sql –C
- ○ D. db2advis –d sales –i wkld.sql –m ALL

Question 15

Which of the following components make up the IBM BCU v2.1 for AIX?

- ○ A. IBM System x 575, IBM DS Series Storage, and DB2 Enterprise Server Edition.
- ○ B. IBM System x 575, IBM DS Series Storage, and DB2 Data Warehouse Edition.
- ○ C. IBM System p 575, IBM DS Series Storage, and DB2 Enterprise Server Edition.
- ○ D. IBM System p 575, IBM DS Series Storage, and DB2 Data Warehouse Edition.

Question 16

Which of the following is NOT a valid statement about the IBM BCU v2.1?

- ○ A. The IBM System x 3455 houses the database partitions in a BCU v2.1 for Linux configuration.
- ○ B. Each data BCU contains eight DB2 database partitions.
- ○ C. The IBM System p 575 houses the database partitions in a BCU v2.1 for AIX configuration.
- ○ D. All backup and recovery operations are performed using Tivoli Storage Manager.

Answers

Question 1

The correct answer is **B**. Before you create a partitioned database, you must decide which partition will act as the catalog partition for the database. Once the partition that will serve as the catalog partition has been selected, you must then create the database directly from that partition or from a remote client that is attached to that partition—the database partition to which you attach and execute the CREATE DATABASE command (or invoke the Create Database Wizard) becomes the catalog partition for the new database. (The catalog partition will be the partition using port number 0 on the server where the CREATE DATABASE command is executed.) In this example, partition 4 is the first partition on server Svr2 so that is the partition that will contain the system catalog for the database.

Keep in mind that on Linux and UNIX, the db2nodes.cfg file is formatted as follows:

```
[PartitionNumber]  [HostName]  [LogicalPort]  [NetName]  [ResourceSetName]
```

And on Windows, the db2nodes.cfg file is formatted as follows:

```
[PartitionNumber] [HostName] [ComputerName] [LogicalPort] [NetName]
```

Question 2

The correct answer is **D**. Intra-partition parallelism refers to the ability to break up a database operation into multiple parts and execute those parts simultaneously within a single DB2 instance. Inter-partition parallelism refers to the ability to break up a database operation into multiple parts, many or all of which can be run in parallel across multiple partitions of a partitioned database.

On Linux and UNIX, the db2nodes.cfg file is formatted as follows:

```
[PartitionNumber]  [HostName]  [LogicalPort]  [NetName]  [ResourceSetName]
```

And on Windows, the db2nodes.cfg file is formatted as follows:

```
[PartitionNumber] [HostName] [ComputerName] [LogicalPort] [NetName]
```

In this example, the db2nodes.cfg file shown in answers A and B indicate that the DB2 instance spans four database partitions that reside on four different servers (hosts)—this illustrates the use of inter-partition parallelism. The db2nodes.cfg file shown in answer C indicates that the DB2 instance spans four database partitions that reside on the same server—this illustrates the use of intra-partition parallelism. The db2nodes.cfg file shown in answer D indicates that the DB2 instance spans two database partitions that reside on one server and two partitions that reside on another server—this illustrates the use of both inter- and intra-partition parallelism. (To support both inter- and intra-partition parallelism, an instance must span multiple partitions that reside on two or more different servers or logical partitions [LPARs].).

Question 3

The correct answers are **B** and **D**. New database partitions can be added to a partitioned database system by executing the ADD DBPARTITIONNUM command. New database partitions can also be created by starting an instance in such a way that a new database partition is defined at instance startup. This is done by executing the START DATABASE MANAGER command with the ADD DBPARTITIONNUM option specified.

When you use the ADD DBPARTITIONNUM command or the ADD DBPARTITIONNUM option of the START DATABASE MANAGER command to add a new database partition to the system, all existing databases in the instance are expanded to the new database partition. However, data cannot be stored on the new partition until one or more database partition groups have been altered to include the new database partition. New partitions are added to an existing database partition group by executing the ALTER DATABASE PARTITION GROUP command.

Question 4

The correct answer is **C**. When the ADD DBPARTITIONNUM option is used with the START DATABASE MANAGER command to add a new database partition to an instance that spans multiple partitions, the db2nodes.cfg file is not updated with information about the new database partition until the instance is stopped and restarted; likewise, the new database partition does not become part of the partitioned database system until the instance is stopped and restarted.

Question 5

The correct answer is **A**. The syntax for the form of the ALTER DATABASE PARTITION GROUP SQL statement that is used to add new database partitions to an existing database partition group is:

```
ALTER DATABASE PARTITION GROUP [PartGroupName]
ADD DBPARTITIONNUM<S>
  ([StartPartitionNum] <TO [EndPartitionNum]> ,...)
<LIKE DBPARTITIONNUM [SrcPartitionNum] |
  WITHOUT TABLESPACES>
```

where:

PartGroupName   Identifies, by name, the database partition group that is to be modified.

StartPartitionNum   Identifies, by partition number, one or more database partitions that are to be added to the database partition group specified.

EndPartitionNum   Identifies, by partition number, a database partition that, together with the database partition number specified in the *StartPartitionNum* parameter, identify a range of database partitions that are to be added to the database partition group specified. (The partition number specified in this parameter must be greater than the partition number specified in the *StartPartitionNum* parameter.)

SrcPartitionNum   Identifies, by partition number, a database partition that is to be used as a reference when defining containers on the database partition being added for table spaces that already exist in the partition group being altered. (The database partition number specified must correspond to a partition that existed in the database partition group being altered before the ALTER DATABASE PARTITION GROUP statement was executed.)

If the WITHOUT TABLESPACES option is specified, containers for table spaces in the database partition group being altered are not created for the database partition(s) added; if this option is used, the ALTER TABLESPACE statement must be executed in order to define table space containers to be used by the table spaces that have been defined in the partition group–before the table spaces can be used. If neither the LIKE DBPARTRTIONNUM option nor the WITHOUT TABLESPACES option is specified when adding a database partition to a database partition group, the containers used for table spaces on the database partition(s) being added will be the same as the containers found on the lowest numbered database partition in the partition group.

So, in this example, the lowest numbered database partition in the database partition group PG1 is 2 and neither the LIKE DBPARTITIONNUM option nor the WITHOUT TABLESPACES option is specified, so new database partitions will be added as if the option LIKE DBPARTITIONNUM 2 had been specified; the table space containers on database partition number 2 will be used as a model for the table space containers created on database partition number 6.

Question 6

The correct answer is **B**. The partitioning key for a table is defined as part of the table creation process by using the PARTITION BY clause of the CREATE TABLE SQL statement. If a partitioning key is not explicitly specified (and the table is being created in a table space that resides in multi-partition database partition group), the partitioning key for the table will be defined as follows:

- If a primary key is defined for the table, the first column of the primary key will be the partitioning key,

- If the table is a typed table, the object identifier column for the table will be the partitioning key,

- The first column whose data type is not a LOB, LONG VARCHAR, LONG VARGRAPHIC, XML, structured data type, or a distinct data type based on one of these data types will be the partitioning key; otherwise,

- The table will be created without a partitioning key—in this case, the table can only be created in a table space that has been defined on a single-partition database partition group. (A single-partition database partition group is a partition group that only spans one database partition.)

Question 7

The correct answer is **D**. Data from a given table is partitioned into multiple storage objects based on the specifications provided in the PARTITION BY clause of the CREATE TABLE statement. Multidimensional clustering tables are created by specifying the ORGANIZE BY DIMENSIONS clause of the CREATE TABLE SQL statement when a table is created. So in this example, the table SALES is partitioned by the YEAR_DAY column and clustered by the ITEM_NUMBER column. The (STARTING 200801 ENDING 200812 EVERY 3) partitioning range indicates that data will be partitioned every three months - a one year period was specified and the keyword EVERY along with the value 3 indicates 3 months of a 12 month period.

Question 8

The correct answer is **D**. To create the best design for an MDC table, perform the following tasks, in the order shown:

1. Identify candidate dimensions for the table by examining typical workload queries. Columns that are referenced in one or more of the following ways should be considered:

    - Range, equality, or IN-list predicates

    - Roll-in or roll-out of data

    - Group-by and order-by clauses

    - Join clauses (especially in star schema environments)

2. Identify how many potential cells are possible if the table is organized along a set of candidate dimensions identified in Step 1. (In other words, determine the number of unique combinations of the dimension values that can occur in the data.)

3. Estimate the space occupancy (cell density).

4. Take the following items into consideration:

    - When identifying candidate dimensions, search for attributes that are not too granular, thereby enabling more rows to be stored in each cell. This will make better use of block level indexes.

    - Higher data volumes may improve population density.

    - It may be beneficial to load the data into a non-MDC table for analysis before creating and loading an MDC table.

- The table space extent size and page size are critical parameters for efficient space utilization.

- Although a smaller extent size will provide the most efficient use of disk space, the I/O for the queries should also be considered.

- A larger extent will normally reduce I/O cost, since more data will be read at a time, all other things being equal. This in turn makes for smaller dimension block indexes, since each dimension value will need fewer blocks. In addition, inserts will be quicker, since new blocks will be needed less often.

- Although an MDC table may require a greater initial understanding of the data, the payback is that query times will likely improve.

- Some data may be unsuitable for MDC tables and would be a better candidate for a standard clustering index.

Because the columns MODEL and MANUFACTURER are referenced in equality predicates of frequently executed queries in this example, they make the ideal clustering dimensions for the table. If those two columns are used as the dimensions of the table, all sales with the same MODEL and MANUFACTURER will be stored together. Having YEAR or PRICE in the dimensions will actually mean that DB2 will need to read more blocks of data to retrieve the desired data.

Question 9

The correct answer is **B**. Multidimensional clustering (MDC) is primarily intended to be used with large tables in data warehousing and large database environments.

Question 10

The correct answer is **A**. When designing an MDC table, it is important to choose the right set of dimensions (for clustering) and the optimum block (extent) size and page size (for space utilization). If these two items are selected appropriately, the resulting clustering can translate into significant performance increases and ease of maintenance. On the other hand, if an incorrect dimension and/or block size is chosen, performance can be negatively impacted and the space required to store the table's data could increase dramatically.

The best criteria to use for determining which clustering dimensions are ideal for a given table, is a set of frequently executed queries that might benefit from clustering at the block level. Columns, especially those with low cardinalities, that are involved in equality or range predicate queries will show the greatest benefit from, and should be considered as candidates for, clustering dimensions. Foreign keys in a fact table that is involved in star joins with other dimension tables are also good candidates for clustering.

Because column COL1 has a high cardinality, it is not a good MDC dimension candidate. Its use is likely to lead to sparse dimensions, which can increase the storage requirements of the table.

Question 11

The correct answer is **A**. Partitioned table data can be rolled in or out of a partitioned table by executing an ALTER TABLE SQL statement with either the ATTACH PARTITION or the DETACH PARTITION option specified. In this example, suppose you want to update the information stored in a table named SALES_RECORDS by removing the data for May 2001 and replacing it with data for May 2008. To perform this roll-out and roll-in of data, you would complete the following steps, in the order shown:

1. Remove the May 2001 data from the SALES_RECORDS table and copy it to another table by executing an ALTER TABLE statement that looks something like this:

   ```
   ALTER TABLE sales_records DETACH PARTITION may01 INTO tab0501
   ```

2. Load the data for May 2008 into the table used to store the data for May 2001 by executing a LOAD command that looks like this:

   ```
   LOAD FROM may08.del OF DEL REPLACE INTO tab0501;
   ```

   (Executing the LOAD command with the REPLACE option causes existing data to be overwritten; you must run the SET INTEGRITY statement to disable constraint checking before you can load the detached table.)

3. If appropriate, perform any data cleansing activities needed. Data cleansing activities include:

   - Filling in missing values

   - Deleting inconsistent and incomplete data

   - Removing redundant data arriving from multiple sources

   - Transforming data

     ○ Normalization (Data from different sources that represents the same value in different ways must be reconciled as part of rolling the data into a data warehouse.)

     ○ Aggregation (Raw data that is too detailed to store in a data warehouse must be pre-aggregated during roll-in.)

4. Attach the table containing the data for May 2008 (TAB0501) to the SALES_RECORDS table as a new partition by executing an ALTER TABLE statement that looks something like this:

```
ALTER TABLE sales_records
ATTACH PARTITION may08
STARTING '05/01/2008' ENDING '05/31/2008'
FROM tab0501;
```

(Attaching a data partition terminates queries and invalidates packages.)

5. Update indexes and other dependent objects by executing a SET INTEGRITY SQL statement that looks something like this:

```
SET INTEGRITY FOR sales_records
ALLOW WRITE ACCESS
IMMEDIATE CHECKED FOR EXCEPTION IN sales_records
  USE salesrecs_ex;
```

Question 12

The correct answer is **B**. Range-clustered tables are created by specifying the ORGANIZE BY KEY SEQUENCE clause of the CREATE TABLE SQL statement; Range-partitioned tables are created by specifying the PARTITION BY RANGE clause of the CREATE TABLE SQL statement; and multidimensional clustering (MDC) tables are created by specifying the ORGANIZE BY DIMENSIONS clause of the CREATE TABLE SQL statement. PARTITION BY DIMENSIONS is not a valid data organization scheme.

Question 13

The correct answer is **C**. Columns, especially those with low cardinalities, that are involved in equality or range predicate queries will show the greatest benefit from, and should be considered as candidates for, clustering dimensions (distribution keys). Foreign keys in a fact table that is involved in star joins with other dimension tables are also good candidates for clustering. Columns that are referenced in one or more of the following ways should be considered:

- Range, equality, or IN-list predicates

- Roll-in or roll-out of data

- Group-by and order-by clauses

- Join clauses (especially in star schema environments)

Question 14

The correct answer is **A**. The Design Advisor is invoked by executing the db2advis command. The basic syntax for this command is:

```
db2advis [-d | -db] [DatabaseName]
<-w [WorkloadName]>
<-s "[SQLStatement]">
<-i [InFile]>
<-g>
<-qp>
<-a [UserID] </[Password]>
<-m [AdviseType ,...]>
<-l [DiskLimit]>
<-t "[MaxAdviseTime]">
<-k [HIGH | MED | LOW | OFF]>
<-h>
<-p>
<-o [OutFile]>
```

where:

DatabaseName	Identifies, by name, the database with which the Design Advisor is to interact.
WorkloadName	Identifies the name of a workload that is to be analyzed to determine whether new indexes/MQTs/MDCs should be created.
SQLStatement	Identifies a single SQL statement that is to be analyzed to determine whether new indexes/MQTs/MDCs should be created.
InFile	Identifies the name assigned to an ASCII format file that contains a set of SQL statements that are to be analyzed to determine whether new indexes/MQTs/MDCs should be created.
UserID	Identifies the authentication ID (or user ID) that is to be used to establish a connection to the database specified.
Password	Identifies the password that is to be used to establish a connection to the database specified.
AdviseType	Specifies one or more types of recommendations for which the Design Advisor is to analyze. Valid values for this parameter include the following: I (index), M (materialized query tables [MQTs] and indexes on the MQTs), C (convert standard tables to multidimensional clustering [MDC] tables), and P (repartitioning of existing tables).
DiskLimit	Identifies the maximum amount of storage space, in megabytes, that is available for all indexes/MQTs/MDCs in the existing schema.

MaxAdviseTime Identifies the maximum amount of time, in minutes, in which the Design Advisor will be allowed to conduct an analysis. When this time limit is reached, the Design Advisor will stop all processing.

OutFile Identifies the name of the file to which the DDL that is needed to create the indexes/MQTs/MDCs recommended is to be written.

If you want advice for all types of objects, you must use -m MICP, not -m ALL.

Question 15

The correct answer is **D**. The components that make up the IBM BCU v2.1 for AIX are one or more IBM System p 575 servers, one or more IBM DS4800 or IBM DS8100 storage systems, and DB2 Data Warehouse Edition (DB2 DWE) V9.1.1 or V9.5.

Question 16

The correct answer is **A**. The BCU for Linux is based on the IBM eServer 326m, which is a 1U server that uses two AMD dual-core Opteron CPUs. Users may upgrade from the IBM eServer 326m to the IBM System x3455; model 2218 (2.6 GHz AMD dual-core Opteron CPUs) has been validated with the BCU for Linux, but models with the faster 2.8 GHz processors are also supported. The BCU for AIX v2.1 uses an IBM System p5 575 server with 8 POWER5+ processors and 32 GB of memory. In general data BCUs host eight database partitions.

All customers should implement some form of backup solution. To provide this functionality, a Tivoli Storage Manager (TSM) server is recommended, but not required.

CHAPTER 4

High Availability and Diagnostics

Twenty percent (20%) of the DB2 9 for Linux, UNIX, and Windows Advanced Database Administration exam (Exam 734) is designed to evaluate your knowledge of transactions and transaction logging, to test your ability to back up and restore a database using the various methods of backup and recovery available, and to test your ability to use some of the diagnostic tools available with DB2. The questions that make up this portion of the exam are intended to evaluate the following:

- Your ability to manage database logs for recovery

- Your knowledge of the types of database recovery available (crash, version, and roll-forward) and your ability to demonstrate when and how each is used

- Your ability to use advanced backup and recovery features

- Your knowledge of high availability disaster recovery (HADR)

- Your ability to use some of the DB2 diagnostic tools available

This chapter is designed to introduce you to the backup and recovery tools that are available with DB2 and to show you how to both back up a database on a regular basis and restore a database if it becomes damaged or corrupted. This chapter is also designed to introduce you to some of the basic diagnostic tools that are available with DB2.

Transactions

A transaction (also known as a unit of work) is a sequence of one or more SQL statements or operations grouped together as a single unit, usually within an application process. The initiation and termination of a single transaction defines points of data consistency within a database; either the effects of all operations performed within a transaction are applied to the database and made permanent (committed) or the effects of all operations performed are backed out (rolled back), and the database is returned to the state it was in before the transaction started.

In most cases, transactions are initiated the first time an executable SQL statement is executed after a connection to a database has been made or immediately after a preexisting transaction has ended or has been terminated. Once initiated, transactions can be implicitly terminated using a feature known as "automatic commit." If automatic commit is turned on, each executable SQL statement is treated as a single transaction, and any changes made by that statement are applied to the database if the statement executes successfully. If a statement fails, the changes are rolled back. Transactions can be explicitly terminated by executing the COMMIT or the ROLLBACK SQL statement. The basic syntax for these two statements is:

```
COMMIT <WORK>
```

and

```
ROLLBACK <WORK>
```

When the COMMIT statement is used to terminate a transaction, all changes made to the database since the transaction began are made permanent. On the other hand, when the ROLLBACK statement is used, all changes made are backed out, and the database is returned to the state it was in just before the transaction began.

Transaction Logging

Transaction logging is the process used to keep track of changes made to a database (by transactions) *as they occur*. Each time an update or a delete operation is performed, the page containing the record to be updated/deleted is retrieved from storage and copied to the appropriate buffer pool, where it is then modified by the update/delete operation. If a new record is created by an insert operation, that record is created directly in the appropriate buffer pool. (In some cases, for example when a referential constraint is enforced, an insert operation can also require that one or more pages be retrieved from disk.) Once the record has been modified (or inserted), a record reflecting the modification/insertion is written to the log buffer, which is simply another designated storage area in memory. (The actual amount of memory reserved for the log buffer is controlled by the *logbufsiz* database configuration parameter.) If an insert operation is performed, a record containing the new row is written to the log buffer; if a delete operation is performed, a record containing the row's original values is written to the log buffer; and if an update operation is performed, a record containing some or all of the row's original values, combined with the row's corresponding new values, is written to the log buffer. (If replication has not been enabled, an exclusive OR operation is performed using the "before" and "after" rows and the results are written to the log buffer.) These kinds of records, along with records that indicate whether the transactions that were responsible for making changes were committed or rolled back, make up the majority of the records stored in the log buffer.

When the log buffer becomes full, all records stored in the buffer are immediately written to one or more log files stored on disk. In addition, whenever buffer pool I/O page cleaners are activated, the log buffer becomes full, or a transaction is terminated (by being committed or rolled back), all records stored in the log buffer are immediately written to one or more log files stored on disk. This is done to minimize the number of log records that might get lost in the event a system failure occurs. As soon as all log records associated with a particular transaction have been externalized to one or more log files, the effects of the transaction itself are recorded in the database (i.e., executed against the appropriate table space containers for permanent storage). The modified data pages remain in memory, where they can be quickly accessed if necessary—eventually they will be overwritten as newer pages are retrieved from storage. This is what is known as "write-ahead logging," and this process can be seen in Figure 4–1.

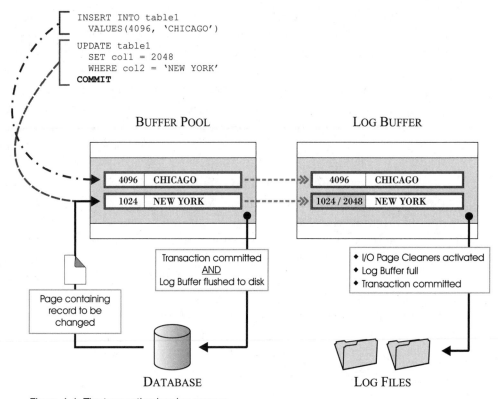

Figure 4–1: The transaction logging process.

Because multiple transactions may be working with a database at any given point in time, a single log file may contain log records that belong to several different transactions. Therefore, to keep track of which log records belong to which transactions, every log record is assigned a special "transaction identifier" that ties it to the transaction that created it. By using transaction IDs, log records associated with a particular transaction can be written to one or more log files at any time without impacting data consistency—eventually the execution of the COMMIT or ROLLBACK statement that terminates the transaction will be logged as well.

Because log records are externalized frequently and because changes made by a particular transaction are only externalized to the database when the transaction itself is successfully committed, the ability to return a database to a consistent state after a failure occurs is guaranteed—when the database is restarted, log records are analyzed, and each record that has a corresponding COMMIT record is reapplied to the database; every record that does not have a corresponding COMMIT record is either ignored or backed out (which is why "before" and "after" information is recorded for all update operations).

Logging Strategies

When a database is first created, three log files, known as primary log files, are allocated as part of the creation process. On Linux and UNIX platforms these log files are 1,000 4K (kilobyte) pages in size; on Windows platforms these log files are 250 4K pages in size. However, the number of primary log files used, along with the amount of data each is capable of holding, can be controlled via the *logprimary* and *logfilsiz* parameters in the database's configuration file. The way in which primary log files are created and used is determined by the logging strategy chosen for the database. Two very different strategies, known as circular logging and archival logging, are available.

Circular Logging

When circular logging is used, records stored in the log buffer are written to primary log files in a circular sequence. Log records are written to the current "active" log file, and when that log file becomes full, it is marked as "unavailable." At that point, DB2 makes the next log file in the sequence the active log file and begins writing log records to it; when that log file becomes full, the process is repeated. In the meantime, as transactions are terminated and their effects are externalized to the database, their corresponding log records are released because they are no longer needed. When all records stored in an individual log file are released, that file is marked as being "reusable," and the next time it becomes the active log file, its contents are overwritten with new log records.

Although primary log files are not marked reusable in any particular order (they are marked reusable when they are no longer needed), they must be written to in sequence. So what happens when the logging process cycles back to a primary log file that was marked as being "unavailable"? When this occurs, DB2 will allocate what is known as a secondary log file and begin writing log records to it. As soon as the secondary log file becomes full, DB2 will poll the primary log file again, and if its status is still "unavailable," another secondary log file is allocated and filled. This process will continue until either the desired primary log file becomes "reusable" or the number of secondary log files created matches the number of secondary log files allowed (designated by the *logsecond* database configuration parameter). If the former occurs, DB2 will begin writing log records to the appropriate primary log file, and logging will pick up where it left off in the logging sequence. In the

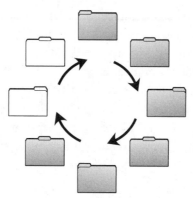

PRIMARY LOG FILES

When a primary log file becomes full,
the next file in the sequence is used
(provided it is marked "reusable").

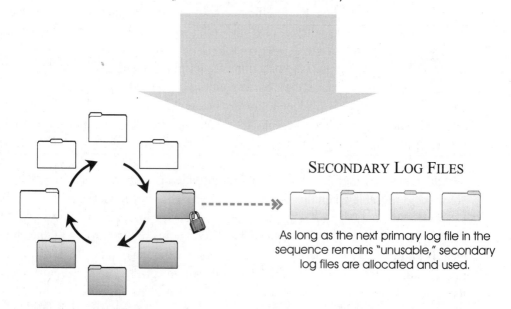

SECONDARY LOG FILES

As long as the next primary log file in the
sequence remains "unusable," secondary
log files are allocated and used.

Figure 4–2: Circular logging.

meantime, log records stored in the secondary log files are eventually released, and when all connections to the database have been terminated, any secondary log files that were created are destroyed. On the other hand, if the maximum number of secondary log files allowed has been allocated, and the desired primary log file is still unavailable, all database activity will stop, and the following message will be generated:

`SQL0964C The transaction log for the database is full.`

With the default configuration, up to two secondary log files will be created if necessary and their size will be the same as that of each primary log file used. Circular logging is illustrated in Figure 4–2.

By default, when a new database is created, circular logging is the logging strategy used.

Archival Logging

Like circular logging, when archival logging (also known as log retention logging) is used, log records stored in the log buffer are written to the primary log files that have been preallocated. However, unlike with circular logging, these log files are never reused. Instead, when all records stored in an individual log file are released, that file is marked as being "archived" rather than as being "reusable," and the only time it is used again is if it is needed for a roll-forward recovery operation. As soon as an active log file becomes full, DB2 allocates a new log file, in sequence, and that file can be used as a primary or a secondary log file, depending on what is needed when that sequence number is hit. This process continues as long as there is sufficient disk space available. A database can be configured to use archival logging by assigning the value LOGRETAIN to the *logarcmeth1* or *logarcmeth2* database configuration parameter.

Because any number of primary log files can exist when archival logging is used, they are classified according to their current state and storage location. Log files containing records associated with transactions that have not yet been committed or rolled back are known as active log files and reside in the active log directory (or device). Log files containing records associated with completed transactions (i.e., transactions that have been externalized to the database) that reside in the active log directory are known as online archive log files. Log files containing records that are associated with completed transactions that have been moved to a storage location other than the active log directory are known as offline archive log files. Offline archive files can be moved to their storage location automatically by assigning the appropriate value (USEREXIT, DISK, TSM, or VENDOR) to the *logarcmeth1* or *logarcmeth2* database configuration parameter. (In this case, DB2 will attempt to move log files to the archive location specified as soon as they become full.) Archival logging is illustrated in Figure 4–3.

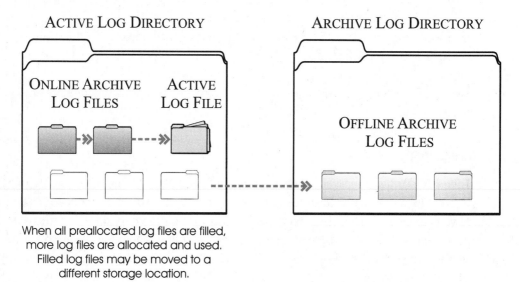

ACTIVE LOG DIRECTORY

ONLINE ARCHIVE LOG FILES ACTIVE LOG FILE

ARCHIVE LOG DIRECTORY

OFFLINE ARCHIVE LOG FILES

When all preallocated log files are filled, more log files are allocated and used. Filled log files may be moved to a different storage location.

Figure 4–3: Archival logging.

The name of the current active log file (also referred to as the first active log file) can be obtained by executing the GET DATABASE CONFIGURATION command and examining the contents of the *loghead* database configuration parameter. (This will appear as "First active log file" in the list of information returned by the GET DATABASE CONFIGURATION command.)

Other Logging Considerations

Along with specifying the logging strategy to employ, several database configuration parameters can be used to control a database's logging behavior. The following items should be taken into consideration when configuring a database for transaction log management.

Infinite Logging

You would think that you could avoid running out of log space simply by configuring a database to use a large number of secondary log files if needed. However, the maximum number of primary and secondary log files allowed (*logprimary* + *logsecond*) is 256, and if the size of your log files is relatively small, you can still run out of log space quickly when transaction workloads become heavy. Furthermore, you want to avoid allocating a large number of secondary log files if possible because performance is impacted each time a log file has to be allocated. Ideally, you want to allocate enough primary log files to handle most situations, and you want to use just enough secondary log files to handle peaks in transaction workloads. If you are concerned about running out of log space, and you want to avoid allocating a large number of secondary log files, you can configure a database to use what is known as infinite logging. To enable infinite logging for a database, you simply set the *logsecond* database configuration parameter to -1.

In order to use infinite logging, a database must be configured to use archival logging. This means that if a problem occurs and a long running transaction needs to be rolled back, DB2 may have to access one or more log files that have already been archived, which, in turn, will negatively impact performance. And if the database needs to be restarted and some of the log files needed have been archived, the recovery process may take longer. To control the impact infinite logging can have on rollback and recovery operations, you can limit the number of logs or total log space that an active transaction can use by assigning appropriate values to the *max_log* and *num_log_span* database configuration parameters.

The *max_log* configuration parameter is used to control the maximum percentage of the total active log space available that any one transaction can consume. This configuration parameter prevents transactions from consuming all of the available active log space, thereby preventing other applications from running. By default, if a running transaction exceeds this threshold, the offending transaction is rolled back and the application that the transaction is running under will be forced to terminate. (This behavior can be overridden by setting the DB2_FORCE_APP_ON_MAX_LOG registry variable to FALSE; if this registry variable is set to FALSE, only work performed by the current statement will be rolled back—the application can still commit the work completed by previous statements in the transaction, or it can roll back the work completed to undo the effects of the transaction.)

The *num_log_span* configuration parameter is used to set a limit on the number of log files any single running transaction can span. When a transaction is started, a record is written to the current active log file and as DB2 processes the transaction (as well as other transactions) log files are filled and closed. If the number of log files filled exceeds the limit established before the transaction is committed or rolled back, then by default the transaction is rolled back and the application the transaction was running under will be terminated. This behavior can also be overridden by setting the DB2_FORCE_APP_ON_MAX_LOG registry variable to FALSE.

Although the *max_log* and *num_log_span* database configuration parameters are used primarily with infinite logging, they can be used with any type of logging; the behavior will be the same regardless of the logging method used.

Mirrored Logging

With DB2 Version 8.1 and later, you have the ability to configure a database such that DB2 will simultaneously create and update active log files in two different locations. If you store active log files in one location and mirror them in another, separate, location, database activity can continue if a disk failure or human error causes log files in one location to become inaccessible. (Mirroring log files may also aid in database recovery.) To enable log file mirroring, you simply assign the fully qualified name of the mirror log location (path) to the *mirrorlogpath* database configuration parameter. Alternately, on UNIX systems, you can assign the value 1 to the DB2_NEWLOGPATH registry variable—in this case, the name of the mirror log location is generated by appending the character "2" to the current value of the *logpath* database configuration parameter. Ideally, the mirror log path used should refer to a physical location (disk) that does not see a large amount of disk I/O and that is separate from the physical location used to store primary log files.

If an error is encountered during attempts to write to either the active log path or the mirror log path, DB2 will mark the failing path as "bad," write a message to the administration notification log, and write subsequent log records to the remaining "good" log path only. When DB2 allocates storage for its next primary log file, it will make a second attempt to write to both log paths. If successful, dual logging will continue. If not, DB2 will not attempt to use the "bad" path again until the next log file is accessed for the first time. There is no attempt to synchronize the log paths, but DB2 keeps track of each access error that occurs so that the correct paths will be used when log files are archived. If a failure occurs while writing to the remaining "good" path, the database shuts down.

The DB2_NEWLOGPATH registry variable is a temporary registry variable and should be used with caution. The preferred method for enabling dual logging is by assigning the fully qualified name of the mirror log location to the *mirrorlogpath* database configuration parameter.

Log File Size

The size of the log files used has an impact on overall performance since there is a cost associated with switching from one log file to another. So, from an optimum performance perspective, the larger the log file, the better. However, when archival logging is used, large log files are not necessarily better because larger log files may cause a delay in log archival or log shipping. If you use a single large log file, you increase the time required to archive it, and if the storage media containing the log file fails, some transaction information will most likely be lost. Decreasing the log file size increases the frequency of archiving but can reduce the amount of information lost in case of a media failure because logs will be archived more frequently and will contain fewer transaction records.

Assuming that you have an application that keeps the database open, or the database has been activated to minimize connection processing time, the best possible log file size to use should be determined by the amount of time it takes to make offline archived log copies. Minimizing log file loss is also an important factor to take into consideration when deciding on an appropriate log file size to use.

Reducing logging with NOT LOGGED INITIALLY

If your application creates and populates work tables from master tables, and you are not concerned about the recoverability of these work tables because they can be easily recreated from the master tables, you may want to specify the NOT LOGGED INITIALLY option with the CREATE TABLE SQL statement used to create the work tables. You can achieve the same result for existing tables by executing the ALTER TABLE SQL statement with the NOT LOGGED INITIALLY option specified.

Because changes to a table (including insert, update, delete, or index creation operations) are not logged (if the table is configured as NOT LOGGED INITIALLY), the following should be taken into consideration when deciding whether or not to use the NOT LOGGED INITIALLY table attribute:

- All changes made to the table will be flushed to disk at commit time. This means that commits may take longer.

- If the NOT LOGGED INITIALLY attribute is activated and an activity occurs that is not logged, the entire transaction will be rolled back if an SQL statement fails or a ROLLBACK TO SAVEPOINT operation is executed.

- You cannot recover these tables when rolling forward. If the roll-forward recovery operation encounters a table that was created or altered with the NOT LOGGED INITIALLY option, the table is marked as unavailable. After the database is recovered, any attempt to access the table returns an error.

- When a table is created, row locks are held on the catalog tables until the transaction that created the table is committed. All catalog changes and storage related information are logged, as are all operations that are performed on the table in subsequent transactions.

Log File Truncation

Whenever an online backup operation is initiated, the last active log file used is truncated, closed, and made available to be archived. This ensures that every online backup image created has a complete set of archived logs available for recovery.

When a log file is truncated as a result of an online backup (or because the ARCHIVE LOG command has been executed), DB2 does not rename the file and save it. Instead, the truncated log file is deleted as soon as it becomes inactive, and a new log file is created to replace it. As a result, each time an active log file is truncated, the Log Sequence Number (LSN) is incremented by an amount proportional to the space that was truncated.

The only way to avoid log file truncation during online backup operations is to not include the transaction logs with the backup image being created. You might also want to avoid closing the last active log file if you find you are receiving log full messages a short time after completing an online backup. (When a log file is truncated, the reserved active log space is incremented by the amount proportional to the size of the truncated log and this log space is freed once the truncated log file is reclaimed. The reclamation process takes place a short time after the log file becomes inactive, but during the short interval between these two events, you may receive log full messages.)

Log file truncation can be avoided by assigning the value ON to the DB2_DISABLE_FLUSH_LOG registry variable. However, during any backup operation in which logs are included in the backup image produced, this registry variable is ignored since the active log file must be truncated and closed in order for the backup image to include the log files.

Storing Log Files on a Raw Device

One of the nice features of DB2 is its ability to store transaction log files on a raw device. Often, by storing log files on raw devices, database performance for logging intensive operations (such as inserts and updates) can be significantly increased. However, this increase in performance does not come without some downsides— some of the disadvantages of storing transaction logs on a raw device include:

- The device used cannot be shared with other applications (i.e., the entire device must be assigned to DB2).

- The device cannot be operated upon by any operating system utility or third-party tool that would backup or copy from the device.

- You can easily wipe out the file system on an existing device if you specify the wrong physical device ID when setting up raw device logging.

If you combine multiple disks at the operating system level to create a single log device, the striping that results can improve performance and provide faster I/O throughput. It can also increase the amount of space available for logs; however, DB2 does not support raw devices larger than 2GB unless large file support has been enabled. (DB2 will make an operating system call to determine the size of the device in 4K pages.) In this case, DB2 will attempt to use all pages, up to the supported limit. The amount of device space that DB2 can write to is referred to as the d*evice-size-available*. The first 4K page of any device is not used by DB2 (it is generally used by the operating system), therefore the total space available to DB2 is *device-size-available* -1.

When using raw devices for storing transaction logs, secondary logs are not used. Log records are still grouped into extents, and log extents are placed in the raw device, one after another. Therefore, the device used must be large enough to support the active log space. That is, the number of log extents available must be greater than (or equal to) the value specified for the *logprimary* database configuration parameter. If a user exit program is used, ensure that the raw device can hold a few more log files than the value specified for the *logprimary* database configuration parameter. This will compensate for the delay incurred when the user exit program archives a log file.

When you are using archival logging but not a user exit program, if the number of log extents available are used up, then all operations that result in an update will receive a log full error. At that time, you must shut down the database and take a full offline backup to ensure recoverability. After the database backup operation is complete, log records written to the raw device are lost. This means that you cannot use an earlier backup image to restore the database and then roll it forward. (If you take a database backup before the number of available log extents are used up, you can restore the database and roll it forward.)

If you are using archival logging in conjunction with a user exit program, the user exit program is called each time a log extent is filled with log records. Thus, the user exit program must be able to read the device and store the archived log extent as an external file. DB2 will not call a user exit program to retrieve log files from a raw device. Instead, during a roll-forward recovery operation, DB2 will read the extent headers to determine if the raw device contains the required log file. If the required log file is not found in the raw device, DB2 will search the overflow log path. If the log file is still not found, DB2 will call the user exit program to retrieve the log file into the overflow log path. If you do not specify an overflow log path for the roll-forward recovery operation, DB2 will not call the user exit program to retrieve the log file.

Database Recovery Concepts

Over time, a database can encounter any number of problems, including power interruptions, storage media failure, and application abends. All of these can result in database failure, and each failure scenario requires a different recovery action.

It is important to protect your data against the possibility of loss by having a well documented and well rehearsed recovery strategy in place. Some of the questions that you should answer when developing a recovery strategy are:

- Should the database be nonrecoverable or recoverable?

- Is version recovery sufficient, or will the database require roll-forward recovery?

- How much time can be spent recovering the database?

- How long can the database be out of service?

- How much time will pass between backup operations?

- How much storage space can be allocated for backup copies and archived logs?

- Will table space level backups be sufficient, or will full database backups be necessary?

Data that is easily recreated can be stored in a nonrecoverable database. This includes data from an outside source that is used for read-only applications and tables that are not often updated, for which the small amount of logging does not justify the added complexity of managing log files and performing roll-forward recovery operations. Data that cannot be easily recreated should be stored in a recoverable database. This includes data whose source is destroyed after the data is loaded, data that is manually entered into tables, and data that is modified by application programs or users after it is loaded into a database.

A database recovery strategy should ensure that all information is available when it is needed for database recovery. It should include a regular schedule for taking backups and, in the case of partitioned database systems, include backups when the system is scaled (i.e., when database partitions are added or dropped). The overall strategy should also include procedures for recovering command scripts, applications, and user-defined functions (UDFs), as well as stored procedure code in the operating system libraries and load copies.

The concept of backing up a database is the same as that of backing up any other set of data files: you make a copy of the data and store it on a different medium where it can be accessed in the event the original becomes damaged or destroyed. The simplest way to back up a database is to shut it down to ensure that no further transactions are processed and then back it up using the Backup utility provided with DB2. Once a backup image has been created, you can use it to rebuild the database if for some reason the database becomes damaged or corrupted.

The process of rebuilding a database is known as recovery, and three types of recovery are available with DB2:

- Crash recovery

- Version recovery

- Roll-forward recovery

Crash Recovery

When an event or condition that causes a database or the DB2 Database Manager to end abnormally takes place, one or more transaction failures may result. Conditions that can cause transaction failure include the following:

- A power failure at the server where the DB2 Database Manager is running

- A serious operating system error

- A hardware failure, such as memory corruption, disk failure, CPU failure, or network failure

When a transaction failure takes place, all work done by partially completed transactions that have not yet been externalized to the database is lost. As a result, the database may be left in an inconsistent state (and therefore will be unusable). Crash recovery is the process used to return such a database to a consistent and usable state. Crash recovery is performed by using information stored in the transaction log files to complete any committed transactions that were in memory (but had not yet been externalized to storage) when the failure occurred, roll back any incomplete transactions found, and purge any uncommitted transactions from memory. Once a database is returned to a consistent and usable state, it has attained what is known as a "point of consistency." Crash recovery is illustrated in Figure 4–4.

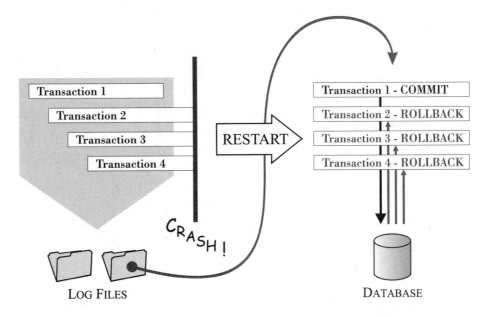

Figure 4–4: Crash recovery.

A crash recovery operation is initiated by executing the RESTART DATABASE command.

Version Recovery

Version recovery is the process used to return a database to the state it was in at the time a particular backup image was made. Version recovery is performed by replacing the current version of a database with a previous version, using a copy that was made with a backup operation—the entire database is rebuilt using a backup image that was created earlier. Unfortunately, when a version recovery operation is performed, all changes made to the database since the backup image used was created are lost. Version recovery is illustrated in Figure 4–5.

A version recovery operation is initiated by executing the RESTORE DATABASE command; database backup images needed for version recovery operations are generated by executing the BACKUP DATABASE command.

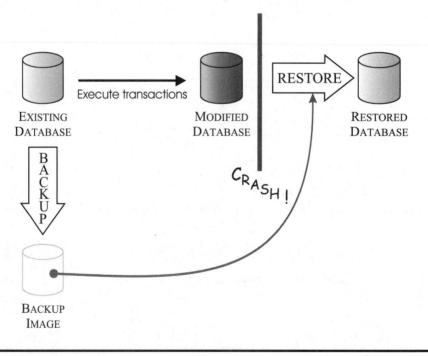

Figure 4–5: Version recovery.

Roll-Forward Recovery

Roll-forward recovery takes version recovery one step farther by rebuilding a database or one or more individual table spaces using a backup image and replaying information stored in transaction log files to return the database/table spaces to the state they were in at an exact point in time. In order to perform a roll-forward recovery operation, you must have archival logging enabled, you must have either a full backup image of the database or a complete set of table space backup images available, and you must have access to all archived log files that have been created since the backup image(s) were made. Roll-forward recovery is illustrated in Figure 4–6.

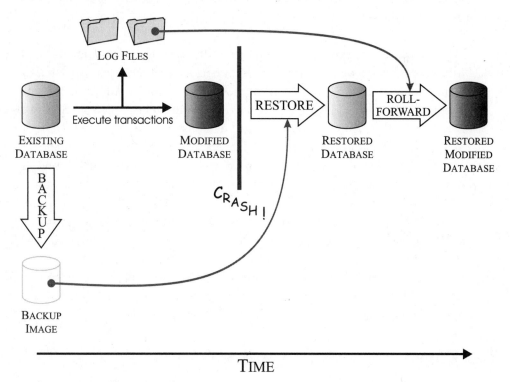

Figure 4–6: Roll-forward recovery.

A roll-forward recovery operation is initiated by executing the ROLLFORWARD DATABASE command.

Online Versus Offline Backup and Recovery

From a backup and recovery perspective, a database is considered to be either online or offline: when a database is offline, other applications and users cannot gain access to it; when a database is online, just the opposite is true. Backup operations can only be performed against a nonrecoverable database (that is, a database that has been configured to use circular logging) while it is offline; recoverable databases (i.e., databases that use archival logging) can be backed up at any time, regardless of whether the database is offline or online. However, before a database (recoverable or nonrecoverable) can be restored, it must first be taken offline. (Individual table spaces can be both backed up and restored while a database remains online.)

When an online backup operation is performed, archival logging ensures that *all* changes made while the backup image is being made are captured and can be recreated with a roll-forward recovery operation. Additionally, online backup operations can be performed against individual table spaces as well as entire databases. And, unlike when full database version recovery operations are performed, table space version recovery operations and table space roll-forward recovery operations can be performed while a database remains online—provided the table space that contains the system catalog is not the table space being recovered. While an online table space backup operation is performed, the table space being backed up remains available for use, and all modifications to the data stored in that table space are recorded in the transaction log files. However, when an online restore or online roll-forward recovery operation is performed against a table space, the table space itself is taken offline and is not available for use until the restore/roll-forward recovery operation is complete.

Incremental and Delta Backup and Recovery

As the size of a database grows, the time and hardware needed to back up and recover the database also grows substantially. Thus, creating full database and table space backup images is not always the best approach when dealing with large databases because the storage requirements for multiple copies of such backup images can be enormous. A better alternative is to create a full backup image periodically and one or more incremental backup images on a more frequent basis. An incremental backup is a backup image that contains only pages that have been updated since the previous backup image was made. Along with updated data and index pages, each incremental backup image also contains all of the initial database metadata (such as database configuration, table space definitions, recovery history file, etc.) that is normally found in a full database backup image.

Two types of incremental backup images can be produced: incremental and delta. An incremental backup image is a copy of all database data that has changed since the most recent, successful, full backup image was created. An incremental backup image is also known as a cumulative backup image because the last incremental backup image in a series of incremental backup images made over a period of time will contain the contents of all of the previous incremental backup images. The predecessor of an incremental backup image is always the most recent successful full backup image of the same object.

A delta backup image, on the other hand, is a copy of all database data that has changed since the last successful backup (full, incremental, or delta) of the database or table space in question. For this reason, a delta backup image is also known as a differential, or noncumulative, backup image. The predecessor of a delta backup image is the most recent successful backup image that contains a copy of each of the objects found in the delta backup image.

The one thing that incremental and delta backup images have in common is that before either type of backup image can be created; a full backup image must already exist. Where they differ can be seen both in their creation (usually, delta backup images are smaller and can be created faster than incremental backup images) and in how they are used for recovery. When incremental backup images are taken, database recovery involves restoring the database using the most recent full backup image available and applying the most recent incremental backup image produced. On the other hand, when delta backup images are taken, database recovery involves restoring the database using the most recent full backup image available and applying each delta backup image produced since the full backup image used was made, in the order in which they were created.

Deciding How, and How Often to Back Up

A database recovery plan should allow for regularly scheduled backup operations. Because backing up a database requires time and system resources, your plan may include a combination of full database backups and incremental backup operations.

You should take full database backups regularly, even if you archive the logs. It is more time consuming to rebuild a database from a collection of table space backup images than it is to recover the database from a full database backup image. (Table space backup images are useful for recovering from an isolated disk failure or an application error.) You should also consider keeping at least two full database backup images and their associated logs available as an added precaution.

To reduce the amount of time that the database is not available, consider performing online backup operations. (Offline backup operations can be performed much faster than online backup operations, but database access is blocked while they are running.) Keep in mind that online backup operations are only supported if archival logging is used. If archival logging is being used and you have a complete set of recovery logs available, you can rebuild the database to any point in time, should the need arise. However, you can only use an online backup image for recovery if you have the logs that span the time during which the backup operation was running.

If the amount of time needed to apply archived logs when recovering and rolling a very active database forward is a major concern, consider backing up the database more frequently. This reduces the number of archived logs you need to apply when performing a roll-forward recovery operation.

You can also save time by taking backups of different table spaces at different times, as long as the frequency of changes to them is not the same. If long field or large object (LOB) data is not changed as frequently as the other data, you can back up these table spaces less frequently. If long field and LOB data are not required for recovery, you can also consider not backing up the table space that contains that data. (If the LOB data can be reproduced from a separate source, choose the NOT LOGGED column option when creating or altering a table to include LOB columns.)

Testing your overall recovery plan will assist you in determining whether the time required to recover the database is reasonable given your business requirements. Following each test, you should determine if the recovery time needed is acceptable; if it is too long, you may want to increase the frequency with which you take backups.

Storage Considerations

When deciding which recovery method to use, consider the storage space required for each. To prevent media failure from destroying a database and your ability to rebuild it, keep database backups, archived logs, the database logs, and the database itself on different physical devices. If you are concerned about the possibility of damaged data or logs due to a disk crash, consider the use of some form of disk fault tolerance. Generally, this is accomplished through the use of a RAID-protected disk array or disk/file system mirroring.

Version recovery requires additional space to hold backup copies of the database. Roll-forward recovery requires storage space to hold both backup copies of the database or its table spaces and archived transaction log files. (Database logs can use up a large amount of storage; if you plan to use roll-forward recovery, you must decide how to manage the archived logs.)

If a table contains long field or LOB columns, you should consider placing this data into a separate table space. This will impact your storage space requirements, as well as affect your plan for recovery. By using a separate table space to store long field and LOB data, and knowing the time required to back up long field and LOB data, you may decide to only make backups of this table space occasionally. You may also choose, when creating or altering a table to include LOB columns, not to log changes to those columns. This will reduce the size of the log space required, as well as the space needed to store archived log files.

Performing a Crash Recovery Operation

Earlier, we saw that whenever transaction processing is interrupted by an unexpected event (such as a power failure), the database with which the transaction was interacting at the time is placed in an inconsistent state.

Such a database will remain in an inconsistent state and will be unusable until a crash recovery operation returns it to some point of consistency. (An inconsistent database will notify users and applications that it is unusable via a return code and error message that is generated each time an attempt to activate it or establish a connection to it is made.)

One way to initiate a crash recovery operation is by executing the RESTART DATABASE command from the DB2 Command Line Processor (CLP). The basic syntax for this command is:

```
RESTART [DATABASE | DB] [DatabaseAlias]
<USER [UserName] <USING [Password]>>
<DROP PENDING TABLESPACES ([TS_Name], ...)>
<WRITE RESUME>
```

where:

DatabaseAlias   Identifies the alias assigned to the database that is to be returned to a consistent and usable state.

UserName   Identifies the name assigned to a specific user under whose authority the crash recovery operation is to be performed.

Password   Identifies the password that corresponds to the name of the user under whom the crash recovery operation is to be performed.

TS_Name   Identifies the name assigned to one or more table spaces that are to be disabled and placed in "Drop Pending" state during the crash recovery process.

If a problem occurs with a table space container during the restart process, the DROP PENDING TABLESPACES ([TS_Name]) option can be used to place one or more table spaces in "Drop Pending" state. This allows the database to be successfully restarted, after which the offending table space(s) can be dropped and, if necessary, recreated. A list of troubled table space names can be found in the administration notification log if a database restart operation fails because of table space container problems.

If all database I/O happened to be suspended at the time a crash occurred, the WRITE RESUME option of the RESTART command can be used to resume database I/O as part of the crash recovery process.

Thus, if you wanted to perform a crash recovery operation on an unusable database named SAMPLE, you could do so by executing a RESTART command that looks something like this:

```
RESTART DATABASE sample
```

On the other hand, if you wanted to perform a crash recovery operation on a database named SAMPLE and place a table space named TEMPSPACE1 in "Drop Pending" state, you could do so by executing a RESTART command that looks something like this:

```
RESTART DATABASE sample
DROP PENDING TABLESPACES (TEMPSPACE1)
```

You can also initiate a crash recovery operation for a particular database by selecting the Restart action from the Databases menu found in the Control Center. Figure 4–7 shows the Control Center menu items that must be selected in order to perform a crash recovery operation on an unusable database.

It is possible to configure a database in such a way that crash recovery will automatically be performed, if necessary, when an application or user attempts to establish a connection to it. This is done by assigning the value ON to the *autorestart* database configuration parameter. (This is the default setting for this configuration parameter.) If the *autorestart* database configuration parameter is set to ON, DB2 checks the state of a database the first time an attempt to establish a connection to the database is made, and if it determines that the database is in an inconsistent state, it executes the RESTART command automatically.

It is important to note that if a crash recovery operation is performed on a recoverable database (i.e., a database that has been configured to support forward recovery operations), and an error occurs during the recovery process that is attributable to an individual table space, that table space will be taken offline and will no longer be accessible until it is repaired. This has no effect on crash recovery itself, and upon completion of the crash recovery operation, all other table spaces in the database will be accessible and connections to the database can be established— provided the table space that is taken offline is not the table space that contains the system catalogs. If the table space containing the system catalogs is taken offline, it must be repaired before any connections to the database will be permitted.

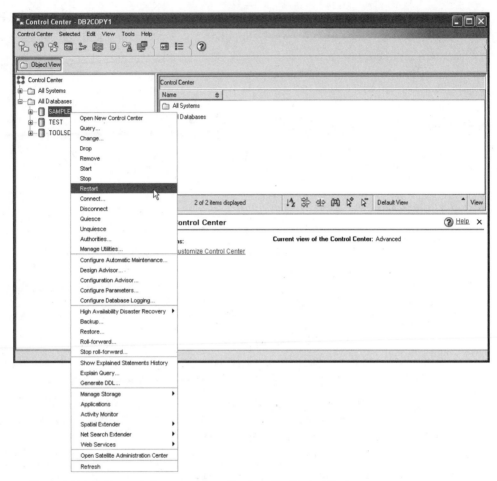

Figure 4–7: Initiating a crash recovery operation from the Control Center.

A Word About Soft Checkpoints

It was mentioned earlier that crash recovery is performed by using information stored in the transaction log files to roll back all incomplete transactions found and complete any committed transactions that were still in memory (but had not yet been externalized to storage) when the transaction failure occurred. As you might imagine, if the transaction log files for a database are large, it could take quite a while to scan the entire log and check for corresponding rows in the database. However, it is usually not necessary to scan the entire log because records recorded at the beginning of a log file are usually associated with transactions that have been completed and have already been externalized to the database. Furthermore, if these records can be skipped, the amount of time required to recover a crashed database can be greatly reduced.

That's where a mechanism known as the soft checkpoint comes in. DB2 uses a log control file to determine which records from a specific log file need to be applied to the database. This log control file is written to disk periodically, and the frequency at which this file is updated is determined by the value of the *softmax* database configuration parameter. Once the log control file is updated, the soft checkpoint information stored in it establishes where in a transaction log file crash recovery should begin; all records in a log file that precede the soft checkpoint are assumed to be associated with transactions that have already been written to the database and are ignored.

Backup and Recovery

Although crash recovery can be used to resolve inconsistency problems that result from power interruptions or application failures, it cannot be used to handle problems that arise when the storage media being used to hold a database's files becomes corrupted or fails. In order to handle these types of problems, some kind of backup (and recovery) program must be put in place.

A database recovery strategy should include a regular schedule for making database backup images and, in the case of partitioned database systems, include making backup images whenever the system is scaled (i.e., whenever database partition servers are added or dropped). Additionally, the strategy used should ensure that all information needed is available when database recovery is necessary, and it should include procedures for restoring command scripts, applications, user-defined functions (UDFs), stored procedure code in operating system libraries, and load copies as well as database data. To help with such a strategy, DB2 provides four utilities that are used to facilitate backing up and restoring a database:

- The Backup utility
- The Restore utility
- The Roll-forward utility
- The Recover utility

The DB2 Backup Utility

The single most important item that will prevent catastrophic data losses in the event storage media becomes corrupted or fails is a database backup image. A database backup image is essentially a copy of an entire database that includes its metadata, its objects, its data, and, optionally, its transaction logs. Once created, a backup image can be used at any time to return a database to the exact state it was in at the time the backup image was made (version recovery). A good database recovery strategy should ensure that backup images are created on a regular basis and that backup copies of critical data are retained in a secure location and on different storage media from that used to house the database. Depending on the logging method used (circular or archival), database backup images can be made when a database is offline or while other users and applications are connected to it. (In order to backup a database while it is online, archival logging must be enabled.)

A backup image of a DB2 database, or a table space within a DB2 database, can be created by executing the BACKUP DATABASE command. The basic syntax for this command is:

```
BACKUP [DATABASE | DB] [DatabaseAlias]
<USER [UserName] <USING [Password]>>
<TABLESPACE ([TS_Name],...)
<ONLINE>
<INCREMENTAL <DELTA>>
<TO [Location] |
    USE TSM <OPTIONS [TSMOptions]>
    <OPEN [NumSessions] SESSIONS>>
<WITH [NumBuffers] BUFFERS>
<BUFFER [BufferSize]>
<PARALLELISM [ParallelNum]>
<UTIL_IMPACT_PRIORITY [Priority]>
<EXCLUDE LOGS | INCLUDE LOGS>
<WITHOUT PROMPTING>
```

where:

DatabaseAlias   Identifies the alias assigned to the database for which a backup image is to be created.

UserName   Identifies the name assigned to a specific user under whose authority the backup operation is to be performed.

Password	Identifies the password that corresponds to the name of the user under whom the backup operation is to be performed.
TS_Name	Identifies the name assigned to one or more specific table spaces for which backup images are to be created.
Location	Identifies the directory or device where the backup image created is to be stored.
TSMOptions	Identifies options that are to be used by Tivoli Storage Manager (TSM) during the backup operation.
NumSessions	Specifies the number of I/O sessions to be created between DB2 and TSM. (This parameter has no effect when backing up to tape, disk, or another local device.)
NumBuffers	Identifies the number of buffers that are to be used to perform the backup operation. (By default, two buffers are used if this option is not specified.)
BufferSize	Identifies the size, in pages, that each buffer used to perform the backup operation will be. (By default, the size of each buffer used by the Backup utility is determined by the value of the *backbufsz* DB2 Database Manager configuration parameter.)
ParallelNum	Identifies the number of table spaces that can be read in parallel during the backup operation.
Priority	Indicates that the Backup utility is to be throttled such that it executes at a specific rate so that its effect on concurrent database activity can be controlled. This parameter can be assigned a numerical value within the range of 1 to 100, with 100 representing the highest priority and 1 representing the lowest.

If the INCREMENTAL option is specified, an incremental backup image will be produced—an incremental backup image is a copy of all data that has changed since the last successful, full backup image was produced. If the INCREMENTAL DELTA option is specified, a delta backup image will be produced—a delta backup image is a copy of all data that has changed since the last successful backup image of any type (full, incremental, or delta) was produced.

Thus, if you wanted to create a full backup image of a database named SAMPLE that is currently offline and store the image created in a directory named BACKUPS on logical disk drive E:, you could do so by executing a BACKUP DATABASE command that looks something like this:

```
BACKUP DATABASE sample
USER db2admin USING ibmdb2
TO E:\backups
```

On the other hand, if you wanted to backup a database named SAMPLE to a TSM server, using two concurrent TSM client sessions and four buffers, you could do so by executing a BACKUP DATABASE command that looks more like this:

```
BACKUP DATABASE sample
USER db2admin USING ibmdb2
USE TSM OPEN 2 SESSIONS WITH 4 BUFFERS
```

Finally, if you wanted to create an incremental backup image of a table space named TBSP1 and store the image created in a directory named BACKUPS on logical disk drive E: while the database it is associated with (named SAMPLE) remains online, you could do so by executing a BACKUP DATABASE command that looks something like this:

```
BACKUP DATABASE sample
USER db2admin USING ibmdb2
TABLESPACE (tbsp1) ONLINE INCREMENTAL TO E:\backups
```

Keep in mind that table space backup images can be created only if archival logging is being used; if circular logging is used instead, table space backups are not supported.

You can also create a backup image of a database or one or more table spaces using the Backup Wizard, which can be activated by selecting the Backup action from the Databases menu found in the Control Center. Figure 4–8 shows the Control Center menu items that must be selected to activate the Backup Wizard; Figure 4–9 shows how the first page of the Backup Wizard might look immediately after it is activated.

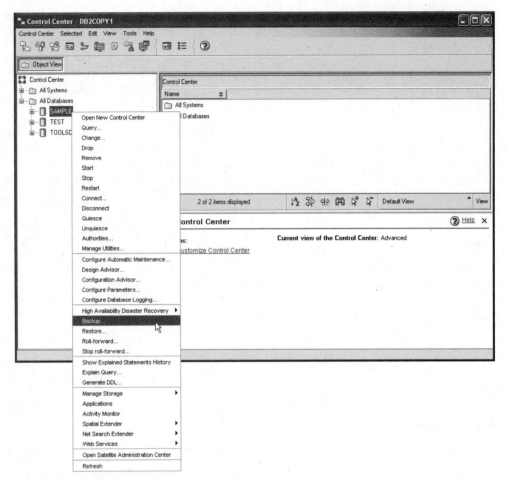

Figure 4–8: Invoking the Backup Wizard from the Control Center.

Only users with System Administrator (SYSADM) authority, System Control (SYSCTRL) authority, or System Maintenance (SYSMAINT) authority are allowed to back up a database or its table spaces.

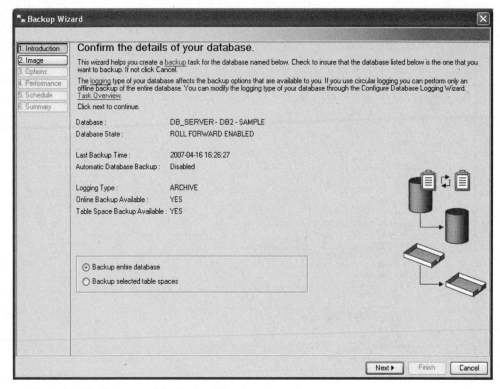

Figure 4–9: The first page of the Backup Wizard.

The DB2 Restore Utility

Earlier, we saw that version recovery is the process that returns a database to the state it was in at the time a backup image was made. This means that in order to perform a version recovery operation, at least one backup image must exist and be available. So just how is a version recovery operation initiated? The most common way is by executing the RESTORE DATABASE command. The basic syntax for this command is:

```
RESTORE [DATABASE | DB] [DatabaseAlias]
<USER [UserName] <USING [Password]>>
[TABLESPACE ([TS_Name] ,... ) <ONLINE> |
    HISTORY FILE <ONLINE>> |
    COMPRESSION LIBRARY <ONLINE>> |
    LOGS <ONLINE>]
<INCREMENTAL <AUTO | AUTOMATIC | ABORT>>
<FROM [SourceLocation] |
        USE TSM <OPTIONS [TSMOptions]>
        <OPEN [NumSessions] SESSIONS>>
```

```
<TAKEN AT [Timestamp]>
<TO [TargetLocation] | DBPATH ON [TargetPath]>
<INTO [TargetAlias]> <LOGTARGET [LogsLocation]>
<NEWLOGPATH [LogsLocation]>
<WITH [NumBuffers] BUFFERS>
<BUFFER [BufferSize]>
<REPLACE HISTORY FILE>
<REPLACE EXISTING>
<REDIRECT <GENERATE SCRIPT [ScriptFile]>>
<PARALLELISM [ParallelNum]>
<WITHOUT ROLLING FORWARD>
<WITHOUT PROMPTING>
```

or

```
RESTORE [DATABASE | DB] [DatabaseAlias]
<USER [UserName] <USING [Password]>>
<REBUILD WITH [TABLESPACE ([TS_Name] ,... )] |
    [ALL TABLESPACES IN [DATABASE | IMAGE]]
        <EXCEPT TABLESPACE ([TS_Name] ,... )>>
<INCREMENTAL <AUTO | AUTOMATIC | ABORT>>
<FROM [SourceLocation] |
        USE TSM <OPTIONS [TSMOptions]>
        <OPEN [NumSessions] SESSIONS>>
<TAKEN AT [Timestamp]>
<TO [TargetLocation] | DBPATH ON [TargetPath]>
<INTO [TargetAlias]> <LOGTARGET [LogsLocation]>
<NEWLOGPATH [LogsLocation]>
<WITH [NumBuffers] BUFFERS>
<BUFFER [BufferSize]>
<REPLACE HISTORY FILE>
<REPLACE EXISTING>
<REDIRECT <GENERATE SCRIPT [ScriptFile]>>
<PARALLELISM [ParallelNum]>
<WITHOUT ROLLING FORWARD>
<WITHOUT PROMPTING>
```

or

```
RESTORE [DATABASE | DB] [DatabaseName]
[CONTINUE | ABORT]
```

where:

DatabaseAlias	Identifies the alias assigned to the database associated with the backup image that is to be used to perform a version recovery operation.
UserName	Identifies the name assigned to a specific user under whom the version recovery operation is to be performed.
Password	Identifies the password that corresponds to the name of the user under whom the version recovery operation is to be performed.
TS_Name	Identifies the name assigned to one or more specific table spaces that are to be restored from a backup image. (If the table space name has changed since the backup image was made, the new name should be specified.)
SourceLocation	Identifies the directory or device where the backup image to be used for version recovery is stored.
TSMOptions	Identifies options that are to be used by Tivoli Storage Manager (TSM) during the version recovery operation.
NumSessions	Specifies the number of I/O sessions to be created between DB2 and TSM. (This parameter has no effect when restoring from tape, disk, or another local device.)
Timestamp	Identifies a timestamp that is to be used as search criterion when looking for a particular backup image to use for version recovery. (If no timestamp is specified, it is assumed that there is only one backup image stored at the source location specified.)
TargetLocation	Identifies the directory where the storage containers for the database that will be created are to be stored—if the backup image is to be used to create a new database and automatic storage is used.
TargetPath	Identifies the directory where the metadata for the database that will be created is to be stored—if the backup image is to be used to create a new database and automatic storage is used.

TargetAlias   Identifies the alias to be assigned to the new database to be created.

LogsLocation   Identifies the directory or device where log files for the new database are to be stored.

NumBuffers   Identifies the number of buffers that are to be used to perform the version recovery operation. (By default, two buffers are used if this option is not specified.)

BufferSize   Identifies the size, in pages, that each buffer used to perform the backup operation will be. (By default, the size of each buffer used by the RESTORE utility is determined by the value of the *restbufsz* DB2 Database Manager configuration parameter.)

ScriptFile   Identifies the name of a file to which all commands needed to perform a redirected restore operation are to be written.

ParallelNum   Identifies the number of table spaces that can be read in parallel during the version recovery operation.

If the INCREMENTAL option is specified without additional parameters, a manual cumulative restore operation will be initiated—during a manual cumulative restore, the RESTORE DATABASE command must be executed for each backup image needed to restore the database. (During such a recovery operation backup images must be restored in the following order: last full backup, last incremental, first delta, second delta, third delta, and so on up to and including the last delta backup image made.) If the INCREMENTAL AUTO or the INCREMENTAL AUTOMATIC option is specified, an automatic cumulative restore operation will be initiated and no user intervention will be required to apply incremental and delta restores.

Thus, if you wanted to restore a database named SAMPLE (which already exists), using a full backup image stored in a directory named BACKUPS on logical disk drive E:, you could do so by executing a RESTORE DATABASE command that looks something like this:

```
RESTORE DATABASE sample
USER db2admin USING ibmdb2
FROM E:\backups
REPLACE EXISTING
WITHOUT PROMPTING
```

On the other hand, if you wanted to restore a table space named TBSP1 from an incremental backup image stored in a directory named BACKUPS on logical disk drive E: while the database it is associated with (named SAMPLE) remains online, you could do so by executing a RESTORE DATABASE command that looks more like this:

```
RESTORE DATABASE sample
USER db2admin USING ibmdb2
TABLESPACE (tbsp1) ONLINE
INCREMENTAL
FROM E:\backups
```

Finally, if you wanted to perform an automatic cumulative restore operation to restore a database named SAMPLE from a full backup image and a set of incremental delta backup images stored in a directory named BACKUPS on logical disk drive E:, you could do so by executing a RESTORE DATABASE command that looks something like this:

```
RESTORE DATABASE sample
INCREMENTAL AUTOMATIC
FROM E:\backups
TAKEN AT 20081230234149
```

Each full database backup image contains, among other things, a copy of the database's recovery history file (which we will look at shortly). However, when an existing database is restored from a full database backup image, the existing recovery history file is not overwritten. But what if the recovery history file for the database happens to be corrupted? Can the recovery history file be restored as well given that a copy exists in the database backup image? The answer is yes. A special form of the RESTORE DATABASE command can be used to restore just the recovery history file from a database backup image. Such a RESTORE DATABASE command looks something like this:

```
RESTORE DATABASE sample
HISTORY FILE
FROM E:\backups
```

It is also possible to create an entirely new database from a full database backup image, effectively cloning an existing database. For example, you could create a new database named SAMPLE_2 that is an exact duplicate of a database named SAMPLE, using a backup image stored in a directory named BACKUPS on logical disk drive E: by executing a RESTORE DATABASE command that looks something like this:

```
RESTORE DATABASE sample
USER db2admin USING ibmdb2
FROM E:\backups
INTO sample_2
```

It is important to note that if a backup image is used to create a new database, the recovery history file stored in the backup image will become the recovery history file for the new database. Also, if the original database was created using automatic storage, the restore operation will maintain the storage path definitions used. If you want to change the storage path definitions, you must do so explicitly when restoring the database.

You can also perform any of the restore/recovery operations just described (along with many others) using the Restore Data Wizard, which can be activated by selecting the Restore action from the Databases menu found in the Control Center. Figure 4–10 shows the Control Center menu items that must be selected to activate the Restore Data Wizard; Figure 4–11 shows how the first page of the Restore Data Wizard might look immediately after it is activated.

Only users with System Administrator (SYSADM) authority, System Control (SYSCTRL) authority, or System Maintenance (SYSMAINT) authority are allowed to restore a database or any of its table spaces from a backup image; only users with SYSADM authority or SYSCTRL authority are allowed to create a new database from a backup image.

Redirected Restore

As you might imagine, a full backup image of a database contains, among other things, information about all table spaces that have been defined for the database,

Figure 4–10: Invoking the Restore Data Wizard from the Control Center.

including specific information about each table space container being used at the time the backup image was made. During a version recovery operation, a check is performed to verify that all table space containers referenced by the backup image exist and are accessible. If this check determines that one or more of the table space containers needed is no longer available/accessible, the recovery operation will fail, and the database will not be restored. When this happens, any invalid table space containers encountered can be redefined at the beginning of the recovery process by performing what is known as a redirected restore.

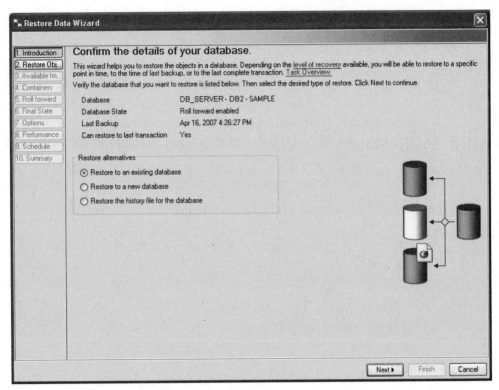

Figure 4–11: The first page of the Restore Data Wizard.

Unavailable/inaccessible table space containers are redefined by executing the SET TABLESPACE CONTAINERS command. The basic syntax for this command is:

```
SET TABLESPACE CONTAINERS FOR [TS_ID] USING
[(PATH '[Container]' ,...) |
  ([FILE | DEVICE] '[Container]' [ContainerSize] ,...)]
```

where:

> *TS_ID* Identifies the identification number assigned to the table space for which new storage containers are to be provided.
>
> *Container* Identifies one or more containers that are to be used to store the data associated with the table space specified.
>
> *ContainerSize* Identifies the number of pages to be stored in the table space container specified.

The steps used to perform a redirected restore operation are as follows:

1. Start the redirected restore operation by executing the RESTORE DATABASE command with the REDIRECT option specified. (When this option is specified, each invalid table space container encountered is flagged, and all table spaces that reference invalid table space containers are placed in the "Restore Pending" state. A list of all table spaces affected can be obtained by executing the LIST TABLESPACES command.) At some point, you should see a message that looks something like this:

    ```
    SQL1277W A redirected restore operation is being performed. Table space
    configuration can now be viewed and table spaces that do not use automatic
    storage can have their containers reconfigured.
    DB20000I The RESTORE DATABASE command completed successfully.
    ```

2. Specify new table space containers for each table space placed in the "Restore Pending" state by executing a SET TABLESPACE CONTAINERS command for each appropriate table space. (Keep in mind that SMS table spaces can use only PATH containers, whereas DMS table spaces can use only FILE or DEVICE containers.)

3. Complete the redirected restore operation by executing the RESTORE DATABASE command again with the CONTINUE option specified.

    To simplify things, all of these steps can be coded in a UNIX shell script or Windows batch file, which can then be executed from a system prompt. Such a file would look something like this:

    ```
    db2 "RESTORE DATABASE sample FROM C:\backups TO D:\DB_DIR INTO sample_2
    REDIRECT"

    db2 "SET TABLESPACE CONTAINERS FOR 0 USING
    (PATH 'D:\DB_DIR\SYSTEM')"

    db2 "SET TABLESPACE CONTAINERS FOR 1 USING
    (PATH 'D:\DB_DIR\TEMP')"

    db2 "SET TABLESPACE CONTAINERS FOR 2 USING
    (PATH 'D:\DB_DIR\USER')"

    db2 "RESTORE DATABASE sample CONTINUE"
    ```

With DB2 9, the RESTORE DATABASE command can be used to take a lot of the work out of creating such a script file. You simply execute the RESTORE DATABASE command with the REDIRECT GENERATE SCRIPT option specified, modify the script produced, and then run the script to perform the redirected restore operation. For example, to generate a redirected restore script based on an existing backup image of a database named SAMPLE that resides on an AIX server, you would execute a RESTORE DATABASE command that looks something like this:

```
RESTORE DATABASE sample FROM /home/db2inst1/backups
TAKEN AT 20080514093000
REDIRECT GENERATE SCRIPT redir_rest.sh
```

 A redirected restore operation can also be used to restore a backup image to a target machine that is different than the source machine or to store table space data in a different physical location.

You can also perform a redirected restore by assigning new table space containers to existing table spaces on the Containers page of the Restore Data Wizard. Figure 4–12 shows how this page looks.

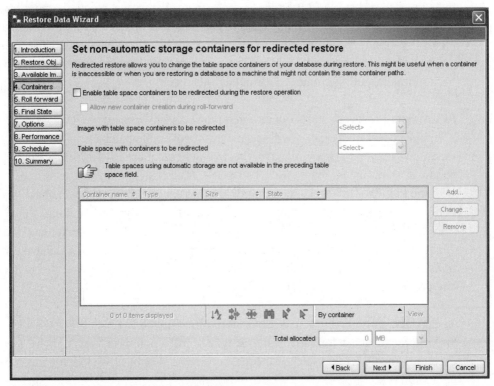

Figure 4–12: The Containers page of the Restore Data Wizard (used when performing a redirected restore operation).

In addition to providing new storage containers for table spaces when older table space containers are inaccessible or are no longer present, a redirected restore can also be used to add new containers to existing SMS table spaces. (The ALTER TABLESPACE command does not allow you to add new storage containers to existing SMS table spaces; a redirected restore provides a workaround to this limitation.)

The DB2 Roll-Forward Utility

When a backup image is used to restore a damaged or corrupted database, the database can be returned only to the state it was in at the time the backup image was made. Therefore, all changes that were made to the database after the backup image was created will be lost when a version recovery operation is performed. To return a database to the state it was in at any given point in time, roll-forward recovery must be used instead. And in order to perform a roll-forward recovery operation, the database must be recoverable (that is, the database must be configured to use archival logging), you must have a full backup image of the database available, and you must have access to all archived log files that have been created since the last backup image (full, incremental, or delta) was made.

Roll-forward recovery starts out as a version recovery operation. However, whereas a version recovery operation will leave a nonrecoverable database in "Normal" state, the same operation will leave a recoverable database in "Roll-forward pending" state (unless the WITHOUT ROLLING FORWARD option was specified with the RESTORE DATABASE command that was used to recover the database). At that point, either the database can be taken out of "Roll-forward pending" state (in which case all changes made to the database since the backup image used for version recovery was made will be lost), or information stored in the database's transaction log files can be replayed to return the database to the state it was in at any given point in time.

The process of replaying transactions stored in archived log files is known as "rolling the database forward," and one way to roll a database forward is by executing the ROLLFORWARD DATABASE command. The basic syntax for this command is:

```
ROLLFORWARD [DATABASE | DB] [DatabaseAlias]
<USER [UserName] <USING [Password]>>
<TO [PointInTime] <USING [UTC | LOCAL] TIME>
              <AND [COMPLETE | STOP]> |
   END OF BACKUP <AND [COMPLETE | STOP]> |
   END OF LOGS <AND [COMPLETE | STOP]> |
   COMPLETE |
   STOP |
   CANCEL |
   QUERY STATUS <USING [UTC | LOCAL] TIME>>
<TABLESPACE ONLINE |
   TABLESPACE <( [TS_Name] ,... )> <ONLINE>>
<OVERFLOW LOG PATH ([LogDirectory] ,...)>
<RECOVER DROPPED TABLE [TableID] TO [Location]>
```

where:

DatabaseAlias Identifies the alias assigned to the database that is to be rolled forward.

UserName Identifies the name assigned to a specific user under whom the roll-forward operation is to be performed.

Password Identifies the password that corresponds to the name of the user under whom the roll-forward operation is to be performed.

PointInTime Identifies a specific point in time, identified by a timestamp value in the form *yyyy-mm-dd-hh.mm.ss.nnnnnn* (year, month, day, hour, minutes, seconds, microseconds), to which the database is to be rolled forward. (Only transactions that took place before and up to the date and time specified will be reapplied to the database.)

TS_Name Identifies the name assigned to one or more specific table spaces that are to be rolled forward. (If the table space name has changed since the backup image used to restore the database was made, the new name must be specified.)

LogDirectory Identifies the directory that contains offline archived log files that are to be used to perform the roll-forward operation.

TableID Identifies a specific table (by ID) that was dropped earlier that is to be restored as part of the roll-forward operation. (The table ID can be obtained by examining the database's recovery history file.)

Location   Identifies the directory to which files containing dropped table data are to be written when the table is restored as part of the roll-forward operation.

If the AND COMPLETE, AND STOP, COMPLETE, or STOP option is specified, the database will be returned to "Normal" state when the roll-forwsard operation has completed. Otherwise, the database will remain in "Roll-forward pending state." (When a recoverable database is restored from a backup image, it is automatically placed in "Roll-forward pending" state unless the WITHOUT ROLLING FORWARD option is used with the RESTORE DATABASE command; while a database is in "Roll-forward pending" state, it cannot be accessed by users and applications.)

If the QUERY STATUS option is specified, a list of the log files that have been used to perform the roll-forward recovery operation, along with the next archive file required, and the time stamp of the last committed transaction since roll-forward processing began is returned.

Thus, if you wanted to perform a roll-forward recovery operation on a database named SAMPLE that was just restored from a backup image, you could do so by executing a ROLLFORWARD DATABASE command that looks something like this:

```
ROLLFORWARD DATABASE sample TO END OF LOGS AND STOP
```

On the other hand, if you wanted to perform a roll-forward recovery operation on a table space named DATA_TBSP in a database named SAMPLE by reapplying transactions that were performed against the table space on or before April 1, 2008 (04/01/2008), you could do so by executing a ROLLFORWARD DATABASE command that looks something like this:

```
ROLLFORWARD DATABASE sample TO 2008-04-01-00.00.00.0000
AND STOP TABLESPACE (data_tbsp)
```

It is important to note that the time value specified is interpreted as a Coordinated Universal Time (UTC)—otherwise known as Greenwich Mean Time (GMT)—value. If a ROLLFORWARD DATABASE command that looks something like the following had been executed instead, the time value specified would have been interpreted as a local time value:

```
ROLLFORWARD DATABASE SAMPLE TO 2008-04-01-00.00.00.0000 USING LOCAL TIME
AND STOP TABLESPACE (data_tbsp)
```

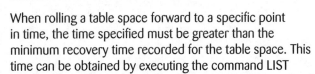

When rolling a table space forward to a specific point
in time, the time specified must be greater than the
minimum recovery time recorded for the table space. This
time can be obtained by executing the command LIST
TABLESPACES SHOW DETAIL. Among other things, this command
returns the earliest point in time to which each table space can
be rolled forward. The minimum recovery time is updated when
data definition language (DDL) statements are run against a table
space or against tables stored in a table space. A table space must
be rolled forward to at least the minimum recovery time so that it
becomes synchronized with the information in the system catalog
tables. If recovering more than one table space, each table space
must be rolled forward to at least the highest minimum recovery
time of all the table spaces being recovered.

If you want to roll a table space forward to a specific point in time, and a table in
the table space participates in a referential integrity constraint with another table
that resides in another table space, you should roll both table spaces
forward simultaneously to the same point in time. If you do not, the child table
in the referential integrity relationship will be placed in "Set integrity pending"
state at the end of the roll-forward recovery operation, and constraint checking
will have to be performed on the table before it can be used.

You can also initiate a roll-forward recovery operation using the Roll-forward
Wizard, which can be activated by selecting the Roll-forward action from the
Databases menu found in the Control Center. Figure 4–13 shows the Control
Center menu items that must be selected to activate the Roll-forward Wizard;
Figure 4–14 shows how the first page of the Roll-forward Wizard might look
immediately after it is activated.

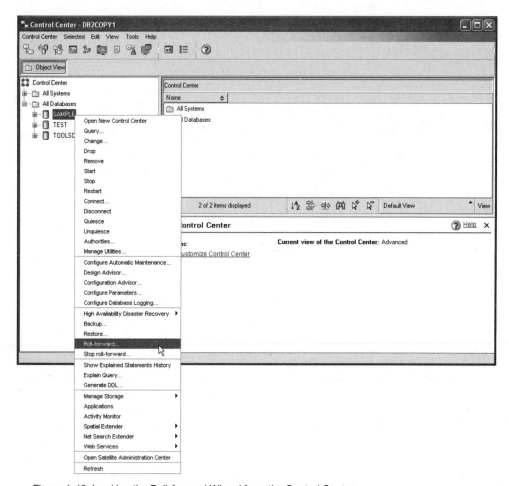

Figure 4–13: Invoking the Roll-forward Wizard from the Control Center.

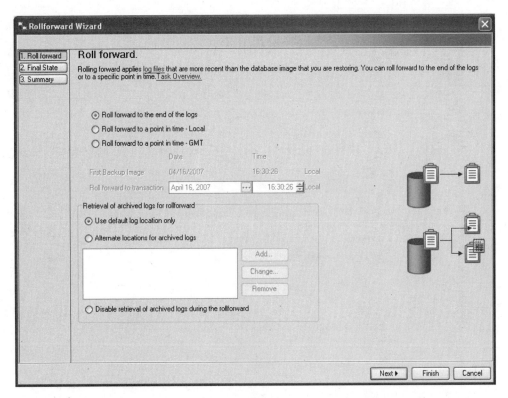

Figure 4–14: The first page of the Roll-forward Wizard.

Because a roll-forward recovery operation is typically performed immediately after a database is restored from a backup image, a roll-forward recovery operation can also be initiated by providing the appropriate information on the Roll-forward page of the Restore Data Wizard. Figure 4–15 shows how the Roll forward page of the Restore Data Wizard normally looks.

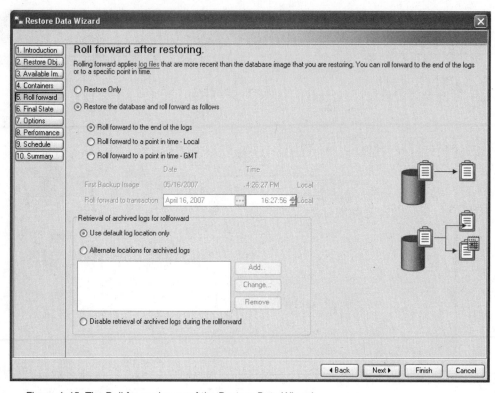

Figure 4–15: The Roll forward page of the Restore Data Wizard.

Only users with System Administrator (SYSADM) authority, System Control (SYSCTRL) authority, or System Maintenance (SYSMAINT) authority are allowed to perform a roll-forward recovery operation.

A Word About the Recovery History File

When a new DB2 database is created, a special file known as the recovery history file is built as part of the database creation process. This file is used to log historical information about specific actions that are performed against the database with which the file is associated. Specifically, records are written to the recovery history file whenever any of the following actions are performed:

- A backup image of any type is created

- A version recovery operation is performed either on the database or on one of its table spaces

- A table is loaded using the Load utility

- A roll-forward recovery operation is performed either on the database or on one of its table spaces

- A table space is altered

- A table space is quiesced

- Data in a table is reorganized using the REORG utility

- Statistics for a table are updated using the RUNSTATS utility

- A table is deleted (dropped)

In addition to identifying the event that was performed, each entry in the recovery history file identifies the date and time the event took place, how the event took place, and the table spaces and tables that were affected. If the action was a backup operation, it will also include the location where the backup image produced was stored, along with information on how to access this image. And because the recovery history file contains image location information for each backup image available, it acts as a tracking and verification mechanism during version recovery operations.

Because the recovery history file sits quietly in the background and DB2 is responsible for managing its contents, a database administrator rarely has to interact with it. However, two commands—LIST HISTORY and PRUNE HISTORY—provide a way to both view the contents of a database's recovery history file and remove one or more entries stored in it. Additionally, if the recovery history file for a database becomes corrupt, it is possible to restore just the recovery history file from a database backup image.

The DB2 Recover Utility

While the RESTORE DATABASE command can be used to return a database to the state it was in at the time a backup image was made and the ROLLFORWARD DATABASE command can be used to replay information recorded in a database's transaction log files to return a database to the state it was in at a specific point in time, if you are restoring a database from a full database backup image and several incremental backup images, delta backup images, or table space backup images, the process can be a little complicated. However, if you have a current recovery history file available, you can take advantage of DB2's Recover utility.

Introduced in DB2 9, the Recover utility performs the necessary restore and roll-forward operations to recover a database to a specific point in time based on information found in the recovery history file. The Recovery utility is invoked by executing the RECOVER DATABASE command. The basic syntax for this command is:

```
RECOVER [DATABASE | DB] [DatabaseAlias]
<TO [PointInTime] <USING [UTC | LOCAL] TIME>>
<ON ALL DBPARTITIONNUMS>
<USER [UserName] <USING [Password]>>
<USING HISTORY FILE ([HistoryFile])>
<OVERFLOW LOG PATH ([LogDirectory] ,...)>
<RESTART>
```

> or

```
RECOVER [DATABASE | DB] [DatabaseAlias]
<TO END OF LOGS
    <ON ALL DBPARTITIONNUMS |
     ON DBPARTITIONNUM<S> ([PartitionNum],...)>>
<USER [UserName] <USING [Password]>>
<USING HISTORY FILE ([HistoryFile])>
<OVERFLOW LOG PATH ([LogDirectory] ,...)>
<RESTART>
```

where:

DatabaseAlias   Identifies the alias assigned to the database associated with the backup image that is to be used to perform a version recovery operation.

PointInTime   Identifies a specific point in time, identified by a timestamp value in the form *yyyy-mm-dd-hh.mm.ss.nnnnnn* (year, month, day, hour, minutes, seconds, microseconds), to which the database is to be rolled forward. (Only transactions that took place before and up to the date and time specified will be reapplied to the database.)

PartitionNum   Identifies, by number, one or more database partitions (identified in the db2nodes.cfg file) that transactions are to be rolled forward on. In a partitioned database environment, the Recover utility must be invoked from the catalog partition of the database.

UserName   Identifies the name assigned to a specific user under whom the recovery operation is to be performed.

Password   Identifies the password that corresponds to the name of the user under whom the recovery operation is to be performed.

HistoryFile   Identifies the name assigned to the recovery history log file that is to be used by the Recovery utility.

LogDirectory   Identifies the directory that contains offline archived log files that are to be used to perform the roll-forward portion of the recovery operation.

If the RESTART option is specified, any previous recover operations are ignored; the RESTART option forces the RECOVER utility to execute a fresh restore operation and then roll the database forward to the point in time specified.

Thus, if you wanted to perform a full recovery operation on a database named SAMPLE (which already exists) using information stored in the recovery history file, you could do so by executing a RECOVER DATABASE command that looks something like this:

```
RECOVER DATABASE sample
TO END OF LOGS
```

On the other hand, if you wanted to restore a database named SAMPLE and roll it forward to an extremely old point in time that is no longer contained in the current recovery history file, you could do so by executing a RECOVER DATABASE command that looks something like this (assuming you have a copy of an older recovery history file available):

```
RECOVER DATABASE sample
TO 2005-01-31-04.00.00
USING HISTORY FILE (/home/user/old2005files/db2rhist.asc)
```

It is important to note that if the Recover utility successfully restores a database, but for some reason fails while attempting to roll it forward, the Recover utility will attempt to continue the previous recover operation without redoing the restore phase. If you want to force the Recover utility to redo the restore phase, you need to execute the RECOVER DATABASE command with the RESTART option specified. There is no way to explicitly restart a recovery operation from a point of failure.

 The Recover utility is designed to restore complete databases—not individual table spaces. If the Recover utility is used in an attempt to restore a damaged table space, the database will be restored first and then an attempt will be made to make as much of the table space available as possible.

Backing Up and Restoring a Partitioned Database

In a partitioned database environment, database partitions are backed up (and restored) individually—backup operations are local to the database partition server upon which the Backup utility is invoked. However, by using the db2_all command, you can create backup images for multiple partitions (which you identify by node number) from a single database partition server. (The LIST NODES command can be used to identify the nodes, or database partition servers, that have user tables on them.) For example, if you wanted to create a set of online incremental backup images for every partition on which a database named SAMPLE is stored, you could do so by executing a db2_all command that looks something like this:

```
db2_all "db2 BACKUP DATABASE sample ONLINE INCREMENTAL"
```

In this example, the BACKUP DATABASE command was executed on every partition. However, there may be times when you only want to perform a backup or recovery operation on one or more specific database partitions. Because of this, the db2_all command has two prefix sequences that can be used to limit the execution of specified operations to individual database partition servers. These prefix sequences are:

- <<-*nnn*<

  The operation is to be performed on all database partition servers identified in the db2nodes.cfg file *except* the database partition server whose node number is *nnn*.

- <<+*nnn*<

  The operation is *only* to be performed on the database partition server in the db2nodes.cfg file whose database partition number is *nnn*.

When using the <<-*nnn*< and <<+*nnn*< prefix sequences, *nnn* can be any 1-, 2-, or 3-digit database partition number; however, the number specified must have a matching nodenum value in the db2nodes.cfg file.

Thus, if you wanted to create a set of online incremental backup images for every partition that a database named SAMPLE is stored on except partition number 2, you could do so by executing a db2_all command that looks something like this:

```
db2_all "<<-2< db2 BACKUP DATABASE sample ONLINE
    INCREMENTAL TO C:/backups"
```

On the other hand, if you wanted to perform an online table space-level backup of all table spaces for a database named SAMPLE that reside on partition number 3, you could do so by executing a db2_all command that looks more like this:

```
db2_all "<<+3< db2 BACKUP DATABASE sample TABLESPACE (tbsp1, tbsp2) ONLINE
TO /backup_dir"
```

Restore operations are performed in a similar manner. Thus, if you wanted to restore a database named SAMPLE that has been defined on four database partitions numbered 0 through 3, using backup images available in a location that is accessible from all database partitions, you could do so by executing a set of db2_all commands that look something like this:

```
db2_all "<<+0< db2 RESTORE DATABASE sample FROM /backup_dir
    TAKEN AT 20080515234149
    INTO sample REPLACE EXISTING";
db2_all "<<+1< db2 RESTORE DATABASE sample FROM /backup_dir
    TAKEN AT 20080515234427
    INTO sample REPLACE EXISTING";
db2_all "<<+2< db2 RESTORE DATABASE sample FROM /backup_dir
    TAKEN AT 20080515234828
    INTO sample REPLACE EXISTING";
db2_all "<<+3< db2 RESTORE DATABASE sample FROM /backup_dir
    TAKEN AT 20080515235235
    INTO sample REPLACE EXISTING"
```

In this case, the catalog partition would be restored first, followed by all other database partitions of the SAMPLE database. As with the BACKUP command, the db2_all command issues the RESTORE command to each specified database partition.

It is important to note that when performing a restore operation using the db2_all command, you should always specify the REPLACE EXISTING and/or the WITHOUT PROMPTING option. Otherwise, if there is prompting, the restore operation will stop until user input is provided.

> Backing up multiple database partitions one partition at a time can be time consuming and prone to error. Additionally, if you back up a partitioned database one partition at a time, the timestamp for each database partition backup image is slightly different and you cannot include transaction log files in the backup image produced. Because the backup timestamp is different for each database partition, identifying all database partitions that belong to the same backup is difficult, as is determining the minimum recovery time for a backup that contains all database partitions. Using the db2_all command simplifies backing up partitioned databases somewhat, but the timestamp issue and log restrictions still apply.
>
> In DB2 Version 9.5, when you perform a backup operation from the catalog node of a partitioned database, you can specify which partitions to include in the backup or you can specify that all database partitions should be included. The partitions specified will be backed up simultaneously, and the backup timestamp associated with all specified database partitions will be the same. Also, you can include database logs with the backup; including logs in backup images is the default behavior for snapshot backup operations. Finally, when you restore from a "single system view" backup image, you can specify to roll forward to end of logs, which is the minimum recovery time as calculated by DB2.

Testing the Integrity of a Backup Image

Because backup images are a vital part of any disaster recovery plan, it is important that every backup image created is valid and can be used to recover a database. But how can you know whether a backup image is good unless you try to use it to restore a damaged or corrupted database? That's where the DB2 Check Backup utility comes in. This utility can be used to test the integrity of a backup image, or multiple parts of a backup image, and to determine whether or not the image can be used to restore a damaged or corrupted database. It can also be used to display the metadata stored in the backup header (such as log path used, instance name, type of backup image, etc.).

The DB2 Check Backup utility is invoked by executing the db2ckbkp command. The syntax for this command is:

```
db2ckbkp
[ <-a>
  <-c>
  <-d>
  <-e>
  <-h>
  <-l>
  <-n>
  <-o>
  <-p>
  <-s>
  <-t>
  <-cl [DecompressLib]>
  <-co [DecompressOpts]> ,... ]
[FileName ,...]
```

or

```
db2ckbkp -H [FileName ,...]
```

or

```
db2ckbkp -S [FileName ,...]
```

or

```
db2ckbkp -T [FileName ,...]
```

where:

DecompressLib	Specifies the library, by name, that is to be used to decompress the backup image. (If this parameter is not specified, DB2 will attempt to use the library stored in the image. If the backup image was not compressed, the value of this parameter will be ignored; if the backup image was compressed and the specified library cannot be loaded, the operation will fail.)

DecompressOpts Describes a block of binary data that will be passed to the initialization routine in the decompression library. DB2 will pass this string directly from the client to the server, so any issues of byte reversal or code page conversion will have to be handled by the decompression library. If the first character of the data block is '@', the remainder of the data will be interpreted by DB2 as the name of a file residing on the server. DB2 will then replace the contents of the string with the contents of that file and will pass this new value to the initialization routine instead.

FileName Identifies, by name, one or more backup image files that are to be analyzed. When checking multiple parts of a backup image, the first backup image object (.001) must be specified first.

All other options shown with this command are described in Table 4.1.

Table 4.1 db2ckbkp Command Options	
Option	**Meaning**
-a	Specifies that all information available about the backup image is to be collected and displayed.
-c	Specifies that checkbit and checksum information is to be collected and displayed.
-d	Specifies that information stored in the headers of DMS table space data pages is to be collected and displayed.
-e	Specifies that pages are to be extracted from the backup image and written to a file. To extract pages, you need an input file and an output file. The default input file is called *extractPage.in* and the default output file is called *extractPage.out*. You can override the default input file name using the DB2LISTFILE environment variable; you can override the default output file name using the DB2EXTRACTFILE environment variable.
-h	Specifies that media header information, including the name and path of the backup image, is to be collected and displayed.
-l	Specifies that log file header (LFH) and mirror log file header (MFH) information is to be collected and displayed.
-n	Indicates that the user is to be prompted whenever a tape needs to be mounted. (Assumes one tape per device.)
-o	Specifies that object header information is to be collected and displayed.

Table 4.1 db2ckbkp Command Options (Continued)	
Option	**Meaning**
-p	Specifies that information about the number of pages of each object type found in the backup image is to be collected and displayed. This option will not show the number of pages for all different object types if the backup was done for DMS table space data—instead, it will show the total of all pages; LOB data pages and long data pages will not be returned.
-s	Specifies that information about the automatic storage paths used is to be collected and displayed.
-t	Displays table space details, including container information, for all table spaces in the backup image.
-H	Specifies that only the 4K media header information stored at the beginning of the backup image is to be collected and displayed; does not validate the image. This option cannot be used in combination with any other options.
-S	Specifies that information about the automatic storage paths used is to be collected and displayed; does not validate the image. This option cannot be used in combination with any other options.
-T	Displays table space details, including container information, for all table spaces in the backup image; does not validate the image. This option cannot be used in combination with any other options.

Thus, if you wanted to display automatic storage path information found in an existing backup image named TEST.0.DB2.NODE0000.CATN0000.20081215130904.001, you could do so by executing a db2ckbkp command that looks something like this:

```
db2ckbkp -S TEST.0.DB2.NODE0000.CATN0000.20081215130904.001
```

And the results produced should look something like this:

```
Automatic storage enabled: Yes
 Number of storage paths: 2
            storage path: C:
            storage path: F:
        Header:
                flavour:  1
                version:  0
        Storage Group:
                flavour:  2
                version:  0
             stateFlags:  0x0
                lastLSN:  0000000000000000
             initialLSN:  0000000000000000
Storage group information dumped -- NO VERIFICATION PERFORMED.
```

On the other hand, if you wanted to determine whether or not an existing backup image named TEST.0.DB2.NODE0000.CATN0000.20081215131853.001 was created using the COMPRESS option of the BACKUP DATABASE command, you could do so by executing a db2ckbkp command that looks something like this:

```
db2ckbkp -h TEST.0.DB2.NODE0000.CATN0000.20081215131853.001
```

This time the results produced should look something like this:

```
=====================
MEDIA HEADER REACHED:
=====================
        Server Database Name        -- TEST
        Server Database Alias       -- TEST
        Client Database Alias       -- TEST
        Timestamp                   -- 20081215131853
        Database Partition Number   -- 0
        Instance                    -- DB2
        Sequence Number             -- 1
        Release ID                  -- B00
        Database Seed               -- 4773F9E6
        DB Comment's Codepage (Volume) -- 2020
        DB Comment (Volume)         --
        DB Comment's Codepage (System) -- 2020
        DB Comment (System)         --
        Authentication Value        -- 32
        Backup Mode                 -- 0
        Includes Logs               -- 0
        Compression                 -- 1
        Backup Type                 -- 0
        Backup Gran.                -- 0
        Status Flags                -- 1
        System Cats inc             -- 1
        Catalog Partition Number    -- 0
        DB Codeset                  -- IBM-1252
        DB Territory                --
        LogID                       -- 1197742728
        LogPath                     -- C:\LOGS\NODE0000\
        Backup Buffer Size          -- 16777216
        Number of Sessions          -- 1
        Platform                    -- 5
    The proper image file name would be:
        TEST.0.DB2.NODE0000.CATN0000.20081215131853.001

[1] Buffers processed:  ####

Image Verification Complete - successful.
```

(In this case, because the "Compression" attribute is set to 1, the COMPRESS option of the BACKUP DATABASE command was specified when the backup image was created.)

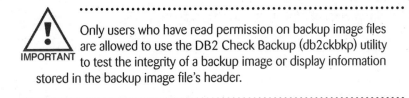

Only users who have read permission on backup image files are allowed to use the DB2 Check Backup (db2ckbkp) utility to test the integrity of a backup image or display information stored in the backup image file's header.

Backing Up a Database with Split Mirroring

It was mentioned earlier that as databases increase in size and as heavy usage demands require databases to be available 24 hours a day, 7 days a week, the time and hardware needed to back up and restore a database can increase substantially. Backing up an entire database or several table spaces of a large database can put a strain on system resources, require a considerable amount of additional storage space (to hold the backup images), and reduce the availability of the database system (particularly if the system has to be taken offline in order to be backed up). Therefore, a popular alternative to creating and maintaining backup images of high-availability databases is to use what is known as a split mirror.

A *split mirror* is an "instantaneous" copy of a database that is made by mirroring the disk or disks that contain the database's data and splitting the mirror when a backup copy of the database is required. *Mirroring* is the process of writing all database data to two separate disks (or disk subsystems) simultaneously; one disk/subsystem holds the database data while the other holds an exact copy (known as a mirror) of the primary disk/subsystem being used. Splitting a mirror simply involves separating the primary and secondary copies of the database from each other. Split mirroring provides the following advantages:

- The overhead required to create backup images of the database is eliminated.

- Entire systems can be cloned very quickly.

- It provides a fast implementation of idle standby failover.

To further enhance split mirroring, DB2 provides a way to temporarily suspend (and later resume) all database I/O so that a mirror can be split without having to take a database offline. The command that provides this functionality is the SET WRITE command, and the syntax for this command is:

```
SET WRITE [SUSPEND | RESUME] FOR [DATABASE | DB]
```

Therefore, if you wanted to temporarily suspend all I/O for a database, you would do so by establishing a connection to that database and executing a SET WRITE command that looks like this:

```
SET WRITE SUSPEND FOR DATABASE
```

When executed, the SET WRITE SUSPEND FOR DATABASE command causes DB2 to suspend all write operations to table space containers and log files that are associated with the current database. (The suspension of writes to table spaces and log files is intended to prevent partial page writes from occurring until the suspension is removed.) All operations, apart from online backup and restore operations, will function normally while database writes are suspended. That's because read-only transactions are not suspended and are able to continue working with a write-suspended database provided they do not require I/O processing; applications can continue to perform insert, update, and delete operations with data that has been cached in the database's buffer pool(s), but new pages cannot be read from disk. Additionally, new database connections can be established to a write-suspended database provided the system catalog pages required to authenticate the connections already reside in a buffer pool.

I/O for a write-suspended database can be resumed at any time by executing a SET WRITE command that looks like this:

```
SET WRITE RESUME FOR DATABASE
```

When executed, the SET WRITE RESUME FOR DATABASE command causes DB2 to lift all write suspensions and to allow write operations to table space containers and log files that are associated with the current database to continue.

It is recommended that I/O for a write-suspended database be resumed from the same connection from which I/O was suspended. Otherwise, subsequent connection attempts might hang if they require flushing dirty pages from the buffer pool to disk. If your connection attempts are hanging, and it has become impossible to resume I/O from the connection that was used to suspend I/O, then you will have to run the RESTART DATABASE command with the WRITE RESUME option specified to resume I/O for the database.

Initializing a Split Mirror with db2inidb

Before a split mirror copy of a DB2 database can be used, it must first be initialized; a split mirror database copy is initialized by executing the system command db2inidb. The syntax for this command is:

```
db2inidb [DatabaseAlias]
AS [SNAPSHOT | MIRROR | STANDBY]
<RELOCATE USING [ConfigFile]>
```

where:

DatabaseAlias   Identifies the alias assigned to the database that the split mirror copy to be initialized references.

ConfigFile   Indicates that the database files contained in the split mirror copy are to be relocated according to information stored in the configuration file specified.

As you can see, a split mirror database copy can be initialized in one of three ways:

SNAPSHOT. The split mirror copy of the database will be initialized as a read-only clone of the primary database.

MIRROR. The split mirror copy of the database will be initialized as a backup image that can be used to restore the primary database.

STANDBY. The split mirror copy of the database will be initialized and placed in roll-forward pending state so that it can be continuously synchronized with the primary database. (New logs from the primary database can be retrieved and applied to the copy of the database at any time.) The standby copy of the database can then be used in place of the primary database if, for some reason, the primary database goes down.

Thus, if you wanted to initialize a split mirror copy of a database named SAMPLE and make it a backup image that can be used to restore the primary database, you could do so by executing a db2inidb command that looks like this:

```
db2inidb SAMPLE AS MIRROR
```

Managing Log files With a User Exit Program

When a DB2 9 database is configured to support roll-forward recovery, DB2 can call a special program, known as a user exit program, to move archived log files from the active log directory/device to a specific storage location when they are no longer needed to support transaction logging. So just what is a user exit program? Essentially, a user exit program is a user-supplied application that is invoked by DB2 whenever an open log file is closed, a database is closed (i.e., all connections to the database are terminated), or the ROLLFORWARD DATABASE command/API is executed (to perform a roll-forward recovery operation on a DB2 9 database).

Earlier, we saw that changes made to a database are recorded in log files and that when archival logging is used, log files are allocated and filled as they are needed. Each time a full log file is closed and a new log file is allocated, DB2 calls the user exit program (provided one exists and the database has been configured to take advantage of it) and passes it an ARCHIVE request along with the name of the oldest filled log file that currently resides in the active log directory. The user exit program then copies the log file specified to a designated archive log file storage area (the user exit program runs as a background process) and returns control to DB2, which then removes the log file just copied from the active log file directory—provided it is no longer needed. At times, a log file may exist in both the active log file directory and the archive log file storage area. That's because DB2 does not remove a log file from the active log file directory as long as it contains records that are associated with a running transaction. (If a long-running transaction needs to be rolled back, information stored in the log file may be needed and user exit programs are not invoked by rollback operations.) When the database is closed, all log files in the active log file directory are closed, and in some cases, the user exit program is called again (with an ARCHIVE request) to copy all remaining log files to the designated archive log file storage area.

When a roll-forward recovery operation is to be performed on a database whose archive log files reside somewhere other than the active log file directory, the log files must either be copied to the active log file directory so that they are available for the roll-forward recovery operation or the location where the archived log files reside must be specified in the OVERFLOW LOG PATH option of the ROLLFORWARD DATABASE command (which is the command that is used to initiate a roll-forward recovery operation). If you are using a user exit program and if the database's transaction log files are not stored on a raw device, the user exit program will automatically move transaction log files to the active log directory for you. Here's how it works. Each time a log file that does not reside in the active log file directory is needed, DB2 calls the user exit program and passes it a RETRIEVE request along with the name of the log file the roll-forward recovery operation is looking for. The user exit program then copies the specified log file to the active log file directory. (To see which log files are actually needed, you can execute the ROLLFORWARD DATABASE command with the QUERY STATUS option specified). Log records stored in the log file copied will then be replayed against the database; once all records stored in the log file have been processed, DB2 removes the copy from the active log file directory.

Because archived log files can be moved from the active log directory to a specific storage location automatically by assigning the value DISK or TSM to the *logarcmeth1* or *logarcmeth2* database configuration parameter, user exits are rarely necessary.

Constructing a User Exit Program

Basically, there are two approaches you can take to develop a DB2 9 user exit program—you can modify one of the sample user exit programs provided with DB2 or you can construct your own. A number of sample user exit programs are provided with DB2 9 that demonstrate how user exit programs that interact with different devices and software interfaces are to be coded. These programs can be used "as is" or they can be modified to meet your specific needs. (When used "as is" you must provide values for some constants that are used by the program and you must compile it to create an executable application.) Comments within these programs provide technical information on how they are constructed.

On the other hand, if you understand the basic requirements for constructing a user exit program, you can create your own from the ground up. (If you decide to go this route, you may find it beneficial to use one of the sample user exit programs provided as a model to aid you in your development efforts.) By taking this approach, you can construct a user exit program that has been customized to work closely with your server environment and any hardware/software interfaces necessary. You can also construct a single user exit routine that works with multiple databases.

Four sample user exit programs are provided with DB2 9 for Linux, UNIX, and Windows. They are named as follows:

db2uext2.ctsm Uses the Tivoli Storage Manager (TSM) utility to archive and retrieve database log files.

db2uext.ctape Designed to archive and retrieve database log files to/from tape media.

db2uexit.cdisk Uses the system copy command (COPY or cp) to archive and retrieve database log files to/from disk media.

db2uexit.cxbsa Uses the XBSA Draft 0.8 published by the X/Open group, to archive and retrieve database log files. (This sample user exit program is only applicable for DB2 for AIX.)

All of these sample user exit programs are written in C and they can be found in the /sqllib/samples/c subdirectory of the current instance directory. However, whereas the sample user exit programs provided are written in C, user exit programs can be written in a wide variety of programming languages.

Regardless of which programming language is used, all user exit programs must be structured such that they perform three distinct tasks:

1. First, they must accept and parse the input parameters that will be sent to them when they are called by DB2. The calling format used is:

```
db2uext2
    -OS[OperatingSystem]
    -RL[DB2ReleaseLevel]
    -RQ[Request]
    -DB[DatabaseName]
    -NN[NodeNumber]
    -LP[LogFilePath]
    -LN[LogFileName]
    -AP[TSMPassword]
    -SP[LogExtentStartPage]
    -LS[LogExtentSize]
```

where:

OperatingSystem	Identifies the platform that the DB2 instance is running on (Linux, AIX, Solaris, HP-UX, or Windows).
B2ReleaseLevel	Identifies the DB2 product release level of DB2 that called the user exit program.
Request	Identifies the action being requested—ARCHIVE or RETRIEVE.
DatabaseName	Identifies the database, by name, that the log file is associated with.
NodeNumber	Identifies the local node number.
LogFilePath	Specifies the fully qualified path that identifies where active log files are located.
LogFileName	Identifies the name of a log file to be archived or retrieved.
TSMPassword	Specifies the password needed by the Tivoli Storage Manager utility.
LogExtentStartPage	Identifies the starting page where log information needed can be found (if the log file is stored on a raw device).
LogExtentSize	Identifies the size, in 4K pages, of the requested log extent (if the log file is stored on a raw device).

2. Then, they must perform whatever processing is needed in order to manipulate data according to the action/request received. In some cases, this involves copying a log file from one location to another using the system copy command. In other cases, this involves communicating with a special hardware component using a vendor-supplied interface.

3. Finally, they must exit with an appropriate return code that DB2 knows how to process. In order for DB2 to react properly to any error encountered during user exit program execution, all user exit programs must be coded so that they always exit with one of the following return code values:

   - 0 - Success

   - 4 - Resource error encountered

   - 8 - Operator intervention required

   - 12 - Hardware error

   - 16 - Software error

   - 20 - Error with one or more parameters passed

   - 24 - User Exit program not found

   - 28 - I/O failure

   - 32 - Operator terminated

If DB2 receives a return code of 4 or 8, it waits five minutes before attempting to perform the operation again. If DB2 receives a return code of 12 or greater, the request is suspended for five minutes and any additional requests are ignored. After five minutes have elapsed, an attempt to process the request is made again—if successful, all pending requests are also processed; if unsuccessful and a return code of 8 or greater is returned, the five minute suspensions continue until the problem is corrected or the database is stopped and restarted.

Whether you decide to modify an existing sample user exit program or create one from the ground up, you must convert it to a format that can be executed by DB2 on the database server. This means that unless the user exit program is written in REXX, it must be compiled and linked to produce an executable program. On

Linux and UNIX platforms, the file containing the source code for the user exit program should be compiled and linked to produce an executable program named db2uext2; on Windows platforms, the file containing the source code for the user exit program should be compiled and linked to produce a file named db2uext2.exe.

Configuring a DB2 Database to Use a User Exit Program

Once the source code file for a user exit program has been compiled and linked to produce an executable program, two actions must be performed before it can actually be used: the executable form of the user exit program must be copied to a specific location and the *logarcmeth1* or *logarcmeth2* database configuration parameter for the appropriate database(s) must be assigned the value USEREXIT.

Because DB2 calls a user exit program on behalf of a database, and because a database can reside in a wide variety of locations, DB2 looks for a user exit program in one specific location. Therefore, it is your responsibility to ensure that the executable form of your user exit program resides in that location. On UNIX platforms, user exit programs should be stored in either the /sqllib/bin or the /sqllib/adm subdirectory of the current instance directory (which is where the other DB2 executable programs are stored). On Windows platforms, user exit programs must be stored in the \sqllib\bin subdirectory of the current instance directory (again, where the other DB2 executable programs are stored).

Storing an executable form of the user exit program in the appropriate location is just the first step. Whether or not a user exit program will actually be invoked on behalf of a database is determined by the value of that database's *logarcmeth1* or *logarcmeth2* database configuration parameter: if either parameter is set to USEREXIT, archival logging is performed and DB2 interacts with the user exit program as described earlier.

User Exit Program Considerations

When a user exit program is used to archive and retrieve transaction log files, the following items need to be taken into consideration:

- Only one user exit program can be called by a DB2 instance. Therefore, each program used must be designed to handle all actions/requests it may need to perform for each database within the instance.

- The log file size used has an impact on how well a user exit program executes; if a small log file size is used, the user exit routine will be called more often but may execute faster.

- In some cases, if a database is closed before a user exit program processing an archive request returns a positive response, another archive request will be sent as soon as the database is reopened. Thus a log file may be archived more than once.

- If two or more databases are using the same log storage device at the same time and that device uses changeable media (for example, a tape drive), and if one of the databases needs to perform a roll-forward recovery operation, a log file needed may not exist on the medium currently being used by the device.

- A user exit program does not guarantee that a database can be rolled forward to the point in time that a failure occurred; instead, it attempts to make the recovery window smaller. Should a disk containing online archive log files fail before the active log file is filled or before all log files are archived to a new location, those log files will be lost.

- User exit programs are not called as part of a rollback operation or when a database is restarted as part of crash recovery.

- If a user exit program receives a request to archive a log file that does not exist (because multiple requests to archive the file were made and the file has already been moved, copied, and deleted) or to retrieve a log file that does not exist (because it is located in another directory or the end of the logs has been reached), it should ignore the request and return a successful return code.

- A user exit program should allow for the existence of different log files that have the same name after a database recovery operation has been performed. In addition, a user exit program should be written to preserve both log files and to associate those log files with the correct database.

High Availability Disaster Recovery (HADR)

High availability disaster recovery (HADR) is a DB2 database replication feature that provides a high availability solution for both partial and complete site failures. HADR protects against data loss by replicating data changes from a source database, called the primary, to a target database, called the standby. In an HADR environment, applications can access the current primary database—synchronization with the standby database occurs by rolling forward transaction log data that is generated on the primary database and shipped to the standby database. And with HADR, you can choose the level of protection you want from potential loss of data by specifying one of three synchronization modes: synchronous, near synchronous, or asynchronous.

HADR is designed to minimize the impact to a database system when a partial or a complete site failure occurs. A partial site failure can be caused by a hardware, network, or software (DB2 or operating system) malfunction. Without HADR, a partial site failure requires restarting the server and the instance where one or more DB2 databases reside. The length of time it takes to restart the server and the instance is unpredictable. If the transaction load was heavy at the time of the partial site failure, it can take several minutes before a database is returned to a consistent state and made available for use. With HADR, the standby database can take over in seconds. Furthermore, you can redirect the clients that were using the original primary database to the standby database (which is now the new primary database) by using Automatic Client Reroute or retry logic in the applications that interact with the database. After the failed original primary server is repaired, it can rejoin the HADR pair as a standby database if both copies of the database can be made consistent. Once the original primary database is reintegrated into the HADR pair as the standby database, you can switch the roles so that the original primary database once again functions as the primary database. (This is known as failback operation).

A complete site failure can occur when a disaster, such as a fire, causes the entire site to be destroyed. Because HADR uses TCP/IP to communicate between a primary and a standby database, the databases can reside in two different locations. For example, your primary database might be located at your head office in one city, whereas your standby database is located at your sales office in another city. If a disaster occurs at the primary site, data availability is maintained by having the remote standby database take over as the primary database.

Requirements for HADR Environments

To achieve optimal performance with HADR, the system hosting the standby database should consist of the same hardware and software as the system where the primary database resides. If the system hosting the standby database has fewer resources than the system hosting the primary database, the standby database may not be able to keep up with the transaction load generated by the primary database. This can cause the standby database to fall behind or the performance of the primary database to suffer. More importantly, if a failover situation occurs, the new primary database may not have the resources needed to adequately service the client applications. And because buffer pool operations performed on the primary database are replayed on the standby database, it is important that the primary and standby database servers have the same amount of memory.

IBM recommends that you use similar host computers for the HADR primary and standby databases. (If possible, they should be from the same vendor and have the same architecture. This will ensure consistent performance on the two servers.) Furthermore, the operating system on the primary and standby database servers should be the same version, including patch level. You can violate this rule for a short time during a rolling upgrade, but use extreme caution when doing so. A TCP/IP interface must also be available between the HADR host machines, and a high-speed, high-capacity network should be used to connect the two.

The DB2 software installed on both the primary and the standby database server must have the same bit size (32 or 64), and the version of DB2 used for the primary and standby databases must be identical; for example, both must be either version 8 or version 9. During rolling upgrades, the modification level (for example, the fix pack level) of the database system for the standby database can be later than that of the primary database for a short while. However, you should not keep this configuration for an extended period of time. The primary and standby databases will not connect to each other if the modification level of the database system for the primary database is later than that of the standby database. Therefore, fix packs must always be applied to the standby database system first.

Both the primary and the standby database must be a single-partition database, and they both must have the same database name; however, they do not have to be stored on the same database path. The amount of storage space allocated for transaction log files should also be the same on both the primary and the standby database server; the use of raw devices for transaction logging is not supported. (Archival logging is performed only by the current primary database.)

Table space properties such as table space name, table space type (DMS, SMS, or Automatic Storage), table space page size, table space size, container path, container size, and container type (raw device, file, or directory) must be identical on the primary and standby databases. When you issue a table space statement such as CREATE TABLESPACE, ALTER TABLESPACE, or DROP TABLESPACE on the primary database, it is replayed on the standby database. Therefore, you must ensure that the table space containers involved with such statements exist on both systems before you issue the table space statement on the primary database. (If you create a table space on the primary database, and log replay fails on the standby database because the containers are not available, the primary database does not receive an error message stating that the log replay failed.) Automatic storage databases are fully supported, including replication of ALTER DATABASE statements. Similar to table space containers, the storage paths specified must exist on both the primary and the standby server.

Additionally, once an HADR environment has been established, the following restrictions apply:

- Clients cannot connect to the standby database.

- Self Tuning Memory Manager (STMM) can be run only on the current primary database.

- Backup operations cannot be performed on the standby database.

- Redirected restore is not supported. That is, HADR does not support redirecting table space containers. However, database directory and log directory changes are supported.

- Load operations with the COPY NO option specified are not supported.

Setting Up an HADR Environment

The process of setting up an HADR environment is fairly straightforward. After ensuring that the systems to be used as primary and secondary server are identical and that a TCP/IP connection exists between them, you simply perform the following tasks in the order shown:

1. Determine the host name, host IP address, and the service name or port number for both the primary and the secondary database server.

If a server has multiple network interfaces, ensure that the HADR host name or IP address maps to the intended interface. You will need to allocate separate HADR ports for each protected database—these cannot be the same as the ports that have been allocated to the instance. The host name can map to only one IP address.

2. Create the standby database by restoring a backup image or initializing a split mirror copy of the database that is to serve as the primary database.

It is recommended that you do not issue the ROLLFORWARD DATABASE command on the standby database after the restore operation or split mirror initialization. The results of performing a roll-forward recovery operation might differ slightly from replaying the logs on the standby database using HADR. If the primary and standby databases are not identical when HADR is started, an error will occur.

When setting up the standby database using the RESTORE DATABASE command, it is recommended that the REPLACE HISTORY FILE option be used; use of the following options must be avoided: TABLESPACE, INTO, REDIRECT, and WITHOUT ROLLING FORWARD.

When setting up the standby database using the db2inidb utility, do not use the SNAPSHOT or MIRROR options. You can specify the RELOCATE USING option to change one or more of the following configuration attributes: instance name, log path, and database path. However, you must not change the database name or the table space container paths.

3. Set the HADR configuration parameters on both the primary and the standby databases.

After the standby database has been created, but before HADR is started, the HADR configuration parameters shown in Table 4.2 need to be set.

Table 4.2 HADR-Specific Configuration Parameters		
Parameter	**Value Range / Default**	**Description**
hadr_db_role	N/A	Read-only. Indicates the current role of the database, if it is part of a high availability disaster recovery (HADR) environment. Valid values are STANDARD, PRIMARY, or STANDBY.
hadr_local_host	Any valid character string Default: NULL	Specifies the local host for high availability disaster recovery (HADR) TCP communication. Either a host name or an IP address can be used.
hadr_local_svc	Any valid character string Default: NULL	Specifies the TCP service name or port number for which the local high availability disaster recovery (HADR) process accepts connections.
hadr_remote_ host	Any valid character string Default: NULL	Specifies the TCP/IP host name or IP address of the remote HADR node.
hadr_remote_ inst	Any valid character string Default: NULL	Specifies the instance name of the remote server. Administration tools, such as the Control Center, use this parameter to contact the remote server. HADR also checks whether a remote database requesting a connection belongs to the declared remote instance.
hadr_remote_svc	Any valid character string Default: NULL	Specifies the TCP service name or port number that will be used by the remote HADR node.

hadr_remote_ svc	SYNC, NEARSYNC, ASYNC Default: NEARSYNC	Specifies the synchronization mode to use for HADR. This determines how primary log writes are synchronized with the standby database when the systems are in peer state. Valid values for this configuration parameter are:
		
		• SYNC (Synchronous)
		    This mode provides the greatest protection against transaction loss, and using it results in the longest transaction response time among the three modes. In this mode, log writes are considered successful only when log records have been written to log files on the primary database and when the primary database has received acknowledgement from the standby database that the log records have also been written to log files on the standby database. The log data is guaranteed to be stored at both sites.
		
		• NEARSYNC (Near Synchronous)
		    Although this mode has a shorter transaction response time than synchronous mode, it also provides slightly less protection against transaction loss. In this mode, log writes are considered successful only when log records have been written to the log files on the primary database and when the primary database has received acknowledgement from the standby system that the log records have also been written to main memory on the standby system. Loss of data occurs only if both sites fail simultaneously and if the target site has not transferred all of the log data that it has received to nonvolatile storage.

Table 4.2 HADR-Specific Configuration Parameters		
Parameter	**Value Range / Default**	**Description**
		• ASYNC (Asynchronous) This mode has the highest chance of transaction loss if the primary system fails. It also has the shortest transaction response time among the three modes. In this mode, log writes are considered successful only when log records have been written to the log files on the primary database and have been delivered to the TCP layer of the primary system's host machine. Because the primary system does not wait for acknowledgement from the standby system, transactions might be considered committed when they are still on their way to the standby system.
hadr_timeout	1–4,294,967,295 Default: 120	Specifies the time (in seconds) that the HADR process waits before considering a communication attempt to have failed. (The value assigned to this configuration parameter must be the same for both the primary and the standby database.)

4. Connect to the standby instance and start HADR on the standby database.

    HADR is started by executing the START HADR command. The basic syntax for this command is:

    ```
    START HADR ON [DATABASE | DB] [DatabaseAlias]
    <USER [UserName] <USING [Password]>>
    AS [PRIMARY <BY FORCE> | SECONDARY]
    ```

where:

> *DatabaseAlias* Identifies the alias assigned to the database for which HADR is to be started.

> *DatabaseAlias* Identifies the alias assigned to the database for which HADR is to be started.

> *UserName* Identifies the name assigned to a specific user under whom HADR is to be started.

> *Password* Identifies the password that corresponds to the name of the user under whom HADR is to be started.

Thus, if you wanted to start HADR on a database named SAMPLE and indicate that it is to act as a standby database, you could do so by executing a START HADR command that looks something like this:

```
START HADR ON DATABASE sample AS STANDBY
```

5. Connect to the primary instance and start HADR on the primary database.

   In this case, you would execute a START HADR command that looks something like this:

```
START HADR ON DATABASE sample AS PRIMARY
```

You can also set up an HADR environment using the Set Up HADR Databases Wizard, which can be activated by selecting the High Availability Disaster Recovery action from the Databases menu found in the Control Center. Figure 4–16 shows the Control Center menu items that must be selected to activate the Set Up HADR Databases Wizard; Figure 4–17 shows how the first page of the Set Up HADR Databases Wizard might look immediately after it is activated.

Once an HADR environment has been established, the following operations will be replicated automatically in the standby database whenever they are performed on the primary database:

- Execution of Data Definition Language (DDL) statements (CREATE, ALTER, DROP)

- Execution of Data Manipulation Language (DML) statements (INSERT, UPDATE, DELETE)

- Buffer pool operations

- Table space operations (as well as storage-related operations performed on automatic storage databases)

- Online reorganization

- Offline reorganization

- Changes to metadata (system catalog information) for stored procedures and user-defined functions (UDFs)

HADR does not replicate stored procedure and UDF object and library files. If this type of replication is needed, you must physically create the files on identical paths on both the primary and standby databases. (If the standby database cannot find the

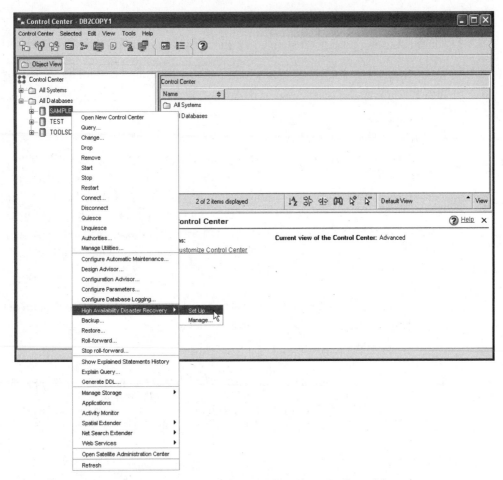

Figure 4–16: Invoking the Set Up HADR Databases Wizard from the Control Center.

referenced object or library file, the stored procedure or UDF invocation will fail on the standby database.)

Nonlogged operations, such as changes to database configuration parameters and to the recovery history file, are not replicated to the standby database.

Automatic Client Reroute and HADR

Automatic Client Reroute is a DB2 feature that allows client applications to recover from a loss of communication with the server so that the application can continue

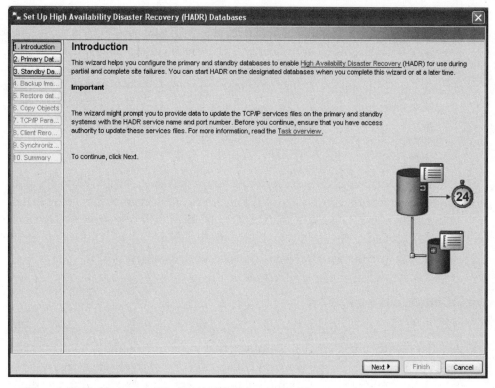

Figure 4–17: The first page of the Set Up HADR Databases Wizard.

its work with minimal interruption. (If automatic client reroute is not enabled, client applications will receive an error message indicating that a connect attempt has failed due to a timeout and no further attempts will be made to establish a connection with the server.) However, rerouting is only possible when an alternate database location has been specified at the server and the TCP/IP protocol is used.

The automatic client reroute feature can be used with HADR to make client applications connect to the new primary database immediately after a takeover operation. In fact, if you set up HADR using the Set Up High Availability Disaster Recovery (HADR) Databases Wizard, automatic client reroute is enabled by default. If you set up HADR manually, you can enable the automatic client reroute feature by executing the UPDATE ALTERNATE SERVER FOR DATABASE command; automatic client reroute does not use the values stored in the *hadr_remote_host* and *hadr_remote_svc* database configuration parameters.

For example, suppose you have cataloged a database named SALES on a client workstation as being located at host named SVR1. Database SALES is the primary database in an HADR environment and its corresponding standby database, also named SALES, resides on a host named SVR2 and listens on port number 456. To enable automatic client reroute, you simply specify an alternate server for the SALES database stored on host SVR1 by executing the following command:

```
UPDATE ALTERNATE SERVER FOR DATABASE sales
USING HOSTNAME svr2 PORT 456
```

Once this command is executed, the client must connect to host SVR1 to obtain the alternate server information. Then, if a communication error occurs between the client and the SALES database at host SVR1, the client will first attempt to reconnect to the SALES database on host SVR1. If this fails, the client will then attempt to establish a connection with the standby SALES database located on host SVR2.

Load Operations and HADR

Load operations present a special problem for HADR. Because load operations are not recorded in a database's transaction log files, whether a load operation can be duplicated is dependent on whether a copy of the loaded data was saved as part of the load process (which is the case if the COPY YES option of the LOAD command is specified). If a load operation is performed on the primary database with the COPY YES option specified, the command will execute on the primary database, and the data will be replicated to the standby database—provided the load copy image created can be accessed by the standby database via the path or device provided with the LOAD command. If the standby database cannot access the load copy image, the table space in which the table is stored is marked invalid on the standby database, and the standby database will stop replaying log records that pertain to this table space. To ensure that the load operation can access the copy on the standby database, it is recommended that you use a shared location for the load copy image output file location specified with the COPY YES option. Alternatively, you can deactivate the standby database while the load operation is performed, perform the load operation on the primary database, place a copy of the load copy image produced in the standby path, and then activate the standby database.

If a load operation is executed on the primary database with the NONRECOVERABLE option specified, data will be loaded into the appropriate table in the primary database, the corresponding table on the standby database will be marked invalid, and the standby database will stop replaying log records that pertain to this table. You can reissue the LOAD command with the COPY YES and REPLACE options specified to restore the table on the standby database, or you can drop the table and recover the space.

Because executing a load operation with the COPY NO option specified is not supported by HADR, an attempt to perform such an operation is automatically converted to a load operation that behaves as if the NONRECOVERABLE option was specified. To prevent this behavior, you can set the DB2_LOAD_COPY_NO_OVERRIDE registry variable on the primary database to COPY YES, in which case all load operations performed will behave as if the COPY YES option were specified. When setting this variable, make sure that the device or directory specified on the primary database can be accessed by the standby database using the same path, device, or load library.

Load operations against primary databases in an HADR environment can have an impact on indexes as well as tables and table spaces. If a load operation is performed on the primary database with the COPY YES option specified, affected indexes will be replicated as follows:

- If the indexing mode is set to REBUILD, and the table being loaded has been assigned the LOG INDEX BUILD attribute, or if the table being loaded has been assigned the DEFAULT attribute, and the *logindexbuild* database configuration parameter on the primary database is set to ON, the primary database will include the rebuilt index object in the copy file so that the standby database can replicate the index object. If the index object on the standby database is marked invalid before the load operation is performed, it will become usable again after the load operation as a result of the index rebuild.

- If the indexing mode is set to INCREMENTAL and the table being loaded has been assigned the LOG INDEX BUILD attribute, or if the table being loaded has been assigned the NULL attribute and the *logindexbuild* database configuration parameter on the primary database is set to ON, the index object on the standby database is updated only if it is not marked invalid before the load operation. Otherwise, the index is marked invalid on the standby database.

IBM recommends you set the *logindexbuild* database configuration parameter to ON for HADR databases to ensure that complete information is logged for index creation, re creation, and reorganization. Although this means that index builds might take longer on the primary system and that more log space may be required, the indexes will be rebuilt on the standby system during HADR log replay and will be available when a failover takes place. If index operations on the primary system are not logged and a failover occurs, any invalid indexes that remain after the failover is complete will have to be rebuilt before they can be accessed—while indexes are being recreated, they cannot be accessed by any application.

Problem Determination Tools

Along with creating database backup images on a regular basis, database monitoring is a vital activity that, when performed, provides continuous feedback on the health of a database system. And because database monitoring is such an integral part of database administration, DB2 comes equipped with a built-in monitoring utility known as the Database System Monitor. Although the name "Database System Monitor" suggests that only one monitoring tool is available, in reality the Database System Monitor is composed of two distinct tools (a snapshot monitor and one or more event monitors) that can be used to capture and return system monitor information.

The snapshot monitor is designed to collect information about the state of a DB2 instance and the databases it controls at a specific point in time (i.e., at the time the snapshot is taken). Additionally, the snapshot monitor can be tailored to retrieve specific types of monitoring data (for example, it could be configured to collect just information about buffer pools). Snapshots can be taken by executing the GET SNAPSHOT command from the DB2 Command Line Processor (CLP) by using the snapshot administrative views and/or snapshot table functions, or by embedding the snapshot monitor APIs in a C or C++ application. Snapshots are useful for determining the status of a database system and, when taken at regular intervals, can provide valuable information that can be used to observe trends and identify potential problem areas.

Although the snapshot monitor provides a method for recording information about the state of database activity at a given point in time, an event monitor can be used to record information about database activity when an event or transition in database activity occurs. (Such a transition takes place when a connection is established, a deadlock cycle is encountered, an SQL statement is executed, and a transaction is started or stopped.) Thus, event monitors provide a way to collect monitor data when events or activities that cannot be monitored using the snapshot monitor occur. Unlike the snapshot monitor, which resides in the background and is always available, event monitors are special objects that must be created. Event monitors are created by executing the CREATE EVENT MONITOR SQL statement and event monitors are activated (or deactivated) by executing the SET EVENT MONITOR SQL statement. When an event monitor is activated (started), it sits quietly in the background and waits for one of the events it is associated with to occur. Immediately after an event being monitored takes place, the event monitor collects monitor data associated with the event that triggered it and writes all data collected to the event monitor's target location. Thus, the event itself controls when monitor data is collected—unlike with the snapshot monitor, no special steps are required to capture the monitor data.

Along with the database system monitor, several other tools are available to help a database administrator isolate and identify problems with a system, database, or application. Some of the more popular problem determination tools are the DB2 memory tracker utility and the DB2 Problem Determination tool.

The DB2 Memory Tracker

The DB2 memory tracker utility is used to produce a complete report of memory status for instances, databases, and agents. This utility provides the following information about memory pool allocation:

- Current size

- Maximum size (hard limit)

- Largest size (high water mark)

- Type (identifier indicating function for which memory will be used)

- Agent who allocated pool (only if the pool is private)

(This information is also available from the snapshot monitor.)

The DB2 memory tracker is invoked by executing the db2mtrk command. The syntax for this command is:

```
db2mtrk
<-i>
<-d>
<-p>
<-m | -w>
<-r [Interval] <Count>>
<-v>
<-h>
```

where:

Interval Identifies the number of seconds to wait between subsequent calls to the DB2 memory tracker.

Count Identifies the number of times to repeat calls to the DB2 memory tracker.

All other options shown with this command are described in Table 4.2.

Table 4.2 db2mtrk Command Options	
Option	**Meaning**
-i	Specifies that information about instance level memory is to be collected and displayed.
-d	Specifies that information about database level memory is to be collected and displayed.
-p	Specifies that information about private memory is to be collected and displayed.
-m	Specifies that maximum values for each memory pool is to be collected and displayed.
-w	Specifies that high water mark values for each memory pool are to be collected and displayed.
-v	Indicates that verbose output is to be returned.
-h	Displays help information. When this option is specified, all other options are ignored, and only the help information is displayed.

Thus, if you wanted to see how memory is utilized by the active databases on a system, and you wanted to capture and view this information every two minutes, you could do so by executing a db2mtrk command that looks something like this:

```
db2mtrk -d -r 120
```

Assuming a database named SAMPLE is active at the time the db2mtrk command is issued, the results produced should look something like this:

```
Tracking Memory on: 2008/05/21 at 14:00:38

Memory for database: SAMPLE

    utilh     pckcacheh catcacheh bph (1)   bph (S32K) bph (S16K) bph (S8K)
    64.0K     128.0K    64.0K     1.2M      704.0K     448.0K     320.0K


    bph (S4K) shsorth   lockh     dbh       other
    256.0K    0         320.0K    4.3M      128.0K
```

The DB2 Problem Determination Tool

The DB2 Problem Determination tool is used to obtain quick and immediate information from the DB2 database system memory sets without acquiring any latches. Two benefits to collecting information without latching include faster data retrieval and no competition for engine resources. However, because the DB2 Problem Determination tool works directly with memory, it is possible to retrieve information that is changing as it is being collected; hence, the data retrieved might not be completely accurate. A signal handler is used to prevent the DB2 Problem Determination tool from aborting abnormally when changing memory pointers are encountered. However, this can result in messages such as "Changing data structure forced command termination" appearing in the output produced. Nonetheless, this tool can be extremely helpful for problem determination.

The DB2 Problem Determination tool is invoked by executing the db2pd command. The basic syntax for this command is:

```
db2pd
<- version | -v >
<-inst>
<[-database | -db] [DatabaseName] ,...>
<-alldatabases | -alldbs>
<-full>
<-everything>
<-hadr [-db [DatabaseName] | -alldbs]>
<-utilities>
<-applications [-db [DatabaseName] | -alldbs]>
```

```
<-agents>
<-transactions [-db [DatabaseName] | -alldbs]>
<-bufferpools [-db [DatabaseName] | -alldbs]>
<-logs [-db [DatabaseName] | -alldbs]>
<-tablespaces [-db [DatabaseName] | -alldbs]>
<-dynamic [-db [DatabaseName] | -alldbs]>
<-static [-db [DatabaseName] | -alldbs]>
<-fcm>
<-memsets>
<-mempools>
<-memblocks>
<-dbmcfg>
<-dbcfg [-db [DatabaseName] | -alldbs]>
<-catalogcache [-db [DatabaseName] | -alldbs]>
<-tcbstats [-db [DatabaseName] | -alldbs]>
<-reorg [-db [DatabaseName] | -alldbs]>
<-recovery [-db [DatabaseName] | -alldbs]>
<-reopt [-db [DatabaseName] | -alldbs]>
<-osinfo>
<-storagepaths [-db [DatabaseName] | -alldbs]>
<-pages [-db [DatabaseName] | -alldbs]>
<-stack [all | [ProcessID]]>
<-repeat [Interval] <[Count]>>
<-command [CmdFileName]>
<-file [OutFileName]>
<-interactive>
<-h | -help>
```

where:

DatabaseName	Identifies, by name, the database with which the DB2 Problem Determination tool is to interact.
ProcessID	Identifies the process, by ID, for which a stack trace file is to be produced.
Interval	Identifies the number of seconds to wait between subsequent calls to the DB2 Problem Determination tool.
Count	Identifies the number of time to repeat calls to the DB2 Problem Determination tool.
CmdFileName	Identifies the name assigned to an ASCII format file that contains DB2 Problem Determination tool command options that are to be used.

OutFile   Identifies the name of the file to which information returned by the DB2 Problem Determination tool is to be written.

All other options shown with this command are described in Table 4.3.

Table 4.3 db2pd Command Options	
Option	Meaning
-version | -v	Specifies that the current version and service level of the installed DB2 product is to be collected and displayed.
-inst	Specifies that all instance level information available is to be collected and displayed.
-alldatabases | -alldbs	Specifies that the utility is to attach to all memory sets of all available databases.
-full	Specifies that all output is to be expanded to its maximum length. (If this option is not specified, output is truncated to save space on the display.)
-everything	Specifies that all options are to be used and that information is to be collected and displayed for all databases on all database partition servers that are local to the server.
-hadr	Specifies that information about HADR is to be collected and displayed.
-utilities	Specifies that information about utilities is to be collected and displayed.
-applications	Specifies that information about applications is to be collected and displayed.
-agents	Specifies that information about agents is to be collected and displayed.
-transactions	Specifies that information about active transactions is to be collected and displayed.
-bufferpools	Specifies that information about buffer pools is to be collected and displayed.
-logs	Specifies that information about transaction log files is to be collected and displayed.
-locks	Specifies that information about locks is to be collected and displayed.
-tablespaces	Specifies that information about table spaces is to be collected and displayed.
-dynamic	Specifies that information about the execution of dynamic SQL statements is to be collected and displayed.
-static	Specifies that information about the execution of static SQL and packages is to be collected and displayed.
-fcm	Specifies that information about the fast communication manager is to be collected and displayed.

Table 4.3 db2pd Command Options (Continued)	
Option	**Meaning**
-memsets	Specifies that information about memory sets is to be collected and displayed.
-mempools	Specifies that information about memory pools is to be collected and displayed.
-memblocks	Specifies that information about memory blocks is to be collected and displayed.
-dbmcfg	Specifies that information about current DB2 Database Manager configuration parameter settings is to be collected and displayed.
-dbcfg	Specifies that information about current database configuration parameter settings is to be collected and displayed.
-catalogcache	Specifies that information about the catalog cache is to be collected and displayed.
-tcbstats	Specifies that information about tables and indexes is to be collected and displayed.
-reorg	Specifies that information about table and data partition reorganization is to be collected and displayed.
-recovery	Specifies that information about recovery activity is to be collected and displayed.
-reopt	Specifies that information about cached SQL statements that were reoptimized using the REOPT ONCE option is to be collected and displayed.
-osinfo	Specifies that operating system information is to be collected and displayed.
-storagepaths	Specifies that information about the automatic storage paths defined for the database is to be collected and displayed.
-pages	Specifies that information about buffer pool pages is to be collected and displayed.
-stack	Specifies that stack trace information is to be collected and displayed.
-repeat	Specifies that the command is to be repeated after the specified number of seconds for the specified number of times.
-command	Specifies that db2pd commands that are stored in the specified file are to be executed.
-file	Specifies that all information collected is to be written to the specified file.
-interactive	Indicates that values specified for the DB2PDOPT environment variable are to be overridden when running the db2pd command.
-help | -h	Displays help information. When this option is specified, all other options are ignored, and only the help information is displayed.

So if you wanted to determine which indexes are actually being used for accessing data in a database named SAMPLE, you could do so by executing a db2pd command that looks something like this:

```
db2pd -tcbstats -db sample
```

On the other hand, if you wanted to obtain a list of applications that are currently connected to a database named SAMPLE, you could do so by executing the LIST APPLICATIONS command from the DB2 Command Line Processor, or by executing a db2pd command that looks something like this:

```
db2pd -applications -db sample
```

There is no minimum connection requirement for executing the db2pd command. However, if a database-level option is specified, that database must be active before the requested information can be returned.

Practice Questions

Question 1

Which of the following commands must be executed in order to configure a database named SAMPLE for infinite logging?

○ A. UPDATE DB CFG FOR sample USING LOGARCHMETH1 LOGRETAIN LOGARCHMETH2 -1

○ B. UPDATE DB CFG FOR sample USING LOGARCHMETH1 LOGRETAIN LOGARCHMETH2 INFINITE

○ C. UPDATE DB CFG FOR sample USING LOGARCHMETH1 LOGRETAIN LOGSECOND -1

○ D. UPDATE DB CFG FOR sample USING USING LOGARCHMETH1 LOGRETAIN LOGSECOND INFINITE

Question 2

A database administrator executes the following command:

```
GET DB CFG FOR sample
```

Assuming the database named SAMPLE has been configured to use archival logging, which of the following information can be obtained from output produced?

○ A. The RID of the last record written to an active log file.

○ B. The name of the first active log file.

○ C. The transaction ID of the last transaction written to an active log file.

○ D. The number of archived log files created.

Question 3

Which two of the following commands can be used to enable dual logging for a database named SAMPLE? (Select two)

❑ A. db2set DB2_NEWLOGPATH=D:\logs_copy

❑ B. db2set DB2_NEWLOGPATH=1

❑ C. UPDATE DB CFG FOR sample USING failarchpath D:\ logs_copy

❑ D. UPDATE DB CFG FOR sample USING mirrorlogpath D:\ logs_copy

❑ E. UPDATE DB CFG FOR sample USING logarchmeth2 MIRRORPATH: D:\ logs_copy

Question 4

A database administrator would like to configure a database named PAYROLL such that whenever a log file becomes full, DB2 will attempt to archive it automatically. Which of the following commands will achieve this objective?

○ A. UPDATE DB CFG FOR payroll USING LOGARCHMETH1 USEREXIT

○ B. UPDATE DB CFG FOR payroll USING LOGARCHMETH1 LOGRETAIN

○ C. UPDATE DB CFG FOR payroll USING LOGARCHMETH2 OFF

○ D. UPDATE DB CFG FOR payroll USING LOGARCHMETH2 AUTOARCHIVE

Question 5

If the following commands are executed:

```
db2set -g DB2_FORCE_APP_ON_MAX_LOG=FALSE;
UPDATE DB CFG FOR sample USING LOGFILSIZ 10000;
UPDATE DB CFG FOR sample USING MAX_LOG 10;
```

What will happen if an application with a long running transaction consumes more than 100,000 log pages?

○ A. The transaction will be rolled back and the application will be forced to terminate.

○ B. The transaction will be rolled back, but the application will be allowed to continue.

○ C. The work performed by the current statement will be rolled back; the application will be allowed to commit or roll back the work performed by other statements in the transaction.

○ D. The work performed by the current statement and all previous statements in the transaction will be rolled back; the application will be allowed to commit or rollback any remaining statements in the transaction.

Question 6

Which of the following commands will display only the media header information for an existing backup image?

○ A. db2 inspect –h

○ B. db2 inspect –H

○ C. db2ckbkp -h

○ D. db2ckbkp -H

Question 7

Which command will back up a database named ACCOUNTING to a Tivoli Storage Manager (TSM) server using 4 concurrent TSM client sessions and 8 buffers?

- ○ A. BACKUP DATABASE accounting USE TSM WITH 4 SESSIONS OPEN 8 BUFFERS
- ○ B. BACKUP DATABASE accounting USE TSM WITH 4 SESSIONS 8 BUFFERS
- ○ C. BACKUP DATABASE accounting USE TSM OPEN 4 SESSIONS WITH 8 BUFFERS
- ○ D. BACKUP DATABASE accounting USE TSM OPTIONS 4 SESSIONS WITH 8 BUFFERS

Question 8

A database named TEST was backed up to disk and a database administrator needs to determine if this backup was taken with using the INCLUDE LOGS option of the BACKUP DATABASE command.

How can the database administrator accomplish this?

- ○ A. Examine the output from the command LIST HISTORY BACKUP ALL FOR test.
- ○ B. Check the value of the BKUPLOGS database configuration parameter.
- ○ C. Examine the header information stored in the backup image using the db2ckbkp command.
- ○ E. Check the value of the DB2_BKUP_INCLLOGS registry variable.

Question 9

A database named SALES was created across 8 database partitions. Then, 12 tables were created and populated using the default table spaces provided – no additional table spaces were created.

Which of the following commands can be used to backup just the user tables on database partition 5 while the database remains online?

- ○ A. db2_all "<<+5< db2 BACKUP DATABASE sales TABLESPACE (*) ONLINE TO /backup_dir"
- ○ B. db2_all "<<+5< db2 BACKUP DATABASE sales TABLESPACE (userspace1) ONLINE TO /backup_dir"
- ○ C. db2_all "<<-5< db2 BACKUP DATABASE sales TABLESPACE (*) ONLINE TO /backup_dir"
- ○ D. db2_all "<<-5< db2 BACKUP DATABASE sales TABLESPACE (userspace1) ONLINE TO /backup_dir"

Question 10

Which of the following statements about incremental (cumulative) backups is NOT true?

- ○ A. The predecessor of an incremental backup image is always the most recent successful full backup image of the same object (database or table space).
- ○ B. Database recovery involves restoring the database using the most recent full backup image available and applying each incremental backup image produced since the last full backup, in the order in which they were created.
- ○ C. Before an incremental backup image can be created, a full backup image must already exist.
- ○ D. Along with updated data and index pages, each incremental backup image also contains all of the initial database metadata that is normally found in a full database backup image.

Question 11

Which of the following statements about the DB2 Check Backup utility (db2ckbkp) is NOT true?

- ○ A. Only users who have read permission on backup image files are allowed to use the db2ckbkp utility.
- ○ B. Multiple backup images can be analyzed with a single db2ckbkp command.
- ○ C. Only users who have System Administrator authority are allowed to use the db2ckbkp utility.
- ○ D. If a backup image was compressed when it was created, the library used to compress the data must be accessible to the db2ckbkp utility.

Question 12

A database named PRODDB has a weekly full backup taken on Sunday, and non-cumulative (delta) backups taken daily. A database crash occurs on Wednesday.

What is the best way to return the database to the state it was in when the last backup image was made?

- ○ A. RESTORE DATABASE proddb TAKEN AT (Sunday);
  RESTORE DATABASE proddb INCREMENTAL TAKEN AT (Tuesday);
- ○ B. RESTORE DATABASE proddb TAKEN AT (Sunday);
  RESTORE DATABASE proddb INCREMENTAL AUTO TAKEN AT (Tuesday);
- ○ C. RESTORE DATABASE proddb TAKEN AT (Sunday);
  RESTORE DATABASE proddb INCREMENTAL AUTO TAKEN AT (Monday);
  RESTORE DATABASE proddb INCREMENTAL AUTO TAKEN AT (Tuesday);
- ○ D. RESTORE DATABASE proddb INCREMENTAL AUTO TAKEN AT (Tuesday);

Question 13

While cleaning up files stored on an older AIX server, a database administrator found a shell script that contained the following commands:

```
db2 "RESTORE DATABASE sample FROM C:\backups TO D:\DB_DIR INTO sample_2
REDIRECT"

db2 "SET TABLESPACE CONTAINERS FOR 0 USING
(PATH 'D:\DB_DIR\SYSTEM')"

db2 "SET TABLESPACE CONTAINERS FOR 1 USING
(PATH 'D:\DB_DIR\TEMP')"

db2 "SET TABLESPACE CONTAINERS FOR 2 USING
(PATH 'D:\DB_DIR\USER')"

db2 "RESTORE DATABASE sample CONTINUE"
```

What was this file designed to perform?

- ○ A. A multiple table space recovery operation.
- ○ B. A reverted restore operation.
- ○ C. A partial table space reconstruction operation.
- ○ D. A redirected restore operation.

Question 14

A database named PAYROLL was created using automatic storage, with the following storage paths: /path1, /path2, /path3. Later, the database was backed up using the following command:

```
BACKUP DATABASE payroll TO /backups
```

If the PAYROLL database needs to be cloned, which of the following commands will re-create it in a new location while maintaining the original storage paths?

- ○ A. RESTORE DB payroll FROM /backups INTO /path1, /path3, /path3 DBPATH /payroll2
- ○ B. RECOVER DB payroll FROM /backups INTO /path1, /path3, /path3 DBPATH /payroll2
- ○ C. RESTORE DB payroll FROM /backups INTO payroll2
- ○ D. RECOVER DB payroll FROM /backups INTO payroll2

Question 15

A database administrator attempted to recover a database named SAMPLE by executing the following command:

`RECOVER DATABASE sample TO END OF LOGS;`

During the roll-forward phase of recovery, an error occurred. Once the problem is corrected, which of the following commands should be executed to force the recovery process to start over at the beginning?

- ○ A. RECOVER DATABASE sample RESTART;
- ○ B. RECOVER DATABASE sample TO END OF LOGS RESTART;
- ○ C. RECOVER DATABASE sample RESTART AND CONTINUE;
- ○ D. RECOVER DATABASE sample START AT RESTORE AND CONTINUE;

Question 16

Which of the following is NOT a requirement for an HADR environment?

- ○ A. The operating system on the primary server and the standby server must be the same (including fix pack level).
- ○ B. The database path on the primary server and the standby server must be the same.
- ○ C. The DB2 software version and bit size (32 or 64) used on the primary server and the standby server must be the same.
- ○ D. Table spaces and table space containers on the primary server and the standby server must be identical.

Question 17

Which of the following is NOT replicated in an HADR environment?

- ○ A. Data Definition Language (DDL) statements
- ○ B. Buffer pool operations
- ○ C. Database configuration parameter changes
- ○ D. System catalog information for stored procedures

Question 18

A system administrator wants to configure an HADR environment so that whenever an application issues a COMMIT, data in the log buffers will be written to the log files on the primary server and then be sent to the standby server and written to the log files there, before a return code will be sent to the application.

Which of the following commands can be used to accomplish this?

- ○ A. UPDATE DB CFG FOR sales USING HADR_SYNCMODE SYNC
- ○ B. UPDATE DB CFG FOR sales USING HADR_SYNCMODE NEARSYNC
- ○ C. UPDATE DB CFG FOR sales USING HADR_SYNCMODE ASYNC
- ○ D. UPDATE DB CFG FOR sales USING HADR_SYNCMODE INSYNC

Question 19

Two database servers have been enabled for synchronous HADR. If the HADR_TIMEOUT configuration parameter on the primary server is set to 30, which two of the following statements are true? (Select two)

- ❑ A. When HADR is started on the secondary server, HADR must be started, within 30 seconds, on the primary server.
- ❑ B. The HADR_TIMEOUT configuration parameter on the secondary server must also be set to 30.
- ❑ C. If the primary server does not receive acknowledgement of a log buffer within 30 seconds it stops processing all requests.
- ❑ D. The HADR_TIMEOUT configuration parameter on the secondary server must be assigned a value less than 30.
- ❑ E. If the primary server does not receive acknowledgement of a log buffer write within 30 seconds it drops out of peer mode.

Question 20

While setting up an HADR environment, a system administrator executed the following commands at the primary server:

```
db2set DB2COMM=TCPIP;
UPDATE ALTERNATE SERVER FOR DATABASE sales
    USING HOSTNAME svr2 PORT 456;
```

What will happen if a failover event occurs while a client application is connected to the SALES database on the primary server?

○ A. The client application will receive an error message indicating that a connect attempt has failed due to a timeout and no further attempts will be made to establish a connection with the server.

○ B. The client application will receive an error message indicating that a connect attempt has failed due to a timeout and the system administrator will have to manually switch over to the standby server SVR2 before further attempts are made to establish a connection with the server.

○ C. The client application will automatically connect to the standby database on SVR2 and that database will become the primary database.

○ D. The client application will automatically connect to the standby database on SVR2 and that database will become the primary database – provided the HADR_REMOTE_HOST and HADR_REMOTE_SVC database configuration parameters have been set appropriately.

Question 21

Which two commands can be used to list all applications that are currently connected to a database named PAYROLL? (Select two)

❑ A. db2pd –connections –db payroll

❑ B. db2pd –list applications –db payroll

❑ C. LIST APPLICATIONS FOR payroll

❑ D. GET APPLICATION SNAPSHOT FOR payroll

❑ E. SELECT * FROM TABLE(SNAP_GET_APPLICATIONS('payroll',-1)) AS applications

Question 22

Which command will take 10 different snapshots of how memory is used by all active databases in the DB2 instance every 5 minutes?

○ A. db2mtrk –d –i 5 10

○ B. db2mtrk –d –r 5 –c 10

○ C. db2mtrk –d –i 300 –c 10

○ D. db2mtrk –d –r 300 10

Question 23

A db2mtrk command was used to produce the results shown below:

```
Tracking Memory on: 2008/05/21 at 14:00:38

Memory for database: SAMPLE

    utilh     pckcacheh catcacheh bph (1)  bph (S32K) bph (S16K) bph (S8K)
    64.0K     128.0K    64.0K     1.2M     704.0K     448.0K     320.0K

    bph (S4K) shsorth   lockh     dbh      other
    256.0K    0         320.0K    4.3M     128.0K
```

Which option was specified when the db2mtrk command was executed?

- ○ A. –d
- ○ B. –i
- ○ C. –p
- ○ D. –w

Question 24

When the following command was executed from the DB2 Command Line Processor:

```
db2pd -tablespaces -db SAMPLE
```

The following information was displayed:

```
Database Partition 0 -- Database SAMPLE -- Active -- Up 25 days 08:32:31

Tablespace Configuration:
Address    Id    Type Content PageSz ExtentSz Auto Prefetch BufID
BufIDDisk FSC NumCntrs MaxStripe  LastConsecPg Name
0x7F91C230 0     DMS  Regular 8192   4        Yes  4        1     1
Off 1         0         3        SYSCATSPACE
0x7F91CA20 1     SMS  SysTmp  8192   32       Yes  32       1     1
On  1         0         31       TEMPSPACE1
0x7F91F1E0 2     DMS  Large   8192   32       Yes  32       1     1
Off 1         0         31       USERSPACE1
0x7F91F9D0 3     DMS  Large   8192   32       Yes  32       1     1
Off 1         0         31       IBMDB2SAMPLEREL
0x7EBAD220 4     DMS  Large   8192   32       Yes  32       1     1
Off 1         0         31       TBSP1
```

```
Tablespace Statistics:
Address     Id   TotalPgs    UsablePgs   UsedPgs   PndFreePgs FreePgs  HWM
State       MinRecTime NQuiescers
0x7F91C230 0     8192        8188        6852      0          1336     6852
0x00000000 0                0
0x7F91CA20 1     1           1           1         0          0        0
0x00000000 0                0
0x7F91F1E0 2     4096        4064        1760      0          2304     1760
0x00000000 0                0
0x7F91F9D0 3     4096        4064        608       0          3456     608
0x00000000 0                0
0x7EBAD220 4     200         160         156       0          0        156
0x00000000 0                0

Tablespace Autoresize Statistics:
Address     Id   AS  AR  InitSize     IncSize       IIP MaxSize LastResize
LRF
0x7F91C230 0     Yes Yes 33554432     -1            No  None         None
                     No
0x7F91CA20 1     Yes No  0            0             No  0            None
                     No
0x7F91F1E0 2     Yes Yes 33554432     -1            No  None         None
                     No
0x7F91F9D0 3     Yes Yes 33554432     -1            No .None         None
                     No
0x7EBAD220 4     No  No  0            0             No  0            None
                     No

Containers:
Address    TspId ContainNum Type  TotalPgs UseablePgs StripeSet Container
0x7F91C8B0 0     0          File  8192     8188       0
C:\DB2\NODE0000\SAMPLE\T0000000\C0000000.CAT
0x7F91D050 1     0          Path  1        1          0
C:\DB2\NODE0000\SAMPLE\T0000001\C0000000.TMP
0x7F91F860 2     0          File  4096     4064       0
C:\DB2\NODE0000\SAMPLE\T0000002\C0000000.LRG
0x7EF220D0 3     0          File  4096     4064       0
C:\DB2\NODE0000\SAMPLE\T0000003\C0000000.LRG
0x7EBADF30 4     0          File  200      160        0
C:\DB295_ESE\tbsp1.dat
```

Based on this information, which of the following is a valid statement?

○ A. Table space SYSCATSPACE has been resized 5 times

○ B. Table space IBMDB2SAMPLEREL is an SMS table space

○ C. Table space USERSPACE1 cannot be accessed until it has been rolled forward

○ D. Table space TBSP1 is about to run out of storage space

Answers

Question 1

The correct answer is **C**. If you are concerned about running out of log space, and you want to avoid allocating a large number of secondary log files, you can configure a database to use what is known as infinite logging. To enable infinite logging for a database, you simply set the *logsecond* database configuration parameter to -1. However, in order to use infinite logging, a database must be configured to use archival logging. This is done by assigning the value LOGRETAIN to the *logarcmeth1* or *logarcmeth2* database configuration parameter.

Question 2

The correct answer is **B**. The name of the current active log file (also referred to as the first active log file) can be obtained by executing the GET DATABASE CONFIGURATION command and examining the contents of the *loghead* database configuration parameter. (This will appear as "First active log file" in the list of information returned by the GET DATABASE CONFIGURATION command.). Other log-related information returned by the GET DATABASE CONFIGURATION command includes:

• Log buffer size (4KB)	*logbufsz*
• Log file size (4KB)	*logfilsiz*
• Number of primary log files	*logprimary*
• Number of secondary log files	*logsecond*
• Path to log files	*logpath*
• Overflow log path	*overflowlogpath*
• Mirror log path	*mirrorlogpath*
• Block log on disk full	*blk_log_dsk_ful*
• Percent max primary log space by transaction	*max_log*
• Num. of active log files for 1 active UOW	*num_log_span*
• First log archive method	*logarchmeth1*
• Options for logarchmeth1	*logarchopt1*
• Second log archive method	*logarchmeth2*
• Options for logarchmeth2	*logarchopt2*
• Failover log archive path	*failarchpath*
• Number of log archive retries on error	*numarchretry*
• Log archive retry Delay (secs)	*archretrydelay*

Question 3

The correct answers are **B** and **D**. To enable log file mirroring, you simply assign the fully qualified name of the mirror log location (path) to the *mirrorlogpath* database configuration parameter. Alternately, on UNIX systems, you can assign the value 1 to the DB2_NEWLOGPATH registry variable—in this case, the name of the mirror log location is generated by appending the character "2" to the current value of the *logpath* database configuration parameter. Ideally, the mirror log path used should refer a physical location (disk) that does not see a large amount of disk I/O and that is separate from the physical location used to store primary log files.

Question 4

The correct answer is **A**. When a DB2 9 database is configured to support roll-forward recovery, DB2 can call a special program, known as a user exit program, to move archived log files from the active log directory/device to a specific storage location when they are no longer needed to support transaction logging. So just what is a user exit program? Essentially, a user exit program is a user-supplied application that is invoked by DB2 whenever an open log file is closed, a database is closed (i.e., all connections to the database are terminated), or the ROLLFORWARD DATABASE command/API is executed (to perform a roll-forward recovery operation on a DB2 9 database).

Once the source code file for a user exit program has been compiled and linked to produce an executable program, two actions must be performed before it can actually be used: the executable form of the user exit program must be copied to a specific location and the *logarcmeth1* or *logarcmeth2* database configuration parameter for the appropriate database(s) must be assigned the value USEREXIT.

It is important to note that IBM is recommending users move away from user exit programs. An easier method for moving log files from the active log directory to an archive log storage location is to assign the value DISK:, followed by the desired location path to the *logarchmeth1* or *logarcmeth2* database configuration parameter.

Question 5

The correct answer is **C**. The *max_log* configuration parameter is used to control the maximum percentage of the total active log space available that any one transaction can consume. This configuration parameter prevents transactions from consuming all of the available active log space, thereby preventing other applications from running. By default, if a running transaction exceeds this threshold, the offending transaction is rolled back and the application that the transaction is running under will be forced to terminate. (This behavior can be overridden by setting the DB2_FORCE_APP_ON_MAX_LOG registry variable to FALSE; if this registry variable is set to FALSE, only work performed by the current statement will be rolled back—the application can still commit the work completed by previous statements in the transaction, or it can roll back the work completed to undo the effects of the transaction.)

The *num_log_span* configuration parameter is used to set a limit on the number of log files any single running transaction can span. When a transaction is started, a record is written to the current active log file and as DB2 processes the transaction (as well as other transactions) log files are filled and closed. If the number of log files filled exceeds the limit established before the transaction is committed or rolled back, then by default the transaction is rolled back and the application the transaction was running under will be terminated. This behavior can also be overridden by setting the DB2_FORCE_APP_ON_MAX_ LOG registry variable to FALSE.

Question 6

The correct answer is **D**. The DB2 Check Backup utility can be used to test the integrity of a backup image, or multiple parts of a backup image, and to determine whether or not the image can be used to restore a damaged or corrupted database. It can also be used to display the metadata stored in the backup header (such as log path used, instance name, type of backup image, etc.).

The DB2 Check Backup utility is invoked by executing the db2ckbkp command. The syntax for this command is:

```
db2ckbkp
[ <-a>
  <-c>
  <-d>
  <-e>
  <-h>
  <-l>
  <-n>
  <-o>
  <-p>
  <-s>
  <-t>
  <-cl [DecompressLib]>
  <-co [DecompressOpts]> ,... ]
[FileName ,...]
```

   or

```
db2ckbkp -H [FileName ,...]
```

or

```
db2ckbkp -S [FileName ,...]
```

or

```
db2ckbkp -T [FileName ,...]
```

where:

DecompressLib   Specifies the library, by name, that is to be used to decompress the backup image. (If this parameter is not specified, DB2 will attempt to use the library stored in the image. If the backup image was not compressed, the value of this parameter will be ignored; if the backup image was compressed and the specified library cannot be loaded, the operation will fail.)

DecompressOpts   Describes a block of binary data that will be passed to the initialization routine in the decompression library. DB2 will pass this string directly from the client to the server, so any issues of byte reversal or code page conversion will have to be handled by the decompression library. If the first character of the data block is '@', the remainder of the data will be interpreted by DB2 as the name of a file residing on the server. DB2 will then replace the contents of the string with the contents of that file and will pass this new value to the initialization routine instead.

FileName   Identifies, by name, one or more backup image files that are to be analyzed. When checking multiple parts of a backup image, the first backup image object (.001) must be specified first.

All other options shown with this command are described in Table 4.1.

Table 4.1 db2ckbkp Command Options	
Option	**Meaning**
-a	Specifies that all information available about the backup image is to be collected and displayed.
-c	Specifies that checkbit and checksum information is to be collected and displayed.
-d	Specifies that information stored in the headers of DMS table space data pages is to be collected and displayed.
-e	Specifies that pages are to be extracted from the backup image and written to a file. To extract pages, you need an input file and an output file. The default input file is called extractPage.in and the default output file is called extractPage.out. You can override the default input file name using the DB2LISTFILE environment variable; you can override the default output file name using the DB2EXTRACTFILE environment variable.

	Table 4.1 db2ckbkp Command Options (Continued)	
Option	**Meaning**	
-h	Specifies that media header information, including the name and path of the backup image, is to be collected and displayed.	
-l	Specifies that log file header (LFH) and mirror log file header (MFH) information is to be collected and displayed.	
-n	Indicates that the user is to be prompted whenever a tape needs to be mounted. (Assumes one tape per device.)	
-o	Specifies that object header information is to be collected and displayed.	
-p	Specifies that information about the number of pages of each object type found in the backup image is to be collected and displayed. This option will not show the number of pages for all different object types if the backup was done for DMS table space data—instead, it will show the total of all pages; LOB data pages and long data pages will not be returned.	
-s	Specifies that information about the automatic storage paths used is to be collected and displayed.	
-t	Displays table space details, including container information, for all table spaces in the backup image.	
-H	Specifies that only the 4K media header information stored at the beginning of the backup image is to be collected and displayed; does not validate the image. This option cannot be used in combination with any other options.	
-S	Specifies that information about the automatic storage paths used is to be collected and displayed; does not validate the image. This option cannot be used in combination with any other options.	
-T	Displays table space details, including container information, for all table spaces in the backup image; does not validate the image. This option cannot be used in combination with any other options.	

Thus, if you wanted to display only the media header information for an existing backup image named TEST.0.DB2.NODE0000.CATN0000.20081215130904.001, you could do so by executing a db2ckbkp command that looks something like this:

```
db2ckbkp -H TEST.0.DB2.NODE0000.CATN0000.20081215130904.001
```

(The –h option tells the tool to display header information along with other information; the –H options tells the tool to display ONLY header information.)

Question 7

The correct answer is **C**. A backup image of a DB2 database, or a table space within a DB2 database, can be created by executing the BACKUP DATABASE command. The basic syntax for this command is:

```
BACKUP [DATABASE | DB] [DatabaseAlias]
<USER [UserName] <USING [Password]>>
<TABLESPACE ([TS_Name],...)
<ONLINE>
<INCREMENTAL <DELTA>>
<TO [Location] |
    USE TSM <OPTIONS [TSMOptions]>
    <OPEN [NumSessions] SESSIONS>>
<WITH [NumBuffers] BUFFERS>
<BUFFER [BufferSize]>
<PARALLELISM [ParallelNum]>
<UTIL_IMPACT_PRIORITY [Priority]>
<EXCLUDE LOGS | INCLUDE LOGS>
<WITHOUT PROMPTING>
```

where:

DatabaseAlias Identifies the alias assigned to the database for which a backup image is to be created.

UserName Identifies the name assigned to a specific user under whose authority the backup operation is to be performed.

Password Identifies the password that corresponds to the name of the user under whom the backup operation is to be performed.

TS_Name Identifies the name assigned to one or more specific table spaces for which backup images are to be created.

Location Identifies the directory or device where the backup image created is to be stored.

TSMOptions Identifies options that are to be used by Tivoli Storage Manager (TSM) during the backup operation.

NumSessions Specifies the number of I/O sessions to be created between DB2 and TSM. (This parameter has no effect when backing up to tape, disk, or another local device.)

NumBuffers Identifies the number of buffers that are to be used to perform the backup operation. (By default, two buffers are used if this option is not specified.)

BufferSize Identifies the size, in pages, that each buffer used to perform the backup operation will be. (By default, the size of each buffer used by the Backup utility is determined by the value of the backbufsz DB2 Database Manager configuration parameter.)

ParallelNum Identifies the number of table spaces that can be read in parallel during the backup operation.

Priority   Indicates that the Backup utility is to be throttled such that it executes at a specific rate so that its effect on concurrent database activity can be controlled. This parameter can be assigned a numerical value within the range of 1 to 100, with 100 representing the highest priority and 1 representing the lowest.

Thus, if you wanted to backup a database named ACCOUNTING to a TSM server, using four concurrent TSM client sessions and eight buffers, you could do so by executing a BACKUP DATABASE command that looks something like this:

```
BACKUP DATABASE accounting
USER db2admin USING ibmdb2
USE TSM OPEN 4 SESSIONS WITH 8 BUFFERS
```

Question 8

The correct answer is **C**. If you wanted to determine whether or not an existing backup image for a database named TEST was created using the INCLUDE LOGS option of the BACKUP DATABASE command, you could do so by executing a db2ckbkp command that looks something like this (assuming the name of the backup image created is TEST.0.DB2. NODE0000.CATN0000.20081215131853.001):

```
db2ckbkp -h TEST.0.DB2.NODE0000.CATN0000.20081215131853.001
```

The results produced should look something like this:

```
======================
MEDIA HEADER REACHED:
======================
          Server Database Name           -- TEST
          Server Database Alias          -- TEST
          Client Database Alias          -- TEST
          Timestamp                      -- 20081215131853
          Database Partition Number      -- 0
          Instance                       -- DB2
          Sequence Number                -- 1
          Release ID                     -- B00
          Database Seed                  -- 4773F9E6
          DB Comment's Codepage (Volume) -- 2020
          DB Comment (Volume)            --
          DB Comment's Codepage (System) -- 2020
          DB Comment (System)            --
          Authentication Value           -- 32
          Backup Mode                    -- 0
          Includes Logs                  -- 0
          Compression                    -- 1
          Backup Type                    -- 0
```

```
          Backup Gran.                 -- 0
          Status Flags                 -- 1
          System Cats inc              -- 1
          Catalog Partition Number     -- 0
          DB Codeset                   -- IBM-1252
          DB Territory                 --
          LogID                        -- 1197742728
          LogPath                      -- C:\LOGS\NODE0000\
          Backup Buffer Size           -- 16777216
          Number of Sessions           -- 1
          Platform                     -- 5

      The proper image file name would be:
          TEST.0.DB2.NODE0000.CATN0000.20081215131853.001

      [1] Buffers processed:  ####

      Image Verification Complete - successful.
```

(In this case, because the "Include Logs" attribute is set to 0, the INCLUDE LOGS option of the BACKUP DATABASE command was NOT specified when the backup image was created.)

The LIST HISTORY command will tell you what type of backup image was created (F = Offline, N = Online, I = Incremental offline, O = Incremental online, D = Delta offline, E = Delta online, R = Rebuild), when the backup image was created, where the backup image was stored, and the earliest log and current log files used. However, it will not tell you if the log files were included in the backup image.

Question 9

The correct answer is **B**. In a partitioned database environment, database partitions are backed up (and restored) individually—backup operations are local to the database partition server upon which the Backup utility is invoked. However, by using the db2_all command, you can create backup images for multiple partitions (which you identify by node number) from a single database partition server. (The LIST NODES command can be used to identify the nodes, or database partition servers, that have user tables on them.) For example, if you wanted to create a set of online incremental backup images for every partition on which a database named SAMPLE is stored, you could do so by executing a db2_all command that looks something like this:

```
    db2_all "db2 BACKUP DATABASE sample ONLINE INCREMENTAL"
```

In this example, the BACKUP DATABASE command was executed on every partition. However, there may be times when you only want to perform a backup or recovery operation on one or more specific database partitions. Because of this, the db2_all command has two prefix sequences that can be used to limit the execution of specified operations to individual database partition servers. These prefix sequences are:

- <<-*nnn*<

   The operation is to be performed on all database partition servers identified in the db2nodes.cfg file except the database partition server whose node number is *nnn*.

- <<+*nnn*<

   The operation is only to be performed on the database partition server in the db2nodes.cfg file whose database partition number is *nnn*.

When using the <<-*nnn*< and <<+*nnn*< prefix sequences, nnn can be any 1-, 2-, or 3-digit database partition number; however, the number specified must have a matching nodenum value in the db2nodes.cfg file.

Thus, if you wanted to perform an online table space-level backup of the table space USERSPACE1 (which is the default table space used to hold user tables) for a database named SALES that resides on partition number 5, you could do so by executing a db2_all command that looks something like this:

```
db2_all "<<+5< db2 BACKUP DATABASE sample
    TABLESPACE (userspace1) ONLINE TO /backup_dir".
```

Question 10

The correct answer is **B**. When incremental (cumulative) backup images are taken, database recovery involves restoring the database using the most recent full backup image available and applying the most recent incremental backup image produced. On the other hand, when incremental delta backup images are taken, database recovery involves restoring the database using the most recent full backup image available and applying each delta backup image produced since the full backup image used was made, in the order in which they were created.

Question 11

The correct answer is **C**. No special authority is required to run the DB2 Check Backup (db2ckbkp) utility, however, in order to use this utility, you must have read permission on the backup image files that are to be analyzed.

Question 12

The correct answer is **D**. When the RESTORE DATABASE command is executed, if the INCREMENTAL option is specified without additional parameters, a manual cumulative restore operation will be initiated—during a manual cumulative restore, the RESTORE DATABASE command must be executed for each backup image needed to restore the database. During such a recovery operation backup images must be restored in the following order: last full backup, last incremental, first delta, second delta, third delta, and so on up to and including the last delta backup image made.

If the INCREMENTAL AUTO or the INCREMENTAL AUTOMATIC option is specified, an automatic cumulative restore operation will be initiated and no user intervention will be required to apply incremental and delta restores.

Question 13

The correct answer is **D**. When invalid table space containers are encountered, they can be redefined at the beginning of the recovery process by performing what is known as a *redirected restore*. (A redirected restore operation can also be used to restore a backup image to a target machine that is different than the source machine, or to store table space data into a different physical location.)

The steps used to perform a redirected restore operation are as follows:

1. Start the redirected restore operation by executing the RESTORE DATABASE command with the REDIRECT option specified. (When this option is specified, each invalid table space container encountered is flagged, and all table spaces that reference invalid table space containers are placed in the "Restore Pending" state. A list of all table spaces affected can be obtained by executing the LIST TABLESPACES command.) At some point, you should see a message that looks something like this:

   ```
   SQL1277N Restore has detected that one or more table space
   containers are inaccessible, or has set their state to 'storage must
   be defined'.
   DB20000I The RESTORE DATABASE command completed successfully.
   ```

2. Specify new table space containers for each table space placed in "Restore Pending" state by executing a SET TABLESPACE CONTAINERS command for each appropriate table space. (Keep in mind that SMS table spaces can only use PATH containers, while DMS table spaces can only use FILE or DEVICE containers.)

3. Complete the redirected restore operation by executing the RESTORE DATABASE command again with the CONTINUE option specified.

To simplify things, all of these steps can be coded in a UNIX shell script or Windows batch file, which can then be executed from a system prompt. Such a file would look something like this:

```
db2 "RESTORE DATABASE sample FROM C:\backups TO D:\DB_DIR INTO sample_2
REDIRECT"

db2 "SET TABLESPACE CONTAINERS FOR 0 USING
(PATH 'D:\DB_DIR\SYSTEM')"

db2 "SET TABLESPACE CONTAINERS FOR 1 USING
(PATH 'D:\DB_DIR\TEMP')"

db2 "SET TABLESPACE CONTAINERS FOR 2 USING
(PATH 'D:\DB_DIR\USER')"

db2 "RESTORE DATABASE sample CONTINUE"
```

Question 14

The correct answer is **C**. The RESTORE DATABASE command can be used to create an entirely new database from a full database backup image, effectively cloning an existing database. For example, you could create a new database named PAYROLL2 that is an exact duplicate of a database named PAYROLL, using a backup image stored in a directory named BACKUPS by executing a RESTORE DATABASE command that looks something like this:

```
RESTORE DATABASE payroll
FROM /backups
INTO payroll2
```

If the PAYROLL database was created using automatic storage, the restore operation will maintain the storage path definitions used. So simply restoring the database will not alter the storage paths used; if you want to change the storage path definitions, you must do so explicitly when restoring the database.

(The RECOVER DATABASE command cannot be used to create an entirely new database.)

Question 15

The correct answer is **B**. The basic syntax for the RECOVER DATABASE command is:

```
RECOVER [DATABASE | DB] [DatabaseAlias]
<TO [PointInTime] <USING [UTC | LOCAL] TIME>>
<ON ALL DBPARTITIONNUMS>
<USER [UserName] <USING [Password]>>
<USING HISTORY FILE ([HistoryFile])>
<OVERFLOW LOG PATH ([LogDirectory] ,...)>
<RESTART>
```

or

```
RECOVER [DATABASE | DB] [DatabaseAlias]
<TO END OF LOGS
    <ON ALL DBPARTITIONNUMS |
     ON DBPARTITIONNUM<S> ([PartitionNum],...)>>
<USER [UserName] <USING [Password]>>
<USING HISTORY FILE ([HistoryFile])>
<OVERFLOW LOG PATH ([LogDirectory] ,...)>
<RESTART>
```

where:

DatabaseAlias   Identifies the alias assigned to the database associated with the backup image that is to be used to perform a version recovery operation.

PointInTime   Identifies a specific point in time, identified by a timestamp value in the form *yyyy-mm-dd-hh.mm.ss.nnnnnn* (year, month, day, hour, minutes, seconds, microseconds), to which the database is to be rolled forward. (Only transactions that took place before and up to the date and time specified will be reapplied to the database.)

PartitionNum   Identifies, by number, one or more database partitions (identified in the db2nodes.cfg file) that transactions are to be rolled forward on. In a partitioned database environment, the Recover utility must be invoked from the catalog partition of the database.

UserName   Identifies the name assigned to a specific user under whom the recovery operation is to be performed.

Password   Identifies the password that corresponds to the name of the user under whom the recovery operation is to be performed.

HistoryFile   Identifies the name assigned to the recovery history log file that is to be used by the Recovery utility.

LogDirectory   Identifies the directory that contains offline archived log files that are to be used to perform the roll-forward portion of the recovery operation.

If the RESTART option is specified, any previous recover operations are ignored; the RESTART option forces the Recover utility to execute a fresh restore operation and then roll the database forward to the point in time specified.

It the Recover utility successfully restores a database, but for some reason fails while attempting to roll it forward, the Recover utility will attempt to continue the previous recover operation without redoing the restore phase. If you want to force the Recover utility to redo the restore phase, you need to execute the RECOVER DATABASE command with the RESTART option specified. There is no way to explicitly restart a recovery operation from a point of failure.

Question 16

The correct answer is **B**. Both the primary and the standby database must be a single-partition database and they both must have the same database name; however, they do not have to be stored on the same database path.

IBM recommends that you use identical host computers for the HADR primary and standby databases. (If possible, they should be from the same vendor and have the same architecture.) Furthermore, the operating system on the primary and standby database servers should be the same version, including patch level. You can violate this rule for a short time during a rolling upgrade, but use extreme caution when doing so. A TCP/IP interface must also be available between the HADR host machines, and a high-speed, high-capacity network should be used to connect the two.

The DB2 software installed on both the primary and the standby database server must have the same bit size (32 or 64) and the version of DB2 used for the primary and standby databases must be identical; for example, both must be either version 8 or version 9. During rolling upgrades, the modification level (for example, the fix pack level) of the database system for the standby database can be later than that of the primary database for a short while. However, you should not keep this configuration for an extended period of time. The primary and standby databases will not connect to each other if the modification level of the database system for the primary database is later than that of the standby database. Therefore, fix packs must always be applied to the standby database system first.

The amount of storage space allocated for transaction log files should also be the same on both the primary and the standby database server; the use of raw devices for transaction logging is not supported. (Archival logging is only performed by the current primary database.) Table space properties such as table space name, table space type (DMS, SMS, or Automatic Storage), table space page size, table space size, container path, container size, and container type (raw device, file, or directory) must be identical on the primary and standby databases. When you issue a table space statement such as CREATE TABLESPACE, ALTER TABLESPACE, or DROP TABLESPACE on the primary database, it is replayed on the standby database. Therefore, you must ensure that the table space containers involved such statements exist on both systems before you issue the table space statement on the primary database. (If you create a table space on the primary database and log replay fails on the standby database because the containers are not available, the primary database does not receive an error message stating that the log replay failed.) Automatic storage databases are fully supported, including replication of ALTER DATABASE statements. Similar to table space containers, the storage paths specified must exist on both the primary and the standby server.

Question 17

The correct answer is **C**. Once an HADR environment has been established, the following operations will be replicated automatically in the standby database whenever they are performed on the primary database:

- Execution of Data Definition Language (DDL) statements (CREATE, ALTER, DROP)

- Execution of Data Manipulation Language (DML) statements (INSERT, UPDATE, DELETE)

- Buffer pool operations

- Table space operations (as well as storage-related operations performed on automatic storage databases)

- Online reorganization

- Offline reorganization

- Changes to metadata (system catalog information) for stored procedures and user-defined functions (UDFs)

HADR does not replicate stored procedure and UDF object and library files. If this type of replication is needed, you must physically create the files on identical paths on both the primary and standby databases. (If the standby database cannot find the referenced object or library file, the stored procedure or UDF invocation will fail on the standby database.)

Additionally, non-logged operations, such as changes to database configuration parameters and to the recovery history file, are not replicated to the standby database.

Question 18

The correct answer is **A**. The *hadr_syncmode* database configuration parameter is used to specify the synchronization mode to use for HADR. The value assigned to this parameter determines how primary log writes are synchronized with the standby database when the systems are in peer state. Valid values for this configuration parameter are:

- **SYNC (Synchronous)** This mode provides the greatest protection against transaction loss, and using it results in the longest transaction response time among the three modes. In this mode, log writes are considered successful only when log records have been written to log files on the primary database and when the primary database has received acknowledgement from the standby database that the log records have also been written to log files on the standby database. The log data is guaranteed to be stored at both sites.

- **NEARSYNC (Near Synchronous)** Although this mode has a shorter transaction response time than synchronous mode, it also provides slightly less protection against transaction loss. In this mode, log writes are considered successful only when log records have been written to the log files on the primary database and when the primary database has received acknowledgement from the standby system that the log records have also been written to main memory on the standby system. Loss of data occurs only if both sites fail simultaneously and if the target site has not transferred all of the log data that it has received to nonvolatile storage.

- **ASYNC (Asynchronous)** This mode has the highest chance of transaction loss if the primary system fails. It also has the shortest transaction response time among the three modes. In this mode, log writes are considered successful only when log records have been written to the log files on the primary database and have been delivered to the TCP layer of the primary system's host machine. Because the primary system does not wait for acknowledgement from the standby system, transactions might be considered committed when they are still on their way to the standby system.

Question 19

The correct answers are **B** and **E**. The *hadr_timeout* database configuration parameter is used to specify the time (in seconds) that the HADR process waits before considering a communication attempt to have failed. Therefore, when the *hadr_timeout* database configuration parameter on the primary server is set to 30, if the primary server does not receive acknowledgement of a log buffer write within 30 seconds it assumes there was a communications error and drops out of peer mode.

The value assigned to the *hadr_timeout* database parameter must be the same for both the primary and the standby database.

Question 20

The correct answer is **C**. Automatic Client Reroute is a DB2 feature that allows client applications to recover from a loss of communication with the server so that the application can continue its work with minimal interruption. (If automatic client reroute is not enabled, client applications will receive an error message indicating that a connect attempt has failed due to a timeout and no further attempts will be made to establish a connection with the server.) However, rerouting is only possible when an alternate database location has been specified at the server and the TCP/IP protocol is used.

The automatic client reroute feature can be used with HADR to make client applications connect to the new primary database immediately after a takeover operation. In fact, if you set up HADR using the Set Up High Availability Disaster Recovery (HADR) Databases

Wizard, automatic client reroute is enabled by default. If you set up HADR manually, you can enable the automatic client reroute feature by executing the UPDATE ALTERNATE SERVER FOR DATABASE command; automatic client reroute does not use the values stored in the *hadr_remote_host* and *hadr_remote_svc* database configuration parameters.

For example, suppose you have cataloged a database named SALES on a client workstation as being located at host named SVR1. Database SALES is the primary database in an HADR environment and its corresponding standby database, also named SALES, resides on a host named SVR2 and listens on port number 456. To enable automatic client reroute, you simply specify an alternate server for the SALES database stored on host SVR1 by executing the following command:

```
UPDATE ALTERNATE SERVER FOR DATABASE sales
USING HOSTNAME svr2 PORT 456
```

Once this command is executed, the client must connect to host SVR1 to obtain the alternate server information. Then, if a communication error occurs between the client and the SALES database at host SVR1, the client will first attempt to reconnect to the SALES database on host SVR1. If this fails, the client will then attempt to establish a connection with the standby SALES database located on host SVR2.

Question 21

The correct answers are **B** and **C**. if you wanted to obtain a list of applications that are currently connected to a database named PAYROLL, you could do so by executing the LIST APPLICATIONS command from the DB2 Command Line Processor, or by executing a db2pd command that looks something like this:

```
db2pd -applications -db payroll
```

You could obtain information about connected applications using the DB2 snapshot monitor, but the query used to do so would look like this:

```
SELECT * FROM TABLE(SNAP_GET_APPL('payroll',-1)) AS applications
```

It is important to note that if the DB2 server is not responding and appears to be hung, the ONLY way to obtain a list of applications that are currently connected to the database is by using the db2pd utility.

Question 22

The correct answer is **D**. The DB2 memory tracker utility is used to produce a complete report of memory status for instances, databases, and agents. This utility provides the following information about memory pool allocation:

- Current size

- Maximum size (hard limit)

- Largest size (high water mark)

- Type (identifier indicating function for which memory will be used)

- Agent who allocated pool (only if the pool is private)

(This information is also available from the snapshot monitor.)

The DB2 memory tracker is invoked by executing the db2mtrk command. The syntax for this command is:

```
db2mtrk
<-i>
<-d>
<-p
<-m | -w>
<-r [Interval] <Count>>
<-v>
<-h>
```

where:

Interval Identifies the number of seconds to wait between subsequent calls to the DB2 memory tracker.

Count Identifies the number of times to repeat calls to the DB2 memory tracker.

All other options shown with this command are described in Table 4.2.

Table 4.2 db2mtrk Command Options	
Option	**Meaning**
-i	Specifies that information about instance level memory is to be collected and displayed.
-d	Specifies that information about database level memory is to be collected and displayed.
-p	Specifies that information about private memory is to be collected and displayed.
-m	Specifies that maximum values for each memory pool is to be collected and displayed.
-w	Specifies that high water mark values for each memory pool are to be collected and displayed.
-v	Indicates that verbose output is to be returned.
-h	Displays help information. When this option is specified, all other options are ignored, and only the help information is displayed.

Thus, if you wanted to see how memory is utilized by the active databases on a system, and you wanted to capture and view this information ten times, updating it every five minutes, you could do so by executing a db2mtrk command that looks something like this:

```
db2mtrk -d -r 300 10
```

(The –d option tells db2mtrk to collect and display information for all databases; the –r 300 10 option tells db2mtrk to collect the information every 300 seconds – which is 5 minutes – a total of 10 times.)

Question 23

The correct answer is **A**. If you wanted to see how memory is utilized by the active databases on a system, you could do so by executing a db2mtrk command that looks something like this:

```
db2mtrk -d
```

Assuming a database named SAMPLE is active at the time the db2mtrk command is issued, the results produced should look something like this:

```
Tracking Memory on: 2008/05/21 at 14:00:38

Memory for database: SAMPLE

    utilh      pckcacheh  catcacheh  bph (1)    bph (S32K)  bph (S16K)  bph (S8K)
    64.0K      128.0K     64.0K      1.2M       704.0K      448.0K      320.0K

    bph (S4K)  shsorth    lockh      dbh        other
    256.0K     0          320.0K     4.3M       128.0K
```

Question 24

The correct answer is **D**. Because table space TBSP1 has 160 useable pages and 156 of them have already been used, there are only 4 free pages remaining. Therefore, table space TBSP1 is about to run out of storage space.

Table space SYSCATSPACE is a resizable DMS table space, however, it has NOT been resized yet; table space IBMDB2SAMPLEREL is an autoresizing DMS table space; and the state of table space USERSPACE1 is "Normal" – not "Roll-forward pending".

CHAPTER 5

Performance and Scalability

Thirty-three percent (33%) of the DB2 9 for Linux, UNIX, and Windows Advanced Database Administration exam (Exam 734) is designed to test your ability to tune a database for optimal performance by modifying registry variables and configuration parameters, creating the right indexes, and generating and analyzing data access plans. The questions that make up this portion of the exam are intended to evaluate the following:

- Your ability to identify and set DB2 registry variables that can affect database system performance

- Your ability to identify and set configuration parameters that can affect instance and database performance

- Your ability to manage and tune instance, database, and application memory usage and I/0

- Your ability to use DB2's self-tuning memory manager

- Your ability to manage a large number of users and connections

- Your knowledge of query optimizer concepts

- Your ability to analyze and influence the optimizer's selection of data access plans

- Your ability to exploit parallelism

- Your ability to create appropriate indexes

- Your ability to analyze performance problems

- Your ability to use deep compression

This chapter is designed to provide you with an inside-out look at performance tuning, starting with an overview of the DB2 registry variables and configuration parameters that have the greatest impact on performance, followed by an in-depth look at using the self-tuning memory manager, taking advantage of parallelism, creating appropriate indexes, controlling locking at the application level, and taking control of a server. This chapter will also show you how the DB2 optimizer works, how to analyze data access plans created by the optimizer, and how to take advantage of deep compression.

Basic Performance Tuning

DB2 9 runs in environments that range from simple standalone systems to complex client-server environments running a wide variety of applications. And, regardless of which environment is used, one of the most important aspects from a user's point of view is how well (or how poorly) database applications perform. But, just what is "performance," and how do you know if it is good or bad? And if it is bad, what can be done to improve it?

In its simplest terms, performance is the way a computer system behaves while it is executing a given task. Performance is typically measured in terms of system response time, throughput, and/or availability. Each of these metrics can be affected by several factors, including the following:

- Type of hardware being used

- System (server and storage) used

- Database and Operating System configuration

- Type of and number of users working concurrently

- Workload performed by each user's application

After you have decided that a system is performing poorly, there are usually several things you can do to tune it. However, because a wide variety of tuning options are available, tuning should always be done in an organized, concise manner with a specific goal in mind. To be successful, the goal must be realistic, quantitative, and measurable; otherwise, performance tuning becomes a hit-or-miss exercise. The following performance-tuning guidelines can help you get started:

1. Check for known hardware and software problems.

   Some performance problems can be corrected simply by applying service packs to your software, upgrading your hardware, or both. Why spend the time and effort monitoring and tuning other parts of your system when a simple service might resolve the problem? With that said, make sure you understand the problem before you upgrade your hardware. If you decide to add another network interface card (NIC) only to discover the system needs more memory, you have just made a costly mistake that did nothing to improve performance.

2. Consider the whole system.

   Usually, tuning one aspect of a system affects at least one other part of that system. Before you make changes, consider how those changes might affect the system as a whole.

3. Measure and reconfigure by levels.

   Never tune more than one level of your system at a time. Even if you are sure that all the changes you plan to make are beneficial, you have no way to evaluate how much each change contributes to any performance improvements that you might see. However, if you are wrong and performance goes down instead of up, you have no way of determining which change had the negative effect. In a database server environment, the following system levels should be evaluated:

   - Hardware
   - Operating system
   - Communications software
   - Database

- SQL statements

- Applications

4. Change one thing at a time.

For the same reasons that you should tune only one system level at a time, you must change only one thing at a time as you tune each system level. This is one of the most important things for you to take away from this chapter. If you change three things, two of them could improve your performance, whereas the third could reduce performance significantly. The result would be that you would think that the three things you changed caused poor performance.

5. Put tracking and fallback procedures in place before you start.

Unfortunately, performance tuning is not an exact science, and some changes that you make are likely to have a negative effect on performance. When such a situation occurs, you can avoid spending time trying to get the system back to an earlier state if you have a way to back out of every change made. Likewise, if you are forced to back out several changes, be prepared to reapply every change made.

6. Do not tune just for the sake of tuning.

Tune your system only when you are trying to resolve an existing or impending problem. If you tune resources that are not directly related to the primary cause of the problem that you are trying to solve, the tuning will have no noticeable effect until the primary problem itself has been resolved. And in some cases, such actions can actually make subsequent tuning much more difficult.

7. Remember the law of diminishing returns.

Keep in mind that the greatest performance tuning gains usually come from your initial efforts. Subsequent tuning usually results in progressively smaller gains and requires progressively greater amounts of work.

Tuning the DB2 System Environment

During normal operation, the behavior of the DB2 instance is controlled, in part, by a collection of values that define the DB2 operating environment. Some of these values are operating system environment variables, and others are special DB2-specific system-level values known as environment or registry variables. Registry variables provide a way to centrally control the database environment. Three different registry profiles are available, and each controls the database environment at a different level. The registry profiles available are as follows:

The DB2 Global-Level Profile Registry. All machine-wide environment variable settings are kept in this registry; one global-level profile registry exists on each DB2 server. If an environment variable is to be set for all instances on the server, this profile registry is used.

The DB2 Instance-Level Profile Registry. The environment variable settings for a particular instance are kept in this registry; this is where the majority of the DB2 environment variables are set. (Values defined in this profile registry override any corresponding settings in the global-level profile registry.)

The DB2 Instance Node-Level Profile Registry. This profile registry level contains variable settings that are specific to a partition (node) in a multi-partitioned database environment. (Values defined in this profile registry override any corresponding settings in the global-level and instance-level profile registries.)

DB2 looks for environment variable values in the DB2 global-level profile registry first, then in the DB2 instance-level profile registry, and finally, in the DB2 instance node–level profile registry. Additional values may be set in individual sessions, in which case DB2 will consider these values last.

A wide variety of registry variables are available, and they vary depending on the operating system being used. A complete listing can be found in Appendix B of the *IBM DB2 Version 9 Performance Guide* product documentation.

So how do you determine which registry variables have been set and what their values are? Or more importantly, how do you assign values to one or more registry variables? You can do both by executing the db2set system command. The basic syntax for this command is:

```
db2set
<[Variable] = [Value]>
<-g | -gl | -i [InstanceName]>
<-all>
<-null>
<-r [InstanceName]>
<-n [DASNode] <-u [UserID] <-p [Password]>>>
<-l | -lr>
<-v>
<-ul | -ur>
<-h | -?>
```

where:

Variable	Identifies the registry variable whose value is to be displayed, set, or removed.
Value	Identifies the value that is to be assigned to the registry variable specified. If no value is provided, but a registry variable is specified, the registry variable specified is deleted.
InstanceName	Identifies the instance profile with which the specified registry variable is associated.
DASNode	Identifies the name of the node where the DB2 Administration Server instance resides.
UserID	Identifies the authentication ID that will be used to attach to the DB2 Administration Server instance.
Password	Identifies the password (for the authentication ID) that will be used to attach to the DB2 Administration Server instance.

All other options shown with this command are described in Table 5.1.

Table 5.1 db2set Command options	
Option	**Meaning**
-g	Indicates that a global profile variable is to be displayed, set, or removed.
-gl	Indicates that a global profile variable stored in LDAP is to be displayed, set, or removed. This option is only effective if the registry variable DB2_ENABLE_LDAP has been set to YES.
-i	Indicates that an instance profile variable is to be displayed, set, or removed.
-all	Indicates that all occurrences of the registry variable, as defined in the following, are to be displayed: • The environment (denoted by [e]) • The node-level registry (denoted by [n]) • The instance-level registry (denoted by [i]) • The global-level registry (denoted by [g])
-null	Indicates that the value of the variable at the specified registry level is to be set to NULL.
-r	Indicates that the profile registry for the given instance is to be reset.
-n	Indicates that a remote DB2 Administration Server instance node name is specified.
-u	Indicates that an authentication ID that will be used to attach to the DB2 Administration Server instance is specified.
-p	Indicates that a password for the authentication ID specified is provided.
-l	Indicates that all instance profiles will be listed.
-lr	Indicates that all registry variables supported will be listed.
-v	Indicates that the db2set command is to be executed in verbose mode.
-ul	Accesses the user profile variables. (This parameter is supported only on Windows operating systems.)
-ur	Refreshes the user profile variables. (This parameter is supported only on Windows operating systems.)
-h | -?	Displays help information. When this option is specified, all other options are ignored, and only the help information is displayed.

If the db2set command is executed without options specified, a list containing every registry variable that has been set for the current (default) instance, along with their values, will be returned.

Thus, if you wanted to find out which registry variables have been set for each profile available, you could do so by executing a db2set command that looks like this:

```
db2set -all
```

When this command is executed, the output will look something like:

```
[e] DB2PATH=C:\DB2_ESE\SQLLIB
[i] DB2_ENABLE_AUTOCONFIG_DEFAULT=NO
[i] DB2_XML_RUNSTATS_PATHVALUE_K=300
[i] DB2_XML_RUNSTATS_PATHID_K=300
[i] DB2ACCOUNTNAME=db_server\db2admin
[i] DB2INSTOWNER=db_server
[i] DB2PORTRANGE=60000:60003
[i] DB2INSTPROF=C:\DB2_ESE\SQLLIB
[i] DB2COMM=TCPIP, NPIPE
[g] DB2_EXTSECURITY=YES
[g] DB2SYSTEM=DB_SERVER
[g] DB2PATH=C:\DB2_ESE\SQLLIB
[g] DB2INSTDEF=DB2
[g] DB2ADMINSERVER=DB2DAS00
```

On the other hand, if you wanted to see the current value of the DB2COMM registry variable for all DB2 instances, you could do so by executing the db2set command that looks something like this:

```
db2set -l DB2COMM
```

And finally, if you wanted to assign a value to the DB2COMM registry variable for all DB2 instances on a server, you could do so by executing a db2set command that looks something like this:

```
db2set -g DB2COMM=[Protocol, ...]
```

where:

Protocol Identifies one or more communications protocols that are to be started when the DB2 instance is started. Any combination of the following values is valid: NPIPE, TCPIP, and SSL.

Thus, if you wanted to set the DB2COMM instance level registry variable such that the DB2 instance would start the TCP/IP communication manager each time any instance is started, you could do so by executing a db2set command that looks like this:

```
db2set -g DB2COMM=TCPIP
```

You can remove the value assigned to any registry variable by providing just the variable name and the equal sign as input to the db2set command. Thus, if you wanted to disable the DB2COMM instance level registry variable for an instance named PAYROLL, you could do so by executing a db2set command that looks like this:

```
db2set -i Payroll DB2COMM=
```

Another way to view and/or change registry variable settings is by using a tool known as the DB2 Registry management tool. The DB2 Registry management tool is activated by selecting the DB2 Registry action from the Configure menu found in the Configuration Assistant. Figure 5–1 shows the Configuration Assistant menu items that must be selected in order to activate the DB2 Registry management tool; Figure 5–2 shows how the main dialog of the DB2 Registry management tool might look after it has been activated.

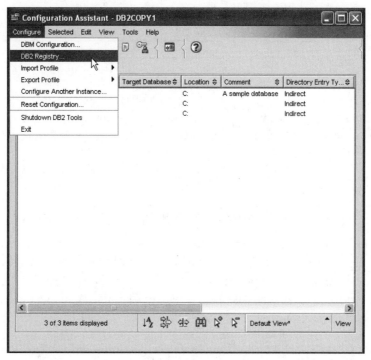

Figure 5–1: Invoking the DB2 Registry management tool from the Configuration Assistant.

Figure 5–2: The DB2 Registry management tool dialog.

 Although registry variables can be set at any time, the DB2 instance must be stopped and restarted before any changes or new settings will take effect.

Registry Variables that Impact Performance

Earlier, it was mentioned that a wide variety of registry variables are available and they vary depending on the operating system being used. Some of these registry variables can have a significant impact on performance, whereas others have little or no impact whatsoever. The DB2 9 registry variables that can have the greatest impact on performance are shown in Table 5.2.

Table 5.2 DB2 registry variables that have the greatest impact on performance		
Parameter	**Value Range / Default**	**Description**
DB2_ALLOCATION_ SIZE	64 KB – 256 MB Default: 128 KB	Specifies the size of memory allocations for buffer pools.
DB2_APM_ PERFORMANCE	ON, OFF Default: OFF	Specifies whether performance-related changes in the access plan manager (APM) that affect the behavior of the SQL cache (package cache) are to be made. Also specifies whether the global SQL cache is to operate without package locks, which are internal system locks that prevent cached package entries from being inadvertently removed. This registry variable should only be set to ON in a nonproduction environment. When set to ON, "Out of package cache" errors are possible and memory usage might increase. Furthermore, operations that invalidate packages, operations that make packages inoperable, and PRECOMPILE, BIND, and REBIND operations cannot be performed.
DB2ASSUMEUPDATE	ON, OFF Default: OFF	Specifies whether the DB2 database system is to assume that all fixed-length columns provided in an UPDATE statement are being changed. When set to ON, the need for the DB2 database system to compare existing column values to new values to determine if the column is actually changing is eliminated.
DB2_AVOID_ PREFETCH	ON, OFF Default: OFF	Specifies whether or not prefetching should be used during crash recovery. When set to ON, prefetching is not used.
DB2BPVARS	Path to file Default: Current path	Specifies the location of a file that contains parameter values that are to be used when tuning buffer pools.

Table 5.2 DB2 registry variables that have the greatest impact on performance (Continued)		
Parameter	**Value Range / Default**	**Description**
		Supported parameters include: NO_NT_SCATTER, NT_SCATTER_ DMSFILE, NT_SCATTER_DMSDEVICE, NT_ SCATTER_SMS, NUMPREFETCHQUEUES, and PREFETCHQUEUESIZE. For each of the _SCATTER parameters, the default value is 0 (or OFF) and the possible values are: 0 (or OFF) and 1 (or ON). For NUMPREFETCHQUEUES, the default value is 1 and the range of values is 1 to NUM_IOSERVERS. And for PREFETCHQUEUESIZE, the default value is whichever is the largest— 100 or 2 * NUM_IOSERVERS—and the range is 1 to 32,767.
		Each _SCATTER parameter is used to turn scatter read on/off for the respective type of table space containers used (or to turn scatter read off for all containers). The remaining parameters can be used to improve buffer pool data prefetching.
		Note: A _SCATTER parameter can only be set to ON if DB2NTNOCACHE is set to ON and the Windows operating system is being used.
DB2CHKPTR	ON, OFF Default: OFF	Specifies whether or not pointer checking for input is required.
DB2CHKSQLDA	ON, OFF Default: ON	Specifies whether or not SQLDA checking for input is required.
DB2_ENABLE_BUFPD	ON, OFF Default: ON	Specifies whether or not the DB2 instance uses intermediate buffering to improve query performance. (Buffering may not improve query performance in all environments—testing should be done to determine individual query performance improvements.)
DB2_ EVALUNCOMMITTED	ON, OFF Default: OFF	Specifies whether, where possible, table or index access scans are to defer or avoid row locking until a data record is known to satisfy predicate evaluation. (Predicate evaluation may occur on uncommitted data.)

Table 5.2 DB2 registry variables that have the greatest impact on performance (Continued)		
Parameter	**Value Range / Default**	**Description**
DB2_EXTENDED_IO_ FEATURES (AIX only)	ON, OFF, ONLINE_BACKUP_ IOPRIORITY=[HIGH | MEDIUM | LOW] Default: OFF	Specifies whether features that enhance I/O performance are enabled. Enhancements include improving the hit rate of memory cache as well as reducing the latency on high priority I/O. These enhancements are only available with certain combinations of software and hardware configurations. The minimum configuration requirements are: • Database version: DB2 V9.1 • RAW device must be used for database containers (container on file systems is not supported) • Operating system: AIX 5.3 TL4 • Storage subsystem: IBM DS8000 or IBM DS6000 If you set this registry variable to ON, you can optionally use the ONLINE_BACKUP_ IOPRIORITY keyword to set the I/O priority for online backups to HIGH, MEDIUM, or LOW.
DB2_EXTENDED_ OPTIMIZATION	ON, OFF, ENHANCED_ MULTIPLE_DISTINCT Default: OFF	Specifies whether the query optimizer will use optimization extensions to improve query performance.
DB2_IO_PRIORITY_ SETTING (AIX only)	HIGH:n, MEDIUM:n, LOW:n, where n is a value between 1 and 15	This variable is used in combination with the DB2_EXTENDED_IO_FEATURES registry variable and provides a means to override the default HIGH, MEDIUM, and LOW I/O priority settings for the DB2 database system, which are 3, 8, and 12, respectively.
DB2_KEEP_AS_AND_ DMS_CONTAINERS_ OPEN	YES, NO Default: NO	Specifies whether each DMS table space container is to have a file handle opened until the database is deactivated. If this parameter is assigned the value YES, query performance might improve because the overhead required to open table space containers is eliminated. You should use this registry only in pure DMS environments, otherwise performance of queries against SMS table spaces might be negatively impacted.

Parameter	Value Range / Default	Description
Table 5.2 DB2 registry variables that have the greatest impact on performance (Continued)		
DB2_KEEPTABLELOCK	ON, OFF, TRANSACTION, CONNECTION Default: OFF	Specifies whether the DB2 database system is to maintain table locks when an Uncommitted Read or Cursor Stability isolation level scan is closed. The table lock that is kept is released at the end of the transaction, just as it would be released for Read Stability and Repeatable Read scans.
DB2_LARGE_PAGE_MEM (64-bit AIX, Linux, & Windows 2003 only)	*, DB, DBMS, FCM, PRIVATE Default: NULL	Specifies whether one or more applicable memory regions should use large page memory.
DB2MAXFSCRSEARCH	-1, 1–33, 554 Default: 5	Specifies the number of free-space control records to search when a record is being added to a table so that you can balance insert speed with space reuse. Use small values to optimize for insert speed; use large values to optimize for space reuse. If this registry variable is set to -1, the DB2 instance searches all free-space control records.
DB2_MAX_INACT_STMTS	up to 4 GB Default: Not set	Overrides the default limit on the number of inactive statements kept by any one application.
DB2_MAX_NON_TABLE_LOCKS	Maximum number of tables expected to be accessed by any connection Default: YES	Specifies the maximum number of NON table locks a transaction can have before it releases all of these locks. NON table locks are table locks that are kept in the hash table and transaction chain even when the transaction has finished using them. Because transactions often access the same table more than once, retaining locks and changing their state to NON can improve performance.
DB2_MDC_ROLLOUT	IMMEDIATE, OFF, DEFER Default: IMMEDIATE	Specifies whether a performance enhancement known as "roll out" for deletions from MDC tables is enabled. Roll out is a faster way of deleting rows in an MDC table, when entire cells (intersections of dimension values) are deleted in a search DELETE statement. The benefits are reduced logging and more efficient processing.

Parameter	Value Range / Default	Description
Table 5.2 DB2 registry variables that have the greatest impact on performance (Continued)		
		Valid values for this parameter are: OFF—no rollout; IMMEDIATE—immediate rollout; and DEFER—rollout with deferred index cleanup.
DB2MEMDISCLAIM (AIX only)	YES, NO Default: YES	Specifies whether the AIX operating system is to stop paging memory so that it no longer occupies any real storage. Setting DB2MEMDISCLAIM to YES tells DB2 to disclaim some or all memory after it is freed, depending on the value specified with the DB2MEMMAXFREE registry variable. If DB2MEMMAXFREE is null, then all of the memory is disclaimed after it is freed. If DB2MEMMAXFREE is given a value, then only some of the memory is disclaimed (up to the value given in DB2MEMMAXFREE). This ensures that the memory is made readily available for other processes as soon as it is freed.
DB2MEMMAXFREE	0–2.0e+32 bytes Default: 8,388,608 bytes	Specifies the amount of free memory that each DB2 agent retains.
DB2_MEM_TUNING_ RANGE	A sequence of percentages—[Minfree, Maxfree] Default: NULL	Specifies the amount of physical memory left free by a given instance (and its active databases) when self tuning of database shared memory is enabled. It is recommended to set this variable only when using the self-tuning memory manager (STMM) and the *database_ memory* database configuration parameter is set to AUTOMATIC, or insufficient system memory problems are occurring.
DB2_MMAP_READ (AIX only)	ON, OFF Default: OFF	Used with DB2_MMAP_WRITE so that DB2 can use mmap as an alternate method of I/O. In most environments, MMAP is used to avoid operating system locks when multiple processes are reading from different sections of the same file.
DB2_MMAP_WRITE (AIX only)	ON, OFF Default: ON	Used with DB2_MMAP_READ so that DB2 can use mmap as an alternate method of I/O. In most environments, MMAP is used to avoid operating system locks when multiple processes are writing to different sections of the same file.

Table 5.2 DB2 registry variables that have the greatest impact on performance (Continued)		
Parameter	**Value Range / Default**	**Description**
		When these variables are set to ON, data that is read to and written from the DB2 buffer pools bypasses the AIX memory cache.
DB2_NO_FORK_CHECK (UNIX only)	ON, OFF Default: OFF	Specifies whether the DB2 runtime client minimizes checks to determine if the current process is a result of a fork call. This can improve performance of DB2 applications that do not use the fork() API.
DB2_NO_MPFA_FOR_NEW_DB	YES Default: Not set	Specifies whether databases created with the CREATE DATABASE command or the equivalent API have multipage file allocation (MPFA) enabled.
DB2NTMEMSIZE (Windows only)	DBMS: [*NumberOfBytes*] FCM: [*NumberOfBytes*] DBAT: [*NumberOfBytes*] APLD: [*NumberOfBytes*] Default: DBMS:16,777,216; FCM:22,020,096; DBAT: 3,554,432; APLD: 16,777,216	Windows NT requires that all shared memory segments be reserved at DLL initialization time to ensure matching addresses across processes. This registry variable is used to override the DB2 defaults in Windows NT if necessary. (In most situations, the default values are sufficient.)
DB2NTNOCACHE (Windows only)	ON, OFF Default: OFF	Specifies whether file system caching is performed. This applies to all data except long data or LOB data. When you eliminate system caching, more memory becomes available to the database so that the buffer pool or *sortheap* can be increased.
DB2_OVERRIDE_BPF	A positive number of 4 KB pages Default: Null	Specifies the size of the buffer pool, in pages, that is to be created at database activation, or the first time a connection is established. This registry variable is useful when failures resulting from memory constraints occur during database activation or the first time a connection is established. Such a memory constraint could arise either because of a real memory shortage (which is rare) or because of an attempt by the DB2 instance to allocate large, inaccurately configured buffer pools.

Table 5.2 DB2 registry variables that have the greatest impact on performance (Continued)		
Parameter	**Value Range / Default**	**Description**
DB2_PINNED_BP (AIX, HP-UX, Linux only)	YES, NO Default: NO	Specifies whether the database global memory used (including buffer pool memory) is to be kept in system main memory.
		Database performance is more consistent when database global memory is kept in main memory.
		On 64-bit DB2 for AIX, setting this variable to YES means that self tuning for database shared memory (activated by setting the *database_memory* database configuration parameter to AUTOMATIC) cannot be enabled.
DB2PRIORITIES	Values are platform dependent Default: Not set	Controls the priorities of DB2 processes and threads.
DB2_RESOURCE_ POLICY	Values are platform dependent Default: Not set	Defines a resource policy that can be used to limit what operating system resources are used by the DB2 database OR specifies rules for assigning specific operating system resources to specific DB2 database objects. For example, on AIX, Linux, or Windows operating systems, this registry variable can be used to limit the set of processors that the DB2 database system uses. The extent of resource control varies depending on the operating system.
DB2_SET_MAX_ CONTAINER_SIZE	-1, any positive integer greater than 65 536 bytes Default: Not set	Specifies the maximum size individual containers for automatic storage table spaces with the AUTORESIZE feature enabled can be.
DB2_SKIPDELETED	ON, OFF Default: OFF	Specifies whether statements using either Cursor Stability or Read Stability isolation levels are allowed to unconditionally skip deleted keys during index access and deleted rows during table access. With DB2_EVALUNCOMMITTED enabled, deleted rows are automatically skipped, but uncommitted pseudo-deleted keys in type-2 indexes are not skipped unless DB2_SKIPDELETED is also enabled.

Table 5.2 DB2 registry variables that have the greatest impact on performance (Continued)

Parameter	Value Range / Default	Description
DB2_SKIPINSERTED	ON, OFF Default: OFF	When the DB2_SKIPINSERTED registry variable is enabled, this registry variable allows statements using either Cursor Stability or Read Stability isolation levels to skip uncommitted inserted rows as if they had not been inserted.
DB2_SMS_TRUNC_ TMPTABLE_THRESH	-1, 0–*n*, where n is the number of extents per temporary table in an SMS table space container that are to be maintained Default: 0	Specifies a minimum file size threshold at which a temporary table (file) is maintained in an SMS table space. By default, this variable is set to 0, which means no special threshold handling is done. Instead, once a temporary table is no longer needed, its file is truncated to 0 extents. When the value of this variable is greater than 0, a larger file is maintained. If this variable is set to -1, the file is not truncated and is allowed to grow indefinitely, restricted only by system resources. This reduces some of the system overhead involved in dropping and recreating the file each time a temporary table is used.
DB2_SORT_AFTER_TQ	YES, NO Default: NO	Specifies how the DB2 optimizer works with directed table queues in a partitioned database environment when the receiving end requires the data to be sorted and the number of receiving nodes is equal to the number of sending nodes. When this registry variable is set to NO, the DB2 optimizer sorts at the sending end and merges the rows at the receiving end; when set to YES, the DB2 optimizer transmits the rows unsorted and sorts the rows at the receiving end after receiving all the rows.
DB2_SELUDI_COMM_ BUFFER	ON, OFF Default: OFF	Specifies whether the result of a query can be stored in a temporary table. This variable is used during the processing of blocking cursors over SELECT from UPDATE, INSERT, or DELETE (UDI) queries. If the parameter is set to ON during the OPEN processing of a blocking cursor for a SELECT from UDI query, the DB2 database system attempts to buffer the entire result of the query directly into the communications buffer memory area.

Table 5.2 DB2 registry variables that have the greatest impact on performance (Continued)		
Parameter	**Value Range / Default**	**Description**
DB2_TRUSTED_BINDIN	ON, OFF, CHECK Default: OFF	Specifies whether there is conversion from the external SQLDA format to an internal DB2 format during the binding of SQL and XQuery statements contained within an embedded unfenced stored procedure. If this parameter is set to ON, no conversion will take place, which will speed up the processing of the embedded SQL and XQuery statements
DB2_USE_ ALTERNATE_PAGE_ CLEANING	ON, OFF Default: Not set	Specifies whether a DB2 database uses an alternate set of page cleaning algorithms or the default method of page cleaning. When this variable is set to ON, the DB2 system writes changed pages to disk, keeping ahead of LSN_GAP and proactively finding victims. Doing this allows the page cleaners to better utilize available disk I/O bandwidth. (When this variable is set to ON, the *chngpgs_thresh* database configuration parameter no longer controls page cleaner activity.)

Because changes that are made to registry and environment variables affect the entire system, consider them carefully before you make them.

A Word About The DB2_PARALLEL_IO Registry Variable

When reading data from table spaces, DB2 will automatically attempt to use parallel I/O if the table space spans more than one container. However, there are situations when it would be beneficial to have parallel I/O enabled for single container table spaces. For example, if the container is created on a RAID device that consists of more than one physical disk, performance may be improved if read operations are performed in parallel. That is where the DB2_PARALLEL_IO registry variable comes in.

The DB2_PARALLEL_IO registry variable is used to force DB2 LUW to use parallel I/O for table spaces that only have one container or for table spaces whose containers reside on more than one physical disk. If this registry variable is not set, the level of I/O parallelism used is equal to the number of containers used by the table space.

On the other hand, if this registry variable is assigned a value, the level of I/O parallelism used is equal to the number of containers used multiplied by the value stored in the DB2_PARALLEL_IO registry variable. (Another way of saying this is that the parallelism of the table space is equal to the prefetch size divided by the extent size of the table space.)

For example, if the DB2_PARALLEL_IO registry variable has not been set and a table space that uses four containers issues a prefetch request, that request will be broken into four extent-sized prefetch requests (and each request will be executed in parallel). Or, if a table space has two containers and its prefetch size is four times the extent size, every prefetch request will be broken into two requests and each request will be for two extents. If, in this example, each table space container resided on a single, dedicated disk, setting the DB2_PARALLEL_IO registry variable could result in contention on both disks because two prefetchers could attempt to access both disks used at the same time. On the other hand, if both table space containers were striped across multiple disks, setting the DB2_PARALLEL_IO registry variable could potentially allow access to multiple disks at the same time.

If the DB2_PARALLEL_IO registry variable is assigned a value and the prefetch size of a table space is not AUTOMATIC, the degree of parallelism used by the table space is the prefetch size divided by the extent size. Thus, if the DB2_PARALLEL_IO registry variable has been set for a table space that has a prefetch size of 160 and an extent size of 32 pages, each prefetch request will be broken into five extent-sized prefetch requests (160 / 32 = 5).

Often, the DB2_PARALLEL_IO registry variable is assigned the asterisk (*) value to indicate that every table space in the database is to use parallel I/O. (The asterisk value implies that each table space container used spans six physical disk spindles.) Such an assignment is made by executing a db2set command that looks something like this:

```
db2set DB2_PARALLEL_IO=*
```

However, this is not a correct setting to use when a table space container does not span six physical disk spindles. In those cases, the DB2_PARALLEL_IO registry variable should be set by executing a db2set command that looks more like this:

```
db2set DB2_PARALLEL_IO=[TS_ID]:[DisksPerCtr] ,...
```

where:

TS_ID   Identifies one or more individual table spaces, by their numeric table space ID.

DisksPerCtr   Identifies the number of physical disks used by each table space container that is assigned to the table space specified.

Thus, if you wanted to set the DB2_PARALLEL_IO registry variable for a table space whose numeric ID is 1 to reflect that its storage containers reside on a RAID-5 3+1 group (3 data disk spindles), you could do so by executing a db2set command that looks something like this:

```
db2set DB2_PARALLEL_IO=1:3
```

On the other hand, if you wanted to set the DB2_PARALLEL_IO registry variable to indicate that the storage containers for all table spaces reside on a RAID-5 7+1 group (7 data disk spindles), you could do so by executing a db2set command that looks something like this:

```
db2set DB2_PARALLEL_IO=*:7
```

If the DB2_PARALLEL_IO registry variable is set, and the prefetch size of a table space is AUTOMATIC, DB2 calculates the prefetch size using the following equation:

prefetch size = number of containers * number of disks per container * extent size

Configuring Instances and Databases

Along with the comprehensive set of registry variables available, DB2 also uses an extensive array of configuration parameters to control how system resources are allocated and utilized on behalf of a DB2 instance and any database(s) under the instance's control. Initially, the default values provided for many of these configuration parameters were produced with very simple systems in mind. (The goal was for DB2 to run out of the box, on virtually any platform, not for DB2 to run optimally on the platform on which it is installed.) Now you can run the DB2 Configuration Advisor (which we will look at shortly) and answer some simple questions about the workload, database size, and number of users, and DB2 will use this information as well as information about the server to determine optimum values to assign many configuration parameters.

Although the default configuration values are sufficient to meet most database needs, you can usually improve overall system and application performance by changing the values of one or more configuration parameters. In fact, the values assigned to DB2 configuration parameters should always be modified if your database environment contains one or more of the following:

- Large databases

- Databases that service large numbers of concurrent connections

- One or more special applications that have high performance requirements

- A special hardware configuration

- Unique query or transaction loads

- Unique query or transaction types

The Database Manager (DB2 Instance) Configuration

Whenever an instance is created, a corresponding DB2 Database Manager (or instance) configuration file is created and initialized as part of the creation process. Each DB2 Database Manager configuration file is made up of approximately 85 different parameter values, and most control the amount of system resources that are allocated to the DB2 instance. The DB2 9 instance configuration parameters that have the greatest impact on performance are listed in Table 5.3.

Table 5.3 DB2 instance configuration parameters that have the greatest impact on performance		
Parameter	**Value Range/Default**	**Description**
agentpri	-1, 41–128 4K Pages or 0–6 4K Pages, depending on the operating system being used. Default: -1	Specifies the execution priority that is to be given, by the operating system scheduler, both to all agents and to other DB2 instance processes and threads.
aslheapsz	1–524,288 4K Pages Default: 15	Specifies the amount of memory (in pages) that is to be shared between a local client application and a DB2 agent. The application support layer heap represents a communication buffer between the local application and its associated agent. This buffer is allocated as shared memory by each DB2 agent that is started.
audit_buf_sz	0–65,000 4K Pages Default: 0	Specifies the amount of memory (in pages) that is to be used to store audit records that are generated by the audit facility. If this parameter is set to 0, no audit buffer is used.
intra_parallel	SYSTEM, YES, NO Default: NO	Specifies whether the DB2 instance can use intra-partition parallelism.
java_heap_sz	0–524,288 4K Pages Default: 2,048 or 4,096 (HP-UX only)	Specifies the maximum amount of memory (in pages) that is to be used by the Java interpreter to service Java DB2 stored procedures and user-defined functions.
max_connections	AUTOMATIC, -1, 1–64,000 Default: -1 (*max_coordagents*)	Specifies the maximum number of applications that can be connected to the instance.
max_coordagents	AUTOMATIC, -1, 1–64,000 Default: 200	Specifies the maximum number of coordinating agents that can exist on a node at one time. This parameter is used to limit the number of coordinating agents or to control the workload in a database.

Table 5.3 DB2 instance configuration parameters that have the greatest impact on performance (Continued)		
Parameter	**Value Range/Default**	**Description**
maxfilop	2–1,950 (UNIX), 2–32,768 (Windows) Default: 64	Specifies the maximum number of files that can be open per application. The value specified in this parameter defines the total database and application file handles that can be used by a specific process connected to a database. (Because DB2 is thread based in Version 9.5, this configuration parameter is used to specify the number of files that can be open per <u>database</u> in DB2 9.5.)
max_querydegree	ANY, 1–32,767 Default: ANY	Specifies the maximum degree of intra-partition parallelism that is to be used for any SQL statement executing on this instance of the DB2 instance.
num_poolagents	AUTOMATIC, 0–64,000 Default: 100	Specifies the size to which the idle agent pool is allowed to grow. As an agent becomes free, it is added to the idle agent pool, where at some point the DB2 Database Manager evaluates whether it should be terminated or not. At the time when the Database Manager considers terminating the agent, if the total number of idle agents pooled is greater than the value assigned to the *num_poolagents* configuration parameter, the agent will be terminated.
rqrioblk	4,096–65,535 Bytes Default: 32,767	Specifies the size (in bytes) of the buffer that is used for communication between remote applications and their corresponding database agents on the database server.
sheapthres	0–2,097,152 4K Pages Default: 0	Specifies the instance-wide soft limit on the total amount of memory (in pages) that is to be made available for private sorting operations.
util_impact_lim	1–100 Percent Default: 10	Specifies the percentage that the execution of a throttled utility will impact a database workload. For example, a value of 10 indicates that a throttled backup operation will not impact the current database workload by more than 10 percent.

The contents of the Database Manager configuration file for a particular instance can be displayed by attaching to the instance and executing the GET DATABASE MANAGER CONFIGURATION command. The syntax for this command is:

```
GET [DATABASE MANAGER | DB MANAGER | DBM]
[CONFIGURATION | CONFIG | CFG]
<SHOW DETAIL>
```

Thus, if you wanted to view the contents of the Database Manager configuration file for the current instance, you could do so by executing a GET DATABASE MANAGER CONFIGURATION command that looks like this:

```
GET DBM CFG
```

You can change the value assigned to a particular Database Manager configuration file parameter by attaching to the instance and executing the UPDATE DATABASE MANAGER CONFIGURATION command. The syntax for this command is:

```
UPDATE [DATABASE MANAGER | DB MANAGER | DBM]
[CONFIGURATION | CONFIG | CFG]
USING [[Parameter] [Value] |
       [Parameter] [Value] AUTOMATIC |
       [Parameter] AUTOMATIC |
       [Parameter] MANUAL ,...]
<IMMEDIATE | DEFERRED>
```

where:

Parameter   Identifies one or more DB2 instance configuration parameters (by keyword) whose values are to be modified. (In many cases, the keyword for a parameter is the same as the parameter name itself.)

Value   Identifies the new value or values that are to be assigned to the DB2 instance configuration parameter(s) specified.

If the AUTOMATIC keyword is specified as the value for a particular parameter, DB2 will automatically adjust the parameter value to reflect the current resource requirements. (Refer to Table 5.3 to identify the configuration parameters that can be assigned the AUTOMATIC keyword.) If a value is specified along with the AUTOMATIC keyword, the value specified may influence the automatic calculations performed.

If the DEFERRED clause is specified with the UPDATE DATABASE MANAGER CONFIGURATION command, changes made to the DB2 instance configuration file will not take effect until the instance is stopped and restarted. If the IMMEDIATE clause is specified instead, or if neither clause is specified, all changes made to the DB2 instance configuration file will take effect immediately—provided the necessary resources required are available.

So if you wanted to configure the current instance such that the maximum number of applications that can be executing concurrently at any given point in time is 100, you could do so by executing an UPDATE DATABASE MANAGER CONFIGURATION command that looks like this:

```
UPDATE DBM CFG USING MAXCAGENTS 100
```

Or, if you wanted to specify the name of the TCP/IP port that the current instance is to use to receive communications from remote clients, you could do so by executing an UPDATE DATABASE MANAGER CONFIGURATION command that looks like this:

```
UPDATE DBM CFG USING SVCENAME db2c_db2inst1
```

If you wanted to update both the MAXCAGENTS and the SVCENAME configuration parameters at the same time, you could do so by executing an UPDATE DATABASE MANAGER CONFIGURATION command that looks like this:

```
UPDATE DBM CFG USING MAXCAGENTS 100 SVCENAME db2c_db2inst1
```

The values assigned to all Database Manager configuration file parameters can be returned to their factory settings at any time by attaching to the appropriate instance and executing the RESET DATABASE MANAGER CONFIGURATION command. The syntax for this command is:

```
RESET [DATABASE MANAGER | DB MANAGER | DBM]
[CONFIGURATION | CONFIG | CFG]
```

Thus, if you wanted to return the Database Manager configuration file parameters for the current instance to their system default settings, you could do so by executing a RESET DATABASE MANAGER CONFIGURATION command that looks like this:

```
RESET DBM CFG
```

The contents of a Database Manager configuration file can also be viewed or altered using the DBM Configuration dialog, which can be activated by selecting the Configure Parameters action from the Instances menu found in the Control Center. Figure 5–3 shows the Control Center menu items that must be selected to activate the DBM Configuration dialog; Figure 5–4 shows how this dialog might look after it has been activated.

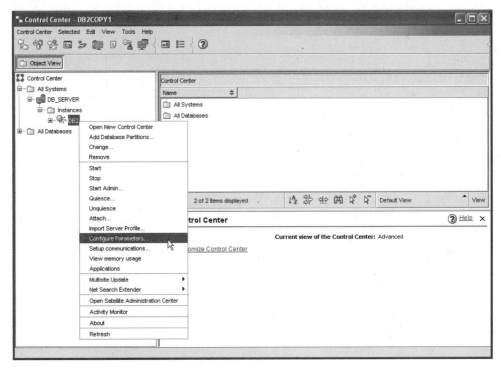

Figure 5–3: Invoking the DBM Configuration dialog from the Control Center.

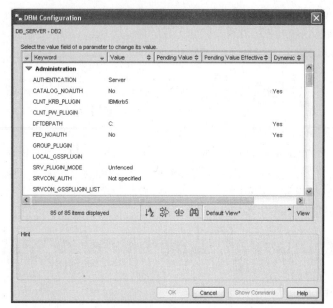

Figure 5–4: The DBM Configuration dialog.

Database Configurations

Just as a Database Manager configuration file is created and initialized whenever a new instance is created, a database configuration file is created and initialized each time a new database is created. Each database configuration file is made up of approximately 105 different parameters, and just as most Database Manager configuration parameters control the amount of system resources that will be allocated to a single DB2 instance, many of the database configuration file parameters control the amount of system resources that will be allocated to a database during normal operation. The DB2 9 database configuration parameters that have the greatest impact on performance are shown in Table 5.4.

Table 5.4 *Database configuration parameters that have the greatest impact on performance*		
Parameter	**Value Range / Default**	**Description**
avg_appls	AUTOMATIC, 1–*maxappls* Default: AUTOMATIC	Specifies the average number of active applications that normally access the database. The SQL optimizer uses this parameter to help estimate how much buffer pool memory will be available for the chosen access plan at application run time.
catalogcache_sz	-1, 8–524,288 4K Pages Default: -1	Specifies the amount of memory (in pages) that is to be used to cache system catalog information.
chngpgs_thresh	5–99 percent Default: 60	Specifies the level (percentage) of changed pages in the buffer pools at which the asynchronous page cleaners will be triggered if they are not currently active.
database_memory	AUTOMATIC, COMPUTED, 1– 4,294,967,295 Default: AUTOMATIC	Specifies how memory requirements for the database are to be defined for STMM. When STMM is enabled, you can set the *database_memory* configuration parameter to AUTOMATIC or a specific value. If it is set to AUTOMATIC, STMM determines the overall memory requirements for the database and increases or decreases the amount of memory allocated for database shared memory depending on the current database requirements. For example, if the current database requirements are high, and there is sufficient free memory on the system, more memory will be consumed by database shared memory. Once the database memory requirements drop, or the amount of free memory on the system drops too low, some database shared memory is released. When the *database_memory* configuration parameter is not set to AUTOMATIC, the entire database will use the specified amount of memory, distributing it across the database memory consumers as required. In this case the amount of memory used by the database can be specified in two ways: by setting the *database_memory* configuration parameter to a numeric value or by setting it to COMPUTED. In the second case, the total amount of memory is computed based on the sum of the initial values of the database memory heaps at database startup time.

Table 5.4 Database configuration parameters that have the greatest impact on performance (Continued)		
Parameter	**Value Range / Default**	**Description**
dft_degree	ANY, -1, 1–32,767 Default: 1	Specifies the default value for the CURRENT DEGREE special register and the DEGREE bind option.
locklist	AUTOMATIC, 4–524,288 4K Pages Default: AUTOMATIC	Specifies the maximum amount of memory (in pages) that is to be allocated and used to hold the lock list.
logbufsz	4–4,096 (32-bit), 4–65,535 (64-bit) 4KPages Default: 8	Specifies the amount of memory (in pages) that is to be used to buffer log records before they are written to disk. (Increasing the size of the log buffer can improve performance if transactions must wait for log data to be written to disk.)
maxlocks	AUTOMATIC, 1–100 percent Default: AUTOMATIC	Specifies a percentage of the lock list held by an application that must be filled before the DB2 instance performs lock escalation.
min_dec_div_3	YES, NO Default: NO	Specifies whether the results of decimal division arithmetic operations are to always have a scale of at least 3.
mincommit	1–25 Default: 1	Specifies the number of COMMIT SQL statements that are to be processed before log records are written to disk.
num_iocleaners	AUTOMATIC, 0–255 Default: AUTOMATIC	Specifies the number of asynchronous page cleaners that are to be used by the database.
num_ioservers	AUTOMATIC, 1–255 Default: AUTOMATIC	Specifies the number of I/O servers that are to be used on behalf of database agents to perform prefetch I/O and asynchronous I/O needed by utilities such as backup and restore.
pckcachesz	AUTOMATIC, 32–128,000(32-bit), 32–524,288 (64-bit) 4K Pages Default: AUTOMATIC	Specifies the amount of application memory (in pages) that will be used to cache packages for static and dynamic SQL statements and XQuery expressions.
self_tuning_mem	ON, OFF Default: ON for a single-partition database, OFF for a multi-partition database.	Specifies whether or not self-tuning memory manager (STMM) is to be enabled for the database. (When STMM is enabled, the memory tuner dynamically distributes available memory resources as required between all memory consumers that are enabled for self-tuning.)

Table 5.4 Database configuration parameters that have the greatest impact on performance (Continued)		
Parameter	**Value Range / Default**	**Description**
		In DB2 9, STMM is automatically enabled (for non-partitioned databases) when you create a new database. That is, the *self_tuning_mem* configuration parameter is set to ON, and the database parameters for the buffer pools, package cache, lock list, sort memory, and total database shared memory are set to AUTOMATIC. For existing databases migrated from earlier versions of DB2, self-tuning memory needs to be enabled manually. Rather than have all of the database memory resources managed automatically, you can also choose to set just the desired memory resources (parameters) to AUTOMATIC.
seqdetect	YES, NO Default: YES	Specifies whether the DB2 instance can monitor I/O and, if sequential page reading is occurring, can activate I/O prefetching on behalf of the database.
sheapthres_shr	AUTOMATIC, 0, 250–2,097,152 (32-bit), 250–2,147,483,647 (64-bit) 4K Pages Default: AUTOMATIC	Specifies the maximum amount of memory (in pages) that is to be used at any one time to perform sort operations. When this parameter is set to 0, all sort operations are performed in shared memory.
sortheap	AUTOMATIC, 16–524,288 (32-bit), 16–4,194,303 4K Pages Default: AUTOMATIC	Specifies the maximum number of private memory pages to be used for private sorts or the maximum number of shared memory pages to be used for shared sorts.

The contents of the database configuration file for a particular database can be displayed by executing the GET DATABASE CONFIGURATION command. The syntax for this command is:

```
GET [DATABASE | DB] [CONFIGURATION | CONFIG | CFG]
FOR [DatabaseAlias]
<SHOW DETAIL>
```

where:

DatabaseAlias   Identifies the alias assigned to the database that configuration information is to be displayed for.

Thus, if you wanted to view the contents of the database configuration file for a database named SAMPLE, you could do so by executing a GET DATABASE CONFIGURATION command that looks like this:

```
GET DB CFG FOR sample
```

The value assigned to a particular database configuration file parameter can be changed by executing the UPDATE DATABASE CONFIGURATION command. The syntax for this command is:

```
UPDATE [DATABASE | DB]
[CONFIGURATION | CONFIG | CFG]
FOR [DatabaseAlias]
USING [[Parameter] [Value] |
       [Parameter] [Value] AUTOMATIC |
       [Parameter] AUTOMATIC |
       [Parameter] MANUAL ,...]
<IMMEDIATE | DEFERRED>
```

where:

DatabaseAlias	Identifies the alias assigned to the database for which configuration information is to be modified.
Parameter	Identifies one or more database configuration parameters (by keyword) whose values are to be modified. (In many cases, the keyword for a parameter is the same as the parameter name itself.)
Value	Identifies the new value(s) that are to be assigned to the database configuration parameter(s) specified.

If the AUTOMATIC keyword is specified as the value for a particular parameter, DB2 will automatically adjust the parameter value to reflect the current resource requirements. (Refer to Table 5.4 to identify the configuration parameters that can be set using the AUTOMATIC keyword.) If a value is specified along with the AUTOMATIC keyword, the value specified will influence any other automatic memory allocations.

If the DEFERRED clause is specified with the UPDATE DATABASE CONFIGURATION command, changes made to the database configuration file will not take effect until all connections to the corresponding database have been terminated and a new connection is established. If the IMMEDIATE clause is specified instead, or if neither clause is specified, all changes made to the database configuration file will take effect immediately—provided the necessary resources are available. (Applications running against a database at the time database configuration changes are made will see the change the next time an SQL statement is executed.)

So if you wanted to configure a database named SAMPLE such that any application connected to the database will wait up to 10,000 seconds to acquire a lock before rolling back the current transaction, you could do so by executing an UPDATE DATABASE CONFIGURATION command that looks like this:

```
UPDATE DB CFG FOR sample USING LOCKTIMEOUT 10000
```

Or if you wanted to configure a database named SAMPLE to use archival logging and instruct it to store a second copy of the active log files in a directory named MIRRORLOGS that resides on drive E:, you could do so by executing an UPDATE DATABASE CONFIGURATION command that looks like this:

```
UPDATE DB CFG FOR sample USING LOGARCHMETH1 LOGRETAIN MIRRORLOGPATH
  E:/mirrorlogs
```

The values assigned to all database configuration file parameters can be returned to their system defaults by executing the RESET DATABASE CONFIGURATION command. The syntax for this command is:

```
RESET [DATABASE | DB]
[CONFIGURATION | CONFIG | CFG]
FOR [DatabaseAlias]
```

where:

DatabaseAlias   Identifies the alias assigned to the database whose configuration
                   information is to be modified.

Therefore, if you wanted to return the database configuration file parameters for a database named SAMPLE to their system default settings (thereby loosing any configuration changes that have been made), you could do so by executing a RESET DATABASE CONFIGURATION command that looks like this:

```
RESET DB CFG FOR sample
```

You can also view or alter the contents of a database configuration file by using the Database Configuration dialog, which can be activated by selecting the Configure Parameters action from the Databases menu found in the Control Center. Figure 5–5 shows the Control Center menu items that must be selected to activate the Database Configuration dialog; Figure 5–6 shows how this dialog might look after it has been activated.

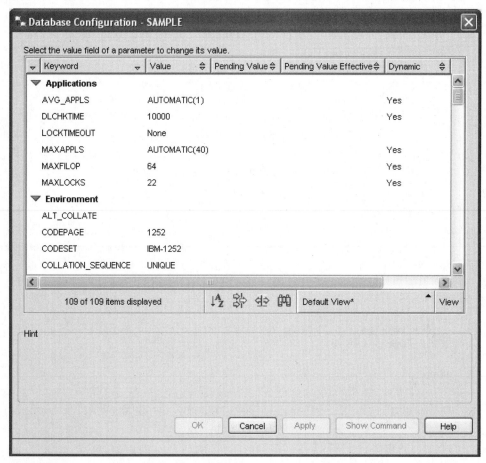

Figure 5–5: Invoking the Database Configuration dialog from the Control Center.

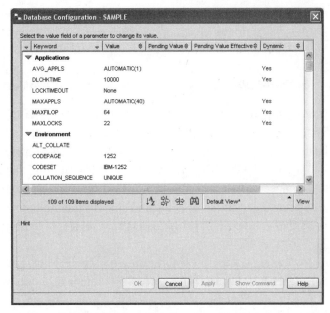

Figure 5–6: The Database Configuration dialog.

A Word About the NUM_IOSERVERS Database Configuration Parameter

I/O servers, also called prefetchers, are used on behalf of database agents to perform prefetch I/O and asynchronous I/O for utilities such as the Backup utility and the Restore utility. The *num_ioservers* database configuration parameter is used to specify the number of I/O servers that can be in progress for a database at any given point in time. (An I/O server waits while an I/O operation that it initiated is in progress.) Non-prefetch I/Os are scheduled directly from database agents and as a result are not constrained by the value assigned to the *num_ioservers* database configuration parameter.

In order to fully exploit all the I/O devices in a database that is using automatic storage, a good value to assign to this configuration parameter is the value AUTOMATIC.

If you are not using automatic storage or the value AUTOMATIC is not recognized (as is the case with earlier versions of DB2), this configuration parameter should be assigned a number that is one or two more than the number of physical devices on which the database resides. It is better to configure a few additional I/O servers and not use them, than to not configure enough since there is a minimal amount of overhead associated with each one; any unused I/O servers will remain idle.

A Word About the NUM_IOCLEANERS Database Configuration Parameter

DB2 uses asynchronous page cleaners to write changed pages found in a buffer pool to disk before space in a buffer pool is acquired on behalf of a database agent. Ideally, database agents should not have to wait for changed pages to be written to disk before they will have sufficient space in a buffer pool. If that is indeed the case, overall performance of database applications is improved. The *num_iocleaners* database configuration parameter is used to specify the number of asynchronous page cleaners that can be in progress for a database at any given point in time.

If the *num_iocleaners* database configuration parameter is assigned the value zero (0), no page cleaners are started and as a result, database agents will be required to perform page writes from buffer pool to disk. This can have a significant impact on performance, particularly for a database stored across many physical storage devices. Additionally, if no page cleaners are configured, applications might encounter periodic log full conditions.

If applications running against the database consist primarily of transactions that update data, increasing the number of page cleaners used will speed up performance. Increasing the amount of page cleaners used will also shorten recovery time from soft failures, such as power outages, because the contents of the database on disk will be more up-to-date at any given point in time.

A good value to assign to this configuration parameter is the value AUTOMATIC. If this parameter is set to AUTOMATIC, the number of page cleaners started will be based on the number of CPUs found on the current machine, as well as the number of local logical database partitions used (in a partitioned database environment). There will always be at least one page cleaner started when this parameter is set to AUTOMATIC.

If you choose not to assign the *num_iocleaners* database configuration parameter the value AUTOMATIC, the following factors should be taken into consideration when deciding on an appropriate value to use:

- **Application type**.

  ○ If the database is a read-only database that will not be updated, set this parameter to zero (0). The exception would be if the query work load results in many TEMP tables being created (you can determine this by using the Explain utility).

  ○ If transactions are run against the database, set this parameter to a value between one and the number of physical storage devices used for the database.

- **Workload**. Environments with high update transaction rates might require more page cleaners to be configured.

- **Buffer pool sizes**. Environments with large buffer pools might require more page cleaners to be configured.

The Configuration Advisor

With such a broad range of configuration parameters to choose from, deciding where to start and what changes to make can be difficult. Fortunately, DB2 comes packaged with a tool to help you get started; that tool is the Configuration Advisor. The Configuration Advisor is a GUI application that makes it easy to tune and balance the resource requirements of a single database within an instance—you provide specific information about your database environment and the Configuration Advisor makes suggestions about which configuration parameters should be modified and provides recommended values for each. You can then elect to have the Configuration Advisor apply all changes recommended, or you can apply them yourself however you see fit.

You can activate the Configuration Advisor by selecting the Configuration Advisor action from the Databases menu found in the Control Center. Figure 5–7 shows the Control Center menu items that must be selected to activate the Configuration Advisor; Figure 5–8 shows how the Configuration Advisor looks when it is first activated.

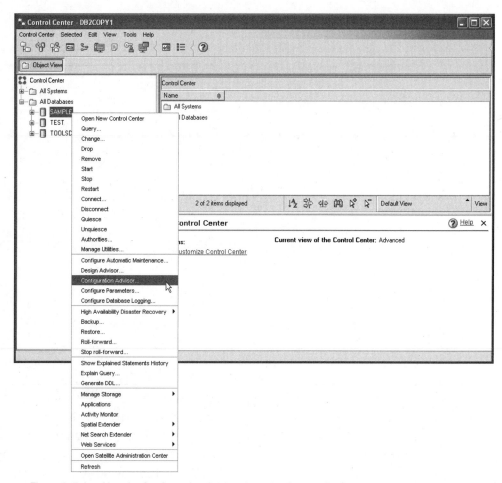

Figure 5–7: Invoking the Configuration Advisor from the Control Center.

Once the Configuration Advisor wizard is activated, you simply follow the directions shown on each panel presented to describe your server environment and to explain what a typical transaction workload for your database looks like. When you have provided the information requested, the Configuration Advisor will recommend changes that should improve overall performance if made to instance and/or database configuration parameters. At that time, the "Finish" push button displayed in the lower right corner of the wizard (see Figure 5–8) will be enabled, and when this button is selected, the recommended configuration parameter changes may be applied.

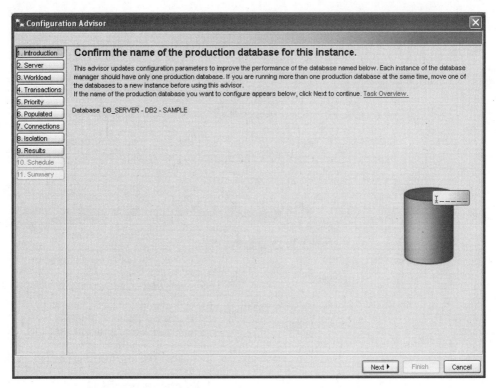

Figure 5–8: The Configuration Advisor dialog.

In DB2 9, the Configuration Advisor is automatically invoked whenever you create a database using the Create Database Wizard. (This behavior can be changed by assigning the value NO to the DB2_ENABLE_AUTOCONFIG_DEFAULT registry variable.)

The AUTOCONFIGURE Command

If you prefer to work with commands instead of GUI tools, the functionality provided by the Configuration Advisor can also be obtained by executing the AUTOCONFIGURE command (which calls the Configuration Advisor under the covers). The basic syntax for this command is:

```
AUTOCONFIGURE
USING [[Keyword] [Value] ,...]
APPLY [DB ONLY | DB AND DBM | NONE]
```

where:

Keyword   One or more special keywords that are recognized by the
AUTOCONFIGURE command. Valid values include mem_percent,
workload_type, num_stmts, tpm, admin_priority, is_populated, num_
local_apps, num_remote_apps, isolation, and bp_resizable.

Value   Identifies the value associated with the keyword provided. Table 5.5
lists the values that are valid for each keyword recognized by the
AUTOCONFIGURE command.

Table 5.5 AUTOCONFIGURE Command Keywords and Values		
Keyword	**Valid Values / Default**	**Description**
mem_percent	1–100 Default: 25	Percentage of available server memory (RAM) the DB2 instance is to use when performing database operations.
workload_type	simple, complex, mixed Default: mixed	The type of workload that is usually run against the database. Valid values are as follows: **simple**—workloads tend to be I/O-intensive and mostly transactions (for example, order entry and OLTP); **complex**—workloads tend to be CPU-intensive and mostly queries (for example, decision support and data warehousing); and **mixed**—workloads tend to be a combination of the two.
num_stmts	1–1,000,000 Default: 10	Average number of SQL statements executed within a single transaction (i.e., between commits). NOTE: If unknown, choose a number greater than 10.
tpm	1–200,000 Default: 60	Average number of transactions executed per minute (estimated). NOTE: The DB2 Performance Monitor can help you get a more accurate TPM measurement.

Table 5.5 AUTOCONFIGURE Command Keywords and Values (Continued)		
Keyword	**Valid Values / Default**	**Description**
admin_priority	performance, recovery, both Default: both	Type of activity for which the database should be optimized. Valid values include the following: **performance**—database should be optimized for transaction performance (slower backup/recovery); **recovery**—database should be optimized for backup and recovery (slower transaction performance); or **both**—database should be optimized for both transaction performance and backup/recovery (both are equally important).
is_populated	yes, no Default: yes	Indicates whether the database currently contains data. Valid values are as follows: **yes**—the database contains data; and **no**—the database does not contain data.
num_local_apps	0–5,000 Default: 0	Number of local applications that will be connected to the database at one time.
num_remote_apps	0–5,000 Default: 10	Number of remote applications that will be connected to the database at one time. Allocating memory to handle all connections needed (both local and remote) ensures that users never have to wait for an existing connection to be terminated before they can get connected. However, over allocating memory for connections can result in wasted resources. The DB2 Performance Monitor can help you determine how many connections are actually acquired within a specified time frame.
isolation	RR, RS, CS, UR Default: RR	Isolation level used by most applications that access the database. Valid values include the following: **RR**—Repeatable Read (large number of locks acquired for long periods of time); **RS**—Read Stability (small number of locks acquired for long periods of time); **CS**—Cursor Stability (large number of locks acquired for short periods of time); and **UR**—Uncommitted Read (no locks acquired).
bp_resizeable	yes, no Default: yes	Are buffer pools resizable?

If the APPLY DB ONLY clause is specified with the AUTOCONFIGURE command, database configuration and buffer pool changes recommended by the Configuration Advisor will be applied to the appropriate database configuration file; if the APPLY DB AND DBM clause is specified, database configuration and buffer pool changes recommended will be applied to the database configuration file, and instance configuration changes recommended will be applied to the appropriate DB2 instance configuration file. If the APPLY NONE clause is specified instead, change recommendations will be displayed but not applied.

Thus, if you wanted to determine the best configuration to use for an OLTP database named SAMPLE that uses resizable buffer pools and is populated, and you wanted to review any configuration changes recommended before applying them to the appropriate database configuration file, you could do so by executing an AUTOCONFIGURE command that looks like this:

```
AUTOCONFIGURE USING workload_type complex,
  is_populated yes,
  bp_resizable yes
APPLY NONE
```

Or if you wanted to determine the best configuration to use if 60 percent of a system's memory will be available for the DB2 instance to use when performing database operations, and if the instance controlled only one database (named SAMPLE) and you wanted to automatically update the appropriate configuration files to reflect any configuration changes recommended, you could do so by executing an AUTOCONFIGURE command that looks like this:

```
AUTOCONFIGURE USING mem_percent 60 APPLY DB AND DBM
```

On the other hand, if you wanted to determine the optimum configuration to use if 60 percent of a system's memory will be available for a DB2 instance, and the instance controls two active databases that need to use memory equally, you could see this configuration by executing an AUTOCONFIGURE command that looks like this *for each database*:

```
AUTOCONFIGURE USING mem_percent 30 APPLY DB AND DBM
APPLY NONE
```

> The AUTOCONFIGURE command (and the Design Advisor) will always recommend that a database be configured to take advantage of the Self-Tuning Memory Manager. However, if you run the AUTOCONFIGURE command against a database that resides in an instance where the SHEAPTHRES configuration parameter has been assigned a value other than zero, the sort memory heap database configuration parameter (SORTHEAP) will not be configured for automatic tuning. Therefore, you must execute the command UPDATE DATABASE MANAGER CONFIGURATION USING SHEAPTHRES 0 before you execute the AUTOCONFIGURE command if you want to enable sort memory tuning.

Self-Tuning Memory Manager

In DB2 9, a new memory tuning feature, known as the Self-Tuning Memory Manager (STMM), simplifies the task of configuring memory-related database parameters by automatically setting values for these parameters after measuring and analyzing how well each DB2 memory consumer is using the allocated memory available. The following database memory pools can be enabled for self-tuning, either entirely or individually:

- Buffer pools (controlled by the ALTER BUFFERPOOL and CREATE BUFFERPOOL statements)

- Package cache (controlled by the *pckcachesz* configuration parameter)

- Locking memory (controlled by the *locklist* and *maxlocks* configuration parameters)

- Sort memory (controlled by the *sheapthres_shr* and the *sortheap* configuration parameter)

- Database shared memory (controlled by the *database_memory* configuration parameter)

When a database is not configured to take advantage of STMM, it will use a specified amount of memory, distributing it across all database memory consumers. However, when a database has been configured to take advantage of STMM, the memory tuner responds to changes in database workload characteristics and response times, adjusting the values of memory configuration parameters and buffer pool sizes to optimize performance. If the current workload requirements are high, and there is sufficient free memory on the system, more memory will be consumed by the database. It can also move memory between the different DB2 memory segments, for example, from the sort heap to a buffer pool.

Once the workload's memory requirements drop, or if the amount of free memory available on the system becomes too low, some database shared memory is released. It is important to note that because STMM bases its tuning decisions on database workload and response times, workloads with changing memory characteristics limit its ability to tune effectively. If a workload's memory characteristics are constantly changing, self-tuning memory will tune memory less frequently.

Self-tuning is enabled for a database by assigning the value ON to the *self_tuning_ mem* database configuration parameter. (By default, the *self_tuning_mem* database configuration parameter is assigned the value ON for single-partition databases and OFF for multi-partition databases.) Specific memory areas that are controlled by a memory configuration parameter can then be enabled for self-tuning by assigning the appropriate configuration parameter the value AUTOMATIC; buffer pools can be enabled for self-tuning by setting their size to AUTOMATIC. (Self-tuning can be disabled for the entire database by assigning the value OFF to the *self_tuning_mem* database configuration parameter; when self-tuning is disabled, configuration parameters and buffer pools that have been set to AUTOMATIC remain AUTOMATIC and their corresponding memory areas remain at their current size.)

If a new buffer pool is created (by executing the CREATE BUFFERPOOL statement) after STMM has been enabled, DB2 will attempt to create the buffer pool immediately (unless the DEFERRED clause was specified with the CREATE BUFFERPOOL statement used) by allocating the memory requested from shared database memory. If the memory needed is not available, the buffer pool will be created, but no memory will be allocated until all connections to the database the buffer pool is to be created for have been terminated and the database has been deactivated (i.e., the database is stopped and restarted).

Because the memory tuner trades memory resources between different memory consumers, there must be at least two memory consumers enabled for self-tuning in order for STMM to be effective. The one exception to this rule is when the sort heap (*sortheap* database configuration parameter) is enabled for self-tuning; in this case, STMM will balance the number of private memory pages used for private sorts and the number of shared memory pages used for shared sorts.

Once a database and two or more memory consumers have been configured for self-tuning, the current memory configuration for the database can be obtained by executing the GET DATABASE CONFIGURATION command with the SHOW DETAIL option specified. Changes made by self-tuning are recorded in memory tuning log files, which reside in the *stmmlog* subdirectory of the instance. (The first file created will be assigned the name *stmm.0.log*, the second will be assigned the name *stmm.1.log*, and so on.) Each memory tuning log file contains summaries of the resource demands for each memory consumer at the time a tuning operation was performed. Tuning intervals can be determined by examining the timestamps for the entries made in the memory tuning log files.

Using the Self-Tuning Memory Manager in a Partitioned Database Environment

When the self-tuning memory manager is enabled in a partitioned database environment, a single database partition, known as the "tuning partition," is responsible for monitoring the memory configuration and usage patterns and determining if changes could improve performance. If the tuning partition deems a change should be made, it propagates the appropriate configuration changes to all other database partitions to maintain a consistent configuration across all database partitions used.

The tuning partition is selected based on the number of database partitions and the number of buffer pools that have been defined. You can determine which database partition is the current tuning partition by executing the following procedure call:

```
CALL SYSPROC.ADMIN_CMD('get stmm tuning dbpartitionnum')
```

If desired, you can change the tuning partition by calling the same procedure as follows:

```
CALL SYSPROC.ADMIN_CMD('update stmm tuning dbpartitionnum
[DBPartitionNum]')
```

where:

DBPartitionNum   Specifies, by number, the database partition that is to act as the tuning partition.

Thus, if you wanted database partition number 4 to be the tuning partition, you would execute a procedure call that looks like this:

```
CALL SYSPROC.ADMIN_CMD('update stmm tuning dbpartitionnum
   4)
```

On the other hand, if you have specified that a particular database partition is to act as the tuning partition and you want STMM to automatically re-select the tuning partition, you would make this change by executing a procedure call that looks like this:

```
CALL SYSPROC.ADMIN_CMD('update stmm tuning dbpartitionnum
   -1)
```

When you change the tuning partition by executing either of these procedure calls, the tuning partition will be updated asynchronously or the next time the database is stopped and restarted.

Since there can be different database configurations for each database partition in a partitioned database environment, STMM can be enabled or disabled at the partition level. To disable self tuning for a subset of database partitions, set the *self_tuning_ mem* database configuration parameter to OFF for the database partitions that are not to take advantage of STMM. You can also disable self tuning for a subset of the memory pools controlled by configuration parameters on a particular database partition by setting the value of the relevant configuration parameter or buffer pool size on that partition to MANUAL or a specific value. However, it is recommended that STMM configuration parameter values be consistent across all partitions used.

Indexes

An index is an object that contains an ordered set of pointers that refer to rows in a base table. Each index is based on one or more columns in the base table to which it refers (known as keys); however, indexes are stored as separate entities. Figure 5–9 shows the structure of a simple index, along with its relationship to a base table.

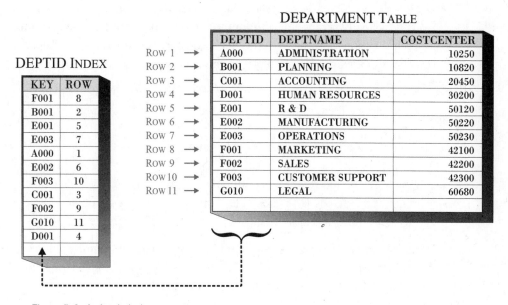

Figure 5–9: A simple index.

Indexes are important because they do the following:

- Provide a fast, efficient method for locating specific rows of data in very large tables. (In some cases, all the information needed to resolve a query may be found in the index itself, in which case the actual table data does not have to be accessed.)

- Provide a logical ordering of the rows of a table. (Data is stored in a table in no particular order; when indexes are used, the values of one or more columns can be sorted in ascending or descending order. This is very beneficial when processing queries that contain ORDER BY and GROUP BY clauses.)

- Improve overall query performance. (If no index exists on a table, a table scan must be performed for each table referenced in a query. The larger the table, the longer a table scan takes because a table scan requires each table row to be accessed sequentially.)

- Enforce the uniqueness of records stored in a table.

- Can require a table to use clustering storage, which causes the rows of a table to be physically arranged according to the ordering of their index column values. (Although all indexes provide a logical ordering of data, only a clustering index provides a physical ordering of data.)

- Can provide greater concurrency in multi-user environments. (Because records can be located faster, acquired locks do not have to be held as long.)

However, there is a price to pay for these benefits:

- Each index created requires additional storage or disk space. The exact amount of space needed is dependent on the size of the associated table, along with the size and number of columns contained in the index.

- Every insert and update operation performed on a table requires additional updating of the indexes associated with that table. This is also true when data is bulk-loaded into a table using DB2's LOAD utility.

- Each index potentially adds an alternative access path that the DB2 Optimizer must consider when generating the optimum access plan to use to resolve a query. This in turn increases compilation time when static queries are embedded in an application program.

Although some indexes are created implicitly to provide support for a table's definition (for example, to provide support for a primary key), indexes are typically created explicitly, using tools available with DB2. One way to explicitly create an index is by executing the CREATE INDEX SQL statement. The basic syntax for this statement is:

```
CREATE <UNIQUE> INDEX [IndexName]
ON [TableName] ([PriColumnName] <ASC | DESC> ,...)
<INCLUDE ([SecColumnName] ,...)>
<CLUSTER>
<PCTFREE 10 | PCTFREE [PercentFree]>
<ALLOW REVERSE SCANS | DISALLOW REVERSE SCANS>
```

where:

IndexName   Identifies the name that is to be assigned to the index to be created.

TableName   Identifies the name assigned to the base table with which the index to be created is to be associated.

PriColumnName Identifies one or more primary columns that are to be part of the index's key. (The combined values of each primary column specified will be used to enforce data uniqueness in the associated base table.)

SecColumnName Identifies one or more secondary columns whose values are to be stored with the values of the primary columns specified but are not to be used to enforce data uniqueness.

PercentFree   Specifies a percentage of each index page to leave as free space when building the index.

Thus, if you wanted to create an index for a base table named EMPLOYEE such that the index key consists of a column named EMPNO and employee numbers are stored in descending order, you could do so by executing a CREATE INDEX statement that looks something like this:

```
CREATE INDEX empno_indx
ON employee (empno DESC)
```

Indexes can also be created using the Create Index wizard, which can be activated by selecting the appropriate action from the Indexes menu found in the Control Center. Figure 5–10 shows the Control Center menu items that must be selected to activate the Create Indexes dialog; Figure 5–11 shows how the Create Index wizard might look when it is first activated.

The primary purpose of an index is to help DB2 quickly locate records stored in a table. Therefore, creating an index for frequently accessed columns in a table usually improves performance for data access and update operations. Indexes also allow for greater concurrency when multiple transactions need to access the same table at the same time— row retrieval is faster and locks are acquired more quickly and don't have to be held as long. But, as we saw earlier, these benefits come with a price.

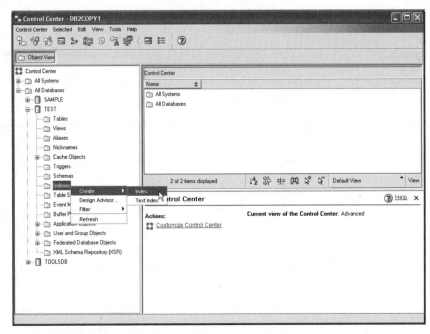

Figure 5–10: Invoking the Create Index dialog from the Control Center.

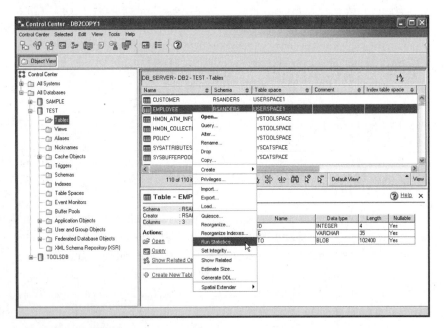

Figure 5–11: The Create Index wizard.

To ensure that the benefits outweigh the costs, you must analyze how data is frequently accessed to determine which columns should be indexed and which should not. Identifying columns that are frequently joined and/or searched is a good place to start:

1. Consider creating a clustering index on the column most frequently searched and/or joined, based on the data order. Consider nonclustering indexes on searched or joined columns in which less than 10 percent of the rows will be scanned/joined.

2. Refine this analysis with an estimate of the percentage of the rows that will be inserted, updated, and/or deleted over a given period of time. Minimize the number of indexes used when inserting, updating, and deleting data frequently.

3. Composite indexes (i.e., indexes with more than one column) are most beneficial when columns are frequently accessed together.

4. Consider the cardinality of the columns, particularly for composite indexes. Indexes on columns with a low cardinality are not very selective and do not enhance performance as much as indexes on columns with high cardinalities.

Any number of indexes can be created for a table, using a wide variety of combinations of columns. However, it is important to keep in mind that if a large number of indexes are created for a table that is modified frequently, overall performance will decrease rather than increase for all operations *except* data retrieval. Tables that are used for data mining, business intelligence, business warehousing, and other applications that execute many (and often complex) queries while rarely modifying data are prime targets for multiple indexes. On the other hand, tables that are used in On-Line Transactional Processing (OLTP) environments or other environments where data throughput is high should use indexes sparingly.

How can you tell whether creating an index will improve performance? One way is by using the Design Advisor. You may recall that in Chapter 3, "Data Partitioning and Clustering," we saw that the Design Advisor is a special tool that is designed to identify indexes, materialized query tables (MQTs), and multidimensional clustering tables that could help improve query performance in your database environment. Using current database statistics, the DB2 Optimizer, snapshot monitor information, and/or a specific query or set of SQL statements (known as a workload) you provide, the Design Advisor recommends one or more indexes that would improve query/workload performance. The Design Advisor looks at a workload rather than at individual queries, and so it can examine the effect that any index it recommends will have on the *entire workload*. This is important because a particular index might improve the performance of one or more queries but negatively impact others.

Unique Indexes

One of the best ways to optimize query performance with an index is by using a unique index. A unique index is created by specifying the UNIQUE clause with the CREATE INDEX statement. When the CREATE INDEX statement is executed with the UNIQUE clause specified, rows in the table associated with the index being created must not have two or more occurrences of the same values in the set of columns that make up the index key. If the table for which the index is to be created contains data, uniqueness is checked when DB2 attempts to create the index specified—if records with duplicate values for the index key are found, the index will not be created; if no duplicates are found, the index is created, and uniqueness is enforced each time an insert or update operation is performed against the table. Any time the uniqueness of the index key is compromised, the insert or update operation will fail, and an error will be generated.

Thus, if you wanted to create a unique index for a table named EMPLOYEE that will guarantee that no two employees will have the same social security number, you could do so by executing a CREATE INDEX statement that looks something like this:

```
CREATE UNIQUE INDEX empssn_indx
ON employee (ssn)
```

It is important to note that if you have a query that accesses multiple columns in a table, you cannot simply combine the columns accessed into one unique index, because that may not enforce the uniqueness you want. For example, suppose you have a table named CUSTOMER that contains the following columns: CUSTID, FNAME, LNAME, SALUTATION, ADDRESS, PHONE, and EMAIL. You want to ensure that the CUSTID column will contain unique values, but a close look reveals that many of your applications execute queries that look something like this:

```
SELECT salutation, lname FROM customer
WHERE custid = 19002
```

Without an index, this query will require that the entire table be scanned in order to retrieve the desired data. On the other hand, if you create a unique index on the CUSTID column, DB2 will have to scan the index to locate the record, and then read the corresponding data page to retrieve the customer's last name and salutation. But, if you create a unique index on CUSTID, and include the SALUTATION and LNAME columns, DB2 can get the data for the query using index only access. Therefore, you might be tempted to create a unique index for the CUSTOMER table by executing a CREATE INDEX statement that looks like this:

```
CREATE UNIQUE INDEX custinfo_indx
ON customer (custid, salutation, lname)
```

However, this index does not ensure that the CUSTID column will contain unique values. Instead, it ensures that the *combination* of CUSTID, SALUTATION, and LNAME will be unique. To create a unique index on CUSTID, and include the SALUTATION and LNAME columns so that DB2 can get the data for the query using index only access, you would need to create the index by executing a CREATE INDEX statement that looks like this:

```
CREATE UNIQUE INDEX custid_indx
ON customer (custid)
INCLUDE (salutation, lname)
```

Clustering Indexes

When an index is created, only keys and record IDs are stored in the resulting index structure and each record ID points to a corresponding row in the data pages. However, when a clustered index is created, DB2 attempts to store the data in the data pages in the same order as the corresponding keys appear in the index pages. DB2 will also attempt to insert rows with similar key values onto the same pages. (Because of this, only one clustering index can be defined for a table.) A clustering index is most useful for columns that have range predicates because it allows better sequential access of data in the table. Clustering indexes can also improve performance when a query needs to access a large percentage of the rows in the table, particularly when the rows are retrieved in order.

A clustering index is created by specifying the CLUSTER option with the CREATE INDEX SQL statement. Thus, if you wanted to create a clustering index for a table named EMPLOYEE so that its rows in the data pages will be ordered by employee names, last name first, you could do so by executing a CREATE INDEX statement that looks something like this:

```
CREATE INDEX empno_cindx
ON employee (lname, fname)
CLUSTER
```

In order for DB2 to maintain the clustering of the data and the index as records are inserted or updated, you must leave free space on the data pages to provide room for additional rows. The PCTFREE option of the CREATE INDEX SQL statement is used to control how much space is reserved on data pages for future insert, update, load, and reorganization operations. Specify a higher PCTFREE value at index creation time to reduce the likelihood that index page splits will occur when records are added to the table. (The default is 10 percent, but you should increase this to between 20 and 35 percent for tables that have a heavy volume of insert/update/delete operations.)

When deciding whether to use a clustering index, consider the following:

- The optimizer is likely to use a clustering index, if one is available, to avoid sorting data for ORDER BY, GROUP BY, DISTINCT, and join processing—so a column where these operations are often performed is a good candidate for a clustering index.

- Columns frequently searched or joined over a range of values using the operators BETWEEN, >, <, and LIKE are good candidates for clustering. A clustering index means that values are maintained in sequence on the data pages. A matching index scan can be used followed by a nonmatching index scan to satisfy a range predicate. DB2 can use sequential prefetch to scan the data pages and the leaf pages.

- A column with a low cardinality (i.e., a few distinct values) is a good candidate for clustering if an index is required on the column at all. Generally it is not a good idea to create an index on a column with a low cardinality because the index does not narrow the search. However, if an index is required, a clustering index on such a column is a good choice because all like values are grouped (clustered) together on the data pages.

- For best performance, create a clustering index over small data types (such as INTEGER and CHAR(10)), unique columns, and columns most often used in range searches.

- Do not create a clustered index on a volatile table because the index will not be used. A volatile table is a table that is updated very frequently and that changes size dramatically within a short period of time. To tell the optimizer to use an index scan for this type of table, you can mark it as being volatile when you create it (by specifying the VOLATILE option with the CREATE TABLE SQL statement used to create it), or if it already exists, you can mark it as being volatile (by executing an ALTER TABLE statement with the VOLATILE option specified; for example, ALTER TABLE sales VOLATILE).

Clustering Indexes and Partitioned Tables

Clustering indexes offer the same benefits for partitioned tables as they do for regular tables. However, to achieve well-maintained clustering with good performance, there should be a correlation between the index columns used and the table partitioning key columns. One way to ensure such correlation is to prefix the index columns with the table partitioning key columns, as shown in the following example:

```
CREATE TABLE monthly_sales
    (sales_date   DATE,
        sales_month INT GENERATED ALWAYS AS
                    (MONTH(sales_date)),
    region        CHAR(20),
    department    CHAR(20),
    amount        DECIMAL(8,2))
  PARTITION BY RANGE (sales_month)
   (STARTING FROM 1 ENDING AT 12 EVERY 1);

CREATE INDEX msales_cindx
ON monthly_sales (sales_month, region)
CLUSTER;
```

Although DB2 does not enforce this correlation, there is an expectation that all keys in the index are grouped together by partition IDs to achieve good clustering. For example, if a table is partitioned on a column named SALES_MONTH (as in the previous example), and a clustering index is defined on a column named SALES_DATE, because a relation between month and date exists, optimal clustering of the data can be achieved because all keys of any data partition are grouped together within the index.

Improving Insert Performance

The first time an application attempts to insert a record into a table, a special algorithm will search the Free Space Control Records (FSCRs) in an effort to locate a page that has enough free space to hold the new record. (The value assigned to the DB2MAXFSCRSEARCH registry variable determines the number of FSCRs that are searched; the default value for this registry variable is 5). If no space is found within the specified number of FSCRs searched, the record is appended to the end of the table. To optimize insert performance, subsequent records are also appended to the end of the table until two extents have been written. Once two extents have been filled, the next insert operation will resume searching FSCRs where the last search left off and the whole process is repeated. After all FSCRs in the entire table have been searched in this way, records are automatically appended and no additional searching is performed. In fact, searching using the FSCRs is not done again until space is created somewhere in the table by deleting one or more records.

To optimize a table for insert performance, at the possible expense of faster table growth, consider assigning a small number to the DB2MAXFSCRSEARCH registry variable. (To optimize for space reuse at the possible expense of insert performance, assign a larger number to the DB2MAXFSCRSEARCH registry variable; setting the value to -1 forces the DB2 Database Manager to search all FSCRs.) Another option is to define a clustering index for the table. As we have just seen, if a clustering index exists, DB2 will attempt to insert records on the same page as other records with similar index key values. If there is no space on that page, an attempt is made to put the record into one of the surrounding pages. If this is not possible, the FSCR search algorithm is used, except in this case, a worst-fit approach is used instead of a first-fit approach—this worst-fit approach tends to choose pages with more free space. The end result is that a new clustering area for rows with this key value is established. Keep in mind that using the PCTFREE option of the CREATE INDEX statement to specify the percentage of free space that should remain on a data page increases the probability that an insert operation will find free space on the appropriate page and the FSCR search algorithm will not have to be invoked.

Another way to optimize for insert performance is to place a table into what is known as append mode. Regular tables are placed into append mode by executing an ALTER TABLE SQL statement that looks like this:

```
ALTER TABLE [TableName] APPEND ON
```

where:

TableName   Identifies the table, by name, that is to be placed into append mode.

So, to place a table named PAYROLL.EMPLOYEE into append mode, you would execute the following ALTER TABLE statement:

```
ALTER TABLE payroll.employee APPEND ON
```

Once a table is placed in append mode, new rows are always appended to the end of the table—no searching or maintenance of FSCRs takes place. Append mode is best used for tables where clustering to any specific index is not important, the insert rate is high, and there are few or no delete operations performed.

> A table with a clustering index should normally not be placed in append mode. If it is, DB2 will be unable to maintain the index/data clustering. However, if you are doing batch updates to the table, and plan on reorganizing and capturing statistics on the table afterward, you can use append mode to speed up insert processing.

Object Statistics and the RUNSTATS Utility

The DB2 optimizer (which we will look at shortly), relies on object statistics when determining the cost of using different access plans to retrieve data in response to a query. The object statistics contain information such as the number of rows stored in a table, the way tables and indexes utilize storage space, and the number of unique values found in a particular column. In order to choose the optimum access plan, the optimizer needs good statistics. If this information is missing or out of date, the access plan chosen may cause the SQL statement to take longer to execute than necessary. Having valid information available becomes more crucial as the complexity of the SQL statement increases—with simple statements, there are usually a limited number of choices available; with complex statements, the number of choices available increases dramatically.

Prior to DB2 Version 9, object statistics information was not updated automatically as changes were made to a database. Instead, this information had to be updated periodically by manually running DB2's RUNSTATS utility. Starting with DB2 Version 9, automatic statistics collection (part of DB2's Automated Table Maintenance feature) is enabled by default when a new database is created. As long as automatic statistics collection remains enabled, DB2 will automatically execute the RUNSTATS utility in the background to ensure that the most current object statistics are available.

If automatic statistics collection is disabled, the RUNSTATS utility can be invoked manually by executing the RUNSTATS command. The basic syntax for this command is:

```
RUNSTATS ON TABLE [TableName]
USE PROFILE
<UTIL_IMPACT_PRIORITY [Priority]>
```

    or

```
RUNSTATS ON TABLE [TableName] FOR
<<SAMPLED> DETAILED>
[INDEXES | INDEX]
[[IndexName,...] | ALL]
<EXCLUDING XML COLUMNS>
<ALLOW READ ACCESS | ALLOW WRITE ACCESS>
<SET PROFILE NONE | SET PROFILE <ONLY> | UPDATE PROFILE
    <ONLY>>
<UTIL_IMPACT_PRIORITY [Priority]>
```

    or

```
RUNSTATS ON TABLE [TableName]
<ON ALL COLUMNS |
    ON KEY COLUMNS> |
    ON COLUMNS [ColumnName ,...] |
    ON ALL COLUMNS AND COLUMNS [ColumnName ,...] |
    ON KEY COLUMNS AND COLUMNS [ColumnName ,...]>
<WITH DISTRIBUTION>
<EXCLUDING XML COLUMNS>
```

```
<AND <<SAMPLED> DETAILED>
    [INDEXES | INDEX]
    [[IndexName,...] | ALL]>
<EXCLUDING XML COLUMNS>
<ALLOW READ ACCESS | ALLOW WRITE ACCESS>
<SET PROFILE NONE | SET PROFILE <ONLY> | UPDATE PROFILE
    <ONLY>>
<UTIL_IMPACT_PRIORITY [Priority]>
```

where:

TableName	Identifies the name assigned to the table for which statistical information is to be collected. This can be any base table, including a volatile table.
IndexName	Identifies the name assigned to one or more associated indexes for which statistical information is to be collected.
ColumnName	Identifies the name assigned to one or more columns for which statistical information is to be collected.
Priority	Indicates that the RUNSTATS utility is to be throttled such that it executes at a specific rate so that its effect on concurrent database activity can be controlled. This parameter can be assigned a numerical value within the range of 1 to 100, with 100 representing the highest priority and 1 representing the lowest.

Thus, if you wanted to collect statistics for a table named EMPLOYEE (which resides in a schema named PAYROLL) along with all of its associated indexes and allow read-only access to the table while statistics are being gathered, you could do so by executing a RUNSTATS command that looks something like this:

```
RUNSTATS ON TABLE payroll.employee
FOR INDEXES ALL
ALLOW READ ACCESS
```

On the other hand, if you only wanted to collect basic statistics and distribution statistics for all eligible columns of a table named DEPARTMENT (which resides in a schema named PAYROLL), you could do so by executing a RUNSTATS command that looks something like this:

```
RUNSTATS ON TABLE payroll.department
ON ALL COLUMNS
WITH DISTRIBUTION DEFAULT
```

Statistics can be gathered for all, some, or just a few selected columns. (Columns with data types such as LONG VARCHAR and CLOB are not examined by RUNSTATS.) You can also tell the tool to only capture statistics on key columns or on a specific list of highly accessed columns.

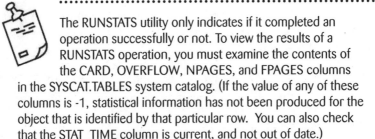

The RUNSTATS utility only indicates if it completed an operation successfully or not. To view the results of a RUNSTATS operation, you must examine the contents of the CARD, OVERFLOW, NPAGES, and FPAGES columns in the SYSCAT.TABLES system catalog. (If the value of any of these columns is -1, statistical information has not been produced for the object that is identified by that particular row. You can also check that the STAT_TIME column is current, and not out of date.)

Statistical information for tables and indexes can also be collected using the Run Statistics dialog, which can be activated by selecting the appropriate action from the Tables menu found in the Control Center. Figure 5–12 shows the Control Center menu items that must be selected in order to activate the Run Statistics dialog; Figure 5–13 shows how the Run Statistics dialog typically looks when it is first activated.

So just how often should you run the RUNSTATS utility? Ideally, the RUNSTATS utility should be run against a table immediately after any of the following occur:

- A large number of insert, update, merge, or delete operations are performed against the table.

- An import or load operation is performed.

- One or more columns are added to an existing table.

- A new index is created.

- A table or index is reorganized.

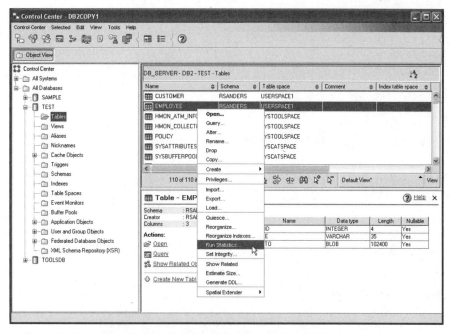

Figure 5–12: Invoking the Run Statistics dialog from the Control Center.

Figure 5–13: The Run Statistics dialog.

It is also a good idea to run the RUNSTATS utility before running the REORGCHK utility; if query response is slow because of fragmentation, and statistics are not up to date, the REORGCHK utility may report that a table/index reorganization operation is unnecessary when it really is.

Statistical Views

Unlike a table, a view normally does not have statistics associated with it. Instead, DB2 will make assumptions about a view's statistics based on the object statistics for the underlying table(s) the view is based on. The accuracy of these estimates depends on the predicates used to create the view and the availability of table statistics.

Statistical views are views with associated statistics that can be used to improve cardinality estimates for queries in which the view definition overlaps with the query definition. Statistical views allow the DB2 optimizer to compute more accurate cardinality estimates. (Cardinality estimation is the process where the optimizer uses statistics to determine the size of partial query results after predicates are applied or aggregation is performed.) The accuracy of cardinality estimates depends on the predicates used and the available statistics. Statistics are available to represent the distribution of data values within a column, which can improve cardinality estimates when the data values are unevenly distributed. Statistics are also available to represent the number of distinct values in a set of columns, which can improve cardinality estimates when columns are statistically correlated. However, quite often these statistics are not able to represent anything other than predicates or aggregation involving independent attributes and simple comparison operations.

Before statistics can be captured for a view, the view must first be enabled for optimization. A view can be enabled for optimization by executing the ALTER VIEW statement with the ENABLE OPTIMIZATION clause specified. A view that has been enabled for optimization can subsequently be disabled for optimization by executing the ALTER VIEW statement with the DISABLE OPTIMIZATION clause specified. For example, to enable the view ORG_VIEW for optimization, you would execute an ALTER VIEW statement that looks like this:

```
ALTER VIEW org_view ENABLE QUERY OPTIMIZATION
```

Once a view has been enabled for optimization, statistics are collected by executing the RUNSTATS command with the view name specified in place of a table name. Thus, to collect statistics for the view named ORG_VIEW that was enabled for optimization earlier, you would execute a RUNSTATS command that looks something like this:

```
RUNSTATS ON TABLE org_view WITH DISTRIBUTION
```

After the RUNSTATS command is executed, the system catalogs will be populated with the view statistics. However, only statistics that characterize the data distribution of the query that defines the view itself are taken into account by the optimizer. The following statistics associated with view records can be collected and utilized by the DB2 optimizer.

Table statistics (SYSCAT.TABLES, SYSSTAT.TABLES)

- **CARD**—The number of rows in the view result.

Column statistics (SYSCAT.COLUMNS, SYSSTAT.COLUMNS)

- **COLCARD**—The number of distinct values of a column in the view result
- **AVGCOLLEN**—Average length of column in the view result
- **HIGH2KEY**—Second highest value of a column in the view result
- **LOW2KEY**—Second lowest value of a column in the view result
- **NUMNULLS**—Number of NULLs in a view result column
- **SUB_COUNT**—Average number of subelements in a view result column
- **SUB_DELIM_LENGTH**—Average length of each delimiter separating each subelement

Column Distribution Statistics (SYSCAT.COLDIST, SYSSTAT.COLDIST)

- **DISTCOUNT**—If **TYPE** is **Q**, the number of distinct values that are less than or equal to **COLVALUE** statistics
- **SEQNO**—Frequency ranking of a sequence number to help uniquely identify the row in the table

- **COLVALUE**—Data value for which frequency or quantile statistic is collected

- **VALCOUNT**—Frequency with which the data value occurs in view column, or for quantiles, the number of values less than or equal to the data value (**COLVALUE**)

This information can then be included as part of the information the optimizer uses when determining the costs for executing qualified queries, which do not even need to reference the view directly. This will result in more accurate costing and more optimal access plans.

Another Look at Parallelism

You may recall that in Chapter 3, "Data Partitioning and Clustering," we saw that intra-partition parallelism refers to the ability to break up a database operation into multiple parts and execute those parts simultaneously within a single DB2 instance and that inter-partition parallelism refers to the ability to break up a database operation into multiple parts, many or all of which can be run in parallel across multiple partitions of a partitioned database. Both types of parallelism can provide a significant benefit in overall database performance as well as the execution of normal administrative tasks.

Types of Parallelism Supported

The degree of parallelism used is largely determined by the number of database partitions created and how database partition groups have been defined. So just where should each type of parallelism be used? As we saw in Chapter 3, that is determined primarily by the hardware configuration used. Some of the more common hardware configurations available, along with the type of parallelism that is best suited for each, can be seen in Table 5.6.

Table 5.6 Types of Parallelism Possible in Common Hardware Environments			
		Intra-Query Parallelism	
Hardware Configuration	I/O Parallelism	Intra-partition Parallelism	Inter-partition Parallelism
Single Database Partition, Single Processor	Yes	No	No
Single Database Partition, Multiple Processors (SMP)	Yes	Yes	No
Multiple Database Partitions, One Processor (MPP)	Yes	No	Yes
Multiple Database Partitions, Multiple Processors (cluster of SMPs)	Yes	Yes	Yes
Logical Database Partitions	Yes	Yes	Yes

Keep in mind that each database partition can reside on its own machine and have its own processor, memory, and disks. A logical database partition differs from a physical partition in that it is not given control of an entire machine—although the machine has shared resources, logical database partitions do not share these resources. Processors are shared but disks and memory are not.

Connections and Connection Pooling

When an application connects to a nonpartitioned database, the connection is assigned to a coordinating agent (named db2agent in Linux and UNIX environments), and all subsequent SQL statements and DB2 commands are executed by this agent on behalf of the application. When the application disconnects, the corresponding coordinating agent can be terminated; however, this is inefficient because the overhead of continually terminating existing agent processes and starting new ones when needed can be quite high. A better approach is to let DB2 keep unused (idle) agents around and allow them to be reused by other applications.

Idle agents reside in an agent pool. These agents are available for requests from coordinating agents operating on behalf of client applications, or from subagents operating on behalf of existing coordinating agents. When the maximum number of connections supported (determined by the value assigned to the *max_connections* Database Manager configuration parameter) is equal to or less than the maximum number of coordinating agents allowed (determined by the value assigned to the *max_coordagents* configuration parameter), the size of the idle agent pool is determined by the maximum number of agents allowed. All idle agents, regardless of whether they are coordinating agents or subagents, count toward this limit; if the workload causes this limit to be exceeded, the agents needed are created to support the workload and then terminated as soon as they finish executing their current request.

Having an appropriately sized idle agent pool can help performance in configurations that have significant application workloads because idle agents can be immediately used as needed, rather than having to allocate a completely new agent for each application connection, which involves creating a thread and allocating and initializing memory and other resources. Starting with version 9.5, DB2 can also automatically manage the size of the idle agent pool if so desired.

DB2's connection concentrator allows servers to provide support for thousands of users simultaneously executing business transactions while drastically reducing the resources required. It accomplishes this by concentrating the workload from all active applications in a much smaller number of database server connections. The connection concentrator is enabled when the maximum number of connections supported (determined by the value assigned to the *max_connections* Database Manager configuration parameter) is greater than the maximum number of coordinating agents allowed (determined by the value assigned to the *max_coordagents* configuration parameter). When the connection concentrator is enabled, the value assigned to the *max_coordagents* configuration parameter is used as a guideline for determining how large the agent pool will be when the system workload is low. In this case, an idle agent will always be returned to the pool, no matter what the *max_coordagents* configuration parameter has been set to, and DB2's connection concentrator technology will be enabled.

The connection concentrator uses logical agents (LAs) to handle the application context while database agents (DAs) handle the actual DB2 connections. When a new application connects to a database, it is assigned an LA. Because a DA is needed to pass SQL statements to the DB2 server for processing, one is assigned to perform the work for the LA as soon as a new transaction is initiated. The key to this architecture is the fact that the DA is disassociated from the LA and is returned to the agent pool when a transaction completes.

Applications and Intra-Partition Parallelism

When an SQL statement is executed in an environment where intra-partition parallelism is enabled, the agent assigned to handle the connection (the coordinating agent) will determine the degree of parallelism that is to be used to execute the statement based on the access plan chosen and the values assigned to various instance and database configuration parameters. The coordinating agent will then make n copies of the access plan (where n is the degree of parallelism used) and distribute database requests to the appropriate number of subagents for processing. (In this case, coordinating subagents that perform requests on the database are named db2agntp; subagents that are associated with an application but are currently idle are identified by the name db2agnta.) Thus, for an access plan with a degree of parallelism of eight, one coordinating agent and eight subagents will be used to execute the plan and return the data. Such subagents are called *associated* because they have an affiliation with the coordinating agent and have control blocks and shared inter-process communication (IPC) blocks set up to communicate with the coordinating agent.

When a coordinating agent finishes executing its current SQL statement, its associated subagents will become idle but will remain associated with the coordinating agent. Subagents remain associated with a coordinating agent because there is a chance that they may be needed in the future for processing a subsequent statement and it is inefficient to break a subagent's association, release it back to the idle agent pool, and then associate it with the coordinating agent again.

If the current SQL statement being executed by a coordinating agent completes, and the next statement to be executed has a higher degree of parallelism than the previous one, the coordinating agent must activate and/or acquire a number of additional subagents. The activation and acquiring of these subagents will be done in the following order to help ensure the optimal usage of the agents and available resources:

1. Convert any idle subagents currently associated to the coordinating agent to active.

2. Convert any idle subagents not currently associated to another coordinating agent to active.

3. Convert any idle subagents currently associated to another coordinating agent to active.

4. Create a new agent process.

For large, complex queries, result sets can normally be returned much quicker when intra-partition parallelism is used. However, the insertion of a single row does not require a large number of agents. In a typical OLTP environment there are normally hundreds (if not more) applications running in parallel. If each of them were assigned a large number of agent processes to handle their simple tasks, there would be far too many agent processes running on the system, causing a great deal more system overhead than is required. Therefore, a thorough knowledge of the database workload is required before you can decide whether or not to use intra-partition parallelism.

A Word About Table Queues

When queries are executed in a database environment that has been designed to take advantage of parallelism, a table queue is used to pass table data from one database agent to another. When inter-partition parallelism is used, table queues facilitate the passing of table data from one database partition to another; when intra-partition parallelism is used they aid in the passing of table data within a single database partition. Each table queue passes data in a single direction. The SQL compiler decides where table queues are required and includes them in the access plan; when the plan is executed, connections between the database partitions open the table queues needed. Table queues are closed automatically as processes end.

Several types of table queues are available, including:

- **Local table queues (sometimes referred to as LTQ)**. These table queues are used to pass data between database agents within a single database partition. Local table queues (LTQ) are used for intra-partition parallelism.

- **Asynchronous table queues.** These table queues are known as asynchronous because they read rows in advance of any FETCH statement issued by an application. When the FETCH statement is issued, the row is retrieved from the table queue. Asynchronous table queues are used when you specify the FOR FETCH ONLY clause on a SELECT statement. If you are only fetching rows, the asynchronous table queue is faster.

- **Synchronous table queues.** These table queues are known as synchronous because they read one row for each FETCH statement issued by an application. Synchronous table queues are used when you do not specify the FOR FETCH ONLY clause on a SELECT statement. In a partitioned database environment, if you are updating rows, the Database Manager will use the synchronous table queues.

- **Merging table queues.** These table queues preserve order.

- **Nonmerging table queues.** These table queues, also known as "regular" table queues, do not preserve order.

- **Listener table queues.** These table queues are used with correlated subqueries. Correlation values are passed down to the subquery and the results are passed back up to the parent query block using this type of table queue.

- **Directed table queues (sometimes referred to as DTQ).** These table queues are used in join operations. With directed table queues, rows are hashed to one of the receiving database partitions.

- **Broadcast table queues (sometimes referred to as BTQ).** These table queues are also used in join operations. With broadcast table queues, rows are sent to all of the receiving database partitions but are not hashed.

The DB2 Optimizer

The DB2 Optimizer is the component of the SQL compiler that is responsible for choosing the access plan to use for processing data manipulation language (DML) SQL statements. It does this by modeling the execution cost of many alternative access plans and choosing the one with the minimal estimated cost.

The first thing that the DB2 Optimizer does when it is invoked is accept and parse the SQL statement received. As an SQL statement is parsed, the optimizer begins to construct a graphical representation of the access plan needed. This graphical representation is then refined in subsequent steps and eventually becomes the section in the access plan chosen.

Once the SQL statement has been parsed, the optimizer then attempts to verify that all objects referenced in the statement do, in fact, exist in the database. (This is referred to as checking or validating the semantics.) For example, if the following SQL statement was submitted to the DB2 Optimizer for processing:

```
SELECT * FROM payroll.employees
```

the table named EMPLOYEES, stored in the schema named PAYROLL, must exist in the database in order for the statement to pass the semantics check. If the table and/or schema specified do not exist, there is no need to perform any additional work because a valid access plan cannot be created.

After semantics checking is complete, the DB2 Optimizer will use its powerful query rewrite facility to examine the statement and try to determine if there are better ways to write the statement. The query rewrite facility can also perform the following functions, if applicable:

- Automatically redirect a query to use a materialized query table if one can be used to satisfy the query

- Pre-compute constant expressions

- Optimize aggregates

- Remove or replace subselects

- Eliminate redundant operations

For example, suppose a table named T1 has two columns named C1 and C2 and a unique index exists for column C1. If the following query is executed:

```
SELECT DISTINCT (C1) FROM T1
```

the DISTINCT clause is considered to be redundant. If the DB2 Optimizer were to leave this clause in, a sort would need to be performed to ensure that no duplicate values are returned. However, by examining the statement and the statistics for the table the optimizer can eliminate the DISTINCT clause and take advantage of the unique index to make the final access plan chosen more efficient.

Once the query rewrite step is complete, the DB2 Optimizer will enumerate different plan options available and evaluate each one. Depending on the optimization level used and the instance and database configuration settings found, some techniques may or may not be allowed. As each allowed plan is enumerated, the cost of the plan is evaluated; once the optimizer has analyzed all possible plans, the plan with the lowest cost is chosen. Once a plan is chosen, the code for that plan is built into a package, which is then stored in the system catalog of the database (if the statement was static) or the package cache (if the statement was dynamic).

Optimizer Techniques

Of the most basic techniques that the optimizer can use when deciding on an optimal access plan is whether an index can be used to access the data or a table scan will be required. In general, the fastest way to access data is to use an index; indexes are structured in a way that increases the efficiency of finding rows of data. By simply traversing an index from the root to the leaf page, DB2 can quickly find a record, and therefore the page, where the data for the record exists.

An index cannot be used if one does not exist, and certain types of SQL statements simply are best satisfied with a simple table scan. For example, consider the following SQL statement:

```
SELECT * FROM PAYROLL.EMPLOYEES
```

In this case an index would not be beneficial because the query is returning all columns in all rows from the table. Even if a WHERE clause was added to the query, the DB2 optimizer might still determine that a table scan (or sequential scan) will outperform an index scan.

Why would nonindexed access outperform indexed access when the primary reason indexes exist in the first place is to improve performance? Well, in some cases, it is possible that indexed access will be slower. For example, reading all of the pages for a very small table may be faster than first reading the index page(s) and then reading the data page(s). Even for larger tables, the organization of an index could require additional I/O to satisfy a query. When an index is not used to satisfy a query, the resulting access path uses a table scan (or table space scan).

A table scan generally reads every page of a table. However, in certain circumstances, DB2 can be smart enough to limit the number of pages that are scanned. Additionally, DB2 can invoke sequential prefetching to read pages before they have been requested. Sequential prefetching is particularly useful when an SQL request needs to access rows sequentially, in the order in which they were stored on disk. The optimizer will signal that sequential prefetch should be used when it determines that a query will sequentially read data pages. As you might imagine, table scans frequently benefit from the read ahead processing of sequential prefetching because in most cases, needed data will already be in memory when it is requested by a query.

Writing Better Queries

Earlier, we saw that when the DB2 Optimizer compiles SQL statements, it may rewrite them into a form that can be optimized more easily. The optimizer then generates a number of alternative execution plans for satisfying the SQL statement, estimates the execution cost of each alternative plan using the statistics available, and chooses the plan with the lowest estimated execution cost.

Because the optimizer must choose an access plan that will produce a result data set for the query that was submitted, it is important to develop queries that only request data that is needed. The following guidelines, when used while writing queries, will help ensure that the optimizer will choose the best access plan.

Only Retrieve Data That Is Needed

Specify only those columns that are needed in the SELECT list used. Although it may be simpler to specify all columns with an asterisk (*), the processing and returning of unneeded columns can result in slower query response time.

Limit the Number of Rows Returned

Limit the number of rows retrieved by using predicates to restrict the answer set to only those rows that you require. Four types of predicates, each with its own distinct method of processing and associated cost, can be used for this purpose. These predicates, ordered in terms of performance, starting with the most favorable, are:

1. Range delimiting predicates

2. Index SARGable predicates

3. Data SARGable predicates

4. Residual predicates

Range delimiting predicates are used to define the start key and/or stop key for an index search. Index SARGable predicates are not used to define the start/stop key for an index search but can be evaluated from the index because the columns involved in the predicate are part of the index key. For example, suppose you have a table named STAFF and an index defined on columns NAME, DEPT and SVC_YEARS in the table. For the following query:

```
SELECT name, job, salary
  FROM staff
  WHERE name = 'Alyssa' AND
        dept = 23 AND
        svc_years > 5
```

the predicates NAME = 'Alyssa' and DEPT = 23 would be range delimiting predicates, whereas SVC_YEARS > 5 would be evaluated as an index sargable predicate because the start key value for the index search cannot be determined by the information provided. The start key value may be 6, 10, or even higher.

If the query were written as follows:

```
SELECT name, job, salary
  FROM staff
  WHERE name = 'Alyssa' AND
        dept = 23 AND
        svc_years >= 5
```

SVC_YEARS >=5 can now be evaluated using a range delimiting predicate because the index search can start from the key value 5.

DB2 will make use of the index when evaluating range delimiting predicates and index sargable predicates, rather than reading the base table. As a result, these predicates reduce the number of data pages that must be accessed by reducing the set of rows that need to be read from the table. Index sargable predicates do not affect the number of index pages that are accessed.

Data sargable predicates are predicates that cannot be evaluated using the index and must be evaluated by reading the data. Typically, these predicates require the access of individual rows from a base table. DB2 will retrieve the columns needed to evaluate the predicate, as well as any others to satisfy the columns in the SELECT list that could not be obtained from the index. For example, assume that a table named PROJECT has an index defined on the PROJNUM column in the table. For the following query:

```
SELECT projnum, projname, repemp
  FROM project
  WHERE dept = 'D11'
  ORDER BY projnum
```

the predicate DEPT = 'D11' will be processed as a data sargable predicate because there are no indexes defined on the DEPT column, and the base table must be accessed to evaluate that predicate.

Residual predicates, typically, are those predicates that require I/O beyond the simple accessing of a base table. Examples of residual predicates include those using quantified subqueries (subqueries with ANY, ALL, SOME, or IN) or those that require reading LONG VARCHAR or LOB data. Residual predicates are the most expensive of the four types of predicates. Residual predicates and data sargable predicates require more resources and cost more than range delimiting predicates and index sargable predicates; therefore, you should limit the number of rows qualified by range delimiting predicates and index sargable predicates whenever possible.

Use the FOR UPDATE Clause

If a cursor is used and there is a chance that the data retrieved will be updated, specify the FOR UPDATE clause in the SELECT statement used to define the cursor. By doing this, DB2 can choose appropriate locking levels (i.e., an Update lock instead of a Shared lock) to prevent having to perform a lock conversion when the update operation is performed.

Use the OPTIMIZE FOR n ROWS Clause

Specify the OPTIMIZE FOR *n* ROWS clause in the SELECT statement when the number of rows required is less than the total number of rows that could be returned. Row blocking is a technique that reduces overhead by retrieving a number of rows in a single operation. These rows are stored in a cache, and each FETCH request in the application retrieves the next row from the cache. When used, the OPTIMIZE FOR n ROWS clause will determine the number of records to be blocked. For example, if OPTIMIZE FOR 10 ROWS is specified, the block of rows returned will contain ten rows. Use of the OPTIMIZE FOR clause influences query optimization based on the assumption that the first *n* rows should be retrieved quickly, whereas the application can wait for the remaining rows.

Keep in mind that the OPTIMIZE FOR n ROWS clause does not limit the number of rows that can be fetched or affect the result in any way other than performance. Using this clause can improve performance if no more than *n* rows are retrieved but may degrade performance if more than *n* rows are retrieved.

Use the FETCH FIRST n ROWS Clause

Specify the FETCH FIRST *n* ROWS ONLY clause if the application should not retrieve more than *n* rows, regardless of how many rows there might be in the result set produced when this clause is not specified. For example, the following query will retrieve the first five rows from the result set, not the entire result set:

```
SELECT projnum, projname, repemp
FROM project
WHERE dept = 'D11'
FETCH FIRST 5 ROWS ONLY
```

The FETCH FIRST *n* ROWS ONLY clause also determines the number of rows that are blocked in the communication buffer. If both the FETCH FIRST *n* ROWS ONLY and the OPTIMIZE FOR *n* ROWS clauses are specified, the lower of the two values is used to determine the number of rows to be blocked. This clause cannot be specified with the FOR UPDATE clause.

Use the FOR FETCH ONLY Clause

If a cursor is used and the data retrieved will not be updated, specify the FOR FETCH ONLY clause in the SELECT statement used to define the cursor. This can improve performance by allowing the query to take advantage of record blocking. This can also improve concurrency since exclusive locks will never be obtained when this clause is specified.

The FOR READ ONLY clause is equivalent to the FOR FETCH ONLY clause.

Avoid Data Type Conversions

Data type conversions (particularly numeric data type conversions) should be avoided whenever possible. When two values are compared, it is more efficient to compare rows with the same data type. For example, suppose a table named EMPLOYEE and a table named DEPARTMENT are to be joined using column DEPTID in the EMPLOYEE table and column ID in the DEPARTMENT table. If the columns DEPTID and ID are the same data type, no data type conversion is required. If they are not the same data type, a data type conversion is required in order to compare the values at run time, and this will affect the performance of the query.

A Word About Joins

When joining two tables, no matter which join method is being used, one table will be selected to be the outer table and the other table will be the inner table. The optimizer decides which will be the outer table and which will be the inner table based on the calculated cost and the join method selected. The outer table will be accessed first and will only be scanned once. The inner table may be scanned multiple times, depending on the type of join and the indexes that are present on the tables. It is also important to remember that even though an SQL statement may join more than two tables, the optimizer will only join two tables at a time and keep the intermediate results if necessary.

There are three basic join techniques that the optimizer can choose between for a single partition database:

- Nested Loop Join
- Merge Join
- Hash Join

In a partitioned database, there are three more basic join techniques:

- Collocated Join
- Directed Join
- Broadcast Join

A collocated table join is most efficient because there is no need to send data between partitions. A directed join will send data from one table to the partition where the data in the other table resides using a directed table queue (DTQ). As the name implies, a broadcast join will send a whole table to all partitions where the other table resides using a broadcast table queue (BTQ).

These partitioned and nonpartitioned join techniques are covered in detail in Appendix E.

Locking

Locking also has a direct influence on the access plan that the optimizer will choose for a particular query. A *lock* is a mechanism that is used to associate a data resource with a single transaction, for the sole purpose of controlling how other transactions interact with that resource while it is associated with the transaction that has it locked. (The transaction that has a data resource associated with it is said to "hold" or "own" the lock.) Essentially, locks in a database environment serve the same purpose as they do in a house or a car: they determine who can and cannot gain access to a particular resource—which can be one or more table spaces, tables, and/or rows. The DB2 instance imposes locks to prohibit "owning" transactions from accessing uncommitted data that has been written by other transactions and/or to prevent other transactions from making data modifications that might adversely affect the owning transaction. When an owning transaction is terminated (by being committed or by being rolled back), any changes made to the resource that was locked are either made permanent or removed, and all locks on the resource that had been acquired by the owning transaction are released. Once unlocked, a resource can be locked again and manipulated by another active transaction. Figure 5–14 illustrates the principles of transaction/resource locking.

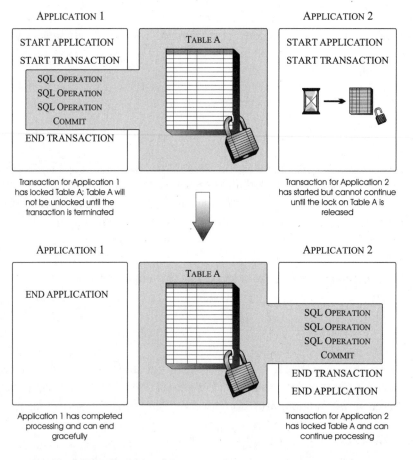

Figure 5–14: How DB2 prevents uncontrolled concurrent access to a resource through the use of locks.

How Locks Are Acquired

A DB2 instance implicitly acquires locks as they are needed; once acquired, these locks remain under the instance's control until they are no longer needed. By default, DB2 always attempts to acquire row-level locks. However, it is possible to control whether the DB2 instance will attempt to acquire row-level locks or table-level locks on a specific table resource by executing a special form of the ALTER TABLE SQL statement. The syntax for this form of the ALTER TABLE statement is:

```
ALTER TABLE [TableName] LOCKSIZE [ROW | TABLE]
```

where:

TableName   Identifies the name of an existing table for which the level of locking that all transactions are to use when accessing it is to be specified.

For example, when executed, the SQL statement

```
ALTER TABLE employee LOCKSIZE ROW
```

will force the DB2 instance to acquire row-level locks for every transaction that accesses a table named EMPLOYEE. (This is the default behavior.) On the other hand, if the SQL statement

```
ALTER TABLE employee LOCKSIZE TABLE
```

is executed, the DB2 instance will attempt to acquire table-level locks for every transaction that accesses the EMPLOYEE table.

But what if you don't want every transaction that works with a particular table to acquire table-level locks? What if instead you want one specific transaction to acquire table-level locks and all other transactions to acquire row-level locks when working with that particular table? In this case, you leave the default locking behavior alone (row-level locking) and use the LOCK TABLE SQL statement to acquire a table-level lock for the appropriate individual transaction. The syntax for the LOCK TABLE statement is:

```
LOCK TABLE [TableName] IN [SHARE | EXCLUSIVE] MODE
```

where:

TableName   Identifies the name of an existing table to be locked.

As you can see, the LOCK TABLE statement allows a transaction to acquire a table-level lock on a particular table in one of two modes: SHARE mode and EXCLUSIVE mode. If a table is locked using the SHARE mode, a table-level Share (S) lock is acquired on behalf of the requesting transaction, and other concurrent transactions are allowed to read, but not change, data stored in the locked table. On the other hand, if a table is locked using the EXCLUSIVE mode, a table-level Exclusive (X) lock is acquired, and other concurrent transactions can neither access nor modify data stored in the locked table.

For example, if executed, the SQL statement

```
LOCK TABLE employee IN SHARE MODE
```

would acquire a table-level Share (S) lock on the EMPLOYEE table on behalf of the current transaction (provided no other transaction holds a lock on this table), and other concurrent transactions would be allowed to read, but not change, the data stored in the table. On the other hand, if the statement

```
LOCK TABLE employee IN EXCLUSIVE MODE
```

were executed, a table-level Exclusive (X) lock would be acquired, and no other transaction would be allowed to read or modify data stored in the EMPLOYEE table until the owning transaction is terminated—unless the other transaction is running under the Uncommitted Read (UR) isolation level.

Lock Granularity and Concurrency

When it comes to deciding whether to use row-level locks or table-level locks, it is important to keep in mind that any time a transaction holds a lock on a particular resource, other transactions may be denied access to that resource until the owning transaction is terminated. Therefore, row-level locks are usually better than table-level locks because they restrict access to a much smaller resource. However, because each lock acquired requires some amount of storage space (to hold) and some degree of processing time (to manage), often there is considerably less overhead involved when a single table-level lock is acquired, rather than several individual row-level locks.

To a certain extent, lock granularity (row-level locking vs. table-level locking) can be controlled through the use of the ALTER TABLE and LOCK TABLE SQL statements—the ALTER TABLE statement controls granularity at a global level, whereas the LOCK TABLE statement controls granularity at an individual transaction level. So when is it more desirable to control granularity at the global level rather than at an individual transaction level? It all depends on the situation.

Suppose you have a read-only lookup table that is to be accessed by multiple concurrent transactions. Forcing the DB2 instance to globally acquire Share (S) table-level locks for every transaction that attempts to access this table might improve overall performance because the locking overhead required would be greatly reduced. On the other hand, suppose you have a table that needs to be accessed frequently by read-only transactions and periodically by a single transaction designed to perform basic maintenance. Forcing the DB2 instance to only acquire an Exclusive (X) table-level lock at the transaction level whenever the maintenance transaction executes makes more sense than forcing the DB2 instance to globally acquire Exclusive (X) table-level locks for every transaction that needs to access the table. If this approach is used, the read-only transactions are only locked out of the table whenever the maintenance transaction runs, but in all other situations, they can access the table concurrently while requiring very little locking overhead.

Analyzing DB2 Query Access Plans

Earlier, we saw that when a DML SQL statement is submitted to DB2 for processing, it is analyzed by the DB2 optimizer to produce what is known as an access plan. Each access plan contains detailed information about the strategy that will be used to execute the statement (such as whether indexes will be used; what sort methods, if any, are required; what locks are needed; and what join methods, if any, will be used). If the SQL statement is coded in an application, the access plan is generated at precompile time (or at bind time if deferred binding is used), and an executable form of the access plan produced is stored in the system catalog as an object known as a package. If, however, the statement is submitted from the Command Line Processor, or if the statement is a dynamic SQL statement in an application program (i.e., an SQL statement that is constructed at application run time), the access plan is generated at the time the statement is prepared for execution and is stored temporarily in memory (in the global package cache) rather than in the system catalog.

The Explain Facility

In order to see how an SQL statement was optimized, you must be able to capture and view the information stored in the access plan that was produced for the statement. That's where the Explain Facility comes in. The Explain Facility allows you to capture and view detailed information about the access plan chosen for a particular SQL statement. By analyzing this information, you can identify poorly written statements or a weakness in your database design.

Before Explain information can be captured, a special set of tables, known as the Explain tables, must be created. Typically, Explain tables are used in a development database to aid in application design but not in production databases, where application code remains fairly static. Therefore, they are not created along with the system catalog tables as part of the database creation process. Instead, Explain tables must be created manually in the database with which the Explain Facility will be used. To create the Explain tables, simply establish a connection to the appropriate database and execute a script named EXPLAIN.DDL (using the DB2 Command Line Processor), which can be found in the misc subdirectory of the sqllib directory where the DB2 software was installed. (Comments in the header of this file provide information on how it is to be executed.)

Once Explain tables have been created, there are a variety of ways in which Explain data can be collected. These methods include:

- Executing the EXPLAIN SQL statement

- Setting the CURRENT EXPLAIN MODE special register

- Setting the CURRENT EXPLAIN SNAPSHOT special register

- Using the EXPLAIN bind option with the PRECOMPILE or BIND command

- Using the EXPLSNAP bind option with the PRECOMPILE or BIND command

After Explain data has been collected (or an access plan has been produced) you can use one of the following tools to present Explain information in a meaningful format:

- **The db2expln tool.** Used to produce information about the access plans that have been chosen for packages for which Explain data has not been captured. Can describe the implementation of the final access plan chosen; cannot provide information on how a particular SQL statement was optimized.

- **The dynexpln tool.** Used to produce information about the access plan that was chosen for a specified SQL statement.

- **The db2exfmt tool.** Used to query the Explain tables for information, format the results, and produce a text-based report, as well as a graphical representation of the access plan chosen, that can be displayed directly on the terminal or written to an ASCII-formatted file.

- **Visual Explain.** A GUI tool that provides the ability to view a graphical representation of the access plan that has been chosen for a particular SQL statement. Can only be used to view Explain snapshot data; the db2exfmt tool must be used to view detailed Explain data that has been collected and written to the Explain tables.

Understanding db2exfmt Output

Before we take a look at how to analyze a DB2 query access plan, let's spend a few moments examining the output produced by the db2exfmt tool, which is the tool that is often used by DBAs to examine Explain data. As mentioned earlier, the db2exfmt tool is designed to work directly with comprehensive Explain or Explain snapshot data that has been collected and stored in the Explain tables. Given a database name and other qualifying information, the db2exfmt tool will query the Explain tables for information, format the results, and produce a text-based report that can be displayed directly on the terminal or written to an ASCII-formatted file.

For example, if you wanted to generate a detailed report consisting of all Explain data that has been collected and stored in the SAMPLE database provided with DB2, you could do so by executing a db2exfmt command that looks something like this:

```
db2exfmt -d sample -1 -o F:\db2exfmt.out
```

When this command is executed, a report will be produced and written to a file named db2exfmt.out (that resides on the F: drive), and you should see a message that looks something like this:

```
DB2 Universal Database Version 9.1, 5622-044 (c) Copyright IBM Corp.
  1991, 2006
Licensed Material - Program Property of IBM
IBM DATABASE 2 Explain Table Format Tool


Connecting to the Database.
Connect to Database Successful.
Output is in F:/db2exfmt.out.
Executing Connect Reset -- Connect Reset was Successful.
```

The file produced (db2exfmt.out) can then be viewed in any ASCII text editor. The following sections describe how to interpret the information stored in this file.

Overview Area

The beginning of the output file created by the db2exfmt tool is referred to as the overview area because it provides general overview information, such as the version and release level of DB2 used, as well as the date and time the tool was run. The overview area typically looks something like this:

```
DB2 Universal Database Version 9.1, 5622-044 (c) Copyright IBM Corp.
  1991, 2006
Licensed Material - Program Property of IBM
IBM DATABASE 2 Explain Table Format Tool

******************** EXPLAIN INSTANCE ********************

DB2_VERSION:           09.01.0
SOURCE_NAME:           SQLC2FOA
SOURCE_SCHEMA:         NULLID
SOURCE_VERSION:
EXPLAIN_TIME:          2008-04-02-09.20.14.687000
EXPLAIN_REQUESTER:     DSNOW
```

Database Context Area

The database context area follows the overview area and contains information about the parameters that have the biggest impact on the performance of the database and its applications, including:

- Parallelism

- CPU speed

- Communication Speed

- Buffer pool size

- Sort heap size

- Database heap size

- Lock list size

- Maximum lock list

- Average number of applications

- Locks available

The database context area looks something like this:

```
Database Context:
----------------
        Parallelism:             None
        CPU Speed:               3.621306e-007
        Comm Speed:              100
        Buffer Pool size:        15250
        Sort Heap size:          256
        Database Heap size:      600
        Lock List size:          50
        Maximum Lock List:       22
        Average Applications:    1
        Locks Available:         935
```

Package Context Area

The package context area follows the database context area and contains information about whether the SQL processed was dynamic or static, as well as the optimization level, isolation level, and degree of intra-partition parallelism used to process the statement. The package context area looks something like this:

```
Package Context:
---------------
     SQL Type:                  Dynamic
     Optimization Level:        5
     Blocking:                       Block All Cursors
     Isolation Level:                Cursor Stability


--------------- STATEMENT 1  SECTION 203 ----------------
     QUERYNO:                   1
     QUERYTAG:
     Statement Type:            Select
     Updatable:                 No
     Deletable:                 No
     Query Degree:        1
```

Original Statement Area

The original statement area follows the package context area and contains the SQL statement as it was originally received by the Explain Facility. The original statement area will look something like this:

```
Original Statement:
------------------
select count (*)
from alyssa.address
```

Optimized Statement Area

The optimized statement area follows the original statement area and contains the rewritten SQL statement that was produced by the query rewrite facility within the optimizer. The query rewrite facility can also perform the following functions if applicable:

- Automatically redirect the query to a materialized query table if one can be used to satisfy the query

- Precomputate constant expressions

- Optimize aggregates

- Embed or remove subselects

The optimized statement area looks something like this:

```
Optimized Statement:
-------------------
SELECT Q3.$C0
FROM
     (SELECT COUNT(*)
     FROM
          (SELECT $RID$
          FROM ALYSSA.ADDRESS AS Q1) AS Q2) AS Q3
```

The internal names shown in this example (Q1, Q2, and Q3) represent the table or subselect's position in the query list.

Access Plan Area

The access plan area follows the optimized statement area and contains an ASCII/text graphical representation of the access plan chosen for the SQL statement provided. The access plan area will look something like this:

```
Access Plan:
-----------
Total Cost:          876.373
Query Degree:        1

       Rows
     RETURN
     (   1)
      Cost
       I/O
        |
        1
     GRPBY
     (   2)
     876.373
       735
        |
     196904
     TBSCAN
     (   3)
     858.547
       735
        |
     196904
  TABLE: ALYSSA.ADDRESS
```

The elements of the access plan are read from the bottom up. Starting at the bottom of this access plan we see that the base table accessed by the query is the ADDRESS table and that it has a cardinality of 196904 rows. The table is accessed via a table scan (relation scan) and the data is then grouped on the return column before being returned to the application. In this access plan, the operators TBSCAN, GRPBY, and RETURN are used to identify either an action that must be performed on data or output produced. A wide variety of operators can appear in an access plan; the operators used by DB2 and their meanings can be seen in Table 5.7.

Table 5.7 Access Plan Operators		
Category	**Definition**	**Description**
Scan/Fetch	TBSCAN	Table Scan—Retrieves rows by reading all required data directly from the data pages.
	IXSCAN	Index Scan—Scans an index of a table with optional start/stop conditions, producing an ordered stream of rows.
	FETCH	Fetch From Table—Fetches columns from a table using a specific record identifier.
	EISCAN	Extended Index Scan—Scans a user-defined index to produce a reduced stream of rows.
	RIDSCN	Row Identifier Scan—Scans a list of row identifiers (RIDs) obtained from one or more indexes.
Joins	MSJOIN	Merge Scan Join—A join where both outer and inner tables must be in join-predicate order.
	NLJOIN	Nested Loop Join—A join that accesses an inner table once for each row of the outer table.
	HSJOIN	Hash Join—A join where two or more tables are hashed on the join columns.
Aggregation	GRPBY	Group By—Groups rows by common values of designated columns or functions and evaluates set functions.
	SUM	Sum—Summation of numeric data values for GROUP BY clause.
	AVG	Average—Average of numeric data values for GROUP BY clause.
	MIN	Minimum—Minimum of numeric data values for GROUP BY clause.
	MAX	Maximum—Maximum of numeric data values for GROUP BY clause.
	GENROW	Generate Rows—Generates rows of data (for example, for an INSERT statement or for some IN-lists that are transformed into joins).

Table 5.7 Access Plan Operators (Continued)		
Category	**Definition**	**Description**
Temporary/Sort	TEMP	Insert Into Temporary Table—Stores data in a temporary table to be read back out (possibly multiple times).
	SORT	Sort—Sorts rows in the order of specified columns and optionally eliminates duplicate entries.
DML operations	INSERT	Insert—Inserts rows into a table.
	UPDATE	Update—Updates rows in a table.
	DELETE	Delete—Deletes rows from a table.
Table queues	LTQ	Local Table Queue—A table queue used to pass data between database agents within a single database partition. (Used for intra-partition parallelism.)
	DTQ	Directed Table Queue—A table queue in which rows are hashed to one of the receiving database partitions.
	BTQ	Broadcast Table Queue—A table queue in which rows are sent to all of the receiving database partitions, but are not hashed.
	MDTQ	Merge Directed Table Queue—A table queue in which rows are hashed to one of the receiving database partitions and order is preserved.
	MBTQ	Merge Broadcast Table Queue—A table queue in which rows are sent to all of the receiving database partitions but are not hashed and order is preserved.
Special operations	IXAND	Index AND—ANDs together the row identifiers (RIDs) from two or more index scans.
	FILTER	Filter—Filters data by applying one or more predicates to it.
	SHIP	Ship—Retrieves data from a remote database source. Used in the federated system.
	RETURN	Return—Represents the return of data from the query to the user.
	UNION	Union—Concatenates streams of rows from multiple tables.
	UNIQUE	Unique—Eliminates rows with duplicate values for specified columns.

Another Access Plan—With Details

Consider the following portion of an access plan graph:

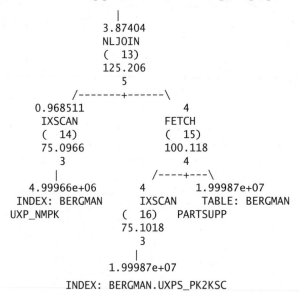

```
                         |
                      3.87404
                      NLJOIN
                      (  13)
                      125.206
                         5
                /-------+------\
           0.968511              4
           IXSCAN              FETCH
           (  14)             (  15)
           75.0966            100.118
              3                  4
              |              /----+---\
         4.99966e+06        4          1.99987e+07
        INDEX: BERGMAN    IXSCAN      TABLE: BERGMAN
        UXP_NMPK          (  16)       PARTSUPP
                          75.1018
                             3
                             |
                         1.99987e+07
                   INDEX: BERGMAN.UXPS_PK2KSC
```

As before, the path of execution is read from the bottom up and from left to right. In this particular plan, each row found by the index scan (IXSCAN) in step 14 is passed to the nested loop join (NLJOIN) in step 13. The nested loop join (NLJOIN) then accesses an inner table based on the join predicates and local predicates (if any) returned by the fetch (FETCH) in step 15—based on the index scan (IXSCAN) in step 16. Each joined row is then returned from the nested loop join (NLJOIN) to the next operator in the access plan. Execution continues until the entire outer stream is exhausted.

Unfortunately, this graph does not provide all of the details. It is important to know why the fetch is required on the inner table and what columns the tables are being joined on. This information can be found in the access plan details.

Access Plan Details—Cost

The cost information in the access plan details for the nested loop join in step 13 is as follows:

```
13) NLJOIN: (Nested Loop Join)
           Cumulative Total Cost:        125.206
           Cumulative CPU Cost:          164264
           Cumulative I/O Cost:          5
           Cumulative Re-Total Cost:     0.062461
           Cumulative Re-CPU Cost:       49744
           Cumulative Re-I/O Cost:       0
           Cumulative First Row Cost:    125.204
           Estimated Bufferpool Buffers: 6
```

The total cumulative cost is 125.206 timerons. This is not the elapsed time but rather a measurement that is based on the elapsed time in a parallel environment. Elapsed time could be different because of parallel I/O and overlap between CPU and I/O operations in a serial environment.

The Re-Total Cost is the estimated cost to re-execute this subplan. The Cumulative First Row Cost is the estimated cost to return the first row of the result set. The cost model used is based on resource consumption (i.e., total CPU and I/O resources consumed); communication costs are considered in a parallel environment. Keep in mind that plan costs are cumulative—in general, each plan operator adds cost to the plan.

The Estimated Bufferpool Buffers is the expected number of buffer pool pages required by this operator.

Access Plan Details—Arguments

The arguments information in the access plan details for the nested loop join in step 13 shows the following:

```
Arguments:
---------
EARLYOUT: (Early Out flag)                FALSE
FETCHMAX: (Override for FETCH MAXPAGES)   IGNORE
ISCANMAX: (Override for ISCAN MAXPAGES)   IGNORE
```

- EARLYOUT: Indicates whether or not the optimizer will get the next outer row after finding the first match on the inner row. This guarantees one match on the inner.

- FETCHMAX: Specifies the maximum number of pages to prefetch for a fetch or index scan.

- ISCANMAX: A nested loop join can override the original settings if it is an ordered nested loop join.

Access Plan Details—Predicates

The predicates information in the access plan details for the nested loop join in step 13 shows the following:

```
13) NLJOIN: (Nested Loop Join)
Predicates:
----------
16) Predicate used in Join
      Relational Operator:          Equal (=)
      Subquery Input Required:      No
      Filter Factor:                           5.00034e-08

    Predicate Text:
    --------------
    (Q1.PS_PARTKEY = Q2.P_PARTKEY)
```

The predicate information includes the estimated selectivity of the predicate used based on the table and column statistics as well as the predicate being applied by the operator. In this case the columns being joined are the PS_PARTKEY column in table Q1 and the P_PARTKEY column in table Q2.

Access Plan Details—Input Stream(s)

The input stream information in the access plan details for the nested loop join in step 13 shows the following:

```
13) NLJOIN: (Nested Loop Join)
Input Streams:
-------------
       5) From Operator #14
          Estimated number of rows:    0.968511
                 Partition Map ID:          1
                 Partitioning:              (MULT )
                                            Multiple Partitions
             Number of columns:          3
             Subquery predicate ID:                  Not Applicable
```

```
              Column Names:
              ------------
              +$RID$+P_PARTKEY+P_NAME

              Partition Column Names:
              ----------------------
              +1: PS_PARTKEY

     13) NLJOIN: (Nested Loop Join)
     Input Streams:
     -------------
          9) From Operator #15
          Estimated number of rows:     4
          Partition Map ID:             1
          Partitioning:                            (MULT )
                                        Multiple Partitions
          Number of columns:            4
          Subquery predicate ID:                Not Applicable

          Column Names:
          ------------
          +PS_PARTKEY(A)+PS_SUPPKEY(A)+$RID$+PS_AVAILQTY

          Partition Column Names:
          ----------------------
          +1: PS_PARTKEY
```

This shows that the join will have two input streams, one for the inner table and one for the outer table. The estimated stream cardinality from operator 14 in this case is .968511, and it is returning three columns. In addition, the operation is occurring on multiple partitions in the database; the partitioning key is PS_PARTKEY. The estimated stream cardinality from operator 15 is 4, and it is returning four columns. This operation is also occurring on multiple partitions, and the partitioning key is PS_PARTKEY.

Access Plan Details—FETCH

The detailed information in the access plan for the fetch operation in step 15 is as follows:

```
15) FETCH : (Fetch)
      Arguments:
      ---------
   ...
      Input Streams:
      -------------
              7) From Operator #16
                          Column Names:
                          ------------
                          +PS_PARTKEY(A)+PS_SUPPKEY(A)+$RID$

          8) From Object BERGMAN.PARTSUPP
                          Column Names:
                          ------------
                          +PS_AVAILQTY
```

This shows that the columns PS_PARTKEY and PS_SUPPKEY are being passed to the fetch from the index scan in operation 16 and that the fetch is then retrieving the PS_AVAILQTY column from the table PARTSUPP. The PS_AVAILQTY column must be retrieved from the table because it is not contained in the index used in operator 16.

Access Plan Details—Index Scan

The detailed information in the access plan for the index scan operation in step 16 is as follows:

```
16) IXSCAN: (Index Scan)
            Predicates:
            ----------
            16) Start Key Predicate
                    Relational Operator:         Equal (=)
                    Subquery Input Required:     No
                    Filter Factor:                     5.00034e-08

                    Predicate Text:
                    --------------
                    (Q1.PS_PARTKEY = Q2.P_PARTKEY)

            16) Stop Key Predicate
                    Relational Operator:         Equal (=)
                    Subquery Input Required:     No
                    Filter Factor:                     5.00034e-08

                    Predicate Text:
                    --------------
                    (Q1.PS_PARTKEY = Q2.P_PARTKEY)
```

In this example, the optimizer is applying a start and stop predicate to the index scan. The scan will only read the index leaf pages where Q1.PS_PARTKEY = Q2.P_ PARTKEY, therefore it does not need to scan the entire index. The estimated number of rows returned by the index scan operation in step 16 is four.

Access Plan Details—Sort

The detailed information in the access plan for the sort operation in step 16 is as follows:

```
3.65665e+07
        TBSCAN
        (  15)
     6.87408e+06
     1.45951e+06
          |
     3.65665e+07
        SORT
        (  16)
     6.14826e+06
     1.30119e+06
          |
     3.65665e+07
        TBSCAN
        (  17)
     2.00653e+06
     1.14286e+06
          |
     3.74999e+07
    TABLE: BERGMAN
    ORDERS
```

These details indicate that I/O occurred during the sort operation. Therefore, the sort must have overflowed and could not be accomplished within the sort heap.

Access Plan Details—Table Scan

The detailed information in the access plan about the table scan operation in step 15 is as follows:

```
15) TBSCAN: (Table Scan)
                .
                .
                .

        Estimated Bufferpool Buffers:          163976
```

This detailed information lists the estimated number of buffer pool buffers needed, which gives an estimate for the size of the overflowed temporary table. In this example, the estimated size of the overflowed sort table will be 163,976 pages.

Recognizing List Prefetch

List prefetch, or list sequential prefetch, is a way to access data pages efficiently even when the data pages needed are not contiguous. (List prefetch may be used in conjunction with single or multiple index access.) The following access plan graph shows an example of list prefetch:

```
                455.385
                FETCH
                (   9)
                308.619
                61.2878
             /----+---\
    455.385          15009
    RIDSCN     TABLE: BERGMAN
    (  10)     L_SUMMARY2
    219.093
    17.4697
       |
    455.385
    SORT
    (  11)
    219.091
    17.4697
       |
    455.385
    IXSCAN
    (  12)
    218.559
    17.4697
       |
      15009
    INDEX: BERGMAN
  L_SUMMARY2_IDX
```

In step 12, the index scan is applying the predicates and returning the row identifiers (RIDs) to the sort operation in step 11. The RIDs are then sorted based on the page number and passed to the RID Scan (RIDSCN) operation in step 10. The RID scan will build a list of the pages and call the prefetchers to retrieve the pages into the buffer pool. The fetch operation in step 9 can then fetch and process the pages; they should already be in the buffer pool due to the work of the prefetchers.

Recognizing Index ORing

In some cases, the DB2 optimizer might find that all data that a query requires from a table can be retrieved from an index that has been defined for the table. In other cases, the optimizer might choose to scan multiple indexes on the same table. For example, suppose a table named DEPARTMENT has the following two index definitions:

```
INDEX IX2:  DEPT    ASC
INDEX IX3:  JOB     ASC, YEARS    ASC
```

If the following predicates are used in a query against the DEPARTMENT table, they can be satisfied by using the two indexes:

```
WHERE DEPT = :hv1
   OR (JOB   = :hv2 AND YEARS >= :hv3)
```

Scanning index IX2 will produce a list of row IDs (RIDs) that satisfy the DEPT = : hv1 predicate. Scanning index IX3 will produce a list of RIDs satisfying the JOB = : hv2 AND YEARS >= :hv3 predicate. These two lists of RIDs can then be combined and any duplicates found can be removed to produce the result data set desired. This process is known as index ORing. Index ORing may be used for predicates specified in a WHERE clause or an IN clause.

The following access plan graph shows an example of index ORing:

```
             59537.2
              FETCH
              (  3)
             62819.1
             37361.7
           /----+---\
      59537.2      1.50002e+08
```

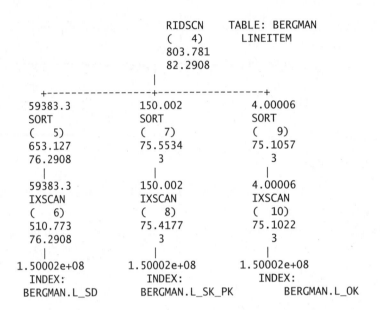

```
                        RIDSCN     TABLE: BERGMAN
                        (    4)        LINEITEM
                        803.781
                        82.2908
                           |
        +----------------+----------------+
     59383.3          150.002          4.00006
      SORT             SORT             SORT
     (    5)          (    7)          (    9)
     653.127          75.5534          75.1057
     76.2908             3                3
        |                |                |
     59383.3          150.002          4.00006
     IXSCAN           IXSCAN           IXSCAN
     (    6)          (    8)          (   10)
     510.773          75.4177          75.1022
     76.2908             3                3
        |                |                |
   1.50002e+08      1.50002e+08      1.50002e+08
     INDEX:           INDEX:           INDEX:
   BERGMAN.L_SD     BERGMAN.L_SK_PK    BERGMAN.L_OK
```

In steps 6, 8, and 10, the index scan is applying the predicates and returning the row identifiers (RIDs) to the sort operations shown. The RIDs are then sorted based on the page number, any duplicates are eliminated, and the results are then passed to the RID Scan (RIDSCN) operation in step 4. The RID scan will build a list of the pages and call the prefetchers to retrieve the pages into the buffer pool. The fetch operation in step 3 can then fetch and process the pages because they should already be in the buffer pool due to the work of the prefetchers. In this case the fetch operation must reapply the predicates due to the OR predicates.

Recognizing Index ANDing

Although the purpose of index ORing is to eliminate duplicate RIDs, the objective of index ANDing is to find common RIDs. Index ANDing might occur in situations where multiple indexes exist on corresponding columns in the same table and a query using multiple AND predicates is run against that table. Multiple index scans against each indexed column in such a query produce values that are hashed to create bitmaps. The second bitmap is then used to probe the first bitmap to generate the qualifying rows that are fetched to create the final result data set returned. For example, suppose a table named EMPLOYEE has the following two index definitions:

```
INDEX IX4: SALARY   ASC
INDEX IX5: COMM     ASC
```

If the following predicates are used in a query against the EMPLOYEE table, they can be satisfied by using the two indexes:

```
WHERE SALARY BETWEEN 20000 AND 30000
  AND COMM BETWEEN 1000 AND 3000
```

In this example, scanning index IX4 produces a bitmap satisfying the SALARY BETWEEN 20000 AND 30000 predicate. Scanning IX5 and probing the bitmap for IX4 results in the list of qualifying RIDs that satisfy both predicates. This is known as "dynamic bitmap ANDing" and it occurs only if the table has sufficient cardinality and the columns have sufficient values in the qualifying range, or sufficient duplication if equality predicates are used.

The following access plan graph shows an example of index ANDing.

```
                          |
                        4.4314
                        FETCH
                        (   3)
                        5475.6
                        1952.4
                     /----+---\
                886.281       1.50002e+08
                RIDSCN        TABLE: BERGMAN
                (   4)           LINEITEM
                4027.9
                1100.96
                   |
                886.281
                 SORT
                (   5)
                4027.9
                1100.96
                   |
                886.281
                IXAND
                (   6)
                4026.01
                1100.96
             /------+-----\
        248752          534445
        IXSCAN          IXSCAN
        (   7)          (   8)
```

```
    1480.95          2509.07
    430.024          670.935
       |                |
   1.50002e+08      1.50002e+08
  INDEX: BERGMAN    INDEX: BERGMAN
  L_OK             L_SD
```

In steps 7 and 8, the index scan is applying the predicates and returning the row identifiers (RIDs) from the index. The index ANDing (IXAND) operation then hashes the RIDs into the dynamic bitmap, and starts returning the RIDs as it works on the last index. The RIDs are then sorted based on the page number, any duplicates are eliminated, and the results are then passed to the RID scan (RIDSCN) operation in step 4. The RID scan will build a list of the pages and call the prefetchers to retrieve the pages into the buffer pool. The fetch operation in step 3 can then fetch and process the pages; they should already be in the buffer pool due to the work of the prefetchers. In this case the fetch operation must reapply the predicates because the bitmap used is a reducing bitmap, and not all "qualified" rows are truly qualified.

Index ANDing is considered when there are a large number of rows to process, but the expected result set is relatively small. In this case the indexes scanned had approximately 250,000 rows and 500,000 rows, respectively, but the expected number of rows returned by the fetch is only four.

Taking Control of The Server

Because any number of clients can access a server, and in turn, any number of users can be granted the privileges needed to work with a particular database, it can be difficult, if not impossible, to coordinate the work efforts of everyone using a specific database at any given point in time. This can create a problem because there are times when a Database Administrator will need all users to stop using a particular instance or database so that routine maintenance operations can be performed. If your organization is small, it may be possible to contact each database user and ask them to disconnect long enough to perform any necessary maintenance operations. But what if your organization consists of several hundred users? Or what if an employee went home early and inadvertently left an instance attachment or database connection open? How can you find out which users and applications are interacting with the instance or database you need exclusive access to?

Finding Out Who Is Using an Instance or a Database

If you have System Administrator (SYSADMN) or System Control (SYSCTRL) authority for a DB2 database server, you can find out who is using an instance or a database on that server by executing the LIST APPLICATIONS command. The basic syntax for this command is:

```
LIST APPLICATIONS
<FOR [DATABASE | DB] [DatabaseAlias]>
<SHOW DETAIL>
```

where:

DatabaseAlias   Identifies the alias assigned to the database for which application information is to be obtained.

Thus, if you wanted to find out what applications are currently connected to a database named SAMPLE (along with the authorization IDs associated with the users running those applications), you could do so by executing a LIST APPLICATIONS command that looks something like this:

```
LIST APPLICATIONS FOR DATABASE sample
```

And when this command is executed, you might see output that looks something like this:

```
Auth Id  Application Appl.   Application Id            DB     # of
         Name        Handle                           Name   Agents
-------- ----------- ------- ------------------------ ------ -----
RSANDERS db2taskd    148     *LOCAL.DB2.070601164915  SAMPLE 1
RSANDERS db2stmm     147     *LOCAL.DB2.070601164914  SAMPLE 1
RSANDERS db2bp.exe   146     *LOCAL.DB2.070601164913  SAMPLE 1
```

You can also find out what applications are attached to an instance (or connected to a database within that instance) by selecting the Applications action from the Databases menu found in the Control Center. Figure 5–15 shows the Control Center menu items that must be selected in order to activate the Applications dialog. Figure 5–16 shows how this dialog might look if an application is connected to a database within the instance specified.

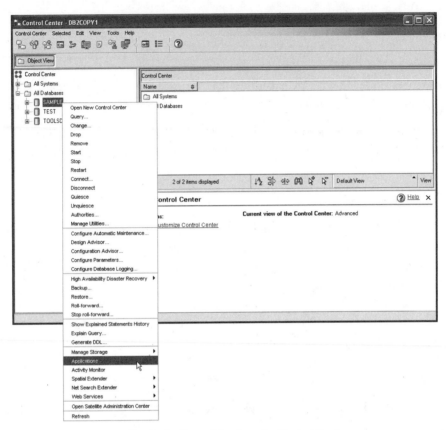

Figure 5–15: Invoking the Applications dialog from the Control Center.

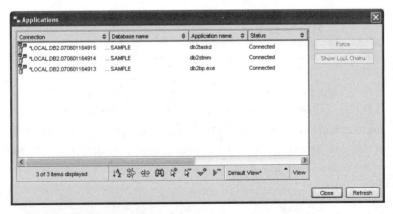

Figure 5–16: The Applications dialog.

The FORCE APPLICATION Command

Once you know what applications are using a particular instance or database, you can terminate one or more of those applications prematurely by executing the FORCE APPLICATION command (assuming you have SYSADMN or SYSCTRL authority). The basic syntax for this command is:

```
FORCE APPLICATION ALL
```

or

```
FORCE APPLICATION ([ApplicationHandle] ,...)
```

where:

ApplicationHandle Identifies the handle associated with one or more applications whose instance attachments or database connections are to be terminated.

Thus, if you wanted to force all users and applications connected to databases stored on a server named DB_SERVER to terminate their database connections, you could do so by executing a FORCE APPLICATION command that looks something like this:

```
FORCE APPLICATION ALL
```

On the other hand, if you wanted to force a specific application whose handle is 148 (refer to the sample output shown for the LIST APPLICATIONS command to see where this value came from) to terminate its connection to a database named SAMPLE, you could do so by executing a FORCE APPLICATION command that looks something like this:

```
FORCE APPLICATION (148)
```

It is important to note that when an application's instance attachment or database connection is terminated by the FORCE APPLICATION command, any SQL operations that have been performed by the application but have not yet been committed are rolled back.

In order to preserve database integrity, only applications that are idle or that are performing interruptible database operations can be terminated when the FORCE APPLICATION command is processed. (For example, applications in the process of creating or backing up a database would not be terminated; applications in the process of restoring a database would be terminated; and the restore operation would have to be rerun before the database would be usable). In addition, the DB2 instance cannot be stopped during a force operation; the DB2 instance must remain active so that subsequent instance-level operations can be handled without having to restart the instance. Finally, because the FORCE APPLICATION command is run asynchronously, other applications or users can attach to the instance or connect to a database within the instance after this command has been executed. Multiple FORCE APPLICATION commands may be required to completely terminate all instance attachments and database connections.

If you are using the Applications dialog to see which users or applications are currently attached to an instance or connected to a database, you can terminate instance attachments and database connections by highlighting one or more entries in the list shown on the Applications dialog and selecting the "Force" push button located in the upper right corner of the screen (refer to Figure 5–16).

Deep Compression

Along with table partitioning and pureXML, one of the most prominent features introduced in DB2 9 is the ability to reduce the amount of storage needed to store table data using what is known as deep compression. Although the primary purpose of deep compression is to save storage space, it can lead to significant disk I/O savings and higher buffer pool hit ratios as well. (More data can be cached in memory.) All of this can lead to an increase in performance, but not without some cost—extra CPU cycles are needed to compress and decompress the data. The storage savings and performance impact of deep compression are tied directly to the characteristics of the data within the database, the design of the database itself, how well the database has been tuned, and application workloads.

Believe it or not, as the volume of data increases, the cardinality tends to drop. As it turns out, there just aren't that many truly "unique" things in the world. Things may be unique when used in combination, but the basic elements themselves aren't all that varied. Consider the periodic table of elements—everything in our world is made up of combinations of a rather small set of elements. Apply the concept to data, and you find the same is true. For instance, according to the last U.S. census, there are about 300 million people living in the United States. But there are only about 78,800 unique last names, resulting in very low cardinality with huge "clumps" in certain name sets. First names are even worse, coming in at around 6,600 (4,400 unique first names for females and 2,200 for males). The names of cities, streets, and addresses, not to mention product names, descriptions, and attributes, also tend to be highly redundant with low cardinality.

Deep compression works by searching for repeating patterns in the data and replacing the patterns with 12-bit symbols, which are stored along with the pattern they represent in a static dictionary. Once this dictionary is created, it is stored in the table along with the compressed data and loaded into memory whenever data in the table is accessed to aid in decompression. DB2 9 scans an entire table looking for repeating column values and repeating patterns that span multiple columns in a row. DB2 also looks for repeating patterns that are substrings of a given column. However, just because a repeating pattern is found doesn't mean that the data is automatically compressed—data is compressed only when storage savings will be realized. In any case, the entire row is stored as a set of 12-bit symbols; rows are never partially compressed. Figure 5–17 illustrates how deep compression works.

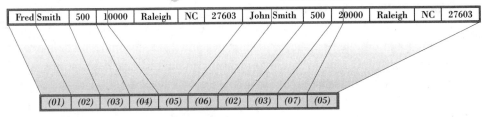

EMPLOYEE TABLE

NAME	DEPT	SALARY	CITY	STATE	ZIPCODE
Fred Smith	500	10000	Raleigh	NC	27603
John Smith	500	20000	Raleigh	NC	27603

UNCOMPRESSED DATA ROWS ON DISK

| Fred | Smith | 500 | 10000 | Raleigh | NC | 27603 | John | Smith | 500 | 20000 | Raleigh | NC | 27603 |

| (01) | (02) | (03) | (04) | (05) | (06) | (02) | (03) | (07) | (05) |

COMPRESSED DATA ROWS ON DISK

COMPRESSION DICTIONARY

SYMBOL	PATTERN
01	Fred
02	Smith
03	500
04	1
05	0000 Raleigh NC 27603
06	John
07	2

Figure 5–17: How deep compression works.

With DB2 9, it is not possible to compress long, large object, or XML data. With DB2 9.5, inline XML documents can be compressed as long as they are less than 32K in size.

In order to use deep compression with a table, two prerequisites must be satisfied:

1. Compression must be enabled at the table level.

2. A compression dictionary for the table must exist.

Enabling a Table for Deep Compression

Compression is enabled at the table level by executing either the CREATE TABLE SQL statement or the ALTER TABLE statement with the COMPRESS YES option specified. For example, if you wanted to create a new table named EMPLOYEE and enable it for deep compression, you could do so by executing a CREATE TABLE statement that looks something like this:

```
CREATE TABLE employee
    (name      VARCHAR(60),
     dept      CHAR(3),
     salary    DECIMAL(7,2),
     city      VARCHAR(25),
     state     CHAR(2),
     zipcode   VARCHAR(10))
  COMPRESS YES
```

On the other hand, if you wanted to enable an existing table named EMPLOYEE for deep compression, you could do so by executing an ALTER TABLE statement that looks like this:

```
ALTER TABLE employee COMPRESS YES
```

Building a Compression Dictionary

Although you can enable a table for deep compression at any time by setting its COMPRESS attribute to YES, compression of the data cannot occur until a compression dictionary has been built. A compression dictionary is built (and existing data in the table is compressed) by performing an offline (classic) table reorganization operation; such an operation is initiated by executing the REORG command with either the KEEPDICTIONARY or the RESETDICTIONARY option specified. If the REORG command is executed with either option specified, and a compression dictionary does not exist, a new dictionary will be built. If the REORG command is executed with either option specified, and a compression dictionary already exists, the existing dictionary will either be recreated (RESETDICTIONARY) or left as it is (KEEPDICTIONARY), and data in the table will be reorganized and compressed.

Thus, if you wanted to create a new compression dictionary (and compress the existing data) for a table named EMPLOYEE that has been enabled for deep compression, you could do so by executing a REORG command that looks like this:

```
REORG TABLE employee RESETDICTIONARY
```

When this command is executed, data stored in the EMPLOYEE table will be analyzed, a compression dictionary will be constructed and stored at the beginning of the table, and all existing data will be compressed and written to the table directly behind the compression dictionary. Figure 5–18 illustrates how the EMPLOYEE table would look before and after deep compression is applied.

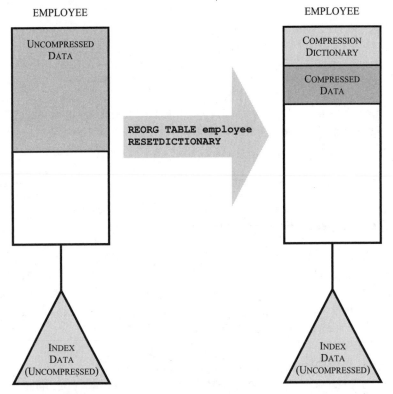

Figure 5–18: How data in a table is altered when a compression dictionary is built and deep compression is applied.

It is important to note that index data is not affected by deep compression; only data stored on a page in a base table can be compressed. However, because records in a compressed table are moved between storage and memory in compressed form, records for compressed tables that are written to transaction log files are compressed as well. (The compression dictionary is loaded into memory when the table is accessed so that compression and decompression can take place.)

> To delete a compression dictionary from a table, set the COMPRESS attribute for the table to NO and execute the REORG command with the RESETDICTIONARY option specified; reorg processing will remove the compression dictionary and the rows in the newly reorganized table will be in non-compressed format. (If the COMPRESS attribute for a table is set to NO and the REORG command is executed with the KEEPDICTIONARY option specified, reorg processing will preserve the compression dictionary and all rows in the newly reorganized table will be in non-compressed format.)

Estimating Storage Savings from Deep Compression

Because an offline reorganization operation is needed to construct a compression dictionary and perform data compression, the initial overhead required to compress data can be quite high. Therefore, it can be helpful to know which tables will benefit the most from deep compression and which tables will not. With DB2 9, the Inspect utility can help you make that determination. The Inspect utility is invoked by executing the INSPECT command, and if this command is executed with the ROWCOMPESTIMATE option specified, the Inspect utility will examine each row in the table specified, build a compression dictionary from the data found, and then use this dictionary to estimate how much space will be saved if the data in the table is compressed.

Thus, if you wanted to estimate how much storage space would be saved if the data in a table named EMPLOYEE is compressed, you could do so by executing an INSPECT command that looks something like this:

```
INSPECT ROWCOMPESTIMATE TABLE NAME employee
```

And when this command is executed, the information returned might look something like this:

```
DATABASE: TEST
VERSION: SQL09000
2007-06-06-12.35.58.14.296000

Action: ROWCOMPESTIMATE TABLE
Schema name: PAYROLL
Table name: EMPLOYEE
Tablespace ID: 4 Object ID: 6
Result file name: emp
  Table phase start (ID Signed: 6, Unsigned: 6; Tablespace
    ID:4) PAYROLL.EMPLOYEE
  Data phase start. Object: 6 Tablespace : 4
  Row compression estimate results:
  Percentage of pages saved from compression: 46
  Percentage of bytes saved from compression: 46
  Percentage of rows ineligible for compression due to
    smallrow size: 0
  Compression dictionary size: 13312 bytes.
  Expansion dictionary size: 10240 bytes.
  Data phase end.
  Table phase end.
```

If a table is enabled for deep compression (that is, the COMPRESS attribute is set to YES) before the INSPECT command is executed, the compression dictionary that is built and used to estimate space savings will be written to the table, at the end of the existing data—provided a compression dictionary doesn't already exist. (Otherwise, the compression dictionary created to estimate space savings will be destroyed.) Figure 5–19 shows a table before and after the Inspect utility was used to estimate storage savings that was enabled for deep compression before the estimate was acquired.

Regardless of the method used to create it, once a compression dictionary has been constructed and written to a table, new records added to that table will automatically be compressed. If the compression dictionary was created by the Inspect utility, preexisting records in the table will remain uncompressed until an offline table reorganization operation is performed or the preexisting records are updated (in which case each record modified will be compressed)

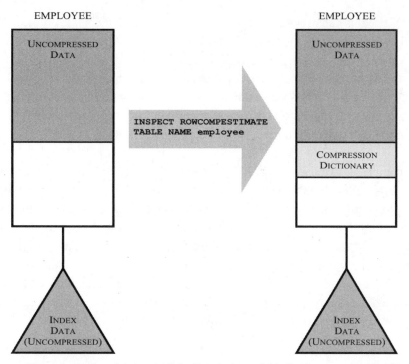

Figure 5–19: How data in a table is altered when a table that has been enabled for deep compression is evaluated by the Inspect utility.

Automatic Dictionary Creation (ADC)

As you might imagine, optimal compression ratios are achieved when a compression dictionary is built from an all-inclusive set of data. When a compression dictionary is built by reorganizing a table (or by using the Inspect utility), a high compression ratio results because every row in the table is used. However, testing at IBM has shown that a good compression ratio is also possible when just a small amount of representative data is analyzed. (In some cases, evaluating less than 1 percent of the total number of rows available yielded a compression ratio of 45 percent.) This concept forms the basis for a new compression feature that was introduced in DB2 9.5 called Automatic Dictionary Creation (ADC).

Beginning with DB2 9.5, if a table is enabled for compression at the time it's created, ADC will cause a compression dictionary to be built automatically once a sufficient amount of data has been stored in the table. The threshold at which ADC kicks in and begins constructing the compression dictionary depends on the table's size. Dictionary construction typically begins when 1 to 2MBs of pages have been allocated to the table. At that point, ADC will check to see how much user data is contained within the table—if at least 700KB of data is present, a compression dictionary will be built. (It is important to note that these values are set internally and can't be altered.) Operations that can trigger ADC include inserts, imports, loads, and the redistribution of data across partitions.

Like the compression dictionary built by the Inspect utility, the dictionary created via ADC is stored in the table at the end of the existing data. The table's preexisting records remain uncompressed until an offline table reorganization operation is performed or until the preexisting records are updated (in which case each record modified is compressed when the changes are saved). New records are compressed as they're added. (One of the goals of ADC is to build a compression dictionary that will yield a decent compression ratio without leaving a large amount of uncompressed data in the table.) Figure 5–20 shows what a table that was enabled for compression during creation would look like before, during, and after a compression dictionary is built by ADC.

If compression is enabled for a table that is already populated (by setting the COMPRESS attribute to ON), a compression dictionary is not created automatically. Rather, the next time a table growth action occurs, ADC will be triggered and a small number of records at the beginning of the table will be used to construct a compression dictionary for the table. Once the dictionary is created, data added to the table by subsequent insert, import, load, and redistribution operations will be compressed; preexisting data will remain uncompressed.

As you can see, the automatic creation of a compression dictionary is controlled, in part, by a table's compression attribute. If you want to prevent ADC behavior, don't enable a table for compression until you're ready to manually build a compression dictionary and compress the data. On the other hand, if you elect to take advantage of ADC, remember that the compression ratio for the dictionary produced may not be as optimal as one created by an offline table reorganization. Also, because the table will remain online while the compression dictionary is built, the transaction that causes ADC to be initiated will experience a slight impact on performance when ADC is triggered.

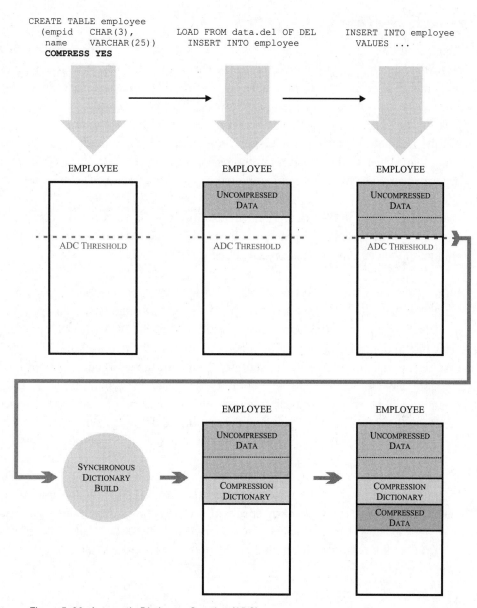

Figure 5–20: Automatic Dictionary Creation (ADC).

Deep Compression and the Load Utility

Another significant change in DB2 9.5 is how load operations behave when they are performed against tables enabled for deep compression. In DB2 9, if a compression dictionary had been created for a table, the Load utility would use that dictionary to compress data as it was being loaded. However, if no compression dictionary was present, the Load utility would not build one as part of the load operation. In DB2 9.5, the Load utility can construct a compression dictionary provided that the table being loaded has been enabled for compression and that a LOAD REPLACE operation is performed. Such an operation is initiated by executing the LOAD command with either the REPLACE KEEPDICTIONARY or the REPLACE RESETDICTIONARY option specified. (A LOAD INSERT operation can also result in the creation of a compression dictionary if the table being loaded has been configured for compression and the amount of data coming in causes ADC to be triggered.)

If the LOAD command is executed with either the REPLACE KEEPDICTIONARY or the REPLACE RESETDICTIONARY option specified, and a compression dictionary doesn't exist, a new dictionary will be created. If the KEEPDICTIONARY option is used, the amount of data that will be required to build the compression dictionary is subject to the policies of ADC. Therefore, some of the data will be stored in the table uncompressed; once the dictionary is created, the remaining data that is loaded will be compressed using the new dictionary. On the other hand, if the RESETDICTIONARY option is specified, the amount of data required to build the dictionary is not subject to the policies of ADC and a compression dictionary can be built after loading just one row.

If the LOAD command is executed with either the REPLACE KEEPDICTIONARY or the REPLACE RESETDICTIONARY option specified, and a compression dictionary already exists, the existing dictionary will either be recreated (RESETDICTIONARY) or left as it is (KEEPDICTIONARY) and data in the table will be compressed using the existing or new dictionary.

Thus, if you wanted to create a new compression dictionary for a compression-enabled table named EMPLOYEE while performing a load operation, you would execute a command similar to this one:

```
LOAD FROM datafile.del OF DEL REPLACE RESETDICTIONARY
INTO employee
```

When this command is executed, assuming no compression dictionary exists for the EMPLOYEE table, a few records found in the file DATAFILE.DEL will be loaded into the EMPLOYEE table uncompressed. As soon as 1 to 2MB of data has been loaded, ADC will construct a compression dictionary using that data, and the remaining records will be compressed and written to the table directly behind the compression dictionary as they are loaded.

The Deep Compression Administrative View and Table Function

To aid in evaluating the effects of deep compression on a table, the ADMINTABCOMPRESSINFO administrative view and the ADMIN_GET_TAB_COMPRESS_INFO() table function were also introduced in DB2 9.5. Table 5.8 shows the structure of the ADMINTABCOMPRESSINFO administrative view.

Table 5.8 The ADMINTABCOMPRESSINFO administrative view		
Column Name	Data Type	Description
TABSCHEMA	VARCHAR(128)	Schema name.
TABNAME	VARCHAR(128)	Table name.
DBPARTITIONNUM	SMALLINT	Database partition number.
DATA_PARTITION_ID	INTEGER	Data partition number.
COMPRESS_ATTR	CHAR(1)	The state of the COMPRESS attribute on the table, which can be one of the following: 'Y' = Row compression is set to YES 'N' = Row compression is set to NO
DICT_BUILDER	VARCHAR(30)	Code path taken to build the compression dictionary, which can be one of the following: 'NOT BUILT' = no dictionary available 'INSPECT' = INSPECT ROWCOMPESTIMATE 'LOAD' = LOAD INSERT/REPLACE 'REDISTRIBUTE' = REDISTRIBUTE 'REORG' = REORG RESETDICTIONARY
DICT_BUILD_ TIMESTAMP	TIMESTAMP	Date and time the compression dictionary was built. (If no dictionary is available, the timestamp is NULL.)
COMPRESS_DICT_ SIZE	BIGINT	Size of compression dictionary, measured in bytes.

Table 5.8 The ADMINTABCOMPRESSINFO administrative view (Contiuned)		
Column Name	**Data Type**	**Description**
EXPAND_DICT_SIZE	BIGINT	Size of expansion dictionary, measured in bytes.
ROWS_SAMPLED	INTEGER	Number of records that contributed to building the dictionary. Migrated tables with compression dictionaries will return NULL in this column.
PAGES_SAVED_ PERCENT	SMALLINT	Percentage of pages saved from compression. This information is based on the record data in the sample buffer only. Migrated tables with compression dictionaries will return NULL in this column.
BYTES_SAVED_ PERCENT	SMALLINT	Percentage of bytes saved from compression. This information is based on the record data in the sample buffer only. Migrated tables with compression dictionaries will return NULL in this column.
AVG_COMPRESS_ REC_LENGTH	SMALLINT	Average compressed record length of the records contributing to building the dictionary. Migrated tables with compression dictionaries will return NULL in this column.

The ADMIN_GET_TAB_COMPRESS_INFO() table function provides a programmatic interface to the ADMINTABCOMPRESSINFO administrative view that can be embedded in an SQL query. The syntax for this function is:

```
ADMIN_GET_TAB_COMPRESS_INFO (TableSchema, TableName, ExecMode)
```

where:

TableSchema   Identifies by name the schema where the table for which compression information is to be obtained resides.

TableName   Identifies by name the table for which compression information is to be obtained.

ExecMode   Identifies the mode to use when executing this function. If this parameter is assigned the value REPORT (the default), compression statistics that were collected at the time the table was compressed will be retrieved. If this parameter is assigned the value ESTIMATE, new compression statistics will be generated based on current data in the table specified, and the results returned will reflect what the compression statistics would look like if you were to compress the table right now.

Therefore, to retrieve and display compression statistics that were generated at the time a table named PAYROLL.STAFF was compressed, you would execute a query similar to this one:

```
SELECT * FROM TABLE (SYSPROC.ADMIN_GET_TAB_COMPRESS_INFO('payroll',
'staff', 'REPORT')) AS comp_info
```

On the other hand, to estimate and display compression statistics for a table named PAYROLL.STAFF using data stored in the table right now, you would execute a query like this one:

```
SELECT * FROM TABLE (SYSPROC.ADMIN_GET_TAB_COMPRESS_INFO('payroll',
'staff', 'ESTIMATE')) AS comp_info
```

The first query will tell you the effects of the last compression operation performed; the second will tell you whether compression can be improved by generating a new compression dictionary and recompressing the data. By executing both queries on a regular basis, you can gauge the effectiveness of compression as your data evolves and changes over time.

Practice Questions

Question 1

Which DB2 registry variable can be used to prevent DB2 from performing prefetching during restart operations?

- ○ A. DB2_PREFETCH
- ○ B. DB2_LIMIT_PREFETCH
- ○ C. DB2_AVOID_PREFETCH
- ○ D. DB2_RESTRICT_PREFETCH

Question 2

A 250GB transactional database is running on a 64-bit Linux server that has only 2GB of memory available. If self tuning memory is enabled, which of the following registry variables can be used to prevent "Insufficient System Memory" errors from occurring?

- ○ A. DB2_MEM_LIMIT
- ○ B. DB2_MEM_TUNING
- ○ C. DB2_MEM_TUNING_LIMIT
- ○ D. DB2_MEM_TUNING_RANGE

Question 3

Which of the following is NOT true about the DB2_PINNED_BP registry variable?

- ○ A. When this variable is set to YES, buffer pools will remain in system main memory.
- ○ B. When this variable is set to YES, database performance can be somewhat inconsistent.
- ○ C. When this variable is set to YES, all database global memory will be kept in the system main memory.
- ○ D. When this variable is set to YES, self-tuning for database shared memory cannot be enabled on 64-bit AIX.

Question 4

Which description is correct when discussing the DB2_SMS_TRUNC_TMPTABLE_THRESH registry variable?

- ○ A. Setting this variable to -1 will reduce the system overhead involved in dropping and recreating a temporary table in an SMS table space.
- ○ B. Setting this variable to 50 will ensure that no temporary table created in an SMS table space will contain more than 50 rows.
- ○ C. Setting this variable to 10 will restrict the number of temporary tables that can be created in an SMS table space to 10.
- ○ D. Setting this variable to 0 will ensure that once a temporary table in an SMS table space is no longer needed, its file will be truncated to 1 extent.

Question 5

Which of the following is NOT a true statement about the SHEAPTHRES configuration parameter?

○ A. The SHEAPTHRES configuration parameter sets an instance-wide soft limit on the total amount of memory that can be consumed by private sorts at any given time.

○ B. The SHEAPTHRES configuration parameter specifies the maximum amount of memory (in pages) that is to be used at any one time to perform sort operations.

○ C. If the SHEAPTHRES configuration parameter is assigned a value other than zero, the sort memory heap database configuration parameter (SORTHEAP) cannot not be configured for automatic tuning.

○ D. The SHEAPTHRES configuration parameter is an instance level configuration parameter; therefore its setting affects all databases under an instance's control.

Question 6

A DB2 system supporting a critical application with many concurrent medium to long running transactions that use a small amount of log space appears to be running slowly.

Current parameter settings are:

```
DBHEAP      512
LOGBUFSZ    128
MINCOMMIT   1
MAX_LOG     40
```

If the length of each individual transaction is not important, what parameter can be changed to minimize the number of times the log buffer is flushed to disk?

○ A. LOGARCHMETH1

○ B. MAX_LOG

○ C. LOGBUFSZ

○ D. MINCOMMIT

Question 7

A database with a default configuration is performing poorly on a Linux system. During peak operation a database snapshot was taken that contains the following information:

```
                Database Snapshot
Database name                        =  SAMPLE
First database connect timestamp     =  05/23/2008 13:40:09.704208
Snapshot timestamp                   =  05/23/2008 13:41:44.556973
Direct reads                         =  2134
Direct writes                        =  0
Direct read requests                 =  11
Direct write requests                =  0
Direct reads elapsed time (ms)       =  155
Direct write elapsed time (ms)       =  0
Database files closed                =  51782
```

Which of the following commands, when executed, should improve performance?

○ A. UPDATE DB CFG FOR sample USING MAXFILOP 2048

○ B. UPDATE DB CFG FOR sample USING BUFFPAGE 200000

○ C. UPDATE DB CFG FOR sample USING LOGFILSIZ 4096

○ D. UPDATE DB CFG FOR sample USING MAXAPPLS 2048

Question 8

In which case would executing the statement "ALTER TABLE payroll VOLATILE" be beneficial?

○ A. The number of records in the PAYROLL table does not change, but approximately 10 percent of its data is updated every day.

○ B. An index associated with the PAYROLL table has values ranging from 1 to 1,000,000,000,000,000.

○ C. The PAYROLL table is loaded every day with the exact same data.

○ D. The PAYROLL table is loaded every day with drastically varying amounts of data.

Question 9

Which of the following is NOT a valid statement about clustering indexes?

○ A. Columns frequently searched or joined over a range of values using the operators BETWEEN, >, <, and LIKE are good candidates for a clustering index.

○ B. In order for DB2 to maintain the clustering of the data and the index as records are inserted or updated, you must leave free space on the data pages to provide room for additional rows.

○ C. When creating a clustering index in a DPF environment, the index columns specified should be prefixed with the partitioning key columns.

○ D. Specify a lower PCTFREE value at index creation time to reduce the likelihood that index page splits will occur when records are added to the table.

Question 10

Place the following steps in the correct order as they are performed by the DB2 optimizer when generating an access plan for a SQL statement.

1. check semantics
2. parse query
3. generate package
4. rewrite query
5. generate access plan

○ A. 1, 2, 4, 3, 5
○ B. 1, 2, 4, 5, 3
○ C. 2, 1, 4, 5, 3
○ D. 2, 1, 4, 3, 5

Question 11

Which statement correctly describes the purpose of statistical views?

○ A. Statistical views provide the optimizer with more accurate collocation estimates.
○ B. Statistical views provide the optimizer with more accurate cardinality estimates.
○ C. Statistical views provide the optimizer with more accurate free space estimates.
○ D. Statistical views provide the optimizer with more accurate I/O estimates.

Question 12

Which of the following correctly describes the objective of index ANDing?

○ A. Find common RIDs
○ B. Eliminate duplicate RIDs
○ C. Generate duplicate RIDs
○ D. Map RIDs to data pages

Question 13

Which type of table queue is used to pass table data from one database agent to another when the FOR FETCH ONLY clause is not specified with a SELECT statement?

○ A. Local table queue
○ B. Merging table queue
○ C. Synchronous table queue
○ D. Asynchronous table queue

Question 14

A database administrator created a table named HISTORY and a trigger to insert records into the HISTORY table each time an employee's salary is modified in a table named EMPLOYEE. If the first column in the HISTORY table is a continually increasing sequential key, which of the following, if executed, will increase the performance of the trigger inserts?

○ A. db2set DB2MAXFSCRSEARCH -1
○ B. ALTER TABLE history APPEND ON
○ C. db2set DB2MAXFSCRSEARCH 1000
○ D. ALTER TABLE history FREESPACE 1000

Question 15

The service level agreement for an application that performs a large number of update operations on a table named EMPLOYEE states that the application must complete its work as quickly as possible to ensure that other dependant workloads can execute within a nightly maintenance window.

Which two of the following statements can be added to the beginning of the application to help it execute quickly? (Select two)

❏ A. LOCK TABLE employee FOR APPLICATION.
❏ B. LOCK TABLE employee IN EXCLUSIVE MODE
❏ C. ALTER TABLE employee LOCKSIZE ROW
❏ D. ALTER TABLE employee LOCKSIZE TABLE
❏ E. ALTER TABLE employee LOCKSIZE APPLICATION

Question 16

If a database routinely services workloads that consist primarily of transactions that update data, which database configuration parameter should be assigned a high value or the value AUTOMATIC to improve performance?

○ A. NUM_IOCLEANERS
○ B. LOGBUFSIZ
○ C. NUM_IOSERVERS
○ D. CATALOGCACHE_SZ

Question 17

Which of the following commands will force DB2 to perform all sort operations in shared memory?

○ A. UPDATE DB CFG FOR sample USING SHEAPTHRES_SHR -2

○ B. UPDATE DB CFG FOR sample USING SHEAPTHRES_SHR -1

○ C. UPDATE DB CFG FOR sample USING SHEAPTHRES_SHR 0

○ D. UPDATE DB CFG FOR sample USING SHEAPTHRES_SHR 250

Question 18

Which configuration parameter is used to specify the number of prefetchers that are available to a database?

○ A. NUM_IOCLEANERS

○ B. NUM_IOSERVERS

○ C. NUM_IOAGENTS

○ D. NUM_IOFSCRS

Question 19

A database administrator executed the following SQL statement:

```
CREATE BUFFERPOOL bp1 SIZE 1000 AUTOMATIC PAGESIZE 8K
```

If this statement was executed against a database with self tuning memory enabled, what will DB2 do?

○ A. Check available memory, and create the buffer pool if there is enough memory available; if there is not enough memory available, return an error message and do not create the buffer pool.

○ B. Check available memory, and create the buffer pool if there is enough memory available; if there is not enough memory available, monitor system resources and as soon as there is enough free memory available on the server, create the buffer pool.

○ C. Check available memory, and create the buffer pool if there is enough memory available; if there is not enough memory available, wait until all activations and connections to the database are closed, and then allocate the buffer pool on the next activation or connection.

○ D   Check available memory, and create buffer pool BP1 if there is enough memory available; if there is not enough memory available, wait until the DB2 instance is stopped and allocate the buffer pool when the instance is restarted.

Question 20

When setting up the Self-Tuning Memory Manager (STMM), at least two memory areas should be configured for self-tuning so that memory can be redistributed between them. However, one DB2 memory areas can be enabled for self tuning by itself and still have the STMM automatically redistribute memory on its behalf. Which memory tuning area is this?

- ○ A. Buffer pools
- ○ B. Lock list
- ○ C. Package cache
- ○ D. Sort heap

Question 21

A database administrator executed the following commands and statements in the order shown:

```
CREATE DATABASE db1 ON /mnt/db2fs2, /mnt/db2fs3 DBPATH /mnt/db2fs1;

UPDATE DB CFG FOR db1 USING DATABASE_MEMORY AUTOMATIC;
UPDATE DB CFG FOR db1 USING PCKCACHESZ AUTOMATIC;
UPDATE DB CFG FOR db1 USING LOCKLIST AUTOMATIC;
UPDATE DB CFG FOR db1 USING MAXLOCKS AUTOMATIC;
UPDATE DB CFG FOR db1 USING SHEAPTHRES_SHR AUTOMATIC;
UPDATE DB CFG FOR db1 USING SORTHEAP AUTOMATIC;

CONNECT TO db1;
ALTER BUFFERPOOL ibmdefaultbp SIZE AUTOMATIC;
CONNECT RESET;
```

If database DB1 is a partitioned database, which of the following is a valid statement?

- ○ A. Database DB1 has been configured to take advantage of the Self-Tuning Memory Manager (STMM) and STMM has been enabled for the database.
- ○ B. Database DB1 has been configured to take advantage of the Self-Tuning Memory Manager (STMM); however STMM has not been enabled for the database.
- ○ C. If the amount of free memory available on the system becomes too low, some of the database shared memory that has been reserved for database DB1 will be released.
- ○ D. Memory consumed by database DB1 can be moved between the different DB2 memory segments, for example, from the sort heap to a buffer pool.

Question 22

Which of the following correctly describes how the Self-Tuning Memory Manager (STMM) monitors and tunes memory in a partitioned database environment?

- ○ A. All memory tuning decisions are based on memory and workload characteristics of the catalog partition; memory adjustments are made on this partition first and then distributed to all other partitions.
- ○ B. All memory tuning decisions are based on memory and workload characteristics of the coordinator partition; memory adjustments are made on this partition first and then distributed to all other partitions.
- ○ C. All memory tuning decisions are based on memory and workload characteristics of a single partition that has been designated as the tuning partition; memory adjustments are made on this partition first and then distributed to all other partitions.
- ○ D All memory tuning decisions are based on memory and workload characteristics of the entire database; memory adjustments are made on individually on each partition.

Question 23

If the following statement is executed:

```
ALTER TABLE employee COMPRESS YES
```

Which of the following commands will NOT build a compression dictionary for the EMPLOYEE table?

- ○ A. INSPECT RESETDICTIONARY TABLE NAME employee
- ○ B. INSPECT ROWCOMPESTIMATE TABLE NAME employee
- ○ C. REORG TABLE employee RESETDICTIONARY
- ○ D. REORG TABLE employee KEEPDICTIONARY

Question 24

After being enabled for deep compression and having a compression dictionary built, the following command was used to alter a table named EMPLOYEE:

```
ALTER TABLE employee COMPRESS NO
```

Which of the following commands can be used to remove the compression dictionary from the EMPLOYEE table?

- ○ A. DELETE
- ○ B. REORG
- ○ C. INSPECT
- ○ D. RUNSTATS

Question 25

A table named PARTS was created in a DB2 9 database by executing the following CREATE TABLE statement:

```
CREATE TABLE parts
     (itemid         INT NOT NULL,
      description    VARCHAR(250),
      price          DECIMAL(7,2),
      photo          BLOB(2000),
      warranty_info  XML)
   COMPRESS YES
```

Once a compression dictionary has been built for the PARTS table, which column should yield the greatest amount of compression?

- ○ A. PHOTO
- ○ B. ITEMID
- ○ C. DESCRIPTION
- ○ D. WARRANTY_INFO

Question 26

A table named ITEMS has the following columns and cardinalities:

```
ID             1000000
TYPE           10
NAME           50000
DESCRIPTION    50000
```

If the following query is executed on a regular basis:

```
SELECT * FROM items WHERE type = 1 AND id = 10
```

Which of the following set of statements would provide the fastest response time for the query?

- ○ A. CREATE INDEX items_ix1 ON items (type, id);
       RUNSTATS ON TABLE items FOR INDEX items_ix1;
- ○ B. CREATE INDEX items_ix1 ON items(type);
       RUNSTATS ON TABLE items FOR INDEX items_ix1;
- ○ C. CREATE INDEX items_ix1 ON items(id);
       RUNSTATS ON TABLE items FOR INDEX items_ix1;
- ○ D. CREATE INDEX items_ix1 ON items(id, type);
       RUNSTATS ON TABLE items FOR INDEX items_ix1;

Question 27

A LIST APPLICATIONS command returned the following output:

```
Auth Id  Application Appl.   Application Id             DB     # of
         Name        Handle                            Name   Agents
-------- ----------- ------- ------------------------- ------ -----
RSANDERS db2taskd    148     *LOCAL.DB2.070601164915 SAMPLE   1
RSANDERS db2stmm     147     *LOCAL.DB2.070601164914 SAMPLE   1
RSANDERS db2bp.exe   146     *LOCAL.DB2.070601164913 SAMPLE   1
```

Which two of the following commands will terminate all of the applications that are currently running?

○ A. FORCE APPLICATION (146, 147, 148)

○ B. FORCE APPLICATION (LOCAL.DB2.070601164915, LOCAL.DB2.070601164914, LOCAL.DB2.070601164913)

○ C. FORCE APPLICATION (db2taskd, db2stmm, db2bp.exe)

○ D. FORCE APPLICATION ALL

○ E. FORCE ALL APPLICATIONS

Question 28

A table space named TBSP1 (with the table space ID 5) is deployed on a storage array that is using RAID-5 4+1 protection.

Which command would optimize I/O for all tables and indexes stored in table space TBSP1?

○ A. db2set DB2_PARALLEL_IO=4:4

○ B. db2set DB2_PARALLEL_IO=5:4

○ C. db2set DB2_PARALLEL_IO=5:5

○ D. db2set DB2_PARALLEL_IO=4:5

Question 29

User USER1 needs to sort a table that has an average row length of 450. The table resides is in a database named DB1 that has intra-partition parallelism disabled; the cardinality of the table is 2500.

Which command(s) will prevent a sort heap overflow from occurring when the table is sorted?

○ A. UPDATE DBM CFG USING SHEAPTHRES 1500000

○ B. UPDATE DB CFG FOR db1 USING SORTHEAP 300

○ C. UPDATE DBM CFG USING SHEAPTHRES 1500000;
  UPDATE DB CFG FOR db1 USING SORTHEAP 300;

○ D. UPDATE DBM CFG USING SHEAPTHRES 0;
  UPDATE DB CFG FOR db1 USING SORTHEAP AUTOMATIC;

Question 30

If the following sequence of commands and statements are issued from the DB2 Command Line Processor immediately after an instance is started:

```
ACTIVATE DATABASE sample;
CONNECT TO sample;
SELECT * FROM org;
TERMINATE;
```

What will happen to the agent that was used to provide the results for the query when the TERMINATE command is processed?

- ○ A. The agent process/thread will be suspended.
- ○ B. The agent process/thread will be terminated or killed.
- ○ C. The agent process/thread will be placed in the idle agent pool if enough space is available in the pool.
- ○ D. The agent process/thread will remain active provided the MAXAGENTS setting has not been exceeded.

Question 31

Which of the following is NOT a valid statement about the connection concentrator?

- ○ A. The connection concentrator is enabled when the maximum number of connections supported is equal to or less than the maximum number of coordinating agents allowed.
- ○ B. The connection concentrator uses logical agents (LAs) to handle the application context while database agents (DAs) handle the actual DB2 connections.
- ○ C. The connection concentrator is enabled when the maximum number of connections supported is greater than the maximum number of coordinating agents allowed.
- ○ D. The connection concentrator allows servers to provide support for thousands of users simultaneously executing business transactions while drastically reducing the resources required.

Question 32

When an application connects to a nonpartitioned database stored on a Linux server, what is responsible for executing all subsequent SQL statements and DB2 commands on behalf of the application?

- ○ A. A subagent named db2agntp
- ○ B. A connection agent db2agntc
- ○ C. A director agent named db2agent
- ○ D. A coordinating agent named db2agent

Question 33

A table named PARTS was created as follows:

```
CREATE TABLE parts
    (partnumber      INT NOT NULL,
     description     VARCHAR(25),
     price           DECIMAL(7,2),
     weight          DECIMAL(3,2))
```

If column PARTNUMBER is unique and queries typically access columns PARTNUMBER, PRICE and DESCRIPTION together, which statement will create an index that will provide optimal query performance?

- ○ A. CREATE UNIQUE INDEX parts_idx1 ON parts (partnumber, price)
- ○ B. CREATE UNIQUE INDEX parts_idx1 ON parts (partnumber, price, description)
- ○ C. CREATE UNIQUE INDEX parts_idx1 ON parts (partnumber) INCLUDE (price, description)
- ○ D. CREATE UNIQUE INDEX parts_idx1 ON parts (partnumber, price) INCLUDE description)

Question 34

A table named STAFF was created by executing the following statement:

```
CREATE TABLE staff
    (emp_id      INTEGER ,
     name        VARCHAR (40) ,
     dept        VARCHAR (40) ,
     salary      DECIMAL (15,2))
```

The following query is frequently run against the STAFF table:

```
SELECT name, dept
FROM staff
WHERE salary > (SELECT MAX (salary *.95) FROM staff)
```

Which statement will create an index that will provide optimal performance for this query?

- ○ A. CREATE INDEX staffx1 ON staff (salary ASC)
- ○ B. CREATE INDEX staffx1 ON staff (salary DESC)
- ○ C. CREATE INDEX staffx1 ON staff (salary, name, dept)
- ○ D. CREATE INDEX staffx1 ON staff (salary ASC, name ASC, dept DESC)

Question 35

A table named EMPLOYEE was created by executing the following statement:

```
CREATE TABLE employee
     (emp_id    INTEGER NOT NULL,
      name      VARCHAR (40) NOT NULL ,
      dept_id   INTEGER NOT NULL)
```

Immediately after creation, the table was populated with 250,000 rows. If the following query is frequently run against the EMPLOYEE table:

```
ELECT emp_id, dept_id, name
FROM employee
WHERE emp_id  = 50 AND dept_id = 10
```

Which statement will create an index that will provide optimal performance for this query?

O A. CREATE INDEX emp_idx1 ON employee (emp_id)

O B. CREATE INDEX emp_idx1 ON employee (dept_id)

O C. CREATE INDEX emp_idx1 ON employee (emp_id, dept_id)

O D. CREATE INDEX emp_idx1 ON employee (emp_id) INCLUDE (dept_id)

Question 36

Which of the following statements will tell the DB2 optimizer to use an index scan on a table named TAB1 regardless of any catalog statistics that might have been collected, because the table varies in size dramatically from one minute to the next?

O A. ALTER TABLE tab1 VOLATILE

O B. ALTER TABLE tab1 USE INDEX tab1_idx

O C. ALTER TABLE tab1 DISTRIBUTION SCAN

O D. ALTER TABLE tab1 REFRESH CARDINALITY

Question 37

Which two of the following determine the degree of inter-partition parallelism used?

❑ A. The number of database partitions.

❑ B. The value of the INTER_PARALLEL Database Manager configuration parameter.

❑ C. The definition of database partition groups.

❑ D. The number of CPUs/cores per database partition.

❑ E. The amount of memory available per database partition.

Question 38

In which environment would intra-partition parallelism be used by DB2?

- ○ A. The server has two CPUs and one DB2 instance.
- ○ B. The server has one CPU and one DB2 instance.
- ○ C. The server has one CPU and two DB2 instances.
- ○ D. The server has one CPU and four DB2 instances.

Question 39

Which statement correctly describes intra-partition parallelism?

- ○ A. Intra-partition parallelism refers to the ability to break up a database operation into multiple parts, many or all of which can be run in parallel across multiple partitions of a partitioned database.
- ○ B. Intra-partition parallelism refers to the ability to break up a database operation into multiple parts and execute those parts simultaneously within a single DB2 instance.
- ○ C. Intra-partition parallelism refers to the ability of the database to accept queries from multiple applications at the same time; each query runs independently of the others, but DB2 runs all of them simultaneously.
- ○ D. Intra-partition parallelism refers to the ability to merge multiple database operations into a single operation that can be processed across multiple partitions of a partitioned database.

Question 40

Which of the following would indicate an access plan is using inter-partition parallelism?

- ○ A. Local table queues
- ○ B. Merging table queues
- ○ C. Listener table queues
- ○ D. Broadcast table queues

Question 41

Which of the following would indicate an access plan is using intra-partition parallelism?

- ○ A. Local table queues
- ○ B. Merging table queues
- ○ C. Directed table queues
- ○ D. Synchronous table queues

Question 42

Which of the following is NOT a valid statement regarding the Configuration Advisor?

○ A. The Configuration Advisor is a GUI application that makes it easy to tune and balance the resource requirements of a single database within an instance.

○ B. In DB2 9, the Configuration Advisor is automatically invoked whenever you create a database using the Create Database Wizard.

○ C. The Configuration Advisor takes information you provide about a database and its anticipated workload and produces a set of recommended configuration parameters changes.

○ D The Configuration Advisor takes information you provide about a server and produces a set of recommended registry variable settings.

Answers

Question 1

The correct answer is **C**. The DB2_AVOID_PREFETCH registry variable is used to specify whether or not prefetching should be used during crash recovery. Valid values for this variable are ON and OFF - OFF is the default. Setting the DB2_AVOID_PREFETCH registry variable to ON tells DB2 NOT to perform normal prefetching during crash recovery (restart) operations.

Question 2

The correct answer is **D**. The DB2_MEM_TUNING_RANGE registry variable is used to specify the amount of physical memory that is to be left free by a given instance (and its active databases) when self tuning of database shared memory is enabled. Essentially, the DB2_MEM_TUNING_RANGE sets the limits for automatic memory tuning within DB2, and can be used to prevent a database from consuming all of the system memory available.

Keep in mind that it is recommended to set this variable only when using the DB2 self-tuning memory manager (STMM) and the *database_memory* database configuration parameter has been set to AUTOMATIC, or if insufficient system memory problems are occurring.

Question 3

The correct answer is **B**. The DB2_PINNED_BP registry variable is used to specify whether the database global memory used – including buffer pool memory – is to be kept in system main memory. Valid values for this variable are YES and NO - NO is the default. When set to YES, the DB2_PINNED_BP variable will keep the database global memory "pinned" or resident in real memory; database performance is more consistent when database global memory is kept in main memory.

On 64-bit DB2 for AIX, setting this variable to YES means that self tuning for database shared memory (activated by setting the *database_memory* database configuration parameter to AUTOMATIC) cannot be enabled.

Question 4

The correct answer is **A**. The DB2_SMS_TRUNC_TMPTABLE_THRESH registry variable is used to specify a minimum file size threshold at which a temporary table (file) is maintained in an SMS table space. By default, this variable is set to 0, which means no special threshold handling is done. Instead, once a temporary table is no longer needed, its file is truncated to 0 extents. When the value of this variable is greater than 0, a larger file is maintained. If this variable is set to -1, the file is not truncated and is allowed to grow indefinitely, restricted only by system resources. This reduces some of the system overhead involved in dropping and recreating the file each time a temporary table is used.

Question 5

The correct answer is **B**. The *sheapthres_shr* configuration parameter—not the *sheapthres* configuration parameter—is used to specify the maximum amount of memory (in pages) that is to be used at any one time to perform sort operations.

The *sheapthres* Database Manager configuration parameter is used to specify an instance-wide soft limit on the total amount of memory that can be consumed by private sorts at any given time. When the limit is reached it does not prevent more sorts, it just reduces the memory each sort can consume until other sorts complete.

If you run the AUTOCONFIGURE command against a database that resides in an instance where the *sheapthres* configuration parameter has been assigned a value other than zero, the sort memory heap database configuration parameter (*sortheap*) will not be configured for automatic tuning. (You must execute the command UPDATE DATABASE MANAGER CONFIGURATION USING SHEAPTHRES 0 before you execute the AUTOCONFIGURE command if you want to enable sort memory tuning.)

Question 6

The correct answer is **D**. The *mincommit* database configuration parameter is used to specify the number of COMMIT SQL statements that are to be processed before log records are written to disk. If individual query response times are not absolutely important, setting *mincommit* to a value of more than one will cause DB2 not to flush the log buffers until there are *mincommit* commits, or the buffer is full (whichever comes first).

The *logarchmeth1* configuration parameter specifies the logging method to use and the media type of the primary destination for archived log files; the *max_log* configuration parameter specifies if there is a limit to the percentage of primary log space that a single transaction can consume, and if so, what that limit is; and the *logbufsz* database configuration parameter is used to specify the amount of memory (in pages) that is to be used to buffer log records before they are written to disk.

Changing the logging method used or limiting the amount of log space available to a single transaction will not help in this situation. Increasing the size of the log buffer can improve performance if transactions must wait for log data to be written to disk, but in this example, very few log records appear to be written and the log buffer size appears to be sufficient so changing the frequency at which COMMITs are processed and log record are flushed to disk is the best solution.

Question 7

The correct answer is **A**. The *maxfilop* Database Manager configuration parameter is used to specify the maximum number of files that can be open per application. (Because DB2 is thread based and not process based in Version 9.5, the *maxfilop* configuration parameter is used to specify the number of files that can be open per database in DB2 9.5.) The value specified in this parameter defines the total database and application file handles that can be used by a specific process connected to a database. In this scenario, we can see that there were over 51000 files closed and opened in a very short period of time. By increasing the value assigned to *maxfilop*, you allow DB2 to maintain more file handles, so it will not have to spend time opening and closing files to get work done.

Question 8

The correct answer is **D**. A volatile table is a table that is updated very frequently and that changes size dramatically within a short period of time. To tell the optimizer to use an index scan for this type of table, you can mark it as being volatile when you create it (by specifying the VOLATILE option with the CREATE TABLE SQL statement used to create it), or if it already exists, you can mark it as being volatile by executing an ALTER TABLE statement with the VOLATILE option specified; for example, ALTER TABLE payroll VOLATILE.

Declaring a table as being volatile is very important if there are very different numbers of rows in the table at different times, so that gathering statistics, while possible, is not feasible.

Question 9

The correct answer is **D**. When an index is created, only keys and record IDs are stored in the resulting index structure and each record ID points to a corresponding row in the data pages. However, when a clustered index is created, DB2 attempts to store the data in the data pages in the same order as the corresponding keys appear in the index pages. DB2 will also attempt to insert rows with similar key values onto the same pages. A clustering index is most useful for columns that have range predicates because it allows better sequential access of data in the table. (Columns frequently searched or joined over a range of values using the operators BETWEEN, >, <, and LIKE are good candidates for clustering.) Clustering indexes can also improve performance when a query needs to access a large percentage of the rows in the table, particularly when the rows are retrieved in order.

In order for DB2 to maintain the clustering of the data and the index as records are inserted or updated, you must leave free space on the data pages to provide room for additional rows. The PCTFREE option of the CREATE INDEX SQL statement is used to control how much space is reserved on data pages for future insert, update, load, and reorganization operations. Specify a higher PCTFREE value at index creation time to reduce the likelihood that index page splits will occur when records are added to the table. (The default is 10 percent, but you should increase this to between 20 and 35 percent for tables that have a heavy volume of insert/update/delete operations.)

Clustering indexes offer the same benefits for partitioned tables as they do for regular tables. However, to achieve well-maintained clustering with good performance, there should be a correlation between the index columns used and the table partitioning key columns. One way to ensure such correlation is to prefix the index columns with the table partitioning key columns.

Question 10

The correct answer is **C**. The DB2 optimizer is the component of the SQL compiler that is responsible for choosing the access plan to use for processing data manipulation language (DML) SQL statements. It does this by modeling the execution cost of many alternative access plans and choosing the one with the minimal estimated cost.

The first thing that the DB2 optimizer does when it is invoked is accept and parse the SQL statement received. Once the SQL statement has been parsed, the optimizer then attempts to verify that all objects referenced in the statement do, in fact, exist in the database. (This is referred to as checking or validating the semantics.) After semantics checking is complete, the DB2 optimizer will use its powerful query rewrite facility to examine the statement and try to determine if there are better ways to write the statement. Once the query rewrite step is complete, the DB2 optimizer will enumerate different plan options available and evaluate each one. Depending on the optimization level used and the instance and database configuration settings found, some techniques may or may not be allowed. As each allowed plan is enumerated, the cost of the plan is evaluated; once the DB2 optimizer has analyzed all possible plans, the plan with the lowest cost is chosen. Once a plan is chosen, the code for that plan is built into a package, which is then stored in the system catalog of the database (if the statement was static) or the package cache (if the statement was dynamic).

Question 11

The correct answer is **B**. Statistical views allow the DB2 optimizer to compute more accurate cardinality estimates. (Cardinality estimation is the process where the optimizer uses statistics to determine the size of partial query results after predicates are applied or aggregation is performed.) The accuracy of cardinality estimates depends on the predicates used and the available statistics. Statistics are available to represent the distribution of data values within a column, which can improve cardinality estimates when the data values are unevenly distributed. Statistics are also available to represent the number of distinct values in a set of columns, which can improve cardinality estimates when columns are statistically correlated.

Question 12

The correct answer is **A**. The objective of index ANDing is to find common RIDs. Index ANDing might occur in situations where multiple indexes exist on corresponding columns in the same table and a query using multiple AND predicates is run against that table. (The purpose of index ORing is to eliminate duplicate RIDs.)

Question 13

The correct answer is **C**. When queries are executed in a database environment that has been designed to take advantage of parallelism, a table queue is used to pass table data from one database agent to another. When inter-partition parallelism is used, table queues facilitate the passing of table data from one database partition to another; when intra-partition parallelism is used they aid in the passing of table data within a single database partition. Each table queue passes data in a single direction. The SQL compiler decides where table queues are required and includes them in the access plan; when the plan is executed, connections between the database partitions open the table queues needed. Table queues are closed automatically as processes end.

Synchronous table queues read one row for each FETCH statement issued by an application. Synchronous table queues are used when you do not specify the FOR FETCH ONLY clause on a SELECT statement. In a partitioned database environment, if you are updating rows, the database manager will use the synchronous table queues.

Other types of table queues available include:

- *Local table queues (sometimes referred to as LTQ).* These table queues are used to pass data between database agents within a single database partition. Local table queues (LTQ) are used for intra-partition parallelism.

- *Asynchronous table queues.* These table queues are known as asynchronous because they read rows in advance of any FETCH statement issued by an application. When the FETCH statement is issued, the row is retrieved from the table queue. Asynchronous table queues are used when you specify the FOR FETCH ONLY clause on a SELECT statement. If you are only fetching rows, the asynchronous table queue is faster.

- *Merging table queues.* These table queues preserve order.

- *Nonmerging table queues.* These table queues, also known as "regular" table queues, do not preserve order.

- *Listener table queues.* These table queues are used with correlated subqueries. Correlation values are passed down to the subquery and the results are passed back up to the parent query block using this type of table queue.

- *Directed table queues* (*sometimes referred to as DTQ*). These table queues are used in join operations. With directed table queues, rows are hashed to one of the receiving database partitions.

- *Broadcast table queues (sometimes referred to as BTQ).* These table queues are also used in join operations. With broadcast table queues, rows are sent to all of the receiving database partitions but are not hashed.

Question 14

The correct answer is **B**. The first time an application attempts to insert a record into a table, a special algorithm will search the Free Space Control Records (FSCRs) in an effort to locate a page that has enough free space to hold the new record. (The value assigned to the DB2MAXFSCRSEARCH registry variable determines the number of FSCRs that are searched; the default value for this registry variable is five). If no space is found within the specified number of FSCRs searched, the record is appended to the end of the table. To optimize insert performance, subsequent records are also appended to the end of the table until two extents have been written. Once two extents have been filled, the next insert operation will resume searching FSCRs where the last search left off and the whole process is repeated. After all FSCRs in the entire table have been searched in this way, records are automatically appended and no additional searching is performed. In fact, searching using the FSCRs is not done again until space is created somewhere in the table by deleting one or more records.

To optimize a table for insert performance, at the possible expense of faster table growth, consider assigning a small number to the DB2MAXFSCRSEARCH registry variable. (To optimize for space reuse at the possible expense of insert performance, assign a larger number to the DB2MAXFSCRSEARCH registry variable; setting the value to -1 forces the DB2 Database Manager to search all FSCRs.)

Another way to optimize for insert performance is to place a table into what is known as append mode. Regular tables are placed into append mode by executing an ALTER TABLE SQL statement that looks like this:

```
ALTER TABLE [TableName] APPEND ON
```

where:

TableName   Identifies the table, by name, that is to be placed into append mode.

So in this example, the SQL statement "ALTER TABLE history APPEND ON" is the best choice for improving insert performance on the HISTORY table. Setting the DB2MAXFSCRSEARCH registry variable to 1000 or -1 can actually degrade insert performance.

Question 15

The correct answers are **B** and **D**. When it comes to deciding whether to use row-level locks or table-level locks, it is important to keep in mind that any time a transaction holds a lock on a particular resource, other transactions may be denied access to that resource until the owning transaction is terminated. Therefore, row-level locks are usually better than table-level locks because they restrict access to a much smaller resource. However, because each lock acquired requires some amount of storage space (to hold) and some degree of processing time (to manage), often there is considerably less overhead involved when a single table-level lock is acquired, rather than several individual row-level locks.

By default, DB2 always attempts to acquire row-level locks. However, it is possible to force DB2 to acquire table-level locks on a specific table by executing a special form of the ALTER TABLE SQL statement. The syntax for this form of the ALTER TABLE statement is:

```
ALTER TABLE [TableName] LOCKSIZE TABLE
```

where:

TableName   Identifies the name of an existing table for which the level of locking that all transactions are to use when accessing it is to be specified.

For example, when executed, the SQL statement

```
ALTER TABLE employee LOCKSIZE TABLE
```

is executed, DB2 will attempt to acquire table-level locks for every transaction that accesses the EMPLOYEE table.

But what if you don't want every transaction that works with a particular table to acquire table-level locks? What if instead you want one specific transaction to acquire table-level locks and all other transactions to acquire row-level locks when working with that particular table? In this case, you leave the default locking behavior alone (row-level locking) and use the LOCK TABLE SQL statement to acquire a table-level lock for the appropriate individual transaction. The syntax for the LOCK TABLE statement is:

```
LOCK TABLE [TableName] IN [SHARE | EXCLUSIVE] MODE
```

where:

TableName   Identifies the name of an existing table to be locked.

As you can see, the LOCK TABLE statement allows a transaction to acquire a table-level lock on a particular table in one of two modes: SHARE mode and EXCLUSIVE mode. If a table is locked using the SHARE mode, a table-level Share (S) lock is acquired on behalf of the requesting transaction, and other concurrent transactions are allowed to read, but not change, data stored in the locked table. On the other hand, if a table is locked using the EXCLUSIVE mode, a table-level Exclusive (X) lock is acquired, and other concurrent transactions can neither access nor modify data stored in the locked table.

Question 16

The correct answer is **A**. DB2 uses asynchronous page cleaners to write changed pages found in a buffer pool to disk before space in a buffer pool is acquired on behalf of a database agent. Ideally, database agents should not have to wait for changed pages to be written to disk before they will have sufficient space in a buffer pool. If that is indeed the case, overall performance of database applications is improved. The *num_iocleaners* database configuration parameter is used to specify the number of asynchronous page cleaners that can be in progress for a database at any given point in time.

If applications running against the database consist primarily of transactions that update data, increasing the number of page cleaners used will speed up performance. Increasing the amount of page cleaners used will also shorten recovery time from soft failures, such as power outages, because the contents of the database on disk will be more up-to-date at any given point in time.

A good value to assign to this configuration parameter is the value AUTOMATIC. If this parameter is set to AUTOMATIC, the number of page cleaners started will be based on the number of CPUs found on the current machine, as well as the number of local logical database partitions used (in a partitioned database environment).

Question 17

The correct answer is **C**. The *sheapthres_shr* database configuration parameter is used to specify the maximum amount of memory (in pages) that is to be used at any one time to perform sort operations. When this parameter is set to 0, all sort operations are performed in shared memory. Otherwise, sort operations are performed in private sort memory.

Question 18

The correct answer is **B**. I/O servers, also called prefetchers, are used on behalf of database agents to perform prefetch I/O and asynchronous I/O for utilities such as the Backup utility and the Restore utility. The *num_ioservers* database configuration parameter is used to specify the number of I/O servers that can be in progress for a database at any given point in time. (An I/O server waits while an I/O operation that it initiated is in progress.) Non-prefetch I/Os are scheduled directly from database agents and as a result are not constrained by the value assigned to the *num_ioservers* database configuration parameter.

Question 19

The correct answer is **C**. If a new buffer pool is created (by executing the CREATE BUFFERPOOL statement) after the self tuning memory manager (STMM) has been enabled, DB2 will attempt to create the buffer pool immediately (unless the DEFERRED clause was specified with the CREATE BUFFERPOOL statement used) by allocating the memory requested from shared database memory. If the memory needed is not available, the buffer pool will be created, but no memory will be allocated until all connections to the database the buffer pool is to be created for have been terminated and the database has been deactivated (i.e., the database is stopped and restarted).

Question 20

The correct answer is **D**. The Self-Tuning Memory Manager (STMM) simplifies the task of configuring memory-related database parameters by automatically setting values for these parameters after measuring and analyzing how well each DB2 memory consumer is using the allocated memory available. The following database memory pools can be enabled for self-tuning, either entirely or individually:

- Buffer pools (controlled by the ALTER BUFFERPOOL and CREATE BUFFERPOOL statements)
- Package cache (controlled by the *pckcachesz* configuration parameter)
- Locking memory (controlled by the *locklist* and *maxlocks* configuration parameters)
- Sort memory (controlled by the *sheapthres_shr* and the *sortheap* configuration parameter)
- Database shared memory (controlled by the *database_memory* configuration parameter)

When a database has been configured to take advantage of STMM, the memory tuner responds to changes in database workload characteristics and response times, adjusting the values of memory configuration parameters and buffer pool sizes to optimize performance. If the current workload requirements are high, and there is sufficient free memory on the system, more memory will be consumed by the database. It can also move memory between the different DB2 memory segments, for example, from the sort heap to a buffer pool.

Because the memory tuner trades memory resources between different memory consumers, there must be at least two memory consumers enabled for self-tuning in order for STMM to be effective. The one exception to this rule is when the sort heap (*sortheap* database configuration parameter) is enabled for self-tuning; in this case, STMM will balance the number of private memory pages used for private sorts and the number of shared memory pages used for shared sorts.

Question 21

The correct answer is **B**. Self-tuning is enabled for a database by assigning the value ON to the *self_tuning_mem* database configuration parameter. (By default, the *self_tuning_mem* database configuration parameter is assigned the value ON for single-partition databases and OFF for multi-partition databases.) Specific memory areas that are controlled by a memory configuration parameter can then be enabled for self-tuning by assigning the appropriate configuration parameter the value AUTOMATIC; buffer pools can be enabled for self-tuning by setting their size to AUTOMATIC.

In this example, the *self_tuning_mem* database configuration parameter was not set to ON, so even though the database DB1 was configured to take advantage of the Self-Tuning Memory Manager (STMM), STMM was been enabled for the database. If the database DB1 had been a single-partition database OR if the statement "UPDATE DB CFG FOR db1 USING SELF_TUNING_MEM ON" had been included in the set of commands, answers A, C, and D would have been valid statements and answer B would have been incorrect.

Question 22

The correct answer is **C**. When the Self-Tuning Memory Manager (STMM) is enabled in a partitioned database environment, a single database partition, known as the "tuning partition," is responsible for monitoring the memory configuration and usage patterns and determining if changes could improve performance. If the tuning partition deems a change should be made, it propagates the appropriate configuration changes to all other database partitions to maintain a consistent configuration across all database partitions used.

Question 23

The correct answer is **A**. A compression dictionary is built (and existing data in the table is compressed) by performing an offline (classic) table reorganization operation; such an operation is initiated by executing the REORG command with either the KEEPDICTIONARY or the RESETDICTIONARY option specified. If the REORG command is executed with either option specified, and a compression dictionary does not exist, a new dictionary will be built. If the REORG command is executed with either option specified, and a compression dictionary already exists, the existing dictionary will either be recreated (RESETDICTIONARY) or left as it is (KEEPDICTIONARY), and data in the table will be reorganized and compressed.

If the INSPECT command is executed with the ROWCOMPESTIMATE option specified, the Inspect utility will examine each row in the table specified, build a compression dictionary from the data found, and then use this dictionary to estimate how much space will be saved if the data in the table is compressed. If a table is enabled for deep compression (that is, the COMPRESS attribute is set to YES) before the INSPECT command is executed, the compression dictionary that is built and used to estimate space savings will be written to the table, at the end of the existing data—provided a compression dictionary doesn't already exist. Otherwise, the compression dictionary created to estimate space savings will be destroyed.

Question 24

The correct answer is **B**. To delete a compression dictionary from a table, set the COMPRESS attribute for the table to NO and execute the REORG command with the RESETDICTIONARY option specified; reorg processing will remove the compression dictionary and the rows in the newly reorganized table will be in non-compressed format. (If the COMPRESS attribute for a table is set to NO and the REORG command is executed with the KEEPDICTIONARY option specified, reorg processing will preserve the compression dictionary and all rows in the newly reorganized table will be in non-compressed format.)

Question 25

The correct answer is **C**. Deep compression works by searching for repeating patterns in the data and replacing the patterns with 12-bit symbols, which are stored along with the pattern they represent in a static dictionary. Once this dictionary is created, it is stored in the table along with the compressed data and loaded into memory whenever data in the table is accessed to aid in decompression. DB2 9 scans an entire table looking for repeating column values and repeating patterns that span multiple columns in a row. DB2 also looks for repeating patterns that are substrings of a given column. However, just because a repeating pattern is found doesn't mean that the data is automatically compressed—data is compressed only when storage savings will be realized.

Since it is not possible to compress long, large object, or XML data in DB2 9, only ITEMID, DESCRIPTION, and PRICE information can be compressed. Because DESCRIPTION is character string of up to 250 characters, it should yield the greatest amount of compression. (With DB2 9.5, inline XML documents can be compressed as long as they are less than 32K in size.)

Question 26

The correct answer is **D**. The primary purpose of an index is to help DB2 quickly locate records stored in a table. Therefore, creating an index for frequently accessed columns in a table usually improves performance for data access and update operations. Indexes also allow for greater concurrency when multiple transactions need to access the same table at the same time— row retrieval is faster and locks are acquired more quickly and don't have to be held as long.

In this scenario, creating an index on columns ID and TYPE will be the best choice since the first key (ID) cardinality is much higher, allowing much faster selection of the RIDs that match the query predicates. And ideally, the RUNSTATS utility should be run against a table immediately after any a new index is created.

Question 27

The correct answers are **A** and **D**. You can terminate one or more running applications prematurely by executing the FORCE APPLICATION command (assuming you have SYSADMN or SYSCTRL authority). The basic syntax for this command is:

```
FORCE APPLICATION ALL
```

or

```
FORCE APPLICATION ( [ApplicationHandle] , . . . )
```

where:

ApplicationHandle   Identifies the handle associated with one or more applications whose instance attachments and/or database connections are to be terminated.

Thus, if you wanted to force all users and applications connected to databases stored on a server named DB_SERVER to terminate their database connections, you could do so by executing a FORCE APPLICATION command that looks something like this:

```
FORCE APPLICATION ALL
```

On the other hand, if you wanted to force a specific application whose handle is 148 to terminate its processing, you could do so by executing a FORCE APPLICATION command that looks like this:

```
FORCE APPLICATION (148)
```

Question 28

The correct answer is **B**. The DB2_PARALLEL_IO registry variable is used to force DB2 to use parallel I/O for table spaces that only have one container or for table spaces whose containers reside on more than one physical disk. If this registry variable is not set, the level of I/O parallelism used is equal to the number of containers used by the table space. On the other hand, if this registry variable is assigned a value, the level of I/O parallelism used is equal to the number of containers used multiplied by the value stored in the DB2_PARALLEL_IO registry variable.

Often, the DB2_PARALLEL_IO registry variable is assigned the asterisk (*) value to indicate that every table space in the database is to use parallel I/O. (The asterisk value implies that each table space container used spans six physical disk spindles.) Such an assignment is made by executing a db2set command that looks something like this:

```
db2set DB2_PARALLEL_IO=*
```

However, this is not a correct setting to use when a table space container does not span six physical disk spindles. In those cases, the DB2_PARALLEL_IO registry variable should be set by executing a db2set command that looks more like this:

```
db2set DB2_PARALLEL_IO=[TS_ID]:[DisksPerCtr] ,...
```

where:

TS_ID	Identifies one or more individual table spaces, by their numeric table space ID.
DisksPerCtr	Identifies the number of physical disks used by each table space container that is assigned to the table space specified.

Thus, if you wanted to set the DB2_PARALLEL_IO registry variable for a table space whose numeric ID is 5 to reflect that its storage containers reside on a RAID-5 4+1 group (4 data disk spindles), you could do so by executing a db2set command that looks something like this:

```
db2set DB2_PARALLEL_IO=5:4
```

Question 29

The correct answer is **D**. The *sheapthres* Database Manager configuration parameter is used to set an instance-wide soft limit on the total amount of memory (in pages) that is to be made available for private sorting operations. The *sortheap* database configuration parameter is used to specify the maximum number of private memory pages to be used for private sorts or the maximum number of shared memory pages to be used for shared sorts.

If you set the sort heap threshold configuration parameter (*sheapthres*) to 0 and the sort heap (*sortheap*) database configuration to AUTOMATIC, DB2 will automatically adjust the size of the sort heap to keep sorts resident in memory and to keep sort heap overflows from occurring.

Question 30

The correct answer is **C**. When an application connects to a nonpartitioned database, the connection is assigned to a coordinating agent (named db2agent), and all subsequent SQL statements and DB2 commands are executed by this agent on behalf of the application. When the application disconnects, the corresponding coordinating agent can be terminated;

however, a better approach is to let DB2 keep unused (idle) agents around and allow them to be reused by other applications.

Idle agents reside in an agent pool. These agents are available for requests from coordinating agents operating on behalf of client applications, or from subagents operating on behalf of existing coordinating agents. When the maximum number of connections supported (determined by the value assigned to the *max_connections* Database Manager configuration parameter) is equal to or less than the maximum number of coordinating agents allowed (determined by the value assigned to the *max_coordagents* configuration parameter), the size of the idle agent pool is determined by the maximum number of agents allowed. All idle agents, regardless of whether they are coordinating agents or subagents, count toward this limit; if the workload causes this limit to be exceeded, the agents needed are created to support the workload and then terminated as soon as they finish executing their current request.

In this example, because the database was activated, an agent pool was created so the idle agent for the query will be placed in the agent pool as long as the pool has not reached its maximum size.

Question 31

The correct answer is **A**. DB2's connection concentrator allows servers to provide support for thousands of users simultaneously executing business transactions while drastically reducing the resources required. It accomplishes this by concentrating the workload from all active applications in a much smaller number of database server connections. The connection concentrator is enabled when the maximum number of connections supported (determined by the value assigned to the *max_connections* Database Manager configuration parameter) is greater than the maximum number of coordinating agents allowed (determined by the value assigned to the *max_coordagents* configuration parameter) maximum number of connections supported is greater than the maximum number of coordinating agents allowed). When the connection concentrator is enabled, the value assigned to the *max_coordagents* configuration parameter is used as a guideline for determining how large the agent pool will be when the system workload is low. In this case, an idle agent will always be returned to the pool, no matter what the *max_coordagents* configuration parameter has been set to, and DB2's connection concentrator technology will be enabled.

The connection concentrator uses logical agents (LAs) to handle the application context while database agents (DAs) handle the actual DB2 connections. When a new application connects to a database, it is assigned an LA. Because a DA is needed to pass SQL statements to the DB2 server for processing, one is assigned to perform the work for the LA as soon as a new transaction is initiated. The key to this architecture is the fact that the DA is disassociated from the LA and is returned to the agent pool when a transaction completes.

Question 32

The correct answer is **D**. When an application connects to a nonpartitioned database, the connection is assigned to a coordinating agent (named db2agent in Linux and UNIX environments), and all subsequent SQL statements and DB2 commands are executed by this agent on behalf of the application.

Question 33

The correct answer is **C**. If you have a query that accesses multiple columns in a table, you cannot simply combine the columns accessed into one unique index, because that may not enforce the uniqueness you want. In this example, you want to ensure that the PARTNUMBER column will contain unique values, yet provide optimum performance for a queries that look something like this:

```
SELECT partnumber, price, description FROM parts
WHERE partnumber = 19002
```

Without an index, this query will require that the entire table be scanned in order to retrieve the desired data. On the other hand, if you create a unique index on the PARTNUMBER column, DB2 will have to scan the index to locate the record, and then read the corresponding data page to retrieve the price and description. But, if you create a unique index on PARTNUMBER, and include the PRICE and DESCRIPTION columns, DB2 can get the data for the query using index only access. Therefore, you might be tempted to create a unique index for the PARTS table by executing a CREATE INDEX statement that looks like this:

```
CREATE UNIQUE INDEX parts_idx1
    ON parts (partnumber, price, description)
```

However, this index does not ensure that the PARTNUMBER column will contain unique values. Instead, it ensures that the *combination* of PARTNUMBER, PRICE, and DESCRIPTION will be unique. To create a unique index on PARTNUMBER, and include the PRICE and DESCRIPTION columns so that DB2 can get the data for the query using index only access, you would need to create the index by executing a CREATE INDEX statement that looks like this:

```
CREATE UNIQUE INDEX parts_idx1 ON parts (partnumber) INCLUDE (price,
    description)
```

Question 34

The correct answer is **B**. The primary purpose of an index is to help DB2 quickly locate records stored in a table. Therefore, creating an index for frequently accessed columns in a table usually improves performance for data access and update operations. To ensure that an index will be beneficial, you must analyze how data is frequently accessed to determine which columns should be indexed and which should not. Identifying columns that are frequently joined and/or searched is a good place to start:

1. Consider creating a clustering index on the column most frequently searched and/or joined, based on the data order. Consider nonclustering indexes on searched or joined columns in which less than 10 percent of the rows will be scanned/joined.

2. Refine this analysis with an estimate of the percentage of the rows that will be inserted, updated, and/or deleted over a given period of time. Minimize the number of indexes used when inserting, updating, and deleting data frequently.

3. Composite indexes (i.e., indexes with more than one column) are most beneficial when columns are frequently accessed together.

4. Consider the cardinality of the columns, particularly for composite indexes. Indexes on columns with a low cardinality are not very selective and do not enhance performance as much as indexes on columns with high cardinalities.

In this example, the SALARY column is accessed both in the query and the subquery so it is the best candidate for an index. And by making the index on salary a descending index, the first key contain the highest salary so no further work is required on that index to find the 95% of max salary value.

Question 35

The correct answer is **C**. The primary purpose of an index is to help DB2 quickly locate records stored in a table. Therefore, creating an index for frequently accessed columns in a table usually improves performance for data access and update operations. To ensure that an index will be beneficial, you must analyze how data is frequently accessed to determine which columns should be indexed and which should not. Identifying columns that are frequently joined and/or searched is a good place to start:

1. Consider creating a clustering index on the column most frequently searched and/or joined, based on the data order. Consider nonclustering indexes on searched or joined columns in which less than 10 percent of the rows will be scanned/joined.

2. Refine this analysis with an estimate of the percentage of the rows that will be inserted, updated, and/or deleted over a given period of time. Minimize the number of indexes used when inserting, updating, and deleting data frequently.

3. Composite indexes (i.e., indexes with more than one column) are most beneficial when columns are frequently accessed together.

4. Consider the cardinality of the columns, particularly for composite indexes. Indexes on columns with a low cardinality are not very selective and do not enhance performance as much as indexes on columns with high cardinalities.

In this example, both the EMP_ID column and the DEPT_ID column are frequently accessed together so a composite index of the two columns should provide optimal performance for the query.

Question 36

The correct answer is **A**. A volatile table is a table that is updated very frequently and that changes size dramatically within a short period of time. To tell the optimizer to use an index scan for this type of table, you can mark it as being volatile when you create it (by specifying the VOLATILE option with the CREATE TABLE SQL statement used to create it), or if it already exists, you can mark it as being volatile (by executing an ALTER TABLE statement with the VOLATILE option specified; for example, ALTER TABLE tab1 VOLATILE).

Question 37

The correct answers are **A** and **C**. The degree of parallelism used is largely determined by the number of database partitions created and how database partition groups have been defined.

Question 38

The correct answer is **A**. Where each type of parallelism available should be used is determined primarily by the hardware configuration used. Some of the more common hardware configurations available, along with the type of parallelism that is best suited for each, can be seen in Table 5.1.

Table 5.1 Types of Parallelism Possible in Common Hardware Environ-ments			
		Intra-Query Parallelism	
Hardware Configuration	I/O Parallel-ism	Intra-partition Parallelism	Inter-partition Parallelism
Single Database Partition, Single Processor	Yes	No	No
Single Database Partition, Multi-ple Processors (SMP)	Yes	Yes	No
Multiple Database Partitions, One Processor (MPP)	Yes	No	Yes
Logical Database Partitions	Yes	Yes	Yes

Keep in mind that each database partition can reside on its own machine and have its own processor, memory, and disks.

Question 39

The correct answer is **B**. Intra-partition parallelism refers to the ability to break up a database operation into multiple parts and execute those parts simultaneously within a single DB2 instance; inter-partition parallelism refers to the ability to break up a database operation into multiple parts, many or all of which can be run in parallel across multiple partitions of a partitioned database. Both types of parallelism can provide a significant benefit in overall database performance as well as the execution of normal administrative tasks.

Question 40

The correct answer is **D**. The use of broadcast table queues (sometimes referred to as BTQ) and/or directed table queues (sometimes referred to as DTQ) signifies inter-partition parallelism and the movement of data between database partitions. Broadcast table queues and directed table queues are used in join operations. With broadcast table queues, rows are sent to all of the receiving database partitions but are not hashed; with directed table queues, rows are hashed to one of the receiving database partitions.

Question 41

The correct answer is **A**. Local table queues (sometimes referred to as LTQ) are used to pass data between database agents within a single database partition. Local table queues (LTQ) are used for intra-partition parallelism.

Question 42

The correct answer is **D**. The Configuration Advisor is a GUI application that makes it easy to tune and balance the resource requirements of a single database within an instance—you provide specific information about your database environment and the Configuration Advisor makes suggestions about which configuration parameters should be modified and provides recommended values for each. You can then elect to have the Configuration Advisor apply all changes recommended, or you can apply them yourself however you see fit.

In DB2 9, the Configuration Advisor is automatically invoked whenever you create a database using the Create Database Wizard. (This behavior can be changed by assigning the value NO to the DB2_ENABLE_AUTOCONFIG_DEFAULT registry variable.)

The Configuration Advisor only makes recommendations for DB2 Database Manager and database configuration parameters; it has no affect on environment registry variables.

CHAPTER 6

Security

E ight percent (8%) of the DB2 9 for Linux, UNIX, and Windows Advanced Database Administration exam (Exam 734) is designed to test your knowledge about the mechanisms DB2 uses to protect data and database objects against unauthorized access and/or modification and track all attempts to access data stored in a database. The questions that make up this portion of the exam are intended to evaluate the following:

- Your ability to identify the methods that can be used to restrict access to data stored in a DB2 database

- Your knowledge of the external authentication mechanisms that are used by DB2

- Your knowledge of the mechanisms and steps needed to implement data encryption

- Your knowledge of the mechanisms and steps needed to implement label-based access control (LBAC)

- Your ability to use DB2's Audit facility

This chapter is designed to introduce you to the various authorizations, authorities, and privileges that are available with DB2 9 and to the ways in which one or more authorities and/or privileges are granted to various users and groups. This chapter will also show you how to use encryption to further protect sensitive data, how to implement LBAC to control access to columns and rows in a table, and how to track all data access using an audit trail.

Controlling Database Access

Identity theft—a crime in which someone wrongfully obtains another person's personal data (such as a Social Security number, bank account number, and credit card number) and uses it in some way that involves fraud or deception for economic gain—is the fastest-growing crime in our nation today. Criminals are stealing information by overhearing conversations made on cell phones, by reading faxes and emails, by hacking into computers, by waging telephone and email scams, by stealing wallets and purses, by taking discarded documents from trash bins, by stealing mail, and by taking advantage of careless online shopping and banking habits. But more frightening is the fact that studies show that up to 70 percent of all identity theft cases are inside jobs—perpetrated by a coworker or an employee of a business you patronize. In these cases, all that is needed is access to your personal data, which can often be found in a company database.

Every database management system must be able to protect data against unauthorized access and modification. DB2 uses a combination of external security services and internal access control mechanisms to perform this vital task. In most cases, three different levels of security are employed: The first level controls access to the instance under which a database was created, the second controls access to the database itself, and the third controls access to the data and data objects that reside within the database.

Authentication

The first security portal most users must pass through on their way to gaining access to a DB2 instance or database is a process known as authentication. The purpose of authentication is to verify that users really are who they say they are. Normally, authentication is performed by an external security facility that is not part of DB2. This security facility may be part of the operating system (as is the case with AIX, Solaris, Linux, HP-UX, Windows 2000/XP/Vista, and many others), may be a separate add-on product (for example, Lightweight Directory Access

Protocol [LDAP]), or may not exist at all (which was the case with earlier versions of Windows). If a security facility does exist, it must be presented with two specific items before a user can be authenticated: a unique user ID and a corresponding password. The user ID identifies the user to the security facility, and the password, which is information known only by the user and the security facility, is used to verify that the user is indeed who he or she claims to be.

> Because passwords are a very important tool for authenticating users, you should always require passwords at the operating system level if you want the operating system to perform the authentication for your database. Keep in mind that on most UNIX operating systems, undefined passwords are treated as NULL, and any user who has not been assigned a password will be treated as having a NULL password. From the operating system's perspective, if no password is provided when a user attempts to log on, this will evaluate to being a valid match.

Where Does Authentication Take Place?

Because DB2 can reside in environments composed of multiple clients, gateways, and servers, each of which may be running on a different operating system and server, deciding where authentication is to take place can be a daunting task. To simplify things, DB2 uses two parameters in each DB2 Database Manager configuration file (the *authentication* parameter and the *srvcon_auth* parameter) to determine how and where users are authenticated. Such a file is associated with every instance, and a value, often referred to as the authentication type, is assigned to each parameter when an instance is first created. The *authentication* configuration parameter defines the authentication type that will be used for database connections and instance attachments as well as for performing local instance operations; the *srvcon_auth* parameter can be used to override the authentication type used for connections/attachments. Thus, an instance can be configured to use two different authentication types—one for connections/attachments and one for local instance operations. On the server side, the authentication type assigned to the *authentication* configuration parameter is specified during the instance creation process; on the client side, the authentication type is specified when a remote database is cataloged. With DB2 9, the following authentication types are available:

SERVER. Authentication occurs at the server where the DB2 instance is running, using the security facility provided by the server's operating system. (The user ID and password provided by the user wishing to attach to an instance or connect to a database are compared to the user ID and password combinations stored at the server to determine whether the user is permitted to access the instance or database.) By default, this is the authentication type used when an instance is first created.

SERVER_ENCRYPT. Authentication occurs at the server where the DB2 instance is running, using the security facility that is provided by the server's operating system. However, the password provided by the user wishing to attach to an instance or connect to a database stored on the server may be encrypted at the client workstation before it is sent to the server for validation.

CLIENT. Authentication occurs at the client workstation or database partition where a client application is invoked, using the security facility that is provided by the client's operating system, assuming one is available. If no security facility is available, authentication is handled in a slightly different manner. The user ID and password provided by the user wishing to attach to an instance or connect to a database are compared to the user ID and password combinations stored at the client or node to determine whether the user is permitted to access the instance or the database.

KERBEROS. Authentication occurs at the server where the DB2 instance is running, using a security facility that supports the Kerberos security protocol. This protocol performs authentication as a third-party service by using conventional cryptography to create a shared secret key, which is a 56-bit encrypted key that is generated using the Data Encryption Standard (DES) algorithm. The key becomes the credentials that are used to verify the identity of the user whenever local or network services are requested; this eliminates the need to pass a user ID and password across the network as ASCII text. (If both the client and the server support the Kerberos security protocol, the user ID and password provided by the user wishing to attach to an instance or connect to a database are encrypted at the client workstation and sent to the server for validation.) It should be noted that the KERBEROS authentication type is supported only on clients and servers that are using the AIX, Linux IA 32-bit, Linux AMD 64-bit, Sun Solaris, and select versions of the Windows operating system. In addition, in Windows environments, both client and server workstations must either belong to the same Windows domain or belong to trusted domains. In UNIX and Linux environments, the client will need to use the same KDC server releam or use the same cross releam for authentication.

KRB_SERVER_ENCRYPT. Authentication occurs at the server where the DB2 instance is running, using either the KERBEROS or the SERVER_ENCRYPT authentication method. If the client's authentication type is set to KERBEROS, authentication is performed at the server using the Kerberos security system. On the other hand, if the client's authentication type is set to anything other than KERBEROS, or if the Kerberos authentication service is unavailable, the server acts as if the SERVER_ENCRYPT authentication type was specified, and the rules of this authentication method apply.

DATA_ENCRYPT. Authentication occurs at the server where the DB2 instance is running, using the SERVER_ENCRYPT authentication method. In addition, the following data is encrypted before it is passed from client to server and from server to client:

- SQL and XQuery statements

- SQL program variable data

- Output data from the server processing of an SQL statement or XQuery expression, including a description of the data

- Some or all of the result data set data produced in response to a query

- Large object (LOB) data streaming

- SQLDA descriptors

DATA_ENCRYPT_CMP. Authentication occurs at the server where the DB2 instance is running, using the SERVER_ENCRYPT authentication method; all user data is encrypted before it is passed from client to server and from server to client. In addition, this authentication type provides compatibility for down-level products that do not support the DATA_ENCRYPT authentication type. Such products connect using the SERVER_ENCRYPT authentication type, and user data is not encrypted.

GSSPLUGIN. Authentication occurs at the server where the DB2 instance is running, using a Generic Security Service Application Program Interface (GSS-API) plug-in. If the client's authentication type is not specified, the server returns a list of server-supported plug-ins, including any Kerberos plug-ins listed in the *srvcon_gssplugin_list* DB2 Database Manager configuration parameter, to the client. The client then selects the first plug-in found in the client plug-in directory that is also on the list; if the client does not support any plug-in in the list, the client cannot be authenticated.

GSS_SERVER_ENCRYPT. Authentication occurs at the server where the DB2 instance is running, using either the GSSPLUGIN or the SERVER_ENCRYPT authentication method. That is, if client authentication occurs through a GSS-API plug-in, the client is authenticated using the first client-supported plug-in found in the list of server-supported plug-ins. If the client authentication is not specified and an implicit connect is performed (that is, the client does not supply a user ID and password when making the connection), the server returns a list of server-supported plug-ins, and the client is authenticated using the first supported plug-in found in the client plug-in directory—if the client does not support any of the plug-ins that are in the list, the client will not be authenticated and the connection will fail because of a missing password. A client supports the Kerberos authentication scheme if a DB2-supplied Kerberos plug-in exists for the operating system, or a Kerberos-based plug-in is specified for the *srvcon_gssplugin_list* database manager configuration parameter. If the client authentication is not specified and an explicit connection is performed (that is, both the user ID and password are supplied), the authentication type is equivalent to SERVER_ENCRYPT.

It is important to note that if the authentication type used by the client workstation encrypts user ID and password information before sending it to a server for authentication (i.e., SERVER_ENCRYPT, KRB_SERVER_ENCRYPT, etc.), the server must be configured to use a compatible authentication method. Otherwise, it will not be able to process the encrypted data received, and an error will occur.

It is also important to note that if the authentication type is not specified for a client workstation, the SERVER_ENCRYPT authentication method is used by default. If such a client tries to communicate with a server that does not support the SERVER_ENCRYPT authentication method, the client will attempt to use the authentication type that is being used by the server—provided the server has been configured to use only one authentication type. If the server supports multiple authentication types, an error may be generated.

For example, if a server is configured to use the KRB_SERVER_ENCRYPT authentication method and the authentication type is not specified for a client, whether an error will be generated is dependant upon on whether a user ID and password are provided. If a user ID and/or password are not provided, DB2 will initially request CLIENT authentication, the server will reject it, and DB2 will then request to use either KERBEROS or SERVER_ENCRYPT authentication.
If the client supports Kerberos, KERBEROS authentication will be used. Otherwise, an error will be generated because SERVER_ENCRYPT cannot be used if a user ID and password are not provided by the client. On the other hand, if a user ID and password are provided, DB2 will request SERVER_ENCRYPT authentication by default and the server will accept the connection using SERVER_ENCRYPT authentication. This could cause a problem if it is thought that the connection is actually using Kerberos authentication. In this case, it would be better to explicitly configure the client to use KERBEROS authentication to avoid any confusion.

> Although the value assigned to the *authentication* DB2 Database Manager (DBM) configuration parameter determines how and where user authentication takes place, this value can be overridden for a particular server by assigning a different value to the *srvcon_auth* configuration parameter. (The *srvcon_auth* DBM configuration parameter is used to specify how and where authentication is to take place when handling connections at the server; if this parameter is not assigned a value, DB2 uses the current value of the *authentication* configuration parameter.)

Security Plug-ins

In DB2 9, authentication is done using security plug-ins. A security plug-in is a dynamically loadable library that provides authentication security services; DB2 9 supports two mechanisms for plug-in authentication:

- User ID/password authentication

  This involves authentication using a user ID and password. The following authentication types are implemented using user ID/password authentication plug-ins:

    - CLIENT
    - SERVER
    - SERVER_ENCRYPT
    - DATA_ENCRYPT
    - DATA_ENCRYPT_CMP

- GSS-API authentication

  GSS-API is formally known as Generic Security Service Application Program Interface, Version 2 (IETF RFC2743), and Generic Security Service API Version 2: C-Bindings (IETF RFC2744). The following authentication types are implemented using GSS-API authentication plug-ins:

    - KERBEROS
    - GSSPLUGIN
    - KRB_SERVER_ENCRYPT
    - GSS_SERVER_ENCRYPT

Unless otherwise specified, the DB2 Kerberos plug-in library IBMkrb5 is used on AIX, Linux, Sun Solaris, and Windows operating systems when the client is authenticated using KERBEROS or KRB_SERVER_ENCRYPT authentication. If the client is authenticated using KRB_SERVER_ENCRYPT or GSS_SERVER_ ENCRYPT, both GSS-API authentication and user ID/password authentication can be used; however, GSS-API authentication is the authentication type preferred.

Each plug-in can be used independently or in conjunction with one or more of the other plug-ins available. For example, you might specify only a server authentication plug-in to use and allow DB2 to use the defaults for client and group authentication. Alternatively, you might specify only a group or client authentication plug-in. The only situation where both a client and server plug-in are required is for GSS-API authentication. (In some cases—for example, if you are using Microsoft Active Directory to validate a user—you may need to create your own custom security plug-in and make it available for DB2 to use.)

The default behavior for DB2 9 is to use a user ID/password plug-in that implements an operating-system-level mechanism for authentication.

A Word About LDAP Security Plug-ins

DB2 9 and DB2 Connect support LDAP-based authentication and group lookup functionality through the use of LDAP security plug-in modules. LDAP security plug-in modules allow DB2 to authenticate users defined in an LDAP directory, removing the requirement that users and groups be defined to the operating system. Supported platforms are AIX, Linux on IA32, Linux on x64, Linux on zSeries, Solaris, and Windows. DB2 LDAP security plug-in modules are available for server-side authentication, client-side authentication, and group lookup. Depending on your specific environment, you may need to use one, two, or all three types of plug-ins available.

The server authentication plug-in module performs server validation of user IDs and passwords supplied by clients when connections or attachments are made. It also provides a way to map LDAP user IDs to DB2 authorization IDs, if required. The server plug-in module is generally required if you want users to authenticate to the DB2 Database Manager using their LDAP user ID and password.

The client authentication plug-in module is used where user ID and password validation occurs on the client system; that is, where the DB2 server is configured for CLIENT authentication. The client validates any user IDs and passwords supplied when connections or attachments are made and sends the user ID to the DB2 server. It is important to note that CLIENT authentication is difficult to secure and not generally recommended.

The group lookup plug-in module retrieves group membership information from the LDAP server for a particular user. It is required if you want to use LDAP to store your group definitions.

When the LDAP security plug-in modules are used, all users associated with the database must be defined on the LDAP server. This includes both the DB2 instance owner ID as well as the fenced user. (These users are typically defined in the operating system, but must also be defined in LDAP.) Similarly, if you use the LDAP group plug-in module, any groups required for authorization must be defined on the LDAP server. This includes the System Administrator (SYSADM), System Maintenance (SYSMAINT), System Control (SYSCTRL), and System Monitor (SYSMON) groups that are defined in the DB2 Database Manager Configuration file.

Trusted Clients Versus Untrusted Clients

If both the server and the client are configured to use the CLIENT authentication type, authentication occurs at the client workstation, using the security facility provided by the client workstation's operating system; if you are connecting from a server running a database partition in a DPF configuration, authentication will occur at the database partition from which the connection is established. But what happens if the client workstation is using an operating system that does not contain a tightly integrated security facility, and no separate add-on security facility has been made available? Does such a configuration compromise security? The answer is no. However, in such environments, the DB2 Database Manager for the instance at the server must be able to determine which clients will be responsible for validating users and which clients will be forced to let the server handle user authentication. To make this distinction, clients that use an operating system that contains a tightly integrated security facility (for example, zOS, OS/390, VM, VSE, MVS, AS/400, iOS, Windows NT, Windows XP, Windows Vista, Windows 2000, and all supported versions of Linux and UNIX) are classified as trusted clients, whereas clients that use an operating system that does not provide an integrated security facility (for example, Windows 95, Windows 98, and Windows Millennium Edition) are treated as untrusted clients.

The trust_allclnts parameter of the DB2 Database Manager configuration file helps DB2 anticipate whether its clients are to be treated as trusted or untrusted. If this configuration parameter is set to YES (which is the default), DB2 assumes that any client that accesses the instance is a trusted client and that some form of authentication will take place at the client. However, if this configuration parameter is set to NO, DB2 assumes that one or more untrusted clients will try to access the server; therefore, all users must be authenticated at the server. (If this configuration parameter is set to DRDAONLY, only MVS, zOS, OS/390, VM, VSE, iOS, and OS/400 clients will be treated as trusted clients.) It is important to note that, regardless of how the trust_allclnts parameter is set, whenever an untrusted client attempts to access an instance or a database, user authentication always takes place at the server.

In some situations, it may be desirable to authenticate users at the server, even when untrusted clients will not be accessing an instance or database. In such situations, the trust_clntauth configuration parameter of the DB2 Database Manager configuration file can be used to control where trusted clients are to be validated. When the default value for this parameter (which is CLIENT) is accepted, authentication for trusted clients will take place at the client workstation. If, however, the value for this parameter is changed to SERVER, authentication for all trusted clients will take place at the server.

Authentication Considerations for Remote Clients

When cataloging a database for remote access, the authentication type may be specified during the cataloging process; however an authentication type is not required. If an authentication type is not provided, the client will use the SERVER authentication type if the remote database will be accessed using DB2 Connect. If DB2 Connect is not used, the client will use the SERVER_ENCRYPT authentication type by default.

If a client using SERVER_ENCRYPT authentication attempts to connect to a server that does not support SERVER_ENCRYPT, KRB_SERVER_ENCRYPT, or GSS_ SERVER_ENCRYPT, the client will be unable to connect to the server. If the server supports KRB_SERVER_ENCRYPT and/or GSS_SERVER_ENCRYPT authentication types, the client will use the SERVER_ENCRYPT behavior of these authentication types.

If an authentication type is specified when a remote database is cataloged, authentication can begin immediately provided the authentication type specified matches the authentication type used by the server. If a mismatch is detected, DB2 will attempt to recover. Recovery may result in more flows to reconcile the difference, or in an error if DB2 cannot recover. In the case of a mismatch, the authentication type used by the server is assumed to be correct.

In a partitioned database environment with multiple servers, all servers must have the same set of users and groups defined. If the user and group definitions are not the same, a user may be authorized to perform different operations on different partitions. Additionally, if a connection is made to a server that is part of a DPF cluster, that server is treated as a local client, thus no user ID and password are required.

Authorities and Privileges

Once a user has been authenticated, and an attachment to an instance or a connection to a database has been established, DB2 evaluates any authorities and privileges that have been assigned to the user to determine what operations the user is allowed to perform. Privileges convey the rights to perform certain actions against specific database resources (such as tables and views). Authorities convey a set of privileges or the right to perform high-level administrative and maintenance/utility operations on an instance or a database. Authorities and privileges can be assigned directly to a user, or they can be obtained indirectly from the authorities and privileges that have been assigned to a group of which the user is a member. Together, authorities and privileges act to control access to DB2 for an instance, to one or more databases running under that instance's control, and to a particular database's objects. Users can work only with those objects for which they have been given the appropriate authorization—that is, the required authority or privilege. Figure 6–1 provides a hierarchical view of the authorities and privileges that are recognized by DB2 9.

Authorities

DB2 9 uses seven different levels of authority to control how users perform administrative and maintenance operations against an instance or a database:

- System Administrator (SYSADM) authority
- System Control (SYSCTRL) authority

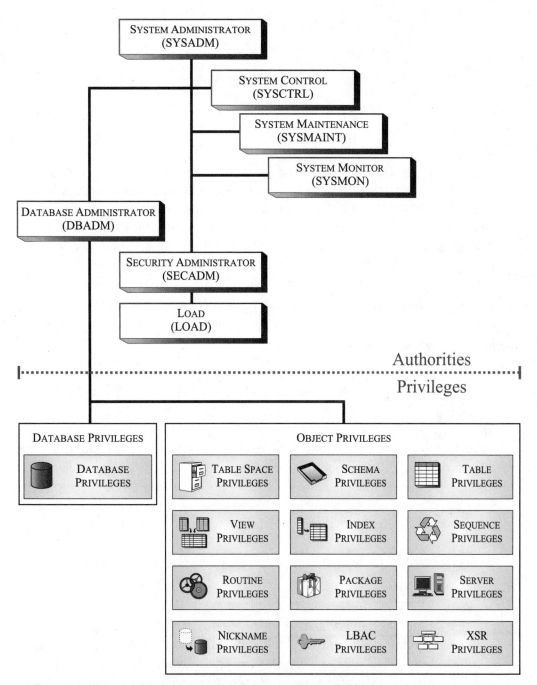

Figure 6–1: Hierarchy of the authorities and privileges available with DB2 9.

- System Maintenance (SYSMAINT) authority

- System Monitor (SYSMON) authority

- Database Administrator (DBADM) authority

- Security Administrator (SECADM) authority

- Load (LOAD) authority

Four of these levels apply to the instance (and to all databases that are under that instance's control), whereas three apply only to specific databases within a particular instance. The instance-level authorities can be assigned only to groups; the names of the groups that are assigned these authorities are stored in the DB2 Database Manager configuration file that is associated with the instance. Conversely, the database-level authorities can be assigned to individual users and, in some cases, groups; groups and users that have been assigned database-level authorities are recorded in the system catalog tables of the database to which the authority applies.

System Administrator Authority

System Administrator (SYSADM) authority is the highest level of administrative authority available. Users who have been given this authority are allowed to run any DB2 utility, execute any DB2 command, and perform any SQL/XQuery operation that does not attempt to access data protected by label-based access control (LBAC). Users with this authority also have the ability to control all database objects within an instance, including databases, database partition groups, buffer pools, table spaces, schemas, tables, views, indexes, aliases, servers, data types, functions, procedures, triggers, packages, and event monitors. Additionally, users who have been given this authority are allowed to perform the following tasks:

- Upgrade (migrate) an existing database from a previous version of DB2 to DB2 9.

- Modify the parameter values of the DB2 Database Manager configuration file associated with an instance—including specifying which groups have System Administrator, System Control, System Maintenance, and System Monitor authority. (The DB2 Database Manager configuration file is used to control the amount of system resources allocated to a single instance.)

- Give (grant) Database Administrator authority and Security Administrator authority to individual users and/or groups.

- Revoke Database Administrator authority and/or Security Administrator authority from individual users and/or groups.

System Administrator authority can be assigned only to a group; this assignment is made by storing the appropriate group name in the sysadm_group parameter of the DB2 Database Manager configuration file associated with an instance. (This is done by executing an UPDATE DATABASE MANAGER CONFIGURATION (or UPDATE DBM CFG) command with the SYSADM_GROUP parameter specified, along with the name of the group that is to receive System Administrator authority.) Individual membership in the group itself is controlled through the security facility provided by the operating system used on the workstation where the instance has been defined. Users who possess System Administrator authority are responsible both for controlling the DB2 Database Manager associated with an instance and for ensuring the safety and integrity of the data contained in databases that fall under the instance's control.

Users who hold System Administrator authority are implicitly given the rights granted by System Control, System Maintenance, System Monitor, and Database Administrator authority. However, they are not implicitly given the rights granted by Security Administrator authority.

System Control Authority

System Control (SYSCTRL) authority is the highest level of system or instance control authority available. Users who have been given this authority are allowed to perform maintenance and utility operations both on a DB2 instance and on any databases that fall under that instance's control. However, because System Control authority is designed to allow special users to maintain an instance that contains sensitive data that they most likely do not have the right to view or modify, users who are granted this authority do not implicitly receive authority to access the data stored in the databases that are controlled by the instance. On the other hand, because a connection to a database is required in order to perform some of the utility operations available, users who are granted System Control authority for a particular instance also receive the privileges needed to connect to each database under that instance's control.

Users with System Control authority (or higher) are allowed to perform the following tasks:

- Update a database, node, or distributed connection services (DCS) directory (by cataloging/uncataloging databases, nodes, or DCS databases).

- Modify the parameter values in one or more database configuration files. (A database configuration file is used to control the amount of system resources that are allocated to a single database during normal operation.)

- Force users off the system.

- Create or destroy (drop) a database.

- Create, alter, or drop a table space.

- Make a backup image of a database or a table space.

- Restore an existing database using a backup image.

- Restore a table space using a backup image.

- Create a new database from a database backup image.

- Perform a roll-forward recovery operation on a database.

- Start or stop an instance.

- Run a trace on a database operation.

- Take database system monitor snapshots of an instance or any database under the instance's control.

- Query the state of a table space.

- Update recovery history log files.

- Quiesce (restrict access to) a table space.

- Reorganize a table.

- Collect catalog statistics using the RUNSTATS utility.

Like System Administrator authority, System Control authority can be assigned only to a group. This assignment is made by storing the appropriate group name in the sysctrl_group parameter of the DB2 Database Manager configuration file that is associated with a particular instance. (This is done by executing an UPDATE DATABASE MANAGER CONFIGURATION command with the SYSCTRL_GROUP parameter specified, along with the name of the group that is to receive System Control authority.) Again, individual membership in the group itself is controlled through the security facility that is used on the DB2 server.

System Maintenance Authority

System Maintenance (SYSMAINT) authority is the second highest level of system or instance control authority available. Users who have been given this authority are allowed to perform maintenance and utility operations both on an instance and on any databases that fall under that instance's control. System Maintenance authority is designed to allow special users to maintain a database that contains sensitive data that they most likely do not have the right to view or modify. Therefore, users who are granted this authority do not implicitly receive authority to access the data stored in the databases on which they are allowed to perform maintenance operation. However, because a connection to a database must exist before some utility operations can be performed, users who are granted System Maintenance authority for a particular instance automatically receive the privileges needed to connect to each database that falls under that instance's control.

Users with System Maintenance authority (or higher) are allowed to perform the following tasks:

- Modify the parameter values of one or more DB2 database configuration files
- Make a backup image of a database or a table space
- Restore an existing database using a backup image
- Restore a table space using a backup image
- Perform a roll-forward recovery operation on a database
- Start or stop an instance
- Run a trace on a database operation

- Take database system monitor snapshots of an instance or any database under the instance's control

- Query the state of a table space

- Update recovery log history files

- Quiesce (restrict access to) a table space

- Reorganize a table

- Collect catalog statistics using the RUNSTATS utility

Like System Administrator and System Control authority, System Maintenance authority can be assigned only to a group. This assignment is made by storing the appropriate group name in the sysmaint_group parameter of the DB2 Database Manager configuration file that is associated with a particular instance. (This is done by executing an UPDATE DATABASE MANAGER CONFIGURATION command with the SYSMAINT_GROUP parameter specified, along with the name of the group that is to receive System Maintenance authority.) Again, individual membership in the group itself is controlled through the security facility that is used on the DB2 server.

System Monitor Authority

System Monitor (SYSMON) authority is the third highest level of system or instance control authority available with DB2. Users who have been given this authority are allowed to take system monitor snapshots for an instance and/or for one or more databases that fall under that instance's control. System Monitor authority is designed to allow special users to monitor the performance of a database that contains sensitive data that they most likely do not have the right to view or modify. Therefore, users who are granted this authority do not implicitly receive authority to access the data stored in the databases on which they are allowed to collect snapshot monitor information. However, because a connection to a database must exist before the snapshot monitor SQL table functions can be used, users who are granted System Monitor authority for a particular instance automatically receive the privileges needed to connect to each database under that instance's control.

Users with System Monitor authority (or higher) are allowed to perform the following tasks:

- Obtain the current settings of the snapshot monitor switches

- Modify the settings of one or more snapshot monitor switches

- Reset all counters used by the snapshot monitor

- Obtain a list of active databases

- Obtain a list of active applications, including DCS applications

- Collect snapshot monitor data

- Use the snapshot monitor SQL table functions

Like System Administrator, System Control, and System Maintenance authority, System Monitor authority can be assigned only to a group. This assignment is made by storing the appropriate group name in the sysmon_group parameter of the DB2 Database Manager configuration file that is associated with a particular instance. (This is done by executing an UPDATE DATABASE MANAGER CONFIGURATION command with the SYSMON_GROUP parameter specified, along with the name of the group that is to receive System Monitor authority.) Again, individual membership in the group itself is controlled through the security facility that is used on the DB2 server.

Database Administrator Authority

Database Administrator (DBADM) authority is the second highest level of administrative authority available (just below System Administrator authority). Users who have been given this authority are allowed to run most DB2 utilities, issue database-specific DB2 commands, perform most SQL/XQuery operations, and access data stored in any table in a database—provided that data is not protected by LBAC. (To access data protected by LBAC, a user must have the appropriate LBAC credentials.) However, they can perform these functions only on the database for which Database Administrator authority is held.

Additionally, users with Database Administrator authority (or higher) are allowed to perform the following tasks:

- Read database log files

- Create, activate, and drop event monitors

- Query the state of a table space

- Update recovery history log files

- Quiesce (restrict access to) a table space

- Reorganize a table

- Collect catalog statistics using the RUNSTATS utility

Unlike System Administrator, System Control, System Maintenance, and System Monitor authority, Database Administrator authority can be assigned to both individual users and groups. This assignment is made by executing the appropriate form of the GRANT SQL statement (which we will look at shortly). When a user is given Database Administrator authority for a particular database, they automatically receive all database privileges available for that database as well.

Any time a user with SYSADM or SYSCTRL authority creates a new database, that user automatically receives DBADM authority on that database. Furthermore, if a user with SYSADM or SYSCTRL authority creates a database and is later removed from the SYSADM or SYSCTRL group (i.e., the user's SYSADM or SYSCTRL authority is revoked), the user retains DBADM authority for that database until it is explicitly removed (revoked).

Security Administrator Authority

Security Administrator (SECADM) authority is a special database level of authority that is designed to allow special users to configure various label-based access control (LBAC) elements to restrict access to one or more tables that contain data to which they most likely do not have access themselves. Users who are granted this authority do not implicitly receive authority to access the data stored in the databases for which they manage data access. In fact, users with Security

Administrator authority are allowed to perform only the following tasks:

- Create and drop security policies.

- Create and drop security labels.

- Grant and revoke security labels to and from individual users using the GRANT SECURITY LABEL and REVOKE SECURITY LABEL SQL statements.

- Grant and revoke LBAC rule exemptions.

- Grant and revoke SETSESSIONUSER privileges using the GRANT SETSESSIONUSER SQL statement.

- Transfer ownership of any object not owned by the Security Administrator by executing the TRANSFER OWNERSHIP SQL statement. (The TRANSFER OWNERSHIP SQL statement provides the Security Administrator or the database object owner with the ability to change the ownership of a database object. For example, if an employee is leaving a company, all objects that he or she owns can be transferred to a different user. The TRANSFER OWNERSHIP SQL statement automatically grants the new owner the same privileges that the previous owner had when the object was created.)

No other authority, including System Administrator authority, provides a user with these abilities.

Security Administrator authority can be assigned only to individual users; it cannot be assigned to groups (including the group PUBLIC). This assignment is made by executing the appropriate form of the GRANT SQL statement, and only users with System Administrator authority are allowed to grant this authority.

Load Authority

Load (LOAD) authority is a special database level of administrative authority that has a much smaller scope than DBADM authority. Users that have been given this authority, along with INSERT and in some cases DELETE privileges, on a particular table are allowed to bulk-load data into that table, using either the LOAD command or the db2Load API. Load authority is designed to allow special users to perform bulk-load operations against a database with which they most likely cannot do anything else. This authority provides a way for database administrators to allow more users to perform special database operations, such as Extraction-Transform-Load (ETL) operations, without having to sacrifice control.

In addition to being able to load data into a database table, users with Load authority (or higher) are allowed to perform the following tasks:

- Query the state of a table space using the LIST TABLESPACES command.

- Quiesce (restrict access to) a table space.

- Perform bulk-load operations using the LOAD utility. (If exception tables are used as part of a load operation, the user must have INSERT privilege on the exception tables used as well as INSERT privilege on the table being loaded.)

- Collect catalog statistics using the RUNSTATS utility.

Like Database Administrator authority, Load authority can be assigned to both individual users and groups. This assignment is made by executing the appropriate form of the GRANT SQL statement.

Privileges

As mentioned earlier, privileges are used to convey the rights to perform certain actions on specific database resources to both individual users and groups. With DB2 9, two distinct types of privileges exist: database privileges and object privileges.

Database Privileges

Database privileges apply to a database as a whole, and in many cases, they act as a second security checkpoint that must be cleared before access to data is provided. Figure 6–2 shows the different types of database privileges available.

As you can see in Figure 6–2, eight different database privileges exist. They are:

CONNECT. Allows a user to establish a connection to the database.

QUIESCE_CONNECT. Allows a user to establish a connection to the database while it is in a quiesced state (i.e., while access to it is restricted).

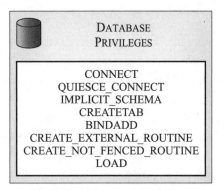

Figure 6–2: Database privileges available with DB2 9.

IMPLICIT_SCHEMA. Allows a user to create a new schema in the database implicitly by creating an object and assigning that object a schema name that is different from any of the schema names that already exist in the database.

CREATETAB. Allows a user to create new tables in the database.

BINDADD. Allows a user to create packages in the database (by precompiling embedded SQL application source code files against the database or by binding application bind files to the database).

CREATE_EXTERNAL_ROUTINE. Allows a user to create user-defined functions (UDFs) and/or stored procedures and define them inside the database so that they can be used by other users and applications.

CREATE_NOT_FENCED_ROUTINE. Allows a user to create unfenced UDFs and/or stored procedures and define them inside the database. (Unfenced UDFs and stored procedures are UDFs/procedures that are considered "safe" enough to be run in the DB2 operating environment's process or address space. Unless a UDF/procedure is registered as unfenced, DB2 insulates the UDF/procedure's internal resources in such a way that they cannot be run in the DB2 address space.)

LOAD. Allows a user to bulk-load data into one or more existing tables in the database.

At a minimum, a user must have CONNECT privilege on a database before he or she can work with any object contained in that database.

Object Privileges

Unlike database privileges which apply to a database as a whole, object privileges apply only to specific objects within a database. These objects include table spaces, schemas, tables, views, indexes, sequences, routines, packages, servers, and nicknames. Because the nature of each database object available varies, the individual privileges that exist for each object can vary as well. The following sections describe the different sets of object privileges that are available with DB2 9.

Table space privileges. Table space privileges control what users can and cannot do with a particular table space. (Table spaces are used to control where data in a database physically resides.) Figure 6–3 shows the only table space privilege available.

Figure 6–3: Table space privilege
available with DB2 9.

As you can see in Figure 6–3, only one table space privilege exists. That privilege is the USE privilege, which, when granted, allows a user to create tables and indexes in the table space. The owner of a table space (usually the individual who created the table space) automatically receives USE privilege for that table space.

The USE privilege cannot be used to provide a user with the ability to create tables in the SYSCATSPACE table space or in any system temporary table space that might exist.

Schema privileges. Schema privileges control what users can and cannot do with a particular schema. (A schema is an object that is used to logically classify and group other objects in the database; most objects are named using a naming convention that consists of a schema name, followed by a period, followed by the object name.) For example, DB2 creates a series of catalog tables and assigns them names such as SYSIBM.SYSTABLES, SYSIBM.SYSINDEXES, etc. Figure 6–4 shows the different types of schema privileges available.

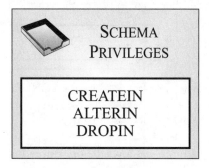

Figure 6–4: Schema privileges
available with DB2 9

As you can see in Figure 6–4, three different schema privileges exist. They are:

CREATEIN. Allows a user to create objects within the schema.

ALTERIN. Allows a user to change the comment associated with any object in the schema or to alter any object that resides within the schema.

DROPIN. Allows a user to remove (drop) any object within the schema.

Objects that can be manipulated within a schema include tables, views, indexes, packages, user-defined data types, user-defined functions, triggers, stored procedures, and aliases. The owner of a schema (usually the individual who created the schema) automatically receives all privileges available for that schema, along with the right to grant any combination of those privileges to other users and groups.

Table privileges. Table privileges control what users can and cannot do with a particular table in a database. (A table is a logical structure used to present data as a collection of unordered rows with a fixed number of columns.) Figure 6–5 shows the different types of table privileges available.

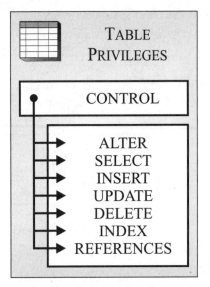

Figure 6–5: Table privileges available with DB2 9.

As you can see in Figure 6–5, eight different table privileges exist. They are:

CONTROL. Provides a user with every table privilege available, allows the user to remove (drop) the table from the database, and gives the user the ability to grant and revoke one or more table privileges (except the CONTROL privilege) to and from other users and groups.

ALTER. Allows a user to execute the ALTER TABLE SQL statement against the table. In other words, allows a user to add columns to the table, add or change comments associated with the table or any of its columns, create or drop a primary key for the table, create or drop a unique constraint for the table, create or drop a check constraint for the table, and create or drop triggers for the table (provided the user holds the appropriate privileges for every object referenced by the trigger).

SELECT. Allows a user to execute a SELECT SQL statement against the table. In other words, this privilege allows a user to retrieve data from a table, create a view that references the table, and run the Export utility against the table.

INSERT. Allows a user to execute the INSERT SQL statement against the table. In other words, this privilege allows a user to add data to the table and run the Import utility against the table.

UPDATE. Allows a user to execute the UPDATE SQL statement against the table. In other words, this privilege allows a user to modify data in the table. (This privilege can be granted for the entire table or limited to one or more columns within the table.)

DELETE. Allows a user to execute the DELETE SQL statement against the table. In other words, allows a user to remove rows of data from the table.

INDEX. Allows a user to create an index for the table.

REFERENCES. Allows a user to create and drop foreign key constraints that reference the table in a parent relationship. (This privilege can be granted for the entire table or limited to one or more columns within the table, in which case only those columns can participate as a parent key in a referential constraint.)

The owner of a table (usually the individual who created the table) automatically receives all privileges available for that table (including CONTROL privilege), along with the right to grant any combination of those privileges (except CONTROL privilege) to other users and groups. If the CONTROL privilege is later revoked from the table owner, all other privileges that were automatically granted to the owner for that particular table are not automatically revoked. Instead, they must be explicitly revoked in one or more separate operations.

View privileges. View privileges control what users can and cannot do with a particular view. (A view is a virtual table residing in memory that provides an alternative way of working with data that resides in one or more base tables. For this reason, views can be used to prevent access to select columns in a table.) Figure 6–6 shows the different types of view privileges available.

As you can see in Figure 6–6, five different view privileges exist. They are:

CONTROL. Provides a user with every view privilege available, allows the user to remove (drop) the view from the database, and gives the user the ability to grant and revoke one or more view privileges (except the CONTROL privilege) to and from other users and groups.

SELECT. Allows a user to retrieve data from the view, create a second view that references the view, and run the Export utility against the view.

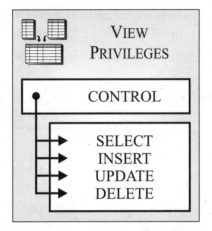

Figure 6–6: View privileges available with DB2 9.

INSERT. Allows a user to execute the INSERT SQL statement against the view. In other words, allows a user to add data to the view.

UPDATE. Allows a user to execute the UPDATE SQL statement against the view. In other words, this privilege allows a user to modify data in the view. (This privilege can be granted for the entire view or limited to one or more columns within the view.)

DELETE. Allows a user to execute the DELETE SQL statement against the view. In other words, this privilege allows a user to remove rows of data from the view.

In order to create a view, a user must hold appropriate privileges (at a minimum, SELECT privilege) on each base table the view references. The owner of a view (usually the individual who created the view) automatically receives all privileges available—with the exception of the CONTROL privilege—for that view, along with the right to grant any combination of those privileges (except CONTROL privilege) to other users and groups. A view owner will receive CONTROL privilege for a view only if he or she also holds CONTROL privilege for every base table the view references.

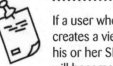

If a user who holds SELECT privilege on one or more tables creates a view based on one or more of those tables and his or her SELECT privileges are later revoked, the view will become inoperative, and any privileges that have been granted for that view will be revoked automatically.

Index privileges. Index privileges control what users can and cannot do with a particular index. (An index is an ordered set of pointers that refer to one or more key columns in a base table; indexes are used to improve query performance.) Figure 6–7 shows the only index privilege available.

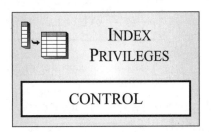

Figure 6–7: Index privilege available with DB2 9.

As you can see in Figure 6–7, only one index privilege exists. That privilege is the CONTROL privilege, which, when granted, allows a user to remove (drop) the index from the database. Unlike the CONTROL privilege for other objects, the CONTROL privilege for an index does not give a user the ability to grant and revoke index privileges to and from other users and groups. That's because the CONTROL privilege is the only index privilege available, and only users who hold System Administrator (SYSADM) or Database Administrator (DBADM) authority are allowed to grant and revoke CONTROL privileges for an object.

The owner of an index (usually the individual who created the index) automatically receives CONTROL privilege for that index.

Sequence privileges. Sequence privileges control what users can and cannot do with a particular sequence. (A sequence is an object that is normally used to generate unique or sequential values automatically. Sequences are ideal for generating unique key values, and they can be used to avoid the possible concurrency and performance problems that can occur when unique counters residing outside the database are used for data generation.) Figure 6–8 shows the different types of sequence privileges available.

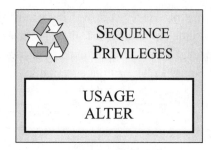

*Figure 6–8: Sequence privileges
available with DB2 9.*

As you can see in Figure 6–8, two different sequence privileges exist. They are:

USAGE. Allows a user to use the PREVIOUS VALUE and NEXT VALUE expressions that are associated with the sequence. (The PREVIOUS VALUE expression returns the most recently generated value for the specified sequence; the NEXT VALUE expression returns the next value for the specified sequence.)

ALTER. Allows a user to perform administrative tasks such as restarting the sequence, changing the increment value for the sequence, and adding or changing the comment associated with the sequence.

The owner of a sequence (usually the individual who created the sequence) automatically receives all privileges available for that sequence, along with the right to grant any combination of those privileges to other users and groups.

Routine privileges. Routine privileges control what users can and cannot do with a particular routine. (A routine can be a user-defined function, a stored procedure, or a method that can be invoked by several different users.) Figure 6–9 shows the only routine privilege available.

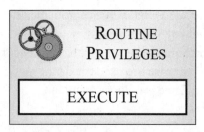

*Figure 6–9: Routine privilege
available with DB2 9.*

As you can see in Figure 6–9, only one routine privilege exists. That privilege is the EXECUTE privilege, which, when granted, allows a user to invoke the routine, create a function that is sourced from the routine (provided the routine is a function), and reference the routine in any Data Definition Language SQL statement (for example, CREATE VIEW and CREATE TRIGGER).

> Before a user can invoke a routine (user-defined function, stored procedure, or method), he or she must hold both EXECUTE privilege on the routine and any privileges required by that routine. Thus, in order to execute a stored procedure that queries a table, a user must hold both EXECUTE privilege on the stored procedure and SELECT privilege on the table against which the query is run.

The owner of a routine (usually the individual who created the routine) automatically receives EXECUTE privilege for that routine.

Package privileges. Package privileges control what users can and cannot do with a particular package. (A package is an object that contains the information needed by DB2 to process SQL statements in the most efficient way possible on behalf of an embedded SQL application.) Figure 6–10 shows the different types of package privileges available.

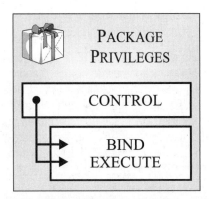

Figure 6–10: Package privileges available with DB2 9.

As you can see in Figure 6–10, three different package privileges exist. They are:

CONTROL. Provides a user with every package privilege available, allows the user to remove (drop) the package from the database, and gives the user the ability to grant and revoke one or more package privileges (except the CONTROL privilege) to and from other users and groups.

BIND. Allows a user to rebind or add new package versions to a package that has already been bound to a database. (In addition to the BIND package privilege, a user must hold the privileges needed to execute the SQL statements that make up the package before the package can be successfully rebound.)

EXECUTE. Allows a user to execute the package. (A user that has EXECUTE privilege for a particular package can execute that package even if the user does not have the privileges that are needed to execute the SQL statements stored in the package. That is because any privileges needed to execute the SQL statements are implicitly granted to the package user. It is important to note that for privileges to be implicitly granted, the creator of the package must hold privileges as an individual user or as a member of the group PUBLIC—not as a member of another named group.)

The owner of a package (usually the individual who created the package) automatically receives all privileges available for that package (including CONTROL privilege), along with the right to grant any combination of those privileges (except CONTROL privilege) to other users and groups. If the CONTROL privilege is later revoked from the package owner, all other privileges that were automatically granted to the owner for that particular package are not automatically revoked. Instead, they must be explicitly revoked in one or more separate operations.

Users who have EXECUTE privilege for a package that contains nicknames do not need additional authorities or privileges for the nicknames in the package; however, they must be able to pass any authentication checks performed at the data source(s) in which objects referenced by the nicknames are stored, and they must hold the appropriate authorizations and privileges needed to access all objects referenced.

Server privileges. Server privileges control what users can and cannot do with a particular federated database server. (A DB2 federated system is a distributed computing system that consists of a DB2 server, known as a federated server, and one or more data sources to which the federated server sends queries. Each data source consists of an instance of some supported relational database management system—such as Oracle—plus the database or databases that the instance supports.) Figure 6–11 shows the only server privilege available.

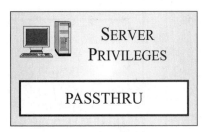

Figure 6–11: Server privilege
available with DB2 9

As you can see in Figure 6–11, only one server privilege exists. That privilege is the PASSTHRU privilege, which, when granted, allows a user to issue Data Definition Language (DDL) and Data Manipulation Language (DML) SQL statements (as pass-through operations) directly to a data source via a federated server.

Nickname privileges. Nickname privileges control what users can and cannot do with a particular nickname. (When a client application submits a distributed request to a federated database server, the server forwards the request to the appropriate data source for processing. However, such a request does not identify the data source itself; instead, it references tables and views within the data source by using nicknames that map to specific table and view names in the data source. Nicknames are not alternate names for tables and views in the same way that aliases are; instead, they are pointers by which a federated server references external objects.) Figure 6–12 shows the different types of nickname privileges available.

As you can see in Figure 6–12, eight different nickname privileges exist. They are:

CONTROL. Provides a user with every nickname privilege available, allows the user to remove (drop) the nickname from the database, and gives the user the ability to grant and revoke one or more nickname privileges (except the CONTROL privilege) to and from other users and groups.

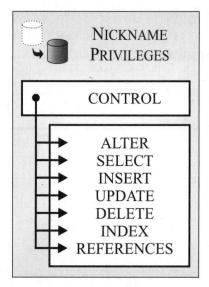

Figure 6–12: Nickname privileges
available with DB2 9.

ALTER. Allows a user to execute the ALTER NICKNAME SQL statement against the nickname. In other words, this privilege allows a user to change column names in the nickname, add or change the DB2 data type to which a particular nickname column's data type maps, and specify column options for a specific nickname column.

SELECT. Allows a user to execute a SELECT SQL statement against the nickname. In other words, this privilege allows a user to retrieve data from the table or view within a federated data source to which the nickname refers.

INSERT. Allows a user to execute the INSERT SQL statement against the nickname. In other words, this privilege allows a user to add data to the table or view within a federated data source to which the nickname refers.

UPDATE. Allows a user to execute the UPDATE SQL statement against the nickname. In other words, this privilege allows a user to modify data in the table or view within a federated data source to which the nickname refers. (This privilege can be granted for the entire table or limited to one or more columns within the table to which the nickname refers.)

DELETE. Allows a user to execute the DELETE SQL statement against the nickname. In other words, allows a user to remove rows of data from the table or view within a federated data source to which the nickname refers.

INDEX. Allows a user to create an index specification for the nickname.

REFERENCES. Allows a user to create and drop foreign key constraints that reference the nickname in a parent relationship.

The owner of a nickname (usually the individual who created the table) automatically receives all privileges available for that nickname (including CONTROL privilege), along with the right to grant any combination of those privileges (except CONTROL privilege) to other users and groups. If the CONTROL privilege is later revoked from the nickname owner, all other privileges that were automatically granted to the owner for that particular table are not automatically revoked. Instead, they must be explicitly revoked in one or more separate operations.

LBAC privileges. Label-based access control (LBAC) privileges control what users can do in regards to changing the current session authorization ID. Figure 6–13 shows the only LBAC privilege available.

Figure 6–13: LBAC privilege available with DB2 9.

As you can see in Figure 6–13, only one server privilege exists. That privilege is the SETSESSIONUSER privilege, which, when granted, allows a user to use the SET SESSION AUTHORIZATION SQL statement to set/change the session authorization ID. Prior to DB2 9, a user with Database Administrator authority could change the session authorization ID to any ID of their choice. This ability was removed with the introduction of LBAC to prevent a user with Database Administrator authority from indirectly gaining access to data in a LBAC-protected table.

XSR privileges. XML schema repository (XSR) privileges control what users can and cannot do with a particular XSR object. (The XML schema repository is a repository for all XML artifacts used to process XML instance documents stored in XML columns. XML instance documents normally contain a reference to a Uniform Resource Identifier or URI that points to an associated XML schema, DTD or other external entity. DB2 manages dependencies on such externally referenced XML artifacts with the XSR without requiring changes to the URI location reference. Without this mechanism to store associated XML schemas, DTDs or other external entities, an external resource may not be accessible when needed by the database. The XSR also removes the additional overhead required to locate external documents, along with any associated performance impact.) Figure 6–14 shows the only XSR privilege available.

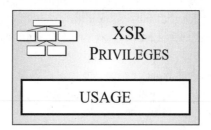

Figure 6–14: XSR privilege available
with DB2 9.

As you can see in Figure 6–14, only one XSR privilege exists. That privilege is the USAGE privilege, which, when granted, allows a user to use a particular XSR object.

A Word About Roles

Security enhancements for DB2 9.5 include support for a new entity known as a role. A role is a database object that groups together one or more privileges. Like privileges, a role can be assigned to users, groups, PUBLIC, or other roles by using a special form of the GRANT statement. Roles simplify the administration and management of privileges by offering a capability equivalent to groups but without incurring the restrictions that are applicable to groups.

Roles provide several advantages that make it easier to manage privileges in a database system:

- Security administrators can control access to their databases in a way that mirrors the structure of their organizations (that is, they can create roles in the database that map directly to the job functions in their organizations).

- Users are granted membership in the roles that reflect their job responsibilities. As their job responsibilities change, their membership in roles can be easily granted and revoked.

- The assignment of privileges is simplified. Instead of granting the same set of privileges to each individual user in a particular job function, the administrator can grant this set of privileges to a role representing that job function and then grant that role to each user in that job function.

- A role's privileges can be updated and all users who have been granted that role receive the update; the administrator does not need to update the privileges for every user on an individual basis.

- The privileges and authorities granted to roles are always used when new database objects are created, whereas privileges and authorities granted to groups (either directly or indirectly) are not. This is because DB2 cannot determine when membership in a group changes because groups are managed by third-party software (for example, the operating system or an LDAP directory). Because roles are managed inside the database, the DB2 database system can determine when authorization changes and act accordingly.

- All the roles assigned to a user are enabled when that user establishes a connection, so all privileges and authorities granted to roles are taken into account when a user connects to a database.

- Roles cannot be explicitly enabled or disabled.

- A role does not have an owner. Therefore a Security Administrator can use the WITH ADMIN OPTION clause of the GRANT statement to delegate management of a role to another user so that the other user can control the role membership.

All DB2 privileges and authorities that can be granted within a database can be granted to a role, with the exception of Security Administrator (SECADM) authority. However, there are a few restrictions when it comes to using roles:

- A role cannot own database objects (even though a role determines whether or not a user is allowed to create database objects).

- A role cannot be granted Security Administrator (SECADM) authority.

- Permissions and roles granted to groups are not considered when the following database objects are created:

  - Packages containing static SQL

  - Views

  - Materialized query tables (MQT)

  - Triggers

  - SQL Routines

A Word About Trusted Contexts

Another security enhancement introduced in DB2 9.5 is a feature known as *trusted contexts*. A trusted context is a database object that describes a trust relationship between a DB2 database and an external entity, such as a Web server, application server, or another DB2 server. When a database connection is established, DB2 compares the attributes of that connection against the definitions of each trusted context object that has been defined for the database. (The Security Administrator is responsible for creating the trusted context objects for a database.) If the connection attributes match the definition of a trusted context object, the connection is referred to as a *trusted connection*. A trusted connection allows the initiator of the connection to acquire additional capabilities that are not available to them outside the scope of the trusted connection. These additional capabilities vary depending on whether the trusted connection is explicit or implicit.

The definition of a trusted context object must contain the following attributes:

- A system authorization ID representing the connection authorization ID that must be used by an incoming connection in order to be trusted.

- A list of IP addresses or domain names representing the IP addresses from which an incoming connection must originate in order to be trusted.

- A data stream encryption value representing the level of encryption (if any) that must be used by an incoming connection in order to be trusted.

DB2 9.5's trusted contexts capability has been designed specifically to address the security concerns around using a 3-tier application model. Traditionally, with this model, all interactions with the database server occurred through a database connection that was established by the middle tier, using a combination of a user ID and a credential that identifies the middle tier to the database server. In other words, the database server uses the database privileges associated with the middle tier's user ID for all authorization checking and auditing that must occur for any database access, including those accesses performed by the middle tier on behalf of a user. With trusted contexts, security is enhanced because the actual user's identity and database privileges are used to perform database activities.

Trusted contexts also introduce the concept of *context-sensitive privileges*. Context-sensitive privileges allow an organization to gain more control of when a privilege becomes available to a user. For example, an organization may want the human resources (HR) manager to acquire the ability to access the payroll table only when they are connected to the database from within the company offices but not when they are connected from home.

Granting Authorities and Privileges

There are three different ways that users (and in some cases, groups) can obtain database-level authorities and database/object privileges. They are:

Implicitly. When a user creates a database, that user implicitly receives Database Administrator authority for that database, along with most database privileges available. Likewise, when a user creates a database object, that user implicitly receives all privileges available for that object, along with the ability to grant any combination of those privileges (with the exception of the CONTROL privilege) to other users and groups. Privileges can also be implicitly given whenever a higher-level privilege is explicitly granted to a user (for example, if a user is explicitly given CONTROL privilege for a table space, the user will implicitly receive the USE privilege for that table space as well). It's important to remember that such implicitly assigned privileges are not automatically revoked when the higher-level privilege that caused them to be granted is revoked.

Indirectly. Indirectly assigned privileges are usually associated with packages; when a user executes a package that requires additional privileges that the user does not have (for example, a package that deletes a row of data from a table requires the DELETE privilege on that table), the user is indirectly given those privileges for the express purpose of executing the package. Indirectly granted privileges are temporary and do not exist outside the scope in which they are granted.

Explicitly. Database-level authorities, database privileges, and object privileges can be explicitly given to or taken from an individual user or a group of users by anyone who has the authority to do so. Users with System Administrator (SYSADM) authority, Database Administrator (DBADM) authority, or ownership privileges (CONTROL) can grant and revoke privileges to and from other users and groups using the GRANT and REVOKE SQL statements (or by using the various authorities and privileges management dialogs that are provided with the Control Center and the Data Studio Administration Console). It is also possible to grant a privilege to another user if that privilege was granted with the WITH GRANT OPTION specified. However, the WITH GRANT OPTION option does not allow the person granting the privilege to revoke the privilege once it is granted. To revoke privileges, a user must have either System Administrator (SYSADM) or Database Administrator (DBADM) authority or CONTROL privilege on an object.

To grant CONTROL privilege for any object, a user must have System Administrator (SYSADM) or Database Administrator (DBADM) authority; to grant System Administrator (SYSADM) or Database Administrator (DBADM) authority, a user must have System Administrator (SYSADM) authority.

Requirements for Granting and Revoking Authorities and Privileges

Not only do authorization levels and privileges control what a user can and cannot do; they also control what authorities and privileges a user is allowed to grant and revoke. A list of the authorities and privileges that a user who has been given a specific authority level or privilege is allowed to grant and revoke can be seen in Table 6.1.

Table 6.1 Requirements for Granting/Revoking Authorities and Privileges.		
If a User Holds...	**The User Can Grant...**	**The User Can Revoke...**
System Administrator (SYSADM) authority	System Control (SYSCTRL) authority System Maintenance (SYSMAINT) authority System Monitor (SYSMON) authority Database Administrator (DBADM) authority Security Administrator (SECADM) authority Load (LOAD) authority Any database privilege, including CONTROL privilege Any object privilege, including CONTROL privilege	System Control (SYSCTRL) authority System Maintenance (SYSMAINT) authority System Monitor (SYSMON) authority Database Administrator (DBADM) authority Security Administrator (SECADM) authority Load (LOAD) authority Any database privilege, including CONTROL privilege Any object privilege, including CONTROL privilege
System Control (SYSCTRL) authority	The USE table space privilege	The USE table space privilege
System Maintenance (SYSMAINT) authority	No authorities or privileges	No authorities or privileges
System Monitor (SYSMON) authority	No authorities or privileges	No authorities or privileges
Database Administrator (DBADM) authority	Any database privilege, including CONTROL privilege Any object privilege, including CONTROL privilege	Any database privilege, including CONTROL privilege Any object privilege, including CONTROL privilege
Security Administrator (SECADM) authority	SETSESSIONUSER privileges and LDAP elements	SETSESSIONUSER privileges and LDAP elements
Load (LOAD) authority	No authorities or privileges	No authorities or privileges
CONTROL privilege on an object (but no other authority)	All privileges available (with the exception of the CONTROL privilege) for the object on which the user holds CONTROL privilege	All privileges available (with the exception of the CONTROL privilege) for the object on which the user holds CONTROL privilege
A privilege on an object that was assigned with the WITH GRANT OPTION option specified	The same object privilege that was assigned with the WITH GRANT OPTION option specified.	No authorities or privileges

Authorities and Privileges Needed to Perform Common Tasks

So far, we have identified the authorities and privileges that are available, and we have examined how these authorities and privileges are granted and revoked. But to use authorities and privileges effectively, you must be able to determine which authorities and privileges are appropriate for an individual user and which are not. Often, a blanket set of authorities and privileges is assigned to an individual, based on his or her job title and job responsibilities. Then, as the individual begins to work with the database, the set of authorities and privileges he or she has is modified as appropriate. Some of the more common job titles used, along with the tasks that usually accompany them and the authorities/privileges needed to perform those tasks, can be seen in Table 6.2.

Table 6.2 Common Job Titles, Tasks and Authorities/Privileges Needed.		
Job Title	**Tasks**	**Authorities/Privileges Needed**
Department Administrator	Oversees the departmental system; designs and creates databases.	System Control (SYSCTRL) authority or System Administrator (SYSADM) authority (if the department has its own instance)
Security Administrator	Grants authorities and privileges to other users and revokes them, if necessary.	System Administrator (SYSADM) authority or Database Administrator (DBADM) authority; Security Administrator (SECADM)authority if label-based access control is used
Database Administrator	Designs, develops, operates, safeguards, and maintains one or more databases.	Database Administrator (DBADM) authority over one or more databases and System Maintenance (SYSMAINT) authority, or in some cases System Control (SYSCTRL) authority, over the instance(s) that control the databases
System Operator	Monitors the database and performs routine backup operations. Also performs recovery operations if needed.	System Maintenance (SYSMAINT) authority or System Monitor (SYSMON) authority
Application Developer/ Programmer	Develops and tests database/DB2 Database Manager application programs; may also create test tables and populate them with data.	CONNECT and CREATE_TAB privilege for one or more databases, BINDADD and BIND privilege on one or more packages, one or more schema privileges for one or more schemas, and one or more table privileges for one or more tables; CREATE_EXTERNAL_ ROUTINE privilege for one or more databases may also be required

Table 6.2 Common Job Titles, Tasks and Authorities/Privileges Needed. (Continued)		
Job Title	**Tasks**	**Authorities/Privileges Needed**
User Analyst	Defines the data requirements for an application program by examining the database structure using the system catalog views.	CONNECT privilege for one or more databases and SELECT privilege on the system catalog views
End User	Executes one or more application programs.	CONNECT privilege for one or more databases and EXECUTE privilege on the package associated with each application used; if an application program contains dynamic SQL statements, SELECT, INSERT, UPDATE, and DELETE privileges for one or more tables may be needed as well
Information Center Consultant	Defines the data requirements for a query user; provides the data needed by creating tables and views and by granting access to one or more database objects.	Database Administrator (DBADM) authority for one or more databases
Query User	Issues SQL statements (usually from the Command Line Processor) to retrieve, add, update, or delete data (may also save results of queries in tables)	CONNECT privilege on one or more databases; SELECT, INSERT, UPDATE, and DELETE privilege on each table used; and CREATEIN privilege on the schema in which tables and views are to be created

Adapted from Table 78 on pages 608–609 of the *IBM DB2 Version 9 for Linux, UNIX, and Windows Administration Guide—Implementation manual.*

Securing Data Using Encryption

In today's environments, there is an increasing need to restrict access to extremely sensitive data, such as social security numbers, bank account numbers, credit card numbers, and anything else that could cause embarrassment or financial loss to a company if it fell into the wrong hands. Most people are aware that transmitting sensitive information without encrypting it first is an invitation for hackers, and as companies move toward doing business over the Internet, they are employing encryption techniques to reduce or eliminate their risk. But few people realize that encryption technology can play a similar role in securing data stored in a database.

DB2 has provided built-in data encryption services since Version 7.2. These services provide a mechanism to safeguard sensitive data by encrypting it as it is stored in a table, and by requiring that the data be decrypted before it can be clearly seen. The algorithm used to encrypt data is an RC2 block cipher with padding; a muli-bit secret key is derived from the user-supplied password using a MD2 message digest. The encryption password is not tied to DB2 authentication and is used for data encryption and decryption only. This enhances the security of DB2 encrypted data because the decryption algorithm is not easily derivable.

DB2 relies on three built-in SQL functions to perform the actual encryption and decryption of sensitive data and an additional function that can be used to produce a hint to help a user remember their password. These functions are:

- ENCRYPT()

- DECRYPT_CHAR()

- DECRYPT_BIN()

- GETHINT()

The built-in encryption and decryption functions ENCRYPT(), DECRYPT_BIN(), and DECRYPT_CHAR() are used to encrypt data in storage. To encrypt data in transit between clients and DB2 databases, you must use either the DATA_ENCRYPT or the SERVER_ENCRYPT authentication type, or alternately, you can configure a DB2 database system for Secure Socket Layer (SSL) support.

Encrypting Data Using the ENCRYPT() Function

The process used to encrypt data is fairly straightforward—you simply include the ENCRYPT() function in a valid INSERT or UPDATE SQL statement. The syntax for the ENCRYPT() function is:

```
ENCRYPT ([Value]
<, [Password]>
<, [Hint]>
)
```

where:

> *Value*   Identifies the value that is to be encrypted.
>
> *Password*   Identifies the password to be used to generate the key that will be used to encrypt and decrypt the data. The password specified must be between 6 and 127 characters in length and must be in the exact case desired because DB2 does not automatically convert passwords into upper case. If the password specified is null or if a password is not provided, the data will be encrypted using the encryption password value that was assigned for the session by the SET ENCRYPTION PASSWORD SQL statement.
>
> *Hint*   Identifies a character string value (up to 32 characters in length) that can be used to help data owners remember the password that was used to encrypt the data. If a hint value is provided, it will be embedded into the result and can be retrieved using the GETHINT() function.

The result data type of the ENCRYPT() function is VARCHAR FOR BIT DATA. Therefore, when creating a table that is to hold encrypted data, each column that is to be encrypted must be assigned the data type VARCHAR FOR BIT DATA. How large an encrypted column must be is determined, in part, by the decision to store password hint information with the encrypted data. If a hint will not be provided, the length of the column must be the length of the unencrypted data + 8 bytes for the password, rounded up to the next 8-byte boundary. For example, if you wanted to encrypt a string that is 11 bytes long and forego providing a password hint, you would need to define a column that is capable of holding 24 bytes (11 + 8 = 17; 17 + 5 to reach the next 8-byte boundary = 24). If a hint will be provided, the length of the column must be the length of the unencrypted data + 8 bytes for the password, rounded up to the next 8-byte boundary + 32 bytes for the hint. Therefore, if you wanted to store a password hint with an 11-byte encrypted string, you would need to define a column that is capable of holding 56 bytes (24 + 32 = 56 bytes). There is *no* password reset option, so making use of hints is good practice, even if it does require additional storage space.

Thus, if a table named EMPLOYEE was created by executing the following CREATE TABLE SQL statement:

```
CREATE TABLE employee
     (name VARCHAR(45), ssn VARCHAR(56) FOR BIT DATA)
```

and you wanted to insert a record into the EMPLOYEE table such that the social
security number information was encrypted using the password "HR_1118", you
could do so by executing an INSERT SQL statement containing the ENCRYPT()
function that looks something like this:

```
INSERT INTO employee(name, ssn)
VALUES ('John Doe', ENCRYPT('111-22-3333', 'HR-1118'))
```

Only fixed-length character string data (CHAR), varying-
length character string data (VARCHAR), and columns
defined as FOR BIT DATA can be encrypted; SQL casting
functions must be used to encrypt any other data types.

On the other hand, if you wanted to insert a record into the EMPLOYEE table, encrypt
the social security number information using the password "HR_1118", and store
the password hint "Dept-Birthdate" with the encrypted data, you could do so by
executing an INSERT SQL statement containing the ENCRYPT() function that looks
more like this:

```
INSERT INTO employee(name, ssn)
VALUES ('John Doe', ENCRYPT('111-22-3333', 'HR-1118', 'Dept-Birthdate'))
```

It is important to note that the encryption of data can have a significant impact on
SQL performance. Furthermore, Unicode databases that store graphic strings are
more likely than ASCII databases to experience serious performance degradation
when using encryption because graphic string data must be converted to character
string data before encryption can occur. In general, you should only encrypt very
sensitive data, such as social security numbers, account numbers, patient names,
etc., to limit the negative impact encryption has on performance. It is also a good
idea to create indexes on columns that contain encrypted data. Keep in mind that
some data values are not very good candidates for encryption. For example,
Boolean values (TRUE and FALSE) or other small sets, such as the integers 1
through 10, are poor candidates. These values along with a meaningful column
name may be easy to guess, thereby counteracting the purpose of encryption.

Decrypting Data Using the DECRYPT_CHAR() and DECRYPT_BIN() Functions

Data that was encrypted using the ENCRYPT() function can be decrypted by including either the DECRYPT_CHAR() or the DECRYPT_BIN() function in a query against a table that contains encrypted data. The syntax for the DECRYPT_CHAR() function is:

```
DECRYPT_CHAR ([EncryptedValue]
<, [Password]>
)
```

and the syntax for the DECRYPT_BIN() function is:

```
DECRYPT_BIN ([EncryptedValue]
<, [Password]>
)
```

where:

> *EncryptedValue*   Identifies a character string value that was encrypted using the ENCRYPT() function.
>
> *Password*   Identifies the password to be used to decrypt the data. The password specified must be between 6 and 127 characters in length and must be in the exact case used to encrypt the data. If the password specified is null or if a password is not provided, the data will be decrypted using the encryption password value that was assigned for the session by the SET ENCRYPTION PASSWORD SQL statement.

Both functions return a value that is the result of the decryption of encrypted data—the DECRYPT_CHAR() function returns a value that is represented in a data type of VARCHAR, whereas the DECRYPT_BIN() function returns a result that is represented by a VARCHAR FOR BIT DATA data type.

Thus, if a table named EMPLOYEE was created by executing the following CREATE TABLE SQL statement:

```
CREATE TABLE employee
    (name VARCHAR(45), ssn VARCHAR(56) FOR BIT DATA)
```

and you wanted to retrieve a record from the EMPLOYEE table, knowing that the social security number information stored in the table was encrypted using the password "HR_1118", you could do so by executing a SELECT SQL statement containing the DECRYPT_CHAR() function that looks something like this:

```
SELECT name, DECRYPT_CHAR(ssn, 'HR-1118')
FROM employee
```

If a password hint was provided when the data was encrypted, the hint is not returned. The length of the resulting value is the length of the data type of encrypted data minus 8 bytes; the actual length of the value returned will match the length of the original string that was encrypted.

It is important to note that users attempting to query a table containing encrypted data without using the DECRYPT_CHAR() or DECRYPT_BIN() function will see sensitive data in its encrypted form, which of course is unreadable. On the other hand, if an attempt is made to query a table containing encrypted data using the DECRYPT_CHAR() or DECRYPT_BIN() function and the incorrect password is provided, the query will fail.

Obtaining Password Hints Using the GETHINT() Function

Earlier, we saw that a phrase that can help data owners remember passwords associated with encrypted data can be provided when data is encrypted using the ENCRYPT() function. If a password hint was provided when data was encrypted, it can be obtained and displayed by executing a query against the encrypted column that contains the GETHINT() function. The syntax for this function is:

```
GETHINT ([EncryptedValue])
```

where:

> *EncryptedValue*   Identifies a character string value that was encrypted using the ENCRYPT() function.

Thus, if a table named EMPLOYEE was created by executing the following CREATE TABLE SQL statement:

```
CREATE TABLE employee
    (name VARCHAR(45), ssn VARCHAR(56) FOR BIT DATA)
```

and a record containing encrypted data and a password hint was inserted into the table by executing an INSERT SQL statement that looks something like this:

```
INSERT INTO employee(name, ssn)
VALUES ('John Doe', ENCRYPT('111-22-3333', 'HR-1118', 'Dept-Birthdate'))
```

the password hint "Dept-Birthdate" could be obtained by executing a query that looks something like this:

```
SELECT GETHINT(ssn) FROM employee
```

Specifying an Encryption Password to Use for the Current Session

Earlier, we saw that if a password is not explicitly provided when data is encrypted using the ENCRYPT() function, data will be encrypted using the encryption password value that was assigned for the session. An encryption password can be set for a session by executing the SET ENCRYPTION PASSWORD SQL statement. The syntax for this statement is:

```
SET ENCRYPTION PASSWORD <=> [Password]
```

where:

> *Password*   Identifies the password to be used to generate the key that will be used to encrypt and decrypt data each time the ENCRYPT(), DECRYPT_CHAR(), and DECRYPT_BIN() functions are executed in the current session. The password specified must be between 6 and 127 characters in length and must be in the exact case desired because DB2 does not automatically convert passwords into upper case. The password specified cannot be null.

Thus, if you wanted to specify that all data encryption and decryption operations performed during the current session are to use the password "HR_1118", you could do so by executing a SET ENCRYPTION PASSWORD SQL statement that looks something like this:

```
SET ENCRYPTION PASSWORD = 'HR-1118'
```

The obvious advantage of using the SET ENCRYPTION PASSWORD statement is to eliminate the need to constantly provide a common password when encrypting and decrypting data. When the same password is used to encrypt all of the rows in one or more tables, the SET ENCRYPTION PASSWORD statement can be quite useful. However, there is one drawback to using this shortcut—if the encryption password is not explicitly supplied when data is encrypted using the ENCRYPT() function, a password hint can not be supplied.

Securing Data with Label-Based Access Control (LBAC)

Earlier, we saw that authentication is performed at the operating system level to verify that users are who they say they are, and authorities and privileges control access to a database and the objects and data that reside within it. Views, which allow different users to see different presentations of the same data, can be used in conjunction with privileges to limit access to specific columns. But what if your security requirements dictate that you create and manage several hundred views? Or, more importantly, what if you want to restrict access to individual rows in a table? If you're using DB2 9, the solution for these situations is label-based access control.

So just what is label-based access control (LBAC)? LBAC is a new security feature that uses one or more security labels to control who has read access and who has write access to individual rows and/or columns in a table. The United States and many other governments use LBAC models in which hierarchical classification labels such as CONFIDENTIAL, SECRET, and TOP SECRET are assigned to data based on its sensitivity. Access to data labeled at a certain level (for example, SECRET) is restricted to those users who have been granted that level of access or higher. With LBAC, you can construct security labels to represent any criteria your company uses to determine who can read or modify particular data values. And LBAC is flexible enough to handle the most simple to the most complex criteria.

One problem with the traditional security methods DB2 uses is that security administrators and DBAs have access to sensitive data stored in the databases they oversee. To solve this problem, LBAC-security administration tasks are isolated from all other tasks—only users with Security Administrator (SECADM) authority are allowed to configure LBAC elements.

Implementing Row-Level LBAC

Before you implement a row-level LBAC solution, you need to have a thorough understanding of the security requirements. Suppose you have a database that contains company sales data and you want to control how senior executives, regional managers, and sales representatives access data stored in a table named SALES. Security requirements might dictate that access to this data should comply with these rules:

- Senior executives are allowed to view, but not update, all records in the table.

- Regional managers are allowed to view and update only records that were entered by sales representatives who report to them.

- Sales representatives are allowed to view and update only records of the sales they made.

Once the security requirements are known, you must then define appropriate security policies and labels, create an LBAC-protected table (or alter an existing table to add LBAC protection), and grant the proper security labels to the appropriate users.

Defining a Security Label Component

Security label components represent criteria that may be used to decide whether a user should have access to specific data. Three types of security label components can exist:

- **SET.** A set is a collection of elements (character string values) where the order in which each element appears is not important.

- **ARRAY.** An array is an ordered set that can represent a simple hierarchy. In an array, the order in which the elements appear is important—the first element ranks higher than the second, the second ranks higher than the third, and so on.

- **TREE.** A tree represents a more complex hierarchy that can have multiple nodes and branches.

To create security label components, you execute one of the following CREATE SECURITY LABEL COMPONENT SQL statements:

```
CREATE SECURITY LABEL COMPONENT [ComponentName]
SET {StringConstant,...}
```

or

```
CREATE SECURITY LABEL COMPONENT [ComponentName]
ARRAY [StringConstant,...]
```

or

```
CREATE SECURITY LABEL COMPONENT [ComponentName]
TREE (StringConstant ROOT < StringConstant UNDER StringConstant >)]
```

where:

ComponentName   Identifies the name that is to be assigned to the security label
component being created.

StringConstant   Identifies one or more string constant values that make up the
valid set, array, or tree of values to be used by the security
label component being created.

Thus, to create a security label component named SEC_COMP that contains a set of
values whose order is insignificant, you would execute a CREATE SECURITY LABEL
COMPONENT statement that looks like this:

```
CREATE SECURITY LABEL COMPONENT sec_comp
SET {'CONFIDENTIAL', 'SECRET', 'TOP_SECRET'}
```

To create a security label component that contains an array of values listed from
highest to lowest order, you would execute a CREATE SECURITY LABEL COMPONENT
statement like this:

```
CREATE SECURITY LABEL COMPONENT sec_comp
ARRAY ['MASTER_CRAFTSMAN', 'JOURNEYMAN', 'APPRENTICE']
```

And to create a security label component that contains a tree of values that describe
a company's organizational chart, you would execute a CREATE SECURITY LABEL
COMPONENT statement that looks something like this:

```
CREATE SECURITY LABEL COMPONENT sec_comp
TREE ('EXEC_STAFF' ROOT,
      'N_MGR' UNDER 'EXEC_STAFF',
      'E_MGR' UNDER 'EXEC_STAFF',
      'S_MGR' UNDER 'EXEC_STAFF',
      'W_MGR' UNDER 'EXEC_STAFF',
      'C_MGR' UNDER 'EXEC_STAFF',
      'SALES_REP1' UNDER 'N_MGR',
      'SALES_REP2' UNDER 'W_MGR')
```

Defining a Security Policy

Security policies determine exactly how a table is to be protected by LBAC. Specifically, a security policy identifies the following:

- What security label components will be used in the security labels that will be part of the policy

- What rules will be used when security label components are compared (at this time, only one set of rules is supported: DB2LBACRULES)

- Which optional behaviors will be used when accessing data protected by the policy

Every LBAC-protected table must have one (and only one) security policy associated with it. Rows and columns in that table can be protected only with security labels that are part of that security policy; all protected data access must adhere to the rules of that policy. You can have multiple security policies within a single database, but you can't have more than one security policy protecting any given table.

Security policies are created by executing the CREATE SECURITY POLICY SQL statement. The syntax for this statement is:

```
CREATE SECURITY POLICY [PolicyName]
COMPONENTS [ComponentName ,...]
WITH DB2LBACRULES
<[OVERRIDE | RESTRICT] NOT AUTHORIZED
    WRITE SECURITY LABEL>
```

where:

PolicyName   Identifies the name that is to be assigned to the security policy being created.

ComponentName   Identifies, by name, one or more security label components that are to be part of the security policy being created.

The [OVERRIDE | RESTRICT] NOT AUTHORIZED WRITE SECURITY LABEL option specifies the action to be taken when a user who is not authorized to write a security label explicitly specified with an INSERT or UPDATE statement attempts to write data to the protected table. By default, the value of a user's security label, rather than an explicitly specified security label, is used for write access during insert and update operations (OVERRIDE NOT AUTHORIZED WRITE SECURITY LABEL). If the RESTRICT NOT AUTHORIZED WRITE SECURITY LABEL option is used, insert and update operations will fail if the user is not authorized to write the explicitly specified security label to the protected table. (We'll see some examples of INSERT statements that contain explicitly specified security labels a little later.)

Therefore, to create a security policy named SEC_POLICY that is based on the SEC_COMP security label component created earlier, you would execute a CREATE SECURITY POLICY statement that looks something like this:

```
CREATE SECURITY POLICY sec_policy
COMPONENTS sec_comp
WITH DB2LBACRULES
```

Defining Security Labels

Security labels describe a set of security criteria and are used to protect data against unauthorized access or modification. Security labels are granted to users who are allowed to access or modify protected data; when users attempt to access or modify protected data, their security label is compared to the security label protecting the data to determine whether the access or modification is allowed. Every security label is part of exactly one security policy, and a security label must exist for each security label component found in the security policy.

Security labels are created by executing the CREATE SECURITY LABEL SQL statement. The syntax for this statement is:

```
CREATE SECURITY LABEL [LabelName]
[COMPONENT [ComponentName] [StringConstant] ,...]
```

where:

    LabelName   Identifies the name that is to be assigned to the security label being created. The name specified must be qualified with a security policy name and must not match an existing security label for the security policy specified.

    ComponentName Identifies, by name, a security label component that is part of the security policy specified as the qualifier for the *LabelName* parameter.

    StringConstant   Identifies one or more string constant values that are valid elements of the security label component specified in the *ComponentName* parameter.

Thus, to create a set of security labels for the security policy named SEC_POLICY that was created earlier, you would execute a set of CREATE SECURITY LABEL statements that looks something like this:

```
CREATE SECURITY LABEL sec_policy.exec_staff
COMPONENT sec_comp 'EXEC_STAFF'

CREATE SECURITY LABEL sec_policy.n_mgr
COMPONENT sec_comp 'N_MGR'

CREATE SECURITY LABEL sec_policy.e_mgr
COMPONENT sec_comp 'E_MGR'

CREATE SECURITY LABEL sec_policy.s_mgr
COMPONENT sec_comp 'S_MGR'

CREATE SECURITY LABEL sec_policy.w_mgr
COMPONENT sec_comp 'W_MGR'

CREATE SECURITY LABEL sec_policy.c_mgr
COMPONENT sec_comp 'C_MGR'

CREATE SECURITY LABEL sec_policy.sales_rep1
COMPONENT sec_comp 'SALES_REP1'
```

```
CREATE SECURITY LABEL sec_policy.sales_rep2
COMPONENT sec_comp 'SALES_REP2'
```

Creating an LBAC-Protected Table

Once you have defined the security policy and labels needed to enforce your
security requirements, you're ready to create a table and configure it for LBAC
protection. To configure a new table for row-level LBAC protection, you include a
column with the data type DB2SECURITYLABEL in the table's definition and associate
a security policy with the table using the SECURITY POLICY clause of the CREATE
TABLE SQL statement.

So to create a table named SALES and configure it for row-level LBAC protection
using the security policy named SEC_POLICY created earlier, you would execute a
CREATE TABLE statement that looks something like this:

```
CREATE TABLE corp.sales (
      sales_rec_id    INTEGER NOT NULL,
      sales_date      DATE WITH DEFAULT,
      sales_rep       INTEGER,
      region          VARCHAR(15),
      manager         INTEGER,
      sales_amt       DECIMAL(12,2),
      margin          DECIMAL(12,2),
      sec_label       DB2SECURITYLABEL)
   SECURITY POLICY sec_policy
```

On the other hand, to configure an existing table named SALES for row-level LBAC
protection using a security policy named SEC_POLICY, you would execute an ALTER
TABLE statement that looks like this:

```
ALTER TABLE corp.sales
   ADD COLUMN sec_label DB2SECURITYLABEL
   ADD SECURITY POLICY sec_policy
```

However, before you can execute such an ALTER TABLE statement, you must be
granted a security label for write access that is part of the security policy that will
be used to protect the table (which, in this case is SEC_POLICY). Otherwise, you
won't be able to create the DB2SECURITYLABEL column.

Granting Security Labels to Users

Once the security policy and labels needed to enforce your security requirements have been defined, and a table has been enabled for LBAC-protection, you must grant the proper security labels to the appropriate users and indicate whether they are to have read access, write access, or full access to data that is protected by that label. Security labels are granted to users by executing a special form of the GRANT SQL statement. The syntax for this form of the GRANT statement is:

```
GRANT SECURITY LABEL [LabelName]
TO USER [UserName]
[FOR ALL ACCESS | FOR READ ACCESS | FOR WRITE ACCESS]
```

where:

LabelName   Identifies the name of an existing security label. The name specified must be qualified with the security policy name that was used when the security label was created.

UserName   Identifies the name of the user to which the security label is to be granted.

Thus, to give a user named USER1 the ability to read data protected by the security label SEC_POLICY.EXEC_STAFF, you would execute a GRANT statement that looks like this:

```
GRANT SECURITY LABEL sec_policy.exec_staff
TO USER user1 FOR READ ACCESS
```

Putting Row-Level LBAC into Action

To enforce the security requirements listed earlier, we must first give users the ability to perform DML operations against the SALES table by executing the following GRANT statements as a user with SYSADM or DBADM authority:

```
GRANT ALL PRIVILEGES ON TABLE corp.sales TO exec_staff;
GRANT ALL PRIVILEGES ON TABLE corp.sales TO n_manager;
GRANT ALL PRIVILEGES ON TABLE corp.sales TO e_manager;
GRANT ALL PRIVILEGES ON TABLE corp.sales TO s_manager;
GRANT ALL PRIVILEGES ON TABLE corp.sales TO w_manager;
```

```
GRANT ALL PRIVILEGES ON TABLE corp.sales TO c_manager;
GRANT ALL PRIVILEGES ON TABLE corp.sales TO sales_rep1;
GRANT ALL PRIVILEGES ON TABLE corp.sales TO sales_rep2;
```

Next, we must grant the proper security labels to the appropriate users and indicate whether they are to have read access, write access, or full access to data that is protected by that label. This is done by executing the following GRANT statements, this time as a user with SECADM authority:

```
GRANT SECURITY LABEL sec_policy.exec_staff
TO USER exec_staff FOR READ ACCESS;

GRANT SECURITY LABEL sec_policy.n_mgr
TO USER n_manager FOR ALL ACCESS;

GRANT SECURITY LABEL sec_policy.e_mgr
TO USER e_manager FOR ALL ACCESS;

GRANT SECURITY LABEL sec_policy.s_mgr
TO USER s_manager FOR ALL ACCESS;

GRANT SECURITY LABEL sec_policy.w_mgr
TO USER w_manager FOR ALL ACCESS;

GRANT SECURITY LABEL sec_policy.c_mgr
TO USER c_manager FOR ALL ACCESS;

GRANT SECURITY LABEL sec_policy.sales_rep1
TO USER sales_rep1 FOR ALL ACCESS;

GRANT SECURITY LABEL sec_policy.sales_rep2
TO USER sales_rep2 FOR ALL ACCESS;
```

Now, suppose user SALES_REP1 adds three rows to the SALES table by executing the following SQL statements:

```
INSERT INTO corp.sales VALUES (1, DEFAULT, 1, 'NORTH', 5,
    1000.50, 500.00,
    SECLABEL_BY_NAME('SEC_POLICY', 'SALES_REP1'));

INSERT INTO corp.sales VALUES (2, DEFAULT, 1, 'NORTH', 5,
    2000.00, 400.00,
    SECLABEL_BY_NAME('SEC_POLICY', 'SALES_REP1'));
```

```
INSERT INTO corp.sales VALUES (3, DEFAULT, 1, 'NORTH', 5,
    4500.90, 850.00,
    SECLABEL_BY_NAME('SEC_POLICY', 'SALES_REP1'));
```

SALES_REP1 has been given read/write access to the table using the SEC_POLICY.
SALES_REP1 security label, so the statements execute successfully. Next, user
SALES_REP2 adds two additional rows to the SALES table by executing the following
SQL statements:

```
INSERT INTO corp.sales VALUES (4, DEFAULT, 1, 'WEST', 20,
    1000.50, 500.00,
    SECLABEL_BY_NAME('SEC_POLICY', 'SALES_REP2'));

INSERT INTO corp.sales VALUES (5, DEFAULT, 1, 'WEST', 20,
    3200.00, 600.00,
    SECLABEL_BY_NAME('SEC_POLICY', 'SALES_REP2'));
```

SALES_REP2 has also been given read/write access to the table using the
SEC_POLICY.SALES_REP2 security label, so the rows are successfully inserted.

Now, when user EXEC_STAFF queries the SALES table, all five records entered will
appear (because the security label SEC_POLICY.EXEC_STAFF is the highest level in the
security policy's security label component tree). However, if user EXEC_STAFF attempts
to insert additional records or update an existing record, an error will be generated
because user EXEC_STAFF is allowed only to read the data (only read access was
granted).

When user N_MANAGER queries the table, only records entered by the user
SALES_REP1 will be displayed; the user W_MANAGER will see only records entered
by the user SALES_REP2; and the users E_MANAGER, S_MANAGER, and C_MANAGER
will not see any records at all. (SALES_REP1 reports to N_MANAGER, SALES_REP2
reports to W_MANAGER, and no other managers have a sales representative
reporting to them.)

And finally, when SALES_REP1 or SALES_REP2 queries the SALES table, they will see
only the records they personally entered. Likewise, they can update only the records
they entered.

· ·

If you want to retrieve values stored in a DB2SECURITYLABEL column and display them in a human-readable format, you can do so by using the SECLABEL_TO_CHAR() scalar function in a SELECT statement—provided you have the LBAC credentials needed to see the row.

Thus, if user EXEC_STAFF executes the following query:

```
SELECT sales_rec_id, sec_label,
    SECLABEL_TO_CHAR('SEC_POLICY', sec_label)
    AS s_l2
FROM corp. sales
```

the following results will be returned:

```
SALES_REC_ID SEC_LABEL             S_L2
------------ -------------------- ----------------
           1 x'0000000000000001 SALES_REP1
           2 x'0000000000000001 SALES_REP1
           3 x'0000000000000001 SALES_REP1
           4 x'0000000000000010 SALES_REP2
           5 x'0000000000000010 SALES_REP2
```

· ·

Implementing Column-Level LBAC

To illustrate how column-level LBAC is employed, let's assume you want to control how Human Resources (HR) staff members, managers, and employees are going to access data stored in a table named EMPLOYEES. For this scenario, the security requirements are as follows:

- Name, gender, department, and phone number information can be viewed by all employees.

- Hire date, salary, and bonus information (in addition to name, gender, department, and phone number information) can be seen only by managers and HR staff members.

- Employee ID and Social Security Number information can be seen only by HR staff members. Additionally, HR staff members are the only users who can create and modify employee records.

Once again, after the security requirements have been identified, the next steps are to define the appropriate security components, policies, and labels; create the table that will house the data; alter the table to add LBAC protection; and grant the proper security labels to the appropriate users.

Defining Security Label Components, Security Policies, and Security Labels

Because an array of values, listed in order from highest to lowest, is the best way to implement the security requirements just outlined, you can create the security component needed by executing a CREATE SECURITY LABEL COMPONENT statement (as a user with SECADM authority) that looks something like this:

```
CREATE SECURITY LABEL COMPONENT sec_comp
ARRAY ['CONFIDENTIAL', 'CLASSIFIED', 'UNCLASSIFIED']
```

After the appropriate security label component has been created, you can create a security policy named SEC_POLICY that is based on the SEC_COMP security label component by executing a CREATE SECURITY POLICY statement (as a user with SECADM authority) that looks like this:

```
CREATE SECURITY POLICY sec_policy
COMPONENTS sec_comp
WITH DB2LBACRULES
```

Earlier, we saw that security labels are granted to users who are allowed to access or modify LBAC-protected data; when users attempt to access or modify protected data, their security label is compared to the security label protecting the data to determine whether the access or modification is allowed. But before security labels can be granted, they must first be defined. To create a set of security labels for the security policy named SEC_POLICY that was just created, you would execute the following set of CREATE SECURITY LABEL statements (as a user with SECADM authority):

```
CREATE SECURITY LABEL sec_policy.confidential
COMPONENT sec_comp 'CONFIDENTIAL'

CREATE SECURITY LABEL sec_policy.classified
COMPONENT sec_comp 'CLASSIFIED'

CREATE SECURITY LABEL sec_policy.unclassified
COMPONENT sec_comp 'UNCLASSIFIED'
```

Keep in mind that every security label is part of exactly one security policy, and a security label must exist for each security label component found in that security policy.

Creating an LBAC-Protected Table and Granting Privileges and Security Labels to Users

Earlier, we saw that in order to configure a new table for row-level LBAC protection, you must associate a security policy with the table being created using the SECURITY POLICY clause of the CREATE TABLE SQL statement. The same is true if column-level LBAC protection is desired. Therefore, to create a table named EMPLOYEES and associate it with a security policy named SEC_POLICY, you would need to execute a CREATE TABLE statement that looks something like this:

```
CREATE TABLE hr.employees (
    emp_id      INTEGER NOT NULL,
    f_name      VARCHAR(20),
    l_name      VARCHAR(20),
    gender      CHAR(1),
    hire_date   DATE WITH DEFAULT,
    dept_id     CHAR(5),
    phone       CHAR(14),
    ssn         CHAR(12),
    salary      DECIMAL(12,2),
    bonus       DECIMAL(12,2))
  SECURITY POLICY sec_policy
```

Then, in order to enforce the security requirements identified earlier, you must give users the ability to perform the appropriate DML operations against the EMPLOYEES table. This is done by executing the following GRANT SQL statements (as a user with SYSADM or DBADM authority):

```
GRANT ALL PRIVILEGES ON TABLE hr.employees TO hr_staff;
GRANT SELECT ON TABLE hr.employees TO manager1;
GRANT SELECT ON TABLE hr.employees TO employee1;
```

Finally, you must grant the proper security label to the appropriate users and indicate whether they are to have read access, write access, or full access to data that is protected by that label. This is done by executing a set of GRANT statements (as a user with SECADM authority) that look something like this:

```
GRANT SECURITY LABEL sec_policy.confidential
TO USER hr_staff FOR ALL ACCESS;

GRANT SECURITY LABEL sec_policy.classified
TO USER manager1 FOR READ ACCESS;

GRANT SECURITY LABEL sec_policy.unclassified
TO USER employee1 FOR READ ACCESS;
```

Creating LBAC-Protected Columns

Once you've defined the security policy and labels needed to enforce your security requirements and have granted the appropriate privileges and security labels to users, you are ready to modify the table associated with the security policy and configure its columns for column-level LBAC protection. This is done by executing an ALTER TABLE statement that looks something like this:

```
ALTER TABLE hr.employees
    ALTER COLUMN emp_id SECURED WITH confidential
    ALTER COLUMN f_name SECURED WITH unclassified
    ALTER COLUMN l_name SECURED WITH unclassified
    ALTER COLUMN gender SECURED WITH unclassified
    ALTER COLUMN hire_date SECURED WITH classified
    ALTER COLUMN dept_id SECURED WITH unclassified
    ALTER COLUMN phone SECURED WITH unclassified
    ALTER COLUMN ssn SECURED WITH confidential
    ALTER COLUMN salary SECURED WITH classified
    ALTER COLUMN bonus SECURED WITH classified;
```

Here is where things get a little tricky. If you try to execute the ALTER TABLE statement shown as a user with SYSADM or SECADM authority, the operation will fail, and you will be presented with an error message that looks something like this:

```
SQL20419N For table "EMPLOYEES", authorization ID " " does not have
LBAC credentials that allow using the security label "CONFIDENTIAL" to
protect column "EMP_ID".  SQLSTATE=42522
```

That's because the only user who can secure a column with the "CONFIDENTIAL" security label is a user who has been granted *write access* to data that is protected by that label. In our scenario, this is the user HR_STAFF. So what happens when user HR_STAFF attempts to execute the preceding ALTER TABLE statement? Now a slightly different error message is produced:

```
SQL20419N For table "EMPLOYEES", authorization ID "HR_STAFF" does not have
LBAC credentials that allow using the security label "UNCLASSIFIED" to
protect column "F_NAME".  SQLSTATE=42522
```

Why? Because, by default, the LBAC rules set associated with the security policy assigned to the EMPLOYEES table allows the user HR_STAFF to write data only to columns or rows that are protected by the same security label that he/she has been granted.

DB2LBACRULES Rules

An LBAC rule set is a predefined set of rules that is used when comparing security labels. Currently, only one LBAC rule set is supported (DB2LBACRULES), and as we have just seen, this rule set prevents both write-up and write-down behavior. (Write-up and write-down apply only to ARRAY security label components and only to write access.) Write-up is when the security label protecting data to which you are attempting to write is higher than the security label you have been granted; write-down is when the security label protecting data is lower.

Which rules are actually used when two security labels are compared is dependent on the type of component used (SET, ARRAY, or TREE) and the type of access being attempted (read or write). Table 6.3 lists the rules found in the DB2LBACRULES rules set, identifies for which component each rule is used, and describes how the rule determines if access is to be blocked.

Table 6.3 Summmary of the DB2LBACRULES Rules			
Rule Name Component	Component	Access	Access is blocked when this condition is met
DB2LBACREADARRAY	ARRAY	Read	The user's security label is lower than the protecting security label.
DB2LBACREADSET	SET	Read	There are one or more protecting security labels that the user does not hold.
DB2LBACREADTREE	TREE	Read	None of the user's security labels are equal to or an ancestor of one of the protecting security labels.
DB2LBACWRITEARRAY	ARRAY	Write	The user's security label is higher than the protecting security label or lower than the protecting security label.

Table 6.3 Summmary of the DB2LBACRULES Rules (Continued)			
Rule Name Component	**Component**	**Access**	**Access is blocked when this condition is met**
DB2LBACWRITESET	SET	Write	There are one or more protecting security labels that the user does not hold.
DB2LBACWRITETREE	TREE	Write	None of the user's security labels are equal to or an ancestor of one of the protecting security labels.
Adapted from Table 78 on pages 608–609 of the *IBM DB2 Version 9 for Linux, UNIX, and Windows Administration Guide—Implementation* manual.			

Granting Exemptions

So how can the remaining columns in the EMPLOYEES table be secured with the appropriate security labels? The Security Administrator must first grant user HR_STAFF an exemption to one or more security policy rules. When a user holds an exemption on a particular security policy rule, that rule is not enforced when the user attempts to access data that is protected by that security policy.

Security policy exemptions are granted by executing the GRANT EXEMPTION ON RULE SQL statement (as a user with SECADM authority). The syntax for this statement is:

```
GRANT EXEMPTION ON RULE [Rule] ,...
FOR [PolicyName]
TO USER [UserName]
```

where:

    Rule   Identifies one or more DB2LBACRULES security policy rules for which exemptions are to be given. The following values are valid for this parameter: DB2LBACREADARRAY, DB2LBACREADSET, DB2LBACREADTREE, DB2LBACWRITEARRAY WRITEDOWN, DB2LBACWRITEARRAY WRITEUP, DB2LBACWRITESET, DB2LBACWRITETREE, and ALL. (If an exemption is held for every security policy rule, the user will have complete access to all data protected by that security policy.)

PolicyName   Identifies the security policy for which the exemption is to be granted.

UserName   Identifies the name of the user to which the exemptions specified are to be granted.

Thus, to grant an exemption to the DB2LBACWRITEARRAY rule in the security policy named SEC_POLICY created earlier to a user named HR_STAFF, you would execute a GRANT EXEMPTION statement that looks something like this:

```
GRANT EXEMPTION ON RULE DB2LBACWRITEARRAY
WRITEDOWN FOR sec_policy
TO USER hr_staff
```

Once this exemption is granted along with the appropriate security label, user HR_STAFF will then be able to execute the ALTER TABLE statement shown earlier without generating an error. (Alternately, the following CREATE TABLE statement could be used to create the EMPLOYEES table and protect each column with the appropriate security label, provided user HR_STAFF has the privileges needed to create the table.)

```
CREATE TABLE hr.employees (
      emp_id     INTEGER NOT NULL SECURED WITH confidential,
      f_name     VARCHAR(20) SECURED WITH unclassified,
      l_name     VARCHAR(20) SECURED WITH unclassified,
      gender     CHAR(1) SECURED WITH unclassified,
      hire_date  DATE WITH DEFAULT SECURED WITH classified,
      dept_id    CHAR(5) SECURED WITH unclassified,
      phone      CHAR(14) SECURED WITH unclassified,
      ssn        CHAR(12) SECURED WITH confidential,
      salary     DECIMAL(12,2) SECURED WITH classified,
      bonus      DECIMAL(12,2) SECURED WITH classified)
   SECURITY POLICY sec_policy
```

Revoking Exemptions

Security policy exemptions that have been granted to a user can be revoked at any time by executing the REVOKE EXEMPTION ON RULE SQL statement (as a user with SECADM authority). The syntax for this statement is:

```
REVOKE EXEMPTION ON RULE [Rule] ,...
FOR [PolicyName]
FROM USER [UserName]
```

where:

Rule	Identifies one or more DB2LBACRULES security policy rules for which exemptions are to be revoked. The following values are valid for this parameter: DB2LBACREADARRAY, DB2LBACREADSET, DB2LBACREADTREE, DB2LBACWRITEARRAY WRITEDOWN, DB2LBACWRITEARRAY WRITEUP, DB2LBACWRITESET, DB2LBACWRITETREE, and ALL.
PolicyName	Identifies the security policy for which the exemption is to be revoked.
UserName	Identifies the name of the user from which the exemptions specified are to be revoked.

So, to revoke an exemption to the DB2LBACWRITEARRAY rule in the security policy named SEC_POLICY that was granted to a user named HR_STAFF, you would execute a REVOKE EXEMPTION statement that looks something like this:

```
REVOKE EXEMPTION ON RULE DB2LBACWRITEARRAY
WRITEDOWN FOR sec_policy
FROM USER hr_staff
```

Putting Column-Level LBAC into Action

Now that we have established a column-level LBAC environment, let's see what happens when different users try to access data stored in protected columns of the EMPLOYEES table. Suppose the user HR_STAFF adds three rows to the EMPLOYEES table by executing the following SQL statements.

```
INSERT INTO hr.employees VALUES(1, 'John', 'Doe', 'M',
    DEFAULT, 'A01', '919-555-1212', '111-22-3333',
    42000.50, 8500.00);

INSERT INTO hr.employees VALUES(2, 'Jane', 'Doe', 'F',
    DEFAULT, 'B02', '919-555-3434', '222-33-4444',
    38000.75, 5000.00);

INSERT INTO hr.employees VALUES(3, 'Paul', 'Smith', 'M',
    DEFAULT, 'C03', '919-555-5656', '333-44-5555',
    39250.00, 3500.00);
```

User HR_STAFF1 has been given read/write access to all columns in the table
(with the SEC_POLICY.CLASSIFIED security label and the DB2LBACWRITEARRAY
WRITEDOWN exemption), so the statements execute successfully. If user HR_STAFF
attempts to query the table, he or she will be able to see every column and every
row because he or she has been granted the highest security level in the array.

Now, when user MANAGER1 attempts to read every column in the table, an error
will be generated stating that he or she does not have "READ" access to the column
"SSN." However, MANAGER1 will be able to execute the following query because he
or she has been granted read access to each column specified:

```
SELECT f_name, l_name, hire_date, salary, bonus
FROM hr.employees
```

If user EMPLOYEE1 attempts to execute the same query, an error will be generated
stating that he or she does not have "READ" access to the column "BONUS." But an
attempt by EMPLOYEE1 to execute the following query
will be successful:

```
SELECT f_name, l_name, gender, dept_id, phone
FROM hr.employees
```

Additionally, if user MANAGER1 or user EMPLOYEE1 attempt to insert additional
records or update existing information, they will get an error stating they do not
have permission to perform the operation against the table.

Combining Row-Level and Column-Level LBAC

There may be times when you would like to limit an individual user's access to a
specific combination of rows and columns. When this is the case, you must include
a column with the data type DB2SECURITYLABEL in the table's definition, add the
SECURED WITH [*SecurityLabel*] option to each column in the table's definition, and
associate a security policy with the table using the SECURITY POLICY clause of the
CREATE TABLE SQL statement or the ADD SECURITY POLICY clause of the ALTER
TABLE statement. Typically, you will also create two security label components—one
for rows and one for columns—and use both components to construct the security
policy and labels needed.

For example, assume that you created two security label components by executing the following commands:

```
CREATE SECURITY LABEL COMPONENT scom_level
ARRAY ['CONFIDENTIAL', 'CLASSIFIED', 'UNCLASSIFIED'];

CREATE SECURITY LABEL COMPONENT scom_country
TREE ('NA' ROOT, 'CANADA' UNDER 'NA', 'USA' UNDER 'NA');
```

You would then create a security policy by executing a CREATE SECURITY POLICY command that looks something like this:

```
CREATE SECURITY POLICY sec_policy
COMPONENTS scom_level, scom_country
WITH DB2LBACRULES
```

Then you could create corresponding security labels by executing commands that look something like this:

```
CREATE SECURITY LABEL sec_policy.confidential
COMPONENT scom_level 'CONFIDENTIAL';

CREATE SECURITY LABEL sec_policy.uc_canada
COMPONENT scom_level 'UNCLASSIFIED'
COMPONENT scom_country 'CANADA';

CREATE SECURITY LABEL sec_policy.uc_us
COMPONENT scom_level 'UNCLASSIFIED'
COMPONENT scom_country 'USA';
```

Finally, after associating the appropriate security labels with individual columns, you would grant the proper security label to each user and conduct a few tests to ensure data access is controlled as expected.

DB2's Audit Facility

So far, we have looked at various methods that can be used to control who can and can not see information stored in a database. But there may be times when you want to monitor and track unauthorized attempts to access data. That's where the DB2 audit facility comes in. The DB2 audit facility monitors database events that you tell it to keep track of, and records information about those events in an audit log file. By analyzing the information stored in the audit log file, you can quickly pinpoint usage patterns that identify system misuse; once identified, you can take appropriate action to minimize or eliminate the problem. The DB2 audit facility works at the instance level, recording both instance-level and database-level activities. Since the DB2 audit facility works independently of the DB2 server, it will continue to run once started, even if the DB2 instance is stopped. In fact, when an instance is stopped, an audit record may be produced and written to the audit log.

The DB2 audit facility is controlled by the db2audit command and the contents of an audit configuration file named db2audit.cfg, which is located in the sqllib/security subdirectory under the instance owner's home directory. (By default the audit log file, db2audit.log, is written to this directory as well.) In order to capture audit records you must start the audit facility, and before audit log files can be examined the audit facility must be stopped. When the audit facility is started, it uses the existing audit configuration file to determine what events to monitor.

By executing the db2audit command, authorized users of the DB2 audit facility can perform the following tasks:

- Start recording auditable events within the DB2 instance.

- Stop recording auditable events within the DB2 instance.

- Configure the behavior of the audit facility, including selecting the categories of the auditable events to be monitored and recorded.

- Request a description of the current audit configuration.

- Flush any pending audit records from memory and write them to the audit log.

- Extract audit records by formatting and copying them from the audit log to a flat file or ASCII delimited file. (Extraction is done for one of two reasons: in preparation for analysis of log records or in preparation for pruning of log records.)

- Prune (remove) audit records from the current audit log.

The syntax for the db2audit command is:

```
db2audit [start | stop | describe | flush |
configure reset]
```

or

```
db2audit [configure scope all |
configure scope [Event],...]
<status [success | failure | both]>
<errortype [audit | normal]>
```

or

```
db2audit [extract file [OutputFile] |
extract <delasc [Delimiter]>]
<category [Event],...]>
<database [DatabaseName]>
<status [success | failure]>
```

or

```
db2audit [prune all |
prune date [Date] <pathname [Path]>]
```

where:

Event	Identifies which category or categories of events are to be monitored by the DB2 audit facility. The following values are valid for this parameter: audit, checking, objmaint, secmaint, sysadmin, validate, and context.
OutputFile	Identifies the name of the file to which extracted audit records are to be placed. If no file name is specified, records are written to a file named db2audit.out in the sqllib/security subdirectory under the instance owner's home directory. If a file name is specified, but no directory is provided, the file is created in the current working directory.
Delimiter	Identifies a single character (for example, '!') or the four-byte string representation of the hexadecimal number for the

character (for example, "0x32") that is to replace the default character string delimiter ("0xff") when records are extracted from the audit log.

DatabaseName Identifies the name of the database for which audit information is to be collected.

Date Identifies a date that is to be used to identify which records are to be removed from the audit log. (All audit records that occurred on or before the date/time specified will be deleted from the audit log.)

Path Identifies the location on disk that the DB2 audit facility is to use as temporary storage space when pruning (removing) records from the audit log. This temporary space allows for the pruning of the audit log when the disk it resides on is full and does not have enough space to allow a pruning operation.

All other options shown with this command are described in Table 6.4.

Table 6.4 db2 audit Command Options	
Option	**Meaning**
start	Indicates that the audit facility is to begin auditing events based on the contents of the db2audit.cfg file. (In a partitioned DB2 database instance, auditing will begin on all database partitions when this option is specified.) If the "audit" category of events has been specified for auditing, an audit record will be logged when the audit facility is started.
stop	Indicates that the audit facility is to stop auditing events. (In a partitioned DB2 database instance, auditing will be stopped on all database partitions when this option is specified.) If the "audit" category of events has been specified for auditing, an audit record will be logged when the audit facility is stopped.
describe	Indicates that current audit configuration information and status information is to be displayed to standard output.
flush	Forces any pending audit records to be written to the audit log. Also, resets the audit state in the engine from "unable to log" to "ready to log" if the audit facility is in an error state.
configure reset	Specifies that the audit configuration file (db2audit.cfg) is to be returned to its original state (where SCOPE is all of the categories except CONTEXT, STATUS is FAILURE, ERRORTYPE is NORMAL, and the audit facility is OFF). This option can also be used to create a new audit configuration file if the original file has been lost or damaged.

Table 6.4 db2 audit Command Options (Continued)	
Option	**Meaning**
configure scope	Specifies which category or categories of events are to be audited. This option also allows a user to focus their auditing and reduce the growth of the audit log. It is recommended that the number and type of events being logged be limited as much as possible; otherwise the audit log will grow rapidly. The default SCOPE is all categories except CONTEXT and may result in records being generated rapidly. The categories selected, in conjunction with the mode used (synchronous or asynchronous), may result in a significant performance reduction and significantly increased disk requirements.
status	Specifies whether only successful or failing events, or both successful and failing events, should be logged. Context events occur before the status of an operation is known. Therefore, such events are logged regardless of the value associated with this parameter.
errortype	Specifies whether audit errors are returned to the user or are ignored. The value for this parameter can be: • **AUDIT**. All errors including errors occurring within the audit facility are managed by DB2 database and all negative SQLCODEs are reported back to the caller. • **NORMAL**. Any errors generated by db2audit are ignored and only the SQLCODEs for the errors associated with the operation being performed are returned to the application.
extract file	Specifies that audit records are to be copied from the audit log to an external file. If no optional clauses are specified, all of the audit records are extracted and placed in a flat report file. (If the output file already exists, an error message is returned.)
extract delasc	Specifies that audit records are to be extracted from the audit log and placed in a delimited ASCII format suitable for loading into DB2 database relational tables. The output is placed in separate files: one for each category. The filenames used are: • audit.del • checking.del • objmaint.del • secmaint.del • sysadmin.del • validate.del • context.del
category	Indicates that just the audit records for the specified categories of audit events are to be extracted. If no categories are specified, records for all categories are eligible for extraction.
database	Indicates that just the audit records for a specified database are to be extracted. If no database is specified, records for all databases are eligible for extraction.

Table 6.4 db2 audit Command Options (Continued)

Option	Meaning
status	Indicates that just the audit records for the specified status are to be extracted. If no status is specified, records for all statuses are eligible for extraction
prune all	Specifies that all of the records in the audit log are to be deleted. If the audit facility is active and the "audit" category of events has been specified for auditing, then an audit record will be logged after the audit log is pruned.

Thus, if you wanted to start the DB2 audit facility on a server using the default configuration (where SCOPE is all of the categories available except CONTEXT, STATUS is FAILURE, and ERRORTYPE is NORMAL), you could do so by executing a db2audit command that looks something like this:

```
db2audit -start
```

On the other hand, if you wanted to stop the DB2 audit facility, you could do so by executing a db2audit command that looks something like this:

```
db2audit -stop
```

Depending upon how the DB2 audit facility has been configured, up to seven different categories of audit records may be produced. The categories that are available, along with information about when audit records are produced for each, can be seen in Table 6.5.

Table 6.5 db2 Audit Record Categories

Category	When Audit Records Are Generated
Audit (AUDIT)	Records are produced when audit settings are changed or the audit log is accessed.
Authorization Checking (CHECKING)	Records are produced when authorization checking is performed in response to an attempt to access or manipulate DB2 database objects or functions.
Object Maintenance (OBJMAINT)	Records are produced when data objects are created or dropped.

Table 6.5 db2 Audit Record Categories (Continued)	
Category	When Audit Records Are Generated
Security Maintenance (SECMAINT)	Records are produced when object/database privileges or Database Administrator (DBADM) authority is granted or revoked and when the security-related DB2 Database Manager configuration parameters (SYSADM_GROUP, SYSCTRL_GROUP, SYSMAINT_GROUP, or SYSMON_GROUP) are modified.
System Administration (SYSADMIN)	Records are produced when operations requiring System Administrator (SYSADM), System Control (SYSCTRL), or System Maintenance (SYSMAINT), authority are performed.
User Validation (VALIDATE)	Records are produced when users are authenticated or system security information is retrieved.
Operation Context (CONTEXT)	Records that show the operation context are produced when a database operation is performed. When used with the log's event correlator field, a group of events can be associated back to a single database operation. For example, a query statement for dynamic queries, a package identifier for static queries, or an indicator of the type of operation being performed, such as CONNECT, can provide needed context when analyzing audit results. It is important to note that because the SQL or XQuery statement providing the operation context is shown in its entirety and this statement might be very long, a single CONTEXT record can be very large.

In a partitioned database environment (DPF), most of these events will occur on the catalog and/or coordinator partitions. However, audit records can be generated by any of the database partitions, so part of each record contains information about the originating partition as well as the coordinator partition.

Any single operation on a database may result in the generation of several audit records. The actual number of records produced and written to the audit log file is dependant on the number of categories of events that are to be monitored and recorded as specified by the audit facility configuration file. Total record count is also dependant upon whether successes, failures, or both, are to be tracked. For this reason, it is important to be selective of the events to audit.

A Word About the AUDIT_BUF_SZ DB2 Database Manager Configuration Parameter

The timing of the writing of audit records to the audit log file can have a significant impact on the performance of databases running in the instance being audited. The writing of the audit records can take place synchronously or asynchronously and the value of the *audit_buf_sz* DB2 Database Manager configuration parameter determines when the writing of audit records is done. If the value of this configuration parameter is zero (0), writing is done synchronously. That is, the event generating the audit record will wait until the record is written to disk. And the wait associated with each record has a negative impact on performance.

If the *audit_buf_sz* configuration parameter is assigned a value that is greater than zero, record writing is done asynchronously. In this case, the value assigned to the *audit_buf_sz* configuration parameter represents the number of 4KB pages to set aside as an internal buffer; the internal buffer is used to cache a number of audit records before a group of them are written out to disk. Thus, the event generating an audit record will not wait until the record is written to disk and can continue its operation.

In the asynchronous case, it could be possible for audit records to remain in an unfilled buffer for some time. To prevent this from happening, DB2 will periodically force the writing of audit records to disk. An authorized user of the DB2 audit facility may also flush the audit buffer with an explicit request.

An audit buffer cannot be allocated dynamically. Instead, DB2 must be stopped and restarted before changes made to the *audit_buf_sz* configuration parameter will take effect.

Enhancements such as new audit categories, separate instance and database logs, and new ways to customize the audit configuration were made to the audit facility in DB2 Version 9.5. With these enhancements, you now have control over exactly which database objects are audited. Therefore, you no longer need to audit events that occur for database objects that you are not interested in. Consequently, the performance of auditing (and its performance impact on other database operations) has been greatly improved.

Enhancements available in DB2 9.5 are as follows:

- New database objects called audit policies can be used to control audit configuration within a database. Individual databases can have their own audit configurations, as can particular objects within a database, such as tables, or even users, groups, and roles.

In addition to providing easier access to the information that you need, this enhancement also improves performance, because less data needs to be written to disk.

- Auditing SQL statements is easier and produces less output. The new audit category, EXECUTE, allows you to audit just the SQL statement that is being run. Previously, you needed to audit the CONTEXT event to capture this detail.

- Audit logs exist for each database. There is now one audit log for the instance and one audit log for each database. This feature simplifies audit reviews.

- The audit log now has a customizable path. Control over the audit log path allows you to place audit logs on a large, high-speed disk, with the option of having separate disks for each node in a database partitioning (DPF) installation. This feature also allows you to archive the audit log offline, without having to extract data from it until necessary.

- You can archive audit logs. Archiving the audit log moves the current audit log to an archive directory while the server begins writing to a new, active audit log. When you extract data from an audit log to a database table, it is from an archived log, not the active audit log. This prevents performance degradation caused by locking of the active audit log.

- The Security Administrator manages the audit for each database. The Security Administrator is solely in control of configuring an audit for a database; the System Administrator no longer has this authority. The Security Administrator also has sufficient access to manipulate the audit log, issue the ARCHIVE command, and extract a log file into a table.

- You can audit new information in each category. The CURRENT CLIENT special registers allow values for a client user ID, accounting string, workstation name, and application name to be set within applications so that these values will be recorded in the audit data. Local and global transaction IDs can be recorded in audit data. This facilitates correlation between the audit log and the transaction log.

Practice Questions

Question 1

If the authentication type for an instance is set to KRB_SERVER_ENCRYPT, where will DB2 first try to authenticate the user?

- ○ A. At the client, using KERBEROS authentication.
- ○ B. At the server, using KERBEROS authentication.
- ○ C. At the client, using SERVER_ENCRYPT authentication.
- ○ D. At the server, using SERVER_ENCRYPT authentication.

Question 2

Which two of the following commands, when executed, will ensure that the Kerberos-based authentication plug-in (IBMKrb5) that is shipped with DB2 9 will be used to authenticate users? (Select two)

- ❑ A. UPDATE DBM CFG USING SRVCON_AUTH NOT_SPECIFIED
- ❑ B. UPDATE DBM CFG USING SRVCON_GSSPLUGIN_LIST IBMKrb5
- ❑ C. UPDATE DBM CFG USING AUTHENTICATION IBMKrb5
- ❑ D. UPDATE DBM CFG USING AUTHENTICATION GSSPLUGIN
- ❑ E. UPDATE DBM CFG USING AUTHENTICATION KRB_SERVER_ENCRYPT

Question 3

The authentication type for an instance has been set to KRB_SERVER_ENCRYPT, but a connection request was made from a client that does not support Kerberos authentication. What type of authentication will be used?

- ○ A. None – access will be denied
- ○ B. CLIENT
- ○ C. SERVER
- ○ D. SERVER_ENCRYPT

Question 4

If the following statement is used to create a table named TAB1:

```
CREATE TABLE tab1
     (col1   DECFLOAT,
      col2   LONG VARCHAR,
      col3   VARCHAR(100) FOR BIT DATA,
      col4   CLOB(100))
```

Which column in the table has been defined in a way that will allow its data to be protected with the ENCRYPT() function?

○ A. COL1

○ B. COL2

○ C. COL3

○ D. COL4

Question 5

User USER1 executed the following statements in the order shown:

```
SET ENCRYPTION PASSWORD = 'EXEC-0409';
INSERT INTO employee(name, ssn)
  VALUES ('John Doe', ENCRYPT('111-22-3333', 'HR-1118', 'Dept-
Birthdate'));
```

Later, if user USER2 attempts to execute the following query:

```
SELECT name, DECRYPT_CHAR(ssn) FROM employee
```

What will happen?

○ A. The query will fail because a password was not provided.

○ B. The query will execute; the value 'HR-1118' will be used as the password.

○ C. The query will execute; the value 'EXEC-0409' will be used as the password.

○ D. The query will execute; the password used to authenticate user USER2 will be used as the password.

Question 6

An application developer plans on using SQL statements that look like the following to populate a table named SALES:

```
INSERT INTO sales (po_number, amount)
  VALUES (ENCRYPT('Q108-7234-1111-2222', 'MyPassWord'), 225.00)
```

Which statement should be used to create the SALES table?

- ○ A. CREATE TABLE sales (po_number VARCHAR(19) FOR BIT DATA, amount DECIMAL(9,2))
- ○ B. CREATE TABLE sales (po_number VARCHAR(20) FOR BIT DATA, amount DECIMAL(9,2))
- ○ C. CREATE TABLE sales (po_number VARCHAR(30) FOR BIT DATA, amount DECIMAL(9,2))
- ○ D. CREATE TABLE sales (po_number VARCHAR(40) FOR BIT DATA, amount DECIMAL(9,2))

Question 7

Which method should be used to construct a Label-Based Access Control (LBAC) security label component that represents a company's organizational chart?

- ○ A. SET
- ○ B. TREE
- ○ C. HIERARCHY
- ○ D. ORGANIZATION

Question 8

A user with Security Administrator (SECADM) authority executes the following statements:

```
CREATE SECURITY LABEL COMPONENT sales_region
    TREE ('SALES_ORG' ROOT,
          'EAST_COAST' UNDER 'SALES_ORG',
          'CENTRAL' UNDER 'SALES_ORG',
          'WEST_COAST' UNDER 'SALES_ORG',
          'CENTRAL_NORTH' UNDER 'CENTRAL',
          'CENTRAL_SOUTH' UNDER 'CENTRAL');

CREATE SECURITY POLICY sales_region_policy
    COMPONENTS sales_region
    WITH DB2LBACRULES
    RESTRICT NOT AUTHORIZED WRITE SECURITY LABEL;

CREATE SECURITY LABEL sales_region_policy.sales_org
    COMPONENT sales_region 'SALES_ORG';
CREATE SECURITY LABEL sales_region_policy.east_coast
    COMPONENT sales_region 'EAST_COAST';
CREATE SECURITY LABEL sales_region_policy.central
    COMPONENT sales_region 'CENTRAL';
CREATE SECURITY LABEL sales_region_policy.central_north
    COMPONENT sales_region 'CENTRAL_NORTH';
CREATE SECURITY LABEL sales_region_policy.central_south
    COMPONENT sales_region 'CENTRAL_SOUTH';
CREATE SECURITY LABEL sales_region_policy.west_coast
    COMPONENT sales_region 'WEST_COAST';
GRANT SECURITY LABEL sales_region_policy.central
    TO USER user1 FOR READ ACCESS;
```

Later, a user with database administrator (DBADM) authority executes the following statements:

```
CREATE TABLE corp.sales
    (sales_date    DATE,
     sales_person  VARCHAR (15),
     region        VARCHAR (15),
     amount        DECIMAL(9,2),
     margin        INTEGER,
     region_tag    DB2SECURITYLABEL)
  SECURITY POLICY sales_region_policy;

GRANT ALL PRIVILEGES ON TABLE corp.sales TO user1;
```

If the table SALES is populated as follows:

SALES_DATE	SALES_PERSON	REGION	AMOUNT	MARGIN	REGION_TAG
06/04/2008	LEE	East-Coast	22000	50	sales_region_policy.east_coast
06/04/2008	SANDERS	West-Coast	18000	40	sales_region_policy.west_coast
07/10/2008	SNOW	Central-South	31000	30	sales_region_policy.central_south
07/12/2008	LEE	Central-North	27500	45	sales_region_policy.central_north

And if user USER1 executes the following query:

```
SELECT sales_date, sales_person, region, amount, margin,
  VARCHAR(SECLABEL_TO_CHAR('SALES_REGION_POLICY', REGION_TAG), 30)
FROM corp.sales
```

How many rows will be returned?

- ○ A. 0
- ○ B. 1
- ○ C. 2
- ○ D. 3

Question 9

Which of the following is NOT a valid statement about the DB2 9 audit facility?

- ○ A. The DB2 audit facility works at the instance level, recording both instance-level and database-level activities.
- ○ B. The DB2 audit facility monitors a set of events that have been defined by IBM, based on problems encountered in the field over the years.
- ○ C. Since the DB2 audit facility works independently of the DB2 server, it will continue to run once started, even if the DB2 instance is stopped.
- ○ D. The DB2 audit facility is controlled by the db2audit command and the contents of an audit configuration file named db2audit.cfg.

Question 10

A database administrator executed the following command before starting the DB2 9 audit facility:

```
UPDATE DBM CFG USING AUDIT_BUF_SZ 200 IMMEDIATE
```

Which two of the following statements are correct? (Select two)

- ❑ A. Two hundred kilobytes of storage will be set aside as an internal buffer to cache audit records.
- ❑ B. Two hundred 4 KB pages will be set aside as an internal buffer to cache audit records.
- ❑ C. Audit records will be written synchronously to the audit log file.
- ❑ D. Audit records will be written asynchronously to the audit log file.
- ❑ E. The change to the audit_buf_sz configuration parameter will take effect immediately.

Answers

Question 1

The correct answer is **B**. If the authentication type for an instance is set to KRB_SERVER_ ENCRYPT, authentication occurs at the server where the DB2 instance is running, using either the KERBEROS or the SERVER_ENCRYPT authentication method. If the client's authentication type is set to KERBEROS, authentication is performed at the server using the Kerberos security system. If the client's authentication type is set to anything other than KERBEROS, or if the Kerberos authentication service is unavailable, the server acts as if the SERVER_ENCRYPT authentication type was specified, and the rules of this authentication method apply.

Question 2

The correct answers are **A** and **E**. Although the value assigned to the *authentication* DB2 Database Manager (DBM) configuration parameter determines how and where user authentication takes place, this value can be overridden for a particular server by assigning a different value to the *srvcon_auth* configuration parameter. (The *srvcon_auth* DBM configuration parameter is used to specify how and where authentication is to take place when handling connections at the server; if this parameter is not assigned a value, DB2 uses the current value of the authentication configuration parameter.

Unless otherwise specified, the DB2 Kerberos plug-in library IBMkrb5 is used on AIX, Linux, Sun Solaris, and Windows operating systems when the client is authenticated using KERBEROS or KRB_SERVER_ENCRYPT authentication. Therefore, to configure an instance to use the Kerberos-based authentication plug-in (IBMKrb5) that is shipped with DB2 9 to authenticate users, you must either assign the value KERBEROS or KRB_SERVER_ENCRYPT to the *srvcon_auth* configuration parameter or assign the value NOT_SPECIFIED to the *srvcon_ auth* configuration parameter and assign the value KERBEROS or KRB_SERVER_ENCRYPT to the *authentication* configuration parameter.

Question 3

The correct answer is **D**. If the authentication type for an instance is set to KRB_SERVER_ ENCRYPT, authentication occurs at the server where the DB2 instance is running, using either the KERBEROS or the SERVER_ENCRYPT authentication method. If the client's authentication type is set to KERBEROS, authentication is performed at the server using the Kerberos security system. If the client's authentication type is set to anything other than KERBEROS, or if the Kerberos authentication service is not supported, the server acts as if the SERVER_ENCRYPT authentication type was specified, and the rules of this authentication method apply.

Question 4

The correct answer is **C**. The result data type of the ENCRYPT() function is VARCHAR FOR BIT DATA. Therefore, when creating a table that is to hold encrypted data, each column that is to be encrypted must be assigned the data type VARCHAR FOR BIT DATA. Column COL3 is the only column in the table TAB1 that has been assigned this data type.

Question 5

The correct answer is **C**. If a password is not explicitly provided when data is encrypted using the ENCRYPT() function, data will be encrypted using the encryption password value that was assigned for the session. (The same is true if a password is not explicitly provided when data is decrypted using the DECRYPT_CHAR() or the DECRYPT_BIN() function.) An encryption password can be set for a session by executing the SET ENCRYPTION PASSWORD SQL statement. The syntax for this statement is:

```
SET ENCRYPTION PASSWORD <=> [Password]
```

where:

Password   Identifies the password to be used to generate the key that will be used to encrypt and decrypt data each time the ENCRYPT(), DECRYPT_CHAR(), and DECRYPT_BIN() functions are executed in the current session. The password specified must be between 6 and 127 characters in length and must be in the exact case desired since DB2 does not automatically convert passwords into upper case. The password specified cannot be null.

Thus, if you wanted to specify that all data encryption and decryption operations performed during the current session are to use the password "EXEC_0409", you could do so by executing a SET ENCRYPTION PASSWORD SQL statement that looks something like this:

```
SET ENCRYPTION PASSWORD = 'EXEC-0409'
```

Question 6

The correct answer is **D**. The result data type of the ENCRYPT() function is VARCHAR FOR BIT DATA. Therefore, when creating a table that is to hold encrypted data, each column that is to be encrypted must be assigned the data type VARCHAR FOR BIT DATA. How large an encrypted column must be is determined, in part by the decision to store password hint information with the encrypted data. If a hint will not be provided, the length of the column must be the length of the unencrypted data + 8 bytes for the password, rounded up to the next 8-byte boundary. For example, if you wanted to encrypt a string that is 11 bytes long and forego providing a password hint, you would need to define a column that is capable of holding 24 bytes (11 + 8 = 17; 17 + 5 to reach the next 8-byte boundary = 24). If a hint will be provided, the length of the column must be the length of the unencrypted data + 8 bytes for the password, rounded up to the next 8-byte boundary + 32 bytes for the hint.

Because in this example, you want to encrypt a string that is 19 bytes long and forego providing a password hint, you would need to define a column that is capable of holding at least 32 bytes (19 + 8 = 27; 27 + 5 to reach the next 8-byte boundary = 32). In answer D, the column PO_NUMBER is assigned the data type VARCHAR FOR BIT DATA and its size is 40 bytes, which is greater than the 32 bytes needed.

Question 7

The correct answer is **B**. Security label components represent criteria that may be used to decide whether a user should have access to specific data. Three types of security label components can exist:

- **SET.** A set is a collection of elements (character string values) where the order in which each element appears is not important.
- **Array.** An array is an ordered set that can represent a simple hierarchy. In an array, the order in which the elements appear is important—the first element ranks higher than the second, the second ranks higher than the third, and so on.
- **TREE.** A tree represents a more complex hierarchy that can have multiple nodes and branches.

Question 8

The correct answer is **C**. When user USER1 queries the SALES table, all records with the security label SALES_REGION_POLICY.CENTRAL_NORTH and SALES_REGION_POLICY.CENTRAL_SOUTH will appear (because the security label SALES_REGION_POLICY.CENTRAL – the security label assigned to user USER1 – is at a higher level in the security policy's security label component tree).

Question 9

The correct answer is **B**. The DB2 audit facility monitors database events that you tell it to keep track of, and records information about those events in an audit log file. By analyzing the information stored in the audit log file, you can quickly pinpoint usage patterns that identify system misuse; once identified, you can take appropriate action to minimize or eliminate the problem. The DB2 audit facility works at the instance level, recording both instance-level and database-level activities. Since the DB2 audit facility works independently of the DB2 server, it will continue to run once started, even if the DB2 instance is stopped. In fact, when an instance is stopped, an audit record may be written to the audit log.

The DB2 audit facility is controlled by the db2audit command and the contents of an audit configuration file named db2audit.cfg, which is located in the sqllib/security subdirectory under the instance owner's home directory. (By default the audit log file, db2audit.log, is written to this directory as well.) In order to capture audit records you must start the audit facility, and before audit log files can be examined the audit facility must be stopped. When the audit facility is started, it uses the existing audit configuration file to determine what events to monitor.

Question 10

The correct answers are **B** and **D**. The value of the *audit_buf_sz* DB2 Database Manager configuration parameter determines when the writing of audit records is performed. If the value of this configuration parameter is zero (0), writing is performed synchronously. That is, the event generating the audit record will wait until the record is written to disk. And the wait associated with each record has a negative impact on performance.

If the *audit_buf_sz* configuration parameter is assigned a value that is greater than zero, record writing is performed asynchronously. In this case, the value assigned to the *audit_buf_sz* configuration parameter represents the number of 4 KB pages to set aside as an internal buffer; the internal buffer is used to cache a number of audit records before a group of them are written out to disk. Thus, the event generating an audit record will not wait until the record is written to disk, and can continue its operation.

An audit buffer cannot be allocated dynamically. Instead, the instance must be stopped and restarted before changes made to the *audit_buf_sz* configuration parameter will take effect.

CHAPTER 7

Connectivity and Networking

Ten percent (10%) of the DB2 9 for Linux, UNIX, and Windows Advanced Database Administration exam (Exam 734) is designed to test your ability to configure client/server connectivity, as well as your ability to manage connections to System z and System i host databases. The questions that make up this portion of the exam are intended to evaluate the following:

- Your ability to configure client/server connectivity

- Your ability to configure and use DB2 Discovery

- Your ability to manage connections to System z and System i host databases

- Your ability to identify and resolve connection problems

This chapter is designed to walk you through the process of configuring communications and the processes of cataloging remote databases, remote servers (nodes), and Database Connection Services (DCS) databases. This chapter is also designed to introduce you to DB2 Discovery and to provide you with the ability to manage connections to System z and System i host databases.

Configuring Communications

In a typical client/server environment, databases stored on a server are accessed by applications stored on remote client workstations using what is known as a distributed connection. In addition to providing client applications with a way to access a centralized database located on a remote server, a distributed connection also provides a way for administrators to manage databases and servers remotely.

In order to communicate with a server, each client must use some type of communications protocol recognized by the server. Likewise, each server must use some type of communications protocol to detect inbound requests from clients. In most cases, the operating system being used on both machines provides the communications protocol support needed; however, in some cases, this support may be provided by a separate add-on product. In either case, both clients and servers must be configured to use a communications protocol recognized by DB2. DB2 9 recognizes the following communications protocols:

- NetBios
- Transmission Control Protocol/Internet Protocol (TCP/IP) (which is used today in an overwhelming majority of cases)
- Named pipe

When DB2 is installed on a client or server, it is automatically configured to take advantage of any communications protocols that have been set up for that particular machine (provided the protocols found are recognized by DB2). At that time, information about each supported communications protocol available is collected and stored in the configuration files for both the DAS instance and the default instance as they are created. Unfortunately, this information is not updated automatically when a new protocol is activated or when an existing protocol is reconfigured. Instead, you must manually configure communications for each instance before such changes will be reflected.

Manually Configuring Communications

The easiest way to manually configure communications or make communications configuration changes is by using the Setup communications dialog, which can be activated by selecting the appropriate action from the Instances menu found in the Control Center. Figure 7–1 shows the Control Center menu items that must be selected in order to activate the Setup communications dialog; Figure 7–2 shows how the Setup communications dialog might be used to configure the TCP/IP protocol for a particular instance.

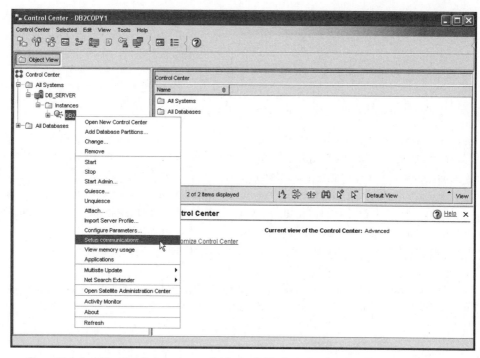

Figure 7–1: Invoking the Setup communications dialog from the Control Center.

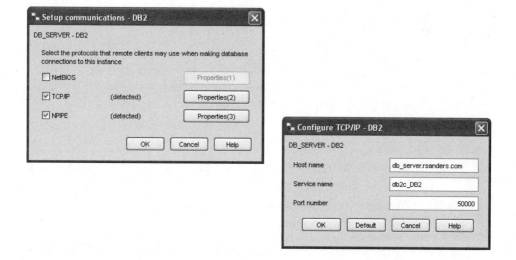

Figure 7–2: The Setup communications dialog and the Configure TCP/IP dialog.

If you choose to configure communications without using the Setup communications dialog, the steps you must follow can vary according to the communications protocol being used. For example, if you wanted to configure a server to use TCP/IP, you would perform the following steps (in any order):

1. Assign the value TCPIP to the DB2COMM registry variable.

   Whenever you manually configure communications for a server, you must update the value of the DB2COMM registry variable before an instance can begin using the desired communications protocol. The value assigned to the DB2COMM registry variable is used to determine which communications managers will be activated when a particular instance is started. (If the DB2COMM registry variable is not set correctly, one or more errors may be generated when DB2 attempts to start protocol support during instance initialization.)

   The DB2COMM registry variable is assigned the value TCPIP by executing a db2set command that looks something like this:

   ```
   db2set DB2COMM=TCPIP
   ```

   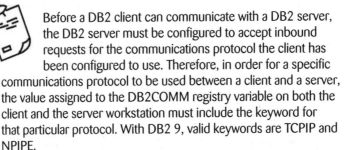

   Before a DB2 client can communicate with a DB2 server, the DB2 server must be configured to accept inbound requests for the communications protocol the client has been configured to use. Therefore, in order for a specific communications protocol to be used between a client and a server, the value assigned to the DB2COMM registry variable on both the client and the server workstation must include the keyword for that particular protocol. With DB2 9, valid keywords are TCPIP and NPIPE.

2. Assign the name of the TCP/IP port that the database server will use to receive communications from remote clients to the *svcename* parameter of the DB2 Database Manager configuration file.

   The svcename parameter should be set to the service name associated with the main connection port, or to the port number itself, so that when the database server is started, it can determine on which port to listen for incoming connection requests. This parameter is set by executing an UPDATE

DATABASE MANAGER CONFIGURATION command that looks something like this:

```
UPDATE DBM CFG USING SVCENAME db2c_db2inst1
```

3. Update the services file on the database server, if appropriate.

The TCP/IP services file identifies the ports on which server applications will listen for client requests. If you specified a service name in the *svcename* parameter of the DB2 Database Manager configuration file, the appropriate service name-to-port number/protocol mapping must be added to the services file on the server. If you specified a port number in the *svcename* parameter, the services file does not need to be updated.

The default location of the services file depends on the operating system being used: on UNIX systems, the services file is named *services* and is located in the */etc* directory; on Windows systems, the services file is located in *%SystemRoot%\system32\drivers\etc*. An entry in the services file for DB2 might look something like this:

```
db2c_db2inst1        50001/tcp
```

DB2's Directory Files

Because databases can reside anywhere on a network, each DB2 instance must know where databases that fall under its control are physically located, as well as how to establish connections to those databases on behalf of users and applications. To keep track of this information, DB2 9 uses a special set of files known as directory files (or directories). Four types of directories exist:

- System database directory
- Local database directory
- Node directory
- Database Connection Services (DCS) directory

The System Database Directory

The system database directory resides in a file named *sqldbdir* that gets created automatically when the first database for an instance is created. Information about the new database is then recorded in the system database directory, and as additional databases are cataloged, information about those databases is recorded as well. Each entry recorded in the system database directory contains the following information:

- The name assigned to the database when the database was created (or explicitly cataloged)

- The alias assigned to the database (which is the same as the database name if no alias was specified when the database was created/cataloged)

- Descriptive information about the database (if that information is available)

- The location of the local database directory file that contains additional information about the database

- The location of the database itself:

  - A *Remote* entry describes a database that resides on another node.

  - An *Indirect* entry describes a database that is local. Databases that reside on the same node as the system database directory are thought to indirectly reference the home entry (to a local database directory), and are considered indirect entries.

  - A *Home* entry indicates that the database directory is on the same path as the local database directory.

  - An *LDAP* entry indicates that the database location information is stored on an LDAP server.

- Other system information, including the code page the database was created under

The contents of the system database directory or a local database directory file can be viewed by executing the LIST DATABASE DIRECTORY command. The syntax for this command is:

```
LIST [DATABASE | DB] DIRECTORY <ON [Location]>
```

where:

Location   Identifies the drive or directory where one or more databases are stored.

If no location is specified when this command is executed, the contents of the system database directory file will be displayed. On the other hand, if a location is specified, the contents of the local database directory file that exists at that particular location will be displayed.

The Local Database Directory

Any time a DB2 9 database is created in a new location (i.e., a drive or a directory), a local database directory file is also created at that location. Information about that database is then recorded in the local database directory, and as other databases are created in that location, information about those databases is recorded in the local database directory as well. Thus, although only one system database directory exists for a particular instance, several local database directories can exist, depending upon how databases have been distributed across the storage available.

Each entry recorded in a local database directory contains the following information:

- The name assigned to the database when the database was created (or explicitly cataloged)

- The alias assigned to the database (which is the same as the database name, if no alias was specified when the database was created/cataloged)

- Descriptive information about the database (if that information is available)

- The name of the root directory of the hierarchical tree used to store information about the database

- Other system information, including the code page the database was created under

As mentioned earlier, the contents of a local database directory file can be viewed by executing the LIST DATABASE DIRECTORY command.

The Node Directory

Unlike the system database directory and the local database directory, which are used to keep track of what databases exist and where they are stored, the node directory contains information that identifies how and where remote systems or instances can be found. A node directory file is created on each client the first time a remote server or instance is cataloged. As other remote instances/servers are cataloged, information about those instances/servers is recorded in the node directory as well. Entries in the node directory are then used in conjunction with entries in the system database directory to make connections and instance attachments to DB2 databases stored on remote servers.

Each entry recorded in the node directory contains the following information:

- The name assigned to the node when the node was explicitly cataloged

- Descriptive information about the node (if that information is available)

- The operating system used at the remote database server

- The communication protocol to be used to communicate between the client workstation and the remote database server

- The TCP/IP hostname or the remote TCP/IP address of the node where the remote database resides (if the protocol used is TCP/IP)

- The TCP/IP service name or the port number of the remote instance (if the protocol used is TCP/IP)

The contents of the node directory file can be viewed by executing the LIST NODE DIRECTORY command. The syntax for this command is:

```
LIST <ADMIN> NODE DIRECTORY <SHOW DETAIL>
```

If the ADMIN option is specified when this command is executed, information about administration servers will be displayed.

The Database Connection Services (DCS) Directory

Using an add-on product called DB2 Connect, it is possible for DB2 for Linux, UNIX, and Windows clients to establish a connection to a DRDA Application Server, such as:

- DB2 for z/OS databases on System z architecture host computers.

- DB2 for VM and VSE databases on System z architecture host computers.

- DB2 databases on Application System/400 (AS/400) and System i computers.

Because the information needed to connect to DRDA host databases is different from the information used to connect to LAN-based databases, information about remote host databases is kept in a special directory known as the Database Connection Services (DCS) directory. If an entry in the DCS directory has a database name that corresponds to the name of a database stored in the system database directory, the specified Application Requester (which, in most cases, is DB2 Connect) can forward SQL requests to the database that resides on a remote DRDA server.

The contents of the DCS directory file can be viewed by executing the LIST DCS DIRECTORY command. The syntax for this command is:

```
LIST DCS DIRECTORY
```

It is important to note that the DCS directory only exists if the DB2 Connect product has been installed.

Cataloging Remote Servers and Databases

Once a server has been configured for communications, any client that wishes to access a database on the server must be configured to communicate with the server. But that's just the first step. Entries for both the server and the remote database must also be added to the system database and node directories on the client. (Entries must also be added to the DCS directory if the client intends to connect to a System z or System i database via DB2 Connect.) Entries are added to DB2's directories using a process known as cataloging.

Cataloging a DB2 Database

Because a database is implicitly cataloged as soon as it is created, most users never have to be concerned with the cataloging process. However, if you want to access a database stored on a remote server, you will need to become familiar with the tools that can be used to catalog DB2 databases. Fortunately, cataloging a database is a relatively straightforward process and can be done using the Control Center or the Configuration Assistant or by executing the CATALOG DATABASE command.

By highlighting the Databases object shown in the objects pane of the Control Center and right-clicking the mouse button, it is possible to bring up a menu that contains a list of options available for database objects. The dialog used to catalog databases (the Add Database dialog) is invoked by selecting "Add . . . " from this menu. Figure 7-3 shows the Control Center menu items that must be selected in order to activate the Add Database dialog; Figure 7-4 shows what the Add Database dialog looks like when it is first activated.

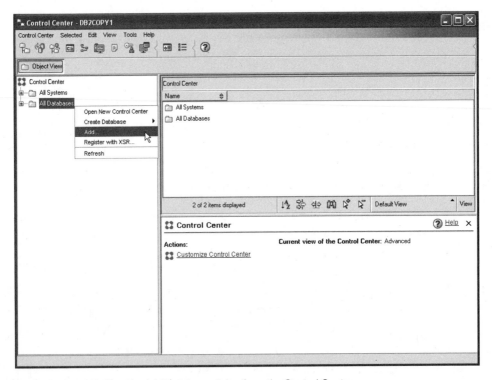

Figure 7–3: Invoking the Add Database dialog from the Control Center.

Figure 7–4: The Add Database dialog.

You can also catalog a database by executing the CATALOG DATABASE command. The syntax for this command is:

```
CATALOG [DATABASE | DB] [DatabaseName]
<AS [Alias]>
<ON [Path] | AT NODE [NodeName]>
<AUTHENTICATION [AuthenticationType]>
<WITH "[Description]">
```

where:

DatabaseName   Identifies the name that has been assigned to the database to be cataloged.

Alias   Identifies the alias that is to be assigned to the database when it is cataloged.

Path	Identifies the location (drive and/or directory) where the directory hierarchy and files associated with the database to be cataloged are physically stored.
NodeName	Identifies the node where the database to be cataloged resides. The node name specified should match an entry in the node directory file (i.e., should correspond to a node that has already been cataloged).
AuthenticationType	Identifies where and how authentication is to take place when a user attempts to access the database. The following values are valid for this parameter: SERVER, CLIENT, SERVER_ENCRYPT, KERBEROS TARGET PRINCIPAL [*PrincipalName*] (where *PrincipalName* is the fully qualified Kerberos principal name for the target server), DATA_ENCRYPT, and GSSPLUGIN.
Description	A comment used to describe the database entry that is to be made in the database directory for the database to be cataloged. The description must be enclosed by double quotation marks.

Thus, if you wanted to catalog a database that physically resides in the directory /home/db2data and that has been given the name "TEST_DB", you could do so by executing a CATALOG DATABASE command that looks something like this:

```
CATALOG DATABASE test_db AS test
ON /home/db2data
AUTHENTICATION SERVER
```

Cataloging a Remote Server (Node)

The process used to catalog nodes (servers) is significantly different from the process used to catalog databases. Instead of being explicitly cataloged as needed, nodes are usually implicitly cataloged whenever a remote database is cataloged via the Configuration Assistant. However, if you desire to explicitly catalog a particular node (server), you can do so by executing the CATALOG . . . NODE command that corresponds to the communications protocol that will be used to access the server being cataloged. Several forms of the CATALOG . . . NODE command are available, including:

- CATALOG LOCAL NODE

- CATALOG LDAP NODE

- CATALOG NAMED PIPE NODE

- CATALOG TCPIP NODE

The syntax for all of these commands is very similar, the major difference being that many of the options available with each are specific to the communications protocol for which the command has been tailored. Because TCP/IP is probably the most common communications protocol in use today, let's take a look at the syntax for that form of the CATALOG . . . NODE command.

The syntax for the CATALOG TCPIP NODE command is:

```
CATALOG <ADMIN> [TCPIP | TCPIP4 | TCPIP6] NODE [NodeName]
REMOTE [IPAddress | HostName]
SERVER [ServiceName | PortNumber]
<SECURITY SOCKS>
<REMOTE INSTANCE [InstanceName]>
<SYSTEM [SystemName]>
<OSTYPE [SystemType]>
<WITH "[Description]">
```

where:

NodeName	Identifies the alias to be assigned to the node to be cataloged. This is an arbitrary name created on the user's workstation and is used to identify the node.
IPAddress	Identifies the IP address of the server where the remote database that you are trying to communicate with resides.
HostName	Identifies the host name, as it is known to the TCP/IP network. (This is the name of the server where the remote database that you are trying to communicate with resides.)
ServiceName	Identifies the service name that the DB2 Database Manager instance on the server uses to communicate.
PortNumber	Identifies the port number that the DB2 Database Manager instance on the server uses to communicate.

InstanceName   Identifies the name of the server instance to which an attachment is to be made.

SystemName   Identifies the DB2 system name used to identify the server workstation.

SystemType   Identifies the type of operating system being used on the server workstation. The following values are valid for this parameter: AIX, WIN, HPUX, SUN, OS390, OS400, VM, VSE, and LINUX.

Description   A comment used to describe the node entry that is to be made in the node directory for the node being cataloged. The description must be enclosed by double quotation marks.

Either the remote TCP/IP hostname or the remote IP address can be used to catalog a node. If a hostname is specified, it must be resolved at the client, either through Domain Name Server (DNS) lookup or by an entry in the local TCP/IP hosts file (i.e., the /etc/hosts file on Linux and UNIX servers). For DB2 for z/OS remote hosts, the hostname can be seen in the DSNL004I message (DOMAIN=hostname) when the Distributed Data Facility (DDF) is started— provided the target database has been set up for TCP/IP communications; if accessing a z/OS data sharing group, the domain name should map to the DB2 group dynamic VIPA address, which routes to the least loaded DB2 member. To access a specific member, use the specific DB2 member dynamic VIPA address and turn off sysplex routing. (Each member DSNL004I message displays the member specific domain name.)

Likewise, either the remote TCP/IP service name or the remote TCP/IP port number can be used when cataloging a node. Port number 446 has been registered as the default port number to use for DRDA connections. For DB2 for z/OS remote hosts, the port number is defined in the Boot Strap Data Set (BSDS) as PORT and can also be seen in the DSNL004I message (TCPPORT=portnumber) when the Distributed Data Facility (DDF) is started.

So, if you wanted to catalog a node for an AIX server named DB2HOST that has a DB2 instance named DB2INST1 that listens on port 60000, and assign it the alias RMT_SERVER, you could do so by executing a CATALOG TCPIP NODE command that looks something like this:

```
CATALOG TCPIP NODE rmt_server
REMOTE db2host
SERVER 60000
OSTYPE AIX
WITH "A remote AIX TCP/IP node"
```

A Word About IPv4 and IPv6

Between 1973 and 1983, while working under contract for the U.S. Department of Defense, Vinton Cerf, Robert Kahn, and others devised a networking system that enabled them to connect dissimilar computer systems. Their work led to the introduction of the Transmission Control Protocol/Internet Protocol (TCP/IP) protocol, which allows data to be broken up into packets and sent from one computer to another over an end-to-end network. TCP/IP is named after two of the most important protocols found in it: the Transmission Control Protocol (TCP) and the Internet Protocol (IP). The sole purpose of the Internet Protocol is to provide unique global computer addressing to ensure that two computers communicating over a network can uniquely identify one another. IPv4 is the fourth iteration of Internet Protocol and the first version of the protocol to be widely deployed. (Version numbers 0 through 3 were development versions used between 1977 and 1979.)

In the beginning, TCP/IP networks were "friendly" environments that used physically secure connections to link computers together. However, the exponential growth of the Internet has brought about a more "hostile" environment, and TCP/IP networks based on IPv4 are vulnerable to a variety of security threats. (Today, most of the Internet uses IPv4, which remains remarkably resilient in spite of its age.) More important, there is a growing shortage of IPv4 addresses, which are needed by every machine that gets added to the Internet.

Aware of the limitations IPv4 imposed on the current Internet infrastructure, the Network Working Group of the Internet Engineering Task Force (IETF) proposed a new suite of protocols in 1998 called Internet Protocol version 6 (IPv6). This new suite of protocols addresses several of the issues that affect IPv4-based networks, including its lack of network level security. Although IPv6 is not an extension of IPv4, but rather an entirely new suite of protocols, it retains many of the design features that have made IPv4 so successful.

The largest improvement provided by IPv6 is the increase in the number of addresses available for networked devices. IPv4 supports about 4.3 billion addresses, which is inadequate for giving even a single address to every living person, let alone supporting embedded and portable devices. IPv6, however, supports 3.4×10^{38} addresses. With such a large address space available, IPv6 nodes can have as many universally scoped addresses as they need, and network address translation is no longer required.

IPv6 is expected to gradually replace IPv4, with the two coexisting for a number of years during a transition period. Because of this, the CATALOG TCPIP NODE command has been designed to handle both IPv4 and IPV6 format addresses. Therefore, if you wanted to catalog a node for a Linux server that has the IPv4 address 192.0.32.67 and a DB2 instance named DB2INST1 that is listening on port 50000, and assign it the alias IPV4_SERVER, you could do so by executing a CATALOG TCPIP NODE command that looks more like this:

```
CATALOG TCPIP4 NODE ipv4_server
REMOTE 192.0.32.67
SERVER 50000
OSTYPE LINUX
WITH "A remote Linux TCP/IP-IPv4 node"
```

On the other hand, if you wanted to catalog a node for a Linux server that has the IPv6 address 1080:0:0:0:8:800:200C:417A and a DB2 instance named DB2INST1 that is listening on port 50000 and assign it the alias IPV6_SERVER, you could do so by executing a CATALOG TCPIP NODE command that looks more like this:

```
CATALOG TCPIP6 NODE ipv6_server
REMOTE 1080:0:0:0:8:800:200C:417A
SERVER 50000
OSTYPE LINUX
WITH "A remote Linux TCP/IP-IPv6 node"
```

Cataloging a DCS Database

Aside from the fact that neither the Control Center nor the Configuration Assistant can be used, the process for cataloging a Database Connection Services (DCS) database is very similar to that used to catalog a regular DB2 database. A DCS database is cataloged by executing the CATALOG DCS DATABASE command. The syntax for this command is:

```
CATALOG DCS [DATABASE | DB] [Alias]
<AS [TargetName]>
<AR [LibraryName]>
<PARMS "[ParameterString]">
<WITH "[Description]">
```

where:

Alias	Identifies the alias of the target database to be cataloged. This name should match an entry in the system database directory associated with the remote node.
TargetName	Identifies the name of the target host database to be cataloged. (If the host database to be cataloged resides on a OS/390 or z/OS server, the *TargetName* specified should refer to a DB2 for z/OS subsystem identified by its LOCATION NAME or one of the alias LOCATION names defined on the z/OS server. The LOCATION NAME can be determined by logging in to TSO and issuing the following SQL query using one of the available query tools: SELECT CURRENT SERVER FROM SYSIBM.SYSDUMMY1.)
LibraryName	Identifies the name of the Application Requester library to be loaded and used to access the remote database listed in the DCS directory.
ParameterString	Identifies a parameter string to be passed to the Application Requestor when it is invoked. The parameter string must be enclosed by double quotation marks.
Description	A comment used to describe the database entry that is to be made in the DCS directory for the database to be cataloged. The description must be enclosed by double quotation marks (").

Thus, if you wanted to catalog a DB2 for z/OS database residing in the DSN_DB_1 subsystem on the z/OS server that has the name PAYROLL and assign it the alias TEST_DB, you could do so by executing a CATALOG DCS DATABASE command that looks something like this:

```
CATALOG DCS DATABASE test_db
AS dsn_db_1
WITH "DB2 for z/OS LOCATION NAME DSN_DB_1"
```

It is important to note that an entry for the database alias TEST_DB also has to exist in the system database directory before the entry in the DCS database directory can be used to connect to the z/OS database.

Configuring Communications to System z and System i Database Servers

Before you can access data stored in a DB2 for z/OS or a DB2 for i5/OS database, you must configure TCP/IP communications between a client that is running DB2 Connect (i.e., a DB2 Connect server) and a System z or System i host. Then you must catalog the remote server and the database. In other words, you must perform the following steps (from the DB2 Connect server):

1. Configure TCP/IP communications on the DB2 Connect server.

2. Catalog the TCP/IP node.

3. Catalog the System z or System i database as a DCS database.

4. Catalog the System z or System i database.

5. Bind utilities and applications to the System z or System i database server.

Most of the steps used to establish a connection between a DB2 Connect and a System z or System i host database are identical to the steps used to configure a client so that it can access a database stored on a remote server. The most significant difference between the two processes is the step that requires the host database to be cataloged as a DCS database and the step that requires DB2 utilities and applications to be bound to the System z or System i host database.

Binding Utilities and Applications

Before DB2-specific utilities and applications such as the Import utility, the Export utility, and the Command Line Processor can be used with a database that resides on a System z or System i host, they must be "bound" to the database. During the "binding" process, a package—an object that includes all of the information needed to process specific SQL statements used by a utility or application—is created and stored in the database. In a network environment, if you are using multiple clients that run on different operating systems or are at different versions or service levels of DB2, you must bind the utilities once for each operating system/DB2 version combination used.

To bind DB2 utilities and applications to a database on a System z or System i server, simply perform the following steps (again, from the DB2 Connect server):

1. Go to the directory on the DB2 Connect server where the DB2-specific utility and application bind files are stored. On Linux and UNIX, these bind files can be found in the *sqllib/bnd* subdirectory of the home directory of the instance user; on Windows, these bind files can be found in the *bnd* subdirectory of the *sqllib* directory where DB2 was installed.

2. Using the Command Editor or the Command Line Processor, establish a connection to the database stored on the System z or System i server by executing a command that looks something like this:

   ```
   CONNECT TO [DatabaseAlias]
   ```

where:

ServerName   Identifies the alias that was assigned to the database on the System z or System i server when the database was cataloged.

3. Bind the DB2-specific utilities and applications to the database stored on the System z or System i server by executing the following commands (from the Command Editor or the Command Line Processor):

   ```
   BIND @db2ubind.lst MESSAGES ubind.msg GRANT PUBLIC;
   BIND @db2cli.lst MESSAGES clibind.msg GRANT PUBLIC;
   ```

   The file db2ubind.lst contains a list of the bind files (.bnd) needed to create packages for DB2's database utilities; the file db2cli.lst contains a list of the bind files (.bnd) needed to create packages for the DB2 Call Level Interface (CLI) and the DB2 ODBC driver. When these two commands are executed, any messages produced by the Bind utility will be written to files named ubind.msg and clibind.msg, and the group PUBLIC will receive EXECUTE and BINDADD privileges for each package produced.

4. Terminate the connection to the database stored on the System z or System i server by executing a command (from the Command Editor or the Command Line Processor) that looks like this:

   ```
   CONNECT RESET;
   ```

If you have BINDADD authority, the first time you use
the DB2 CLI or ODBC driver, the DB2 CLI packages will
be bound automatically. If any applications you are using
require binding, you can use the Configuration Assistant's
Bind facility or the BIND command to bind them to the System z or
System i database.

A Word About the db2schema.bnd Bind File

When a database is created or migrated on a Linux, UNIX, or Windows DB2
server, a file named db2schema.bnd is automatically bound to the database as part
of the database creation/migration process. This bind file exists only on these types
of servers and is used to create a package that provides system catalog function
support. If, for some reason, this package is missing (for example, if a fix pack
was applied on the server, if the package was intentionally dropped by a user, or if
an SQL1088W warning was generated when a database was created or migrated),
the db2schema.bnd file must be rebound to the database (stored locally on the
server).

On Linux and UNIX workstations, the db2schema.bnd bind file can be found in
the *sqllib/bnd* subdirectory of the home directory of the instance user; on Windows
workstations, this bind file can be found in the *bnd* subdirectory of the *sqllib*
directory where DB2 was installed. To bind this file to a database, simply execute
a BIND command that looks something like this:

```
BIND db2schema.bnd BLOCKING ALL GRANT PUBLIC
```

When binding utilities and applications to a System z or System i database server
in order to configure a DB2 Connect server so that it can access a database stored
on a System z or System i host, the db2schema.bnd file should NEVER be
included in the set of files being bound. Attempting to do so may lead to corruption
of data in the host database.

Considerations for System z Sysplex Exploitation

A Sysplex is a collection of System z servers that cooperate, using hardware and
software, to process work. The Sysplex coordinates the cooperation by increasing

the number of processors working together, which increases the amount of work that can be processed. In addition to an increase in processing capability, a Sysplex can provide flexibility in mixing levels of hardware and software and in dynamically adding systems. DB2 Connect support for Sysplex is enabled by default; Sysplex support to a host database can be turned off by removing the SYSPLEX parameter from its DCS directory entry, but the DCS entry itself must not be removed, even if it has no other parameters specified.

When connected to a DB2 for z/OS database server running in a data sharing environment, DB2 Connect will spread the workload among the different DB2 subsystems that make up the data sharing group, based on a prioritized list of Sysplex members that is provided by the Workload Manager (WLM). This list is used by DB2 Connect to handle incoming CONNECT requests by distributing them among the Sysplex members with the highest assigned priorities. (If the DB2 Connect connection concentrator is enabled, this list is also used when determining where to send each transaction.) To assist with load balancing, this Sysplex server list is obtained each time a connection is established.

The Sysplex server list is rendered inaccessible if there are no agents available and if no connections to a host database exist. Therefore, connection pooling must be enabled and at least one agent must be available when working with Sysplex servers. Connection pooling is enabled whenever the maximum number of agents allowed to be pooled on a DB2 instance is greater than zero—this number is determined by the value assigned to the *num_poolagents* DB2 Database Manager configuration parameter.

Thus, if you wanted to enable connection pooling for the default instance on a DB2 Connect server, you could do so by executing a command that looks something like this:

```
UPDATE DBM CFG USING NUM_POOLAGENTS 10
```

However, once this command is executed, the instance will have to be stopped and restarted (by executing the db2stop and db2start commands) before the change will take effect.

DB2 Discovery

It's easy to see how manually configuring communications between clients and servers can become an involved process, especially in complex network environments. And, as we have just seen, establishing communications between clients and servers is only the beginning. Before a client can send requests to a DB2 server for processing, both the server and the database stored on the server must be cataloged on the client as well.

DB2 Discovery allows you to easily catalog a remote server and a database (and set up a distributed connection between a client and a server) without having to know any detailed communication-specific information. Here's how DB2 Discovery works. When invoked from a client, DB2 Discovery broadcasts a discovery request over the network, and each DB2 server on the network that has been configured to support the discovery process responds by returning a list of instances found on the server, information about the communication protocol each instance supports, and a list of databases found within each instance. The Control Center and the Configuration Assistant can then use this information to catalog any instance or database returned by the discovery process.

To process a discovery request, DB2 Discovery can use one of two methods: search and known. When the search discovery method is used, the entire network is searched for valid DB2 servers and databases, and a list of all servers, instances, and databases found is returned to the client, along with the communications information needed to catalog and connect to each. In contrast, when the known discovery method is used, the network is searched for a specific server using a specific communications protocol. (Because the client knows the name of the server and the communications protocol used by that server, the server is said to be "known" by the client.) Again, when the specified server is located, a list of all instances and databases found on the server is returned to the client, along with the information needed to catalog and connect to each one.

 A search discovery can take a very long time (many hours) to complete if the network the client and server are on **WARNING** contains hundreds of machines. Furthermore, some network devices, such as routers, may actually block a search discovery request.

Whether a client can launch a DB2 Discovery request and, if so, how, and whether a particular server will respond and, if so, how, are determined by the values of parameters found in the configuration file for the DAS instance, the DB2 Database Manager configuration file for each instance (both on the client and on the server), and the database configuration file for each database within an instance. Specifically, these parameters control:

- Whether a client can launch a DB2 Discovery request

- Whether a server can be located by DB2 Discovery and, if so, whether the server can be located only when the search discovery method is used or when either the search or known discovery method is used

- Whether an instance can be located with a discovery request

- Whether a database can be located with a discovery request

The DAS instance, DB2 instance, and database configuration parameters that are used to control the behavior of DB2 Discovery are described in Table 7.1.

Table 7.1 Configuration Parameters that Control the Behavior of DB2 Discovery		
Parameter	**Values/Default**	**Description**
Client Instance **(DB2 Database Manager Configuration File)**		
discover	DISABLE, KNOWN, or SEARCH Default: SEARCH	Identifies the DB2 Discovery action to be used by the client instance. If this parameter is set to SEARCH, the client instance can issue either search or known discovery requests; if this parameter is set to KNOWN, the client instance can issue only known discovery requests; if this parameter is set to DISABLE, the client instance cannot issue discovery requests.
discover_inst	ENABLE or DISABLE Default: ENABLE	Specifies whether this instance can be detected by other DB2 Discovery requests.

Table 7.1 Configuration Parameters that Control the Behavior of DB2 Discovery (Continued)		
Parameter	Values/Default	Description
Server DAS Instance (DAS Configuration File)		
discover	DISABLE, KNOWN, or SEARCH Default: SEARCH	Identifies the DB2 Discovery action to be used when the server is started. If this parameter is set to SEARCH, the server will respond to both search and known discovery requests; if this parameter is set to KNOWN, the server will respond only to known discovery requests; if this parameter is set to DISABLE, the server will not respond to discovery requests.
Server Instance (DB2 Database Manager Configuration File)		
discover	DISABLE, KNOWN, or SEARCH Default: SEARCH	Identifies the DB2 Discovery action to be used by the server instance. If this parameter is set to SEARCH, the server instance can issue either search or known discovery requests; if this parameter is set to KNOWN, the server instance can issue only known discovery requests; if this parameter is set to DISABLE, the server instance cannot issue discovery requests.
discover_inst	ENABLE or DISABLE Default: ENABLE	Identifies whether information about a particular instance found on a server will be included in the server's response to a discovery request. If this parameter is set to ENABLE, the server will include information about the instance in its response to both search and known discovery requests. If this parameter is set to DISABLE, the server will not include information about the instance (and will not include information about any databases that come under the instance's control) in its response to discovery requests. This parameter provides a way to hide an instance and all of its databases from DB2 Discovery.
Server Database (Database Configuration File)		
discover_db	ENABLE or DISABLE Default: ENABLE	Identifies whether information about a particular database found on a server will be included in the server's response to a discovery request. If this parameter is set to ENABLE, the server will include information about the database in its response to both search and known discovery requests. On the other hand, if this parameter is set to DISABLE, the server will not include information about the database in its response to discovery requests. This parameter provides a way to hide an individual database from DB2 Discovery.

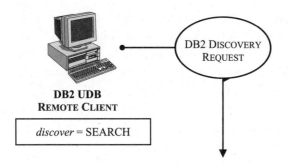

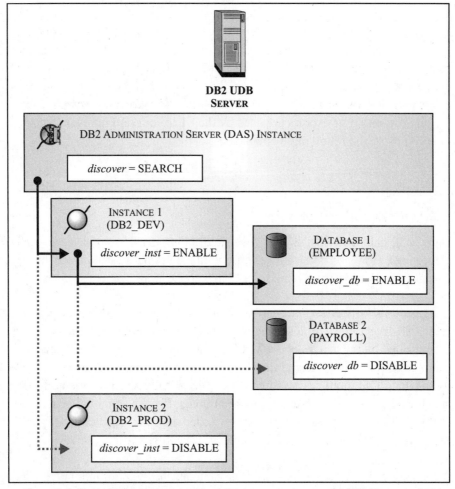

Figure 7–5: Controlling what instances and databases can be seen by DB2 Discovery. In this example, the server, Instance 1, and Database 1 will be returned by a discovery request; Instance 2 and Database 2 will not.

As you can see, it is possible to enable or disable DB2 Discovery at the server level, instance level, and database level, as well as to control how clients (and servers) initiate discovery requests. It is also possible to configure a server so that DB2 Discovery will not see one or more of its instances or databases when discovery requests are made. Figure 7–5 shows how the configuration parameters that control the behavior of DB2 Discovery can be used to prevent DB2 Discovery from seeing certain instances and databases stored on a server.

Fast Communications Manager (FCM) Communications

In a partitioned database environment, most communication between database partitions is handled by the fast communications manager (FCM). During instance creation, a number of ports equal to the number of participating DB2 servers that the instance is capable of supporting will be reserved in the */etc/services* file on Linux and UNIX servers and in the *%SystemRoot%\system32\drivers\etc\services* file on Windows. These ports are used by the FCM for communications and are reserved using the following format:

```
DB2_InstanceName
DB2_InstanceName_1
DB2_InstanceName_2
DB2_InstanceName_END
```

Only the beginning (DB2_*InstanceName*) and ending (*DB2_InstanceName*_END) ports are required. However, if you have defined multiple database partitions on the same host, you must reserve additional ports so that other applications cannot use them.

FCM uses 4K buffers for internal communications between database partitions and database servers; the actual number of 4K buffers used for each database partition is controlled by the *fcm_num_buffers* DB2 Database Manager configuration parameter. By default, this parameter is assigned the value AUTOMATIC, which means that FCM monitors resource usage periodically and incrementally releases resources if they are not used within 30 minutes. If DB2 cannot allocate the number of resources needed when an instance is started, it scales back the configuration values incrementally until the instance is successfully started.

If you have multiple logical nodes on the same machine, you might find it beneficial to assign a value to this parameter. And if you have assigned a value to this parameter, you might find it necessary to increase the value if you run out of message buffers because of the number of users on the system, the number of database partition servers on the system, or the complexity of the applications being used. However, before attempting to manually configure memory for the FCM, it is recommended that you start with the automatic setting for both the *fcm_num_buffers* (number of FCM buffers) and the *fcm_num_channels* (number of FCM channels) DB2 Database Manager configuration parameters. Then use the system monitor to evaluate FCM activity to determine whether this setting is appropriate. System monitor information for FCM can be obtained by executing a query that looks something like this:

```
SELECT * FROM TABLE(SYSPROC.SNAP_GET_FCM(1)) AS T
```

To determine whether the number of FCM buffers being used is appropriate, it is important to look at the current allocation of the number of FCM buffers as well as at the maximum number of FCM buffers that have been allocated. These numbers can then be compared; if the percentage of free FCM buffers drops below ten percent (10%), DB2 may run out of available buffers—indicating that the number of FCM buffers being used should be increased.

It is important to note that if you are using multiple database partitions on the same server, one pool of buffers is shared by all logical database partitions on the same machine. In this case, the size of the pool will be determined by multiplying the *fcm_num_buffers* value by the number of logical database partitions defined on that physical machine.

> Prior to DB2 9, the DB2_FORCE_FCM_BP registry variable could be used to allow DB2 to communicate between database partitions on the same server entirely through shared memory, instead of using the high-speed interconnect. If the DB2_FORCE_FCM_BP registry variable was set to "YES", the FCM communication buffers were created in a separate memory segment so that communication between the FCM daemons for different database partitions on the same server would occur through shared memory. Otherwise, FCM daemons on the same server had to communicate through network sockets using the high-speed interconnect, even though they were on the same server. In DB2 9, the DB2_FORCE_FCM_BP registry variable has been depreciated, and communications between the FCM daemons for different database partitions that reside on the same server automatically occur through shared memory.

Assigning too large a value to the *fcm_num_buffers* configuration parameter can also have negative consequences. Suppose you have four database partitions on a single AIX server that has 2GB of available memory, and suppose that the FCM Buffer Shared Memory segment is 256MB. Because there are a high number of concurrent applications running against the database, the *fcm_num_buffers* configuration parameter has been assigned the value 30,000. Three months later, you add another four database partitions to the same server (for a total of 8 database partitions). But after adding the new partitions, every attempt to start the instance has failed. Why?

When there were only four database partitions, FCM only reserved a total of 30,000 * 4K = 117MB + (20 * 4 partitions) = 197MB on the server, so the instance was able to start successfully. However, when four additional database partitions were added, FCM attempted to reserve a total of 30,000 * 4K = 117 MB + (20 * 8 partitions) = 277 MB, which is greater than the size of the FCM Buffer Shared Memory segment (256 MB), making the instance unable to start. To solve the problem, a value of 24,000 (or lower) would need to be assigned to the *fcm_num_buffers* configuration parameter. (24,000 * 4K) + (20 * 8) = 253 MB.

Troubleshooting Communications Errors

After configuring a client or DB2 Connect server to communicate with a remote database, you should attempt to connect to the database to verify that everything has been configured properly. Assuming everything has been configured correctly, a test connection to the remote database should be successful. However, if a test connection results in an error, take the following actions to determine why the error occurred:

1. **Verify that the remote database is available.** Try connecting to the remote database at the server. If you are unable to connect to the database locally, bring the database online and try connecting to it again from the client. If you can connect to the database locally, the problem is somewhere else.

2. **Ensure that the remote database server is configured to receive incoming connections via the desired protocol.** Ensure that DB2COMM registry variable at both the client and the server have a matching value. (This can be done by executing the command db2set at both machines.) Verify that the *svcename* parameter of the DB2 Database Manager configuration file on the server has

been assigned the correct name of the TCP/IP port that the database server will use to receive communications from remote clients. Finally, make sure the services file on the database server has a matching entry.

If other clients are having problems connecting to this server, chances are good that the DB2COMM registry variable and/or the *svcename* configuration parameter have been set incorrectly—or that the services file does not have a matching entry. If other clients can connect to the server, the problem lies somewhere else.

3. **Verify that the node has been cataloged correctly at the client.** Make sure the port number used to catalog the remote server has a matching entry in the services file on the remote server. (The easiest way to test this is by attaching to the node.)

4. **Verify that the DCS database has been cataloged correctly at the client.** If the remote database resides on a System z or System i server, it must have an entry in the DCS database directory. Check the DCS database directory to see whether the database has been cataloged correctly. (Make sure the local database alias and the remote database names specified were not accidently switched when the DCS database was cataloged; the target database name should refer to the subsystem's LOCATION name on z/OS.)

5. **Verify that the database has been cataloged correctly at the client.** A database must be cataloged in the system database directory on a client before connections can be made to it. Furthermore, if the remote database resides on a System z or System i server, it must be cataloged in both the DCS database directory and the system database directory. Check the system database directory to see whether the database has been cataloged correctly. (Make sure the local database alias and the remote database/DCS database names specified were not accidently switched when the database was cataloged. Also, make sure there is a corresponding node entry in the node directory.)

6. **Verify that DB2 Discovery has been configured correctly at the server.** If you are trying to use DB2 Discovery and are unable to locate a particular server, instance, or database, check the appropriate configuration parameters to determine whether the server, instance, or database can be seen by DB2 Discovery requests.

Practice Questions

Question 1

Which of the following commands will successfully catalog a node for a Linux server that has the IP address 1080:0:0:0:8:800:200C:417A and an instance that is listening on port 50000?

○ A. CATALOG TCPIP NODE rmt_server
         REMOTE 1080:0:0:0:8:800:200C:417A
         SERVER 50000
         OSTYPE LINUX

○ B. CATALOG TCPIP2 NODE rmt_server
         REMOTE 1080:0:0:0:8:800:200C:417A
         SERVER 50000
         OSTYPE LINUX

○ C. CATALOG TCPIP4 NODE rmt_server
         REMOTE 1080:0:0:0:8:800:200C:417A
         SERVER 50000
         OSTYPE LINUX

○ D. CATALOG TCPIP6 NODE rmt_server
         REMOTE 1080:0:0:0:8:800:200C:417A
         SERVER 50000
         OSTYPE LINUX

Question 2

After applying a FixPack to a DB2 server, which two of the following commands should be executed to create new packages for the DB2 utilities and CLI/ODBC driver? (Select two)

❑ A. BIND db2util.bnd BLOCKING ALL GRANT PUBLIC
❑ B. BIND @db2ubind.lst MESSAGES bind.msg GRANT PUBLIC
❑ C. BIND @db2cli.lst MESSAGES bind.msg GRANT PUBLIC
❑ D. BIND @db2odbc.lst MESSAGES bind.msg GRANT PUBLIC
❑ E. BIND db2schema.bnd BLOCKING ALL GRANT PUBLIC

Question 3

A database administrator has established connectivity to a DB2 for z/OS database and wishes to use a System Z Sysplex for load balancing and fault-tolerance.

Which instance-level configuration parameter must be assigned a value that is greater than zero to ensure that enough agents remain allocated to help maintain the Sysplex server list?

○ A. NUM_INITAGENTS
○ B. NUM_IDLE_AGENTS
○ C. NUM_POOLAGENTS
○ D. MAX_AGENTS

Question 4

An instance named DB2INST1 and a database named SAMPLE reside on a server named SVR1. Which two of the following commands must be executed before both the instance and the database can be seen by a DB2 discovery request? (Select two)

❏ A. db2set DISCOVER_INST=ENABLE
❏ B. UPDATE DBM CFG USING DISCOVER_INST ENABLE
❏ C. db2set DISCOVER_DB=ENABLE
❏ D. UPDATE DB CFG FOR sample USING DISCOVER_DB ENABLE
❏ E. UPDATE DBM CFG USING DISCOVER_DATABASE ENABLE

Question 5

Which database configuration parameter must be set to DISABLE if clients are to be prevented from seeing a database with a DB2 discovery request?

○ A. DISCOVER
○ B. DISCOVERY
○ C. DISCOVER_DB
○ D. DISCOVER_DATABASE

Question 6

A database administrator is attempting to catalog a DB2 for z/OS server from a DB2 for Linux, UNIX, and Windows server. The communications protocol that will be used is TCP/IP.

What should the administrator do if he/she cannot connect to a database on the DB2 for z/OS server?

○ A. Ping the server where the DB2 for z/OS database resides and verify that the server has been cataloged correctly.

○ B. Verify the process db2tcpcm is running on the server and that the server has been cataloged correctly.

○ C. Verify that the Distributed Data Facility (DDF) is running and that the server has been cataloged correctly.

○ D. Verify that the Distributed Connection Facility (DCF) is running and that the server has been cataloged correctly.

Question 7

Which two of the following items are NOT required to establish a TCP/IP connection to a DB2 for z/OS database from a DB2 for Linux, UNIX, and Windows server? (Select two)

❑ A. Hostname

❑ B. Port number

❑ C. Database name (target and local)

❑ D. Subsystem ID

❑ E. Logical Unit (LU) name

Question 8

Although everyone else in the HR department can connect to a remote database named PAYROLL from their workstations, one employee cannot, even though he is supplying the correct user ID and password. What is most likely the cause of the problem?

○ A. DB2COMM is not set correctly on the remote database server.

○ B. DB2COMM is not set correctly on the employee's workstation.

○ C. The PAYROLL database was not cataloged correctly on the server.

○ D. The PAYROLL database was not cataloged correctly on the employee's workstation.

Question 9

No one in the HR department can connect to a remote database named PAYROLL from their workstations. Preliminary investigation has shown that there are no problems with the network, the instance on the server is active, TCP/IP is running normally on both the clients and the servers, and users are trying to connect with valid user IDs and passwords. What is most likely the cause of the problem?

○ A. DB2COMM is not set correctly on the remote database server.

○ B. The remote instance's authentication type has not been set to CLIENT.

○ C. The DB2 Administration Server has not been started on the remote database server.

○ D. The PAYROLL database was not cataloged correctly on each employee's workstation.

Question 10

While attempting to connect to a database named TEST_DB (which is a DB2 for z/OS database) from a Windows client, an employee received the following message:

```
SQL1013N The database alias name or database name "TEST_DB" could not
be found.
```

Other employees in the same department can connect to the database without any problem. Close examination shows that the entries for the server and the database in the node and system database directories are the same on everyone's workstation. Which of the following actions should be performed to resolve the problem?

○ A. Stop and restart the instance on the z/OS server.

○ B. Uncatalog and re-catalog the database in the system database directory.

○ C. Catalog the database in the remote database directory.

○ D. Catalog the database in the Database Connection Services (DCS) directory.

Question 11

A database administrator obtained the following information about a UNIX DB2 server:

Instance name: db2inst1

Port number: 50000

Service name: db2c_db2inst1

Host name: hostnm01

Host TCP/IP address: 10.205.15.100

DB2COMM=TCPIP

Database name: PROD_DB

In an attempt to establish connectivity between a Windows client and the DB2 server, the following commands were executed from the Windows client:

```
CATALOG TCPIP NODE node001 REMOTE hostnm01 SERVER 50000;
CATALOG DATABASE prod_db AS prod_db AT NODE node001;
```

However, when an attempt was made to connect to the database, an error occurred. Which of the following actions should be performed to resolve the problem?

- ○ A. Catalog the database PROD_DB in the local database directory.
- ○ B. Add the entry "db2c_db2inst1 50000/tcp" to the services file on the UNIX server.
- ○ C. Catalog the database PROD_DB in the Database Connection Services (DCS) directory.
- ○ D. Add the entry "db2inst1 10.205.15.100" to the services file on the UNIX server.

Question 12

In a DB2 Connect configuration between a Linux client and a z/OS server, the following commands were executed:

```
CATALOG TCPIP NODE node001 REMOTE hostnm01.us.mycorp.com SERVER 446;
CATALOG DATABASE payroll AT NODE node001 AUTHENTICATION DCS;
```

Later, an error occurred while trying to connect to the PAYROLL_DB database in the DSN_DB_1 subsystem on the z/OS server. Close examination shows that the entry for the server in the node directory is correct and that the subsystem's LOCATION NAME on z/OS is DSN_DB_1. Which of the following commands, if executed, should resolve the problem?

- ○ A. CATALOG DCS DATABASE dsn_db_1 AS payroll
- ○ B. CATALOG DCS DATABASE payroll AS dsn_db_1
- ○ C. CATALOG DCS DATABASE payroll_db AS payroll
- ○ D. CATALOG DCS DATABASE payroll AS payroll_db AR dsn_db_1

Answers

Question 1

The correct answer is **D**. Nodes (servers) are usually cataloged implicitly whenever a remote database is cataloged via the Configuration Assistant. However, if you want to explicitly catalog (i.e., add an entry to the node directory for a particular server), you can do so by executing a CATALOG . . . NODE command that corresponds to the communications protocol that will be used to access the server being cataloged. The syntax for the CATALOG TCPIP NODE command is:

```
CATALOG <ADMIN> [TCPIP | TCPIP4 | TCPIP6] NODE [NodeName]
REMOTE [IPAddress | HostName]
SERVER [ServiceName | PortNumber]
<SECURITY SOCKS>
<REMOTE INSTANCE [InstanceName]>
<SYSTEM [SystemName]>
<OSTYPE [SystemType]>
<WITH "[Description]">
```

where:

NodeName   Identifies the alias to be assigned to the node to be cataloged. This is an arbitrary name created on the user's workstation and is used to identify the node.

IPAddress   Identifies the IP address of the server where the remote database that you are trying to communicate with resides.

HostName   Identifies the host name, as it is known to the TCP/IP network. (This is the name of the server where the remote database that you are trying to communicate with resides.)

ServiceName   Identifies the service name that the DB2 Database Manager instance on the server uses to communicate.

PortNumber   Identifies the port number that the DB2 Database Manager instance on the server uses to communicate.

InstanceName   Identifies the name of the server instance to which an attachment is to be made.

SystemName   Identifies the DB2 system name used to identify the server workstation.

SystemType   Identifies the type of operating system being used on the server workstation. The following values are valid for this parameter: AIX, WIN, HPUX, SUN, OS390, OS400, VM, VSE, and LINUX.

Description   A comment used to describe the node entry that is to be made in the node directory for the node being cataloged. The description must be enclosed by double quotation marks.

Thus, if you wanted to catalog a node for a Linux server that has the IPv6 address 1080:0:0:0:8:800:200C:417A and an instance that is listening on port 50000, you could do so by executing a **CATALOG TCPIP NODE** command that looks something like this:

```
CATALOG TCPIP NODE rmt_server
REMOTE 1080:0:0:0:8:800:200C:417A
SERVER 50000
OSTYPE LINUX
```

On the other hand, if you wanted to catalog a node for a Linux server that has the IPv4 address 192.0.32.67 and an instance that is listening on port 50000, you could do so by executing a **CATALOG TCPIP NODE** command that looks like this:

```
CATALOG TCPIP NODE rmt_server
REMOTE 192.0.32.67
SERVER 50000
OSTYPE LINUX
```

Question 2

The correct answers are **B** and **C**. The file db2ubind.lst contains a list of the bind files (.bnd) needed to create packages for DB2's database utilities; the file db2cli.lst contains a list of the bind files (.bnd) needed to create packages for the DB2 Call Level Interface (CLI) and the DB2 ODBC driver. When these two commands are executed, any messages produced by the Bind utility will be written to a file named bind.msg and the group PUBLIC will receive EXECUTE and BINDADD privileges for each package produced.

(The db2schema.bnd bind file is used to create a package that provides system catalog function support and is often used with DB2 Connect.)

Question 3

The correct answer is **C**. The Sysplex server list is rendered inaccessible if there are no agents available and if no connections to a host database exist. Therefore, connection pooling must be enabled and at least one agent must be available when working with Sysplex servers. Connection pooling is enabled whenever the maximum number of agents allowed to be pooled on a DB2 instance is greater than zero—this number is determined by the value assigned to the *num_poolagents* DB2 Database Manager configuration parameter.

Thus, if you wanted to enable connection pooling for the default instance on a DB2 Connect server, you could do so by executing a command that looks something like this:

```
UPDATE DBM CFG USING NUM_POOLAGENTS 10
```

However, once this command is executed, the instance will have to be stopped and restarted (by executing the db2stop and db2start commands) before the change will take effect.

Question 4

The correct answers are **B** and **D**. If the *discover_inst* DB2 Database Manager configuration parameter is set to ENABLE, information about the corresponding instance will be returned in response to both search and known discovery requests. If the *discover_db* database configuration parameter is set to ENABLE, information about the corresponding database will be returned in response to both search and known discovery requests. DB2 Database Manager configuration parameters are set by executing the command "UPDATE DBM CFG [*Parameter*] [*Value*]"; database configuration parameters are set by executing the command "UPDATE DB CFG FOR [*DBAlias*] USING [*Parameter*] [*Value*]".

Question 5

The correct answer is **C**. If the *discover_db* database configuration parameter is set to DISABLE, information about the corresponding database will not be returned in response to a DB2 discovery request. If the *discover_inst* DB2 Database Manager configuration parameter for the instance the database resides under has been set to DISABLE, then this is not required. (If the *discover_inst* DB2 Database Manager configuration parameter is set to DISABLE, information about the corresponding instance will not be returned in response to a DB2 discovery request.)

Question 6

The correct answer is **C**. Once a server has been configured for communications, any client that wishes to access a database on the server must be configured to communicate with the server. In order to catalog a remote server using TCP/IP, you must provide, among other things, the host name, as it is known to the TCP/IP network. (This is the name of the server where the remote database that you are trying to communicate with resides.) When cataloging a DB2 for z/OS remote server, the hostname can be seen in the DSNL004I message (DOMAIN=hostname) when the Distributed Data Facility (DDF) is started—provided the target database has been set up for TCP/IP communications; the Distributed Data Facility (DDF) is required for TCP/IP communications with DB2 on z/OS servers.

Question 7

The correct answers are **D** and **E**. Any client that wishes to access a database on a remote server must be configured to communicate with that server. But that's just the first step. Entries for both the server and the remote database must also be added to the system database and node directories on the client. Entries are added to DB2's directories using a process known as cataloging.

To explicitly catalog a remote server, you execute the CATALOG . . . NODE command that corresponds to the communications protocol that will be used to access the server being cataloged. To catalog a database, you execute the CATALOG DATABASE command.

The syntax for the CATALOG TCPIP NODE command is:

```
CATALOG <ADMIN> [TCPIP | TCPIP4 | TCPIP6] NODE [NodeName]
REMOTE [IPAddress | HostName]
SERVER [ServiceName | PortNumber]
<SECURITY SOCKS>
<REMOTE INSTANCE [InstanceName]>
<SYSTEM [SystemName]>
<OSTYPE [SystemType]>
<WITH "[Description]">
```

where:

NodeName   Identifies the alias to be assigned to the node to be cataloged. This is an arbitrary name created on the user's workstation and is used to identify the node.

IPAddress   Identifies the IP address of the server where the remote database that you are trying to communicate with resides.

HostName   Identifies the host name, as it is known to the TCP/IP network. (This is the name of the server where the remote database that you are trying to communicate with resides.)

ServiceName   Identifies the service name that the DB2 Database Manager instance on the server uses to communicate.

PortNumber   Identifies the port number that the DB2 Database Manager instance on the server uses to communicate.

InstanceName   Identifies the name of the server instance to which an attachment is to be made.

SystemName   Identifies the DB2 system name used to identify the server workstation.

SystemType   Identifies the type of operating system being used on the server workstation. The following values are valid for this parameter: AIX, WIN, HPUX, SUN, OS390, OS400, VM, VSE, and LINUX.

Description   A comment used to describe the node entry that is to be made in the node directory for the node being cataloged. The description must be enclosed by double quotation marks.

The syntax for the CATALOG DATABASE command is:

```
CATALOG [DATABASE | DB] [DatabaseName]
<AS [Alias]>
<ON [Path] | AT NODE [NodeName]>
<AUTHENTICATION [AuthenticationType]>
<WITH "[Description]">
```

where:

DatabaseName   Identifies the name that has been assigned to the database to be cataloged.

Alias   Identifies the alias that is to be assigned to the database when it is cataloged.

Path   Identifies the location (drive and/or directory) where the directory hierarchy and files associated with the database to be cataloged are physically stored.

NodeName   Identifies the node where the database to be cataloged resides. The node name specified should match an entry in the node directory file (i.e., should correspond to a node that has already been cataloged).

AuthenticationType   Identifies where and how authentication is to take place when a user attempts to access the database. The following values are valid for this parameter: SERVER, CLIENT, SERVER_ENCRYPT, KERBEROS TARGET PRINCIPAL [*PrincipalName*] (where *PrincipalName* is the fully qualified Kerberos principal name for the target server), DATA_ENCRYPT, and GSSPLUGIN.

Description   A comment used to describe the database entry that is to be made in the database directory for the database to be cataloged. The description must be enclosed by double quotation marks.

Question 8

The correct answer is **D**. In order to communicate with a server, each client must use some type of communications protocol recognized by the server. Likewise, each server must use some type of communications protocol to detect inbound requests from clients. Both clients and servers must be configured to use a communications protocol recognized by DB2.

Whenever you manually configure communications for a server, you must update the value of the DB2COMM registry variable before an instance can begin using the desired communications protocol. The value assigned to the DB2COMM registry variable is used to determine which communications managers will be activated when a particular instance is started. (If the DB2COMM registry variable is not set correctly, one or more errors may be generated when DB2 attempts to start protocol support during instance initialization.)

Once a server has been configured for communications, any client that wishes to access a database on the server must add entries for both the server and the remote database to the system database and node directories on the client. (Entries must also be added to the DCS directory if the client intends to connect to a System z or System i database via DB2 Connect.) Entries are added to DB2's directories using a process known as cataloging.

In this example, because everyone else in the HR department can connect to the PAYROLL database, the DB2COMM registry variable must be set correctly on the server. The same is true about the way the PAYROLL database was cataloged on the server – since everyone else can connect to the database, the database must be cataloged correctly. The value assigned to the DB2COMM registry variable on the client has no effect since the node directory entry specifies the communications protocol and port number that will be used to connect to the server. So, that's not the problem either. Therefore, the problem must be that either the server (node) or the database has been cataloged incorrectly on the client.

Question 9

The correct answer is **A**. In order to communicate with a server, each client must use some type of communications protocol recognized by the server. Likewise, each server must use some type of communications protocol to detect inbound requests from clients. Both clients and servers must be configured to use a communications protocol recognized by DB2.

Whenever you manually configure communications for a server, you must update the value of the DB2COMM registry variable before an instance can begin using the desired communications protocol. The value assigned to the DB2COMM registry variable is used to determine which communications managers will be activated when a particular instance is started.

In this example, because everyone in the HR department cannot connect to the PAYROLL database, the problem is most likely that the DB2COMM registry variable has not been assigned the value TCPIP.

Question 10

The correct answer is **D**. In order to access a remote database from a client workstation, the database must be cataloged in the system database directory of both the client and the server *and* the server workstation must be cataloged in the client's node directory. (The entry in the node directory tells the DB2 Database Manager how to connect to the server to get access to the database stored there.) Because the information needed to connect to DRDA host databases is different from the information used to connect to LAN-based databases, information about remote host or iSeries databases is kept in a special directory known as the Database Connection Services (DCS) directory. If an entry in the DCS directory has a database name that corresponds to the name of a database stored in the system database directory, the specified Application Requester (which in most cases is DB2 Connect) can forward SQL requests to the database that resides on a remote DRDA server. If there is no record for a zSeries or iSeries database in the DCS directory, no database connection can be established.

Question 11

The correct answer is **B**. If you wanted to configure a server to use TCP/IP, you would perform the following steps (in any order):

1. Assign the value TCPIP to the DB2COMM registry variable.

   The DB2COMM registry variable is assigned the value TCPIP by executing a db2set command that looks something like this:

   ```
   db2set DB2COMM=TCPIP
   ```

2. Assign the name of the TCP/IP port that the database server will use to receive communications from remote clients to the *svcename* parameter of the DB2 Database Manager configuration file.

   This parameter is set by executing an UPDATE DATABASE MANAGER CONFIGURATION command that looks something like this:

   ```
   UPDATE DBM CFG USING SVCENAME db2c_db2inst1
   ```

3. Update the services file on the database server, if appropriate.

   The TCP/IP services file identifies the ports on which server applications will listen for client requests. If you specified a service name in the *svcename* parameter of the DB2

Database Manager configuration file, the appropriate service name-to-port number/ protocol mapping must be added to the services file on the server. If you specified a port number in the *svcename* parameter, the services file does not need to be updated.

The default location of the services file depends on the operating system being used: on UNIX systems, the services file is named *services* and is located in the */etc* directory; on Windows systems, the services file is located in *%SystemRoot%\system32\drivers\etc*. An entry in the services file for DB2 might look something like this:

```
db2c_db2inst1        50001/tcp
```

Once a server has been configured for communications, any client that wishes to access a database on the server must add entries for both the server and the remote database to the system database and node directories on the client.

In this example, because the server and database were cataloged correctly on the Windows client, the most likely cause of the problem was that the services file on the UNIX server did not have an entry for the DB2 service name and port.

Question 12

The correct answer is **B**. A DCS database is cataloged by executing the **CATALOG DCS DATABASE** command. The syntax for this command is:

```
CATALOG DCS [DATABASE | DB] [Alias]
<AS [TargetName]>
<AR [LibraryName]>
<PARMS "[ParameterString]">
<WITH "[Description]">
```

where:

Alias   Identifies the alias of the target database to be cataloged. This name should match an entry in the system database directory associated with the remote node.

TargetName   Identifies the name of the target host database to be cataloged. (If the host database to be cataloged resides on a OS/390 or z/OS server, the TargetName specified should refer to a DB2 for z/OS subsystem identified by its **LOCATION NAME** or one of the alias **LOCATION** names defined on the z/OS server. The **LOCATION NAME** can be determined by logging in to TSO and issuing the following SQL query using one of the available query tools: **SELECT CURRENT SERVER FROM SYSIBM. SYSDUMMY1.**)

LibraryName   Identifies the name of the Application Requester library to be loaded and used to access the remote database listed in the DCS directory.

ParameterString Identifies a parameter string to be passed to the Application Requestor when it is invoked. The parameter string must be enclosed by double quotation marks.

Description   A comment used to describe the database entry that is to be made in the DCS directory for the database to be cataloged. The description must be enclosed by double quotation marks (").

Thus, if you wanted to catalog a DB2 for z/OS database residing in the DSN_DB_1 subsystem on the z/OS server that has the name PAYROLL_DB and assign it the alias PAYROLL, you could do so by executing a CATALOG DCS DATABASE command that looks something like this:

```
CATALOG DCS DATABASE payroll
AS dsn_db_1
WITH "DB2 for z/OS LOCATION NAME DSN_DB_1"
```

DB2 9 for Linux, UNIX, and Windows Advanced Database Administration Exam (Exam 734) Objectives

The DB2 9 for Linux, UNIX, and Windows Advanced Database Administration exam (Exam 734) consists of 51 questions, and candidates have 90 minutes to complete the exam. A score of 64% or higher is required to pass this exam.

The primary objectives that the DB2 9 for Linux, UNIX, and Windows Advanced Database Administration exam (Exam 734) is designed to cover are as follows:

Database Design (14%)

- Ability to design, create, and manage buffer pools
- Ability to design, create, and manage table spaces
- Ability to design and configure federated database access

Data Partitioning and Clustering (15%)

- Ability to design, create, and manage a partitioned database
- Ability to design, create, and manage multi-dimensional clustered tables

- Ability to design, create, and manage table partitioning
- Knowledge of Balance Configuration Unit (BCU)

High Availability and Diagnostics (20%)

- Ability to manage database logs for recovery
- Ability to use advanced backup features
- Ability to use advanced recovery features
- Ability to enhance database availability
- Ability to use diagnostic tools (db2pd, db2mtrk, inspect, db2dart, db2diag)

Performance and Scalability (33%)

- Identify and use DB2 registry variables that affect database system performance
- Identify and use configuration parameters that affect database system performance
- Knowledge of query optimizer concepts
- Ability to manage and tune instance, database, and application memory and I/O
- Ability to use Deep Compression
- Ability to analyze performance problems
- Ability to manage a large number of users and connections
- Ability to determine the more appropriate index
- Ability to exploit parallelism

Security (8%)

- Knowledge of external authentication mechanisms
- Ability to implement data encryption

- Ability to implement Label-Based Access Control (LBAC)

- Ability to use the DB2 Audit facility

Connectivity and Networking (10%)

- Ability to configure client server connectivity (e.g., DB2 Discovery)

- Ability to manage connections to host systems

- Ability to identify and resolve connection problems

Monitoring Buffer Pool Activity

The database monitor can be used to monitor the various buffer pool and prefetching activities. The following entries in the buffer pool snapshot and/or the table space snapshot provide information about the page reads and writes occurring in the database:

Buffer Pool Data Physical Reads: The number of data pages that were physically read from disk into the buffer pool. This includes synchronous reads done by the agents as well as asynchronous reads that are done by the prefetchers.

Buffer Pool Data Logical Reads: The number of data pages that were read from the buffer pool and from disk. To determine the number of read requests that were satisfied by the buffer pool, subtract the buffer pool data physical reads from the buffer pool data logical reads.

Buffer Pool Asynchronous Data Reads: The number of data pages that were read into the buffer pool asynchronously by the prefetchers.

Buffer Pool Index Physical Reads: The number of index pages that were physically read from disk into the buffer pool. This includes synchronous reads done by the agents as well as asynchronous reads that are done by the prefetchers.

Buffer Pool Index Logical Reads: The number of index pages that were read from the buffer pool and from disk. To determine the number of read requests that were satisfied by the buffer pool, subtract the buffer pool index physical reads from the buffer pool index logical reads.

Buffer Pool Asynchronous Index Reads: The number of index pages that were read into the buffer pool asynchronously by the prefetchers.

Buffer Pool Data Writes: The number of data pages that were written out from the buffer pool to disk. This includes synchronous writes done by the agents as well as asynchronous writes done by the page cleaners and agents as a result of victim selection.

Buffer Pool Asynchronous Data Writes: The number of data pages that were written out from the buffer pool to disk asynchronously by the page cleaners as a result of victim selection.

Buffer Pool Index Writes: The number of index pages that were written out from the buffer pool to disk. This includes synchronous writes done by the agents as well as asynchronous writes done by the page cleaners as a result of victim selection.

Buffer Pool Asynchronous Index Writes: The number of index pages that were written out from the buffer pool to disk asynchronously by the page cleaners as a result of victim selection.

Total Buffer Pool Physical Read Time: The total elapsed time spent processing read requests that caused data or index pages to be physically read from disk into the buffer pool. This includes synchronous reads done by the agents as well as asynchronous reads done by the prefetchers.

Buffer Pool Asynchronous Read Time: The total elapsed time spent by the prefetchers processing read requests that caused data or index pages to be physically read from disk into the buffer pool.

Total Buffer Pool Physical Write Time: The total elapsed time spent processing write requests that caused data or index pages to be written out from the buffer pool to disk. This includes synchronous writes done by the agents as well as asynchronous writes done by the page cleaners as a result of victim selection.

Buffer Pool Asynchronous Write Time: The total elapsed time spent writing data or index pages from the buffer pool to disk by page cleaners as a result of victim selection.

Buffer Pool Asynchronous Read Requests: The total number of asynchronous read requests handled by the prefetchers.

Time Waited for Prefetch: The total elapsed time that an agent spent waiting for a prefetcher to finish reading pages into the buffer pool.

Beginning with DB2 Version 8, the snapshot information can also be captured using SQL table functions. For each of the database snapshot monitors there is an equivalent snapshot table function that can be used to obtain the same information. The SQL table functions normally require two input parameters, the database name and the database partition number. However, the database manager snapshot SQL table functions only require the partition number.

If no value is specified for the database name, the information will be captured for the database that the application is currently connected to. If a value of negative one (-1) is specified for the database partition number, the information will be captured for the database partition that the application is currently connected to. If a value of negative two (-2) is specified for the database partition number, the information will be captured for all of the database partitions in the database.

For example:

```
SELECT BP_NAME,
(((1 - ((FLOAT(POOL_INDEX_P_READS + POOL_DATA_P_READS)) / (FLOAT(POOL_
INDEX_L_READS + POOL_DATA_L_READS)))) * 100)) AS bp_hit_ratio
FROM TABLE(SNAPSHOT_BP('sample',-1 )) AS snapshot_bp;
```

will capture the snapshot information for the database partition the application is connected to, and

```
SELECT BP_NAME,
(((1 - ((FLOAT(POOL_INDEX_P_READS + POOL_DATA_P_READS)) / (FLOAT(POOL_
INDEX_L_READS + POOL_DATA_L_READS)))) * 100)) AS bp_hit_ratio
FROM TABLE(SNASHOT_BP('sample',-2 )) AS snapshot_bp;
```

will capture the snapshot information for all database partitions in the database.

Buffer Pool Tuning

After obtaining a buffer pool and/or table space snapshot for the database, the entries described previously need to be analyzed in order to determine if the database is operating efficiently. The information can also be examined using SQL table functions.

The buffer pool hit ratios are measures of the effectiveness of the buffer pool. The hit ratios reflect the number of times that a page request was able to be handled by the buffer pool directly without the need to read the page from disk. The more often that the request for a page can be satisfied from the buffer pool, the better that the overall performance of the system will be.

The following is a sample of the output of the buffer pool snapshot:

```
                  Database Snapshot

Database name                           = SAMPLE
Database path                           = /v1/db2/NODE0000/SQL00001/
Input database alias                    = SAMPLE
Database status                         = Active
Catalog database partition number       = 0
Catalog network node name               =
Operating system running at database server = NT
Location of the database                = Local
First database connect timestamp        = 09-04-2002 13:21:52.797473
Last reset timestamp                    =
Last backup timestamp                   =
Snapshot timestamp                      = 09-04-2002 13:22:16.333042

                  Bufferpool Snapshot

Bufferpool name                         = IBMDEFAULTBP
Database name                           = SAMPLE
Database path                           = /v1/db2/NODE0000/SQL00001/
Input database alias                    = SAMPLE
Buffer pool data logical reads          = 523956
Buffer pool data physical reads         = 33542
Buffer pool data writes                 = 288
Buffer pool index logical reads         = 257949
Buffer pool index physical reads        = 11323
Total buffer pool read time (ms)        = 12012
Total buffer pool write time (ms)       = 720
Asynchronous pool data page reads       = 5227
Asynchronous pool data page writes      = 276
Buffer pool index writes                = 255
```

```
Asynchronous pool index page reads      = 451
Asynchronous pool index page writes     = 239
Total elapsed asynchronous read time    = 819
Total elapsed asynchronous write time   = 663
Asynchronous read requests              = 3553
Direct reads                            = 69664
Direct writes                           = 16902
Direct read requests                    = 2780
Direct write requests                   = 411
Direct reads elapsed time (ms)          = 4830
Direct write elapsed time (ms)          = 979
Database files closed                   = 17
Data pages copied to extended storage   = 0
Index pages copied to extended storage  = 0
Data pages copied from extended storage = 0
Index pages copied from extended storage = 0
Unread prefetch pages                   = 0
Vectored IOs                            = 0
Pages from vectored IOs                 = 0
Block IOs                               = 0
Pages from block IOs                    = 0
Physical page maps                      = 0
```

Buffer Pool Hit Ratio

If DB2 needs to read an index or data page, and the page is already in the buffer pool, the ability to access the page will be much faster than if the page has to be read from disk. The buffer pool hit ratio describes how frequently that a request for an index or data page is handled directly from the buffer pool. The buffer pool hit ratio is calculated using the following formula:

```
BPHR = (1 - ((Data Physical Reads + Index Physical Reads) / ((Data Logical
Reads + Index Logical Reads))) * 100%
```

Based on the preceding buffer pool snapshot, the buffer pool hit ratio would be:

```
BPHR = (1 - ((33542 + 11323) / (523956 + 257949))) * 100%
BPHR = 94.26%
```

In this case 94.26% of the data and index page requests were able to be handled by the buffer pool without the need for a physical I/O request.

The buffer pool hit ratio can also be calculated using the SQL table function as follows:

```
SELECT BP_NAME,
(((1 - ((FLOAT(POOL_INDEX_P_READS + POOL_DATA_P_READS)) / (FLOAT(POOL_
INDEX_L_READS + POOL_DATA_L_READS)))) * 100)) AS bpool_hit_ratio
FROM TABLE(SNAPSHOT_BP('sample',-1 )) AS snapshot_bp;
```

The output of this statement would be the following:

```
BP_NAME                 BPOOL_HIT_RATIO
-------------------- ----------------------
IBMDEFAULTBP            +9.42652009389671E+001

   1 record(s) selected.
```

In order to make the output more readable, the buffer pool hit ratio can be cast as an integer. This will round the value to the integer portion of its value but is close enough for most purposes. In this case, the SQL statement to calculate the buffer pool hit ratio can be changed to:

```
SELECT BP_NAME,
(INT((1 - ((FLOAT(POOL_INDEX_P_READS + POOL_DATA_P_READS)) / (FLOAT(POOL_
INDEX_L_READS + POOL_DATA_L_READS)))) * 100)) AS bpool_hit_ratio
FROM TABLE(SNAPSHOT_BP('SAMPLE',-1 ))
     as SNAPSHOT_BP;
```

The output of this statement would be the following:

```
BP_NAME                 BPOOL_HIT_RATIO
-------------------- ---------------
IBMDEFAULTBP                         68

   1 record(s) selected.
```

Index Hit Ratio

It is also important to examine the individual hit ratios such as the data and index hit ratios. The index hit ratio is calculated using the following formula:

```
IHR = (1 - (Index Physical Reads / Index Logical Reads)) * 100%
```

The index hit ratio can also be calculated using the SQL table function as follows:

```
SELECT BP_NAME,
(INT((1 - ((FLOAT(POOL_INDEX_P_READS)) / (FLOAT(POOL_INDEX_L_READS)))) * 100))
AS index_hit_ratio
FROM TABLE(SNAPSHOT_BP('sample',-1 )) AS snapshot_bp;
```

Data Hit Ratio

The data hit ratio is calculated using the following formula:

```
DHR = (1 - (Data Physical Reads / Data Logical Reads)) * 100%
```

The data hit ratio can also be calculated using the SQL table function as follows:

```
SELECT BP_NAME,
(INT((1 - ((FLOAT(POOL_DATA_P_READS)) / (FLOAT(POOL_DATA_L_READS)))) * 100))
AS data_hit_ratio
FROM TABLE(SNAPSHOT_BP('sample',-1 )) AS snapshot_bp;
```

Based on the preceding buffer pool snapshot, the index and data hit ratios would be:

```
IHR = (1 - (11323) / 257949)) *100%
IHR = 95.61%

DHR = (1 - (33542) / 523956)) *100%
DHR = 93.60%
```

In general a buffer pool hit ratio above 80% is considered good. However, for an OLTP system it is important to have the buffer pool hit ratio as high as possible (especially the index hit ratio) to be able to respond to requests efficiently and quickly. For large DSS systems it is very unlikely that the buffer pool hit ratio will be high due to the vast amounts of data that are normally read. Therefore, it is important to understand the workload on the system when analyzing the buffer pool hit ratios so that they can be examined in the right context.

Asynchronous Read Ratio

Another important aspect of buffer pool performance that can be analyzed using snapshot information is the amount of synchronous vs. asynchronous I/O. The percentage of asynchronous read requests (or Asynchronous Read Ratio) is calculated using the following formula:

```
ARR = ((Asynch Data Reads + Asynch Index Reads) / ((Data Logical Reads +
Index Logical Reads)) * 100%
```

The asynchronous read ratio can also be calculated using the SQL table function as follows:

```
SELECT BP_NAME,
(INT(((FLOAT(POOL_ASYNC_DATA_READS + POOL_ASYNC_INDEX_READS)) /
(FLOAT(POOL_INDEX_L_READS + POOL_DATA_L_READS))) * 100))
AS asynch_read_ratio
FROM TABLE(SNAPSHOT_BP('sample',-1 )) AS snapshot_bp;
```

Based on the preceding buffer pool snapshot, the asynchronous read ratio would be:

```
ARR = ((5227 + 451) / (523956 + 257949)) *100%
ARR = 0.73 %
```

This is a very small value and would indicate that there is very little prefetch activity occurring for this database. This could be due to a number of reasons such as:

1. The workload is reading and writing single rows so cannot take advantage of prefetching.

2. There are too few prefetchers configured for the database.

3. The table spaces in the database are set up with only one container each so that prefetching cannot normally take place.

    a.   Note: If DB2_PARALLEL_IO is set to YES, prefetching can occur within a single container table space if the prefetch size is a multiple of the extent size.

For a system with multiple buffer pools, it is normally a good idea to separate tables with a high percentage of asynchronous reads from those with a low percentage of asynchronous reads. The asynchronous read ratio can also be examined for each table space to help separate the table spaces with high and low asynchronous read ratios. For the following table space snapshot information we see there are four table spaces with different access patterns:

```
Tablespace name                          = TSPC1
  Buffer pool data logical reads         = 1200
  Asynchronous pool data page reads      = 32
  Buffer pool index logical reads        = 3400
  Asynchronous pool index page reads     = 128
Tablespace name                          = TSPC2
  Buffer pool data logical reads         = 15000
  Asynchronous pool data page reads      = 14000
  Buffer pool index logical reads        = 90000
  Asynchronous pool index page reads     = 86000

Tablespace name                          = TSPC3
  Buffer pool data logical reads         = 9000
```

```
Asynchronous pool data page reads      = 8600
Buffer pool index logical reads        = 6250
Asynchronous pool index page reads     = 5975

Tablespace name                        = TSPC4
  Buffer pool data logical reads       = 7200
  Asynchronous pool data page reads    = 1400
  Buffer pool index logical reads      = 800
  Asynchronous pool index page reads   = 770
```

In this case the asynchronous read ratios would be:

```
TBSPC1      3.5%
TBSPC2      95.2%
TBSCP3      95.6%
TBSPC4      27.1%
```

Because table spaces TBSPC1 and TBSPC4 both have low asynchronous read ratios they should not be placed in the same buffer pool as table space TBSPC2 or TBSPC3. Table spaces TBSPC2 and TBSPC3 both have a high asynchronous read ratio, and so they could be placed in the same buffer pool; however, DB2 places an internal limit on the number of pages that can be prefetched into a buffer pool before they are accessed by a DB2 agent, thus, having two table spaces with a high asynchronous read ratio in the same buffer pool may have an adverse effect. It may be more optimal to place the table spaces TBSPC2 and TBSPC3 in their own buffer pools.

Physical Read Rate

The rate at which DB2 is reading pages from disk is also important. This should be calculated for all table spaces and when compared will show if the I/O is spread evenly across all table spaces or if the workload on certain table spaces is causing more I/O than in other table spaces.

The rate at which pages are read from disk (or page read rate) is calculated using the following formula:

```
PRR = (Data Physical Reads + Index Physical Reads) /
        (Time since monitor switches reset or activated)
```

Based on the preceding buffer pool snapshot, the page read rate would be:

```
PRR = (33542 + 11323) / (23.53 seconds)
PRR = 1906.7 reads per second
```

Examining the table space snapshot for the table spaces using the identified buffer pool may provide additional information to help determine which table space, or table spaces, are being read most often. Any table space (or table spaces) with a significantly higher I/O rate than the other table spaces can be examined to determine if the performance could be improved by assigning the table space to its own buffer pool or by adding containers to the table space to improve the I/O bandwidth.

Read Time

For every millisecond that a DB2 agent spends waiting for a page to be read into the buffer pool, the application is also waiting. The database snapshots do not provide information on the amount of time taken by each read request, however, they do provide enough information to calculate the average time taken per read request. The average read time is calculated using the following formula:

```
ART = (Total Buffer Pool Read Time) /
      (Data Physical Reads + Index Physical Reads)
```

The average read time can also be calculated using the SQL table function as follows:

```
SELECT BP_NAME,
(INT(((FLOAT(POOL_READ_TIME)) / (FLOAT(POOL_INDEX_P_READS + POOL_DATA_P_
READS))) * 100))
AS avg_read_time_in_ms
FROM TABLE(SNAPSHOT_BP('sample',-1 )) AS snapshot_bp;
```

The SQL table function can also be used to calculate the buffer pool, data, and index hit ratios as well as the asynchronous read ratio and average read time in one SQL statement. This can be done using the following statement:

```
SELECT BP_NAME,
(INT((1 - ((FLOAT(POOL_INDEX_P_READS + POOL_DATA_P_READS)) / (FLOAT(POOL_
INDEX_L_READS + POOL_DATA_L_READS)))) * 100))
AS bpool_hit_ratio,
(INT((1 - ((FLOAT(POOL_DATA_P_READS)) / (FLOAT(POOL_DATA_L_READS)))) * 100))
AS data_hit_ratio,
(INT((1 - ((FLOAT(POOL_INDEX_P_READS)) / (FLOAT(POOL_INDEX_L_READS)))) * 100))
```

```
AS index_hit_ratio,
(INT(((FLOAT(POOL_ASYNC_DATA_READS + POOL_ASYNC_INDEX_READS)) /
(FLOAT(POOL_INDEX_L_READS + POOL_DATA_L_READS))) * 100))
AS asynch_read_ratio,
(INT(((FLOAT(POOL_READ_TIME)) / (FLOAT(POOL_INDEX_P_READS + POOL_DATA_P_
READS))) * 100))
AS avg_read_time_in_ms
FROM TABLE(SNAPSHOT_BP('sample',-1 )) AS snapshot_bp;
```

The output of this statement looks like the following:

```
BP_NAME               BPOOL_HIT_RATIO DATA_HIT_RATIO INDEX_HIT_RATIO
ASYNCH_READ_RATIO AVG_READ_TIME_IN_MS
-------------------- --------------- -------------- --------------- ------
----------- --------------------
IBMDEFAULTBP                       69             78              63
0                362

  1 record(s) selected.
```

Page Cleaner Triggers

It is also important to understand which of the three triggers are causing the page cleaners to be activated and write dirty pages from the buffer pools to disk. This information is available in the database snapshot information or through an SQL table function. The entries that describe the page cleaner triggers in the database snapshot are:

```
LSN Gap cleaner triggers              = 142
Dirty page steal cleaner triggers     = 2
Dirty page threshold cleaner triggers = 396
```

The SQL table function that will return the page cleaner triggers would look like the following:

```
SELECT DB_NAME,
       POOL_LSNGAP_CLNS,
       POOL_DRTY_PG_STEAL_CLNS,
       POOL_DRTY_PG_THRSH_CLNS
FROM TABLE(SNAPSHOT_DATABASE('sample',-1 ))
  AS snapshot_database
```

The output of the SQL function would look like the following:

```
DB_NAME   POOL_LSN_GAP_CLNS      POOL_DRTY_PG_STEAL_CLNS POOL_DRTY_PG_THRSH_
CLNS
--------  --------------------  ----------------------- --------------------
----
SAMPLE                    142                         2
396
```

   1 record(s) selected.

In this case the page cleaners have been triggered by the "good" triggers, i.e., changed page threshold or LSN gap (softmax) well over 99% of the time. As was explained earlier, a dirty page steal trigger is only done after a number of pages have been synchronously written to disk and their associated clients forced to wait. If the number of "bad" page cleaner triggers (i.e., dirty page steal triggers) is more than a couple percent of the total number of triggers, then the values set for changed page threshold and *softmax* as well as the number of page cleaners should be examined.

The percent bad page cleaner triggers are calculated as follows:

```
PBPCT = ((Dirty page steal cleaner triggers) /
(Dirty page steal cleaner triggers + Dirty page threshold cleaner triggers
+ LSN Gap Cleaner Triggers))* 100%
```

Based on the preceding snapshot information, the percent bad page cleaner triggers equals:

```
PBPCT = ((2) / (142 + 396 + 2)) * 100 %
PBPCT = 0.37 %
```

This ratio is very good and indicates that the system is primarily writing dirty pages to disk using the asynchronous page cleaners.

However, based on the following snapshot information for the page cleaner triggers, the percent bad page cleaner triggers is much higher.

```
DB_NAME   POOL_LSN_GAP_CLNS      POOL_DRTY_PG_STEAL_CLNS POOL_DRTY_PG_THRSH_CLNS
--------  --------------------  ----------------------- -----------------------
SAMPLE                     17                      2034
1192
```

   1 record(s) selected.

The percent bad page cleaner triggers equals:

```
PBPCT = ((2034) / (17 + 1192 + 2034)) * 100 %
PBPCT = 62.7 %
```

In this case the page cleaners are rarely being triggered by the pool LSN gap trigger, which indicates that the *softmax* database configuration parameter may be set too high. To determine the value of the *softmax* configuration variable (on UNIX), use the following command:

```
get db cfg for sample | grep -i softmax
```

This returns the following:

```
Percent log file reclaimed before soft chckpt (SOFTMAX) = 100
```

In this case the page cleaners are being triggered each time a log file is filled. This value is not abnormally high, so next examine the log file size using the following command:

```
get db cfg for sample | grep -i logfilsiz
```

This returns the following:

```
Log file size (4KB)                     (LOGFILSIZ) = 250000
```

The log file size for this database is 250,000 4K pages or 1GB. Therefore the page cleaners are only being triggered after 1GB of log information has been written. If the log file size cannot be reduced, the *softmax* configuration parameter can be reduced to cause the page cleaners to be triggered more frequently. To update the *softmax* configuration parameter to cause the page cleaners to trigger after 10% of a log has been written, use the following command:

```
update db cfg for sample using softmax 10
```

If the log files do not need to be this large and can be reduced, the log file size can be changed to 250 4K pages or 1MB using the following command:

```
update db cfg for sample using logfilsiz 250
```

Asynchronous Pages per Write

When the page cleaners are triggered, it is important that they be writing to disk as efficiently as possible. Having the page cleaners triggered too infrequently and writing a large number of pages to disk will cause the system to slow down. Likewise, having the page cleaners triggered frequently but writing a small number of pages to disk is also inefficient.

The number of pages written per page cleaner trigger is not captured in any of the DB2 snapshots, however, the average number of pages written per asynchronous write request can be calculated using the database base and buffer pool snapshot information. The average pages per asynchronous write can be calculated using the following formula:

```
APPAW = ((Asynchronous pool data page writes + Asynchronous pool index
page writes) / (Dirty page steal cleaner triggers + Dirty page threshold
cleaner triggers + LSN Gap Cleaner Triggers))
```

Based on the following information from the database and buffer pool snapshots:

```
LSN Gap cleaner triggers               = 142
Dirty page steal cleaner triggers      = 2
Dirty page threshold cleaner triggers  = 396

Asynchronous pool data page writes     = 167660
Asynchronous pool index page writes    = 178944
```

The average pages per asynchronous write would be:

```
APPAW = (167660 + 178944) / (142 + 2 + 396)
APPAW = 641.9
```

In this case, the page cleaners wrote an average of 641.9 pages, or 2.5MB, each time they were triggered. This value needs to be examined in the context of the size of the buffer pool that is being examined. For a 1GB buffer pool this is a small value and perhaps the page cleaners are being triggered too aggressively. For a 100MB buffer pool this value is much more reasonable.

Using Materialized Query Tables (MQTs)

A materialized query table (MQT) is a table that is defined based on the result of a query of one or more base tables. Prior to DB2 Version 8, MQTs required an *aggregation =operator* in their defining SQL, and thus were called Automatic Summary Tables. The next section describes how MQTs can provide effective performance improvements in a database.

Avoiding Repeated Calculations

A materialized query table can help to avoid having to repeat calculations, such as SUM, for a number of queries that reference the same base table. For example, a CUSTOMER_ORDER table that stores customer orders for a number of years will grow very large, and applications may run multiple queries on orders only for the year 2007. Only three columns from the table might be used in these queries. For example:

```
SELECT SUM(AMOUNT), TRANS_DT
FROM CUSTOMER_ORDER
WHERE TRANS_DT BETWEEN '1/1/2007' AND '12/31/2007'
GROUP BY TRANS_DT
```

   or

```
SELECT SUM(AMOUNT)' STATUS
FROM CUSTOMER_ORDER
WHERE TRAN S_DT BETWEEN '1/1/2007' AND '12/31/2007'
GROUP BY STATUS
```

Assuming that the table is indexed appropriately, the queries can be executed using index scans. The Explain plan that follows is an excerpt from the first statement, and it shows that the query has an execution cost of 152455 timerons to retrieve only 378 rows.

```
------------------- SECTION ------------------------------
Section = 1


SQL Statement:

   select SUM(AMOUNT), trans_dt
   from db2inst2.CUSTOMER_ORDER
   where trans_dt between '1/1/2007' and '12/31/2007'
   group by trans_dt

Estimated Cost       = 152455
Estimated Cardinality = 378
```

A substantial savings in execution time can be accomplished by creating an MQT that does the following:

- Contains these three columns

- Precomputes the sum

For this example, the MQT should be created as follows:

```
CREATE TABLE SUMMARY_CUST_ORDER_2007 AS
(SELECT SUM(AMOUNT) AS TOTAL_SUM, TRANS_DT, STATUS
FROM CUSTOMER_ORDER
WHERE TRANS_DR BETWEEN '1/1/2007' AND '12/31/2007'
GROUP BY TRANS_DT, STATUS
DATA INITIALLY DEFERRED REFRESH DEFERRED
```

The clause DATA INITIALLY DEFERRED instructs DB2 not to insert the data into the MQT as part of the CREATE TABLE statement. Instead, the DBA will have to perform a REFRESH TABLE statement to populate the MQT. The clause REFRESH DEFERRED indicates that the data in the table only reflects the result of the query as a snapshot at the time the REFRESH TABLE statement was issued. For more information on creating MQTs, see the SQL Reference.

To populate the MQT created previously, issue the following statement:

```
REFRESH TABLE SUMMARY_CUST_ORDER_2007
```

Once the MQT has been populated, queries run against the MQT can run much faster than queries run against the base table because the MQT contains many fewer rows and the SUM has already been precomputed. An excerpt from the execution once the MQT has been created and populated shows a dramatic performance improvement with an estimated cost of 101 timerons versus the original cost of 152455 timerons.

```
-------------------- SECTION ------------------------------
Section = 1

SQL Statement:

    select sum(total_sum), trans_dt
    from db2inst2.summary_customer_order_2007
    where trans_dt between '1/1/2007' and '12/31/2007'
    group by trans_dt

Estimated Cost        = 101
Estimated Cardinality = 25
```

Note that if the data in the CUSTOMER_ORDER table for the year 2007 gets updated after the MQT was refreshed, the MQT may need to be refreshed again.

For an MQT based on a table that changes frequently, it may be best to use the REFRESH IMMEDIATE option when creating the MQT to enable DB2 to automatically update the MQT as the base table is being updated.

Avoiding Resource Intensive Scans

Assume a set of frequently executed reports exist that query sales totals for the year 2007. The reports, which used to run very quickly in January, are now running more and more slowly as the amount of data for the year increases. Assuming that the table is indexed appropriately and the queries are being executed using index scans, MQTs can be used to help improve performance.

However, because the data is being updated all the time and the reports need current data, the MQT cannot be defined using the REFRESH DEFERRED option, because the

MQT will get out of sync with the base table the next time the base table is updated. For an MQT based on a table that changes frequently, the REFRESH IMMEDIATE option should be used when creating the MQT to enable DB2 to automatically update the MQT as the base table is being updated. The MQT can be created as follows:

```
CREATE TABLE SUMMARY_CUSTOMER_ORDER_2007 AS
(SELECT TRANS_DT, STATUS, COUNT(*) AS COUNT)_ALL, SUM(AMOUNT) AS SUM_
AMOUNT, COUNT(AMOUNT) AS COUNT_AMOUNT FROM CUSTOMER_ORDER GROUP BY TRANS_
DT, STATUS)
DATA INITIALLY DEFERRED
REFRESH IMMEDIATE
ENABLE QUERY OPTIMIZATION
```

To allow the optimizer to automatically choose the MQT, even when it is not explicitly referenced in the query, as we did in the preceding example, the ENABLE QUERY OPTIMIZATION must be in effect. This option is the default.

Although the statement is interested only in SUM(AMOUNT), it is best to include the COUNT(*) and COUNT(AMOUNT) in the full select. This helps to optimize the maintenance of the MQT. For example,

If all of the records for a given date are being deleted from the base table, such as the following:

```
DELETE FROM CUSTOMER_ORDER WHERE TRANS_DT = '04/21/2007'
```

DB2 must detect that all of the records for a particular date are now deleted, and delete all of the corresponding records in the MQT. Having the COUNT field allows DB2 to do this quickly, without having to scan either the table or its index. The COUNT(AMOUNT) is required only when the AMOUNT column is nullable.

This table was created with the REFRESH DEFERRED option, therefore the MQT must be populated manually as follows:

```
REFRESH TABLE SUMMARY_CUST_ORDER_2007
```

The table (MQT) has been enabled for optimization, and so it is also good practice to gather statistics on the table as follows:

```
RUNSTATS ON TABLE SUMMARY_CUST_ORDER_2007
        WITH DISTRIBUTION
```

The preceding query can now be routed to the MQT in the query rewrite phase of
the optimization, and its new access plan would look like the following:

```
------------------- SECTION ------------------------------
Section = 1

SQL Statement:

  select SUM(AMOUNT), trans_dt
  from db2inst2.customer_order
  where trans_dt >= '1/1/2007'
  group by trans_dt

Estimated Cost       = 392
Estimated Cardinality = 268
```

The detailed access plan shows that the optimizer is using the MQT (Summary
Table) to resolve this query, even though the query was selected from the
CUSTOMER_ORDER table, not the MQT:

```
Subsection #1:
   Access Summary Table Name = DB2INST2.SUMMARY_CUSTOMER_ORDER_2007  ID = 2,46
   |  #Columns = 2
   |  Relation Scan
```

Whenever the CUSTOMER_ORDER table is modified, an exclusive table lock may be
obtained and held on the MQT SUMMARY_CUSTOMER_ORDER_2007 until the end of
the transaction. That is true only for MQTs with aggregate functions created with the
REFRESH IMMEDIATE option. Therefore, transactions modifying relevant fields in the
CUSTOMER_ORDER table (including all inserts, updates, and deletes) must be kept very
short to reduce lock contention. This issue does not apply to MQTs created with the
REFRESH DEFERRED option, nor to replicated MQTs (described in the next section).

Enabling Collocated Joins Using Replicated MQTs

In a partitioned database, the performance of joins can be greatly enhanced through
collocation of rows of the different tables involved in the join. Figure C-1 describes
such an environment, where the STORE and TRANS tables have both been partitioned
on the STOREID column. An SQL query that requires a join on the STOREID column

will see significant performance benefits from this partitioning scheme because of the greater parallelism achieved through collocated joins.

However, when the CUST table is also involved in the join, a collocated join is not possible, because the CUST table does not have a STOREID column and therefore cannot be partitioned by STOREID. Although DB2 can choose to perform a directed join in this particular case, the performance would be less efficient than that of a collocated join because the movement of data rows occurs during the query execution.

A materialized query table can be used to replicate tables to other database partitions to enable collocated joins even when all of the tables are not joined on the partitioned key. In Figure C-1, the CUST table is replicated to the other database partitions using the materialized query table infrastructure in order to enable collocated joins for superior performance.

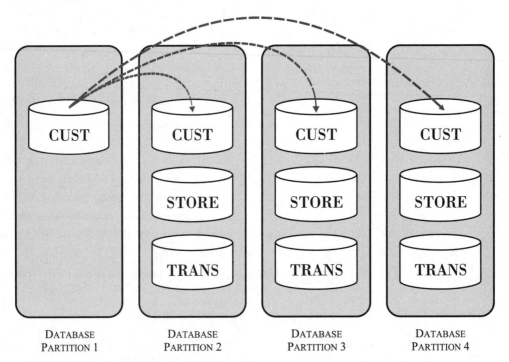

Figure C-1: Replicated Tables for Collocation.

The CUST table can be replicated by creating a replicated MQT.

For another example, the table CUSTOMER_ADDRESS has a reference to another table, ZIP_CODE, but the CUSTOMER_ADDRESS and ZIP_CODE tables are not collocated. However, these two tables are very frequently joined. Without a replicated MQT, the access plan would look like the following:

```
------------------- SECTION ------------------------------
Section = 1

SQL Statement:

  select c.*, z.zip, z.state_name, z.country_name
  from db2inst2.customer_address c join db2inst2.zip_code z on
              c.zip_cd = z.zip_cd

Estimated Cost       = 100975
Estimated Cardinality = 255819

Coordinator Subsection:
   Distribute Subsection #2
   |  Broadcast to Node List
   |  |  Nodes = 0, 1
   Distribute Subsection #1
   |  Broadcast to Node List
   |  |  Nodes = 0, 1
   Access Table Queue  ID = q1  #Columns = 38
   Return Data to Application
   |  #Columns = 38

Subsection #1:
   Access Table Queue  ID = q2  #Columns = 4
   |  Output Sorted
   |  |  #Key Columns = 1
   |  |  |  Key 1: (Ascending)
   Nested Loop Join
   .
   .
   .
   Insert Into Asynchronous Table Queue Completion  ID = q1

Subsection #2:
   Access Table Name = DB2INST2.ZIP_CODE  ID = 2,590
   |  #Columns = 4
   |  Relation Scan
   |  |  Prefetch: Eligible
   .
   .
   .
```

```
|  |  Broadcast to All Nodes of Subsection 1
|  |  Rows Can Overflow to Temporary Table
Insert Into Asynchronous Table Queue Completion  ID = q2

End of section
```

In this case, every time a query is issued that causes the join, it is necessary to broadcast the entire ZIP_CODE table to every database partition.

This may be a good situation in which to use a replicated MQT. A replicated MQT should be created based on a table in a single-partition database partition group that would allow collocated joins if replicated to other database partitions. To create the replicated MQT, use the CREATE TABLE statement with the REPLICATED option as follows:

```
CREATE TABLE SUMMARY_ZIP_CODE AS
(SELECT * FROM ZIP_CODE)
DATA INITIALLY DEFERRED
REFRESH IMMEDIATE
ENABLE QUERY OPTIMIZATION
REPLICATED
```

By default the first column will be hashed and if no table space is defined, USERSPACE1 is used.

Aggregates are not allowed in the definition of a replicated MQT.

If the table ZIP_CODE table has a unique index on ZIP_CD, this index should be created on the MQT as well to let the optimizer know that this column is unique and to allow it to choose an access plan based on this knowledge. To populate the MQT, create an index on it, and update the table's and index's statistics, execute the following commands:

```
REFRESH SUMMARY_ZIP_CODE

CREATE UNIQUE INDEX CU_ZIP_CODE
ON SUMMARY_ZIP_CODE (ZIP_CD)

RUNSTATS ON TABLE SUMMARY_ZIP_CODE
        WITH DISTRIBUTION
        AND DETAILED INDEXES ALL
```

This will allow the optimizer's query rewrite facility to reroute the query to the MQT, eliminating the need to broadcast the ZIP_CODE table to all database partitions every time the query is run. The new access plan would look like the following:

```
------------------ SECTION ------------------------------
Section = 1
SQL Statement:

   select c.*, z.zip, z.state_name, z.country_name
   from db2inst2.customer_address c join db2inst2.zip_code z on
           c.zip_cd = z.zip_cd

Estimated Cost        = 54176
Estimated Cardinality = 255819

Coordinator Subsection:
   Distribute Subsection #1
   |  Broadcast to Node List
   |  |  Nodes = 0, 1
   Access Table Queue  ID = q1  #Columns = 38
   Return Data to Application
   |  #Columns = 38

Subsection #1:
   Access Summary Table Name = DB2INST2.SUMMARY_ZIP_CODE  ID = 2,47
   |  #Columns = 4
   |  Relation Scan
   .
   .
   .
   Nested Loop Join
   |  Access Table Name = DB2INST2.CUSTOMER_ADDRESS  ID = 2,591
   |  |  #Columns = 35
   |  |  Index Scan:  Name = DB2INST2.CU_ZIP_CD  ID = 2
   .
   .
   .
   |  |  Insert Into Asynchronous Table Queue  ID = q1
   |  |  |  Broadcast to Coordinator Node
   |  |  |  Rows Can Overflow to Temporary Table
   Insert Into Asynchronous Table Queue Completion  ID = q1
```

In this case the cost is lower when the optimizer uses the MQT to allow a collocated join, however, if there were more partitions, and the partitions were placed on more than one server, the difference in cost between these access plans would be much greater.

Using replicated MQTs may yield significant performance advantages when the table that is being replicated to the other partitions:

- Is very frequently joined

- Is not heavily updated

- Is not too large

  ○ Infrequently updated larger tables may still make sense to be replicated if the one-time cost of replication can be offset by the performance benefits of collocation

The locking discussed earlier for REFRESH IMMEDIATE MQTs does not apply to REPLICATED MQTs.

Refresh Immediate vs. Refresh Deferred

A REFRESH IMMEDIATE MQTs affects performance of queries in the same manner that an index does. Specifically, it:

- Speeds up the performance of relevant select statements while returning current data

- Is automatically chosen by the optimizer whenever it makes sense

- Can degrade the performance of insert, update, and delete statements

- Cannot be updated directly

- May occupy considerable disk space

- May have exclusive locks held during updates of their base tables

To examine the performance impact of MQTs on updates, first examine the Explain plan for an INSERT statement shown in the following:

```
Section = 1

SQL Statement:
  insert into db2inst2.zip_code(zip_cd, zip, state_cd, state_name,
country_name) values (60606, '60606', 'IL', 'Illinois', 'United States')

Estimated Cost        = 25
Estimated Cardinality = 1
```

Next, examine the Explain plan for the same statement but with a REFRESH IMMEDIATE MQT based on the table as shown:

```
Section = 1

SQL Statement:

  insert into db2inst2.zip_code(zip_cd, zip, state_cd, state_name,
country_name) values (60606,'60606','IL', 'Illinois','United States')

Estimated Cost        = 50
Estimated Cardinality = 1
```

In this example, the estimated cost of inserting a record into the base table is doubled when a REFRESH IMMEDIATE MQT is defined on the table. On the other hand, REFRESH DEFERRED MQTs have no effect on the performance of insert, update, and delete statements.

> Some MQTs cannot be created as REFRESH IMMEDIATE. The exact rules that define when an MQT can and cannot be defined as REFRESH IMMEDIATE are described in the SQL Reference.

As a rule of thumb, use REFRESH IMMEDIATE MQTs in moderation to optimize frequently run queries in which current data is important.

Using MQTs – Let the Optimizer Decide

The optimizer may choose to reroute a query to an MQT defined with the REFRESH IMMEDIATE option instead of its base table, depending on the following:

- The current statistics on the base table, the MQT, and their indexes

- The value of the CURRENT QUERY OPTIMIZATION setting

The optimizer may choose to reroute a query to an MQT defined with the REFRESH DEFERRED option if the CURRENT REFRESH AGE setting is set to ANY.

> The CURRENT QUERY OPTIMIZATION and CURRENT REFRESH AGE options are described in detail in the SQL Reference.

The best practices for using MQTs are as follows:

- Create an appropriate MQT for the queries being executed

- Create appropriate indexes on the base table and MQT

- Keep the statistics current

- Let the optimizer choose whether to use the base table or the MQT; do not explicitly reference the MQT in the SQL

In some cases the optimizer may choose not to use the MQT in place of the base table. In these cases the SQL statement can be rewritten to reference the MQT directly. And the optimizer will use the MQT in the access plan regardless of whether it was defined as REFRESH DEFERRED or REFRESH IMMEDIATE, and regardless of the values of CURRENT REFRESH AGE and CURRENT QUERY OPTIMIZATION.

MQTs are very useful in various situations and can have a significant performance impact. The previous examples illustrate how applying MQTs can significantly improve query performance but can also negatively impact update performance if performed frequently. Although MQTs are very convenient and effective, they do come at a price of additional disk space.

MQTs created with the REFRESH DEFERRED option do not impact the performance of inserts, updates, and deletes on the base tables, but they may not be used by the optimizer as often as MQTs created with the REFRESH IMMEDIATE option.

MQTs and Subdomains

One of the most powerful yet most often overlooked uses of MQTs is to optimize access to frequently used subdomains of the data using a technique sometimes referred to as "Skinny MQTs" or more academically, a domain index or a multi-table index. These MQTs do not contain summarized data, but rather help DB2 quickly boil down the qualifying rows without boiling the ocean, so to speak.

Sure, DB2 can efficiently scan independent indexes and do index ANDing and HASHing, or one could define MQTs for each and every query predicate (NOT a good idea), but often there is a very small set of common query subpredicates (meaning not the entire query predicate, but rather just snippets) and their qualifiers that are executed over and over again. More often than not, several hundred queries can be reduced to a dozen or less very common subpredicates.

Think about this style of MQT as a quick prequalification of the rows involved in a more complex query. There are common domains that are referenced over and over again, resulting from a combination of common JOINs and common subpredicates. For instance, in a reporting system there might be a dozen or more reports that use the domain of data representing "YESTERDAY". One report might look at yesterday's sales overall, while another looks report might look at yesterday's sales region by region, while yet a third report looks at yesterday's sales product by product. Each of these queries likely shares the common subpredicate "WHERE DATE = yesterday", which immediately limits the record set.

Using the summary approach to MQTs, you will end up with three separate MQTs to answer each of these queries, each of which has to be maintained, causing escalating overhead. If on the other hand, you construct an MQT that simply delimits the domain, i.e. "YESTERDAY", and includes the attributes that are not likely to change, such as "Region" and "Product_ID" and create an appropriate index over this single MQT, all queries about "YESTERDAY" can be satisfied. Back JOINs and row fetches are likely to be required, but will use a far smaller subset of the data.

The idea here is simple: make it as fast and easy for DB2 to cut the data involved in the query down to size as quickly as possible, and without having to read several indexes, while at the same time avoiding the proliferation and subsequent overhead of many similar MQTs. And while the roots of MQTs may have been Automatic

Summary Tables, sometimes their best use is to define an index and the subdomains and attributes that help further refine those subdomains over those columns.

Find the common patterns in your queries. Think about them in terms of the domains they express—which attributes are used most often and which attributes will cause the size of the data to be reduced most quickly. These logical sets of data will also tend to have correlations with the physical clustering aspects of MDCs, so don't be surprised if they look familiar. Find the common snippets in your predicates and implement MQTs and indexes on those MQTs to answer those queries.

Joining in DB2

One of the more powerful features of the SELECT statement (and the element that makes data normalization possible) is the ability to retrieve data from two or more tables by performing what is known as a join operation. In its simplest form, the syntax for a SELECT statement that performs a join operation is:

```
SELECT * FROM [ [TableName] | [ViewName] ,...]
```

where:

TableName   Identifies the name(s) assigned to two or more tables that data is to be retrieved from.

ViewName   Identifies the name(s) assigned to two or more views that data is to be retrieved from.

Consequently, if you wanted to retrieve all values stored in two base tables named CL_SCHED and ORG, you could do so by executing a SELECT statement that looks something like this:

```
SELECT * FROM cl_sched, org
```

When such a SELECT statement is executed, the result data set produced will contain all possible combinations of the rows found in each table specified (otherwise known as a Cartesian Product). Every row in the result data set produced is a row from the first table referenced concatenated with a row from the second table referenced, concatenated in turn with a row from the third table referenced, and so on. The total number of rows found in the result data set produced is the product of the number of rows in all the individual table-references. Thus, if the table named CL_SCHED in our previous example contains five rows and the table named ORG contains eight rows, the result data set produced by the statement SELECT * FROM cl_sched, org will consist of 40 rows (5 x 8 = 40).

WARNING A Cartesian product join operation should be used with extreme caution when working with large tables; the amount of resources required to perform such a join operation can have a serious negative impact on performance.

A more common join operation involves collecting data from two or more tables that have one specific column in common and combining the results to create a result data set. The syntax for a SELECT statement that performs this type of join operation is:

```
SELECT
[* | [Expression] <<AS> [NewColumnName]> ,...]
FROM [[TableName] <<AS> [CorrelationName]> ,...]
[JoinCondition]
```

where:

Expression   Identifies one or more columns whose values are to be returned when the SELECT statement is executed. The value specified for this option can be any valid SQL language element; however, corresponding table or view column names are commonly used.

NewColumnName   Identifies a new column name that is to be used in place of the corresponding table or view column name specified in the result data set returned by the SELECT statement.

TableName   Identifies the name(s) assigned to one or more tables that data is to be retrieved from.

CorrelationName Identifies a shorthand name that can be used when referencing the table name specified in the *TableName* parameter.

JoinCondition Identifies the condition to be used to join the tables specified. Typically, this is a WHERE clause in which the values of a column in one table are compared with the values of a similar column in another table.

Thus, a simple join operation could be conducted by executing a SELECT statement that looks something like this:

```
SELECT lastname, deptname
FROM employee e, department d
WHERE e.workdept = d.deptno
```

You cannot join tables using LONG VARCHAR, BLOB, CLOB, DBCLOB, or XML columns

Join Techniques

When joining two tables, one table will be selected to be the outer table and the other table will be the inner table; the DB2 optimizer decides which will be the outer table and which will be the inner table based on the calculated cost and the join method selected. The outer table will be accessed first and will only be scanned once. The inner table may be scanned multiple times, depending on the type of join being performed and the indexes that are present on the tables. It is also important to remember that even though an SQL statement may join more than two tables, the optimizer will only join two tables at a time, keeping the intermediate results if necessary.

There are three basic join techniques that the DB2 optimizer can choose between. They are:

- Nested Loop Join

- Merge Join

- Hash Join

Nested Loop Join

When performing a nested loop join, for each qualifying row in the outer table there are two methods that can be used to find the matching rows in the inner table:

1. **Scan the entire inner table.** Read every row in the inner table and for each row determine if it should be joined with the row from the outer table.

2. **Perform an index lookup of the joined column(s) on the inner table.** This is possible when the predicate used for the join includes a column that is contained in an index on the inner table and can dramatically reduce the number of rows accessed in the inner table.

Figure D–1 illustrates a simple nested loop join.

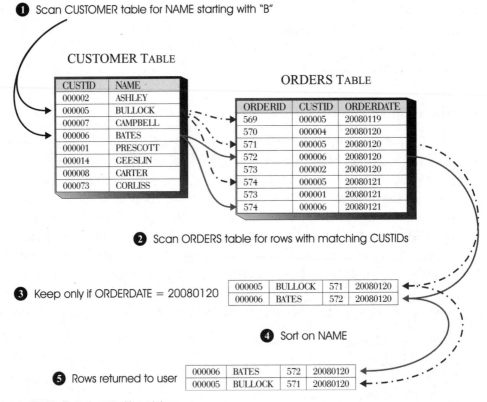

Figure D–1: A nested loop join.

In nested loop joins, the decision of which is the outer table and which is the inner table is very important because the outer table is only scanned once, and the inner table is accessed once for every qualifying row in the outer table. The optimizer uses a cost based model to decide which table will play which role in the join. Some of the factors taken into account by the optimizer when making this decision include:

- Table size
- Buffer pool size
- Predicates
- Ordering requirements
- The presence of indexes

Merge Join

Merge scan joins (or merge joins) require that the SQL statement contain an equality join predicate (i.e., a predicate of the form "table1.column = table2. column"). A merge join also requires that the input tables be sorted on the joined columns. This can be achieved by scanning an existing index or by sorting the tables before proceeding with the join. Figure D–2 illustrates a merge join.

With a merge join, both of the joined tables will be scanned at the same time looking for matching rows. Both the outer and inner tables will be scanned only once unless there are duplicate values in the outer table, in which case some parts of the inner table may be scanned again for each duplicated value. Because the tables are generally scanned only once, the decision on which is the outer and which is the inner table is somewhat less important than with a nested loop join. However, because of the possibility of duplicate values, the optimizer will attempt to choose the table with fewer duplicate values as the outer table.

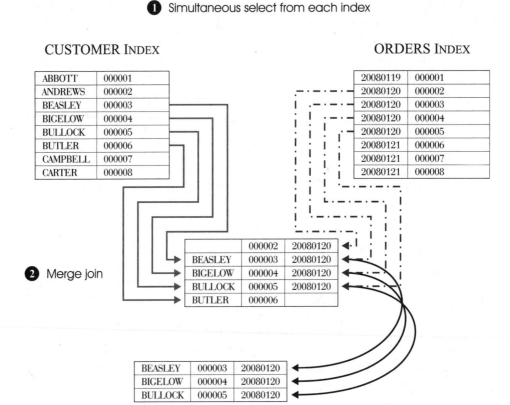

Figure D–2: A merge join.

Hash Join

Hash joins require one or more equality join predicates between the joined tables in which the data types for each of the joined columns must be the same. In the case of CHAR data types, even the length of the column must be the same. In the case of DECIMAL data types, the precision and scale must be the same. The fact that hash joins can handle more than one equality predicate between the joined tables is a distinct advantage over merge joins, which can handle only one equality predicate.

For hash joins, the inner table (also known as the build table) is scanned first, and the qualifying rows are copied into memory buffers. These buffers are divided into partitions based on a hash code computed from the column(s) in the join predicate(s). If there is not enough space in memory to hold the entire build table, some partitions will be written into temporary tables. Then the outer table (also known as the probe table) is scanned. For each row in the probe table the same hashing algorithm is applied to the join column(s). If the hash code obtained matches the hash code of a row in the build table, the actual values in the join columns will be compared. If the partition that matches the probe table row is in memory the comparison can take place immediately. If the partition was written to a temporary table, the probe row will also be written into a temporary table. Finally, the temporary tables containing rows from the same partitions are processed to match the rows. Because of the advantages of keeping the build table in memory, the optimizer will normally choose the smaller table as the build table to avoid having to create a temporary table.

If intra-partition parallelism is enabled the hash join may be executed in parallel. When a hash join is executed in parallel the build table is dynamically partitioned into multiple parallel tuple streams, and each stream is processed by a separate task to enter the build tuples into memory. At the end of processing the build table streams, the hash join process adjusts the contents of memory and performs any needed movement of partitions into or out of memory. Next, multiple parallel tuple streams of the probe table are processed against the in memory partitions and may be spilled for any tuples from hash join partitions that were spilled to temporary tables. Finally, the spilled partitions are processed in parallel, with each task processing one or more of the spilled partitions.

Which Join Technique to Use

We just examined the different join methods available in DB2, and at first glance it may appear that certain join methods seem to be a better choice than others. For example, merge joins have the advantage of scanning the tables only once when compared with nested loop joins that scan the inner table for every row of the outer table. Because of this, a merge join seems to be the better option; however, if the correct index exists on the outer table, a nested loop can end up being a better choice.

Similarly, a hash join seems to be a better option than a merge join because it does not need to sort the input tables before executing. However, if the order of the rows in the outer table needs to be preserved, then a merge join or nested loop join might be a better choice because a hash join cannot guarantee ordering of the output since it may need to spill to disk, which would disrupt the ordering of the rows.

The million-dollar question then is this: How does the optimizer decide which join method to use for a particular join? First, the optimizer must take into account the types of the predicates in the SQL query. After examining the join predicates and the current optimization level, one or more of the join methods may be eliminated. Once the optimizer has determined which of the join methods are possible, it will decide which join method to use based on the calculated costs of the available join methods.

The optimization level is a database configuration parameter that specifies the amount of optimization to be done for any given SQL statement. The higher the optimization level, the more potential access plans that will be examined in search of the best/lowest cost access plan. In DB2 9 the optimization level can be set to 0, 1, 2, 3, 5, 7, or 9.

Some join methods are not available at all optimization levels. For example:

- A nested loop join is available to the optimizer for all optimization levels.

- A merge join is available to the optimizer at optimization level 1 or higher.

- A hash join is available to the optimizer at optimization level 5 or higher.

Joining in a Partitioned Database

When two tables are joined together in a partitioned database, the data being joined must be physically located in the same database partition. If the data is not physically located in the same database partition, DB2 must move the data to a database partition by shipping the data from one partition to another. The movement of data between database partitions can be quite costly when the database is very large. Therefore it is important to examine the largest and most frequently joined tables in the database and choose a partitioning key to minimize the amount of data movement. Once the appropriate data is available in the database partition, DB2 can then determine the optimal join technique to execute the SQL statement.

In general, the best join strategy is to have all of the large, frequently accessed tables partitioned in such a way to resolve the most frequent join requests on their database partitions with minimal data movement. The worst join strategy is to have the large, frequently accessed tables partitioned in such a way as to force the movement of the data to the appropriate partitions for the majority of the joins.

The following sections will look at various access plans to show how the different partitioned join techniques differ. When describing the flow of a particular join strategy, the access plan chosen for the following SQL statement will be used:

```
SELECT o_orderpriority,
    COUNT(DISTINCT(o_orderkey))
FROM orders, lineitem
WHERE l_orderkey = o_orderkey AND
    l_commitdate < l_receiptdate
GROUP BY o_orderpriority
```

In this statement, the two tables involved in the join are ORDERS and LINEITEM. Both tables are defined in the same database partition group, and the partitioning key for each of these tables is listed below:

Table Name	Partitioning Key	Data Type
ORDERS	O_ORDERKEY	Integer
LINEITEM	L_ORDERKEY	Integer

It is important to note that the output of the Explain utility does not explicitly state the type of partitioned join strategy that was chosen by the optimizer, so in some cases you will be shown how you can decipher this information from the Explain -snapshot information presented.

Collocated Table Joins

A collocated join is the best performing partitioned database join strategy. For a collocated join to be possible, all the data needed to perform the join must be located in each of the local database partitions. With a collocated join, no data needs to be shipped to another database partition except to return the answer set to the coordinator partition. The coordinator database partition assembles the answer set for final presentation to the application.

DB2 will perform a collocated join if the following conditions are true:

- For tables residing in a nonpartitioned database partition group —if all the tables reside within a nonpartitioned database partition group, then any join may be resolved on that partition group; therefore, all the tables will be collocated.

- For tables residing in a partitioned database partition group —the joined tables must be defined in the same partition group.

- The partitioning key for each of the joined tables must match, that is, they must have the same number and sequence of columns. For example, assume that a table named CUSTOMER is partitioned on a column named C_CUSTKEY and a table named ORDERS is partitioned on a column named O_CUSTKEY. Each table is partitioned on one column and if the column types are compatible a collocated join can occur. If instead the CUSTOMER table is partitioned on a column named C_CUSTKEY, but the ORDERS table is partitioned on columns O_CUSTKEY and O_ORDERKEY, the CUSTOMER and ORDERS tables no longer have the ability to participate in a collocated join. Once the ORDERS table adds an additional column to the partitioning key, the value that the partitioning key will hash to is now different than when it was just the column O_CUSTKEY. Therefore there is no guarantee that the rows in the CUSTOMER table on any given partition will directly map to those in the ORDERS table on the same partition.

- For each column in the partitioning key of the joined tables, an equijoin predicate must exist. For example, if a table named ORDERS is partitioned on a column named O_ORDERKEY and a table named LINEITEM is partitioned on a column named L_ORDERKEY, in order for these two tables to be eligible for a collocated join, the SQL request must specify that the join columns are equal, that is, that ORDERS.O_ORDERKEY=LINEITEM.L_ORDERKEY.

- Corresponding partitioning key columns must be partition compatible. For example, if the O_ORDERKEY column is defined as SMALLINT in the ORDERS table and L_ORDERKEY is defined as INTEGER in the LINEITEM table, they are still compatible and may be used to join the two tables in a collocated join even though they are defined as different integer types.

Ultimately, the data required to complete the join must be found in the local database partition for DB2 to resolve the join. The collocated table join is the best performing type of join because the data already resides on the local database partition. DB2's goal in all the other join strategies is to relocate the data to the appropriate partition so that it may perform a join on each participating database partition. Figure D–3 illustrates the process flow of a collocated table join.

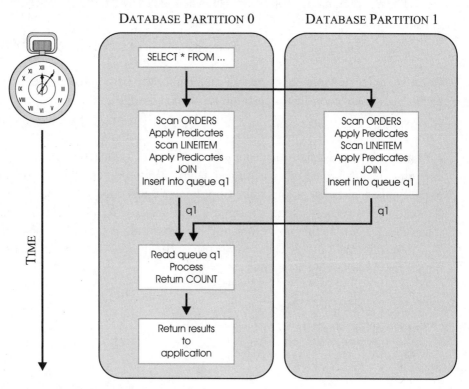

Figure D–3: The flow of a collocated join.

As you can see in Figure D–3, the initial request is sent to the coordinator partition. From there, the request is split across all appropriate database partitions. Each partition scans the ORDERS table, applies the ORDERS predicates, scans the LINEITEM table, applies the LINEITEM predicates, performs the join locally, and inserts the answer set into a table queue. (A table queue is used for communication between database partitions, or between subagents when the optimizer has chosen to do intra-partition parallelism.) The table queue is then sent to the coordinator partition where it is read and processed. The final answer set is then returned to the originating application.

In this case, the optimizer is able to choose a collocated join because all of the requirements for a collocated join have been met:

- The tables reside in the same database partition group
- The partitioning keys for both LINEITEM and ORDERS contain the same number of columns
- The partitioning key for each table is defined as INTEGER; therefore, they are collocatable
- The two tables are joined based on the equijoin of L_ORDERKEY = O_ORDERKEY

Once the collocated join completes on each database partition the answer sets will be returned to the coordinator partition for final assembly and to be returned to the application.

Now, let's examine Explain snapshot information for a collocated join. For each SQL statement executed in a partitioned database environment, the first subsection in the Explain snapshot output is the Coordinator Subsection. The Coordinator Subsection describes steps that the optimizer intends to take to execute the plan that it has decided will be the most efficient. This subsection is the key to the process flow to resolve the request. The Coordinator Subsection of the Explain snapshot output for the following statement:

```
SELECT o_orderpriority,
    COUNT(DISTINCT(o_orderkey))
FROM orders, lineitem
WHERE l_orderkey = o_orderkey AND
    l_commitdate < l_receiptdate
GROUP BY o_orderpriority
```

can be seen in Figure D–4.

```
Coordinator Subsection:
    Distribute Subsection #1      ◄──────────────── Ⓐ
    |   Broadcast to Node List
    |   |   Nodes = 1, 2
    Access Table Queue   ID = q1 #Columns = 3
    |   Output Sorted #Key Columns = 2
    Final Aggregation
    |   Group By
    |   Column Function(s)
    Return Data to Application
    |   #Columns = 2
```

Figure D–4: The Coordinator Subsection Explain snapshot output.

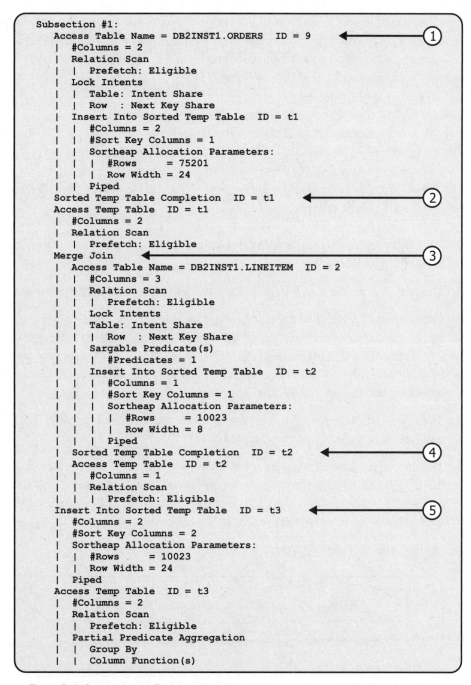

```
Subsection #1:
  Access Table Name = DB2INST1.ORDERS  ID = 9          ←①
  | #Columns = 2
  | Relation Scan
  | | Prefetch: Eligible
  | Lock Intents
  | | Table: Intent Share
  | | Row  : Next Key Share
  | Insert Into Sorted Temp Table  ID = t1
  | | #Columns = 2
  | | #Sort Key Columns = 1
  | | Sortheap Allocation Parameters:
  | | | #Rows     = 75201
  | | | Row Width = 24
  | | Piped
  Sorted Temp Table Completion  ID = t1            ←②
  Access Temp Table  ID = t1
  | #Columns = 2
  | Relation Scan
  | | Prefetch: Eligible
  Merge Join                                        ←③
  | Access Table Name = DB2INST1.LINEITEM  ID = 2
  | | #Columns = 3
  | | Relation Scan
  | | | Prefetch: Eligible
  | | Lock Intents
  | | Table: Intent Share
  | | | Row  : Next Key Share
  | | Sargable Predicate(s)
  | | | #Predicates = 1
  | | Insert Into Sorted Temp Table  ID = t2
  | | | #Columns = 1
  | | | #Sort Key Columns = 1
  | | | Sortheap Allocation Parameters:
  | | | | #Rows     = 10023
  | | | | Row Width = 8
  | | | Piped
  | Sorted Temp Table Completion  ID = t2           ←④
  | Access Temp Table  ID = t2
  | | #Columns = 1
  | | Relation Scan
  | | | Prefetch: Eligible
  Insert Into Sorted Temp Table  ID = t3            ←⑤
  | #Columns = 2
  | #Sort Key Columns = 2
  | Sortheap Allocation Parameters:
  | | #Rows     = 10023
  | | Row Width = 24
  | Piped
  Access Temp Table  ID = t3
  | #Columns = 2
  | Relation Scan
  | | Prefetch: Eligible
  | Partial Predicate Aggregation
  | | Group By
  | | Column Function(s)
```

Figure D–5: Subsection #1 Explain snapshot output.

From the Coordinator Subsection of the previous Explain snapshot, the first step (designated by an A in the Explain snapshot output shown in Figure D–4) is to distribute Subsection #1 to database partitions 1 and 2. The Explain snapshot output for Subsection #1 is shown in Figure D–5.

Node was the old term for database partition, so you will still see it in some places within DB2 utilities, messages, etc.

The processing that takes place in Subsection #1 (designated by numbers 1 through 5 in Figure D–5) is as follows:

1. DB2 will perform a relation scan (also known as a table scan or full table scan) of the ORDERS table.

2. The output from the scan will be placed in a temporary table referred to as t1.

3. The temporary table t1 will then be merge joined with the LINEITEM table on each database partition. The temporary table t1 will be the outer table and the LINEITEM table will be the inner table of the collocated join. Because the join can be directly resolved within each database partition, it is safe to conclude that the optimizer has chosen a collocated join strategy.

4. The output from the merge join of the temporary table t1 and the LINEITEM table will be a new, sorted temporary table, t2.

5. The temporary table t2 will be further processed to resolve any predicates that may be resolved at the partition level. The DISTINCT processing will be performed at the partition level and duplicate rows will be eliminated, with the final partition level answer set placed in the temporary table t3.

Subsection #1 concludes with the steps shown in Figure D–6.

```
    Partial Aggregation Completion
    |  Group By
    |  Column Function(s)
    Insert Into Asynchronous Table Queue   ID = q1        ◄────  ⑥
    |  Broadcast to Coordinator Node
    |  Rows Can Overflow to Temporary Table

End of section
```

Figure D–6: Subsection #1

Once all processing is complete, the rows in the temporary table t3 will be inserted into table queue q1 (designated by number 6 in Figure D–6). Table queue q1 will then be sent back to the coordinator partition where the processing is returned to the coordinator subsection. In the second step, B, the coordinator partition reads from the table queue, q1, performs the final aggregation of the result set received, and returns the final version of the data to the application requestor.

Keep in mind that the activities in Subsection #1 will occur simultaneously on each partition. (That's the case for all joins performed in a partitioned database environment.)

Directed Outer Table Joins

A directed outer table join can only be selected between two partitioned tables when there are equijoin predicates on all columns in the table partitioning keys. With a directed outer table join is chosen, rows of the outer table are directed to other database partitions based on the values of the columns being joined. The data is passed to the target database partition using a directed table queue (DTQ). Once the rows are available on the target database partitions, the join between the two tables will occur. Figure D–7 illustrates the process flow of a directed outer table join.

In Figure D–7 you can see that the process flow for a directed outer table join is as follows:

1. The initial request is sent to the coordinator partition from the originating application.

2. The coordinator partition dispatches the request to all relevant partitions.

3. The partitions scan the table that DB2 has chosen as the outer table and apply any predicates to the interim result set.

4. The partitions hash the join columns of the outer table that correspond to the inner table's partitioning key.

5. Based on the hashing values, the rows are then sent via table queue to the relevant target partitions.

6. The target partitions receive outer table rows via a table queue.

7. The receiving partitions scan the inner table and apply any predicates.

8. The partitions then perform a join of the received outer table rows and inner table.

9. The partitions then send the results of the join back to the coordinator partition.

10. The coordinator partition performs any final aggregation or other necessary processing and returns the final result set to the originating application.

For a directed outer table join, Explain will always show the inner table as a temporary table and the outer table as a table queue that has been hashed to the target database partitions. As noted in the collocated table join strategy section, the Explain snapshot output no longer explicitly states what type of partitioned join strategy is being employed to resolve the request.

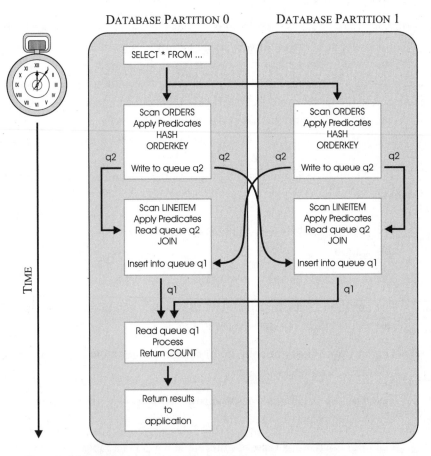

Figure D–7: The flow of a directed outer table join.

Directed Inner Table Joins

With the directed inner join strategy, rows of the inner table are directed to a set of database partitions, based on the hashed values of the joining columns. The data is passed to the target database partition using a directed table queue (DTQ). Once the rows are relocated on the target database partitions, the join between the two tables occurs on these database partitions. As with directed outer join, the directed inner table join may only be chosen as the join strategy when there are equijoin predicates on all partitioning key columns of the two partitioned tables.

The flow of processing for a directed inner table join is identical to the process flow for the directed outer table join except that the table that was directed to the target database partitions based on the hashed value of the joining columns is taken by DB2 as the inner table of the join on the database partition.

In the directed inner table join strategy, Explain will always show the outer table as a temporary table and the inner table as a table queue that has been hashed to the target partitions. So just how does the Explain snapshot for a directed inner table join strategy look? Before we can answer that, we need to execute a query that will produce this type of join. The statement that we used to produce a directed inner table join looks like this:

```
SELECT c_name, COUNT(DISTINCT(o_orderkey))
FROM customer, orders
WHERE c_custkey = o_custkey AND
    c_acctbal > 0 AND
    YEAR(o_orderdate) = 1998
GROUP BY c_name
```

In this statement, the two tables involved in the join are CUSTOMER and ORDERS. The partitioning key for each of these tables is as follows:

Table Name	Partitioning Key	Data Type
CUSTOMER	C_CUSYKEY	Integer
ORDERS	O_ORDERKEY	Integer

The CUSTOMER and ORDERS tables are not joined on their partitioning keys; therefore this join **cannot** be collocated. (The CUSTOMER and ORDERS join predicate from the above SQL statement is C_CUSTKEY = O_CUSTKEY.) An equijoin predicate is required for a directed inner or directed outer table join; therefore, this statement is eligible for a directed table join.

The Coordinator Subsection of the Explain information for this query can be seen in Figure D–8.

```
Coordinator Subsection:
    Distribute Subsection #2         ◄─────────────  Ⓐ
    |   Broadcast to Node List
    |   |   Nodes = 1, 2
    Distribute Subsection #1         ◄─────────────  Ⓑ
    |   Broadcast to Node List
    |   |   Nodes = 1, 2
    Access Table Queue   ID = q1 #Columns = 2  ◄──  Ⓒ
    |   Output Sorted #Key Columns = 2
    Final Aggregation
    |   Group By
    |   Column Function(s)
    Return Data to Application
    |   #Columns = 2
```

Figure D–8: The Coordinator Subsection Explain snapshot output.

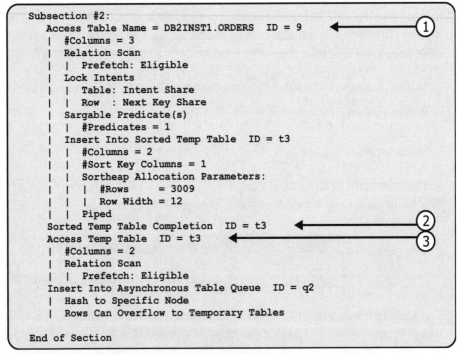

```
Subsection #2:
    Access Table Name = DB2INST1.ORDERS   ID = 9  ◄───  ①
    |   #Columns = 3
    |   Relation Scan
    |   |   Prefetch: Eligible
    |   Lock Intents
    |   |   Table: Intent Share
    |   |   Row  : Next Key Share
    |   Sargable Predicate(s)
    |   |   #Predicates = 1
    |   Insert Into Sorted Temp Table   ID = t3
    |   |   #Columns = 2
    |   |   #Sort Key Columns = 1
    |   |   Sortheap Allocation Parameters:
    |   |   |   #Rows     = 3009
    |   |   |   Row Width = 12
    |   |   Piped
    Sorted Temp Table Completion   ID = t3  ◄──────  ②
    Access Temp Table   ID = t3             ◄──────  ③
    |   #Columns = 2
    |   Relation Scan
    |   |   Prefetch: Eligible
    Insert Into Asynchronous Table Queue   ID = q2
    |   Hash to Specific Node
    |   Rows Can Overflow to Temporary Tables

End of Section
```

Figure D–9: Subsection #2 Explain snapshot output.

Once again, the Coordinator Subsection describes the steps that the optimizer intends to take to obtain the requested results. The first task (designated by letter A of the Explain snapshot output shown in Figure D–8), is to distribute Subsection #2 to database partitions 1 and 2. The activities that occur in Subsection #2 can be seen in Figure D–9 and occur on both database partitions 1 and 2 simultaneously.

The processing that takes place in Subsection #2 (designated by numbers 1 through 3 in Figure D–9) is as follows:

1. DB2 will perform a relation scan (table scan) of the ORDERS table and apply any predicates.

2. The output from the scan and the application of the predicates will be placed in a temporary table, t3.

3. The temporary table t3 will then be read. Rows from temporary table t3 will be inserted into table queue q2 and distributed to the appropriate target partitions based on the hash value of the O_CUSTKEY column that will be used to join to the CUSTOMER table.

The second step performed in the Coordinator Subsection (designated by a B in the Explain snapshot output shown in Figure D–8) is the distribution of Subsection #1 to database partitions 1 and 2. The Explain snapshot output for Subsection #1 can be seen in Figure D–10.

The processing that takes place in Subsection #1 (designated by numbers 4 through 7 in Figure D–10) is as follows:

4. DB2 will perform a relation scan (table scan) of the CUSTOMER table and apply any predicates.

5. The output from the scan and the application of the predicates will be placed in a temporary table, t1.

6. The temporary table t1 will be merge joined to the rows that were hashed to the database partition via the table queue q2. In this example, the temporary table based on the CUSTOMER table is the outer table of the join, and the hashed rows from ORDERS in table queue q2 is the inner table of the join. Based on the

```
Subsection #1:
   Access Table Name = DB2INST1.CUSTOMER  ID = 8         ←———————— ④
   |  #Columns = 3
   |  Relation Scan
   |  |  Prefetch: Eligible
   |  Lock Intents
   |  |  Table: Intent Share
   |  |  Row  : Next Key Share
   |  Sargable Predicate(s)
   |  |  #Predicates = 1
   |  Insert Into Sorted Temp Table  ID = t1
   |  |  #Columns = 2
   |  |  #Sort Key Columns = 1
   |  |  Sortheap Allocation Parameters:
   |  |  |  #Rows     = 6843
   |  |  |  Row Width = 32
   |  |  Piped
   Sorted Temp Table Completion  ID = t1               ←———————— ⑤
   Access Temp Table  ID = t1
   |  #Columns = 2
   |  Relation Scan
   |  |  Prefetch: Eligible
Merge Join
   |  Access Table Queue  ID = q2  #Columns = 2        ←———————— ⑥
   |  |  Output Sorted #Key Columns = 1
   Insert Into Sorted Temp Table  ID = t2
   |  #Columns = 2
   |  #Sort Key Columns = 2
   |  Sortheap Allocation Parameters:
   |  |  #Rows    = 2735
   |  |  Row Width = 32
   |  Piped
   Access Temp Table  ID = t2
   |  #Columns = 2
   |  Relation Scan
   |  |  Prefetch: Eligible
   |  Partial Predicate Aggregation
   |  |  Group By
   Partial Aggregation Completion
   |  Group By
   Insert Into Asynchronous Table Queue  ID = q1       ←———————— ⑦
   |  Broadcast to Coordinator Node
   |  Rows Can Overflow to Temporary Table
```

Figure D–10: Subsection #1 Explain snapshot output.

information in the Explain snapshot output shown, the optimizer has chosen a directed inner table join. Once the merge join is complete, the result set will be further processed to apply any additional predicates and any possible aggregations.

7. The result set is then written to the table queue q1 and broadcast back to the coordinator partition.

When control returns to the Coordinator Subsection the table queue q1 that was sent from each participating partition is read by the coordinator partition (designated by a C in the Explain snapshot output shown in Figure D–8), final aggregation is performed, and the final result set is returned to the originating application.

Directed Inner and Outer Table Joins

The directed inner and outer table join is basically a combination of a directed inner table join and a directed outer table join. With this technique, rows of the outer and inner tables are directed to a set of database partitions, based on the values of the joining columns, where the join will occur.

A directed inner and outer table join may be chosen by the optimizer when the following situation occurs:

- The partitioning keys of both tables are different from the join columns.
- At least one equijoin predicate must exist between the tables being joined in the query.
- Both tables are relatively large.

Figure D–11 illustrates the process flow of a directed inner and outer join strategy.

In Figure D–11 you can see that the process flow for a directed inner and outer table join strategy is as follows:

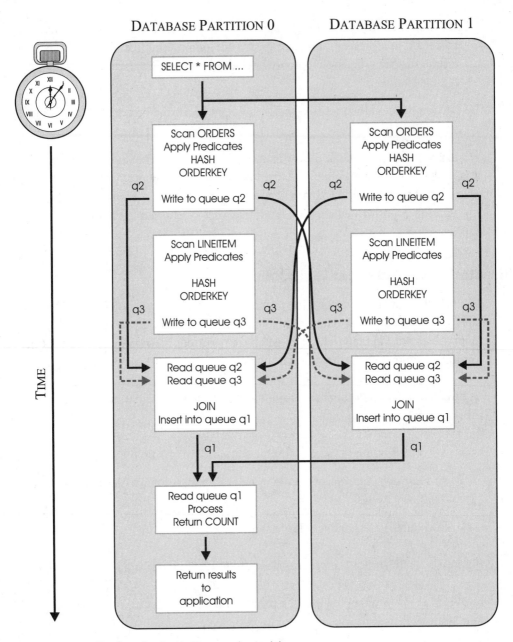

Figure D–11: The flow of a directed inner and outer join.

1. The initial request is sent to the coordinator database partition from the originating application.

2. The coordinator database partition dispatches the request to all relevant nodes.

3. The outer table will be scanned on all nodes that contain the table that DB2 has chosen as the outer table of the join. Predicates will be applied where appropriate.

4. The inner table will be scanned on all database partitions that contain the table that DB2 has chosen as the inner table of the join. Predicates will be applied where appropriate.

5. The outer table database partitions will hash each selected row from the outer table using the join columns specified in the query.

6. The inner table database partitions will hash each selected row from the inner table using the join columns specified in the query.

7. Each participating database partition will send the hashed rows to the appropriate database partition via hashed table queues.

8. The selected database partitions will receive the hashed table queues for the outer table rows.

9. The selected database partitions will receive the hashed table queues for the inner table rows.

10. The nodes perform the join of the received outer table rows to the received inner table rows. Predicates will be applied where appropriate.

11. The results of the join are then sent from the database partitions to the coordinator partition.

12. The coordinator partition performs any additional processing and returns the final result to the originating application.

The directed inner and outer table join strategy is characterized by the local join of two hashed table queues.

Broadcast Table Joins

A broadcast join is always an option for the DB2 optimizer. A broadcast table join will be chosen when the join is not eligible for any of the other join strategies or in the case where the optimizer determines that a broadcast table join is the most economical solution.

A broadcast join may be chosen in the following situations:

- There are no equijoin predicates between the joined tables.

- The optimizer determines that it is the most cost-effective join method.

- When there is one very large table and one very small table, of which neither is partitioned on the join predicate columns. (Rather than relocate the data in both tables, it may be more efficient to broadcast the smaller table to all the database partitions where the larger table resides.)

- The result set from applying the predicates to a large table results in a very small table.

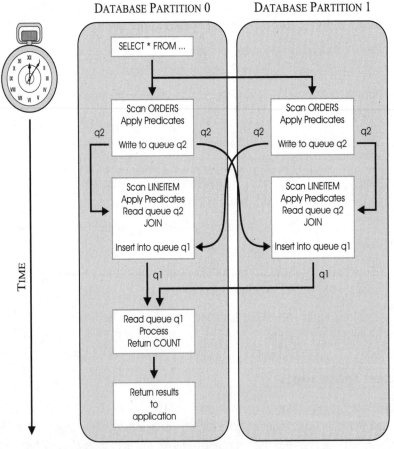

Figure D–12: The flow of a broadcast table join.

Figure D–12 illustrates the process flow of a broadcast table join.

In Figure D–12 you can see that the process flow for a broadcast table join is as follows:

1. The initial request is sent to the coordinator partition from the originating application.

2. The coordinator partition dispatches the request to all relevant nodes.

3. The database partitions scan the table that DB2 has chosen as the outer table and apply any appropriate predicates to the interim result set.

4. The database partitions transmit the full resultant outer table to all relevant database partitions via table queues.

5. The database partitions receive the full resultant outer table via table queue.

6. The receiving database partitions scan the inner table and apply any predicates. The output from this step is placed in a temporary table.

7. The database partitions then perform a join of the received outer table and the local temporary inner table.

8. The database partitions then send the results of the join back to the coordinator partition.

9. The coordinator partition performs any final aggregation or other necessary processing and returns the final result set to the originating application.

With a broadcast outer table join, the rows from the outer table are broadcast to the database partitions where the inner table has rows. With a broadcast inner table join, the rows from the inner table are broadcast to the database partitions where the outer table has rows. Essentially the two broadcast join strategies are equivalent with the inner and outer tables reversed. As with a directed join, a table queue is used to transfer the data between the partitions. But in this case a broadcast table queue (BTQ) is used.

Now, let's lake a look at Explain snapshot information for a broadcast table join. But first, we will need to change the query used once again. The statement that we used to produce a broadcast table join looks like this:

```
SELECT c_name, c_acctbal
FROM customer, nation
WHERE c_nationkey > n_nationkey AND
    c_acctbal > 0
ORDER BY c_name
```

In this statement, the two tables involved in the join are CUSTOMER and NATION. The partitioning key for each of these tables is as follows:

Table Name	Partitioning Key	Data Type
CUSTOMER	C_CUSTKEY	Integer
NATION	N_NATIONKEY	Integer

The CUSTOMER and NATION tables are not partitioned on the same key, therefore this join is not eligible for a collocated join. In addition, the two tables are not joined with an equijoin statement (C_NATIONKEY > N_NATIONKEY), therefore, this join is not eligible for any of the directed joins. The only option left to the optimizer is a broadcast join.

Again, when examining an Explain snapshot, start with the Coordinator Subsection. The Coordinator Subsection of the Explain information for this statement can be seen in Figure D–13.

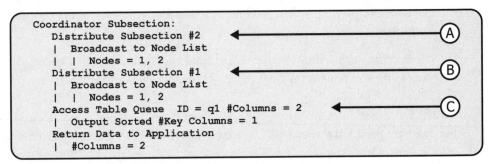

Figure D–13: The Coordinator Subsection Explain snapshot output.

Once again, the first task (designated by letter A of the Explain snapshot output shown in Figure D–13), is to distribute Subsection #2 to database partitions 1 and 2. In Subsection #2, DB2 will perform a relation scan (table scan) of the NATION table. The output from the scan will then be placed in table queue q1 and broadcast to all partitions named in Subsection #1.

The second step performed in the Coordinator Subsection (designated by a B in the Explain snapshot output shown in Figure D–13) is the distribution of Subsection #1 to database partitions 1 and 2. The Explain snapshot output for Subsection #1 can be seen in Figure D–14.

```
Subsection #1:
   Access Table Name = DB2INST1.CUSTOMER   ID = 8      ◄──────── ①
   |  #Columns = 3
   |  Relation Scan
   |  |  Prefetch: Eligible
   |  Lock Intents
   |  |  Table: Intent Share
   |  |  Row  : Next Key Share
   |  Sargable Predicate(s)
   |  |  #Predicates = 1
   |  Insert Into Sorted Temp Table  ID = t1
   |  |  #Columns = 3
   |  |  #Sort Key Columns = 1
   |  |  Sortheap Allocation Parameters:
   |  |  |  #Rows     = 6843
   |  |  |  Row Width = 40
   |  |  Piped
   Sorted Temp Table Completion  ID = t1    ◄──────── ②
   Access Temp Table  ID = t1
   |  #Columns = 3
   |  Relation Scan
   |  |  Prefetch: Eligible
   Nested Loop Join    ◄──────────────── ③
   |  Data Stream 1: Evaluate at Open
   |  |  Not Piped
   |  |  Access Table Queue  ID = q2  #Columns = 1
   |  Insert Into Sorted Temp Table  ID = t2
   |  |  #Columns = 1
   |  End of Data Stream 1
   |  Access Temp Table  ID = t2
   |  |  #Columns = 1
   |  |  Relation Scan
   |  |  |  Prefetch: Eligible
   |  |  Sargable Predicate(s)
   |  |  |  #Predicates = 1
   Insert Into Asynchronous Table Queue  ID = q1   ◄──────── ④
   |  Broadcast to Coordinator Node
   |  Rows Can Overflow to Temporary Table
```

Figure D–14: Subsection #1 Explain snapshot output.

The processing that takes place in Subsection #1 (designated by numbers 1 through 4 in Figure D–14) is as follows:

1. DB2 will perform a relation scan (table scan) of the CUSTOMER table. Any predicates that may be applied are applied at this time.

2. The output from the scan is placed in temporary table t1.

3. The temporary table t1 is then nested loop joined to the received broadcast table queue. Any appropriate predicates are applied at this time.

4. The result set is inserted into table queue q1 and broadcast back to the coordinator partition.

When control returns to the Coordinator Subsection the table queue q1 that was sent from each participating partition is read by the coordinator partition (designated by a C in the Explain snapshot output shown in Figure D–13). The data is then sorted and the final result set is returned to the originating application.

Partitioned Join Strategies and Performance

The table below is a summary of the characteristics of the partitioned database join strategies just discussed.

Join Strategy	Inner Table	Outer Table
Collocated Join	Temporary Table	Temporary Table
Directed Inner Join	Temporary Table	Directed Table Queue
Directed Outer Join	Directed Table Queue	Temporary Table
Directed Inner and Outer Join	Directed Table Queue	Directed Table Queue
Broadcast Inner Join	Temporary Table	Broadcast Table Queue
Broadcast Outer Join	Broadcast Table Queue	Temporary Table

From a performance point of view, the type of partitioned database join strategy that the optimizer chooses can impact performance. With the exception of a collocated join, all of the parallel join strategies require relocation of data across database partitions before the request may be resolved at the partition level. If the larger tables in the database are frequently being broadcast across database partitions, the current partition keys may need to be reevaluated to ensure they are correct for the given workload. The larger the amount of data that is moved between database partitions, the larger the impact on the performance of the query.

Broadcasting small tables to the database partition where they may be joined with your largest tables is desirable. Placing small tables in a single-partition database partition group is often desirable and will force DB2 to perform a broadcast of the table to the database partitions of the larger tables. The goal in a multi-partition database is to perform as much work as possible at the partition level, not at the coordinator partition level.

A Word About Predicate Handling

Query predicates can be handled in two different manners within DB2:

1. When data is being fetched the most straightforward approach is to return one row at a time and wait for the next request to fetch another one. Each returned row is then evaluated to determine whether it matches the given predicate(s). After evaluating the row against the given predicates, the next row is returned, and the same cycle is executed until reaching the end of the table being scanned. Although this approach might be the simplest, it causes a large number of round trips, which can turn into a performance penalty.

2. An alternative is when a record is fetched to reference it in memory and directly evaluate the predicate to determine whether the row qualifies or not. If the row does qualify, it is returned at the end of the predicate evaluation. If the row does not qualify, the next row is fetched immediately.

Definitions and Terminology

A predicate that can be processed using method 2 described previously is known as a sargable predicate (SARG). There are three types of sargable predicates:

- **BLOCK**—These predicates are resolved while scanning the block index scan for an MDC table.

- **INDEX**—These predicates are resolved while performing a conventional index scan.

- **DATA** (or DMS)—These predicates are resolved while scanning the data pages.

All predicates for which method 2 cannot be applied are referred to as residual predicates (RES). In this case the rows must be returned one at a time and evaluated as described in method 1.

Sargable vs. Residual Predicates

Based on the definitions and descriptions given previously, it is evident that residual predicates are systematically more expensive in their processing than sargable predicates. However, it is sometimes impossible to "push down" the evaluation of a predicate to make it sargable, and there are two main reasons for this:

- Data types LOB and LONG VARCHAR cannot be evaluated directly without retrieving the row, because when fetching LOB and LONG VARCHAR only a locator is returned, not the actual data.

- When the evaluation of a predicate requires that more than one page of data be fixed in the buffer pool. As an example, consider a predicate comparing two columns from two different tables: the first row would need to be fetched from the first data page, and then the second row would need to be fetched simultaneously from a different data page before the comparison can be made.

APPENDIX

Explain Tools

For SQL tuning, it is often necessary to determine the access path chosen by the optimizer for the query. Under the Federated Database architecture, the best performance results if the query is passed through to the remote database and all of the steps of the access plan are executed on the remote database.

Explain on the DB2 Enterprise server will show which operations are performed locally and which are performed on the remote server. To see the "real" access plan, it is necessary to run Explain on the remote database. For example, if the query is embedded in a stored procedure, it will be necessary to copy the query out of the stored procedure and replace parameter markers with hard-coded values to run Explain on the query.

The sections that follow describe creating Explain tables, running Explain from the command line, interpreting the output of Explain, and using Visual Explain.

EXPLAIN TABLES

Before Explain information can be captured, a special set of tables, known as the Explain tables, must be created. Each Explain table used, along with the information it is designed to hold, can be seen in Table E.1.

Table E.1 Explain Tables	
Table Name	Contents
EXPLAIN_ARGUMENT	Contains the unique characteristics for each individual operator used, if there are any.
EXPLAIN_INSTANCE	Contains basic information about the source of the SQL statements being explained as well as information about the environment in which the explanation took place. (The EXPLAIN_INSTANCE table is the main control table for all Explain information. Each row of data in the other Explain tables is explicitly linked to one unique row in this table.)
EXPLAIN_OBJECT	Contains information about the data objects that are required by the access plan generated for an SQL statement.
EXPLAIN_OPERATOR	Contains all the operators that are needed by the SQL compiler to satisfy the SQL statement.
EXPLAIN_PREDICATE	Contains information that identifies which predicates are applied by a specific operator.
EXPLAIN_STATEMENT	Contains the text of the SQL statement as it exists for the different levels of Explain information. The original SQL statement as entered by the user is stored in this table along with the version used by the DB2 Optimizer to choose an access plan to satisfy the SQL statement. (The latter version may bear little resemblance to the original because it may have been rewritten or enhanced with additional predicates by the SQL Precompiler.)
EXPLAIN_STREAM	Contains information about the input and output data streams that exist between individual operators and data objects. (The data objects themselves are represented in the EXPLAIN_OBJECT table, and the operators involved in a data stream can be found in the EXPLAIN_OPERATOR table.)

Typically, Explain tables are used in a development database to aid in application design, but they are not used in production databases, where application code remains fairly static. Because of this, they are not created along with the system catalog tables as part of the database creation process. Instead, Explain tables must be created manually in the database with which the Explain Facility will be used. Fortunately, the process used to create the Explain tables is straightforward: using the Command Line Processor, you establish a connection to the appropriate database and execute a script named EXPLAIN.DDL, which can be found in the "misc" subdirectory of the "sqllib" directory where the DB2 software was initially installed. (Comments in the header of this file provide information on how it is to be executed.) On the other hand, if you attempt to invoke the Explain Facility from within the Control Center, and the Explain tables have not been created for the database with which you are interacting, they will be created for you automatically.

The Explain tables must be created for each user ID that will run Explain (on each database).

Collecting Explain Data

The Explain Facility is comprised of several individual tools, and not all tools require the same kind of Explain data. Therefore, two different types of Explain data can be collected:

> **Comprehensive Explain Data.** Contains detailed information about an SQL statement's access plan. This information is stored across several different Explain tables.

> **Explain Snapshot Data.** Contains the current internal representation of an SQL statement, along with any related information. This information is stored in the SNAPSHOT column of the EXPLAIN_STATEMENT Explain table.

As you might imagine, there are a variety of ways in which both types of Explain data can be collected. The methods available for collecting Explain data include the following:

- Executing the EXPLAIN SQL statement

- Setting the CURRENT EXPLAIN MODE special register

- Setting the CURRENT EXPLAIN SNAPSHOT special register

- Using the EXPLAIN bind option with the PRECOMPILE or BIND command

- Using the EXPLSNAP bind option with the PRECOMPILE or BIND command

The Explain SQL Statement

One way to collect both comprehensive Explain information and Explain snapshot data for a single, dynamic SQL statement is by executing the EXPLAIN SQL statement. The basic syntax for this statement is:

```
EXPLAIN [ALL | PLAN | PLAN SELECTION]
<FOR SNAPSHOT | WITH SNAPSHOT>
FOR [SQLStatement]
```

where:

SQLStatement   Identifies the SQL statement for which Explain data or Explain snapshot data is to be collected. (The statement specified must be a valid INSERT, UPDATE, DELETE, SELECT, SELECT INTO, VALUES, or VALUES INTO SQL statement.)

If the FOR SNAPSHOT option is specified with the EXPLAIN statement, only Explain snapshot information will be collected for the dynamic SQL statement specified. On the other hand, if the WITH SNAPSHOT option is specified instead, both comprehensive Explain information and Explain snapshot data will be collected for the dynamic SQL statement specified. However, if neither option is used, only comprehensive Explain data will be collected; no Explain snapshot data will be produced.

Thus, if you wanted to collect only comprehensive Explain data for the SQL statement "SELECT * FROM department," you could do so by executing an EXPLAIN statement that looks like this:

```
EXPLAIN ALL FOR SELECT * FROM department
```

On the other hand, if you wanted to collect only Explain snapshot data for the same SQL statement, you could do so by executing an EXPLAIN statement that looks like this:

```
EXPLAIN ALL FOR SNAPSHOT FOR SELECT * FROM department
```

And finally, if you wanted to collect both comprehensive Explain data and Explain snapshot information for the SQL statement "SELECT * FROM department," you could do so by executing an EXPLAIN statement that looks like this:

```
EXPLAIN ALL WITH SNAPSHOT FOR SELECT * FROM department
```

It is important to note that the EXPLAIN statement does not execute the SQL statement specified, nor does it display the Explain information collected—other Explain Facility tools must be used to view the information collected. (We'll look at those tools shortly.)

Evaluating Explain Data

Both comprehensive and snapshot data is stored in one or more Explain tables as it is collected, thus, you could evaluate Explain data by constructing one or more queries that retrieve data from the Explain tables. A better way to view Explain · information collected is by using one of the Explain Facility tools that have been designed specifically for presenting Explain information in a meaningful format. This set of tools consists of:

- The db2expln tool

- The db2exfmt tool

- Visual Explain

db2expln

When a source code file containing Embedded SQL statements is bound to a database (either as part of the precompile process or during deferred binding), the DB2 Optimizer analyzes each static SQL statement encountered and generates a corresponding access plan, which is then stored in the database in the form of a package. Given the name of the database, the name of the package, the ID of the package creator, and a section number (if the section number 0 is specified, all sections of the package will be processed), the db2expln tool will interpret and describe the access plan information for any package that is stored in a database's system catalog. Because the db2expln tool works directly with a package and not with comprehensive Explain or Explain snapshot data, it is typically used to produce information about the access plans that have been chosen for packages for which Explain data has not been captured. However, because the db2expln tool can only access information that has been stored in a package, it can only describe the implementation of the final access plan chosen; it cannot provide information on how a particular SQL statement was optimized.

To run db2expln, you must have SELECT privilege to the system catalog views as well as EXECUTE authority for the db2expln package.

The db2expln tool can also be used to Explain—and optionally, produce a graph of the access plan chosen by the DB2 Optimizer for—a dynamic SQL statement. For example, suppose you wanted to view the access plan the Optimizer would select for the query "SELECT * FROM department." You could do so by executing a db2expln command that looks something like this:

```
db2expln -d sample -t -g -statement "SELECT * FROM department"
```

And if you executed this command using the SAMPLE database provided with DB2, you would see a report that looks something like this:

```
C:\DB2_ESE\SQLLIB\BIN>

DB2 Universal Database Version 9.1, 5622-044 (c) Copyright IBM Corp.
1991, 2006
Licensed Material - Program Property of IBM
IBM DB2 Universal Database SQL and XQUERY Explain Tool

******************** DYNAMIC *****************************
==================== STATEMENT ============================


   Isolation Level          = Cursor Stability
   Blocking                 = Block Unambiguous Cursors
   Query Optimization Class = 5

   Partition Parallel       = No
   Intra-Partition Parallel = No
   SQL Path                 = "SYSIBM", "SYSFUN", "SYSPROC",
                              SYSIBMADM", "RSANDERS"

Statement:

  SELECT * FROM department

Section Code Page = 1252

Estimated Cost = 7.596399
Estimated Cardinality = 14.000000

Access Table Name = RSANDERS.DEPARTMENT  ID = 2,5
|  #Columns = 5
|  Relation Scan
|  |  Prefetch: Eligible
|  Lock Intents
```

```
|  |  Table: Intent Share
|  |  Row  : Next Key Share
|  Sargable Predicate(s)
|  |  Return Data to Application
|  |  |  #Columns = 5
Return Data Completion


End of section


Optimizer Plan:


    RETURN
    (   1)
       |
    TBSCAN
    (   2)
       |
  Table:
  RSANDERS
  DEPARTMENT
```

The db2expln tool works directly with a package and not with comprehensive Explain or Explain snapshot data, and so you will need to provide the name of the package you want to display Explain information for. The following query can be used to get a list of package names from a database:

```
SELECT SUBSTR(PROCSCHEMA, 1, 8),
       SUBSTR(PROCNAME, 1, 32),
       SUBSTR(IMPLEMENTATION, 1, 8)
   FROM SYSCAT.PROCEDURES
```

If such a query were to show that a package named P7597614 existed in the database, you could view the access plan chosen by the optimizer for that package by executing a db2expln command that looks something like this:

```
db2expln -d sample -c DSNOW -p P7597614 -s 0 -o
db2expln_P7597614.rpt
```

Alternatively, to explain all the packages of schema DSNOW, you can use the wild card character %:

```
db2expln -d sample -c dsnow -p % -s 0 -o
db2expln_all_packages.rpt
```

Finally, to explain a dynamic statement contained in a file named STMT1.SQL, you would execute a db2expln command that looks something like this:

```
db2expln -d sample -stmtfile stmt1.sql 1 -t terminator @ -o
db2expln_ stmt1.rpt
```

db2exfmt

Unlike the db2expln tool, the db2exfmt tool is designed to work directly with comprehensive Explain or Explain snapshot data that has been collected and stored in the Explain tables. Given a database name and other qualifying information, the db2exfmt tool will query the Explain tables for information, format the results, and produce a text-based report that can be displayed directly on the terminal or written to an ASCII-formatted file.

For example, if you wanted to generate a detailed report consisting of all Explain data that has been collected and stored in the SAMPLE database provided with DB2, you could do so by executing a db2exfmt command that looks something like this:

```
db2exfmt -d sample -1 -o F:/db2exfmt.out
```

When this command is executed, a report will be produced and written to a file named db2exfmt.out (that resides on the F: drive), and you should see a message that looks something like this:

```
DB2 Universal Database Version 9.1, 5622-044 (c) Copyright IBM
Corp. 1991, 2006
Licensed Material - Program Property of IBM
IBM DATABASE 2 Explain Table Format Tool


Connecting to the Database.
Connect to Database Successful.
Output is in F:/db2exfmt.out.
Executing Connect Reset -- Connect Reset was Successful.
```

And the beginning of the output file created (db2exfmt.out) should look something like this:

```
DB2 Universal Database Version 9.1, 5622-044 (c) Copyright
IBM Corp. 1991, 2006
Licensed Material - Program Property of IBM
IBM DATABASE 2 Explain Table Format Tool
```

```
******************** EXPLAIN INSTANCE ********************

DB2_VERSION:            09.01.0
SOURCE_NAME:            SYSSH200
SOURCE_SCHEMA:          NULLID
SOURCE_VERSION:
EXPLAIN_TIME:           2007-05-17-16.40.32.188000
EXPLAIN_REQUESTER:      RSANDERS

Database Context:
----------------
        Parallelism:            None
        CPU Speed:              4.762805e-007
        Comm Speed:             100
        Buffer Pool size:       250
        Sort Heap size:         256
        Database Heap size:     600
        Lock List size:         50
        Maximum Lock List:      22
        Average Applications:   1
        Locks Available:        935

Package Context:
---------------
        SQL Type:               Dynamic
        Optimization Level:     5
        Blocking:               Block All Cursors
        Isolation Level:        Cursor Stability

    ...
```

Visual Explain

Visual Explain is a GUI tool that provides database administrators and application developers with the ability to view a graphical representation of the access plan that has been chosen for a particular SQL statement. In addition, Visual Explain allows you to do the following:

- See the database statistics that were used to optimize the SQL statement.

- Determine whether an index was used to access table data. (If an index was not used, Visual Explain can help you determine which columns might benefit from being indexed.)

- View the effects of performance tuning by allowing you to make "before" and "after" comparisons.

- Obtain detailed information about each operation that is performed by the access plan, including the estimated cost of each.

However, Visual Explain can be used to view only Explain snapshot data; to view Explain data that has been collected and written to the Explain tables, the db2exfmt tool must be used instead.

Activating Visual Explain. One of the more common ways to activate Visual Explain is by generating Explain data for a dynamic SQL statement using the Explain Query Statement dialog. (Another is by choosing a query for which Explain data has already been generated from the Explained Statement History dialog.) Figure E–1 shows the Control Center menu items that must be selected to activate Explain Query Statement dialog; Figure E–2 shows how the Explain Query Statement dialog might look when it has been populated with a simple query.

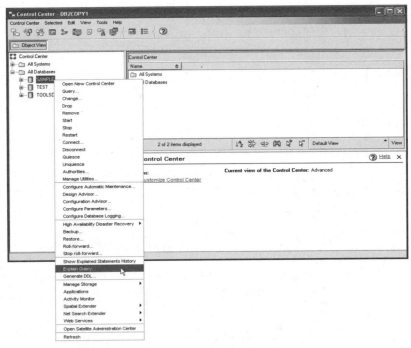

Figure E–1: Invoking the Explain Query dialog from the Control Center.

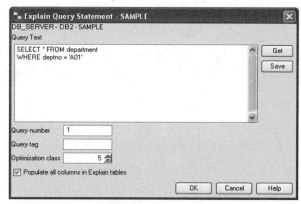

Figure E–2: The Explain Query Statement dialog.

After the Explain Query Statement dialog is opened, any dynamic SQL statement can be entered into the "Query text" entry field. Then, when the "OK" push button located at the bottom of the dialog is selected, Explain snapshot data will be collected for the SQL statement specified. And after all processing is complete, control will be transferred to the Access Plan Graph dialog of Visual Explain, where a graphical view of the access plan chosen for the SQL statement specified will be presented.

Figure E–3 shows how the Access Plan Graph dialog of Visual Explain might look when it is first activated.

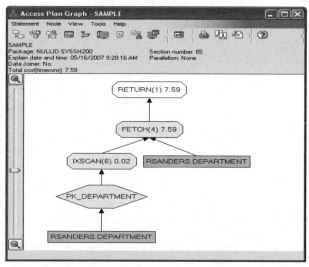

Figure E–3: The Access Plan Graph dialog of Visual Explain.

Visual Explain output. As you can see in Figure E–3, the output provided by Visual Explain consists of a hierarchical graph that represents the various components needed to process the access plan that has been chosen for a particular SQL statement. Each component is represented as a graphical object that is known as a node, and two types of nodes can exist:

Operator. An operator node is used to identify either an action that must be performed on data or output produced from a table or index.

Operand. An operand node is used to identify an entity on which an operation is performed (for example, a table would be the operand of a table scan operator).

Typically, operand nodes are used to identify tables, indexes, and table queues (table queues are used when intrapartition parallelism is used), which are symbolized in the hierarchical graph by rectangles (tables), diamonds (indexes), and parallelograms (table queues). Operator nodes, on the other hand, are used to identify anything from an insert operation to an index or table scan. Operator nodes, which are symbolized in the hierarchical graph by ovals, indicate how data is accessed, how tables are joined, and other factors such as whether a sort operation is to be performed. Table E.2 lists the more common operators that can appear in an access plan hierarchical graph.

Table E.2 Common Operators	
Definition	**Description**
DELETE	Deletes rows from a table.
EISCAN	Scans a user-defined index to produce a reduced stream of rows.
FETCH	Fetches columns from a table using a specific record identifier.
FILTER	Filters data by applying one or more predicates to it.
GRPBY	Groups rows by common values of designated columns or functions and evaluates set functions.
HSJOIN	Represents a hash join, where two or more tables are hashed on the join columns. (Preferred method for joins performed in a decision support environment.)
INSERT	Inserts rows into a table.
IXAND	ANDs together the row identifiers (RIDs) from two or more index scans.

Table E.2 Common Operators (Continued)	
Definition	**Description**
IXSCAN	Scans an index of a table with optional start/stop conditions, producing an ordered stream of rows.
MSJOIN	Represents a merge join, where both outer and inner tables must be in join-predicate order.
NLJOIN	Represents a nested loop join that accesses an inner table once for each row of the outer table. (Preferred method for joins performed in an OLTP environment.)
RETURN	Represents the return of data from the query to the user.
RIDSCN	Scans a list of row identifiers (RIDs) obtained from one or more indexes.
SHIP	Retrieves data from a remote database source. Used in the federated system.
SORT	Sorts rows in the order of specified columns and optionally eliminates duplicate entries.
TBSCAN	Retrieves rows by reading all required data directly from the data pages.
TEMP	Stores data in a temporary table to be read back out (possibly multiple times).
TQUEUE	Transfers table data between database agents.
UNION	Concatenates streams of rows from multiple tables.
UNIQUE	Eliminates rows with duplicate values, for specified columns.
UPDATE	Updates rows in a table.

Arrows that illustrate how data flows from one node to the next connect all nodes shown in the hierarchical graph, and a RETURN operator normally terminates this path. Figure E–3 shows how the hierarchical graph for an access plan that contains three different operator nodes (IXSCAN, FETCH, and RETURN) and two different operand nodes (a table named RSANDERS.DEPARTMENT and an index named PK_DEPARTMENT) might be displayed in Visual Explain.

Detailed information about each operator node shown in an access plan hierarchical graph is also available, and this information can be accessed by placing the mouse pointer over any operator node, right-clicking the mouse button, and selecting the Show Details action from the pop-up menu displayed. Figure E–4 shows the menu items that must be selected to view detailed information about a particular operator node; Figure E–5 shows how the Operator details dialog might look after it has been activated.

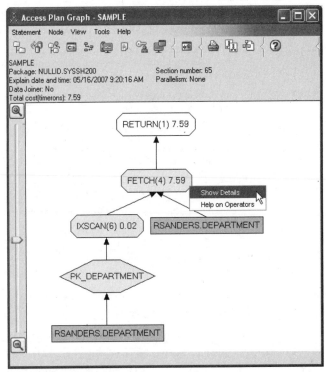

Figure E–4: Invoking the Operator details dialog from Visual Explain.

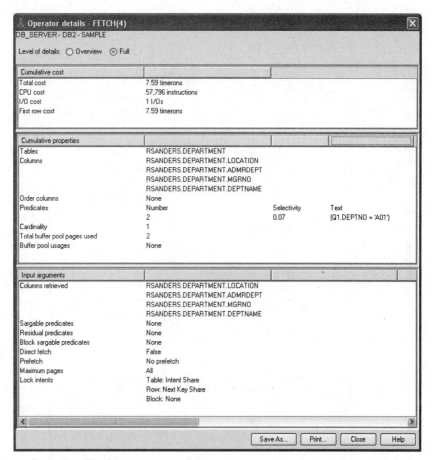

Figure E–5: The Operator details dialog.

Likewise, detailed information about the table or index statistics that were used to select the access plan chosen are available for each operand node shown in an access plan hierarchical graph. This information can be accessed by placing the mouse pointer over any operand node, right-clicking the mouse button, and selecting the Show Statistics action from the menu displayed. Figure E–6 shows the menu items that must be selected to view detailed information about a particular operand node; Figure E–7 shows how the Table/Index Statistics dialog might look after it has been activated.

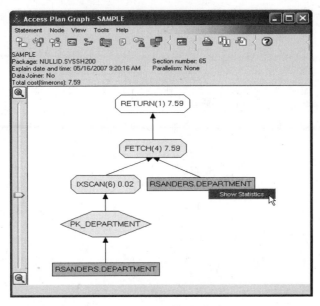

Figure E–6: Invoking the Table/Index Statistics dialog from
Visual Explain.

Figure E–7: The Table/Index Statistics dialog.

APPENDIX F

Sample Test

Welcome to the section that really makes this book unique. One of the best ways to prepare for the DB2 9 for Linux, UNIX, and Windows Advanced Database Administration exam (Exam 734) is by answering sample questions that are presented in the same format that you will see when you take the certification exam. In this section you will find 120 sample questions, along with comprehensive answers for every question. (It's not enough to know which answer is correct; it's also important to know why the answer is correct and why the other choices are wrong!)

If you worked through the Practice Questions presented at the end of each chapter, most of these questions will be familiar; if you skipped that part, all of those questions can all be found here. All of the questions presented here were developed by analyzing the final set of questions that were chosen for the DB2 9 for Linux, UNIX, and Windows Advanced Database Administration exam (Exam 734). (We were members of the team that developed the DB2 9 for Linux, UNIX, and Windows Advanced Database Administration certification exam so we had access to every question!) We hope you find this material helpful.

Roger E. Sanders
Dwaine R. Snow

Database Design

Question 1

A table space named MY_TBSP was created in a database partition group named DBPG1. Later, a decision is made to move this table space to a database partition group named DBPG2. How can this change be made?

○ A. Change the partition group associate with the table space by executing the ALTER TABLESPACE statement.

○ B. Detach the table space from the DBPG1 database partition group and attach it to the DBPG2 database partition group using the DETACH PARTITION and ATTACH PARTITION statements.

○ C. Drop the table space using the DROP statement and recreate it in database partition DBPG2 using the CREATE TABLESPACE statement.

○ D. Move the table space from the database DBPG1 partition group to the DBPG2 database partition group using the REDISTRIBUTE PARTITION GROUP statement.

Question 2

Which of the following commands will create a DMS table space named TBSP1 on all database partitions used by a multi-partition database?

○ A. CREATE TABLESPACE tbsp1 MANAGED BY DATABASE USING (FILE '/db2files/tbsp1/cont1P $N' 5000)

○ B. CREATE TABLESPACE tspc1 MANAGED BY DATABASE USING (FILE '/db2files/ tbsp1/cont1P $NODE' 5000)

○ C. CREATE TABLESPACE tspc1 MANAGED BY DATABASE USING (FILE '/db2files/ tbsp1/cont1P $P' 5000)

○ D. CREATE TABLESPACE tspc1 MANAGED BY DATABASE USING (FILE '/db2files/ tbsp1/cont1P $DBPARTITIONNUM' 5000)

Question 3

While connected to a database that has four partitions, a database administrator executes the following command:

```
CREATE BUFFERPOOL mybp SIZE 3000
```

If 8 MB of memory is available at the time the command is executed, how much memory is immediately consumed?

○ A. 0 MB

○ B. 6 MB

○ C. 8 MB

○ D. 12 MB

Question 4

A database administrator needs to create a federated database and configure access to join data from two Oracle instances, one SQL Server instance, and one DB2 database.

Which objects are needed to establish the specified connections?

- ○ A. 2 Oracle servers, 2 Oracle wrappers, 1 SQL Server server, 1 SQL Server wrapper, and nicknames for all databases.
- ○ B. 2 Oracle servers, 1 Oracle wrapper, 1 SQL Server server, 1 SQL Server wrapper, and nicknames for all databases.
- ○ C. 2 Oracle servers, 2 Oracle wrappers, 1 SQL Server server, 1 SQL Server wrapper, 1 DB2 server, 1 DB2 wrapper, and nicknames for all databases.
- ○ D. 2 Oracle servers, 1 Oracle wrapper, 1 SQL Server server, 1 SQL Server wrapper, 1 DB2 server, 1 DB2 wrapper, and nicknames for all databases.

Question 5

Which CREATE TABLESPACE statement option is used to enable non-buffered I/O?

- ○ A. CONCURRENT IO
- ○ B. NO FILE SYSTEM CACHING
- ○ C. USE DIRECT IO
- ○ D. NO FILE BUFFERING

Question 6

Which two of the following can be successfully performed using the ALTER TABLESPACE statement? (Select two)

- ❑ A. Convert an SMS table space to a DMS table space.
- ❑ B. Change the extent size for a DMS table space.
- ❑ C. Change the prefetch size for an automatic storage table space.
- ❑ D. Resize the containers used by an SMS table space.
- ❑ E. Add a container to an SMS table space on a database partition that currently has no containers

Question 7

If no initial size is specified for a table space that is created in a database that is using automatic storage, how much storage space is preallocated for the table space?

○ A. 32 pages
○ B. 32 MB
○ C. 64 pages
○ D. 64 MB

Question 8

Given a newly created database and sufficient memory, if the following statements are successfully executed on a UNIX server:

```
CREATE BUFFERPOOL bp1 SIZE 60 MB;
CREATE BUFFERPOOL bp2 SIZE 20000 PAGESIZE 16K;
CREATE BUFFERPOOL bp3 SIZE 2000 PAGESIZE 8K;
```

How much memory will be allocated for all buffer pools used by the database?

○ A. 60 MB
○ B. 396 MB
○ C. 400 MB
○ D. 401 MB

Question 9

A database administrator created all of the necessary federated objects for an Oracle data source in a federated system.

Given the following set of steps:

1) Drop the current user mapping
2) Drop the current data type mapping
3) Drop the nickname to the table
4) Create the new user mapping
5) Create the new data type mapping
6) Re-create the nickname to the table

Which steps must be performed if the data types of several columns in the Oracle data source are changed?

○ A. 2, 5
○ B. 3, 5, 6
○ C. 2, 5, 3, 6
○ D. 1, 2, 4, 5, 6

Question 10

A database named MYDB was created using automatic storage and a table space in the database named MY_TBSP is running out of space. Which command will provide more storage space to the table space so more data can be added to it?

- ○ A. ALTER DATABASE ADD STORAGE ON '/db2/dbspace1'
- ○ B. ALTER TABLESPACE my_tbsp EXTEND 100 MB
- ○ C. ALTER DATABASE EXTEND STORAGE FOR my_tbsp 100 MB
- ○ D. ALTER TABLESPACE my_tbsp ADD STORAGE ON '/db2/dbspace1'

Question 11

If the SQL statement shown below is executed:

```
CREATE REGULAR TABLESPACE sales_ts
MANAGED BY DATABASE USING
    (FILE 'C:\TABLESPACES\dms_tbsp.tsf' 1000 M)
```

Assuming DB2 9 is being used, which of the following is NOT a characteristic of the resulting table space?

- ○ A. The page size used is 4K.
- ○ B. File system caching is enabled.
- ○ C. The table space resides in the IBMTEMPGROUP database partition group.
- ○ D. Dropped tables in the specified table space can be recovered using the RECOVER DROPPED TABLE option of the ROLLFORWARD DATABASE command.

Question 12

Given the following statements:

```
CREATE TABLESPACE payroll MANAGED BY DATABASE USING
    (FILE '\home\myfile1' 200 FILE '\home\myfile2' 400);
ALTER TABLESPACE payroll EXTEND (FILE '\home\myfile2' 1000
    FILE '\home\myfile1' 1200);
```

How large are the containers MYFILE1 and MYFILE2?

- ○ A. MYFILE1 = 200 pages, MYFILE2 = 400 pages
- ○ B. MYFILE1 = 1200 pages, MYFILE2 = 1000 pages
- ○ C. MYFILE1 = 1400 pages, MYFILE2 = 1400 pages
- ○ D. MYFILE1 = 1200 pages, MYFILE2 = 1600 pages

Question 13

Given the following sequence of SQL statements:

1) CREATE DATABASE test ON C:
2) CONNECT TO test
3) CREATE BUFFERPOOL bp1 SIZE 2000
4) CREATE TABLESPACE ts1 MANAGED BY DATABASE USING (FILE 'C:\ts1data.dat' 10 M) BUFFERPOOL bp1
5) CREATE TABLE employees(empid INT, fname CHAR(30), lname CHAR(30))

Which two statements are not required in order to create the table named EMPLOYEES? (Select two)

❑ A. 1
❑ B. 2
❑ C. 3
❑ D. 4
❑ E. 5

Question 14

Given the following table spaces, their associated page size, and number of pages:

```
TBSP1          - 16K  page size, 150000 pages
TBSP2          - 8K   page size, 100000 pages
TBSP3          - 4K   page size, 200000 pages
USERSPACE1     - 4K   page size, 500000 pages
```

How many buffer pools must be created before the table spaces listed can be created?

○ A. 1
○ B. 2
○ C. 3
○ D. 4

Question 15

Which two of the following are valid ALTER BUFFERPOOL statements? (Select two)

❑ A. ALTER BUFFERPOOL mybp NUMBLOCKPAGES 32000
❑ B. ALTER BUFFERPOOL mybp TABLESPACE tbsp1
❑ C. ALTER BUFFERPOOL mybp PAGESIZE 8 K
❑ D. ALTER BUFFERPOOL mybp BLOCKSIZE 32
❑ E. ALTER BUFFERPOOL mybp SIZE -1

Question 16

Last week, a database administrator configured a SQL Server data source in a federated database (that references a table named HISTORY). Yesterday, insert operations caused the HISTORY table to double in size. Which of the following steps must be performed in order to update the statistics for the HISTORY table at the federated server?

- ○ A. Perform the SQL Server equivalent of RUNSTATS on the HISTORY table at the SQL Server server.
- ○ B. Perform the SQL Server equivalent of RUNSTATS on the HISTORY table at the SQL Server server; then perform RUNSTATS on the nickname for the HISTORY table at the federated server.
- ○ C. Perform the SQL Server equivalent of RUNSTATS on the HISTORY table at the SQL Server server; then drop and recreate the HISTORY nickname at the federated server.
- ○ D. Perform the SQL Server equivalent of RUNSTATS on the HISTORY table at the SQL Server server; then use the "db2updfedstat" tool to update the statistics at the federated server.

Data Partitioning and Clustering

Question 17

A database named SALES has a database partition group named PG1 that has been defined across partitions 2, 3, 4, and 5.

If the commands shown below are executed:

```
CONNECT TO sales;
ALTER DATABASE PARTITION GROUP pg1 ADD DBPARTITIONNUM (6)
```

Which database partition will DB2 use as a model for table spaces created on partition 6?

- ○ A. Partition 2
- ○ B. Partition 3
- ○ C. Partition 4
- ○ D. Partition 5

Question 18

Given the following CREATE TABLE statement:

```
CREATE TABLE camera_sales
      (model            CHAR(20) NOT NULL,
       price            DECIMAL(9,2) NOT NULL,
       year             CHAR(4) NOT NULL,
       manufacturer     CHAR(20))
```

If the following queries are executed against the resulting table on a regular basis:

```
SELECT * FROM camera_sales WHERE model = 'D300';
SELECT * FROM camera_sales WHERE price < 2000.00;
SELECT * FROM camera_sales WHERE manufacturer = 'NIKON';
```

Which clause could be added to the CREATE TABLE statement to improve performance of the queries shown?

- ○ A. ORGANIZE BY DIMENSIONS (model)
- ○ B. ORGANIZE BY DIMENSIONS (model, price)
- ○ C. ORGANIZE BY DIMENSIONS (price)
- ○ D. ORGANIZE BY DIMENSIONS (model, manufacturer)

Question 19

Which of the following is NOT a true statement about creating distribution keys?

- ○ A. A distribution key should include columns with low cardinality.
- ○ B. A distribution key should include columns most often used in equality or range predicate queries.
- ○ C. A distribution key should include columns most often used in sort operations.
- ○ D. A distribution key should include columns most often used in join operations.

Question 20

A partitioned instance named DB2INST1 uses the following db2nodes.cfg file:

```
 0     Svr1   0
 1     Svr1   1
 2     Svr1   2
 3     Svr1   3
 4     Svr2   0
 5     Svr2   1
 6     Svr2   2
 7     Svr2   3
 8     Svr3   0
 9     Svr4   0
10     Svr4   1
11     Svr4   2
```

If the CREATE DATABASE command is executed from the server Svr2, which partition will be the catalog partition?

- ○ A. 0
- ○ B. 4
- ○ C. 5
- ○ D. 6

Question 21

An active partitioned instance named DB2INST1 uses the following db2nodes.cfg file:

```
0 server1 0
1 server1 1
2 server2 0
3 server2 1
```

If the following command executes without errors:

```
db2start DBPARTITIONNUM 4
     ADD DBPARTITIONNUM HOSTNAME server2 PORT 2
```

Which of the following statements is NOT true regarding instance DB2INST1?

- ○ A. Instance DB2INST1 was started on hosts named SERVER1 and SERVER2.
- ○ B. Partitions 0, 1, 2, and 3 are active and available; partition 4 is not.
- ○ C. An entry for partition 4 was automatically added to the db2nodes.cfg file before the instance DB2INST1 was started.
- ○ D. An entry for partition 4 will not be added to the db2nodes.cfg file until the instance DB2INST1 is stopped and restarted.

Question 22

In which environment should you consider replacing an existing base table with a Multidimensional clustered (MDC) table?

○ A. In an OLTP environment to speed up access to large tables.

○ B. In a data warehouse environment to improve performance and reduce data maintenance overhead for large tables.

○ C. In an OLTP to speed up access to small tables.

○ D. In a data warehouse environment to improve performance and reduce data maintenance overhead for small tables.

Question 23

Which of the following data organization schemes is NOT supported by DB2?

○ A. Partition by range

○ B. Partition by dimensions

○ C. Organize by key sequence

○ D. Organize by dimensions

Question 24

Which of the following is NOT a valid statement about the IBM BCU v2.1?

○ A. The IBM System x 3455 houses the database partitions in a BCU v2.1 for Linux configuration.

○ B. Each data BCU contains eight DB2 database partitions.

○ C. The IBM System p 575 houses the database partitions in a BCU v2.1 for AIX configuration.

○ D. All backup and recovery operations can be performed using Tivoli Storage Manager.

Question 25

Which of the following node configuration files (db2nodes.cfg) indicates that both intra-partition parallelism and inter-partition parallelism is being used?

- ○ A.
  ```
  0   Srv1   0
  1   Srv2   1
  2   Srv3   2
  3   Srv4   3
  ```
- ○ B.
  ```
  0   Srv1   0
  1   Srv2   0
  2   Srv3   0
  3   Srv4   0
  ```
- ○ C.
  ```
  0   Srv1   0
  1   Srv1   1
  2   Srv1   2
  3   Srv1   3
  ```
- ○ D.
  ```
  0   Srv1   0
  1   Srv1   1
  2   Srv2   0
  3   Srv2   1
  ```

Question 26

If the following statement is used to create a table in a multi-partitioned database:

```
CREATE TABLE employee
      (fname       CHAR(30) NOT NULL,
       lname       CHAR(30) NOT NULL,
       empno       INT NOT NULL,
       dept        INT NOT NULL,
       ssn         INT,
    PRIMARY KEY (empno, dept))
```

Which column(s) will be chosen by DB2 to be the table's partitioning key?

- ○ A. FNAME
- ○ B. EMPNO
- ○ C. SSN
- ○ D. EMPNO, DEPT

Question 27

Your company is required to keep exactly 7 years worth of sales history data available in a table named SALES_RECORDS. It is now midnight on April 30th 2008, and you need to remove the data for May 2001 from the table and begin storing sales records for May 2008. Which of the following set of statements will accomplish this?

O A. ALTER TABLE sales_records DETACH PARTITION may01 INTO tab0501;
        LOAD FROM may08.del OF DEL REPLACE INTO tab0501;
        ALTER TABLE sales_records ATTACH PARTITION may08 STARTING
            '05/01/2008' ENDING '05/31/2008' FROM tab0501;
        SET INTEGRITY FOR sales_records ALLOW WRITE ACCESS IMMEDIATE
            CHECKED FOR EXCEPTION IN sales_records USE salesrecs_ex;

O B. ALTER TABLE sales_records DETACH PARTITION may01 INTO tab0501;
        LOAD FROM may08.del OF DEL REPLACE INTO tab0501;
        ALTER TABLE sales_records ATTACH PARTITION may08 STARTING
            '01/01/2008' ENDING '05/31/2008' from tab0501;

O C. ALTER TABLE sales_records DETACH PARTITION may01 into tab0501
        LOAD FROM may08.del OF DEL INSERT INTO tab0501;
        ALTER TABLE sales_records ATTACH PARTITION may08 STARTING
            '05/01/2008' ENDING '05/31/2008' FROM tab0508;
        SET INTEGRITY FOR sales_records ALLOW WRITE ACCESS IMMEDIATE
            CHECKED FOR EXCEPTION IN sales_records USE salesrecs_ex;

O D. ALTER TABLE sales_records DETACH PARTITION may01 into tab0501;
        LOAD FROM may08.del OF DEL INSERT INTO tab0501;
        ALTER TABLE sales_records ATTACH PARTITION may08 STARTING
            '01/01/2008' ENDING '05/31/2008' FROM tab0508;

Question 28

Which of the following components make up the IBM BCU v2.1 for AIX?

O A. IBM System x 575, IBM DS Series Storage, and DB2 Enterprise Server Edition.
O B. IBM System x 575, IBM DS Series Storage, and DB2 Data Warehouse Edition.
O C. IBM System p 575, IBM DS Series Storage, and DB2 Enterprise Server Edition.
O D. IBM System p 575, IBM DS Series Storage, and DB2 Data Warehouse Edition.

Question 29

A database administrator needs to add a new database partition to an existing DB2 instance. Which two of the following SQL statements must be executed before data can be stored in the new partition? (Select two)

❑ A. ADD PARTITION
❑ B. ADD DBPARTITIONNUM
❑ C. ALTER INSTANCE ADD DBPARTITION
❑ D. ALTER DATABASE PARTITION GROUP
❑ E. REDISTRIBUTE DATABASE PARTITION GROUP

Question 30

If the following SQL statements are executed:

```
CREATE TYPE yearday AS INTEGER WITH COMPARISONS;

CREATE TABLE sales
     (year_day        YEARDAY,
      item_number     CHAR(10),
      po_number       CHAR(12),
      amount          NUMERIC(9, 2))
PARTITION BY RANGE (year_day)
     (STARTING 200801 ENDING 200812 EVERY 3)
ORGANIZE BY DIMENSIONS (item_number));
```

Which statement correctly describes the resulting table?

○ A. The table SALES will be partitioned by YEAR_DAY such that 3 days of data will reside on its own partition. Additionally, data will be organized by ITEM_NUMBER such that all rows within any 3 day period are clustered together based on 3 months of data.

○ B. The table SALES will be partitioned by YEAR_DAY such that 3 months of data will reside on its own partition. Additionally, data will be organized by ITEM_NUMBER such that all rows within any 3 day period are clustered together based on 3 months of data.

○ C. The table SALES will be partitioned by YEAR_DAY such that 3 years of data will reside on its own partition. Additionally, data will be organized by ITEM_NUMBER such that all rows within any 3 year period are clustered together based on 12 months of data.

○ D. The table SALES will be partitioned by YEAR_DAY such that 3 months of data will reside on its own partition. Additionally, data will be organized by ITEM_NUMBER such that all rows within any 3 month period are clustered together based on 12 months of data.

Question 31

A table named TAB1 has the following columns and cardinalities:

```
COL1  -  Cardinality 100,000
COL2  -  Cardinality 10,000
COL3  -  Cardinality 1000
COL4  -  Cardinality 100
```

Which columns is NOT a good dimensional candidate for MDC?

○ A. COL1
○ B. COL2
○ C. COL3
○ D. COL4

Question 32

A database administrator captured the entire SQL workload against a database named SALES into an ASCII file names WKLD.SQL. What is the proper command to use to run the Design Advisor so that it will evaluate all information stored in the file WKLD.SQL, and give advice on converting standard tables to multidimensional clustering (MDC) tables?

○ A.   db2advis –d sales –i wkld.sql –m C

○ B.   db2advis –d sales –i wkld.sql –CLUSTERING

○ C.   db2advis –d sales –i wkld.sql –C

○ D.   db2advis –d sales –i wkld.sql –m ALL

High Availbility and Diagnostics

Question 33

A database administrator executes the following command:

```
GET DB CFG FOR sample
```

Assuming the database named SAMPLE has been configured to use archival logging, which of the following information can be obtained from output produced?

○ A.   The RID of the last record written to an active log file.

○ B.   The name of the first active log file.

○ C.   The transaction ID of the last transaction written to an active log file.

○ D.   The number of archived log files created.

Question 34

Which of the following commands will display only the media header information for an existing backup image?

○ A.   db2 inspect –h

○ B.   db2 inspect –H

○ C.   db2ckbkp -h

○ D.   db2ckbkp -H

Question 35

Which of the following statements about incremental (cumulative) backups is NOT true?

○ A. The predecessor of an incremental backup image is always the most recent successful full backup image of the same object (database or table space).

○ B. Database recovery involves restoring the database using the most recent full backup image available and applying each incremental backup image produced since the last full backup, in the order in which they were created.

○ C. Before an incremental backup image can be created, a full backup image must already exist.

○ D. Along with updated data and index pages, each incremental backup image also contains all of the initial database metadata that is normally found in a full database backup image.

Question 36

A database named PAYROLL was created using automatic storage, with the following storage paths: /path1, /path2, /path3. Later, the database was backed up using the following command:

```
BACKUP DATABASE payroll TO /backups
```

If the PAYROLL database needs to be cloned, which of the following commands will recreate it in a new location while maintaining the original storage paths?

○ A. `RESTORE DB payroll FROM /backups INTO /path1, /path3, /path3 DBPATH /payroll2`

○ B. `RECOVER DB payroll FROM /backups INTO /path1, /path3, /path3 DBPATH /payroll2`

○ C. `RESTORE DB payroll FROM /backups INTO /payroll2`

○ D. `RECOVER DB payroll FROM /backups INTO /payroll2`

Question 37

Which of the following is NOT replicated in an HADR environment?

○ A. Data Definition Language (DDL) statements

○ B. Buffer pool operations

○ C. Database configuration parameter changes

○ D. System catalog information for stored procedures

Question 38

Which two commands can be used to list all applications that are currently connected to a database named PAYROLL? (Select two)

❑ A. `db2pd —connections —db payroll`

❑ B. `db2pd —list applications —db payroll`

❑ C. `LIST APPLICATIONS FOR payroll`

❑ D. `GET APPLICATION SNAPSHOT FOR payroll`

❑ E. `SELECT * FROM TABLE(SNAP_GET_APPLICATIONS('payroll',-1)) AS applications`

Question 39

When the following command was executed from the DB2 Command Line Processor:

```
db2pd —tablespaces —db SAMPLE
```

The following information was displayed:

```
Database Partition 0 -- Database SAMPLE -- Active -- Up 25 days
08:32:31
```

Tablespace Configuration:

Address	Id	Type	Content	PageSz	ExtentSz	Auto	Prefetch	BufID	BufIDDisk
FSC	NumCntrs	MaxStripe	Last-ConsecPg	Name					
0x7F91C230	0	DMS	Regular	8192	4	Yes	4	1	1
Off	1	0	3	SYSCATSPACE					
0x7F91CA20	1	SMS	SysTmp	8192	32	Yes	32	1	1
On	1	0	31	TEMPSPACE1					
0x7F91F1E0	2	DMS	Large	8192	32	Yes	32	1	1
Off	1	0	31	USERSPACE1					
0x7F91F9D0	3	DMS	Large	8192	32	Yes	32	1	1
Off	1	0	31	IBMDB2SAMPLEREL					
0x7EBAD220	4	DMS	Large	8192	32	Yes	32	1	1
Off	1	0	31	TBSP1					

Tablespace Statistics:

Address	Id	TotalPgs	UsablePgs	UsedPgs	PndFreePgs	FreePgs	HWM
State	MinRecTime	NQui-escers					
0x7F91C230	0	8192	8188	6852	0	1336	6852
0x00000000	0	0					
0x7F91CA20	1	1	1	1	0	0	0
0x00000000	0	0					
0x7F91F1E0	2	4096	4064	1760	0	2304	1760
0x00000000	0	0					
0x7F91F9D0	3	4096	4064	608	0	3456	608
0x00000000	0	0					
0x7EBAD220	4	200	160	156	0	0	156
0x00000000	0	0					

```
Tablespace Autoresize Statistics:
Address    Id  AS  AR  InitSize    IncSize    IIP MaxSize   LastResize
LRF
0x7F91C230 0   Yes Yes 33554432    -1         No  None      None
No
0x7F91CA20 1   Yes No  0           0          No  0         None
No
0x7F91F1E0 2   Yes Yes 33554432    -1         No  None      None
No
0x7F91F9D0 3   Yes Yes 33554432    -1         No  None      None
No
0x7EBAD220 4   No  No  0           0          No  0         None
No


Containers:
Address    TspId ContainNum Type     TotalPgs  UseablePgs StripeSet
Container
0x7F91C8B0 0     0          File     8192      8188       0
C:\DB2\NODE0000\SAMPLE\T0000000\C0000000.CAT
0x7F91D050 1     0          Path     1         1          0
C:\DB2\NODE0000\SAMPLE\T0000001\C0000000.TMP
0x7F91F860 2     0          File     4096      4064       0
C:\DB2\NODE0000\SAMPLE\T0000002\C0000000.LRG
0x7EF220D0 3     0          File     4096      4064       0
C:\DB2\NODE0000\SAMPLE\T0000003\C0000000.LRG
0x7EBADF30 4     0          File     200       160        0
C:\DB295_ESE\tbsp1.dat
```

Based on this information, which of the following is a valid statement?

- ○ A. Table space SYSCATSPACE has been resized 5 times.
- ○ B. Table space IBMDB2SAMPLEREL is an SMS table space.
- ○ C. Table space USERSPACE1 cannot be accessed until it has been rolled forward.
- ○ D. Table space TBSP1 is about to run out of storage space.

Question 40

A database administrator would like to configure a database named PAYROLL such that whenever a log file becomes full, DB2 will attempt to archive it automatically. Which of the following commands will achieve this objective?

- ○ A. UPDATE DB CFG FOR payroll USING LOGARCHMETH1 USEREXIT
- ○ B. UPDATE DB CFG FOR payroll USING LOGARCHMETH1 LOGRETAIN
- ○ C. UPDATE DB CFG FOR payroll USING LOGARCHMETH2 OFF
- ○ D. UPDATE DB CFG FOR payroll USING LOGARCHMETH2 AUTOARCHIVE

Question 41

A database named TEST was backed up to disk and a database administrator needs to determine if this backup was taken with using the INCLUDE LOGS option of the BACKUP DATABASE command.

How can the database administrator accomplish this?

- ○ A. Examine the output from the command LIST HISTORY BACKUP ALL FOR test.
- ○ B. Check the value of the BKUPLOGS database configuration parameter.
- ○ C. Examine the header information stored in the backup image using the db2ckbkp command.
- ○ D. Check the value of the DB2_BKUP_INCLLOGS registry variable.

Question 42

While cleaning up files stored on an older AIX server, a database administrator found a shell script that contained the following commands:

```
db2 "RESTORE DATABASE sample FROM C:\backups TO D:\DB_DIR INTO sample_2 REDIRECT"

db2 "SET TABLESPACE CONTAINERS FOR 0 USING (PATH 'D:\DB_DIR\SYSTEM')"

db2 "SET TABLESPACE CONTAINERS FOR 1 USING (PATH 'D:\DB_DIR\TEMP')"

db2 "SET TABLESPACE CONTAINERS FOR 2 USING (PATH 'D:\DB_DIR\USER')"

db2 "RESTORE DATABASE sample CONTINUE"
```

What was this file designed to perform?

- ○ A. A multiple table space recovery operation.
- ○ B. A reverted restore operation.
- ○ C. A partial table space reconstruction operation.
- ○ D. A redirected restore operation.

Question 43

A system administrator wants to configure an HADR environment so that whenever an application issues a COMMIT, data in the log buffers will be written to the log files on the primary server and then be sent to the standby server and written to the log files there, before a return code will be sent to the application.

Which of the following commands can be used to accomplish this?

○ A. UPDATE DB CFG FOR sales USING HADR_SYNCMODE SYNC

○ B. UPDATE DB CFG FOR sales USING HADR_SYNCMODE NEARSYNC

○ C. UPDATE DB CFG FOR sales USING HADR_SYNCMODE ASYNC

○ D. UPDATE DB CFG FOR sales USING HADR_SYNCMODE INSYNC

Question 44

Which command will take 10 different snapshots of how memory is used by all active databases in the DB2 instance every 5 minutes?

○ A. db2mtrk –d –i 5 10

○ B. db2mtrk –d –r 5 –c 10

○ C. db2mtrk –d –i 300 –c 10

○ D. db2mtrk –d –r 300 10

Question 45

Which of the following commands must be executed in order to configure a database named SAMPLE for infinite logging?

○ A. UPDATE DB CFG FOR sample USING LOGARCHMETH1 LOGRETAIN LOGARCHMETH2 -1

○ B. UPDATE DB CFG FOR sample USING LOGARCHMETH1 LOGRETAIN LOGARCHMETH2 INFINITE

○ C. UPDATE DB CFG FOR sample USING LOGARCHMETH1 LOGRETAIN LOGSECOND -1

○ D. UPDATE DB CFG FOR sample USING USING LOGARCHMETH1 LOGRETAIN LOGSECOND INFINITE

Question 46

Which two of the following commands can be used to enable dual logging for a database named SAMPLE? (Select two)

- ❏ A. db2set DB2_NEWLOGPATH=D:\logs_copy
- ❏ B. db2set DB2_NEWLOGPATH=1
- ❏ C. UPDATE DB CFG FOR sample USING failarchpath D:\ logs_copy
- ❏ D. UPDATE DB CFG FOR sample USING mirrorlogpath D:\ logs_copy
- ❏ E. UPDATE DB CFG FOR sample USING logarchmeth2 MIRRORPATH: D:\ logs_copy

Question 47

If the following commands are executed:

```
db2set -g DB2_FORCE_APP_ON_MAX_LOG=FALSE;
UPDATE DB CFG FOR sample USING LOGFILSIZ 10000;
UPDATE DB CFG FOR sample USING MAX_LOG 10;
```

What will happen if an application with a long running transaction consumes more than 100,000 log pages?

- ○ A. The transaction will be rolled back and the application will be forced to terminate.
- ○ B. The transaction will be rolled back, but the application will be allowed to continue.
- ○ C. The work performed by the current statement will be rolled back; the application will be allowed to commit or roll back the work performed by other statements in the transaction.
- ○ D. The work performed by the current statement and all previous statements in the transaction will be rolled back; the application will be allowed to commit or rollback any remaining statements in the transaction.

Question 48

Which command will back up a database named ACCOUNTING to a Tivoli Storage Manager (TSM) server using 4 concurrent TSM client sessions and 8 buffers?

- ○ A. BACKUP DATABASE accounting USE TSM WITH 4 SESSIONS OPEN 8 BUFFERS
- ○ B. BACKUP DATABASE accounting USE TSM WITH 4 SESSIONS 8 BUFFERS
- ○ C. BACKUP DATABASE accounting USE TSM OPEN 4 SESSIONS WITH 8 BUFFERS
- ○ D. BACKUP DATABASE accounting USE TSM OPTIONS 4 SESSIONS WITH 8 BUFFERS

Question 49

A database named SALES was created across 8 database partitions. Then, 12 tables were created and populated using the default table spaces provided – no additional table spaces were created.

Which of the following commands can be used to backup just the user tables on database partition 5 while the database remains online?

○ A. db2_all "<<+5< db2 BACKUP DATABASE sales TABLESPACE (*) ONLINE TO /backup_dir"

○ B. db2_all "<<+5< db2 BACKUP DATABASE sales TABLESPACE (userspace1) ONLINE TO /backup_dir"

○ C. db2_all "<<-5< db2 BACKUP DATABASE sales TABLESPACE (*) ONLINE TO /backup_dir"

○ D. db2_all "<<-5< db2 BACKUP DATABASE sales TABLESPACE (userspace1) ONLINE TO /backup_dir"

Question 50

Which of the following statements about the DB2 Check Backup utility (db2ckbkp) is NOT true?

○ A. Only users who have read permission on backup image files are allowed to use the db2ckbkp utility.

○ B. Multiple backup images can be analyzed with a single db2ckbkp command.

○ C. Only users who have System Administrator authority are allowed to use the db2ckbkp utility.

○ D. If a backup image was compressed when it was created, the library used to compress the data must be accessible to the db2ckbkp utility.

Question 51

A database named PRODDB has a weekly full backup taken on Sunday, and non-cumulative (delta) backups taken daily. A database crash occurs on Wednesday.

What is the best way to return the database to the state it was in when the last backup image was made?

○ A. `RESTORE DATABASE proddb TAKEN AT (Sunday);`
`RESTORE DATABASE proddb INCREMENTAL TAKEN AT (Tuesday);`

○ B. `RESTORE DATABASE proddb TAKEN AT (Sunday);`
`RESTORE DATABASE proddb INCREMENTAL AUTO TAKEN AT (Tuesday);`

○ C. `RESTORE DATABASE proddb TAKEN AT (Sunday);`
`RESTORE DATABASE proddb INCREMENTAL AUTO TAKEN AT (Monday);`
`RESTORE DATABASE proddb INCREMENTAL AUTO TAKEN AT (Tuesday);`

○ D. `RESTORE DATABASE proddb INCREMENTAL AUTO TAKEN AT (Tuesday);`

Question 52

A database administrator attempted to recover a database named SAMPLE by executing the following command:

`RECOVER DATABASE sample TO END OF LOGS;`

During the roll-forward phase of recovery, an error occurred. Once the problem is corrected, which of the following commands should be executed to force the recovery process to start over at the beginning?

○ A. `RECOVER DATABASE sample RESTART;`

○ B. `RECOVER DATABASE sample TO END OF LOGS RESTART;`

○ C. `RECOVER DATABASE sample RESTART AND CONTINUE;`

○ D. `RECOVER DATABASE sample START AT RESTORE AND CONTINUE;`

Question 53

Two database servers have been enabled for synchronous HADR. If the HADR_TIMEOUT configuration parameter on the primary server is set to 30, which two of the following statements are true? (Select two)

❑ A. When HADR is started on the secondary server, HADR must be started, within 30 seconds, on the primary server.

❑ B. The HADR_TIMEOUT configuration parameter on the secondary server must also be set to 30.

❑ C. If the primary server does not receive acknowledgement of a log buffer within 30 seconds it stops processing all requests.

❑ D. The HADR_TIMEOUT configuration parameter on the secondary server must be assigned a value less than 30.

❑ E. If the primary server does not receive acknowledgement of a log buffer write within 30 seconds it drops out of peer mode.

Question 54

Which of the following is NOT a requirement for an HADR environment?

○ A. The operating system on the primary server and the standby server must be the same (including fix pack level).

○ B. The database path on the primary server and the standby server must be the same.

○ C. The DB2 software version and bit size (32 or 64) used on the primary server and the standby server must be the same.

○ D. Table spaces and table space containers on the primary server and the standby server must be identical.

Question 55

While setting up an HADR environment, a system administrator executed the following commands at the primary server:

```
db2set DB2COMM=TCPIP;
UPDATE ALTERNATE SERVER FOR DATABASE sales
    USING HOSTNAME svr2 PORT 456;
```

What will happen if a failover event occurs while a client application is connected to the SALES database on the primary server?

○ A. The client application will receive an error message indicating that a connect attempt has failed due to a timeout and no further attempts will be made to establish a connection with the server.

○ B. The client application will receive an error message indicating that a connect attempt has failed due to a timeout and the system administrator will have to manually switch over to the standby server SVR2 before further attempts are made to establish a connection with the server.

○ C. The client application will automatically connect to the standby database on SVR2 and that database will become the primary database.

○ D. The client application will automatically connect to the standby database on SVR2 and that database will become the primary database – provided the HADR_REMOTE_HOST and HADR_REMOTE_SVC database configuration parameters have been set appropriately.

Question 56

A db2mtrk command was used to produce the results shown below:

```
Tracking Memory on: 2008/05/21 at 14:00:38

Memory for database: SAMPLE

    utilh   pckcacheh catcacheh bph (1)  bph (S32K)  bph (S16K) bph (S8K)
    64.0K   128.0K    64.0K     1.2M     704.0K      448.0K     320.0K

    bph (S4K) shsorth  lockh     dbh      other
    256.0K    0        320.0K    4.3M     128.0K
```

Which option was specified when the db2mtrk command was executed?

○ A. −d

○ B. −i

○ C. −p

○ D. −w

Performance and Scalability

Question 57

Which of the following is NOT true about the DB2_PINNED_BP registry variable?

○ A. When this variable is set to YES, buffer pools will remain in system main memory.

○ B. When this variable is set to YES, database performance can be somewhat inconsistent.

○ C. When this variable is set to YES, all database global memory will be kept in the system main memory.

○ D. When this variable is set to YES, self-tuning for database shared memory cannot be enabled on 64-bit AIX.

Question 58

A DB2 system supporting a critical application with many concurrent medium to long running transactions that use a small amount of log space appears to be running slowly.

Current parameter settings are:

```
DBHEAP      512
LOGBUFSZ    128
MINCOMMIT   1
MAX_LOG     40
```

If the length of each individual transaction is not important, what parameter can be changed to minimize the number of times the log buffer is flushed to disk?

- O A. LOGARCHMETH1
- O B. MAX_LOG
- O C. LOGBUFSZ
- O D. MINCOMIT

Question 59

Place the following steps in the correct order as they are performed by the DB2 optimizer when generating an access plan for a SQL statement.

1. check semantics
2. parse query
3. generate package
4. rewrite query
5. generate access plan

- O A. 1, 2, 4, 3, 5
- O B. 1, 2, 4, 5, 3
- O C. 2, 1, 4, 5, 3
- O D. 2, 1, 4, 3, 5

Question 60

A database administrator created a table named HISTORY and a trigger to insert records into the HISTORY table each time an employee's salary is modified in a table named EMPLOYEE. If the first column in the HISTORY table is a continually increasing sequential key, which of the following, if executed, will increase the performance of the trigger inserts?

- O A. db2set DB2MAXFSCRSEARCH -1
- O B. ALTER TABLE history APPEND ON
- O C. db2set DB2MAXFSCRSEARCH 1000
- O D. ALTER TABLE history FREESPACE 1000

Question 61

> Which of the following commands will force DB2 to perform all sort operations in shared memory?
>
> ○ A. UPDATE DB CFG FOR sample USING SHEAPTHRES_SHR -2
>
> ○ B. UPDATE DB CFG FOR sample USING SHEAPTHRES_SHR -1
>
> ○ C. UPDATE DB CFG FOR sample USING SHEAPTHRES_SHR 0
>
> ○ D. UPDATE DB CFG FOR sample USING SHEAPTHRES_SHR 250

Question 62

> Which of the following correctly describes how the Self-Tuning Memory Manager (STMM) monitors and tunes memory in a partitioned database environment?
>
> ○ A. All memory tuning decisions are based on memory and workload characteristics of the catalog partition; memory adjustments are made on this partition first and then distributed to all other partitions.
>
> ○ B. All memory tuning decisions are based on memory and workload characteristics of the coordinator partition; memory adjustments are made on this partition first and then distributed to all other partitions.
>
> ○ C. All memory tuning decisions are based on memory and workload characteristics of a single partition that has been designated as the tuning partition; memory adjustments are made on this partition first and then distributed to all other partitions.
>
> ○ D. All memory tuning decisions are based on memory and workload characteristics of the entire database; memory adjustments are made on individually on each partition.

Question 63

> A LIST APPLICATIONS command returned the following output:
>
> | Auth Id | Application Name | Appl. Handle | Application Id | DB Name | # of Agents |
> |---------|------------------|--------------|----------------|---------|-------------|
> | RSANDERS | db2taskd | 148 | *LOCAL.DB2.070601164915 | SAMPLE | 1 |
> | RSANDERS | db2stmm | 147 | *LOCAL.DB2.070601164914 | SAMPLE | 1 |
> | RSANDERS | db2bp.exe | 146 | *LOCAL.DB2.070601164913 | SAMPLE | 1 |
>
> Which two of the following commands will terminate all of the applications that are currently running?
>
> ❑ A. FORCE APPLICATION (146, 147, 148)
>
> ❑ B. FORCE APPLICATION (LOCAL.DB2.070601164915, LOCAL.DB2.070601164914, LOCAL.DB2.070601164913)
>
> ❑ C. FORCE APPLICATION (db2taskd, db2stmm, db2bp.exe)
>
> ❑ D. FORCE APPLICATION ALL
>
> ❑ E. FORCE ALL APPLICATIONS

Question 64

Which of the following is NOT a valid statement about the connection concentrator?

○ A. The connection concentrator is enabled when the maximum number of connections supported is equal to or less than the maximum number of coordinating agents allowed.

○ B. The connection concentrator uses logical agents (LAs) to handle the application context while database agents (DAs) handle the actual DB2 connections.

○ C. The connection concentrator is enabled when the maximum number of connections supported is greater than the maximum number of coordinating agents allowed.

○ D. The connection concentrator allows servers to provide support for thousands of users simultaneously executing business transactions while drastically reducing the resources required.

Question 65

Which of the following statements will tell the DB2 optimizer to use an index scan on a table named TAB1 regardless of any catalog statistics that might have been collected, because the table varies in size dramatically from one minute to the next?

○ A. `ALTER TABLE tab1 VOLATILE`

○ B. `ALTER TABLE tab1 USE INDEX tab1_idx`

○ C. `ALTER TABLE tab1 DISTRIBUTION SCAN`

○ D. `ALTER TABLE tab1 REFRESH CARDINALITY`

Question 66

Which of the following would indicate an access plan is using intra-partition parallelism?

○ A. Local table queues

○ B. Merging table queues

○ C. Directed table queues

○ D. Synchronous table queues

Question 67

Which DB2 registry variable can be used to prevent DB2 from performing prefetching during restart operations?

○ A. `DB2_PREFETCH`

○ B. `DB2_LIMIT_PREFETCH`

○ C. `DB2_AVOID_PREFETCH`

○ D. `DB2_RESTRICT_PREFETCH`

Question 68

A database with a default configuration is performing poorly on a Linux system. During peak operation a database snapshot was taken that contains the following information:

```
        Database Snapshot
Database name                         = SAMPLE
First database connect timestamp      = 05/23/2008 13:40:09.704208
Snapshot timestamp                    = 05/23/2008 13:41:44.556973
Direct reads                          = 2134
Direct writes                         = 0
Direct read requests                  = 11
Direct write requests                 = 0
Direct reads elapsed time (ms)        = 155
Direct write elapsed time (ms)        = 0
Database files closed                 = 51782
```

Which of the following commands, when executed, should improve performance?

○ A. UPDATE DB CFG FOR sample USING MAXFILOP 2048
○ B. UPDATE DB CFG FOR sample USING BUFFPAGE 200000
○ C. UPDATE DB CFG FOR sample USING LOGFILSIZ 4096
○ D. UPDATE DB CFG FOR sample USING MAXAPPLS 2048

Question 69

Which of the following correctly describes the objective of index ANDing?

○ A. Find common RIDs
○ B. Eliminate duplicate RIDs
○ C. Generate duplicate RIDs
○ D. Map RIDs to data pages

Question 70

If a database routinely services workloads that consist primarily of transactions that update data, which database configuration parameter should be assigned a high value or the value AUTOMATIC to improve performance?

○ A. NUM_IOCLEANERS
○ B. LOGBUFSIZ
○ C. NUM_IOSERVERS
○ D. CATALOGCACHE_SZ

Question 71

When setting up the Self-Tuning Memory Manager (STMM), at least two memory areas should be configured for self-tuning so that memory can be redistributed between them. However, one DB2 memory areas can be enabled for self tuning by itself and still have the Self-Tuning Memory Manager (STMM) automatically redistribute memory on its behalf. Which memory tuning area is this?

○ A. Buffer pools
○ B. Lock list
○ C. Package cache
○ D. Sort heap

Question 72

After being enabled for deep compression and having a compression dictionary built, the following command was used to alter a table named EMPLOYEE:

```
ALTER TABLE employee COMPRESS NO
```

Which of the following commands can be used to remove the compression dictionary from the EMPLOYEE table?

○ A. DELETE
○ B. REORG
○ C. INSPECT
○ D. RUNSTATS

Question 73

A table space named TBSP1 (with the table space ID 5) is deployed on a storage array that is using RAID-5 4+1 protection.

Which command would optimize I/O for all tables and indexes stored in table space TBSP1?

○ A. db2set DB2_PARALLEL_IO=4:4
○ B. db2set DB2_PARALLEL_IO=5:4
○ C. db2set DB2_PARALLEL_IO=5:5
○ D. db2set DB2_PARALLEL_IO=4:5

Question 74

When an application connects to a nonpartitioned database stored on a Linux server, what is responsible for executing all subsequent SQL statements and DB2 commands on behalf of the application?

- ○ A. A subagent named db2agntp
- ○ B. A connection agent db2agntc
- ○ C. A director agent named db2agent
- ○ D. A coordinating agent named db2agent

Question 75

A table named EMPLOYEE was created by executing the following statement:

```
CREATE TABLE employee
    (emp_id    INTEGER NOT NULL,
    name       VARCHAR (40) NOT NULL ,
    dept_id    INTEGER NOT NULL)
```

Immediately after creation, the table was populated with 250,000 rows. If the following query is frequently run against the EMPLOYEE table:

```
SELECT emp_id, dept_id, name
FROM employee
WHERE emp_id = 50 AND dept_id = 10
```

Which statement will create an index that will provide optimal performance for this query?

- ○ A. CREATE INDEX emp_idx1 ON employee (emp_id)
- ○ B. CREATE INDEX emp_idx1 ON employee (dept_id)
- ○ C. CREATE INDEX emp_idx1 ON employee (emp_id, dept_id)
- ○ D. CREATE INDEX emp_idx1 ON employee (emp_id) INCLUDE (dept_id)

Question 76

Which of the following would indicate an access plan is using inter-partition parallelism?

- ○ A. Local table queues
- ○ B. Merging table queues
- ○ C. Listener table queues
- ○ D. Broadcast table queues

Question 77

A 250GB transactional database is running on a 64-bit Linux server that has only 2GB of memory available. If self tuning memory is enabled, which of the following registry variables can be used to prevent "Insufficient System Memory" errors from occurring?

- ○ A. DB2_MEM_LIMIT
- ○ B. DB2_MEM_TUNING
- ○ C. DB2_MEM_TUNING_LIMIT
- ○ D. DB2_MEM_TUNING_RANGE

Question 78

Which of the following is NOT a true statement about the SHEAPTHRES configuration parameter?

- ○ A. The SHEAPTHRES configuration parameter sets an instance-wide soft limit on the total amount of memory that can be consumed by private sorts at any given time.
- ○ B. The SHEAPTHRES configuration parameter specifies the maximum amount of memory (in pages) that is to be used at any one time to perform sort operations.
- ○ C. If the SHEAPTHRES configuration parameter is assigned a value other than zero, the sort memory heap database configuration parameter (SORTHEAP) cannot not be configured for automatic tuning.
- ○ D. The SHEAPTHRES configuration parameter is an instance level configuration parameter; therefore its setting affects all databases under an instance's control.

Question 79

Which type of table queue is used to pass table data from one database agent to another when the FOR FETCH ONLY clause is not specified with a SELECT statement?

- ○ A. Local table queue
- ○ B. Merging table queue
- ○ C. Synchronous table queue
- ○ D. Asynchronous table queue

Question 80

A database administrator executed the following SQL statement:

```
CREATE BUFFERPOOL bp1 SIZE 1000 AUTOMATIC PAGESIZE 8K
```

If this statement was executed against a database with self tuning memory enabled, what will DB2 do?

- ○ A. Check available memory, and create the buffer pool if there is enough memory available; if there is not enough memory available, return an error message and do not create the buffer pool.
- ○ B. Check available memory, and create the buffer pool if there is enough memory available; if there is not enough memory available, monitor system resources and as soon as there is enough free memory available on the server, create the buffer pool.
- ○ C. Check available memory, and create the buffer pool if there is enough memory available; if there is not enough memory available, wait until all activations and connections to the database are closed, and then allocate the buffer pool on the next activation or connection.
- ○ D. Check available memory, and create buffer pool BP1 if there is enough memory available; if there is not enough memory available, wait until all the DB2 instance is stopped and allocate the buffer pool when the instance is restarted.

Question 81

A table named PARTS was created in a DB2 9 database by executing the following CREATE TABLE statement:

```
CREATE TABLE parts
     (itemid        INT NOT NULL,
      description   VARCHAR(250),
      price         DECIMAL(7,2),
      photo         BLOB(2000),
      warranty_info XML)
  COMPRESS YES
```

Once a compression dictionary has been built for the PARTS table, which column should yield the greatest amount of compression?

- ○ A. PHOTO
- ○ B. ITEMID
- ○ C. DESCRIPTION
- ○ D. WARRANTY_INFO

Question 82

If the following sequence of commands and statements are issued from the DB2 Command Line Processor immediately after an instance is started:

```
ACTIVATE DATABASE sample;
CONNECT TO sample;
SELECT * FROM org;
TERMINATE;
```

What will happen to the agent that was used to provide the results for the query when the TERMINATE command is processed?

○ A. The agent process/thread will be suspended.

○ B. The agent process/thread will be terminated or killed.

○ C. The agent process/thread will be placed in the idle agent pool if enough space is available in the pool.

○ D. The agent process/thread will remain active provided the MAXAGENTS setting has not been exceeded.

Question 83

Which two of the following determine the degree of inter-partition parallelism used?

❏ A. The number of database partitions.

❏ B. The value of the INTER_PARALLEL Database Manager configuration parameter.

❏ C. The definition of database partition groups.

❏ D. The number of CPUs/cores per database partition.

❏ E. The amount of memory available per database partition.

Question 84

Which of the following is NOT a valid statement regarding the Configuration Advisor?

○ A. The Configuration Advisor is a GUI application that makes it easy to tune and balance the resource requirements of a single database within an instance.

○ B. In DB2 9, the Configuration Advisor is automatically invoked whenever you create a database using the Create Database Wizard.

○ C. The Configuration Advisor takes information you provide about a database and its anticipated workload and produces a set of recommended configuration parameters changes.

○ D. The Configuration Advisor takes information you provide about a server and produces a set of recommended registry variable settings.

Question 85

Which description is correct when discussing the DB2_SMS_TRUNC_TMPTABLE_THRESH registry variable?

- ○ A. Setting this variable to -1 will reduce the system overhead involved in dropping and recreating a temporary table in an SMS table space.
- ○ B. Setting this variable to 50 will ensure that no temporary table created in an SMS table space will contain more than 50 rows.
- ○ C. Setting this variable to 10 will restrict the number of temporary tables that can be created in an SMS table space to 10.
- ○ D. Setting this variable to 0 will ensure that once a temporary table in an SMS table space is no longer needed, its file will be truncated to 1 extent.

Question 86

In which case would executing the statement "ALTER TABLE payroll VOLATILE" be beneficial?

- ○ A. The number of records in the PAYROLL table does not change, but approximately 10 percent of its data is updated every day.
- ○ B. An index associated with the PAYROLL table has values ranging from 1 to 1,000,000,000,000,000.
- ○ C. The PAYROLL table is loaded every day with the exact same data.
- ○ D. The PAYROLL table is loaded every day with drastically varying amounts of data.

Question 87

Which of the following is NOT a valid statement about clustering indexes?

- ○ A. Columns frequently searched or joined over a range of values using the operators BETWEEN, >, <, and LIKE are good candidates for a clustering index.
- ○ B. In order for DB2 to maintain the clustering of the data and the index as records are inserted or updated, you must leave free space on the data pages to provide room for additional rows.
- ○ C. When creating a clustering index in a DPF environment, the index columns specified should be prefixed with the partitioning key columns.
- ○ D. Specify a lower PCTFREE value at index creation time to reduce the likelihood that index page splits will occur when records are added to the table.

Question 88

Which statement correctly describes the purpose of statistical views?

○ A. Statistical views provide the optimizer with more accurate collocation estimates.

○ B. Statistical views provide the optimizer with more accurate cardinality estimates.

○ C. Statistical views provide the optimizer with more accurate free space estimates.

○ D. Statistical views provide the optimizer with more accurate I/O estimates.

Question 89

The service level agreement for an application that performs a large number of update operations on a table named EMPLOYEE states that the application must complete its work as quickly as possible to ensure that other dependant workloads can execute within a nightly maintenance window.

Which two of the following statements can be added to the beginning of the application to help it execute quickly? (Select two)

❑ A. `LOCK TABLE employee FOR APPLICATION.`

❑ B. `LOCK TABLE employee IN EXCLUSIVE MODE`

❑ C. `ALTER TABLE employee LOCKSIZE ROW`

❑ D. `ALTER TABLE employee LOCKSIZE TABLE`

❑ E. `ALTER TABLE employee LOCKSIZE APPLICATION`

Question 90

Which configuration parameter is used to specify the number of prefetchers that are available to a database?

○ A. NUM_IOCLEANERS

○ B. NUM_IOSERVERS

○ C. NUM_IOAGENTS

○ D. NUM_IOFSCRS

Question 91

A database administrator executed the following commands and statements in the order shown:

```
CREATE DATABASE db1 ON /mnt/db2fs2, /mnt/db2fs3 DBPATH /mnt/db2fs1;

UPDATE DB CFG FOR db1 USING DATABASE_MEMORY AUTOMATIC;
UPDATE DB CFG FOR db1 USING PCKCACHESZ AUTOMATIC;
UPDATE DB CFG FOR db1 USING LOCKLIST AUTOMATIC;
UPDATE DB CFG FOR db1 USING MAXLOCKS AUTOMATIC;
UPDATE DB CFG FOR db1 USING SHEAPTHRES_SHR AUTOMATIC;
UPDATE DB CFG FOR db1 USING SORTHEAP AUTOMATIC;

CONNECT TO db1;
ALTER BUFFERPOOL ibmdefaultbp SIZE AUTOMATIC;
CONNECT RESET;
```

If database DB1 is a partitioned database, which of the following is a valid statement?

- ○ A. Database DB1 has been configured to take advantage of the Self-Tuning Memory Manager (STMM) and STMM has been enabled for the database.
- ○ B. Database DB1 has been configured to take advantage of the Self-Tuning Memory Manager (STMM); however STMM has not been enabled for the database.
- ○ C. If the amount of free memory available on the system becomes too low, some of the database shared memory that has been reserved for database DB1 will be released.
- ○ D. Memory consumed by database DB1 can be moved between the different DB2 memory segments, for example, from the sort heap to a buffer pool.

Question 92

If the following statement is executed:

```
ALTER TABLE employee COMPRESS YES
```

Which of the following commands will NOT build a compression dictionary for the EMPLOYEE table?

- ○ A. INSPECT RESETDICTIONARY TABLE NAME employee
- ○ B. INSPECT ROWCOMPESTIMATE TABLE NAME employee
- ○ C. REORG TABLE employee RESETDICTIONARY
- ○ D. REORG TABLE employee KEEPDICTIONARY

Question 93

A table named ITEMS has the following columns and cardinalities:

```
ID            1000000
TYPE          10
NAME          50000
DESCRIPTION   50000
```

If the following query is executed on a regular basis:

```
SELECT * FROM items WHERE type = 1 AND id = 10
```

Which of the following set of statements would provide the fastest response time for the query?

○ A. CREATE INDEX items_ix1 ON items (type, id);
       RUNSTATS ON TABLE items FOR INDEX items_ix1;

○ B. CREATE INDEX items_ix1 ON items(type);
       RUNSTATS ON TABLE items FOR INDEX items_ix1;

○ C. CREATE INDEX items_ix1 ON items(id);
       RUNSTATS ON TABLE items FOR INDEX items_ix1;

○ D. CREATE INDEX items_ix1 ON items(id, type);
       RUNSTATS ON TABLE items FOR INDEX items_ix1;

Question 94

User USER1 needs to sort a table that has an average row length of 450. The table resides is in a database named DB1 that has intra-partition parallelism disabled; the cardinality of the table is 2500.

Which command(s) will prevent a sort heap overflow from occurring when the table is sorted?

○ A. UPDATE DBM CFG USING SHEAPTHRES 1500000

○ B. UPDATE DB CFG FOR db1 USING SORTHEAP 300

○ C. UPDATE DBM CFG USING SHEAPTHRES 1500000;
       UPDATE DB CFG FOR db1 USING SORTHEAP 300;

○ D. UPDATE DBM CFG USING SHEAPTHRES 0;
       UPDATE DB CFG FOR db1 USING SORTHEAP AUTOMATIC;

Question 95

A table named PARTS was created as follows:

```
CREATE TABLE parts
     (partnumber      INT NOT NULL,
      description     VARCHAR(25),
      price           DECIMAL(7,2),
      weight          DECIMAL(3,2))
```

If column PARTNUMBER is unique and queries typically access columns PARTNUMBER, PRICE, and DESCRIPTION together, which statement will create an index that will provide optimal query performance?

○ A. CREATE UNIQUE INDEX parts_idx1 ON parts (partnumber, price)

○ B. CREATE UNIQUE INDEX parts_idx1 ON parts (partnumber, price, description)

○ C. CREATE UNIQUE INDEX parts_idx1 ON parts (partnumber) INCLUDE (price, description)

○ D. CREATE UNIQUE INDEX parts_idx1 ON parts (partnumber, price) INCLUDE description)

Question 96

A table named STAFF was created by executing the following statement:

```
CREATE TABLE staff
     (emp_id      INTEGER,
      name        VARCHAR (40),
      dept        VARCHAR (40),
      salary      DECIMAL (15,2))
```

The following query is frequently run against the STAFF table:

```
SELECT name, dept
FROM staff
WHERE salary > (SELECT MAX (salary *.95) FROM staff)
```

Which statement will create an index that will provide optimal performance for this query?

○ A. CREATE INDEX staffx1 ON staff (salary ASC)

○ B. CREATE INDEX staffx1 ON staff (salary DESC)

○ C. CREATE INDEX staffx1 ON staff (salary, name, dept)

○ D. CREATE INDEX staffx1 ON staff (salary ASC, name ASC, dept DESC)

Question 97

In which environment would intra-partition parallelism be used by DB2?

○ A. The server has two CPUs and one DB2 instance.

○ B. The server has one CPU and one DB2 instance.

○ C. The server has one CPU and two DB2 instances.

○ D. The server has one CPU and four DB2 instances.

Question 98

Which statement correctly describes intra-partition parallelism?

○ A. Intra-partition parallelism refers to the ability to break up a database operation into multiple parts, many or all of which can be run in parallel across multiple partitions of a partitioned database.

○ B. Intra-partition parallelism refers to the ability to break up a database operation into multiple parts and execute those parts simultaneously within a single DB2 instance.

○ C. Intra-partition parallelism refers to the ability of the database to accept queries from multiple applications at the same time; each query runs independently of the others, but DB2 runs all of them simultaneously.

○ D. Intra-partition parallelism refers to the ability to merge multiple database operations into a single operation that can be processed across multiple partitions of a partitioned database.

Security

Question 99

The authentication type for an instance has been set to KRB_SERVER_ENCRYPT, but a connection request was made from a client that does not support Kerberos authentication. What type of authentication will be used?

○ A. None – access will be denied

○ B. CLIENT

○ C. SERVER

○ D. SERVER_ENCRYPT

Question 100

An application developer plans on using SQL statements that look like the following to populate a table named SALES:

```
INSERT INTO sales (po_number, amount)
    VALUES (ENCRYPT('Q108-7234-1111-2222', 'MyPassWord'), 225.00)
```

Which statement should be used to create the SALES table?

- ○ A. CREATE TABLE sales (po_number VARCHAR(19) FOR BIT DATA, amount DECIMAL(9,2))
- ○ B. CREATE TABLE sales (po_number VARCHAR(20) FOR BIT DATA, amount DECIMAL(9,2))
- ○ C. CREATE TABLE sales (po_number VARCHAR(30) FOR BIT DATA, amount DECIMAL(9,2))
- ○ D. CREATE TABLE sales (po_number VARCHAR(40) FOR BIT DATA, amount DECIMAL(9,2))

Question 101

Which of the following is NOT a valid statement about the DB2 9 audit facility?

- ○ A. The DB2 audit facility works at the instance level, recording both instance-level and database-level activities.
- ○ B. The DB2 audit facility monitors a set of events that have been defined by IBM, based on problems encountered in the field over the years.
- ○ C. Since the DB2 audit facility works independently of the DB2 server, it will continue to run once started, even if the DB2 instance is stopped.
- ○ D. The DB2 audit facility is controlled by the db2audit command and the contents of an audit configuration file named db2audit.cfg.

Question 102

If the authentication type for an instance is set to KRB_SERVER_ENCRYPT, where will DB2 first try to authenticate the user?

- ○ A. At the client, using KERBEROS authentication.
- ○ B. At the server, using KERBEROS authentication.
- ○ C. At the client, using SERVER_ENCRYPT authentication.
- ○ D. At the server, using SERVER_ENCRYPT authentication.

Question 103

If the following statement is used to create a table named TAB1:

```
CREATE TABLE tab1
    (col1   DECFLOAT,
     col2   LONG VARCHAR,
     col3   VARCHAR(100) FOR BIT DATA,
     col4   CLOB(100))
```

Which column in the table has been defined in a way that will allow its data to be protected with the ENCRYPT() function?

○ A. COL1
○ B. COL2
○ C. COL3
○ D. COL4

Question 104

Which method should be used to construct a Label-Based Access Control (LBAC) security label component that represents a company's organizational chart?

○ A. SET
○ B. TREE
○ C. HIERARCHY
○ D. ORGANIZATION

Question 105

A database administrator executed the following command before starting the DB2 9 audit facility:

```
UPDATE DBM CFG USING AUDIT_BUF_SZ 200 IMMEDIATE
```

Which two of the following statements are correct? (Select two)

❑ A. Two hundred kilobytes of storage will be set aside as an internal buffer to cache audit records.
❑ B. Two hundred 4 KB pages will be set aside as an internal buffer to cache audit records.
❑ C. Audit records will be written synchronously to the audit log file.
❑ D. Audit records will be written asynchronously to the audit log file.
❑ E. The change to the *audit_buf_sz* configuration parameter will take effect immediately.

Question 106

User USER1 executed the following statements in the order shown:

```
SET ENCRYPTION PASSWORD = 'EXEC-0409';
INSERT INTO employee(name, ssn)
  VALUES ('John Doe', ENCRYPT('111-22-3333', 'HR-1118', 'Dept-Birthdate'));
```

Later, if user USER2 attempts to execute the following query:

```
SELECT name, DECRYPT_CHAR(ssn) FROM employee
```

What will happen?

- ○ A. The query will fail because a password was not provided.
- ○ B. The query will execute; the value 'HR-1118' will be used as the password.
- ○ C. The query will execute; the value 'EXEC-0409' will be used as the password.
- ○ D. The query will execute; the password used to authenticate user USER2 will be used as the password.

Question 107

Which two of the following commands, when executed, will ensure that the Kerberos-based authentication plug-in (IBMKrb5) that is shipped with DB2 9 will be used to authenticate users? (Select two)

- ❏ A. UPDATE DBM CFG USING SRVCON_AUTH NOT_SPECIFIED
- ❏ B. UPDATE DBM CFG USING SRVCON_GSSPLUGIN_LIST IBMKrb5
- ❏ C. UPDATE DBM CFG USING AUTHENTICATION IBMKrb5
- ❏ D. UPDATE DBM CFG USING AUTHENTICATION GSSPLUGIN
- ❏ E. UPDATE DBM CFG USING AUTHENTICATION KRB_SERVER_ENCRYPT

Question 108

A user with Security Administrator (SECADM) authority executes the following statements:

```
CREATE SECURITY LABEL COMPONENT sales_region
    TREE ('SALES_ORG' ROOT,
                'EAST_COAST' UNDER 'SALES_ORG',
                'CENTRAL' UNDER 'SALES_ORG',
                'WEST_COAST' UNDER 'SALES_ORG',
                'CENTRAL_NORTH' UNDER 'CENTRAL',
                'CENTRAL_SOUTH' UNDER 'CENTRAL');

CREATE SECURITY POLICY sales_region_policy
    COMPONENTS sales_region
    WITH DB2LBACRULES
    RESTRICT NOT AUTHORIZED WRITE SECURITY LABEL;

CREATE SECURITY LABEL sales_region_policy.sales_org_read
    COMPONENT sales_region 'SALES_ORG';

CREATE SECURITY LABEL sales_region_policy.east_coast
    COMPONENT sales_region 'EAST_COAST';

CREATE SECURITY LABEL sales_region_policy.central
    COMPONENT sales_region 'CENTRAL';

CREATE SECURITY LABEL sales_region_policy.central_north
    COMPONENT sales_region 'CENTRAL_NORTH';

CREATE SECURITY LABEL sales_region_policy.central_south
    COMPONENT sales_region 'CENTRAL_SOUTH';

CREATE SECURITY LABEL sales_region_policy.west_coast
    COMPONENT sales_region 'WEST_COAST';

GRANT SECURITY LABEL sales_region_policy.central
    TO USER user1 FOR READ ACCESS;
```

Later, a user with database administrator (DBADM) authority executes the following statements:

```
CREATE TABLE corp.sales
    (sales_date      DATE,
     sales_person    VARCHAR (15),
     region          VARCHAR (15),
     amount          DECIMAL(9,2),
     margin          INTEGER,
     region_tag      DB2SECURITYLABEL)
   SECURITY POLICY sales_region_policy;

GRANT ALL PRIVILEGES ON TABLE corp.sales TO user1;
```

If the table SALES is populated as follows:

SALES_DATE	SALES_PERSON	REGION	AMOUNT	MARGIN	REGION_TAG
06/04/2008	LEE	East-Coast	22000	50	sales_region_policy.east_coast
06/04/2008	SANDERS	West-Coast	18000	40	sales_region_policy.west_coast
07/10/2008	SNOW	Central-South	31000	30	sales_region_policy.central_south
07/12/2008	LEE	Central-North	27500	45	sales_region_policy.central_north

And if user USER1 executes the following query:

```
SELECT sales_date, sales_person, region, amount, margin,
   VARCHAR(SECLABEL_TO_CHAR('SALES_REGION_POLICY', REGION_TAG), 30)
FROM corp.sales
```

How many rows will be returned?

○ A. 0
○ B. 1
○ C. 2
○ D. 3

Connectivity and Networking

Question 109

A database administrator has established connectivity to a DB2 for z/OS database and wishes to use a System Z Sysplex for load balancing and fault-tolerance.

Which instance-level configuration parameter must be assigned a value that is greater than zero to ensure that enough agents remain allocated to help maintain the Sysplex server list?

- O A. NUM_INITAGENTS
- O B. NUM_IDLE_AGENTS
- O C. NUM_POOLAGENTS
- O D. MAX_AGENTS

Question 110

A database administrator is attempting to catalog a DB2 for z/OS server from a DB2 for Linux, UNIX, and Windows server. The communications protocol that will be used is TCP/IP.

What should the administrator do if he/she cannot connect to a database on the DB2 for z/OS server?

- O A. Ping the server where the DB2 for z/OS database resides and verify that the server has been cataloged correctly.
- O B. Verify the process db2tcpcm is running on the server and that the server has been cataloged correctly.
- O C. Verify that the Distributed Data Facility (DDF) is running and that the server has been cataloged correctly.
- O D. Verify that the Distributed Connection Facility (DCF) is running and that the server has been cataloged correctly.

Question 111

No one in the HR department can connect to a remote database named PAYROLL from their workstations. Preliminary investigation has shown that there are no problems with the network, the instance on the server is active, TCP/IP is running normally on both the clients and the servers, and users are trying to connect with valid user IDs and passwords. What is most likely the cause of the problem?

- O A. DB2COMM is not set correctly on the remote database server.
- O B. The remote instance's authentication type has not been set to CLIENT.
- O C. The DB2 Administration Server has not been started on the remote database server.
- O D. The PAYROLL database was not cataloged correctly on each employee's workstation.

Question 112

In a DB2 Connect configuration between a Linux client and a z/OS server, the following commands were executed:

```
CATALOG TCPIP NODE node001 REMOTE hostnm01.us.mycorp.com SERVER 446;
CATALOG DATABASE payroll AT NODE node001 AUTHENTICATION DCS;
```

Later, an error occurred while trying to connect to the PAYROLL_DB database in the DSN_DB_1 subsystem on the z/OS server. Close examination shows that the entry for the server in the node directory is correct and that the subsystem's LOCATION NAME on z/OS is DSN_DB_1. Which of the following commands, if executed, should resolve the problem?

○ A. CATALOG DCS DATABASE dsn_db_1 AS payroll
○ B. CATALOG DCS DATABASE payroll AS dsn_db_1
○ C. CATALOG DCS DATABASE payroll_db AS payroll
○ D. CATALOG DCS DATABASE payroll AS payroll_db AR dsn_db_1

Question 113

Which of the following commands will successfully catalog a node for a Linux server that has the IP address 1080:0:0:0:8:800:200C:417A and an instance that is listening on port 50000?

○ A. CATALOG TCPIP NODE rmt_server
        REMOTE 1080:0:0:0:8:800:200C:417A
        SERVER 50000
        OSTYPE LINUX

○ B. CATALOG TCPIP2 NODE rmt_server
        REMOTE 1080:0:0:0:8:800:200C:417A
        SERVER 50000
        OSTYPE LINUX

○ C. CATALOG TCPIP4 NODE rmt_server
        REMOTE 1080:0:0:0:8:800:200C:417A
        SERVER 50000
        OSTYPE LINUX

○ D. CATALOG TCPIP6 NODE rmt_server
        REMOTE 1080:0:0:0:8:800:200C:417A
        SERVER 50000
        OSTYPE LINUX

Question 114

An instance named DB2INST1 and a database named SAMPLE reside on a server named SVR1. Which two of the following commands must be executed before both the instance and the database can be seen by a DB2 discovery request? (Select two)

- ❑ A. `db2set DISCOVER_INST=ENABLE`
- ❑ B. `UPDATE DBM CFG USING DISCOVER_INST ENABLE`
- ❑ C. `db2set DISCOVER_DB=ENABLE`
- ❑ D. `UPDATE DB CFG FOR sample USING DISCOVER_DB ENABLE`
- ❑ E. `UPDATE DBM CFG USING DISCOVER_DATABASE ENABLE`

Question 115

Although everyone else in the HR department can connect to a remote database named PAYROLL from their workstations, one employee cannot, even though he is supplying the correct user ID and password. What is most likely the cause of the problem?

- ◯ A. DB2COMM is not set correctly on the remote database server.
- ◯ B. DB2COMM is not set correctly on the employee's workstation.
- ◯ C. The PAYROLL database was not cataloged correctly on the server.
- ◯ D. The PAYROLL database was not cataloged correctly on the employee's workstation.

Question 116

A database administrator obtained the following information about a UNIX DB2 server:

```
Instance name        : db2inst1
Port number          : 50000
Service name         : db2c_db2inst1
Host name            : hostnm01
Host TCP/IP address  : 10.205.15.100
DB2COMM              : TCPIP
Database name        : PROD_DB
```

In an attempt to establish connectivity between a Windows client and the DB2 server, the following commands were executed from the Windows client:

```
CATALOG TCPIP NODE node001 REMOTE hostnm01 SERVER 50000;
CATALOG DATABASE prod_db AS prod_db AT NODE node001;
```

However, when an attempt was made to connect to the database, an error occurred. Which of the following actions should be performed to resolve the problem?

- ◯ A. Catalog the database PROD_DB in the local database directory.
- ◯ B. Add the entry "db2c_db2inst1 50000/tcp" to the services file on the UNIX server.
- ◯ C. Catalog the database PROD_DB in the Database Connection Services (DCS) directory.
- ◯ D. Add the entry "db2inst1 10.205.15.100" to the services file on the UNIX server.

Question 117

After applying a FixPack to a DB2 server, which two of the following commands should be executed to create new packages for the DB2 utilities and CLI/ODBC driver? (Select two)

❑ A. `BIND db2util.bnd BLOCKING ALL GRANT PUBLIC`
❑ B. `BIND @db2ubind.1st MESSAGES bind.msg GRANT PUBLIC`
❑ C. `BIND @db2cli.1st MESSAGES bind.msg GRANT PUBLIC`
❑ D. `BIND @db2odbc.1st MESSAGES bind.msg GRANT PUBLIC`
❑ E. `BIND db2schema.bnd BLOCKING ALL GRANT PUBLIC`

Question 118

Which database configuration parameter must be set to DISABLE if clients are to be prevented from seeing a database with a DB2 discovery request?

○ A. DISCOVER
○ B. DISCOVERY
○ C. DISCOVER_DB
○ D. DISCOVER_DATABASE

Question 119

Which two of the following items are NOT required to establish a TCP/IP connection to a DB2 for z/OS database from a DB2 for Linux, UNIX, and Windows server? (Select two)

❑ A. Hostname
❑ B. Port number
❑ C. Database name (target and local)
❑ D. Subsystem ID
❑ E. Logical Unit (LU) name

Question 120

While attempting to connect to a database named TEST_DB (which is a DB2 for z/OS database) from a Windows client, an employee received the following message:

SQL1013N The database alias name or database name "TEST_DB" could not be found.

Other employees in the same department can connect to the database without any problem. Close examination shows that the entries for the server and the database in the node and system database directories are the same on everyone's workstation. Which of the following actions should be performed to resolve the problem?

○ A. Stop and restart the instance on the z/OS server.

○ B. Uncatalog and recatalog the database in the system database directory.

○ C. Catalog the database in the remote database directory.

○ D. Catalog the database in the Database Connection Services (DCS) directory.

Answers

Database Design

Question 1

The correct answer is **C**. Once a table space has been created, there is no way to dynamically change the partition group to which it belongs. Therefore, if you want to change the partition group associated with an existing table space, you must drop the table space (using the DROP statement) and recreate it (using the CREATE TABLESPACE statement) in the new database partition group.

Question 2

The correct answer is **A**. The argument " $N" ([blank]$N) is used to indicate a database partition expression; when used, it is replaced with the actual partition number. A database partition expression can be used anywhere in a container name and expressions can be specified within the same name. To use a partition expression, there must be a space after the container name followed by the expression. The result of the expression following the space will then be appended to the container name. If there is no space character in the container name after the database partition expression, it is assumed that the rest of the string is part of the expression.

Thus, if you wanted to create a DMS table space named TBSP1 in a partitioned database that has five partitions numbered 0 through 4 and you wanted the storage container for the first partition to be a file named CONT1P0, the storage container for the second partition to be a file named CONT1P1, and so on, you could do so by executing a CREATE TABLESPACE command that looks something like this:

```
CREATE TABLESPACE tbsp1
MANAGED BY DATABASE
USING (FILE 'cont1P $N' 5000)
```

Question 3

The correct answer is **A**. If the DEFERRED clause is specified with the CREATE BUFFERPOOL statement, the buffer pool will be created, but no memory will be allocated until all connections to the database the buffer pool is to be created for have been terminated and the database has been deactivated (i.e. the database is stopped and restarted). If the IMMEDIATE clause is specified instead, or if neither clause is specified, the buffer pool will be created and the amount of memory needed will be allocated immediately unless the amount of memory required is unavailable, in which case a warning message will be generated and the buffer pool creation process will behave as if the DEFERRED clause were specified. In this scenario, approximately 12 MB of memory is needed but only 8 MB is available, so no memory will be allocated until the database is stopped and restarted.

Question 4

The correct answer is **D**. Wrappers are mechanisms by which a federated database interacts with data sources. You must register one wrapper for each type of data source you want to have access to. Therefore, if you wanted to access two Oracle database tables, one SQL Server table, and one DB2 for z/OS view, you would need to create one wrapper for the Oracle data source objects, one wrapper for the SQL Server data source object, and one wrapper for the DB2 data source object.

After one or more wrappers have been registered in a federated database, the name used to identify a data source that is associated with a particular wrapper, along with other pertinent information, must be supplied before the data source can be accessed. The data source name, along with other information such as the type and version of the data source, the database name for a relational data source, and metadata that is specific to the data source are collectively called a server definition (or server). You must create one server for every data source that you want to access. Therefore, if you wanted to access two Oracle instances, one SQL Server data source, and one DB2 for z/OS data source, you would need to create one server for each Oracle instance, one server for the SQL Server data source, and one server for the DB2 for z/OS database.

A nickname is an identifier that an application uses to reference a data source object, such as a table or view. Users and applications reference nicknames in SQL statements just as they would reference an alias, a base table, or a view. However, nicknames are not alternative names for data source objects in the same way that aliases are. Instead, they are pointers by which the federated server references these objects. So in order to reference two Oracle database tables, one SQL Server table, and one DB2 for z/OS view in a join operation, you would need to create one nickname for each database (so each database can be referenced in the query performing the join operation).

Question 5

The correct answer is **B**. If the NO FILE SYSTEM CACHING option is used with the CREATE TABLESPACE or ALTER TABLESPACE statement, I/O for the specified table space will not be buffered by the file system (i.e., the table space will use direct I/O). It is important to note that the registry variable DB2_DIRECT_IO, introduced in Version 8.1 FixPak 4, enabled no file system caching for all SMS containers except for long field data, large object data, and temporary table spaces on AIX JFS2. Setting this registry variable in Version 9.1 or later is equivalent to altering all table spaces – SMS and DMS – and specifying the NO FILE SYSTEM CACHING clause. However, using the DB2_DIRECT_IO registry variable is not recommended. Instead, you should enable NO FILE SYSTEM CACHING at the table space level.

Question 6

The correct answers are **C** and **E**. Using the ALTER TABLESPACE statement, an existing table space can be modified as follows:

- A container can be added to an SMS table space on a database partition that currently has no containers.

- Containers can be added to, or dropped from a DMS table space.

- The size of an existing container in a DMS table space can be changed.

- The buffer pool used to cache data for a table space can be changed.

- The amount of data that gets prefetched from a table space (prefetch size) can be changed.

- The I/O controller overhead and disk seek latency time for a table space can be changed.

- The time it takes to transfer one page (4K or 8K) of data from the table space to memory can be changed.

- The file system caching policy used by a table space can be changed.

Question 7

The correct answer is **B**. Unlike when SMS and DMS table spaces are defined, no container definitions are needed for automatic storage table spaces; DB2 assigns containers to automatic storage table spaces automatically. However, an initial size can be specified as part of the table space creation process - if an initial size is not specified, DB2 will use a default value of 32 megabytes.

Question 8

The correct answer is **D**. The amount of memory that will be allocated for all buffer pools is calculated as follows:

Buffer pools specified:

Buffer pool BP1 = 60 MB	= **60 MB**
Buffer pool BP2 = 20,000 pages * 16 KB = 320,000 KB	= **320 MB**
Buffer pool BP3 = 2000 pages * 8 KB = 16,000 KB	= **16 MB**

Default buffer pool (1000 4K pages on UNIX):
Buffer pool IBMDEFAULTBP = 1000 pages * 4KB = 4000 KB =   **4 MB**

DB2's hidden buffer pools:

Hidden buffer pool 1 = 16 pages * 4 KB = 64 KB		**= .064 MB**
Hidden buffer pool 2 = 16 pages * 8 KB = 128 KB		**= .128 MB**
Hidden buffer pool 3 = 16 pages * 16 KB = 256 KB		**= .256 MB**
Hidden buffer pool 4 = 16 pages * 32 KB = 512 KB		**= .512 MB**

Total: **400.96 MB**

The db2mtrk utility can be used to verify the allocation.

Question 9

The correct answer is **B**. In order for a federated server to retrieve data from a data source, the data types used by the data source must map to corresponding DB2 data types. Data type mappings are used to identify how data source-specific data types are to be mapped to DB2 data types. For most relational data sources, default type mappings are included in the wrapper. If you want to override the default data type mappings provided, you can do so by executing one or more CREATE TYPE MAPPING SQL statements.

If after a nickname has been created, the definition of a remote data source object is changed (for example, a column is deleted or a data type is changed), the nickname should be dropped and recreated; otherwise, errors might occur when the nickname is used in SQL statements. Likewise, if you change one or more type mappings for a relational data source after a nickname for an object in that data source has been created, you will need to drop the nickname and recreate it before the type mapping changes will take effect. Thus, in this scenario, you must drop the nickname to the Oracle table, create a new data type mapping to reflect the changes made to the data types used by the Oracle data source, and then re-create the nickname.

Question 10

The correct answer is **A**. If a database is enabled for automatic storage, the container- and space- management characteristics of its table spaces are determined by DB2. Therefore, although the ALTER TABLESPACE command can be used to add new containers to existing DMS table spaces, it cannot be used to add new containers to automatic storage table spaces. Instead, to add new storage paths to the collection of paths that are used for automatic storage table spaces once a database has been created, you must use the ALTER DATABASE statement. The basic syntax for this statement is:

```
ALTER DATABASE [DatabaseName]
ADD STORAGE ON '[Container]' ,...)
```

where:

DatabaseName	Identifies the database, by name, that is to have new containers added to its pool of containers that are used for automatic storage.
Container	Identifies one or more new storage locations (containers) that are to be added to the collection of storage locations that are used for automatic storage table spaces.

Thus, if you wanted to add the storage locations /data/path1 and /data/path2 to a database named SAMPLE that is configured for automatic storage and resides on a UNIX system, you could do so by executing an ALTER DATABASE SQL statement that looks like this:

```
ALTER DATABASE sample
ADD STORAGE '/data/path1', '/data/path2'
```

Question 11

The correct answer is **C**. If no database partition group is specified, the default database partition group IBMDEFAULTGROUP is used for REGULAR, LARGE, and USER TEMPORARY table spaces and the default database partition group IBMTEMPGROUP is used for SYSTEM TEMPORARY table spaces. Unless otherwise specified, pages used by table spaces are 4K in size. If the FILE SYSTEM CACHING option is specified (the default in DB2 9), all I/O for the table space will be buffered by the file system. If the DROPPED TABLE RECOVERY ON option is specified (the default), dropped tables in the specified table space can be recovered using the RECOVER DROPPED TABLE option of the ROLLFORWARD DATABASE command – provided the table space is a regular table space.

Question 12

The correct answer is **C**. If you wanted to increase the size of all containers associated with an existing DMS table space named PAYROLL by 200 megabytes, you could do so by executing an ALTER TABLESPACE SQL statement that looks like this:

```
ALTER TABLESPACE payroll_ts EXTEND (ALL CONTAINERS 200 M)
```

On the other hand, if you wanted to increase the size of individual containers, you could do so by executing an ALTER TABLESPACE SQL statement that looks like this:

```
ALTER TABLESPACE payroll EXTEND (FILE '\home\myfile2' 1000
    FILE '\home\myfile1' 1200);
```

The order of the container names does not matter, so in this example the resulting container sizes would be 200 + 1200 pages or 1400 pages (MYFILE1) and 400 + 1000 or 1400 pages (MYFILE2).

Question 13

The correct answers are **C** and **D**. The database must exist and a connection must be made to it before the EMPLOYEE table can be created with the CREATE TABLE SQL statement shown. However, since no table space is specified with the CREATE TABLE statement used in the sequence of statements provided, the EMPLOYEE table will be created in the USERSPACE1 table space by default. This table space uses the buffer pool IBMDEFAULTBP, so the steps that create a buffer pool named BP1 and a table space named TS1 are unnecessary.

Question 14

The correct answer is **B**. The page size used by a buffer pool determines which table spaces can be used with it – a buffer pool can only be used by a table space that has a corresponding page size. Since one buffer pool with a page size of 4K is created by default (IBMDEFAULTBP), only two additional buffer pools, one with a page size of 8K and one with a page size of 16K, must exist before the table spaces listed can be created.

Question 15

The correct answers are **A** and **D**. The basic syntax for the ALTER BUFFERPOOL statement is:

```
ALTER BUFFERPOOL [BufferPoolName]
<IMMEDIATE | DEFERRED>
<DBPARTITIONNUM [PartionNum]>
SIZE [AUTOMATIC |
    [NumberOfPages] |
    [NumberOfPages] AUTOMATIC]
```

or

```
ALTER BUFFERPOOL [BufferPoolName]
ADD DATABASE PARTITION GROUP [PartitionGroup]
```

or

```
ALTER BUFFERPOOL [BufferPoolName]
NUMBLOCKPAGES [NumBlockPages] <BLOCK SIZE [BlockSize]>
```

or

```
ALTER BUFFERPOOL [BufferPoolName]
BLOCK SIZE [BlockSize]
```

where:

BufferPoolName	Identifies the buffer pool, by name, whose characteristics are to be modified.
PartitionNum	Identifies the database partition on which the size of the buffer pool is to be altered.
NumberOfPages	Enables or disables self-tuning *OR* identifies the new number of pages that are to be allocated for the buffer pool.
PartitionGroup	Identifies a new database partition group that is to be added to the list of database partition groups to which the buffer pool definition is applicable.
NumBlockPages	Specifies the number of pages that are to be created in the block-based area of the buffer pool. (The block-based area of a buffer pool cannot consume more than 98 percent of the total buffer pool.)
BlockSize	Specifies the number of pages that can be stored within a block in the block-based area of the buffer pool. (The *BlockSize* value specified must be between 2 and 256 pages; the default value is 32 pages.)

Therefore, the ALTER BUFFERPOOL statement can be used to change the block size and number of block pages used, but not the table space(s) that use the buffer pool nor the page size. And a size of -1 is not valid.

Question 16

The correct answer is **C**. Currently you cannot execute DB2 utility operations (LOAD, REORG, REORGCHK, IMPORT, RUNSTATS, and so on) on nicknames. If such an operation is required, you must run the equivalent utility at the data source. And in some cases, you may be required to drop and re-create the nickname for the object against which a data source-specific utility was run. In this case, dropping and re-creating the nickname after statistics have been updated at the SQL Server data source will cause DB2 to update the statistics on the federated server.

Data Partitioning and Clustering

Question 17

The correct answer is **A**. The syntax for the form of the ALTER DATABASE PARTITION GROUP SQL statement that is used to add new database partitions to an existing database partition group is:

```
ALTER DATABASE PARTITION GROUP [PartGroupName]
ADD DBPARTITIONNUM<S>
    ([StartPartitionNum] <TO [EndPartitionNum]> ,...)
<LIKE DBPARTITIONNUM [SrcPartitionNum] |
  WITHOUT TABLESPACES>
```

where:

PartGroupName	Identifies, by name, the database partition group that is to be modified.
StartPartitionNum	Identifies, by partition number, one or more database partitions that are to be added to the database partition group specified.
EndPartitionNum	Identifies, by partition number, a database partition that, together with the database partition number specified in the *StartPartitionNum* parameter, identify a range of database partitions that are to be added to the database partition group specified. (The partition number specified in this parameter must be greater than the partition number specified in the *StartPartitionNum* parameter.)
SrcPartitionNum	Identifies, by partition number, a database partition that is to be used as a reference when defining containers on the database partition being added for table spaces that already exist in the partition group being altered. (The database partition number specified must correspond to a partition that existed in the database partition group being altered before the ALTER DATABASE PARTITION GROUP statement was executed.)

If the WITHOUT TABLESPACES option is specified, containers for table spaces in the database partition group being altered are not created for the database partition(s) added; if this option is used, the ALTER TABLESPACE statement must be executed in order to define table space containers to be used by the table spaces that have been defined in the partition group – before the table spaces can be used. If neither the LIKE DBPARTRTIONNUM option nor the WITHOUT TABLESPACES option is specified when adding a database partition to a database partition group, the containers used for table spaces on the database partition(s) being added will be the same as the containers found on the lowest numbered database partition in the partition group.

So, in this example, the lowest numbered database partition in the database partition group PG1 is 2 and neither the LIKE DBPARTITIONNUM option nor the WITHOUT TABLESPACES option is specified, so new database partitions will be added as if the option LIKE DBPARTITIONNUM 2 had been specified; the table space containers on database partition number 2 will be used as a model for the table space containers created on database partition number 6.

Question 18

The correct answer is **D**. To create the best design for an MDC table, perform the following tasks, in the order shown:

1. Identify candidate dimensions for the table by examining typical workload queries. Columns that are referenced in one or more of the following ways should be considered:

    - Range, equality, or IN-list predicates

    - Roll-in or roll-out of data

    - Group-by and order-by clauses

    - Join clauses (especially in star schema environments)

2. Identify how many potential cells are possible if the table is organized along a set of candidate dimensions identified in Step 1. (In other words, determine the number of unique combinations of the dimension values that can occur in the data.)

3. Estimate the space occupancy (cell density).

4. Take the following items into consideration:

    - When identifying candidate dimensions, search for attributes that are not too granular, thereby enabling more rows to be stored in each cell. This will make better use of block level indexes.

    - Higher data volumes may improve population density.

    - It may be beneficial to load the data into a non-MDC table for analysis before creating and loading an MDC table.

    - The table space extent size and page size are critical parameters for efficient space utilization.

    - Although a smaller extent size will provide the most efficient use of disk space, the I/O for the queries should also be considered.

- A larger extent will normally reduce I/O cost, since more data will be read at a time, all other things being equal. This in turn makes for smaller dimension block indexes, since each dimension value will need fewer blocks. In addition, inserts will be quicker, since new blocks will be needed less often.

- Although an MDC table may require a greater initial understanding of the data, the payback is that query times will likely improve.

- Some data may be unsuitable for MDC tables and would be a better candidate for a standard clustering index.

Because the columns MODEL and MANUFACTURER are referenced in equality predicates of frequently executed queries in this example, they make the ideal clustering dimensions for the table. If those two columns are used as the dimensions of the table, all sales with the same MODEL and MANUFACTURER will be stored together. Having YEAR or PRICE in the dimensions will actually mean that DB2 will need to read more blocks of data to retrieve the desired data.

Question 19

The correct answer is **C**. Columns, especially those with low cardinalities, that are involved in equality or range predicate queries will show the greatest benefit from, and should be considered as candidates for, clustering dimensions (distribution keys). Foreign keys in a fact table that is involved in star joins with other dimension tables are also good candidates for clustering. Columns that are referenced in one or more of the following ways should be considered:

- Range, equality, or IN-list predicates

- Roll-in or roll-out of data

- Group-by and order-by clauses

- Join clauses (especially in star schema environments)

Question 20

The correct answer is **B**. Before you create a partitioned database, you must decide which partition will act as the catalog partition for the database. Once the partition that will serve as the catalog partition has been selected, you must then create the database directly from that partition or from a remote client that is attached to that partition – the database partition to which you attach and execute the CREATE DATABASE command (or invoke the Create Database Wizard) becomes the catalog partition for the new database. (The catalog partition will be the partition using port number 0 on the server where the CREATE DATABASE command is executed.) In this example, partition 4 is the first partition on server Svr2 so that is the partition that will contain the system catalog for the database.

Keep in mind that on Linux and UNIX, the db2nodes.cfg file is formatted as follows:

`[PartitionNumber]` `[HostName]` `[LogicalPort]` `[NetName]` `[ResourceSetName]`

And on Windows, the `db2nodes.cfg` file is formatted as follows:

`[PartitionNumber]` `[HostName]` `[ComputerName]` `[LogicalPort]` `[NetName]`

Question 21

The correct answer is **C**. When the ADD DBPARTITIONNUM option is used with the START DATABASE MANAGER command to add a new database partition to an instance that spans multiple partitions, the db2nodes.cfg file is not updated with information about the new database partition until the instance is stopped and restarted; likewise, the new database partition does not become part of the partitioned database system until the instance is stopped and restarted.

Question 22

The correct answer is **B**. Multidimensional clustering (MDC) is primarily intended to be used with large tables in data warehousing and large database environments.

Question 23

The correct answer is **B**. Range-clustered tables are created by specifying the ORGANIZE BY KEY SEQUENCE clause of the CREATE TABLE SQL statement; Range-partitioned tables are created by specifying the PARTITION BY RANGE clause of the CREATE TABLE SQL statement; and multidimensional clustering (MDC) tables are created by specifying the ORGANIZE BY DIMENSIONS clause of the CREATE TABLE SQL statement. PARTITION BY DIMENSIONS is not a valid data organization scheme.

Question 24

The correct answer is **A**. The BCU for Linux is based on the IBM eServer 326m, which is a 1U server that uses two AMD dual-core Opteron CPUs. Users may upgrade from the IBM eServer 326m to the IBM System x3455; model 2218 (2.6 GHz AMD dual-core Opteron CPUs) has been validated with the BCU for Linux, but models with the faster 2.8 GHz processors are also supported. The BCU for AIX v2.1 uses an IBM System p5 575 server with 8 POWER5+ processors and 32 GB of memory. In general data BCUs host eight database partitions.

All customers should implement some form of backup solution. To provide this functionality, a Tivoli Storage Manager (TSM) server is recommended, but not required.

Question 25

The correct answer is **D**. Intra-partition parallelism refers to the ability to break up a database operation into multiple parts and execute those parts simultaneously within a single DB2 instance. Inter-partition parallelism refers to the ability to break up a database operation into multiple parts, many or all of which can be run in parallel across multiple partitions of a partitioned database.

On Linux and UNIX, the db2nodes.cfg file is formatted as follows:

```
[PartitionNumber]  [HostName]  [LogicalPort]  [NetName]  [ResourceSetName]
```

And on Windows, the db2nodes.cfg file is formatted as follows:

```
[PartitionNumber] [HostName] [ComputerName] [LogicalPort] [NetName]
```

In this example, the db2nodes.cfg file shown in answers A and B indicate that the DB2 instance spans four database partitions that reside on four different servers (hosts) – this illustrates the use of inter-partition parallelism. The db2nodes.cfg file shown in answer C indicates that the DB2 instance spans four database partitions that reside on the same server – this illustrates the use of intra-partition parallelism. The db2nodes.cfg file shown in answer D indicates that the DB2 instance spans two database partitions that reside on one server and two partitions that reside on another server – this illustrates the use of both inter- and intra-partition parallelism. (To support both inter- and intra-partition parallelism, an instance must span multiple partitions that reside on two or more different servers or logical partitions [LPARs].).

Question 26

The correct answer is **B**. The partitioning key for a table is defined as part of the table creation process by using the PARTITION BY clause of the CREATE TABLE SQL statement. If a partitioning key is not explicitly specified (and the table is being created in a table space that resides in multi-partition database partition group), the partitioning key for the table will be defined as follows:

- If a primary key is defined for the table, the first column of the primary key will be the partitioning key,

- If the table is a typed table, the object identifier column for the table will be the partitioning key,

- The first column whose data type is not a LOB, LONG VARCHAR, LONG VARGRAPHIC, XML, structured data type, or a distinct data type based on one of these data types will be the partitioning key; otherwise,

- The table will be created without a partitioning key – in this case, the table can only be created in a table space that has been defined on a single-partition database partition group. (A single-partition database partition group is a partition group that only spans one database partition.)

Question 27

The correct answer is **A**. Partitioned table data can be rolled in or out of a partitioned table by executing an ALTER TABLE SQL statement with either the ATTACH PARTITION or the DETACH PARTITION option specified. In this example, suppose you want to update the information stored in a table named SALES_RECORDS by removing the data for May 2001 and replacing it with data for May 2008. To perform this roll-out and roll-in of data, you would complete the following steps, in the order shown:

1. Remove the May 2001 data from the SALES_RECORDS table and copy it to another table by executing an ALTER TABLE statement that looks something like this:

    ```
    ALTER TABLE sales_records DETACH PARTITION may01 INTO tab0501
    ```

2. Load the data for May 2008 into the table used to store the data for May 2001 by executing a LOAD command that looks like this:

    ```
    LOAD FROM may08.del OF DEL REPLACE INTO tab0501;
    ```

    (Executing the LOAD command with the REPLACE option causes existing data to be overwritten; you must run the SET INTEGRITY statement to disable constraint checking before you can load the detached table.)

3. If appropriate, perform any data cleansing activities needed. Data cleansing activities include:

    - Filling in missing values

    - Deleting inconsistent and incomplete data

    - Removing redundant data arriving from multiple sources

    - Transforming data

        o Normalization (Data from different sources that represents the same value in different ways must be reconciled as part of rolling the data into a data warehouse.)

        o Aggregation (Raw data that is too detailed to store in a data warehouse must be pre-aggregated during roll-in.)

4. Attach the table containing the data for May 2008 (TAB0501) to the SALES_RECORDS table as a new partition by executing an ALTER TABLE statement that looks something like this:

```
ALTER TABLE sales_records
ATTACH PARTITION may08
STARTING '05/01/2008' ENDING '05/31/2008'
FROM tab0501;
```

(Attaching a data partition terminates queries and invalidates packages.)

5. Update indexes and other dependent objects by executing a SET INTEGRITY SQL statement that looks something like this:

```
SET INTEGRITY FOR sales_records
ALLOW WRITE ACCESS
IMMEDIATE CHECKED FOR EXCEPTION IN sales_records
  USE salesrecs_ex;
```

Question 28

The correct answer is **D**. The components that make up the IBM BCU v2.1 for AIX are one or more IBM System p 575 servers, one or more IBM DS4800 or IBM DS8100 storage systems, and DB2 Data Warehouse Edition (DB2 DWE) V9.1.1 or V9.5.

Question 29

The correct answers are **B** and **D**. New database partitions can be added to a partitioned database system by executing the ADD DBPARTITIONNUM command. New database partitions can also be created by starting an instance in such a way that a new database partition is defined at instance startup. This is done by executing the START DATABASE MANAGER command with the ADD DBPARTITIONNUM option specified.

When you use the ADD DBPARTITIONNUM command or the ADD DBPARTITIONNUM option of the START DATABASE MANAGER command to add a new database partition to the system, all existing databases in the instance are expanded to the new database partition. However, data cannot be stored on the new partition until one or more database partition groups have been altered to include the new database partition. New partitions are added to an existing database partition group by executing the ALTER DATABASE PARTITION GROUP command.

Question 30

The correct answer is **D**. Data from a given table is partitioned into multiple storage objects based on the specifications provided in the PARTITION BY clause of the CREATE TABLE statement. Multidimensional clustering tables are created by specifying the ORGANIZE BY DIMENSIONS clause of the CREATE TABLE SQL statement when a table is created. So in this example, the table SALES is partitioned by the YEAR_DAY column and clustered by the ITEM_NUMBER column. The (STARTING 200801 ENDING 200812 EVERY 3) partitioning range indicates that data will be partitioned every three months - a one year period was specified and the keyword EVERY along with the value 3 indicates 3 months of a 12 month period.

Question 31

The correct answer is **A**. When designing an MDC table, it is important to choose the right set of dimensions (for clustering) and the optimum block (extent) size and page size (for space utilization). If these two items are selected appropriately, the resulting clustering can translate into significant performance increases and ease of maintenance. On the other hand, if an incorrect dimension and/or block size is chosen, performance can be negatively impacted and the space required to store the table's data could increase dramatically.

The best criteria to use for determining which clustering dimensions are ideal for a given table, is a set of frequently executed queries that might benefit from clustering at the block level. Columns, especially those with low cardinalities, that are involved in equality or range predicate queries will show the greatest benefit from, and should be considered as candidates for, clustering dimensions. Foreign keys in a fact table that is involved in star joins with other dimension tables are also good candidates for clustering.

Because column COL1 has a high cardinality, it is not good MDC dimension candidate. Its use is likely to lead to sparse dimensions, which can increase the storage requirements of the table.

Question 32

The correct answer is **A**. The Design Advisor is invoked by executing the db2advis command. The basic syntax for this command is:

```
db2advis [-d | -db] [DatabaseName]
<-w [WorkloadName]>
<-s "[SQLStatement]">
<-i [InFile]>
<-g>
<-qp>
<-a [UserID] </[Password]>
<-m [AdviseType ,...]>
<-l [DiskLimit]>
<-t "[MaxAdviseTime]">
<-k [HIGH | MED | LOW | OFF]>
<-h>
<-p>
<-o [OutFile]>
```

where:

DatabaseName	Identifies, by name, the database with which the Design Advisor is to interact.
WorkloadName	Identifies the name of a workload that is to be analyzed to determine whether new indexes/MQTs/MDCs should be created.
SQLStatement	Identifies a single SQL statement that is to be analyzed to determine whether new indexes/MQTs/MDCs should be created.
InFile	Identifies the name assigned to an ASCII format file that contains a set of SQL statements that are to be analyzed to determine whether new indexes/MQTs/MDCs should be created.
UserID	Identifies the authentication ID (or user ID) that is to be used to establish a connection to the database specified.
Password	Identifies the password that is to be used to establish a connection to the database specified.
AdviseType	Specifies one or more types of recommendations for which the Design Advisor is to analyze. Valid values for this parameter include the following: I (index), M (materialized query tables [MQTs] and indexes on the MQTs), C (convert standard tables to multidimensional clustering [MDC] tables), and P (repartitioning of existing tables).
DiskLimit	Identifies the maximum amount of storage space, in megabytes, that is available for all indexes/MQTs/MDCs in the existing schema.
MaxAdviseTime	*Identifies* the maximum amount of time, in minutes, in which the Design Advisor will be allowed to conduct an analysis. When this time limit is reached, the Design Advisor will stop all processing.
OutFile	Identifies the name of the file to which the DDL that is needed to create the indexes/MQTs/MDCs recommended is to be written.

If you want advice for all types of objects, you must use –m MICP, not –m ALL.

High Availability and Diagnostics

Question 33

The correct answer is **B**. The name of the current active log file (also referred to as the first active log file) can be obtained by executing the GET DATABASE CONFIGURATION command and examining the contents of the *loghead* database configuration parameter. (This will appear as "First active log file" in the list of information returned by the GET DATABASE CONFIGURATION command.). Other log-related information returned by the GET DATABASE CONFIGURATION command includes:

- Log buffer size (4KB)   *logbufsz*
- Log file size (4KB)   *logfilsiz*
- Number of primary log files   *logprimary*
- Number of secondary log files   *logsecond*
- Path to log files   *logpath*
- Overflow log path   *overflowlogpath*
- Mirror log path   *mirrorlogpath*
- Block log on disk full   *blk_log_dsk_ful*
- Percent max primary log space by transaction   *max_log*
- Num. of active log files for 1 active UOW   *num_log_span*
- First log archive method   *logarchmeth1*
- Options for logarchmeth1   *logarchopt1*
- Second log archive method   *logarchmeth2*
- Options for logarchmeth2   *logarchopt2*
- Failover log archive path   *failarchpath*
- Number of log archive retries on error   *numarchretry*
- Log archive retry Delay (secs)   *archretrydelay*

Question 34

The correct answer is **D**. The DB2 Check Backup utility can be used to test the integrity of a backup image, or multiple parts of a backup image, and to determine whether or not the image can be used to restore a damaged or corrupted database. It can also be used to display the metadata stored in the backup header (such as log path used, instance name, type of backup image, etc.).

The DB2 Check Backup utility is invoked by executing the db2ckbkp command. The syntax for this command is:

```
db2ckbkp
[ <-a>
  <-c>
  <-d>
  <-e>
  <-h>
  <-l>
  <-n>
  <-o>
  <-p>
  <-s>
  <-t>
  <-cl [DecompressLib]>
  <-co [DecompressOpts]> ,... ]
[FileName ,...]
```

or

```
db2ckbkp -H [FileName ,...]
```

or

```
db2ckbkp -S [FileName ,...]
```

or

```
db2ckbkp -T [FileName ,...]
```

where:

DecompressLib	Specifies the library, by name, that is to be used to decompress the backup image. (If this parameter is not specified, DB2 will attempt to use the library stored in the image. If the backup image was not compressed, the value of this parameter will be ignored; if the backup image was compressed and the specified library cannot be loaded, the operation will fail.)
DecompressOpts	Describes a block of binary data that will be passed to the initialization routine in the decompression library. DB2 will pass this string directly from the client to the server, so any issues of byte reversal or code page

conversion will have to be handled by the decompression library. If the first character of the data block is '@', the remainder of the data will be interpreted by DB2 as the name of a file residing on the server. DB2 will then replace the contents of the string with the contents of that file and will pass this new value to the initialization routine instead.

FileName   Identifies, by name, one or more backup image files that are to be analyzed. When checking multiple parts of a backup image, the first backup image object (.001) must be specified first.

All other options shown with this command are described in Table F.1.

Table F.1 db2ckbkp Command Options	
Option	**Meaning**
-a	Specifies that all information available about the backup image is to be collected and displayed.
-c	Specifies that checkbit and checksum information is to be collected and displayed.
-d	Specifies that information stored in the headers of DMS table space data pages is to be collected and displayed.
-e	Specifies that pages are to be extracted from the backup image and written to a file. To extract pages, you need an input file and an output file. The default input file is called *extractPage.in* and the default output file is called *extractPage.out*. You can override the default input file name using the DB2LISTFILE environment variable; you can override the default output file name using the DB2EXTRACTFILE environment variable.
-h	Specifies that media header information, including the name and path of the backup image, is to be collected and displayed.
-l	Specifies that log file header (LFH) and mirror log file header (MFH) information is to be collected and displayed.
-n	Indicates that the user is to be prompted whenever a tape needs to be mounted. (Assumes one tape per device.)
-o	Specifies that object header information is to be collected and displayed.
-p	Specifies that information about the number of pages of each object type found in the backup image is to be collected and displayed. This option will not show the number of pages for all different object types if the backup was done for DMS table space data—instead, it will show the total of all pages; LOB data pages and long data pages will not be returned.
-s	Specifies that information about the automatic storage paths used is to be collected and displayed.
-t	Displays table space details, including container information, for all table spaces in the backup image.

Table F.1 db2ckbkp Command Options (Continued)	
Option	Meaning
-H	Specifies that only the 4K media header information stored at the beginning of the backup image is to be collected and displayed; does not validate the image. This option cannot be used in combination with any other options.
-S	Specifies that information about the automatic storage paths used is to be collected and displayed; does not validate the image. This option cannot be used in combination with any other options.
-T	Displays table space details, including container information, for all table spaces in the backup image; does not validate the image. This option cannot be used in combination with any other options.

Thus, if you wanted to display only the media header information for an existing backup image named TEST.0.DB2.NODE0000.CATN0000.20081215130904.001, you could do so by executing a db2ckbkp command that looks something like this:

```
db2ckbkp –H TEST.0.DB2.NODE0000.CATN0000.20081215130904.001
```

(The –h option tells the tool to display header information along with other information; the –H options tells the tool to display ONLY header information.)

Question 35

The correct answer is **B**. When incremental (cumulative) backup images are taken, database recovery involves restoring the database using the most recent full backup image available and applying the most recent incremental backup image produced. On the other hand, when incremental delta backup images are taken, database recovery involves restoring the database using the most recent full backup image available and applying each delta backup image produced since the full backup image used was made, in the order in which they were created.

Question 36

The correct answer is **C**. The RESTORE DATABASE command can be used to create an entirely new database from a full database backup image, effectively cloning an existing database. For example, you could create a new database named PAYROLL2 that is an exact duplicate of a database named PAYROLL, using a backup image stored in a directory named BACKUPS by executing a RESTORE DATABASE command that looks something like this:

```
RESTORE DATABASE payroll
FROM /backups
INTO payroll2
```

If the PAYROLL database was created using automatic storage, the restore operation will maintain the storage path definitions used. So simply restoring the database will not alter the storage paths used; if you want to change the storage path definitions, you must do so explicitly when restoring the database.

(The RECOVER DATABASE command cannot be used to create an entirely new database.)

Question 37

The correct answer is **C**. Once an HADR environment has been established, the following operations will be replicated automatically in the standby database whenever they are performed on the primary database:

- Execution of Data Definition Language (DDL) statements (CREATE, ALTER, DROP)
- Execution of Data Manipulation Language (DML) statements (INSERT, UPDATE, DELETE)
- Buffer pool operations
- Table space operations (as well as storage-related operations performed on automatic storage databases)
- Online reorganization
- Offline reorganization
- Changes to metadata (system catalog information) for stored procedures and user-defined functions (UDFs)

HADR does not replicate stored procedure and UDF object and library files. If this type of replication is needed, you must physically create the files on identical paths on both the primary and standby databases. (If the standby database cannot find the referenced object or library file, the stored procedure or UDF invocation will fail on the standby database.)

Additionally, non-logged operations, such as changes to database configuration parameters and to the recovery history file, are not replicated to the standby database.

Question 38

The correct answers are **B** and **C**. if you wanted to obtain a list of applications that are currently connected to a database named PAYROLL, you could do so by executing the LIST APPLICATIONS command from the DB2 Command Line Processor, or by executing a db2pd command that looks something like this:

```
db2pd -applications -db payroll
```

You could obtain information about connected applications using the DB2 snapshot monitor, but the query used to do so would look like this:

```
SELECT * FROM TABLE(SNAP_GET_APPL('payroll',-1)) AS applications
```

It is important to note that if the DB2 server is not responding and appears to be hung, the ONLY way to obtain a list of applications that are currently connected to the database is by using the db2pd utility.

Question 39

The correct answer is **D**. Because table space TBSP1 has 160 useable pages and 156 of them have already been used, there are only 4 free pages remaining. Therefore, table space TBSP1 is about to run out of storage space.

Table space SYSCATSPACE is a resizable DMS table space, however, it has NOT been resized yet; table space IBMDB2SAMPLEREL is an autoresizing DMS table space; and the state of table space USERSPACE1 is "Normal" – not "Roll-forward pending".

Question 40

The correct answer is **A**. When a DB2 9 database is configured to support roll-forward recovery, DB2 can call a special program, known as a user exit program, to move archived log files from the active log directory/device to a specific storage location when they are no longer needed to support transaction logging. So just what is a user exit program? Essentially, a user exit program is a user-supplied application that is invoked by DB2 whenever an open log file is closed, a database is closed (i.e., all connections to the database are terminated), or the ROLLFORWARD DATABASE command/API is executed (to perform a roll-forward recovery operation on a DB2 9 database).

Once the source code file for a user exit program has been compiled and linked to produce an executable program, two actions must be performed before it can actually be used: the executable form of the user exit program must be copied to a specific location and the *logarcmeth1 or logarcmeth2* database configuration parameter for the appropriate database(s) must be assigned the value USEREXIT.

It is important to note that IBM is recommending users move away from user exit programs. An easier method for moving log files from the active log directory to an archive log storage location is to assign the value DISK:, followed by the desired location path to the *logarchmeth1* database configuration parameter.

Question 41

The correct answer is **C**. If you wanted to determine whether or not an existing backup image for a database named TEST was created using the INCLUDE LOGS option of the BACKUP DATABASE command, you could do so by executing a db2ckbkp command that looks something like this (assuming the name of the backup image created is TEST.0.DB2. NODE0000.CATN0000.20081215131853.001):

```
db2ckbkp -h TEST.0.DB2.NODE0000.CATN0000.20081215131853.001
```

The results produced should look something like this:

```
=====================
MEDIA HEADER REACHED:
=====================
        Server Database Name             -- TEST
        Server Database Alias            -- TEST
        Client Database Alias            -- TEST
        Timestamp                        -- 20081215131853
        Database Partition Number        -- 0
        Instance                         -- DB2
        Sequence Number                  -- 1
        Release ID                       -- B00
        Database Seed                    -- 4773F9E6
        DB Comment's Codepage (Volume)   -- 2020
        DB Comment (Volume)              --
        DB Comment's Codepage (System)   -- 2020
        DB Comment (System)              --
        Authentication Value             -- 32
        Backup Mode                      -- 0
        Includes Logs                    -- 0
        Compression                      -- 1
        Backup Type                      -- 0
        Backup Gran.                     -- 0
        Status Flags                     -- 1
        System Cats inc                  -- 1
        Catalog Partition Number         -- 0
        DB Codeset                       -- IBM-1252
        DB Territory                     --
        LogID                            -- 1197742728
        LogPath                          -- C:\LOGS\NODE0000\
        Backup Buffer Size               -- 16777216
        Number of Sessions               -- 1
        Platform                         -- 5

    The proper image file name would be:
        TEST.0.DB2.NODE0000.CATN0000.20081215131853.001

    [1] Buffers processed:  ####

    Image Verification Complete - successful.
```

(In this case, because the "Include Logs" attribute is set to 0, the INCLUDE LOGS option of the BACKUP DATABASE command was NOT specified when the backup image was created.)

The LIST HISTORY command will tell you what type of backup image was created (F = Offline, N = Online, I = Incremental offline, O = Incremental online, D = Delta offline, E = Delta online, R = Rebuild), when the backup image was created, where the backup image was stored, and the earliest log and current log files used. However, it will not tell you if the log files were included in the backup image.

Question 42

The correct answer is **D**. When invalid table space containers are encountered, they can be redefined at the beginning of the recovery process by performing what is known as a *redirected restore*. (A redirected restore operation can also be used to restore a backup image to a target machine that is different than the source machine, or to store table space data into a different physical location.)

The steps used to perform a redirected restore operation are as follows:

1. Start the redirected restore operation by executing the RESTORE DATABASE command with the REDIRECT option specified. (When this option is specified, each invalid table space container encountered is flagged, and all table spaces that reference invalid table space containers are placed in the "Restore Pending" state. A list of all table spaces affected can be obtained by executing the LIST TABLESPACES command.) At some point, you should see a message that looks something like this:

```
SQL1277N Restore has detected that one or more table space containers are
inaccessible, or has set their state to 'storage must be defined'.
DB20000I The RESTORE DATABASE command completed successfully.
```

2. Specify new table space containers for each table space placed in "Restore Pending" state by executing a SET TABLESPACE CONTAINERS command for each appropriate table space. (Keep in mind that SMS table spaces can only use PATH containers, while DMS table spaces can only use FILE or DEVICE containers.)

3. Complete the redirected restore operation by executing the RESTORE DATABASE command again with the CONTINUE option specified.

To simplify things, all of these steps can be coded in a UNIX shell script or Windows batch file, which can then be executed from a system prompt. Such a file would look something like this:

```
db2 "RESTORE DATABASE sample FROM C:\backups TO D:\DB_DIR INTO
sample_2 REDIRECT"

db2 "SET TABLESPACE CONTAINERS FOR 0 USING
(PATH 'D:\DB_DIR\SYSTEM')"

db2 "SET TABLESPACE CONTAINERS FOR 1 USING
(PATH 'D:\DB_DIR\TEMP')"

db2 "SET TABLESPACE CONTAINERS FOR 2 USING
(PATH 'D:\DB_DIR\USER')"

db2 "RESTORE DATABASE sample CONTINUE"
```

Question 43

The correct answer is **A**. The *hadr_syncmode* database configuration parameter is used to specify the synchronization mode to use for HADR. The value assigned to this parameter determines how primary log writes are synchronized with the standby database when the systems are in peer state. Valid values for this configuration parameter are:

- **SYNC (Synchronous)** This mode provides the greatest protection against transaction loss, and using it results in the longest transaction response time among the three modes. In this mode, log writes are considered successful only when log records have been written to log files on the primary database and when the primary database has received acknowledgement from the standby database that the log records have also been written to log files on the standby database. The log data is guaranteed to be stored at both sites.

- **NEARSYNC (Near Synchronous)** Although this mode has a shorter transaction response time than synchronous mode, it also provides slightly less protection against transaction loss. In this mode, log writes are considered successful only when log records have been written to the log files on the primary database and when the primary database has received acknowledgement from the standby system that the log records have also been written to main memory on the standby system. Loss of data occurs only if both sites fail simultaneously and if the target site has not transferred all of the log data that it has received to nonvolatile storage.

- **ASYNC (Asynchronous)** This mode has the highest chance of transaction loss if the primary system fails. It also has the shortest transaction response time among the three modes. In this mode, log writes are considered successful only when log records have been written to the log files on the primary database and have been delivered to the TCP layer of the primary system's host machine. Because the primary system does not wait for acknowledgement from the standby system, transactions might be considered committed when they are still on their way to the standby system.

Question 44

The correct answer is **D**. The DB2 memory tracker utility is used to produce a complete report of memory status for instances, databases, and agents. This utility provides the following information about memory pool allocation:

- Current size

- Maximum size (hard limit)

- Largest size (high water mark)

- Type (identifier indicating function for which memory will be used)

- Agent who allocated pool (only if the pool is private)

(This information is also available from the snapshot monitor.)

The DB2 memory tracker is invoked by executing the db2mtrk command. The syntax for this command is:

```
db2mtrk
<-i>
<-d>
<-p>
<-m | -w>
<-r [Interval] <Count>>
<-v>
<-h>
```

where:

Interval   Identifies the number of seconds to wait between subsequent calls to the DB2 memory tracker.

Count   Identifies the number of times to repeat calls to the DB2 memory tracker.

All other options shown with this command are described in Table F.2.

Table F.2 db2mtrk Command Options	
Option	**Meaning**
-i	Specifies that information about instance level memory is to be collected and displayed.
-d	Specifies that information about database level memory is to be collected and displayed.
-p	Specifies that information about private memory is to be collected and displayed.

Table F.2 db2mtrk Command Options (Continued)	
Option	Meaning
-m	Specifies that maximum values for each memory pool is to be collected and displayed.
-w	Specifies that high watermark values for each memory pool are to be collected and displayed.
-v	Indicates that verbose output is to be returned.
-h	Displays help information. When this option is specified, all other options are ignored, and only the help information is displayed.

Thus, if you wanted to see how memory is utilized by the active databases on a system, and you wanted to capture and view this information ten times, updating it every five minutes, you could do so by executing a db2mtrk command that looks something like this:

```
db2mtrk –d –r 300 10
```

(The –d option tells db2mtrk to collect and display information for all databases; the –r 300 10 option tells db2mtrk to collect the information every 300 seconds – which is 5 minutes – a total of 10 times.)

Question 45

The correct answer is **C**. If you are concerned about running out of log space, and you want to avoid allocating a large number of secondary log files, you can configure a database to use what is known as infinite logging. To enable infinite logging for a database, you simply set the *logsecond* database configuration parameter to -1. However, in order to use infinite logging, a database must be configured to use archival logging. This is done by assigning the value LOGRETAIN to the *logarcmeth1* or *logarcmeth2* database configuration parameter.

Question 46

The correct answers are **B** and **D**. To enable log file mirroring, you simply assign the fully qualified name of the mirror log location (path) to the *mirrorlogpath* database configuration parameter. Alternately, on UNIX systems, you can assign the value 1 to the DB2_NEWLOGPATH registry variable - in this case, the name of the mirror log location is generated by appending the character "2" to the current value of the *logpath* database configuration parameter. Ideally, the mirror log path used should refer a physical location (disk) that does not see a large amount of disk I/O and that is separate from the physical location used to store primary log files.

Question 47

The correct answer is **C**. The *max_log* configuration parameter is used to control the maximum percentage of the total active log space available that any one transaction can consume. This configuration parameter prevents transactions from consuming all of the available active log space, thereby preventing other applications from running. By default, if a running transaction exceeds this threshold, the offending transaction is rolled back and the application that the transaction is running under will be forced to terminate. (This behavior can be overridden by setting the DB2_FORCE_APP_ON_MAX_LOG registry variable to FALSE; if this registry variable is set to FALSE, only work performed by the current statement will be rolled back—the application can still commit the work completed by previous statements in the transaction, or it can roll back the work completed to undo the effects of the transaction.)

The *num_log_span* configuration parameter is used to set a limit on the number of log files any single running transaction can span. When a transaction is started, a record is written to the current active log file and as DB2 processes the transaction (as well as other transactions) log files are filled and closed. If the number of log files filled exceeds the limit established before the transaction is committed or rolled back, then by default the transaction is rolled back and the application the transaction was running under will be terminated. This behavior can also be overridden by setting the DB2_FORCE_APP_ON_MAX_ LOG registry variable to FALSE.

Question 48

The correct answer is **C**. A backup image of a DB2 database, or a table space within a DB2 database, can be created by executing the BACKUP DATABASE command. The basic syntax for this command is:

```
BACKUP [DATABASE | DB] [DatabaseAlias]
<USER [UserName] <USING [Password]>>
<TABLESPACE ([TS_Name],...)
<ONLINE>
<INCREMENTAL <DELTA>>
<TO [Location] |
    USE TSM <OPTIONS [TSMOptions]>
    <OPEN [NumSessions] SESSIONS>>
<WITH [NumBuffers] BUFFERS>
<BUFFER [BufferSize]>
<PARALLELISM [ParallelNum]>
<UTIL_IMPACT_PRIORITY [Priority]>
<EXCLUDE LOGS | INCLUDE LOGS>
<WITHOUT PROMPTING>
```

where:

DatabaseAlias   Identifies the alias assigned to the database for which a backup image is to be created.

UserName   Identifies the name assigned to a specific user under whose authority the backup operation is to be performed.

Password   Identifies the password that corresponds to the name of the user under whom the backup operation is to be performed.

TS_Name   Identifies the name assigned to one or more specific table spaces for which backup images are to be created.

Location   Identifies the directory or device where the backup image created is to be stored.

TSMOptions   Identifies options that are to be used by Tivoli Storage Manager (TSM) during the backup operation.

NumSessions   Specifies the number of I/O sessions to be created between DB2 and TSM. (This parameter has no effect when backing up to tape, disk, or another local device.)

NumBuffers   Identifies the number of buffers that are to be used to perform the backup operation. (By default, two buffers are used if this option is not specified.)

BufferSize   Identifies the size, in pages, that each buffer used to perform the backup operation will be. (By default, the size of each buffer used by the Backup utility is determined by the value of the *backbufsz* DB2 Database Manager configuration parameter.)

ParallelNum   Identifies the number of table spaces that can be read in parallel during the backup operation.

Priority   Indicates that the Backup utility is to be throttled such that it executes at a specific rate so that its effect on concurrent database activity can be controlled. This parameter can be assigned a numerical value within the range of 1 to 100, with 100 representing the highest priority and 1 representing the lowest.

Thus, if you wanted to backup a database named ACCOUNTING to a TSM server, using four concurrent TSM client sessions and eight buffers, you could do so by executing a BACKUP DATABASE command that looks something like this:

```
BACKUP DATABASE accounting
USER db2admin USING ibmdb2
USE TSM OPEN 4 SESSIONS WITH 8 BUFFERS
```

Question 49

The correct answer is **B**. In a partitioned database environment, database partitions are backed up (and restored) individually—backup operations are local to the database partition server upon which the Backup utility is invoked. However, by using the db2_all command, you can create backup images for multiple partitions (which you identify by node number) from a single database partition server. (The LIST NODES command can be used to identify the nodes, or database partition servers, that have user tables on them.) For example, if you wanted to create a set of online incremental backup images for every partition on which a database named SAMPLE is stored, you could do so by executing a db2_all command that looks something like this:

```
db2_all "db2 BACKUP DATABASE sample ONLINE INCREMENTAL"
```

In this example, the BACKUP DATABASE command was executed on every partition. However, there may be times when you only want to perform a backup or recovery operation on one or more specific database partitions. Because of this, the db2_all command has two prefix sequences that can be used to limit the execution of specified operations to individual database partition servers. These prefix sequences are:

- *<<-nnn<*
  The operation is to be performed on all database partition servers identified in the db2nodes.cfg file except the database partition server whose node number is nnn.

- *<<+nnn<*
  The operation is only to be performed on the database partition server in the db2nodes.cfg file whose database partition number is *nnn*.

When using the *<<-nnn<* and *<<+nnn<* prefix sequences, *nnn* can be any 1-, 2-, or 3-digit database partition number; however, the number specified must have a matching nodenum value in the db2nodes.cfg file.

Thus, if you wanted to perform an online table space-level backup of the table space USERSPACE1 (which is the default table space used to hold user tables) for a database named SALES that resides on partition number 5, you could do so by executing a db2_all command that looks something like this:

```
db2_all "<<+5< db2 BACKUP DATABASE sample
    TABLESPACE (userspace1) ONLINE TO /backup_dir".
```

Question 50

The correct answer is **C**. No special authority is required to run the DB2 Check Backup (db2ckbkp) utility, however, in order to use this utility, you must have read permission on the backup image files that are to be analyzed.

Question 51

The correct answer is **D**. When the RESTORE DATABASE command is executed, if the INCREMENTAL option is specified without additional parameters, a manual cumulative restore operation will be initiated—during a manual cumulative restore, the RESTORE DATABASE command must be executed for each backup image needed to restore the database. During such a recovery operation backup images must be restored in the following order: last full backup, last incremental, first delta, second delta, third delta, and so on up to and including the last delta backup image made.

If the INCREMENTAL AUTO or the INCREMENTAL AUTOMATIC option is specified, an automatic cumulative restore operation will be initiated and no user intervention will be required to apply incremental and delta restores.

Question 52

The correct answer is **B**. The basic syntax for the RECOVER DATABASE command is:

```
RECOVER [DATABASE | DB] [DatabaseAlias]
<TO [PointInTime] <USING [UTC | LOCAL] TIME>>
<ON ALL DBPARTITIONNUMS>
<USER [UserName] <USING [Password]>>
<USING HISTORY FILE ([HistoryFile])>
<OVERFLOW LOG PATH ([LogDirectory] ,...)>
<RESTART>
```

or

```
RECOVER [DATABASE | DB] [DatabaseAlias]
<TO END OF LOGS
    <ON ALL DBPARTITIONNUMS |
    ON DBPARTITIONNUM<S> ([PartitionNum],...)>>
<USER [UserName] <USING [Password]>>
<USING HISTORY FILE ([HistoryFile])>
<OVERFLOW LOG PATH ([LogDirectory] ,...)>
<RESTART>
```

where:

DatabaseAlias   Identifies the alias assigned to the database associated with the backup image that is to be used to perform a version recovery operation.

PointInTime   Identifies a specific point in time, identified by a timestamp value in the form *yyyy-mm-dd-hh.mm.ss.nnnnnn* (year, month, day, hour, minutes, seconds, microseconds), to which the database is to be rolled forward. (Only transactions that took place before and up to the date and time specified will be reapplied to the database.)

PartitionNum	Identifies, by number, one or more database partitions (identified in the db2nodes.cfg file) that transactions are to be rolled forward on. In a partitioned database environment, the Recover utility must be invoked from the catalog partition of the database.
UserName	Identifies the name assigned to a specific user under whom the recovery operation is to be performed.
Password	Identifies the password that corresponds to the name of the user under whom the recovery operation is to be performed.
HistoryFile	Identifies the name assigned to the recovery history log file that is to be used by the Recovery utility.
LogDirectory	Identifies the directory that contains offline archived log files that are to be used to perform the roll-forward portion of the recovery operation.

If the RESTART option is specified, any previous recover operations are ignored; the RESTART option forces the Recover utility to execute a fresh restore operation and then roll the database forward to the point in time specified.

It the Recover utility successfully restores a database, but for some reason fails while attempting to roll it forward, the Recover utility will attempt to continue the previous recover operation without redoing the restore phase. If you want to force the Recover utility to redo the restore phase, you need to execute the RECOVER DATABASE command with the RESTART option specified. There is no way to explicitly restart a recovery operation from a point of failure.

Question 53

The correct answers are **B** and **E**. The *hadr_timeout* database configuration parameter is used to specify the time (in seconds) that the HADR process waits before considering a communication attempt to have failed. Therefore, when the *hadr_timeout* database configuration parameter on the primary server is set to 30, if the primary server does not receive acknowledgement of a log buffer write within 30 seconds it assumes there was a communications error and drops out of peer mode.

The value assigned to the *hadr_timeout* database parameter must be the same for both the primary and the standby database.

Question 54

The correct answer is **B**. Both the primary and the standby database must be a single-partition database and they both must have the same database name; however, they do not have to be stored on the same database path.

IBM recommends that you use identical host computers for the HADR primary and standby databases. (If possible, they should be from the same vendor and have the same architecture.) Furthermore, the operating system on the primary and standby database servers should be the same version, including patch level. You can violate this rule for a short time during a rolling upgrade, but use extreme caution when doing so. A TCP/IP interface must also be available between the HADR host machines, and a high-speed, high-capacity network should be used to connect the two.

The DB2 software installed on both the primary and the standby database server must have the same bit size (32 or 64) and the version of DB2 used for the primary and standby databases must be identical; for example, both must be either version 8 or version 9. During rolling upgrades, the modification level (for example, the fix pack level) of the database system for the standby database can be later than that of the primary database for a short while. However, you should not keep this configuration for an extended period of time. The primary and standby databases will not connect to each other if the modification level of the database system for the primary database is later than that of the standby database. Therefore, fix packs must always be applied to the standby database system first.

The amount of storage space allocated for transaction log files should also be the same on both the primary and the standby database server; the use of raw devices for transaction logging is not supported. (Archival logging is only performed by the current primary database.) Table space properties such as table space name, table space type (DMS, SMS, or Automatic Storage), table space page size, table space size, container path, container size, and container type (raw device, file, or directory) must be identical on the primary and standby databases. When you issue a table space statement such as CREATE TABLESPACE, ALTER TABLESPACE, or DROP TABLESPACE on the primary database, it is replayed on the standby database. Therefore, you must ensure that the table space containers involved such statements exist on both systems before you issue the table space statement on the primary database. (If you create a table space on the primary database and log replay fails on the standby database because the containers are not available, the primary database does not receive an error message stating that the log replay failed.) Automatic storage databases are fully supported, including replication of ALTER DATABASE statements. Similar to table space containers, the storage paths specified must exist on both the primary and the standby server.

Question 55

The correct answer is **C**. Automatic Client Reroute is a DB2 feature that allows client applications to recover from a loss of communication with the server so that the application can continue its work with minimal interruption. (If automatic client reroute is not enabled, client applications will receive an error message indicating that a connect attempt has failed due to a timeout and no further attempts will be made to establish a connection with the server.) However, rerouting is only possible when an alternate database location has been specified at the server and the TCP/IP protocol is used.

The automatic client reroute feature can be used with HADR to make client applications connect to the new primary database immediately after a takeover operation. In fact, if you set up HADR using the Set Up High Availability Disaster Recovery (HADR) Databases Wizard, automatic client reroute is enabled by default. If you set up HADR manually, you can enable the automatic client reroute feature by executing the UPDATE ALTERNATE SERVER FOR DATABASE command; automatic client reroute does not use the values stored in the *hadr_remote_host* and *hadr_remote_svc* database configuration parameters.

For example, suppose you have cataloged a database named SALES on a client workstation as being located at host named SVR1. Database SALES is the primary database in an HADR environment and its corresponding standby database, also named SALES, resides on a host named SVR2 and listens on port number 456. To enable automatic client reroute, you simply specify an alternate server for the SALES database stored on host SVR1 by executing the following command:

```
UPDATE ALTERNATE SERVER FOR DATABASE sales
USING HOSTNAME svr2 PORT 456
```

Once this command is executed, the client must connect to host SVR1 to obtain the alternate server information. Then, if a communication error occurs between the client and the SALES database at host SVR1, the client will first attempt to reconnect to the SALES database on host SVR1. If this fails, the client will then attempt to establish a connection with the standby SALES database located on host SVR2.

Question 56

The correct answer is **A**. If you wanted to see how memory is utilized by the active databases on a system, you could do so by executing a db2mtrk command that looks something like this:

```
db2mtrk -d
```

Assuming a database named SAMPLE is active at the time the db2mtrk command is issued, the results produced should look something like this:

```
Tracking Memory on: 2008/05/21 at 14:00:38

Memory for database: SAMPLE

    utilh     pckcacheh catcacheh bph (1)   bph (S32K) bph (S16K) bph (S8K)
    64.0K     128.0K    64.0K     1.2M      704.0K     448.0K     320.0K

    bph (S4K) shsorth   lockh     dbh       other
    256.0K    0         320.0K    4.3M      128.0K
```

Performance and Scalability

Question 57

The correct answer is **B**. The DB2_PINNED_BP registry variable is used to specify whether the database global memory used – including buffer pool memory – is to be kept in system main memory. Valid values for this variable are YES and NO – NO is the default. When set to YES, the DB2_PINNED_BP variable will keep the database global memory "pinned" or resident in real memory; database performance is more consistent when database global memory is kept in main memory.

On 64-bit DB2 for AIX, setting this variable to YES means that self tuning for database shared memory (activated by setting the *database_memory* database configuration parameter to AUTOMATIC) cannot be enabled.

Question 58

The correct answer is **D**. The *mincommit* database configuration parameter is used to specify the number of COMMIT SQL statements that are to be processed before log records are written to disk. If individual query response times are not absolutely important, setting *mincommit* to a value of more than one will cause DB2 not to flush the log buffers until there are *mincommit* commits, or the buffer is full (whichever comes first).

The *logarchmeth1* configuration parameter specifies the logging method to use and the media type of the primary destination for archived log files; the *max_log* configuration parameter specifies if there is a limit to the percentage of primary log space that a single transaction can consume, and if so, what that limit is; and the *logbufsz* database configuration parameter is used to specify the amount of memory (in pages) that is to be used to buffer log records before they are written to disk.

Changing the logging method used or limiting the amount of log space available to a single transaction will not help in this situation. Increasing the size of the log buffer can improve performance if transactions must wait for log data to be written to disk, but in this example, very few log records appear to be written and the log buffer size appears to be sufficient so changing the frequency at which COMMITs are processed and log record are flushed to disk is the best solution.

Question 59

The correct answer is **C**. The DB2 optimizer is the component of the SQL compiler that is responsible for choosing the access plan to use for processing data manipulation language (DML) SQL statements. It does this by modeling the execution cost of many alternative access plans and choosing the one with the minimal estimated cost.

The first thing that the DB2 optimizer does when it is invoked is accept and parse the SQL statement received. Once the SQL statement has been parsed, the optimizer then attempts to verify that all objects referenced in the statement do, in fact, exist in the database. (This is referred to as checking or validating the semantics.) After semantics checking is complete, the DB2 optimizer will use its powerful query rewrite facility to examine the statement and try to determine if there are better ways to write the statement. Once the query rewrite step is complete, the DB2 optimizer will enumerate different plan options available and evaluate each one. Depending on the optimization level used and the instance and database configuration settings found, some techniques may or may not be allowed. As each allowed plan is enumerated, the cost of the plan is evaluated; once the DB2 optimizer has analyzed all possible plans, the plan with the lowest cost is chosen. Once a plan is chosen, the code for that plan is built into a package, which is then stored in the system catalog of the database (if the statement was static) or the package cache (if the statement was dynamic).

Question 60

The correct answer is **B**. The first time an application attempts to insert a record into a table, a special algorithm will search the Free Space Control Records (FSCRs) in an effort to locate a page that has enough free space to hold the new record. (The value assigned to the DB2MAXFSCRSEARCH registry variable determines the number of FSCRs that are searched; the default value for this registry variable is five). If no space is found within the specified number of FSCRs searched, the record is appended to the end of the table. To optimize insert performance, subsequent records are also appended to the end of the table until two extents have been written. Once two extents have been filled, the next insert operation will resume searching FSCRs where the last search left off and the whole process is repeated. After all FSCRs in the entire table have been searched in this way, records are automatically appended and no additional searching is performed. In fact, searching using the FSCRs is not done again until space is created somewhere in the table by deleting one or more records.

To optimize a table for insert performance, at the possible expense of faster table growth, consider assigning a small number to the DB2MAXFSCRSEARCH registry variable. (To optimize for space reuse at the possible expense of insert performance, assign a larger number to the DB2MAXFSCRSEARCH registry variable; setting the value to -1 forces the DB2 Database Manager to search all FSCRs.)

Another way to optimize for insert performance is to place a table into what is known as append mode. Regular tables are placed into append mode by executing an ALTER TABLE SQL statement that looks like this:

```
ALTER TABLE [TableName] APPEND ON
```

where:

TableName   Identifies the table, by name, that is to be placed into append mode.

So in this example, the SQL statement "ALTER TABLE history APPEND ON" is the best choice for improving insert performance on the HISTORY table. Setting the DB2MAXFSCRSEARCH registry variable to 1000 or -1 can actually degrade insert performance.

Question 61

The correct answer is **C**. The *sheapthres_shr* database configuration parameter is used to specify the maximum amount of memory (in pages) that is to be used at any one time to perform sort operations. When this parameter is set to 0, all sort operations are performed in shared memory. Otherwise, sort operations are performed in private sort memory.

Question 62

The correct answer is **C**. When the Self-Tuning Memory Manager (STMM) is enabled in a partitioned database environment, a single database partition, known as the "tuning partition," is responsible for monitoring the memory configuration and usage patterns and determining if changes could improve performance. If the tuning partition deems a change should be made, it propagates the appropriate configuration changes to all other database partitions to maintain a consistent configuration across all database partitions used.

Question 63

The correct answers are **A** and **D**. You can terminate one or more running applications prematurely by executing the FORCE APPLICATION command (assuming you have SYSADMN or SYSCTRL authority). The basic syntax for this command is:

```
FORCE APPLICATION ALL
```

or

```
FORCE APPLICATION ( [ApplicationHandle] ,... )
```

where:

ApplicationHandle   Identifies the handle associated with one or more applications whose instance attachments and/or database connections are to be terminated.

Thus, if you wanted to force all users and applications connected to databases stored on a server named DB_SERVER to terminate their database connections, you could do so by executing a FORCE APPLICATION command that looks something like this:

```
FORCE APPLICATION ALL
```

On the other hand, if you wanted to force a specific application whose handle is 148 to terminate its processing, you could do so by executing a FORCE APPLICATION command that looks like this:

```
FORCE APPLICATION (148)
```

Question 64

The correct answer is **A**. DB2's connection concentrator allows servers to provide support for thousands of users simultaneously executing business transactions while drastically reducing the resources required. It accomplishes this by concentrating the workload from all active applications in a much smaller number of database server connections. The connection concentrator is enabled when the maximum number of connections supported (determined by the value assigned to the *max_connections* Database Manager configuration parameter) is greater than the maximum number of coordinating agents allowed (determined by the value assigned to the *max_coordagents* configuration parameter). When the connection concentrator is enabled, the value assigned to the *max_coordagents* configuration parameter is used as a guideline for determining how large the agent pool will be when the system workload is low. In this case, an idle agent will always be returned to the pool, no matter what the *max_coordagents* configuration parameter has been set to, and DB2's connection concentrator technology will be enabled.

The connection concentrator uses logical agents (LAs) to handle the application context while database agents (DAs) handle the actual DB2 connections. When a new application connects to a database, it is assigned an LA. Because a DA is needed to pass SQL statements to the DB2 server for processing, one is assigned to perform the work for the LA as soon as a new transaction is initiated. The key to this architecture is the fact that the DA is disassociated from the LA and is returned to the agent pool when a transaction completes.

Question 65

The correct answer is **A**. A volatile table is a table that is updated very frequently and that changes size dramatically within a short period of time. To tell the optimizer to use an index scan for this type of table, you can mark it as being volatile when you create it (by specifying the VOLATILE option with the CREATE TABLE SQL statement used to create it), or if it already exists, you can mark it as being volatile (by executing an ALTER TABLE statement with the VOLATILE option specified; for example, ALTER TABLE tab1 VOLATILE).

Question 66

The correct answer is **A**. Local table queues (sometimes referred to as LTQ) are used to pass data between database agents within a single database partition. Local table queues (LTQ) are used for intra-partition parallelism.

Question 67

The correct answer is **C**. The DB2_AVOID_PREFETCH registry variable is used to specify whether or not prefetching should be used during crash recovery. Valid values for this variable are ON and OFF – OFF is the default. Setting the DB2_AVOID_PREFETCH registry variable to ON tells DB2 NOT to perform normal prefetching during crash recovery (restart) operations.

Question 68

The correct answer is **A**. The *maxfilop* Database Manager configuration parameter is used to specify the maximum number of files that can be open per application. (Because DB2 is thread based and not process based in Version 9.5, the *maxfilop* configuration parameter is used to specify the number of files that can be open per <u>database</u> in DB2 9.5.) The value specified in this parameter defines the total database and application file handles that can be used by a specific process connected to a database. In this scenario, we can see that there were over 51000 files closed and opened in a very short period of time. By increasing the value assigned to *maxfilop*, you allow DB2 to maintain more file handles, so it will not have to spend time opening and closing files to get work done.

Question 69

The correct answer is **A**. The objective of index ANDing is to find common RIDs. Index ANDing might occur in situations where multiple indexes exist on corresponding columns in the same table and a query using multiple AND predicates is run against that table. (The purpose of index ORing is to eliminate duplicate RIDs.)

Question 70

The correct answer is **A**. DB2 uses asynchronous page cleaners to write changed pages found in a buffer pool to disk before space in a buffer pool is acquired on behalf of a database agent. Ideally, database agents should not have to wait for changed pages to be written to disk before they will have sufficient space in a buffer pool. If that is indeed the case, overall performance of database applications is improved. The *num_iocleaners* database configuration parameter is used to specify the number of asynchronous page cleaners that can be in progress for a database at any given point in time.

If applications running against the database consist primarily of transactions that update data, increasing the number of page cleaners used will speed up performance. Increasing the amount of page cleaners used will also shorten recovery time from soft failures, such as power outages, because the contents of the database on disk will be more up-to-date at any given point in time.

A good value to assign to this configuration parameter is the value AUTOMATIC. If this parameter is set to AUTOMATIC, the number of page cleaners started will be based on the number of CPUs found on the current machine, as well as the number of local logical database partitions used (in a partitioned database environment).

Question 71

The correct answer is **D**. The Self-Tuning Memory Manager (STMM) simplifies the task of configuring memory-related database parameters by automatically setting values for these parameters after measuring and analyzing how well each DB2 memory consumer is using the allocated memory available. The following database memory pools can be enabled for self-tuning, either entirely or individually:

- Buffer pools (controlled by the ALTER BUFFERPOOL and CREATE BUFFERPOOL statements)

- Package cache (controlled by the *pckcachesz* configuration parameter)

- Locking memory (controlled by the *locklist* and *maxlocks* configuration parameters)

- Sort memory (controlled by the *sheapthres_shr* and the *sortheap* configuration parameter)

- Database shared memory (controlled by the *database_memory* configuration parameter)

When a database has been configured to take advantage of STMM, the memory tuner responds to changes in database workload characteristics and response times, adjusting the values of memory configuration parameters and buffer pool sizes to optimize performance. If the current workload requirements are high, and there is sufficient free memory on the system, more memory will be consumed by the database. It can also move memory between the different DB2 memory segments, for example, from the sort heap to a buffer pool.

Because the memory tuner trades memory resources between different memory consumers, there must be at least two memory consumers enabled for self-tuning in order for STMM to be effective. The one exception to this rule is when the sort heap (*sortheap* database configuration parameter) is enabled for self-tuning; in this case, STMM will balance the number of private memory pages used for private sorts and the number of shared memory pages used for shared sorts.

Question 72

The correct answer is **B**. To delete a compression dictionary from a table, set the COMPRESS attribute for the table to NO and execute the REORG command with the RESETDICTIONARY option specified; reorg processing will remove the compression dictionary and the rows in the newly reorganized table will be in non-compressed format. (If the COMPRESS attribute for a table is set to NO and the REORG command is executed with the KEEPDICTIONARY option specified, reorg processing will preserve the compression dictionary and all rows in the newly reorganized table will be in non-compressed format.)

Question 73

The correct answer is **B**. The DB2_PARALLEL_IO registry variable is used to force DB2 to use parallel I/O for table spaces that only have one container or for table spaces whose containers reside on more than one physical disk. If this registry variable is not set, the level of I/O parallelism used is equal to the number of containers used by the table space. On the other hand, if this registry variable is assigned a value, the level of I/O parallelism used is equal to the number of containers used multiplied by the value stored in the DB2_PARALLEL_IO registry variable.

Often, the DB2_PARALLEL_IO registry variable is assigned the asterisk (*) value to indicate that every table space in the database is to use parallel I/O. (The asterisk value implies that each table space container used spans six physical disk spindles.) Such an assignment is made by executing a db2set command that looks something like this:

```
db2set DB2_PARALLEL_IO=*
```

However, this is not a correct setting to use when a table space container does not span six physical disk spindles. In those cases, the DB2_PARALLEL_IO registry variable should be set by executing a db2set command that looks more like this:

```
db2set DB2_PARALLEL_IO=[TS_ID]:[DisksPerCtr] ,...
```

where:

TS_ID   Identifies one or more individual table spaces, by their numeric table space ID.

DisksPerCtr Identifies the number of physical disks used by each table space container that is assigned to the table space specified.

Thus, if you wanted to set the DB2_PARALLEL_IO registry variable for a table space whose numeric ID is 5 to reflect that its storage containers reside on a RAID-5 4+1 group (4 data disk spindles), you could do so by executing a db2set command that looks something like this:

```
db2set DB2_PARAmLLEL_IO=5:4
```

Question 74

The correct answer is **D**. When an application connects to a nonpartitioned database, the connection is assigned to a coordinating agent (named db2agent in Linux and UNIX environments), and all subsequent SQL statements and DB2 commands are executed by this agent on behalf of the application.

Question 75

The correct answer is **C**. The primary purpose of an index is to help DB2 quickly locate records stored in a table. Therefore, creating an index for frequently accessed columns in a table usually improves performance for data access and update operations. To ensure that an index will be beneficial, you must analyze how data is frequently accessed to determine which columns should be indexed and which should not. Identifying columns that are frequently joined and/or searched is a good place to start:

1. Consider creating a clustering index on the column most frequently searched and/or joined, based on the data order. Consider nonclustering indexes on searched or joined columns in which less than 10 percent of the rows will be scanned/joined.

2. Refine this analysis with an estimate of the percentage of the rows that will be inserted, updated, and/or deleted over a given period of time. Minimize the number of indexes used when inserting, updating, and deleting data frequently.

3. Composite indexes (i.e., indexes with more than one column) are most beneficial when columns are frequently accessed together.

4. Consider the cardinality of the columns, particularly for composite indexes. Indexes on columns with a low cardinality are not very selective and do not enhance performance as much as indexes on columns with high cardinalities.

In this example, both the EMP_ID column and the DEPT_ID column are frequently accessed together so a composite index of the two columns should provide optimal performance for the query.

Question 76

The correct answer is **D**. The use of broadcast table queues (sometimes referred to as BTQ) and/or directed table queues (sometimes referred to as DTQ) signifies inter-partition parallelism and the movement of data between database partitions. Broadcast table queues and directed table queues are used in join operations. With broadcast table queues, rows are sent to all of the receiving database partitions but are not hashed; with directed table queues, rows are hashed to one of the receiving database partitions.

Question 77

The correct answer is **D**. The DB2_MEM_TUNING_RANGE registry variable is used to specify the amount of physical memory left free by a given instance (and its active databases) when self tuning of database shared memory is enabled. Essentially, the DB2_MEM_TUNING_RANGE sets the limits for automatic memory tuning within DB2, and can be used to prevent a database from consuming all of the system memory available.

Keep in mind that it is recommended to set this variable only when using the DB2 self-tuning memory manager (STMM) and the *database_memory* database configuration parameter has been set to AUTOMATIC, or if insufficient system memory problems are occurring.

Question 78

The correct answer is **B**. The *sheapthres_shr* configuration parameter – not the *sheapthres* configuration parameter – is used to specify the maximum amount of memory (in pages) that is to be used at any one time to perform sort operations.

The *sheapthres* Database Manager configuration parameter is used to specify an instance-wide soft limit on the total amount of memory that can be consumed by private sorts at any given time. When the limit is reached it does not prevent more sorts, it just reduces the memory each sort can consume until other sorts complete.

If you run the AUTOCONFIGURE command against a database that resides in an instance where the sheapthres configuration parameter has been assigned a value other than zero, the sort memory heap database configuration parameter (sortheap) will not be configured for automatic tuning. (You must execute the command UPDATE DATABASE MANAGER CONFIGURATION USING SHEAPTHRES 0 before you execute the AUTOCONFIGURE command if you want to enable sort memory tuning.)

Question 79

The correct answer is **C**. When queries are executed in a database environment that has been designed to take advantage of parallelism, a table queue is used to pass table data from one database agent to another. When inter-partition parallelism is used, table queues facilitate the passing of table data from one database partition to another; when intra-partition parallelism is used they aid in the passing of table data within a single database partition. Each table queue passes data in a single direction. The SQL compiler decides where table queues are required and includes them in the access plan; when the plan is executed, connections between the database partitions open the table queues needed. Table queues are closed automatically as processes end.

Synchronous table queues read one row for each FETCH statement issued by an application. Synchronous table queues are used when you do not specify the FOR FETCH ONLY clause on a SELECT statement. In a partitioned database environment, if you are updating rows, the database manager will use the synchronous table queues.

Other types of table queues available include:

- **Local table queues (sometimes referred to as LTQ)**. These table queues are used to pass data between database agents within a single database partition. Local table queues (LTQ) are used for intra-partition parallelism.

- **Asynchronous table queues**. These table queues are known as asynchronous because they read rows in advance of any FETCH statement issued by an application. When the FETCH statement is issued, the row is retrieved from the table queue. Asynchronous table queues are used when you specify the FOR FETCH ONLY clause on a SELECT statement. If you are only fetching rows, the asynchronous table queue is faster.

- **Merging table queues.** These table queues preserve order.

- **Nonmerging table queues**. These table queues, also known as "regular" table queues, do not preserve order.

- **Listener table queues**. These table queues are used with correlated subqueries. Correlation values are passed down to the subquery and the results are passed back up to the parent query block using this type of table queue.

- **Directed table queues (sometimes referred to as DTQ)**. These table queues are used in join operations. With directed table queues, rows are hashed to one of the receiving database partitions.

- **Broadcast table queues (sometimes referred to as BTQ).** These table queues are also used in join operations. With broadcast table queues, rows are sent to all of the receiving database partitions but are not hashed.

Question 80

The correct answer is **C**. If a new buffer pool is created (by executing the CREATE BUFFERPOOL statement) after the self tuning memory manager (STMM) has been enabled, DB2 will attempt to create the buffer pool immediately (unless the DEFERRED clause was specified with the CREATE BUFFERPOOL statement used) by allocating the memory requested from shared database memory. If the memory needed is not available, the buffer pool will be created, but no memory will be allocated until all connections to the database the buffer pool is to be created for have been terminated and the database has been deactivated (i.e., the database is stopped and restarted).

Question 81

The correct answer is **C**. Deep compression works by searching for repeating patterns in the data and replacing the patterns with 12-bit symbols, which are stored along with the pattern they represent in a static dictionary. Once this dictionary is created, it is stored in the table along with the compressed data and loaded into memory whenever data in the table is accessed to aid in decompression. DB2 9 scans an entire table looking for repeating column values and repeating patterns that span multiple columns in a row. DB2 also looks for repeating patterns that are substrings of a given column. However, just because a repeating pattern is found doesn't mean that the data is automatically compressed—data is compressed only when storage savings will be realized.

Since it is not possible to compress long, large object, or XML data in DB2 9, only ITEMID, DESCRIPTION, and PRICE information can be compressed. Because DESCRIPTION is character string of up to 250 characters, it should yield the greatest amount of compression. (With DB2 9.5, inline XML documents can be compressed as long as they are less than 32K in size.)

Question 82

The correct answer is **C**. When an application connects to a nonpartitioned database, the connection is assigned to a coordinating agent (named db2agent), and all subsequent SQL statements and DB2 commands are executed by this agent on behalf of the application. When the application disconnects, the corresponding coordinating agent can be terminated; however, a better approach is to let DB2 keep unused (idle) agents around and allow them to be reused by other applications.

Idle agents reside in an agent pool. These agents are available for requests from coordinating agents operating on behalf of client applications, or from subagents operating on behalf of existing coordinating agents. When the maximum number of connections supported (determined by the value assigned to the *max_connections* Database Manager configuration parameter) is equal to or less than the maximum number of coordinating agents allowed (determined by the value assigned to the *max_coordagents* configuration parameter), the size of the idle agent pool is determined by the maximum number of agents allowed. All idle agents, regardless of whether they are coordinating agents or subagents, count toward this limit; if the workload causes this limit to be exceeded, the agents needed are created to support the workload and then terminated as soon as they finish executing their current request.

In this example, because the database was activated, an agent pool was created so the idle agent for the query will be placed in the agent pool as long as the pool has not reached its maximum size.

Question 83

The correct answers are **A** and **C**. The degree of parallelism used is largely determined by the number of database partitions created and how database partition groups have been defined.

Question 84

The correct answer is **D**. The Configuration Advisor is a GUI application that makes it easy to tune and balance the resource requirements of a single database within an instance—you provide specific information about your database environment and the Configuration Advisor makes suggestions about which configuration parameters should be modified and provides recommended values for each. You can then elect to have the Configuration Advisor apply all changes recommended, or you can apply them yourself however you see fit.

In DB2 9, the Configuration Advisor is automatically invoked whenever you create a database using the Create Database Wizard. (This behavior can be changed by assigning the value NO to the DB2_ENABLE_AUTOCONFIG_DEFAULT registry variable.)

The Configuration Advisor only makes recommendations for DB2 Database Manager and database configuration parameters; it has no affect on environment registry variables.

Question 85

The correct answer is **A**. The DB2_SMS_TRUNC_TMPTABLE_THRESH registry variable is used to specify a minimum file size threshold at which a temporary table (file) is maintained in an SMS table space. By default, this variable is set to 0, which means no special threshold handling is done. Instead, once a temporary table is no longer needed, its file is truncated to 0 extents. When the value of this variable is greater than 0, a larger file is maintained. If this variable is set to -1, the file is not truncated and is allowed to grow indefinitely, restricted only by system resources. This reduces some of the system overhead involved in dropping and recreating the file each time a temporary table is used.

Question 86

The correct answer is **D**. A volatile table is a table that is updated very frequently and that changes size dramatically within a short period of time. To tell the optimizer to use an index scan for this type of table, you can mark it as being volatile when you create it (by specifying the VOLATILE option with the CREATE TABLE SQL statement used to create it), or if it already exists, you can mark it as being volatile by executing an ALTER TABLE statement with the VOLATILE option specified; for example, ALTER TABLE payroll VOLATILE.

Declaring a table as being volatile is very important if there are very different numbers of rows in the table at different times, so that gathering statistics, while possible, is not feasible.

Question 87

The correct answer is **D**. When an index is created, only keys and record IDs are stored in the resulting index structure and each record ID points to a corresponding row in the data pages. However, when a clustered index is created, DB2 attempts to store the data in the data pages in the same order as the corresponding keys appear in the index pages. DB2 will also attempt to insert rows with similar key values onto the same pages. A clustering index is most useful for columns that have range predicates because it allows better sequential access of data in the table. (Columns frequently searched or joined over a range of values using the operators BETWEEN, >, <, and LIKE are good candidates for clustering.) Clustering indexes can also improve performance when a query needs to access a large percentage of the rows in the table, particularly when the rows are retrieved in order.

In order for DB2 to maintain the clustering of the data and the index as records are inserted or updated, you must leave free space on the data pages to provide room for additional rows. The PCTFREE option of the CREATE INDEX SQL statement is used to control how much space is reserved on data pages for future insert, update, load, and reorganization operations. Specify a higher PCTFREE value at index creation time to reduce the likelihood that index page splits will occur when records are added to the table. (The default is 10 percent, but you should increase this to between 20 and 35 percent for tables that have a heavy volume of insert/update/delete operations.)

Clustering indexes offer the same benefits for partitioned tables as they do for regular tables. However, to achieve well-maintained clustering with good performance, there should be a correlation between the index columns used and the table partitioning key columns. One way to ensure such correlation is to prefix the index columns with the table partitioning key columns.

Question 88

The correct answer is **B**. Statistical views allow the DB2 optimizer to compute more accurate cardinality estimates. (Cardinality estimation is the process where the optimizer uses statistics to determine the size of partial query results after predicates are applied or aggregation is performed.) The accuracy of cardinality estimates depends on the predicates used and the available statistics. Statistics are available to represent the distribution of data values within a column, which can improve cardinality estimates when the data values are unevenly distributed. Statistics are also available to represent the number of distinct values in a set of columns, which can improve cardinality estimates when columns are statistically correlated.

Question 89

The correct answers are **B** and **D**. When it comes to deciding whether to use row-level locks or table-level locks, it is important to keep in mind that any time a transaction holds a lock on a particular resource, other transactions may be denied access to that resource until the owning transaction is terminated. Therefore, row-level locks are usually better than table-level locks because they restrict access to a much smaller resource. However, because each lock acquired requires some amount of storage space (to hold) and some degree of processing time (to manage), often there is considerably less overhead involved when a single table-level lock is acquired, rather than several individual row-level locks.

By default, DB2 always attempts to acquire row-level locks. However, it is possible to force DB2 to acquire table-level locks on a specific table by executing a special form of the ALTER TABLE SQL statement. The syntax for this form of the ALTER TABLE statement is:

```
ALTER TABLE [TableName] LOCKSIZE TABLE
```

where:

TableName   Identifies the name of an existing table for which the level of locking that all transactions are to use when accessing it is to be specified.

For example, when executed, the SQL statement

```
ALTER TABLE employee LOCKSIZE TABLE
```

is executed, DB2 will attempt to acquire table-level locks for every transaction that accesses the EMPLOYEE table.

But what if you don't want every transaction that works with a particular table to acquire table-level locks? What if instead you want one specific transaction to acquire table-level locks and all other transactions to acquire row-level locks when working with that particular table? In this case, you leave the default locking behavior alone (row-level locking) and use the LOCK TABLE SQL statement to acquire a table-level lock for the appropriate individual transaction. The syntax for the LOCK TABLE statement is:

```
LOCK TABLE [TableName] IN [SHARE | EXCLUSIVE] MODE
```

where:

TableName   Identifies the name of an existing table to be locked.

As you can see, the LOCK TABLE statement allows a transaction to acquire a table-level lock on a particular table in one of two modes: SHARE mode and EXCLUSIVE mode. If a table is locked using the SHARE mode, a table-level Share (S) lock is acquired on behalf of the requesting transaction, and other concurrent transactions are allowed to read, but not change, data stored in the locked table. On the other hand, if a table is locked using the EXCLUSIVE mode, a table-level Exclusive (X) lock is acquired, and other concurrent transactions can neither access nor modify data stored in the locked table.

Question 90

The correct answer is **B**. I/O servers, also called prefetchers, are used on behalf of database agents to perform prefetch I/O and asynchronous I/O for utilities such as the Backup utility and the Restore utility. The *num_ioservers* database configuration parameter is used to specify the number of I/O servers that can be in progress for a database at any given point in time. (An I/O server waits while an I/O operation that it initiated is in progress.) Non-prefetch I/Os are scheduled directly from database agents and as a result are not constrained by the value assigned to the *num_ioservers* database configuration parameter.

Question 91

The correct answer is **B**. Self-tuning is enabled for a database by assigning the value ON to the *self_tuning_mem* database configuration parameter. (By default, the *self_tuning_mem* database configuration parameter is assigned the value ON for single-partition databases and OFF for multi-partition databases.) Specific memory areas that are controlled by a memory configuration parameter can then be enabled for self-tuning by assigning the appropriate configuration parameter the value AUTOMATIC; buffer pools can be enabled for self-tuning by setting their size to AUTOMATIC.

In this example, the *self_tuning_mem* database configuration parameter was not set to ON, so even though the database DB1 was configured to take advantage of the Self-Tuning Memory Manager (STMM), STMM was been enabled for the database. If the database DB1 had been a single-partition database OR if the statement "UPDATE DB CFG FOR db1 USING SELF_TUNING_MEM ON" had been included in the set of commands, answers A, C, and D would have been valid statements and answer B would have been incorrect.

Question 92

The correct answer is **A**. A compression dictionary is built (and existing data in the table is compressed) by performing an offline (classic) table reorganization operation; such an operation is initiated by executing the REORG command with either the KEEPDICTIONARY or the RESETDICTIONARY option specified. If the REORG command is executed with either option specified, and a compression dictionary does not exist, a new dictionary will be built. If the REORG command is executed with either option specified, and a compression dictionary already exists, the existing dictionary will either be recreated (RESETDICTIONARY) or left as it is (KEEPDICTIONARY), and data in the table will be reorganized and compressed.

If the INSPECT command is executed with the ROWCOMPESTIMATE option specified, the Inspect utility will examine each row in the table specified, build a compression dictionary from the data found, and then use this dictionary to estimate how much space will be saved if the data in the table is compressed. If a table is enabled for deep compression (that is, the COMPRESS attribute is set to YES) before the INSPECT command is executed, the compression dictionary that is built and used to estimate space savings will be written to the table, at the end of the existing data—provided a compression dictionary doesn't already exist. Otherwise, the compression dictionary created to estimate space savings will be destroyed.

Question 93

The correct answer is **D**. The primary purpose of an index is to help DB2 quickly locate records stored in a table. Therefore, creating an index for frequently accessed columns in a table usually improves performance for data access and update operations. Indexes also allow for greater concurrency when multiple transactions need to access the same table at the same time— row retrieval is faster and locks are acquired more quickly and don't have to be held as long.

In this scenario, creating an index on columns ID and TYPE will be the best choice since the first key (ID) cardinality is much higher, allowing much faster selection of the RIDs that match the query predicates. And ideally, the RUNSTATS utility should be run against a table immediately after any a new index is created.

Question 94

The correct answer is **D**. The *sheapthres* Database Manager configuration parameter is used to set an instance-wide soft limit on the total amount of memory (in pages) that is to be made available for private sorting operations. The *sortheap* database configuration parameter is used to specify the maximum number of private memory pages to be used for private sorts or the maximum number of shared memory pages to be used for shared sorts.

If you set the sort heap threshold configuration parameter (*sheapthres*) to 0 and the sort heap (*sortheap*) database configuration to AUTOMATIC, DB2 will automatically adjust the size of the sort heap to keep sorts resident in memory and to keep sort heap overflows from occurring.

Question 95

The correct answer is **C**. If you have a query that accesses multiple columns in a table, you cannot simply combine the columns accessed into one unique index, because that may not enforce the uniqueness you want. In this example, you want to ensure that the PARTNUMBER column will contain unique values, yet provide optimum performance for a queries that look something like this:

```
SELECT partnumber, price, description FROM parts
WHERE partnumber = 19002
```

Without an index, this query will require that the entire table be scanned in order to retrieve the desired data. On the other hand, if you create a unique index on the PARTNUMBER column, DB2 will have to scan the index to locate the record, and then read the corresponding data page to retrieve the price and description. But, if you create a unique index on PARTNUMBER, and include the PRICE and DESCRIPTION columns, DB2 can get the data for the query using index only access. Therefore, you might be tempted to create a unique index for the PARTS table by executing a CREATE INDEX statement that looks like this:

```
CREATE UNIQUE INDEX parts_idx1
    ON parts (partnumber, price, description)
```

However, this index does not ensure that the PARTNUMBER column will contain unique values. Instead, it ensures that the *combination* of PARTNUMBER, PRICE, and DESCRIPTION will be unique. To create a unique index on PARTNUMBER, and include the PRICE and DESCRIPTION columns so that DB2 can get the data for the query using index only access, you would need to create the index by executing a CREATE INDEX statement that looks like this:

```
CREATE UNIQUE INDEX parts_idx1 ON parts (partnumber) INCLUDE
(price, description)
```

Question 96

The correct answer is **B**. The primary purpose of an index is to help DB2 quickly locate records stored in a table. Therefore, creating an index for frequently accessed columns in a table usually improves performance for data access and update operations. To ensure that an index will be beneficial, you must analyze how data is frequently accessed to determine which columns should be indexed and which should not. Identifying columns that are frequently joined and/or searched is a good place to start:

1. Consider creating a clustering index on the column most frequently searched and/or joined, based on the data order. Consider nonclustering indexes on searched or joined columns in which less than 10 percent of the rows will be scanned/joined.

2. Refine this analysis with an estimate of the percentage of the rows that will be inserted, updated, and/or deleted over a given period of time. Minimize the number of indexes used when inserting, updating, and deleting data frequently.

3. Composite indexes (i.e., indexes with more than one column) are most beneficial when columns are frequently accessed together.

4. Consider the cardinality of the columns, particularly for composite indexes. Indexes on columns with a low cardinality are not very selective and do not enhance performance as much as indexes on columns with high cardinalities.

In this example, the SALARY column is accessed both in the query and the subquery so it is the best candidate for an index. And by making the index on salary a descending index, the first key contain the highest salary so no further work is required on that index to find the 95% of max salary value.

Question 97

The correct answer is **A**. Where each type of parallelism available should be used is determined primarily by the hardware configuration used. Some of the more common hardware configurations available, along with the type of parallelism that is best suited for each, can be seen in Table F.3.

Table F.3 Types of Parallelism Possible in Common Hardware Environments			
		Intra-Query Parallelism	
Hardware Configuration	I/O Parallelism	Intra-partition Parallelism	Inter-partition Parallelism
Single Database Partition, Single Processor	Yes	No	No
Single Database Partition, Multiple Processors (SMP)	Yes	Yes	No
Multiple Database Partitions, One Processor (MPP)	Yes	No	Yes
Multiple Database Partitions, Multiple Processors (cluster of SMPs)	Yes	Yes	Yes
Logical Database Partitions	Yes	Yes	Yes

Keep in mind that each database partition can reside on its own machine and have its own processor, memory, and disks.

Question 98

The correct answer is **B**. Intra-partition parallelism refers to the ability to break up a database operation into multiple parts and execute those parts simultaneously within a single DB2 instance; inter-partition parallelism refers to the ability to break up a database operation into multiple parts, many or all of which can be run in parallel across multiple partitions of a partitioned database. Both types of parallelism can provide a significant benefit in overall database performance as well as the execution of normal administrative tasks.

Security

Question 99

The correct answer is **D**. If the authentication type for an instance is set to KRB_SERVER_ENCRYPT, authentication occurs at the server where the DB2 instance is running, using either the KERBEROS or the SERVER_ENCRYPT authentication method. If the client's authentication type is set to KERBEROS, authentication is performed at the server using the Kerberos security system. If the client's authentication type is set to anything other than KERBEROS, or if the Kerberos authentication service is not supported, the server acts as if the SERVER_ENCRYPT authentication type was specified, and the rules of this authentication method apply.

Question 100

The correct answer is **D**. The result data type of the ENCRYPT() function is VARCHAR FOR BIT DATA. Therefore, when creating a table that is to hold encrypted data, each column that is to be encrypted must be assigned the data type VARCHAR FOR BIT DATA. How large an encrypted column must be is determined, in part by the decision to store password hint information with the encrypted data. If a hint will not be provided, the length of the column must be the length of the unencrypted data + 8 bytes for the password, rounded up to the next 8-byte boundary. For example, if you wanted to encrypt a string that is 11 bytes long and forego providing a password hint, you would need to define a column that is capable of holding 24 bytes (11 + 8 = 17; 17 + 5 to reach the next 8-byte boundary = 24). If a hint will be provided, the length of the column must be the length of the unencrypted data + 8 bytes for the password, rounded up to the next 8-byte boundary + 32 bytes for the hint.

Because in this example, you want to encrypt a string that is 19 bytes long and forego providing a password hint, you would need to define a column that is capable of holding at least 32 bytes (19 + 8 = 27; 27 + 5 to reach the next 8-byte boundary = 32). In answer D, the column PO_NUMBER is assigned the data type VARCHAR FOR BIT DATA and its size is 40 bytes, which is greater than the 32 bytes needed.

Question 101

The correct answer is **B**. The DB2 audit facility monitors database events that you tell it to keep track of, and records information about those events in an audit log file. By analyzing the information stored in the audit log file, you can quickly pinpoint usage patterns that identify system misuse; once identified, you can take appropriate action to minimize or eliminate the problem. The DB2 audit facility works at the instance level, recording both instance-level and database-level activities. Since the DB2 audit facility works independently of the DB2 server, it will continue to run once started, even if the DB2 instance is stopped. In fact, when an instance is stopped, an audit record may be written to the audit log.

The DB2 audit facility is controlled by the db2audit command and the contents of an audit configuration file named db2audit.cfg, which is located in the sqllib/security subdirectory under the instance owner's home directory. (By default the audit log file, db2audit.log, is written to this directory as well.) In order to capture audit records you must start the audit facility, and before audit log files can be examined the audit facility must be stopped. When the audit facility is started, it uses the existing audit configuration file to determine what events to monitor.

Question 102

The correct answer is **B**. If the authentication type for an instance is set to KRB_SERVER_ ENCRYPT, authentication occurs at the server where the DB2 instance is running, using either the KERBEROS or the SERVER_ENCRYPT authentication method. If the client's authentication type is set to KERBEROS, authentication is performed at the server using the Kerberos security system. If the client's authentication type is set to anything other than KERBEROS, or if the Kerberos authentication service is unavailable, the server acts as if the SERVER_ENCRYPT authentication type was specified, and the rules of this authentication method apply.

Question 103

The correct answer is **C**. The result data type of the ENCRYPT() function is VARCHAR FOR BIT DATA. Therefore, when creating a table that is to hold encrypted data, each column that is to be encrypted must be assigned the data type VARCHAR FOR BIT DATA. Column COL3 is the only column in the table TAB1 that has been assigned this data type.

Question 104

The correct answer is **B**. Security label components represent criteria that may be used to decide whether a user should have access to specific data. Three types of security label components can exist:

- **SET.** A set is a collection of elements (character string values) where the order in which each element appears is not important.

- **ARRAY.** An array is an ordered set that can represent a simple hierarchy. In an array, the order in which the elements appear is important—the first element ranks higher than the second, the second ranks higher than the third, and so on.

- **TREE.** A tree represents a more complex hierarchy that can have multiple nodes and branches.

Question 105

The correct answers are **B** and **D**. The value of the *audit_buf_sz* DB2 Database Manager configuration parameter determines when the writing of audit records is performed. If the value of this configuration parameter is zero (0), writing is performed synchronously. That is, the event generating the audit record will wait until the record is written to disk. And the wait associated with each record has a negative impact on performance.

If the *audit_buf_sz* configuration parameter is assigned a value that is greater than zero, record writing is performed asynchronously. In this case, the value assigned to the *audit_buf_sz* configuration parameter represents the number of 4 KB pages to set aside as an internal buffer; the internal buffer is used to cache a number of audit records before a group of them are written out to disk. Thus, the event generating an audit record will not wait until the record is written to disk, and can continue its operation.

An audit buffer cannot be allocated dynamically. Instead, the instance must be stopped and restarted before changes made to the *audit_buf_sz* configuration parameter will take effect.

Question 106

The correct answer is **C**. If a password is not explicitly provided when data is encrypted using the ENCRYPT() function, data will be encrypted using the encryption password value that was assigned for the session. (The same is true if a password is not explicitly provided when data is decrypted using the DECRYPT_CHAR() or the DECRYPT_BIN() function.) An encryption password can be set for a session by executing the SET ENCRYPTION PASSWORD SQL statement. The syntax for this statement is:

```
SET ENCRYPTION PASSWORD <=> [Password]
```

where:

Password   Identifies the password to be used to generate the key that will be used to encrypt and decrypt data each time the ENCRYPT(), DECRYPT_CHAR(), and DECRYPT_BIN() functions are executed in the current session. The password specified must be between 6 and 127 characters in length and must be in the exact case desired since DB2 does not automatically convert passwords into upper case. The password specified cannot be null.

Thus, if you wanted to specify that all data encryption and decryption operations performed during the current session are to use the password "EXEC_0409", you could do so by executing a SET ENCRYPTION PASSWORD SQL statement that looks something like this:

```
SET ENCRYPTION PASSWORD = 'EXEC-0409'
```

Question 107

The correct answers are **A** and **E**. Although the value assigned to the *authentication* DB2 Database Manager (DBM) configuration parameter determines how and where user authentication takes place, this value can be overridden for a particular server by assigning a different value to the *srvcon_auth* configuration parameter. (The *srvcon_auth* DBM configuration parameter is used to specify how and where authentication is to take place when handling connections at the server; if this parameter is not assigned a value, DB2 uses the current value of the authentication configuration parameter.

Unless otherwise specified, the DB2 Kerberos plug-in library IBMkrb5 is used on AIX, Linux, Sun Solaris, and Windows operating systems when the client is authenticated using KERBEROS or KRB_SERVER_ENCRYPT authentication. Therefore, to configure an instance to use the Kerberos-based authentication plug-in (IBMKrb5) that is shipped with DB2 9 to authenticate users, you must either assign the value KERBEROS or KRB_SERVER_ENCRYPT to the *srvcon_auth* configuration parameter or assign the value NOT_SPECIFIED to the *srvcon_auth* configuration parameter and assign the value KERBEROS or KRB_SERVER_ENCRYPT to the *authentication* configuration parameter.

Question 108

The correct answer is C. When user USER1 queries the SALES table, all records with the security label SALES_REGION_POLICY.CENTRAL_NORTH and SALES_REGION_POLICY.CENTRAL_SOUTH will appear (because the security label SALES_REGION_POLICY.CENTRAL – the security label assigned to user USER1 – is at a higher level in the security policy's security label component tree).

Connectivity and Networking

Question 109

The correct answer is **C.** The Sysplex server list is rendered inaccessible if there are no agents available and if no connections to a host database exist. Therefore, connection pooling must be enabled and at least one agent must be available when working with Sysplex servers. Connection pooling is enabled whenever the maximum number of agents allowed to be pooled on a DB2 instance is greater than zero—this number is determined by the value assigned to the *num_poolagents* DB2 Database Manager configuration parameter.

Thus, if you wanted to enable connection pooling for the default instance on a DB2 Connect server, you could do so by executing a command that looks something like this:

```
UPDATE DBM CFG USING NUM_POOLAGENTS 10
```

However, once this command is executed, the instance will have to be stopped and restarted (by executing the db2stop and db2start commands) before the change will take effect.

Question 110

The correct answer is **C**. Once a server has been configured for communications, any client that wishes to access a database on the server must be configured to communicate with the server. In order to catalog a remote server using TCP/IP, you must provide, among other things, the host name, as it is known to the TCP/IP network. (This is the name of the server where the remote database that you are trying to communicate with resides.) When cataloging a DB2 for z/OS remote server, the hostname can be seen in the DSNL004I message (DOMAIN=hostname) when the Distributed Data Facility (DDF) is started—provided the target database has been set up for TCP/IP communications; the Distributed Data Facility (DDF) is required for TCP/IP communications with DB2 on z/OS servers.

Question 111

The correct answer is **A**. In order to communicate with a server, each client must use some type of communications protocol recognized by the server. Likewise, each server must use some type of communications protocol to detect inbound requests from clients. Both clients and servers must be configured to use a communications protocol recognized by DB2.

Whenever you manually configure communications for a server, you must update the value of the DB2COMM registry variable before an instance can begin using the desired communications protocol. The value assigned to the DB2COMM registry variable is used to determine which communications managers will be activated when a particular instance is started.

In this example, because everyone in the HR department cannot connect to the PAYROLL database, the problem is most likely that the DB2COMM registry variable has not been assigned the value TCPIP.

Question 112

The correct answer is **B**. A DCS database is cataloged by executing the CATALOG DCS DATABASE command. The syntax for this command is:

```
CATALOG DCS [DATABASE | DB] [Alias]
<AS [TargetName]>
<AR [LibraryName]>
<PARMS "[ParameterString]">
<WITH "[Description]">
```

where:

Alias	Identifies the alias of the target database to be cataloged. This name should match an entry in the system database directory associated with the remote node.
TargetName	Identifies the name of the target host database to be cataloged. (If the host database to be cataloged resides on a OS/390 or z/OS server, the *TargetName* specified should refer to a DB2 for z/OS subsystem identified by its LOCATION NAME or one of the alias LOCATION names defined on the z/OS server. The LOCATION NAME can be determined by logging in to TSO and issuing the following SQL query using one of the available query tools: SELECT CURRENT SERVER FROM SYSIBM.SYSDUMMY1.)
LibraryName	Identifies the name of the Application Requester library to be loaded and used to access the remote database listed in the DCS directory.
ParameterString	Identifies a parameter string to be passed to the Application Requestor when it is invoked. The parameter string must be enclosed by double quotation marks.
Description	A comment used to describe the database entry that will be made in the DCS directory for the database to be cataloged. The description must be enclosed by double quotation marks (").

Thus, if you wanted to catalog a DB2 for z/OS database residing in the DSN_DB_1 subsystem on the z/OS server that has the name PAYROLL_DB and assign it the alias PAYROLL, you could do so by executing a CATALOG DCS DATABASE command that looks something like this:

```
CATALOG DCS DATABASE payroll
AS dsn_db_1
WITH "DB2 for z/OS LOCATION NAME DSN_DB_1"
```

Question 113

The correct answer is **D**. Nodes (servers) are usually cataloged implicitly whenever a remote database is cataloged via the Configuration Assistant. However, if you want to explicitly catalog (i.e., add an entry to the node directory for a particular server), you can do so by executing a CATALOG . . . NODE command that corresponds to the communications protocol that will be used to access the server being cataloged. The syntax for the CATALOG TCPIP NODE command is:

```
CATALOG <ADMIN> [TCPIP | TCPIP4 | TCPIP6] NODE [NodeName]
REMOTE [IPAddress | HostName]
SERVER [ServiceName | PortNumber]
<SECURITY SOCKS>
<REMOTE INSTANCE [InstanceName]>
```

```
<SYSTEM [SystemName]>
<OSTYPE [SystemType]>
<WITH "[Description]">
```

where:

NodeName	Identifies the alias to be assigned to the node to be cataloged. This is an arbitrary name created on the user's workstation and is used to identify the node.
IPAddress	Identifies the IP address of the server where the remote database that you are trying to communicate with resides.
HostName	Identifies the host name, as it is known to the TCP/IP network. (This is the name of the server where the remote database that you are trying to communicate with resides.)
ServiceName	Identifies the service name that the DB2 Database Manager instance on the server uses to communicate.
PortNumber	Identifies the port number that the DB2 Database Manager instance on the server uses to communicate.
InstanceName	Identifies the name of the server instance to which an attachment is to be made.
SystemName	Identifies the DB2 system name used to identify the server workstation.
SystemType	Identifies the type of operating system being used on the server workstation. The following values are valid for this parameter: AIX, WIN, HPUX, SUN, OS390, OS400, VM, VSE, and LINUX.
Description	A comment used to describe the node entry that is to be made in the node directory for the node being cataloged. The description must be enclosed by double quotation marks.

Thus, if you wanted to catalog a node for a Linux server that has the IPv6 address 1080:0:0:0:8:800:200C:417A and an instance that is listening on port 50000, you could do so by executing a CATALOG TCPIP NODE command that looks something like this:

```
CATALOG TCPIP NODE rmt_server
REMOTE 1080:0:0:0:8:800:200C:417A
SERVER 50000
OSTYPE LINUX
```

On the other hand, if you wanted to catalog a node for a Linux server that has the IPv4 address 192.0.32.67 and an instance that is listening on port 50000, you could do so by executing a CATALOG TCPIP NODE command that looks like this:

```
CATALOG TCPIP NODE rmt_server
REMOTE 192.0.32.67
SERVER 50000
OSTYPE LINUX
```

Question 114

The correct answers are **B** and **D**. If the *discover_inst* DB2 Database Manager configuration parameter is set to ENABLE, information about the corresponding instance will be returned in response to both search and known discovery requests. If the *discover_db* database configuration parameter is set to ENABLE, information about the corresponding database will be returned in response to both search and known discovery requests. DB2 Database Manager configuration parameters are set by executing the command "UPDATE DBM CFG [*Parameter*] [*Value*]"; database configuration parameters are set by executing the command "UPDATE DB CFG FOR [*DBAlias*] USING [*Parameter*] [*Value*]".

Question 115

The correct answer is **D**. In order to communicate with a server, each client must use some type of communications protocol recognized by the server. Likewise, each server must use some type of communications protocol to detect inbound requests from clients. Both clients and servers must be configured to use a communications protocol recognized by DB2.

Whenever you manually configure communications for a server, you must update the value of the DB2COMM registry variable before an instance can begin using the desired communications protocol. The value assigned to the DB2COMM registry variable is used to determine which communications managers will be activated when a particular instance is started. (If the DB2COMM registry variable is not set correctly, one or more errors may be generated when DB2 attempts to start protocol support during instance initialization.)

Once a server has been configured for communications, any client that wishes to access a database on the server must add entries for both the server and the remote database to the system database and node directories on the client. (Entries must also be added to the DCS directory if the client intends to connect to a System z or System i database via DB2 Connect.) Entries are added to DB2's directories using a process known as cataloging.

In this example, because everyone else in the HR department can connect to the PAYROLL database, the DB2COMM registry variable must be set correctly on the server. The same is true about the way the PAYROLL database was cataloged on the server – since everyone else can connect to the database, the database must be cataloged correctly. The value assigned to the DB2COMM registry variable on the client has no effect since the node directory entry specifies the communications protocol and port number that will be used to connect to the server. So, that's not the problem either. Therefore, the problem must be that either the server (node) or the database has been cataloged incorrectly on the client.

Question 116

The correct answer is **B**. If you wanted to configure a server to use TCP/IP, you would perform the following steps (in any order):

1. Assign the value TCPIP to the DB2COMM registry variable.

   The DB2COMM registry variable is assigned the value TCPIP by executing a db2set command that looks something like this:

   ```
   db2set DB2COMM=TCPIP
   ```

2. Assign the name of the TCP/IP port that the database server will use to receive communications from remote clients to the *svcename* parameter of the DB2 Database Manager configuration file.

   This parameter is set by executing an UPDATE DATABASE MANAGER CONFIGURATION command that looks something like this:

   ```
   UPDATE DBM CFG USING SVCENAME db2c_db2inst1
   ```

3. Update the services file on the database server, if appropriate.

   The TCP/IP services file identifies the ports on which server applications will listen for client requests. If you specified a service name in the *svcename* parameter of the DB2 Database Manager configuration file, the appropriate service name-to-port number/protocol mapping must be added to the services file on the server. If you specified a port number in the *svcename* parameter, the services file does not need to be updated.

   The default location of the services file depends on the operating system being used: on UNIX systems, the services file is named *services* and is located in the */etc* directory; on Windows systems, the services file is located in *%SystemRoot%\system32\drivers\etc*. An entry in the services file for DB2 might look something like this:

   ```
   db2c_db2inst1        50001/tcp
   ```

Once a server has been configured for communications, any client that wishes to access a database on the server must add entries for both the server and the remote database to the system database and node directories on the client.

In this example, because the server and database were cataloged correctly on the Windows client, the most likely cause of the problem was that the services file on the UNIX server did not have an entry for the DB2 service name and port.

Question 117

The correct answers are **B** and **C**. The file db2ubind.lst contains a list of the bind files (.bnd) needed to create packages for DB2's database utilities; the file db2cli.lst contains a list of the bind files (.bnd) needed to create packages for the DB2 Call Level Interface (CLI) and the DB2 ODBC driver. When these two commands are executed, any messages produced by the Bind utility will be written to a file named bind.msg and the group PUBLIC will receive EXECUTE and BINDADD privileges for each package produced.

(The db2schema.bnd bind file is used to create a package that provides system catalog function support and is often used with DB2 Connect.)

Question 118

The correct answer is **C**. If the *discover_db* database configuration parameter is set to DISABLE, information about the corresponding database will not be returned in response to a DB2 discovery request. If the *discover_inst* DB2 Database Manager configuration parameter for the instance the database resides under has been set to DISABLE, then this is not required. (If the *discover_inst* DB2 Database Manager configuration parameter is set to DISABLE, information about the corresponding instance will not be returned in response to a DB2 discovery request.)

Question 119

The correct answers are **D** and **E**. Any client that wishes to access a database on a remote server must be configured to communicate with that server. But that's just the first step. Entries for both the server and the remote database must also be added to the system database and node directories on the client. Entries are added to DB2's directories using a process known as cataloging.

To explicitly catalog a remote server, you execute the CATALOG . . . NODE command that corresponds to the communications protocol that will be used to access the server being cataloged. To catalog a database, you execute the CATALOG DATABASE command.

The syntax for the CATALOG TCPIP NODE command is:

```
CATALOG <ADMIN> [TCPIP | TCPIP4 | TCPIP6] NODE [NodeName]
REMOTE [IPAddress | HostName]
SERVER [ServiceName | PortNumber]
<SECURITY SOCKS>
<REMOTE INSTANCE [InstanceName]>
<SYSTEM [SystemName]>
<OSTYPE [SystemType]>
<WITH "[Description]">
```

where:

NodeName	Identifies the alias to be assigned to the node to be cataloged. This is an arbitrary name created on the user's workstation and is used to identify the node.
IPAddress	Identifies the IP address of the server where the remote database that you are trying to communicate with resides.
HostName	Identifies the host name, as it is known to the TCP/IP network. (This is the name of the server where the remote database that you are trying to communicate with resides.)
ServiceName	Identifies the service name that the DB2 Database Manager instance on the server uses to communicate.
PortNumber	Identifies the port number that the DB2 Database Manager instance on the server uses to communicate.
InstanceName	Identifies the name of the server instance to which an attachment is to be made.
SystemName	Identifies the DB2 system name used to identify the server workstation.
SystemType	Identifies the type of operating system being used on the server workstation. The following values are valid for this parameter: AIX, WIN, HPUX, SUN, OS390, OS400, VM, VSE, and LINUX.
Description	A comment used to describe the node entry that is to be made in the node directory for the node being cataloged. The description must be enclosed by double quotation marks.

The syntax for the CATALOG DATABASE command is:

```
CATALOG [DATABASE | DB] [DatabaseName]
<AS [Alias]>
<ON [Path] | AT NODE [NodeName]>
<AUTHENTICATION [AuthenticationType]>
<WITH "[Description]">
```

where:

DatabaseName	Identifies the name that has been assigned to the database to be cataloged.
Alias	Identifies the alias that is to be assigned to the database when it is cataloged.
Path	Identifies the location (drive and/or directory) where the directory hierarchy and files associated with the database to be cataloged are physically stored.

NodeName	Identifies the node where the database to be cataloged resides. The node name specified should match an entry in the node directory file (i.e., should correspond to a node that has already been cataloged).
AuthenticationType	Identifies where and how authentication is to take place when a user attempts to access the database. The following values are valid for this parameter: SERVER, CLIENT, SERVER_ENCRYPT, KERBEROS TARGET PRINCIPAL [*PrincipalName*] (where *PrincipalName* is the fully qualified Kerberos principal name for the target server), DATA_ ENCRYPT, and GSSPLUGIN.
Description	A comment used to describe the database entry that is to be made in the database directory for the database to be cataloged. The description must be enclosed by double quotation marks.

Question 120

The correct answer is **D**. In order to access a remote database from a client workstation, the database must be cataloged in the system database directory of both the client and the server *and* the server workstation must be cataloged in the client's node directory. (The entry in the node directory tells the DB2 Database Manager how to connect to the server to get access to the database stored there.) Because the information needed to connect to DRDA host databases is different from the information used to connect to LAN-based databases, information about remote host or iSeries databases is kept in a special directory known as the Database Connection Services (DCS) directory. If an entry in the DCS directory has a database name that corresponds to the name of a database stored in the system database directory, the specified Application Requester (which in most cases is DB2 Connect) can forward SQL requests to the database that resides on a remote DRDA server. If there is no record for a zSeries or iSeries database in the DCS directory, no database connection can be established.

Index

Note: Boldface numbers indicate figures; t *indicates tables*

Greenwich Mean Time (GMT), 267
GSS-API authentication, 496
gssplugin authentication, 494, 496, 499
gss_server_encrypt authentication, 494, 499

H

hadr_remote_host database, 299–300
hadr_remote_svc database, 299–300
hashing algorithm, **170**
hash join, 415, 655, 658–659, 660
"hate stacks," 71
Health Monitor, 47
hidden buffer pool, 69–70
hierarchies of databases, 40
High Availability Disaster Recover (HADR)
    Database Wizard, 297, 298, **298–299**, 299
high availability disaster recovery (HADR)
    environment, 223, 290
    Automatic Client Reroute feature of, 298–300
    configuration parameters of, 295–296t
    load operations and, 300–302
    process of setting up, 293–298
    requirements for, 291–293
high-availability, 205, 622
high-priority tables, 72
HIGH2KEY, 401
high-usage tables, 72
high-water mark concept, 100–103, **103**
Hint command, 533
history table, 72
hit ratio, 629–630
home entry, 582
HostName command, 148, 150, 155, 589
HP-UX platform, 8, 11, **149**
human resources (HR) manager, 527

I

IBM, 20
IBMCATGROUP database, 92
IBMCATGROUP group, 161, 162
IBM Certification Agreement, 37
IBM Certification Exam testing software
    exam results panel of, **35–36**
    item (question) review panel of, **31**

refresher course on, 25
screen shot of, **23**
section scores panel of, **35–36**
See also question panels
IBM Certification Group, 37
IBM Certified Advanced Database
    Administrator - DB2 9 for Linux, UNIX, and
    Windows certification, 11, 13, **13**
IBM Certified Application Developer - DB2 9
    Family certification, 8, 10, **11**
IBM Certified Database Administrator - DB2 9
    for Linux, UNIX and Windows certification,
    4–5, 13
IBM Certified Database Administrator - DB2 9
    for z/OS and OS/390 certification, 7, **8**
IBM Certified Database Administrator - DB2
    V8.1 Family certification, 10
IBM Certified Database Administrator - DB2
    V8.1 for Linux, UNIX, and Windows, 4–5,
    5f, **6**
IBM Certified Database Associate - DB2 9 for
    Linux, UNIX and Windows certification,
    2–3, **3**
IBM Certified Database Associate - DB2 9 for
    z/OS certification, 6, 7
"IBM Certified" mark, 37
IBM Certified Solution Designer - DB2 Data
    Warehouse Edition (DWE) V9.1 certification,
    13, 15, **16**
IBM Certified Solution Developer - DB2 9.5
    SQL Procedure Developer certification,
    16–17, **17**
IBMDEFAULTBP buffer pool, 44, 59, 69
    memory of, 70
    table space and, creation of new, 85
IBMDEFAULTGROUP database, 92
IBMDEFAULTGROUP group, 161
IBM InfoSphere Balanced Warehousing, 140
IBM Learning Services, 18
IBM Professional Certification Member Web
    site, 22
IBM pSeries P690, 159, 160
IBMTEMPGROUP database, 92, 162
identity theft, 490
idle agent pooling, 403–405

Note: Boldface numbers indicate figures; t *indicates tables*

J

JDBC programming, 9
join, 414–415
    broadcast table, 675–680
    collocated table, 661–667
    directed inner table, 669–675
    directed outer table, 667–668, 673–675
    hash, 658–659
    merge, 657–658
    nested loop, **656**, 656–657
    partitioned database, strategies, 680–681
    partitioned databases and operation of, 660–661
    replicated materialized query table (MQT)
        and, use of, 643–648
    techniques of, 655, 659–660
    types of, 653–655
JoinCondition command, 655
journal, 72

K

Kahn, Robert, 591
KEEPDICTIONARY command, 445, 447
kerberos authentication, 492–493, 495, 496
Keyword command, 50, 378
krb_server_encrypt authentication, 493, 495, 499

L

label-based access control (LBAC), 13, 489–490
    common-level, 548–549, 555–557
    CREATE SECURITY LABEL
        COMPONENT function of, 549–551
    DB2LBACRULES function of, 552–553
    granting exemptions of, 553–554
    privileges, **523**, 523–524
    protection and use of, 544–545, 551–552
    revoking exemptions of, 554–555
    row-level, 539, 545–548, 556–557
    securing of data with, 538
    security label component of, 539–541
    security labels and, 542–544
    security policy and determination of, 541–542
LabelName command, 543, 545
LAN-based databases, 585
large object (LOB) data, 83, 244

LastPartitionNum command, 61–62
LDAP-based authentication, 497–498
LDAP entry, 582
LibraryName command, 116, 593
Lightweight Directory Access Protocol (LDAP),
    490–491
LIKE DBPARTRTIONNUM option, 156, 164
Linux on IA32, 497
Linux on x64, 497
Linux on zSeries, 497
Linux platform, 8, 11
    Balanced Configuration Unit (BCU) and, 206
    buffer pool, 44, 59
    db2nodes.cfg file and, 148
    prefetching and, 81
    raw device container and, mapping of, 80
    raw devices and, 81
    sqldbdir file and, 46
    user exit program and, 288
list (sequential) prefetch, 434–435
LIST APPLICATIONS command, 309, 439,
    439–440, **440**, 441
LIST DATABASE DIRECTORY command,
    582–583
LIST DCS DIRECTORY command, 585
listener table queues, 407
LIST HISTORY command, 271
LIST NODE DIRECTORY command, 584
LIST NODES command, 274
list prefetching, **107**
LIST TABLESPACES SHOW DETAIL
    command, 267
Load (LOAD) authority, 502, 509–510
load authorities, 509–510
LOAD command, 181
LOAD INSERT option, 452
load library, 301
load operations, 293, 300–302
load privilege, 47, 511
LOAD REPLACE operation, 452
load utility, 146, 270, 386, 452–453
LOB columns, 80
local catalog, 114
local database directory files (directories), 581, 583
local table queue (LTQ), 406

Note: Boldface numbers indicate figures; t *indicates tables*

Windows platform, *continued*
   sqldbdir file and, 46
   user exit programs and, 289
WITHOUT TABLESPACE statement, 156, 164
workload, 375, 389–390
Workload Manager (WLM), 597
WorkloadName command, 197
workstations, 40
WrapperName command, 116, 118
wrappers, 115–117
   defined, 115
   federated systems and, 115–117
   names, predefined, 116t
   types of, 122

"write-ahead logging," 225–226
WRITE RESUME option, 246
write time, 626, 627

X

XBSA Draft 0.8, 286
XML data, **444**
XML schema repository (XSR) privileges, 524
X/Open group, 286
XSR privileges, 524, 524, **524**

Z

zSeries (z/OS, OS/390) platforms, 8

More DB2 Books from MC Press

DB2 9 Fundamentals Certification Study Guide
Exam 730

ISBN: 978-158347-072-5
Author: Roger E. Sanders
http://www.mc-store.com/5088.html

DB2 9 Linux, UNIX, and Windows Database Administration
Exam 731 Certification Study Guide

ISBN: 978-158347-077-0
Author: Roger E. Sanders
http://www.mc-store.com/5090.html

DB2 9 Linux, UNIX, and Windows Advanced Database Administration
Exam 734 Certification Study Guide

ISBN: 978-158347-080-0
Author: Roger E. Sanders
http://www.mc-store.com/5093.html

DB2 9 Linux, UNIX, and Windows Database Administration Upgrade
Exam 736 Certification Study Guide

ISBN: 978-158347-078-7
Author: Roger E. Sanders
http://www.mc-store.com/5091.html

DB2 9 for Developers

ISBN: 978-158347-071-8
Author: Philip K. Gunning
http://www.mc-store.com/5086.html